T0331868

Lecture Notes Series on Computing - Vol. 15

Algorithms

Design Techniques and Analysis

Second Edition

LECTURE NOTES SERIES ON COMPUTING

Editor-in-Chief: D T Lee (*Academia Sinica, Taiwan*)

Published

Vol. 15:   *Algorithms: Design Techniques and Analysis (Second Edition)*
           M H Alsuwaiyel

Vol. 14:   *Algorithms: Design Techniques and Analysis (Revised Edition)*
           M H Alsuwaiyel

Vol. 13:   *Computational Aspects of Algebraic Curves*
           Ed. T Shaska

Vol. 12:   *Planar Graph Drawing*
           T Nishizeki & S Rahman

Vol. 11:   *Geometric Computation*
           Eds. F Chen & D Wang

Vol. 10:   *Computer Mathematics*
           Proceedings of the Sixth Asian Symposium (ASCM 2003)
           Eds. Z Li & W Sit

Vol. 9:   *Computer Mathematics*
           Proceedings of the Fifth Asian Symposium (ASCM 2001)
           Eds. K Yokoyama & K Shirayanagi

Vol. 8:   *Computer Mathematics*
           Proceedings of the Fourth Asian Symposium (ASCM 2000)
           Eds. X-S Gao & D Wang

Vol. 7:   *Algorithms: Design Techniques and Analysis*
           Ed. M H Alsuwaiyel

Vol. 6:   *VLSI Physical Design Automation: Theory and Practice*
           S M Sait & H Youssef

Vol. 5:   *Proceedings of the Conference on*
           Parallel Symbolic Computation — PASCO '94
           Ed. H Hong

Vol. 4:   *Computing in Euclidean Geometry (Second Edition)*
           Eds. D-Z Du & F Hwang

Vol. 3:   *String Searching Algorithms*
           G A Stephen

Vol. 2:   *Algorithmic Aspects of VLSI Layout*
           Eds. D T Lee & M Sarrafzadeh

Vol. 1:   *Computing in Euclidean Geometry*
           Eds. D-Z Du & F Hwang

Lecture Notes Series on Computing - Vol. 15

Algorithms
Design Techniques and Analysis

Second Edition

M. H. Alsuwaiyel
King Fahd University of Petroleum & Minerals (KFUPM), Saudi Arabia

World Scientific

NEW JERSEY • LONDON • SINGAPORE • BEIJING • SHANGHAI • HONG KONG • TAIPEI • CHENNAI • TOKYO

Published by

World Scientific Publishing Co. Pte. Ltd.

5 Toh Tuck Link, Singapore 596224

USA office: 27 Warren Street, Suite 401-402, Hackensack, NJ 07601

UK office: 57 Shelton Street, Covent Garden, London WC2H 9HE

Library of Congress Cataloging-in-Publication Data
Names: Alsuwaiyel, M. H., author.
Title: Algorithms : design techniques and analysis / M.H. Alsuwaiyel,
    King Fahd University of Petroleum & Minerals (KFUPM), Saudi Arabia.
Description: Second edition. | New Jersey : World Scientific, [2022] |
    Series: Lecture notes series on computing, 1793-1223 ; vol. 15 |
    Includes bibliographical references and index.
Identifiers: LCCN 2021038677 | ISBN 9789811238642 (hardcover) |
    ISBN 9789811238659 (ebook) | ISBN 9789811238666 (ebook other)
Subjects: LCSH: Algorithms--Textbooks.
Classification: LCC QA9.58 .A425 2022 | DDC 518/.1--dc23
LC record available at https://lccn.loc.gov/2021038677

British Library Cataloguing-in-Publication Data
A catalogue record for this book is available from the British Library.

For any available supplementary material, please visit
https://www.worldscientific.com/worldscibooks/10.1142/12324#t=suppl

Desk Editors: Balasubramanian Shanmugam/Amanda Yun

Typeset by Stallion Press
Email: enquiries@stallionpress.com

Printed in Singapore

To my wife Noura and my daughter Sara

Preface

The field of computer algorithms has flourished since the early 1960s when the first users of electronic computers started to pay attention to the performance of programs. The limited resources of computers at that time resulted in additional impetus for devising efficient computer algorithms. After extensive research in this field, numerous efficient algorithms for different problems emerged. The similarities among different algorithms for certain classes of problems have resulted in general algorithm design techniques. This book emphasizes most of these algorithm design techniques that have proved their utility in the solution to many problems. It may be considered as an attempt to cover the most common techniques in the design of sequential algorithms. Each technique is presented as follows. First, the context in which that technique can be applied. Second, the special characteristics of that technique that set it apart. Third, comparison with other techniques, whenever possible; finally, and most importantly, illustration of the technique by applying it to several problems.

Although the main theme of the book is algorithm design techniques, it also emphasizes the other major component in algorithmic design: the analysis of algorithms. It covers in detail the analysis of most of the algorithms presented. Appendix A covers most of the mathematical tools that are helpful in analyzing algorithms. Chapter 10 is an introduction to the field of computational complexity, and Chapter 11 covers the basics of establishing lower bounds on the solution of various problems. These chapters are indispensable for the design of efficient algorithms.

The focus of the presentation is on practical applications of the design techniques. Each technique is illustrated by providing an adequate number of algorithms to solve some problems that quite often arise in many applications in science and engineering.

The style of presentation of algorithms is straightforward and uses pseudocode that is similar to the syntax of structured programming languages, e.g., **if-then-else, for** and **while** constructs. The pseudocode is sometimes intermixed with English whenever necessary. Describing a portion of an algorithm in English is indeed instructive; it conveys the idea with minimum effort on the part of the reader. However, sometimes it is both easier and more formal to use a pseudocode statement. For example, the function of the assignment statement

$$B[1..n] \leftarrow A[1..n]$$

is to replace each entry $B[i]$ with $A[i]$ for all $i, 1 \leq i \leq n$. Neither the **for ... end for** construct nor plain English is more concise or easier to state than this notation.

The book is divided into eight parts. Each part consists of chapters that cover those design techniques that have common characteristics or objectives. Part 1 sets the stage for the rest of the book, in addition to providing the background material that is needed in subsequent chapters. Part 2 is devoted to the study of recursive design techniques, which are extremely important, as they emphasize a fundamental tool in the field of computer science: recursion. Part 3 covers two intuitive and natural design techniques: the greedy approach and graph traversals. Part 4 is concerned with those techniques needed to investigate a given problem and the possibility of either coming up with an efficient algorithm for that problem or proving its intractability. This part covers NP-completeness, computational complexity and lower bounds. In Part 5, techniques for coping with hard problems are presented. These include backtracking, randomization and finding approximate solutions that are reasonable and acceptable using a reasonable amount of time. Part 6 introduces the concept of iterative improvement using two important problems that have received extensive attention, which resulted in increasingly efficient algorithms: the problem of finding a maximum flow in a network and the problem of finding a maximum matching in an undirected graph. Part 7 is an introduction to the relatively new field of computational geometry. In one chapter, the widely used technique of geometric sweeping is presented with examples of important problems in that field. In the other chapter, the versatile tool of the Voronoi diagram is covered, and some of its applications are presented. Finally, Part 8 is an introduction to the exciting field of parallel algorithms. It covers material relevant to the most common models of computation: The PRAM, the hypercube and the mesh.

The book is intended as a text in the field of the design and analysis of algorithms. It includes adequate material for two courses in algorithms. Chapters 1–9 provide the core material for an undergraduate course in algorithms at the junior or senior level. Some of the material may be skipped such as the amortized analysis of the union-find algorithms and the linear time algorithms in the case of dense graphs for the shortest path and minimum spanning tree problems. The instructor may find it useful to add some of the material in the following chapters such as backtracking, randomized algorithms, approximation algorithms or geometric sweeping. The rest of the material is intended for a graduate course in algorithms.

The prerequisites for this book have been kept to the minimum; only an elementary background in discrete mathematics and data structures are assumed.

M. H. Alsuwaiyel
Dhahran, Saudi Arabia

About the Author

Muhammad Hamad (M. H.) Alsuwaiyel is a retired Professor of
the Information and Computer Science Department at King Fahd University of Petroleum and Minerals (KFUPM), Dhahran, Saudi Arabia. He
was a member of KFUPM's faculty from 1991 to 2014. Dr Alsuwaiyel
taught both undergraduate and graduate courses on design and analysis of algorithms, computer networks, discrete structures, theory of computing, automata and formal languages, foundations of computer science,
mathematical logic, design and theory of algorithms, combinatorial algorithms optimization, parallel algorithms, theory of automata and formal
languages, computational complexity, and computational geometry. He has
many publications in the design and analysis of algorithms. He holds a B.S.
in Systems Engineering from KFUPM, an M.S. in Computer Science from
University of Colorado at Boulder, USA, and a Ph.D. in Computer Science
from Northwestern University, Illinois, USA.

Acknowledgments

The author is grateful to King Fahd University of Petroleum & Minerals (KFUPM) for their support and providing facilities for the preparation of the manuscript. This book writing project has been funded by KFUPM under Project ics/algorithm/182. The author would like to thank those who have critically read various portions of the manuscript and offered many helpful suggestions, including the students of the undergraduate and graduate Algorithms courses at KFUPM. Special thanks go to S. Albassam, H. Almuallim and S. Ghanta for their valuable comments. Also, thanks go to W. Al-Khatib, M. Almuhammadi and D.T. Lee for valuable discussions.

Contents

Preface   vii

About the Author   xi

Acknowledgments   xiii

Part 1   Basic Concepts and Introduction to Algorithms   1

Chapter 1   Basic Concepts in Algorithmic Analysis   3

1.1	Introduction	3
1.2	Historical Background	4
1.3	Binary Search	6
1.3.1	Analysis of the binary search algorithm	8
1.4	Merging Two Sorted Lists	10
1.5	Selection Sort	12
1.6	Insertion Sort	13
1.7	Bottom-Up Merge Sorting	15
1.7.1	Analysis of bottom-up merge sorting	17
1.8	Time Complexity	19
1.8.1	Order of growth	19
1.8.2	The O-notation	23
1.8.3	The Ω-notation	24
1.8.4	The Θ-notation	26
1.8.5	Examples	27
1.8.6	Complexity classes and the o-notation	30

1.9   Space Complexity 31
1.10   Optimal Algorithms 32
1.11   How to Estimate the Running Time of
        an Algorithm 33
        1.11.1   Counting the number of iterations[c] 33
        1.11.2   Counting the frequency of basic
                 operations 39
        1.11.3   Using recurrence relations 43
1.12   Worst Case and Average Case Analysis 44
        1.12.1   Worst case analysis 45
        1.12.2   Average case analysis 47
1.13   Amortized Analysis 48
1.14   Input Size and Problem Instance 52
1.15   Divide-and-Conquer Recurrences 54
        1.15.1   Expanding the recurrence 54
        1.15.2   Substitution 58
        1.15.3   Change of variables 63
1.16   Practice Problems 66
1.17   Exercises 68
1.18   Bibliographic Notes 78

Chapter 2   Data Structures   **79**

2.1   Introduction 79
2.2   Linked Lists 79
        2.2.1   Stacks and queues 80
2.3   Graphs 80
        2.3.1   Representation of graphs 82
        2.3.2   Planar graphs 83
2.4   Trees 84
2.5   Rooted Trees 84
        2.5.1   Tree traversals 85
2.6   Binary Trees 85
        2.6.1   Some quantitative aspects of binary trees ... 87
        2.6.2   Binary search trees 87
2.7   Practice Problems 88
2.8   Exercises 89
2.9   Bibliographic Notes 91

Chapter 3   Heaps and the Disjoint Sets Data Structures   93

3.1   Introduction 93
3.2   Heaps 93
    3.2.1   Operations on heaps 95
        3.2.1.1   Sift-up 95
        3.2.1.2   Sift-down 96
        3.2.1.3   Insert 97
        3.2.1.4   Delete 98
        3.2.1.5   Delete-max 98
    3.2.2   Creating a heap 99
    3.2.3   Heapsort 102
    3.2.4   Min and max heaps 103
3.3   Disjoint Sets Data Structures 104
    3.3.1   The union by rank heuristic 105
    3.3.2   Path compression 107
    3.3.3   The union-find algorithms 108
    3.3.4   Analysis of the union-find algorithms 110
3.4   Practice Problems 112
3.5   Exercises 113
3.6   Bibliographic Notes 117

Part 2   Techniques Based on Recursion   119

Chapter 4   Induction   121

4.1   Introduction 121
4.2   Finding the Majority Element 122
4.3   Integer Exponentiation 123
4.4   Evaluating Polynomials (Horner's Rule) 124
4.5   Radix Sort 125
4.6   Generating Subsets of a Set 127
    4.6.1   The first algorithm 128
    4.6.2   The second algorithm 129
    4.6.3   Iterative algorithm 131
4.7   Generating Permutations 133
    4.7.1   The first algorithm 133
    4.7.2   The second algorithm 135
    4.7.3   Iterative algorithm 137

4.8   Practice Problems   139
4.9   Exercises   140
4.10   Bibliographic Notes   143

Chapter 5   Divide and Conquer   **145**

5.1   Introduction   145
5.2   Binary Search   147
        5.2.1   Analysis of the recursive binary search
                algorithm   147
5.3   Mergesort   149
        5.3.1   How the algorithm works   150
        5.3.2   Analysis of the mergesort algorithm   152
5.4   The Divide-and-Conquer Paradigm   154
5.5   Selection: Finding the Median and the kth Smallest
        Element   156
        5.5.1   Analysis of the selection algorithm   159
5.6   Quicksort   161
        5.6.1   A partitioning algorithm   162
        5.6.2   The sorting algorithm   164
        5.6.3   Analysis of the quicksort algorithm   166
                5.6.3.1   The worst case behavior   167
                5.6.3.2   The average case behavior   168
        5.6.4   Comparison of sorting algorithms   170
5.7   Quickselect   171
5.8   Multiselection   172
5.9   Multiplication of Large Integers   174
5.10   Matrix Multiplication   175
        5.10.1 The traditional algorithm   176
        5.10.2 Strassen's algorithm   176
                5.10.2.1 Time complexity   177
        5.10.3 Comparison of the two algorithms   177
5.11   The Closest Pair Problem   178
        5.11.1 Time complexity   181
5.12   A Dominance Problem   183
5.13   Practice Problems   184
5.14   Exercises   186
5.15   Bibliographic Notes   192

Chapter 6　Dynamic Programming　　　　　**193**

　6.1　Introduction 193
　6.2　The Longest Common Subsequence Problem 195
　　　6.2.1　The algorithm 196
　6.3　Matrix Chain Multiplication 198
　　　6.3.1　The dynamic programming algorithm 201
　6.4　The Dynamic Programming Paradigm 204
　6.5　The All-Pairs Shortest Path Problem 205
　　　6.5.1　The algorithm 205
　6.6　The Knapsack Problem 207
　　　6.6.1　The algorithm 208
　6.7　Practice Problems 210
　6.8　Exercises 211
　6.9　Bibliographic Notes 215

Part 3　First-Cut Techniques　　　　　**217**

Chapter 7　The Greedy Approach　　　　　**219**

　7.1　Introduction 219
　7.2　The Shortest Path Problem 221
　　　7.2.1　Implementation of the shortest path
　　　　　　algorithm 223
　　　7.2.2　Correctness 224
　　　7.2.3　Time complexity 224
　　　7.2.4　Improving the time bound 225
　7.3　Minimum Cost Spanning Trees
　　　(Kruskal's Algorithm) 227
　　　7.3.1　Implementation of Kruskal's algorithm 229
　　　7.3.2　Correctness 229
　　　7.3.3　Time complexity 230
　7.4　Minimum Cost Spanning Trees (Prim's Algorithm) . . . 231
　　　7.4.1　Implementation of Prim's algorithm 232
　　　7.4.2　Correctness 234
　　　7.4.3　Time complexity 234
　　　7.4.4　Improving the time bound 235

7.5   File Compression 237

      7.5.1   The algorithm 238

      7.5.2   Time complexity 239

7.6   Practice Problems 239

7.7   Exercises 240

7.8   Bibliographic Notes 244

Chapter 8   Graph Traversal   245

8.1   Introduction 245

8.2   Depth-First Search 245

      8.2.1   The case of undirected graphs 247

      8.2.2   The case of directed graphs 247

      8.2.3   Time complexity of depth-first search 249

8.3   Applications of Depth-First Search 250

      8.3.1   Graph acyclicity 250

      8.3.2   Topological sorting 250

      8.3.3   Finding articulation points in a graph 251

      8.3.4   Strongly connected components 254

8.4   Breadth-First Search 255

      8.4.1   Time complexity 257

8.5   Applications of Breadth-First Search 257

8.6   Practice Problems 258

8.7   Exercises 259

8.8   Bibliographic Notes 261

Part 4   Complexity of Problems   263

Chapter 9   NP-Complete Problems   265

9.1   Introduction 265

9.2   The Class P 268

9.3   The Class NP 269

9.4   NP-Complete Problems 271

      9.4.1   The satisfiability problem 272

      9.4.2   Proving NP-completeness 273

      9.4.3   3-Satisfiability 275

9.4.4   Vertex cover, independent set and clique
problems 276

9.4.5   More NP-complete problems 279

9.5   The Class co-NP 280

9.6   The Relationships between the Three Classes 282

9.7   Practice Problems 283

9.8   Exercises 284

9.9   Bibliographic Notes 285

Chapter 10   Introduction to Computational Complexity   287

10.1   Introduction 287

10.2   Model of Computation: The Turing Machine 287

10.3 k-Tape Turing Machines and Time Complexity 288

10.4   Off-line Turing Machines and Space Complexity 291

10.5   Tape Compression and Linear Speed-up 294

10.6   Relationships between Complexity Classes 295

10.6.1   Space and time hierarchy theorems 298

10.6.2   Padding arguments 300

10.7   Reductions 302

10.8   Completeness 306

10.8.1   NLOGSPACE-complete problems 307

10.8.2   PSPACE-complete problems 308

10.8.3   P-complete problems 309

10.8.4   Some conclusions of completeness 311

10.9   The Polynomial Time Hierarchy 313

10.10   Practice Problems 317

10.11   Exercises 318

10.12   Bibliographic Notes 321

Chapter 11   Lower Bounds   323

11.1   Introduction 323

11.2   Trivial Lower Bounds 323

11.3   The Decision Tree Model 324

11.3.1   The search problem 324

11.3.2   The sorting problem 325

11.3.3   Finding the maximum 327

11.3.4   Finding the largest and second largest
            elements 327
            11.3.4.1   Lower bound 327
            11.3.4.2   Optimal algorithm 328
11.4   The Algebraic Decision Tree Model 329
            11.4.1   The element uniqueness problem 331
            11.4.2   The set equality problem 332
            11.4.3   The set inclusion problem 332
            11.4.4   The set disjointness problem 333
11.5   Linear Time Reductions 333
            11.5.1   The convex hull problem 334
            11.5.2   The closest pair problem 335
            11.5.3   The Euclidean minimum spanning
                        tree problem 335
            11.5.4   The diameter of a point set 336
11.6   Practice Problems 337
11.7   Exercises 337
11.8   Bibliographic Notes 339

Part 5   Coping with Hardness   341

Chapter 12   Backtracking   345

12.1   Introduction 345
12.2   The 3-Coloring Problem 345
            12.2.1   The algorithm 347
12.3   The 8-Queens Problem 349
            12.3.1   The algorithm 350
12.4   The General Backtracking Method 352
12.5   Branch and Bound 354
12.6   Practice Problems 359
12.7   Exercises 360
12.8   Bibliographic Notes 362

Chapter 13   Randomized Algorithms   363

13.1   Introduction 363
13.2   Las Vegas and Monte Carlo Algorithms 364

13.3   Two Simple Examples 365
        13.3.1   A Monte Carlo algorithm 365
        13.3.2   A Las Vegas algorithm 366
13.4   Randomized Quicksort 366
        13.4.1   Expected running time of randomized
                 quicksort 368
13.5   Randomized Quickselect 369
        13.5.1   Expected running time of randomized
                 quickselect 369
        13.5.2   The dice problem 372
        13.5.3   Application of the dice problem:
                 Quickselect 374
13.6   Occupancy Problems 375
        13.6.1   Number of balls in each bin 375
        13.6.2   Number of empty bins 376
        13.6.3   Balls falling into the same bin 377
        13.6.4   Filling all bins 378
13.7   Tail Bounds 379
        13.7.1   Markov inequality 379
        13.7.2   Chebyshev inequality 380
        13.7.3   Chernoff bounds 381
                 13.7.3.1   Lower tail 381
                 13.7.3.2   Upper tail 383
13.8   Application of Chernoff Bounds: Multiselection 384
        13.8.1   Analysis of the algorithm 387
13.9   Random Sampling 390
13.10   The Min-Cut Problem 393
13.11   Testing String Equality 395
13.12   Pattern Matching 397
13.13   Primality Testing 400
13.14   Practice Problems 405
13.15   Exercises 406
13.16   Bibliographic Notes 409

Chapter 14   Approximation Algorithms   411

14.1   Introduction 411
14.2   Basic Definitions 411

14.3   Difference Bounds   413
       14.3.1   Planar graph coloring   413
       14.3.2   Hardness result: The knapsack problem   413
14.4   Relative Performance Bounds   414
       14.4.1   The bin packing problem   415
       14.4.2   The Euclidean traveling salesman
                problem   417
       14.4.3   The vertex cover problem   419
       14.4.4   Hardness result: The traveling salesman
                problem   420
14.5   Polynomial Approximation Schemes   422
       14.5.1   The knapsack problem   422
14.6   Fully Polynomial Approximation Schemes   426
       14.6.1   The subset-sum problem   426
14.7   Practice Problems   429
14.8   Exercises   429
14.9   Bibliographic Notes   432

Part 6   Iterative Improvement for Domain-Specific Problems   433

Chapter 15   Network Flow   435

15.1   Introduction   435
15.2   Preliminaries   435
15.3   The Ford–Fulkerson Method   439
15.4   Maximum Capacity Augmentation   440
15.5   Shortest Path Augmentation   442
15.6   Dinic's Algorithm   445
15.7   The MPM Algorithm   448
15.8   Practice Problems   451
15.9   Exercises   451
15.10 Bibliographic Notes   453

Chapter 16   Matching   455

16.1   Introduction   455
16.2   Preliminaries   455

16.3 The Network Flow Method for Bipartite Graphs 458

16.4 The Hungarian Tree Method for Bipartite Graphs . . . 459

16.5 Maximum Matching in General Graphs 462

16.6 An $O(n^{2.5})$ Algorithm for Bipartite Graphs 468

16.7 Practice Problems 473

16.8 Exercises 474

16.9 Bibliographic Notes 476

Part 7 Techniques in Computational Geometry 479

Chapter 17 Geometric Sweeping 481

17.1 Introduction 481

17.2 A Simple Example: Computing the Maximal Points
of a Point Set 481

17.3 Geometric Preliminaries 483

17.4 Computing the Intersections of Line Segments 485

17.5 The Convex Hull Problem 489

17.6 Computing the Diameter of a Set of Points 492

17.7 Practice Problems 496

17.8 Exercises 497

17.9 Bibliographic Notes 499

Chapter 18 Voronoi Diagrams 501

18.1 Introduction 501

18.2 Nearest-Point Voronoi Diagram 501

    18.2.1 Delaunay triangulation 504

    18.2.2 Construction of the Voronoi diagram 506

18.3 Applications of the Voronoi Diagram 509

    18.3.1 Computing the convex hull 509

    18.3.2 All nearest neighbors 510

    18.3.3 The Euclidean minimum spanning tree 511

18.4 Farthest-Point Voronoi Diagram 512

    18.4.1 Construction of the farthest-point Voronoi dia-
gram 513

18.5 Applications of the Farthest-Point Voronoi Diagram . . 515

    18.5.1 All farthest neighbors 516

    18.5.2 Smallest enclosing circle 516

18.6　Practice Problems 517
18.7　Exercises 517
18.8　Bibliographic Notes 519

Part 8　Techniques in Parallel Algorithms　　521

Chapter 19　Parallel Algorithms　　523

19.1　Introduction 523
　　19.1.1　Classifications of parallel architectures 525
19.2　Shared-Memory Computers (PRAM) 525
　　19.2.1　The balanced tree method 526
　　19.2.2　Brent theorem 528
　　19.2.3　Parallel prefix 529
　　　　19.2.3.1　Array packing 531
　　　　19.2.3.2　Parallel quicksort 532
　　19.2.4　Parallel search 533
　　19.2.5　Pointer jumping 535
　　19.2.6　Merging by ranking 536
　　　　19.2.6.1　Computing ranks 536
　　　　19.2.6.2　Merging 540
　　　　19.2.6.3　Parallel bottom-up merge
　　　　　　　　　sorting 540
　　19.2.7　The zero-one principle 541
　　19.2.8　Odd–even merging 542
　　19.2.9　Bitonic merging and sorting 546
　　　　19.2.9.1　Bitonic sorting 551
　　19.2.10　Pipelined merge sort 553
　　　　19.2.10.1　The algorithm 555
　　　　19.2.10.2　Maintaining ranks 557
　　　　19.2.10.3　Analysis of the algorithm 559
　　19.2.11　Selection 560
　　19.2.12　Multiselection 563
　　19.2.13　Matrix multiplication 567
　　19.2.14　Transitive closure 568
　　19.2.15　Shortest paths 569
　　19.2.16　Computing the convex hull of a set
　　　　　　of points 569

19.3 Interconnection-Network Computers 574
19.4 The Hypercube 576
 19.4.1 The butterfly 577
 19.4.2 Embeddings of the hypercube 580
  19.4.2.1 Gray codes 581
  19.4.2.2 Embedding of a linear array into
     the hypercube 582
  19.4.2.3 Embedding of a mesh into
     the hypercube 582
  19.4.2.4 Embedding of a binary tree into
     the hypercube 583
 19.4.3 Broadcasting on the hypercube 584
 19.4.4 Permutation routing in the hypercube 584
  19.4.4.1 The greedy algorithm 585
  19.4.4.2 The randomized algorithm 585
 19.4.5 Permutation routing in the butterfly 588
 19.4.6 Computing parallel prefix on the
     hypercube 590
 19.4.7 Hyperquicksort 591
 19.4.8 Selection on the hypercube 593
 19.4.9 Multiselection on the hypercube 594
 19.4.10 Computing parallel prefix on the
     butterfly 597
19.5 The Linear Array and the Mesh 598
 19.5.1 Broadcasting in the linear array and the mesh 599
 19.5.2 Computing parallel prefix on
     the mesh 600
 19.5.3 Odd–even transposition sort 601
 19.5.4 Shearsort 602
 19.5.5 Odd–even merging and sorting on the mesh . . 604
 19.5.6 Computing the convex hull of a set of points
     on the mesh 606
  19.5.6.1 The first algorithm 607
  19.5.6.2 The second algorithm 608

19.5.7   Three-dimensional mesh   612
          19.5.7.1   Sorting on three-dimensional
                      meshes   613
19.5.8   Fast Fourier transform   616
          19.5.8.1   Implementation on the
                      butterfly   618
          19.5.8.2   Iterative FFT on the butterfly . . .   620
          19.5.8.3   The inverse Fourier transform . . .   622
          19.5.8.4   Applications of FFT   624
          19.5.8.5   Product of polynomials   624
          19.5.8.6   Computing the convolution of
                      two vectors   626
19.6   Systolic Computation   627
        19.6.1   An on-chip bubble sorter   627
19.7   Practice Problems   631
19.8   Exercises   634
19.9   Bibliographic Notes   640
19.10   Solutions   641

Appendix A.   Mathematical Preliminaries   661

A.1   Sets, Relations and Functions   661
       A.1.1   Sets   662
       A.1.2   Relations   663
                A.1.2.1   Equivalence relations   664
       A.1.3   Functions   664
A.2   Proof Methods   665
       A.2.1   Notation   665
       A.2.2   Direct proof   666
       A.2.3   Indirect proof   666
       A.2.4   Proof by contradiction   666
       A.2.5   Proof by counterexample   667
       A.2.6   Mathematical induction   668
A.3   Logarithms   670
A.4   Floor and Ceiling Functions   671
A.5   Factorial and Binomial Coefficients   672
       A.5.1   Factorials   672
       A.5.2   Binomial coefficients   673

A.6   The Pigeonhole Principle 675
A.7   Summations 676
         A.7.1   Approximation of summations
                   by integration 679
A.8   Recurrence Relations 682
         A.8.1   Solution of linear homogeneous
                   recurrences 683
         A.8.2   Solution of inhomogeneous recurrences 685
A.9   Divide-and-Conquer Recurrences 688
A.10   Exercises 688

Appendix B.   Introduction to Discrete Probability   691

B.1   Definitions 691
B.2   Conditional Probability and Independence 691
         B.2.1   Multiplication rule for conditional
                   probability 693
B.3   Random Variables and Expectation 693
B.4   Discrete Probability Distributions 694
         B.4.1   Uniform distribution 694
         B.4.2   Bernoulli distribution 695
         B.4.3   Binomial distribution . . . . ▲. . . 695
         B.4.4   Geometric distribution 696
         B.4.5   Poisson distribution 696

Bibliography   697

Index   709

PART 1

Basic Concepts and Introduction to Algorithms

This part of the book is concerned with the study of the basic tools and prerequisites for the design and analysis of algorithms.

Chapter 1 is intended to set the stage for the rest of the book. In this chapter, we will discuss examples of simple algorithms for solving some of the fundamental problems encountered in almost all applications of computer science. These problems include searching, merging and sorting. Using these example algorithms as a reference, we then investigate the mathematical aspects underlying the analysis of algorithms. Specifically, we will study in detail the analysis of the running time and space required by a given algorithm.

Chapter 2 reviews some of the basic data structures usually employed in the design of algorithms. This chapter is not intended to be comprehensive and detailed. For a more thorough treatment, the reader is referred to standard books on data structures.

In Chapter 3, we investigate in more detail two fundamental data structures that are used for maintaining priority queues and disjoint sets. These two data structures, namely the heap and disjoint set data structures, are used as a building block in the design of many efficient algorithms, especially graph algorithms. In this book, heaps will be used in the design of an efficient sorting algorithm, namely HEAPSORT. We will also make use of heaps in Chapter 7 for designing efficient algorithms for the single-source shortest path problem, the problem of computing minimum cost spanning trees and the problem of finding variable-length code for data compression. Heaps are also used in branch-and-bound algorithms, which is the subject of Sec. 12.5. The disjoint set data structure will be used in Sec. 7.3 in Algorithm KRUSKAL for finding a minimum cost spanning tree of an undirected graph. Both data structures are used extensively in the literature for the design of more complex algorithms.

Chapter 1

Basic Concepts in Algorithmic Analysis

1.1 Introduction

The most general intuitive idea of an *algorithm* is a procedure that consists of a finite set of instructions which, given an *input*, enables us to obtain an *output* if such an output exists or else obtain nothing at all if there is no output for that particular input through a systematic execution of the instructions. The set of possible inputs consists of all inputs to which the algorithm gives an output. If there is an output for a particular input, then we say that the algorithm can be *applied* to this input and *process* it to give the corresponding output. We require that an algorithm halts on every input, which implies that each instruction requires a finite amount of time, and each input has a finite length. We also require that the output of a legal input to be unique, that is, the algorithm is deterministic in the sense that the same set of instructions is executed when the algorithm is initiated on a particular input more than once. In Chapter 13, we will relax this condition when we study randomized algorithms.

The design and analysis of algorithms are of fundamental importance in the field of computer science. As Donald E. Knuth stated "Computer science is the study of algorithms". This should not be surprising, as every area in computer science depends heavily on the design of efficient algorithms. As simple examples, compilers and operating systems are nothing but direct implementations of special-purpose algorithms.

3

The objective of this chapter is twofold. First, it introduces some simple algorithms, particularly related to searching and sorting. Second, it covers the basic concepts used in the design and analysis of algorithms. We will cover in depth the notion of "running time" of an algorithm, as it is of fundamental importance to the design of efficient algorithms. After all, time is the most precious measure of an algorithm's efficiency. We will also discuss the other important resource measure, namely the space required by an algorithm.

Although simple, the algorithms presented will serve as the basis for many of the examples in illustrating several algorithmic concepts. It is instructive to start with simple and useful algorithms that are used as building blocks in more complex algorithms.

1.2   Historical Background

The question of whether a problem can be solved using an *effective procedure*, which is equivalent to the contemporary notion of the algorithm, received a lot of attention in the first part of the 20th century, especially in the 1930s. The focus in that period was on classifying problems as being solvable using an effective procedure or not. For this purpose, the need arose for a model of computation by the help of which a problem can be classified as solvable if it is possible to construct an algorithm to solve that problem using that model. Some of these models are the recursive functions of Gödel, λ-calculus of Church, Post machines of Post and the Turing machines of Turing. The RAM model of computation was introduced as a theoretical counterpart of existing computing machines. By *Church Thesis*, all these models have the same power, in the sense that if a problem is solvable on one of them, then it is solvable on all others.

Surprisingly, it turns out that "almost all" problems are unsolvable. This can be justified easily as follows. Since each algorithm can be thought of as a function whose domain is the set of nonnegative integers and whose range is the set of real numbers, the set of functions to be computed is uncountable. Since any algorithm, or more specifically a program, can be encoded as a binary string, which corresponds to a unique positive integer, the number of functions that can be computed is countable. So, informally, the number of solvable problems is equinumerous with the set of integers (which is countable), while the number of unsolvable problems is equinumerous with the set of real numbers (which is uncountable). As a simple example, no algorithm can be constructed to decide whether seven consecutive 1's occur in the decimal expansion of π. This follows from the definition of an algorithm, which stipulates that the amount of time an algorithm is allowed to run must be finite. Another example is the problem of deciding whether a given equation involving a polynomial with n variables $x_1, x_2, \ldots, x_n$ has integer solutions. This problem is unsolvable, no matter how powerful the computing machine used is. That field which is concerned with decidability and solvability of problems is referred to as *computability theory* or *theory of computation*, although some computer scientists advocate the inclusion of the current field of algorithms as part of this discipline.

After the advent of digital computers, the need arose for investigating those solvable problems. In the beginning, one was content with a simple program that solves a particular problem without worrying about the amount of resources, in particular time, that this program requires. Then, the need for efficient programs that use as few resources as possible evolved as a result of the limited resources available and the need to develop complex algorithms. This led to the evolution of a new area in computing, namely *computational complexity*. In this area, a problem that is classified as solvable is studied in terms of its efficiency, that is, the time and space needed to solve that problem. Later on, other resources were introduced, e.g., communication cost and the number of processors if the problem is analyzed using a parallel model of computation.

Unfortunately, some of the conclusions of this study turned out to be negative: There are many *natural* problems that are *practically* unsolvable due to the need for huge amount of resources, and in particular time. On the other hand, efficient algorithms have been devised to solve many problems. Not only that; it was also proven that those algorithms are optimal in the sense that if any new algorithm to solve the same problem is discovered, then the gain in terms of efficiency is virtually minimal. For example, the problem of sorting a set of elements has been studied extensively; and as a result, several efficient algorithms to solve this problem have been devised, and it was proven that these algorithms are optimal in the sense that no substantially better algorithm can ever be devised in the future.

1.3 Binary Search

Henceforth, in the context of searching and sorting problems, we will assume that the elements are drawn from a linearly ordered set, for example, the set of integers. This will also be the case for similar problems, like finding the median, the kth smallest element, and so forth. Let $A[1..n]$ be a sequence of n elements. Consider the problem of determining whether a given element x is in A. This problem can be rephrased as follows. Find an index $j, 1 \leq j \leq n$, such that $x = A[j]$ if x is in A, and $j = 0$ otherwise. A straightforward approach is to scan the entries in A and compare each entry with x. If after j comparisons, $1 \leq j \leq n$, the search is *successful*, i.e., $x = A[j]$, j is returned; otherwise, a value of 0 is returned indicating an *unsuccessful* search. This method is referred to as *sequential search*. It is also called *linear search*, as the maximum number of element comparisons grows linearly with the size of the sequence. The algorithm is shown as Algorithm LINEARSEARCH.

Algorithm 1.1 LINEARSEARCH
Input: An array $A[1..n]$ of n elements and an element x.
Output: j if $x = A[j], 1 \leq j \leq n$, and 0 otherwise.

1. $j \leftarrow 1$
2. **while** $(j < n)$ **and** $(x \neq A[j])$
3. $j \leftarrow j + 1$
4. **end while**
5. **if** $x = A[j]$ **then return** j **else return** 0

Intuitively, scanning all entries of A is inevitable if no more information about the ordering of the elements in A is given. If we are also given that the elements in A are sorted, say in nondecreasing order, then there is a much more efficient algorithm. The following example illustrates this efficient search method.

Example 1.1   Consider searching the array

$$A[1..14] = \boxed{1\,|\,4\,|\,5\,|\,7\,|\,8\,|\,9\,|\,10\,|\,12\,|\,15\,|\,22\,|\,23\,|\,27\,|\,32\,|\,35}.$$

In this instance, we want to search for element $x = 22$. First, we compare x with the middle element $A[\lfloor (1 + 14)/2 \rfloor] = A[7] = 10$. Since $22 > A[7]$, and since it is known that $A[i] \leq A[i+1], 1 \leq i < 14$, x cannot be in $A[1..7]$, and therefore this portion of the array can be discarded. So, we are left with the subarray

$$A[8..14] = \boxed{12\,|\,15\,|\,22\,|\,23\,|\,27\,|\,32\,|\,35}.$$

Next, we compare x with the middle of the remaining elements $A[\lfloor(8+14)/2\rfloor] = A[11] = 23$. Since $22 < A[11]$, and since $A[i] \leq A[i+1], 11 \leq i < 14$, x cannot be in $A[11..14]$, and therefore this portion of the array can also be discarded. Thus, the remaining portion of the array to be searched is now reduced to

$$A[8..10] = \boxed{12\,|\,15\,|\,22}.$$

Repeating this procedure, we discard $A[8..9]$, which leaves only one entry in the array to be searched, that is, $A[10] = 22$. Finally, we find that $x = A[10]$, and the search is successfully completed.

In general, let $A[low..high]$ be a nonempty array of elements sorted in nondecreasing order. Let $A[mid]$ be the middle element, and suppose that $x > A[mid]$. We observe that if x is in A, then it must be one of the elements $A[mid+1], A[mid+2], \ldots, A[high]$. It follows that we only need to search for x in $A[mid+1..high]$. In other words, the entries in $A[low..mid]$ are discarded in subsequent comparisons since, by assumption, A is sorted in nondecreasing order, which implies that x cannot be in this half of the array. Similarly, if $x < A[mid]$, then we only need to search for x in $A[low..mid-1]$. This results in an efficient strategy which, because of its repetitive halving, is referred to as *binary search*. Algorithm BINARYSEARCH gives a more formal description of this method.

Algorithm 1.2 BINARYSEARCH
Input: An array $A[1..n]$ of n elements sorted in nondecreasing order and an element x.
Output: j if $x = A[j], 1 \leq j \leq n$, and 0 otherwise.

1. $low \leftarrow 1$; $high \leftarrow n$; $j \leftarrow 0$
2. **while** $(low \leq high)$ **and** $(j = 0)$
3. $mid \leftarrow \lfloor(low + high)/2\rfloor$
4.   **if** $x = A[mid]$ **then** $j \leftarrow mid$
5.   **else if** $x < A[mid]$ **then** $high \leftarrow mid - 1$
6.   **else** $low \leftarrow mid + 1$
7. **end while**
8. **return** j

1.3.1 *Analysis of the binary search algorithm*

Henceforth, we will assume that each three-way comparison (if-then-else) counts as one comparison. Obviously, the minimum number of comparisons is 1, and it is achievable when the element being searched for, x, is in the middle position of the array. To find the maximum number of comparisons, let us first consider applying binary search on the array $\boxed{2\ \vert\ 3\ \vert\ 5\ \vert\ 8}$. If we search for 2 or 5, we need two comparisons, whereas searching for 8 costs three comparisons. Now, in the case of unsuccessful search, it is easy to see that searching for elements such as 1, 4, 7 or 9 takes 2, 2, 3 and 3 comparisons, respectively. It is not hard to see that, in general, the algorithm always performs the maximum number of comparisons whenever x is greater than or equal to the maximum element in the array. In this example, searching for any element greater than or equal to 8 costs three comparisons. Thus, to find the maximum number of comparisons, we may assume without loss of generality that x is greater than or equal to $A[n]$.

Example 1.2   Suppose that we want to search for $x = 35$ or $x = 100$ in

$$A[1..14] = \boxed{1\ \vert\ 4\ \vert\ 5\ \vert\ 7\ \vert\ 8\ \vert\ 9\ \vert\ 10\ \vert\ 12\ \vert\ 15\ \vert\ 22\ \vert\ 23\ \vert\ 27\ \vert\ 32\ \vert\ 35}.$$

In each iteration of the algorithm, the bottom half of the array is discarded until there is only one element:

$$\boxed{12\ \vert\ 15\ \vert\ 22\ \vert\ 23\ \vert\ 27\ \vert\ 32\ \vert\ 35} \rightarrow \boxed{27\ \vert\ 32\ \vert\ 35} \rightarrow \boxed{35}.$$

Therefore, to compute the *maximum* number of element comparisons performed by Algorithm BINARYSEARCH, we may assume that x is greater than or equal to all elements in the array to be searched. To compute the number of remaining elements in $A[1..n]$ in the second iteration, there are two cases to consider according to whether n is even or odd. If n is even, then the number of entries in $A[mid + 1..n]$ is $n/2$; otherwise, it is $(n-1)/2$. Thus, in both cases, the number of elements in $A[mid + 1..n]$ is exactly $\lfloor n/2 \rfloor$.

Similarly, the number of remaining elements to be searched in the third iteration is $\lfloor \lfloor n/2 \rfloor /2 \rfloor = \lfloor n/4 \rfloor$ (see Eq. (A.3) on page 672).

In general, in the jth pass through the while loop, the number of remaining elements is $\lfloor n/2^{j-1} \rfloor$. In the last iteration, either x is found or the size of the subsequence being searched reaches 1, whichever occurs first. As a result, the maximum number of iterations needed to search for x is that value of j satisfying the condition

$$\lfloor n/2^{j-1} \rfloor = 1.$$

By the definition of the floor function, this happens exactly when

$$1 \leq n/2^{j-1} < 2,$$

or

$$2^{j-1} \leq n < 2^j,$$

or

$$j - 1 \leq \log n < j.\text{[a]}$$

Since j is integer, we conclude that

$$j = \lfloor \log n \rfloor + 1.$$

Alternatively, the performance of the binary search algorithm can be described in terms of a *decision tree*, which is a binary tree that exhibits the behavior of the algorithm. Figure 1.1 shows the decision tree corresponding to the array given in Example 1.1. The darkened nodes are those compared against x in Example 1.1.

Note that the decision tree is a function of the *number* of the elements in the array only. Figure 1.2 shows two decision trees corresponding to

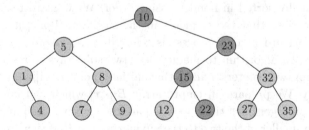

Fig. 1.1.   A decision tree that shows the behavior of binary search.

---

[a]Unless otherwise stated, all logarithms in this book are to the base 2. The natural logarithm of x will be denoted by $\ln x$.

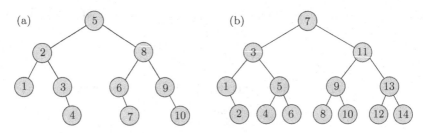

Fig. 1.2.   Two decision trees corresponding to two arrays of sizes 10 and 14.

two arrays of sizes 10 and 14, respectively. As implied by the two figures, the maximum number of comparisons in both trees is 4. In general, the maximum number of comparisons is one plus the height of the corresponding decision tree (see Sec. 2.5 for the definition of height). It can be shown that the height of such a tree is $\lfloor \log n \rfloor$ (Exercise 1.4). Hence, we conclude that the maximum number of comparisons is $\lfloor \log n \rfloor + 1$. We have in effect given two proofs of the following theorem:

Theorem 1.1   *The number of comparisons performed by Algorithm* BINARYSEARCH *on a sorted array of size n is at most $\lfloor \log n \rfloor + 1$.*

1.4   Merging Two Sorted Lists

Suppose we have an array $A[1..m]$ and three indices p, q and r, with $1 \leq p \leq q < r \leq m$, such that both the subarrays $A[p..q]$ and $A[q + 1..r]$ are individually sorted in nondecreasing order. We want to rearrange the elements in A so that the elements in the subarray $A[p..r]$ are sorted in nondecreasing order. This process is referred to as *merging* $A[p..q]$ with $A[q + 1..r]$. An algorithm to merge these two subarrays works as follows. We maintain two pointers s and t that initially point to $A[p]$ and $A[q + 1]$, respectively. We prepare an empty array $B[p..r]$ which will be used as a temporary storage. Each time, we compare the elements $A[s]$ and $A[t]$ and append the smaller of the two to the auxiliary array B; if they are equal we will choose to append $A[s]$. Next, we update the pointers: If $A[s] \leq A[t]$, then we increment s; otherwise, we increment t. This process ends when $s = q + 1$ or $t = r + 1$. In the first case, we append the remaining elements $A[t..r]$ to B, and in the second case, we append $A[s..q]$ to B. Finally, the array $B[p..r]$ is copied back to $A[p..r]$. This procedure is given in Algorithm MERGE.

Algorithm 1.3 MERGE
Input: An array $A[1..m]$ of elements and three indices p, q and r, with
$\qquad 1 \leq p \leq q < r \leq m$, such that both the subarrays $A[p..q]$ and
$\qquad A[q+1..r]$ are sorted individually in nondecreasing order.
Output: $A[p..r]$ contains the result of merging the two subarrays $A[p..q]$ and
$\qquad A[q+1..r]$.

1. **comment:** $B[p..r]$ *is an auxiliary array.*
2. $s \leftarrow p; \quad t \leftarrow q+1; \quad k \leftarrow p$
3. **while** $s \leq q$ **and** $t \leq r$
4. $\quad$ **if** $A[s] \leq A[t]$ **then**
5. $\qquad B[k] \leftarrow A[s]$
6. $\qquad s \leftarrow s+1$
7. $\quad$ **else**
8. $\qquad B[k] \leftarrow A[t]$
9. $\qquad t \leftarrow t+1$
10. $\quad$ **end if**
11. $\qquad k \leftarrow k+1$
12. **end while**
13. **if** $s = q+1$ **then** $B[k..r] \leftarrow A[t..r]$
14. **else** $B[k..r] \leftarrow A[s..q]$
15. **end if**
16. $A[p..r] \leftarrow B[p..r]$

Let n denote the size of the array $A[p..r]$ in the input to Algorithm MERGE, i.e., $n = r - p + 1$. We want to find the number of comparisons that are needed to rearrange the entries of $A[p..r]$. It should be emphasized that from now on when we talk about the number of comparisons performed by an algorithm, we mean *element comparisons*, i.e., the comparisons involving objects in the input data. Thus, all other comparisons, e.g., those needed for the implementation of the **while** loop, will be excluded.

Let the two subarrays be of sizes n_1 and n_2, where $n_1 + n_2 = n$. The least number of comparisons happens if each entry in the smaller subarray is less than all entries in the larger subarray. For example, to merge the two subarrays

$$\boxed{2} \ \boxed{3} \ \boxed{6} \text{ and } \boxed{7} \ \boxed{11} \ \boxed{13} \ \boxed{45} \ \boxed{57},$$

the algorithm performs only three comparisons. On the other hand, the number of comparisons may be as high as $n - 1$. For example, to merge the two subarrays

$$\boxed{2} \; \boxed{3} \; \boxed{66} \text{ and } \boxed{7} \; \boxed{11} \; \boxed{13} \; \boxed{45} \; \boxed{57},$$

seven comparisons are needed. It follows that the number of comparisons done by Algorithm MERGE is at least n_1 and at most $n - 1$.

Observation 1.1 The number of element comparisons performed by Algorithm MERGE to merge two nonempty arrays of sizes n_1 and n_2, where $n_1 \leq n_2$, into one sorted array of size $n = n_1 + n_2$ is between n_1 and $n - 1$. In particular, if the two array sizes are $\lfloor n/2 \rfloor$ and $\lceil n/2 \rceil$, the number of comparisons needed is between $\lfloor n/2 \rfloor$ and $n - 1$.

How about the number of *element assignments* (again here, we mean assignments involving input data)? At first glance, one may start by looking at the **while** loop, the **if** statements, etc. in order to find out how the algorithm works and then compute the number of element assignments. However, it is easy to see that each entry of array B is assigned exactly once. Similarly, each entry of array A is assigned exactly once, when copying B back into A. As a result, we have the following observation:

Observation 1.2 The number of element assignments performed by Algorithm MERGE to merge two arrays into one sorted array of size n is exactly $2n$.

1.5 Selection Sort

Let $A[1..n]$ be an array of n elements. A simple and straightforward algorithm to sort the entries in A works as follows. First, we find the minimum element and store it in $A[1]$. Next, we find the minimum of the remaining $n - 1$ elements and store it in $A[2]$. We continue this way until the second largest element is stored in $A[n-1]$. This method is described in Algorithm SELECTIONSORT.

It is easy to see that the number of element comparisons performed by the algorithm is exactly

$$\sum_{i=1}^{n-1}(n - i) = (n - 1) + (n - 2) + \cdots + 1 = \sum_{i=1}^{n-1} i = \frac{n(n - 1)}{2}.$$

Algorithm 1.4 SELECTIONSORT
Input: An array $A[1..n]$ of n elements.

Output: $A[1..n]$ sorted in nondecreasing order.

1. **for** $i \leftarrow 1$ **to** $n - 1$
2. $k \leftarrow i$
3.   **for** $j \leftarrow i + 1$ **to** n {*Find the ith smallest element.*}
4.   **if** $A[j] < A[k]$ **then** $k \leftarrow j$
5.   **end for**
6.   **if** $k \neq i$ **then** interchange $A[i]$ and $A[k]$
7. **end for**

It is also easy to see that the number of element interchanges is between 0 and $n - 1$. Since each interchange requires three element assignments, the number of element assignments is between 0 and $3(n - 1)$.

Observation 1.3   The number of element comparisons performed by Algorithm SELECTIONSORT is $n(n - 1)/2$. The number of element assignments is between 0 and $3(n - 1)$.

1.6   Insertion Sort

As stated in Observation 1.3 above, the number of comparisons performed by Algorithm SELECTIONSORT is *exactly* $n(n - 1)/2$ regardless of how the elements of the input array are ordered. Another sorting method in which the number of comparisons depends on the order of the input elements is the so-called INSERTIONSORT. This algorithm, which is shown below, works as follows. We begin with the subarray of size 1, $A[1]$, which is already sorted. Next, $A[2]$ is inserted before or after $A[1]$ depending on whether it is smaller than $A[1]$ or not. Continuing this way, in the ith iteration, $A[i]$ is inserted in its proper position in the sorted subarray $A[1..i - 1]$. This is done by scanning the elements from index $i - 1$ down to 1, each time comparing $A[i]$ with the element at the current position. In each iteration of the scan, an element is shifted one position up to a higher index. This process of scanning, performing the comparison and shifting continues until an element less than or equal to $A[i]$ is found or when all the sorted sequence so far is exhausted. At this point, $A[i]$ is inserted in its proper position, and the process of inserting element $A[i]$ in its proper place is complete.

Algorithm 1.5 INSERTIONSORT
Input: An array $A[1..n]$ of n elements.

Output: $A[1..n]$ sorted in nondecreasing order.

1. **for** $i \leftarrow 2$ **to** n
2. $\quad x \leftarrow A[i]$
3. $\quad j \leftarrow i - 1$
4. $\quad$ **while** $(j > 0)$ **and** $(A[j] > x)$
5. $\quad\quad A[j + 1] \leftarrow A[j]$
6. $\quad\quad j \leftarrow j - 1$
7. $\quad$ **end while**
8. $\quad A[j + 1] \leftarrow x$
9. **end for**

Unlike Algorithm SELECTIONSORT, the number of element comparisons done by Algorithm INSERTIONSORT depends on the order of the input elements. It is easy to see that the number of element comparisons is minimum when the array is already sorted in nondecreasing order. In this case, the number of element comparisons is exactly $n - 1$, as each element $A[i]$, $2 \leq i \leq n$, is compared with $A[i - 1]$ only. On the other hand, the maximum number of element comparisons occurs if the array is already sorted in decreasing order and all elements are distinct. In this case, the number of element comparisons is

$$\sum_{i=2}^{n} i - 1 = \sum_{i=1}^{n-1} i = \frac{n(n - 1)}{2},$$

as each element $A[i]$, $2 \leq i \leq n$, is compared with each entry in the subarray $A[1..i - 1]$. This number coincides with that of Algorithm SELECTIONSORT.

As to the number of element assignments, notice that there is an element assignment after each element comparison in the **while** loop. Moreover, there are $n - 1$ element assignments of $A[i]$ to x in Step 2 of the algorithm. It follows that the number of element assignments is equal to the number of element comparisons plus $n - 1$.

Observation 1.4   The number of element comparisons performed by Algorithm INSERTIONSORT is between $n - 1$ and $n(n - 1)/2$. The number of

element assignments is equal to the number of element comparisons plus
$n - 1$.

Notice the correlation of element comparisons and assignments in Algorithm INSERTIONSORT. This is in contrast to the independence of the number of element comparisons in Algorithm SELECTIONSORT related to data arrangement.

1.7 Bottom-Up Merge Sorting

The two sorting methods discussed thus far are both inefficient in the sense that the number of operations required to sort n elements is proportional to n^2. In this section, we describe an efficient sorting algorithm that performs much fewer element comparisons. Suppose we have the following array of eight numbers that we wish to sort:

$$\boxed{9\ |\ 4\ |\ 5\ |\ 2\ |\ 1\ |\ 7\ |\ 4\ |\ 6}.$$

Consider the following method for sorting these numbers (see Fig. 1.3).

First, we divide the input elements into four pairs and merge each pair into one 2-element sorted sequence. Next, we merge each two consecutive 2-element sequences into one sorted sequence of size four. Finally, we merge the two resulting sequences into the final sorted sequence, as shown in the figure.

In general, let A be an array of n elements that is to be sorted. We first merge $\lfloor n/2 \rfloor$ consecutive pairs of elements to yield $\lfloor n/2 \rfloor$ sorted sequences

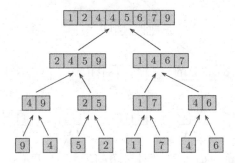

Fig. 1.3. Example of bottom-up merge sorting.

of size 2. If there is one remaining element, then it is passed to the next iteration. Next, we merge $\lfloor n/4 \rfloor$ pairs of consecutive 2-element sequences to yield $\lfloor n/4 \rfloor$ sorted sequences of size 4. If there are one or two remaining elements, then they are passed to the next iteration. If there are three elements left, then two (sorted) elements are merged with one element to form a 3-element sorted sequence. Continuing this way, in the jth iteration, we merge $\lfloor n/2^j \rfloor$ pairs of sorted sequences of size 2^{j-1} to yield $\lfloor n/2^j \rfloor$ sorted sequences of size 2^j. If there are k remaining elements, where $1 \leq k \leq 2^{j-1}$, then they are passed on to the next iteration. If there are k remaining elements, where $2^{j-1} < k < 2^j$, then these are merged to form a sorted sequence of size k.

Algorithm BOTTOMUPSORT implements this idea. The algorithm maintains the variable s which is the size of sequences to be merged. Initially, s is set to 1 and is doubled in each iteration of the outer **while** loop. $i + 1$, $i + s$ and $i + t$ define the boundaries of the two sequences to be merged. Step 8 is needed in the case when n is not a multiple of t. In this case, if the number of remaining elements, which is $n - i$, is greater than s, then one more merge is applied on a sequence of size s and the remaining elements.

Example 1.3   Figure 1.4 shows an example of the working of the algorithm when n is not a power of 2. The behavior of the algorithm can be described as follows.

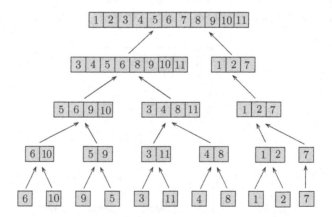

Fig. 1.4.   Example of bottom-up merge sorting when n is not a power of 2.

Algorithm 1.6 BOTTOMUPSORT

Input: An array $A[1..n]$ of n elements.

Output: $A[1..n]$ sorted in nondecreasing order.

1. $t \leftarrow 1$
2. **while** $t < n$
3. $s \leftarrow t; \quad t \leftarrow 2s; \quad i \leftarrow 0$
4.   **while** $i + t \leq n$
5.   MERGE($A, i+1, i+s, i+t$)
6. $i \leftarrow i + t$
7.   **end while**
8.   **if** $i + s < n$ **then** MERGE($A, i+1, i+s, n$)
9. **end while**

---

(1) In the first iteration, $s = 1$ and $t = 2$. Five pairs of 1-element sequences are merged to produce five 2-element sorted sequences. After the end of the inner **while** loop, $i + s = 10 + 1 \not< n = 11$, and hence no more merging takes place.

(2) In the second iteration, $s = 2$ and $t = 4$. Two pairs of 2-element sequences are merged to produce two 4-element sorted sequences. After the end of the inner **while** loop, $i + s = 8 + 2 < n = 11$, and hence one sequence of size $s = 2$ is merged with the one remaining element to produce a 3-element sorted sequence.

(3) In the third iteration, $s = 4$ and $t = 8$. One pair of 4-element sequences is merged to produce one 8-element sorted sequence. After the end of the inner **while** loop, $i + s = 8 + 4 \not< n = 11$, and hence no more merging takes place.

(4) In the fourth iteration, $s = 8$ and $t = 16$. Since $i + t = 0 + 16 \not\leq n = 11$, the inner **while** loop is not executed. Since $i + s = 0 + 8 < n = 11$, the condition of the **if** statement is satisfied, and hence one merge of 8-element and 3-element sorted sequences takes place to produce a sorted sequence of size 11.

(5) Since now $t = 16 > n$, the condition of the outer **while** loop is not satisfied, and consequently the algorithm terminates.

1.7.1 *Analysis of bottom-up merge sorting*

Now, we compute the number of element comparisons performed by the algorithm for the special case when n is a power of 2. In this case, the outer

while loop is executed $k = \log n$ times, once for each level in the sorting tree except the topmost level (see Fig. 1.3). Observe that since n is a power of 2, $i = n$ after the execution of the inner **while** loop, and hence Algorithm MERGE will never be invoked in Step 8. In the first iteration, there are $n/2$ comparisons. In the second iteration, $n/2$ sorted sequences of two elements each are merged in pairs. The number of comparisons needed to merge each pair is either 2 or 3. In the third iteration, $n/4$ sorted sequences of four elements each are merged in pairs. The number of comparisons needed to merge each pair is between 4 and 7. In general, in the jth iteration of the while loop, there are $n/2^j$ merge operations on two subarrays of size 2^{j-1} and it follows, by Observation 1.1, that the number of comparisons needed in the jth iteration is between $(n/2^j)2^{j-1}$ and $(n/2^j)(2^j - 1)$. Thus, if we let $k = \log n$, then the number of element comparisons is at least

$$\sum_{j=1}^{k} \left(\frac{n}{2^j}\right) 2^{j-1} = \sum_{j=1}^{k} \frac{n}{2} = \frac{kn}{2} = \frac{n \log n}{2}$$

and is at most

$$\sum_{j=1}^{k} \frac{n}{2^j} \left(2^j - 1\right) = \sum_{j=1}^{k} \left(n - \frac{n}{2^j}\right)$$

$$= kn - n \sum_{j=1}^{k} \frac{1}{2^j}$$

$$= kn - n \left(1 - \frac{1}{2^k}\right) \qquad \text{(Eq. (A.11), page 678)}$$

$$= kn - n \left(1 - \frac{1}{n}\right)$$

$$= n \log n - n + 1.$$

As for the number of element assignments, there are, by Observation 1.2 applied to each merge operation, $2n$ element assignments in each iteration of the outer **while** loop for a total of $2n \log n$. As a result, we have the following observation:

Observation 1.5   The total number of element comparisons performed by Algorithm BOTTOMUPSORT to sort an array of n elements, where n is a power of 2, is between $(n \log n)/2$ and $n \log n - n + 1$. The total number of element assignments done by the algorithm is exactly $2n \log n$.

1.8 Time Complexity

In this section, we study an essential component of algorithmic analysis, namely determining the running time of an algorithm. This theme belongs to an important area in the theory of computation, namely computational complexity, which evolved when the need for efficient algorithms arose in the 1960s and flourished in the 1970s and 1980s. The main objects of study in the field of computational complexity include the time and space needed by an algorithm in order to deliver its output when presented with legal input. We start this section with an example whose sole purpose is to reveal the importance of analyzing the running time of an algorithm.

Example 1.4 We have shown before that the maximum number of element comparisons performed by Algorithm BOTTOMUPSORT when n is a power of 2 is $n \log n - n + 1$, and the number of element comparisons performed by Algorithm SELECTIONSORT is $n(n-1)/2$. The elements may be integers, real numbers, strings of characters, etc. For concreteness, let us assume that each element comparison takes 10^{-6} seconds on some computing machine. Suppose we want to sort a small number of elements, say 128. Then, the time taken for comparing elements using Algorithm BOTTOMUP-SORT is at most $10^{-6}(128 \times 7 - 128 + 1) = 0.0008$ seconds. Using Algorithm SELECTIONSORT, the time becomes $10^{-6}(128 \times 127)/2 = 0.008$ seconds. In other words, Algorithm BOTTOMUPSORT uses one tenth of the time taken for comparison using Algorithm SELECTIONSORT. This, of course, is not noticeable, especially to a novice programmer whose main concern is to come up with a program that does the job. However, if we consider a larger number, say $n = 2^{20} = 1,048,576$ which is typical of many real-world problems, we find the following: The time taken for comparing elements using Algorithm BOTTOMUPSORT is at most $10^{-6}(2^{20} \times 20 - 2^{20} + 1) = 20$ seconds, whereas, using Algorithm SELECTIONSORT, the time becomes $10^{-6}(2^{20} \times (2^{20} - 1))/2 = 6.4$ days!

The calculations in the above example reveal the fact that time is undoubtedly an extremely precious resource to be investigated in the analysis of algorithms.

1.8.1 *Order of growth*

Obviously, it is meaningless to say that an algorithm A, when presented with input x, runs in time y seconds. This is because the actual time is not only a function of the algorithm used, it is a function of numerous factors, e.g., how and on what machine the algorithm is implemented and in what language or even what compiler or programmer's skills, to mention a few. Therefore, we should be content with only an approximation of the exact time. But, first of all, when assessing an algorithm's efficiency, do we have to deal with exact or even approximate times? It turns out that we really do not need even approximate times. This is supported by many factors, some of which are the following. First, when analyzing the running time of an algorithm, we usually compare its behavior with another algorithm that solves the same problem or even a different problem. Thus, our estimates of times are *relative* as opposed to *absolute*. Second, it is desirable for an algorithm to be not only machine independent but also capable of being expressed in any language, including human languages. Moreover, it should be technology independent, that is, we want our measure of the running time of an algorithm to survive technological advances. Third, our main concern is not in small input sizes; we are mostly concerned with the behavior of the algorithm under investigation on large input instances.

In fact, counting the number of operations in some "reasonable" implementation of an algorithm is more than what is needed. As a consequence of the third factor above, we can take a giant step further: A precise count of the number of all operations is very cumbersome, if not impossible, and since we are interested in the running time for large input sizes, we may talk about the *rate of growth* or the *order of growth* of the running time. For instance, if we can come up with some constant $c > 0$ such that the running time of an algorithm A when presented with an input of size n is at most cn^2, c becomes inconsequential as n gets bigger and bigger. Furthermore, specifying this constant does not bring about extra insight when comparing this function with another one of different order, say dn^3 for an algorithm B that solves the same problem. To see this, note that the ratio between the two functions is dn/c and, consequently, the ratio d/c has virtually no effect as n becomes very large. The same reasoning applies to lower order terms as in the function $f(n) = n^2 \log n + 10n^2 + n$. Here, we observe that the larger the value of n the lesser the significance of the contribution of the lower order terms $10n^2$ and n. Therefore, we may say about the running times of algorithms A and B above to be "*of order*" or "*in the order of*" n^2 and n^3, respectively. Similarly, we say that the function $f(n)$ above is of order $n^2 \log n$.

Once we dispose of lower order terms and leading constants from a function that expresses the running time of an algorithm, we say that we are measuring the *asymptotic running time* of the algorithm. Equivalently, in the analysis of algorithm terminology, we may refer to this asymptotic time using the more technical term "time complexity".

Now, suppose that we have two algorithms A_1 and A_2 of running times in the order of $n \log n$. Which one should we consider to be preferable to the other? Technically, since they have the same time complexity, we say that they have the same running time *within a multiplicative constant*, that is, the ratio between the two running times is constant. In some cases, the constant may be important and more detailed analysis of the algorithm or conducting some experiments on the behavior of the algorithm may be helpful. Also, in this case, it may be necessary to investigate other factors, e.g., space requirements and input distribution. The latter is helpful in analyzing the behavior of an algorithm on average.

Figure 1.5 shows some functions that are widely used to represent the running times of algorithms. Higher-order functions and exponential and

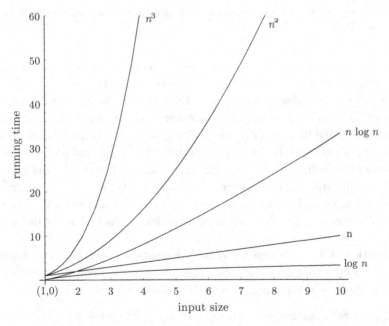

Fig. 1.5. Growth of some typical functions that represent running times.

Table 1.1. Running times for different sizes of input.

n	$\log n$	n	$n \log n$	n^2	n^3	2^n
8	3 nsec	0.01 μ	0.02 μ	0.06 μ	0.51 μ	0.26 μ
16	4 nsec	0.02 μ	0.06 μ	0.26 μ	4.10 μ	65.5 μ
32	5 nsec	0.03 μ	0.16 μ	1.02 μ	32.7 μ	4.29 sec
64	6 nsec	0.06 μ	0.38 μ	4.10 μ	262 μ	5.85 cent
128	0.01 μ	0.13 μ	0.90 μ	16.38 μ	0.01 sec	10^{20} cent
256	0.01 μ	0.26 μ	2.05 μ	65.54 μ	0.02 sec	10^{58} cent
512	0.01 μ	0.51 μ	4.61 μ	262.14 μ	0.13 sec	10^{135} cent
2048	0.01 μ	2.05 μ	22.53 μ	0.01 sec	1.07 sec	10^{598} cent
4096	0.01 μ	4.10 μ	49.15 μ	0.02 sec	8.40 sec	10^{1214} cent
8192	0.01 μ	8.19 μ	106.50 μ	0.07 sec	1.15 min	10^{2447} cent
16384	0.01 μ	16.38 μ	229.38 μ	0.27 sec	1.22 hrs	10^{4913} cent
32768	0.02 μ	32.77 μ	491.52 μ	1.07 sec	9.77 hrs	10^{9845} cent
65536	0.02 μ	65.54 μ	1048.6 μ	0.07 min	3.3 days	10^{19709} cent
131072	0.02 μ	131.07 μ	2228.2 μ	0.29 min	26 days	10^{39438} cent
262144	0.02 μ	262.14 μ	4718.6 μ	1.15 min	7 mnths	10^{78894} cent
524288	0.02 μ	524.29 μ	9961.5 μ	4.58 min	4.6 years	10^{157808} cent
1048576	0.02 μ	1048.60 μ	20972 μ	18.3 min	37 years	10^{315634} cent

Note: "nsec" stands for nanoseconds, "μ" is one microsecond and "cent" stands for centuries.

hyperexponential functions are not shown in the figure. Exponential and hyperexponential functions grow much faster than the ones shown in the figure, even for moderate values of n. Functions of the form $\log^k n, cn, cn^2$ and cn^3 are called, respectively, *logarithmic, linear, quadratic* and *cubic*. Functions of the form n^c or $n^c \log^k n, 0 < c < 1$, are called *sublinear*. Functions that lie between linear and quadratic, e.g., $n \log n$ and $n^{1.5}$, are called *subquadratic*. Table 1.1 shows approximate running times of algorithms with time complexities $\log n, n, n \log n, n^2, n^3$ and 2^n, for $n = 2^3, 2^4, \ldots, 2^{20} \approx$ one million, assuming that each operation takes one nanosecond. Note the explosive running time (measured in centuries) when it is of the order 2^n.

Definition 1.1 We denote by an "elementary operation" any computational step whose cost is always upperbounded by a constant amount of time regardless of the input data or the algorithm used.

Let us take, for instance, the operation of adding two integers. For the running time of this operation to be constant, we stipulate that the size of its operands be fixed no matter what algorithm is used. Furthermore, as we are now dealing with the asymptotic running time, we can freely choose any positive integer k to be the "word length" of our "model of computation". Incidentally, this is but one instance in which the beauty of asymptotic notation shows off; the word length can be any *fixed* positive integer. If we want to add arbitrarily large numbers, an algorithm whose running time is proportional to its input size can easily be written in terms of the elementary operation of addition. Likewise, we can choose from a large pool of operations and apply the fixed-size condition to obtain as many number of elementary operations as we wish. The following operations on *fixed-size* operands are examples of elementary operation.

- Arithmetic operations: addition, subtraction, multiplication and division.
- Comparisons and logical operations.
- Assignments, including assignments of pointers when, say, traversing a list or a tree.

In order to formalize the notions of *order of growth* and *time complexity*, special mathematical notations have been widely used. These notations make it convenient to compare and analyze running times with minimal use of mathematics and cumbersome calculations.

1.8.2 *The O-notation*

We have seen before (Observation 1.4) that the number of elementary operations performed by Algorithm INSERTIONSORT is *at most* cn^2, where c is some appropriately chosen positive constant. In this case, we say that the running time of Algorithm INSERTIONSORT is $O(n^2)$ (read "Oh of n^2" or "big-Oh of n^2"). This can be interpreted as follows. Whenever the number of elements to be sorted is equal to or exceeds some threshold n_0, the running time is *at most* cn^2 for some constant $c > 0$. It should be emphasized, however, that this does not mean that the running time is *always* as large as cn^2, even for large input sizes. Thus, the O-notation provides an *upper bound* on the running time; it *may* not be indicative of the *actual* running time of an algorithm. For example, for any value of n, the running time of Algorithm INSERTIONSORT is $O(n)$ if the input is already sorted in nondecreasing order.

In general, we say that the running time of an algorithm is $O(g(n))$, if whenever the input size is equal to or exceeds some threshold n_0, its running time can be bounded *above* by some positive constant c times $g(n)$. The formal definition of this notation is as follows.[b]

Definition 1.2   Let $f(n)$ and $g(n)$ be two functions from the set of natural numbers to the set of nonnegative real numbers. $f(n)$ is said to be $O(g(n))$ if there exists a natural number n_0 and a constant $c > 0$ such that

$$\forall\, n \geq n_0, \quad f(n) \leq cg(n).$$

Consequently, if $\lim_{n\to\infty} f(n)/g(n)$ exists, then

$$\lim_{n\to\infty} \frac{f(n)}{g(n)} \neq \infty \text{ implies } f(n) = O(g(n)).$$

Informally, this definition says that f grows no faster than some constant times g. The O-notation can also be used in equations as a simplification tool. For instance, instead of writing

$$f(n) = 5n^3 + 7n^2 - 2n + 13,$$

we may write

$$f(n) = 5n^3 + O(n^2).$$

This is helpful if we are not interested in the *details* of the lower-order terms.

1.8.3   *The Ω-notation*

While the O-notation gives an upper bound, the Ω-notation, on the other hand, provides a *lower bound* within a constant factor of the running time. We have seen before (Observation 1.4) that the number of elementary operations performed by Algorithm INSERTIONSORT is *at least* cn, where c is some appropriately chosen positive constant. In this case, we say that the running time of Algorithm INSERTIONSORT is $\Omega(n)$ (read "omega of n",

---

[b]The more formal definition of this and subsequent notations is in terms of sets. We prefer not to use their exact formal definitions, as it only complicates things unnecessarily.

or "big-omega of n"). This can be interpreted as follows. Whenever the number of elements to be sorted is equal to or exceeds some threshold n_0, the running time is *at least* cn for some constant $c > 0$. As in the O-notation, this does not mean that the running time is *always* as small as cn. Thus, the Ω-notation provides a lower bound on the running time; it *may* not be indicative of the *actual* running time of an algorithm. For example, for any value of n, the running time of Algorithm INSERTIONSORT is $\Omega(n^2)$ if the input consists of distinct elements that are sorted in decreasing order.

In general, we say that an algorithm is $\Omega(g(n))$, if whenever the input size is equal to or exceeds some threshold n_0, its running time can be bounded *below* by some positive constant c times $g(n)$.

This notation is widely used to express lower bounds on *problems* as well. In other words, it is commonly used to state a lower bound for *any* algorithm that solves a specific problem. For example, we say that the problem of matrix multiplication is $\Omega(n^2)$. This is a shorthand for saying "any algorithm for multiplying two $n \times n$ matrices is $\Omega(n^2)$". Likewise, we say that the problem of sorting by comparisons is $\Omega(n \log n)$, to mean that no comparison-based sorting algorithm with time complexity that is asymptotically less than $n \log n$ can ever be devised. Chapter 11 is devoted entirely to the study of lower bounds of problems. The formal definition of this notation is symmetrical to that of the O-notation.

Definition 1.3 Let $f(n)$ and $g(n)$ be two functions from the set of natural numbers to the set of nonnegative real numbers. $f(n)$ is said to be $\Omega(g(n))$ if there exists a natural number n_0 and a constant $c > 0$ such that

$$\forall\, n \geq n_0, \quad f(n) \geq cg(n).$$

Consequently, if $\lim_{n \to \infty} f(n)/g(n)$ exists, then

$$\lim_{n \to \infty} \frac{f(n)}{g(n)} \neq 0 \text{ implies } f(n) = \Omega(g(n)).$$

Informally, this definition says that f grows at least as fast as some constant times g. It is clear from the definition that

$$f(n) \text{ is } \Omega(g(n)) \text{ if and only if } g(n) \text{ is } O(f(n)).$$

1.8.4 *The Θ-notation*

We have seen before that the number of element comparisons performed by Algorithm SELECTIONSORT is *always proportional to* n^2 (Observation 1.3). Since each element comparison takes a constant amount of time, we say that the running time of Algorithm SELECTIONSORT is $\Theta(n^2)$ (read "theta of n^2"). This can be interpreted as follows. There exist two constants c_1 and c_2 *associated with the algorithm* with the property that on any input of size $n \geq n_0$, the running time is between $c_1 n^2$ and $c_2 n^2$. These two constants encapsulate many factors pertaining to the details of the implementation of the algorithm and the machine and technology used. As stated earlier, the details of the implementation include numerous factors such as the programming language used and the programmer's skill.

By Observation 1.5, the number of element comparisons performed by Algorithm BOTTOMUPSORT is proportional to $n \log n$. In this case, we say that the running time of Algorithm BOTTOMUPSORT is $\Theta(n \log n)$.

In general, we say that the running time of an algorithm is *of order* $\Theta(g(n))$ if whenever the input size is equal to or exceeds some threshold n_0, its running time can be bounded *below* by $c_1 g(n)$ and *above* by $c_2 g(n)$, where $0 < c_1 \leq c_2$. Thus, this notation is used to express the *exact order* of an algorithm, which implies an *exact bound* on its running time. The formal definition of this notation is as follows.

Definition 1.4 Let $f(n)$ and $g(n)$ be two functions from the set of natural numbers to the set of nonnegative real numbers. $f(n)$ is said to be $\Theta(g(n))$ if there exists a natural number n_0 and two positive constants c_1 and c_2 such that

$$\forall\, n \geq n_0, \quad c_1 g(n) \leq f(n) \leq c_2 g(n).$$

Consequently, if $\lim_{n \to \infty} f(n)/g(n)$ exists, then

$$\lim_{n \to \infty} \frac{f(n)}{g(n)} = c \text{ implies } f(n) = \Theta(g(n)),$$

where c is a *constant strictly greater than* 0.

An important consequence of the above definition is that

$$f(n) = \Theta(g(n)) \text{ if and only if } f(n) = O(g(n)) \text{ and } f(n) = \Omega(g(n)).$$

Unlike the previous two notations, the Θ-notation gives an exact picture of the rate of growth of the running time of an algorithm. Thus, the running time of some algorithms as INSERTIONSORT cannot be expressed using this notation, as the running time ranges from linear to quadratic. On the other hand, the running time of some algorithms like Algorithm SELECTIONSORT and Algorithm BOTTOMUPSORT can be described precisely using this notation.

It may be helpful to think of O as *similar to* $\leq$, Ω as *similar to* $\geq$ and Θ as *similar to* $=$. We emphasized the phrase "similar to" since one should be cautious not to confuse the exact relations with the asymptotic notations. For example $100n = O(n)$ although $100n \geq n$, $n = \Omega(100n)$ although $n \leq 100n$ and $n = \Theta(100n)$ although $n \neq 100n$.

1.8.5 *Examples*

The above O, Ω and Θ notations are not only used to describe the time complexity of an algorithm; they are so general that they can be applied to characterize the asymptotic behavior of any other resource measure, say the amount of space used by an algorithm. Theoretically, they may be used in conjunction with any abstract function. For this reason, we will not attach any measures or meanings with the functions in the examples that follow. We will assume in these examples that $f(n)$ is a function from the set of natural numbers to the set of nonnegative real numbers.

Example 1.5 Let $f(n) = 10n^2 + 20n$. Then, $f(n) = O(n^2)$ since for all $n \geq 1, f(n) \leq 30n^2$. $f(n) = \Omega(n^2)$ since for all $n \geq 1, f(n) \geq n^2$. Also, $f(n) = \Theta(n^2)$ since for all $n \geq 1, n^2 \leq f(n) \leq 30n^2$. We can also establish these three relations using the limits as mentioned above. Since $\lim_{n \to \infty} (10n^2 + 20n)/n^2 = 10$, we see that $f(n) = O(n^2), f(n) = \Omega(n^2)$ and $f(n) = \Theta(n^2)$.

Example 1.6 In general, let $f(n) = a_k n^k + a_{k-1} n^{k-1} + \ldots + a_1 n + a_0$. Then, $f(n) = \Theta(n^k)$. Recall that this implies that $f(n) = O(n^k)$ and $f(n) = \Omega(n^k)$.

Example 1.7 Since

$$\lim_{n \to \infty} \frac{\log n^2}{n} = \lim_{n \to \infty} \frac{2 \log n}{n} = \lim_{n \to \infty} \frac{2}{\ln 2} \frac{\ln n}{n} = \frac{2}{\ln 2} \lim_{n \to \infty} \frac{1}{n} = 0$$

(differentiate both numerator and denominator), we see that $f(n) = \log n^2$ is $O(n)$, but not $\Omega(n)$. It follows that $\log n^2$ is not $\Theta(n)$.

Example 1.8 Since $\log n^2 = 2\log n$, we immediately see that $\log n^2 = \Theta(\log n)$. In general, for any *fixed constant* k, $\log n^k = \Theta(\log n)$.

Example 1.9 Any constant function is $O(1), \Omega(1)$ and $\Theta(1)$.

Example 1.10 It is easy to see that 2^n is $\Theta(2^{n+1})$. This is an example of many functions that satisfy $f(n) = \Theta(f(n+1))$.

Example 1.11 In this example, we give a monotonic increasing function $f(n)$ such that $f(n)$ is not $\Omega(f(n+1))$ and hence not $\Theta(f(n+1))$. Since $(n+1)! = (n+1)n! > n!$, we have that $n! = O((n+1)!)$. Since

$$\lim_{n \to \infty} \frac{n!}{(n+1)!} = \lim_{n \to \infty} \frac{1}{n+1} = 0,$$

we conclude that $n!$ is not $\Omega((n+1)!)$. It follows that $n!$ is not $\Theta((n+1)!)$

Example 1.12 Consider the series $\sum_{j=1}^{n} \log j$. Clearly,

$$\sum_{j=1}^{n} \log j \leq \sum_{j=1}^{n} \log n.$$

That is,

$$\sum_{j=1}^{n} \log j = O(n \log n).$$

Also,

$$\sum_{j=1}^{n} \log j \geq \sum_{j=1}^{\lfloor n/2 \rfloor} \log\left(\frac{n}{2}\right) = \lfloor n/2 \rfloor \log\left(\frac{n}{2}\right) = \lfloor n/2 \rfloor \log n - \lfloor n/2 \rfloor.$$

Thus,

$$\sum_{j=1}^{n} \log j = \Omega(n \log n).$$

It follows that

$$\sum_{j=1}^{n} \log j = \Theta(n \log n).$$

Example 1.13   We want to find an exact bound for the function $f(n) = \log n!$. First, note that $\log n! = \sum_{j=1}^{n} \log j$. We have shown in Example 1.12 that $\sum_{j=1}^{n} \log j = \Theta(n \log n)$. It follows that $\log n! = \Theta(n \log n)$.

Example 1.14   Since $\log n! = \Theta(n \log n)$ and $\log 2^n = n$, we deduce that $2^n = O(n!)$, but $n!$ is not $O(2^n)$. Similarly, since $\log 2^{n^2} = n^2 > n \log n$, and $\log n! = \Theta(n \log n)$ (Example 1.13), it follows that $n! = O(2^{n^2})$, but 2^{n^2} is not $O(n!)$.

Example 1.15   It is easy to see that

$$\sum_{j=1}^{n} \frac{n}{j} \leq \sum_{j=1}^{n} \frac{n}{1} = O(n^2).$$

However, this upper bound is not useful since it is not tight. Example A.16 shows that

$$\frac{\log(n+1)}{\log e} \leq \sum_{j=1}^{n} \frac{1}{j} \leq \frac{\log n}{\log e} + 1.$$

That is

$$\sum_{j=1}^{n} \frac{1}{j} = O(\log n) \quad \text{and} \quad \sum_{j=1}^{n} \frac{1}{j} = \Omega(\log n).$$

It follows that

$$\sum_{j=1}^{n} \frac{n}{j} = n \sum_{j=1}^{n} \frac{1}{j} = \Theta(n \log n).$$

Example 1.16   Consider the brute-force algorithm for primality test given in Algorithm BRUTE-FORCE PRIMALITYTEST.

Algorithm 1.7 BRUTE-FORCE PRIMALITYTEST
Input: A positive integer $n \geq 2$.

Output: *true* if n is prime and *false* otherwise.

1. $s \leftarrow \lfloor \sqrt{n} \rfloor$
2. **for** $j \leftarrow 2$ **to** s
3.   **if** j divides n **then return** *false*
4. **end for**
5. **return** *true*

We will assume here that $\sqrt{n}$ can be computed in $O(1)$ time. Clearly, the algorithm is $O(\sqrt{n})$ since the number of iterations is exactly $\lfloor \sqrt{n} \rfloor - 1$ when the input is prime. Besides, the number of primes is infinite, which means that the algorithm performs exactly $\lfloor \sqrt{n} \rfloor - 1$ iterations for an infinite number of values of n. It is also easy to see that for infinitely many values of n, the algorithm performs only $O(1)$ iterations (e.g., when n is even), and hence the algorithm is $\Omega(1)$. Since the algorithm may take $\Omega(\sqrt{n})$ time on some inputs and $O(1)$ time on some other inputs infinitely often, it is neither $\Theta(\sqrt{n})$ nor $\Theta(1)$. It follows that the algorithm is not $\Theta(f(n))$ for any function f.

1.8.6 *Complexity classes and the o-notation*

Let R be the relation on the set of complexity functions defined by $f \, R \, g$ if and only if $f(n) = \Theta(g(n))$. It is easy to see that R is reflexive, symmetric and transitive, i.e., an equivalence relation (see Sec. A.1.2.1). The equivalence classes induced by this relation are called *complexity classes*. The complexity class to which a complexity function $g(n)$ belongs includes all functions $f(n)$ of order $\Theta(g(n))$. For example, all polynomials of degree 2 belong to the same complexity class n^2. To show that two functions belong to different classes, it is useful to use the o-notation (read "little oh") defined as follows.

Definition 1.5   Let $f(n)$ and $g(n)$ be two functions from the set of natural numbers to the set of nonnegative real numbers. $f(n)$ is said to be $o(g(n))$ if for *every* constant $c > 0$ there exists a positive integer n_0 such that $f(n) < cg(n)$ for all $n \geq n_0$. Consequently, if $\lim_{n\to\infty} f(n)/g(n)$ exists, then

$$\lim_{n\to\infty} \frac{f(n)}{g(n)} = 0 \text{ implies } f(n) = o(g(n)).$$

Informally, this definition says that $f(n)$ becomes insignificant relative to $g(n)$ as n approaches infinity. It follows from the definition that

$$f(n) = o(g(n)) \text{ if and only if } f(n) = O(g(n)), \text{ but } g(n) \neq O(f(n)).$$

For example, $n \log n$ is $o(n^2)$ is equivalent to saying that $n \log n$ is $O(n^2)$, but n^2 is *not* $O(n \log n)$.

We also write $f(n) \prec g(n)$ to denote that $f(n)$ is $o(g(n))$. Using this notation, we can concisely express the following hierarchy of complexity classes.

$$1 \prec \log \log n \prec \log n \prec \sqrt{n} \prec n^{3/4} \prec n \prec n \log n \prec n^2 \prec 2^n \prec n! \prec 2^{n^2}.$$

1.9 Space Complexity

We define the space used by an algorithm to be the number of memory cells (or words) needed to carry out the computational steps required to solve an instance of the problem *excluding the space allocated to hold the input*. In other words, it is only the *work space* required by the algorithm. The reason for not including the input size is basically to distinguish between algorithms that use "less than" linear work space throughout their computation. All definitions of order of growth and asymptotic bounds pertaining to time complexity carry over to *space complexity*. It is clear that the work space cannot exceed the running time of an algorithm, as writing into each memory cell requires at least a constant amount of time. Thus, if we let $T(n)$ and $S(n)$ denote, respectively, the time and space complexities of an algorithm, then $S(n) = O(T(n))$.

To appreciate the importance of space complexity, suppose we want to sort $n = 2^{20} = 1{,}048{,}576$ elements. If we use Algorithm SELECTIONSORT, then we need no extra storage. On the other hand, if we use Algorithm BOTTOMUPSORT, then we need $n = 1{,}048{,}576$ extra memory cells as a temporary storage for the input elements (see Example 1.19).

In the following examples, we will look at some of the algorithms we have discussed so far and analyze their space requirements.

Example 1.17 In Algorithm LINEARSEARCH, only one memory cell is used to hold the result of the search. If we add local variables, e.g., for looping, we conclude that the amount of space needed is $\Theta(1)$. This is also the case in algorithms BINARYSEARCH, SELECTIONSORT and INSERTIONSORT.

Example 1.18 In Algorithm MERGE for merging two sorted arrays, we need an auxiliary amount of storage whose size is exactly that of the input, namely n (Recall that n is the size of the array $A[p..r]$). Consequently, its space complexity is $\Theta(n)$.

Example 1.19 When attempting to compute an estimate of the space required by Algorithm BOTTOMUPSORT, one may find it to be complex at first. Nevertheless, it is not difficult to see that the space needed is no more than n, the size of the input array. This is because we can set aside an array of size n, say $B[1..n]$, to be used by Algorithm MERGE as an auxiliary storage for carrying out the merging process. It follows that the space complexity of Algorithm BOTTOMUPSORT is $\Theta(n)$.

Example 1.20 In this example, we will "devise" an algorithm that uses $\Theta(\log n)$ space. Let us modify the Algorithm BINARYSEARCH as follows. After the search terminates, output a *sorted* list of all those entries of array A that have been compared against x. This means that after we test x against $A[mid]$ in each iteration, we must save $A[mid]$ using an auxiliary array, say B, which can be sorted later. As the number of comparisons is at most $\lfloor \log n \rfloor + 1$, it is easy to see that the size of B should be at most this amount, i.e., $O(\log n)$.

Example 1.21 An algorithm that *outputs* all permutations of a given n characters needs only $\Theta(n)$ space. If we want to keep these permutations so that they can be used in subsequent calculations, then we need at least $n \times n! = \Theta((n+1)!)$ space.

Naturally, in many problems there is a time–space tradeoff: The more space we allocate for the algorithm the faster it runs, and vice versa. This, of course, is within limits: In most of the algorithms that we have discussed so far, increasing the amount of space does not result in a noticeable speedup in the algorithm running time. However, it is almost always the case that decreasing the amount of work space required by an algorithm results in a degradation in the algorithm's speed.

1.10 Optimal Algorithms

In Sec. 11.3.2, we will show that the running time of any algorithm that sorts an array with n entries *using element comparisons* must be $\Omega(n \log n)$ in the worst case (see Sec. 1.12). This means that we cannot hope for an algorithm that runs in time that is asymptotically less than $n \log n$ in the worst case. For this reason, it is commonplace to call any algorithm that sorts using element comparisons in time $O(n \log n)$ *an optimal algorithm for the problem of comparison-based sorting.* By this definition, it follows that Algorithm BOTTOMUPSORT is optimal. In this case, we also say that it is optimal *within a multiplicative constant* to indicate the possibility of the existence of another sorting algorithm whose running time is a *constant* fraction of that of BOTTOMUPSORT. In general, if we can prove that any algorithm to solve problem Π must be $\Omega(f(n))$, then we call any algorithm to solve problem Π in time $O(f(n))$ an *optimal algorithm* for problem Π.

Incidentally, this definition, which is widely used in the literature, does not take into account the space complexity. The reason is twofold. First, as we indicated before, time is considered to be more precious than space so long as the space used is within reasonable limits. Second, most of the existing *optimal* algorithms compare to each other in terms of space complexity in the order of $O(n)$. For example, Algorithm BOTTOMUPSORT, which needs $\Theta(n)$ of space as auxiliary storage, is called optimal, although there are other algorithms that sort in $O(n \log n)$ time and $O(1)$ space. For example, Algorithm HEAPSORT, which will be introduced in Sec. 3.2.3, runs in time $O(n \log n)$ using only $O(1)$ amount of space.

1.11 How to Estimate the Running Time of an Algorithm

As we discussed before, a bound on the running time of an algorithm, be it upper, lower or exact, can be estimated to within a constant factor if we restrict the operations used by the algorithm to those we referred to as *elementary operations*. Now, it remains to show how to analyze the algorithm in order to obtain the desired bound. Of course, we can get a precise bound by summing up all elementary operations. This is undoubtedly ruled out, as it is cumbersome and quite often impossible. There is, in general, no mechanical procedure by the help of which one can obtain a "reasonable" bound on the running time or space usage of the algorithm at hand. Moreover, this task is mostly left to intuition and, in many cases, to ingenuity too. However, in many algorithms, there are some agreed-upon techniques that give a tight bound with straightforward analysis. In the following, we discuss some of these techniques using simple examples.

1.11.1 *Counting the number of iterations*[c]

It is quite often the case that the running time is proportional to the number of passes through **while** loops and similar constructs. Thus, it follows that

---

[c]Some of the ideas in this section were contributed by W. G. Al-Khatib.

counting the number of iterations is a good indicator of the running time of an algorithm. This is the case with many algorithms including those for searching, sorting, matrix multiplication and so forth.

Counting the number of iterations can be achieved by looking for one or more statements in the algorithm that get executed the most and then estimating the number of times they get executed. Assuming that the cost of executing such a statement once is constant, the estimate we compute is asymptotically proportional to the overall cost of the algorithm and can be expressed in terms of $O()$ or $\Theta()$ notation. One way to achieve that is to map the loop to a mathematical summation formula. Call the iterator variable of a loop *simple* if it increases by one. A loop will be called *simple* if its iterator variable is simple. In its simplest form, the simple **for** loop like

---

1. *count* ← 0
2. **for** *i* ← *low* **to** *high*
3.   *count* ← *count* + 1
4. **end for**

---

is mapped to the summation

$$count = \sum_{i=low}^{high} 1.$$

Thus, a simple loop can be mapped to a mathematical summation formula as follows:

- Use the iterator variable in the loop as the summation index.
- Use the starting value of the iterator as the lower limit and the last value of the iterator as the upper limit of the summation formula.
- Each nested loop is mapped to a nested summation.

Example 1.22   Let n be a perfect square, i.e., an integer whose square root is integer. Algorithm COUNT1 computes for each perfect square j between 1 and n the sum $\sum_{i=1}^{j} i$. (Obviously, this sum can be computed more efficiently).

We will assume that $\sqrt{n}$ can be computed in $\Theta(1)$ time. It is obvious that the cost of the algorithm is dominated by the number of times Line 5

Algorithm 1.8 COUNT1
Input: $n = k^2$ for some integer k.
Output: $\sum_{i=1}^{j} i$ for each perfect square j between 1 and n.

1. $k \leftarrow \sqrt{n}$
2. **for** $j \leftarrow 1$ **to** k
3. $sum[j] \leftarrow 0$
4.   **for** $i \leftarrow 1$ **to** j^2
5. $sum[j] \leftarrow sum[j] + i$
6.   **end for**
7. **end for**
8. **return** $sum[1..k]$

---

is executed. Since we have two simple loops, we can immediately map them to the double summation $\sum_{j=1}^{k} \sum_{i=1}^{j^2} 1$ which is computed as follows:

$$\sum_{j=1}^{k} \sum_{i=1}^{j^2} 1 = \sum_{j=1}^{k} j^2 = \frac{k(k+1)(2k+1)}{6} = \Theta(k^3) = \Theta(n^{1.5}).$$

It follows that the running time of the algorithm is $\Theta(n^{1.5})$.

Example 1.23 Consider Algorithm COUNT2, which consists of two nested loops and a variable *count* that counts the number of iterations performed by the algorithm on input n, which is a positive integer.

Algorithm 1.9 COUNT2
Input: A positive integer n.
Output: *count* = number of times Step 5 is executed.

1. $count \leftarrow 0$
2. **for** $i \leftarrow 1$ **to** n
3. $m \leftarrow \lfloor n/i \rfloor$
4.   **for** $j \leftarrow 1$ **to** m
5. $count \leftarrow count + 1$
6.   **end for**
7. **end for**
8. **return** *count*

Again, we have two nested loops that are simple. Hence, the value of *count* is

$$\sum_{i=1}^{n}\sum_{j=1}^{m} 1 = \sum_{i=1}^{n} m = \sum_{i=1}^{n} \left\lfloor \frac{n}{i} \right\rfloor.$$

By the definition of the floor function, we know that

$$\frac{n}{i} - 1 < \left\lfloor \frac{n}{i} \right\rfloor \leq \frac{n}{i}.$$

Hence,

$$\sum_{i=1}^{n} \left(\frac{n}{i} - 1 \right) < \sum_{i=1}^{n} \left\lfloor \frac{n}{i} \right\rfloor \leq \sum_{i=1}^{n} \frac{n}{i} \approx n \ln n.$$

Therefore, we conclude that Step 5 is executed $\Theta(n \log n)$ times As the running time is proportional to *count*, we conclude that it is $\Theta(n \log n)$.

In the previous examples, the mapping was straightforward, as the loops were simple. If at least one loop is not simple, then we need to "devise" a new iterator that is simple in order to include in the summation. This variable is *dependent* on the original iterator, and hence we need to preserve that dependency when evaluating the new summation.

Example 1.24 Consider Algorithm COUNT3, which consists of two nested loops and a variable *count* which counts the number of iterations performed by the algorithm on input $n = 2^k$, for some positive integer k.

Algorithm 1.10 COUNT3
Input: $n = 2^k$, for some positive integer k.
Output: *count* = number of times Step 5 is executed.

1. *count* ← 0
2. i ← 1
3. **while** $i \leq n$
4.   **for** j ← 1 **to** i
5.   *count* ← *count* + 1
6.   **end for**
7. i ← $2i$
8. **end while**
9. **return** *count*

In this case, it is obvious that the **for** loop is simple, but the while loop is not. The iterator of the **while** loop, i, is not simple, as it is doubled in each iteration. The values that iterator i assumes are

$$i = 1, 2, 4, \ldots, n,$$

which can be rewritten as

$$i = 2^0, 2^1, 2^2, \ldots, 2^k = n.$$

Obviously, the exponent of 2 in the original iterator is a simple iterator ranging between 0 and k. Hence, we choose a variable name that is not used by the algorithm as an index in the summation formula. Let us choose index r. Note the following relationship between the new iterator and the original iterator:

$$i = 2^r \quad \text{or} \quad r = \log i.$$

Hence, we can express the number of times Line 5 is executed as

$$\sum_{r=0}^{k}\sum_{j=1}^{i} 1 = \sum_{r=0}^{k} i = \sum_{r=0}^{k} 2^r = \frac{2^{k+1} - 1}{2 - 1} = 2^{\log n + 1} - 1 = 2n - 1 = \Theta(n).$$

It follows that the running time is $\Theta(n)$.

Example 1.25 Consider Algorithm COUNT4, which consists of two nested loops and a variable *count* which counts the number of iterations performed by the algorithm on input $n = 2^k$, for some positive integer k.

Algorithm 1.11 COUNT4
Input: $n = 2^k$, for some positive integer k.

Output: *count* = number of times Step 4 is executed.

1. *count* ← 0
2. **while** $n \geq 1$
3.   **for** $j \leftarrow 1$ **to** n
4.   *count* ← *count* + 1
5.   **end for**
6. $n \leftarrow n/2$
7. **end while**
8. **return** *count*

The **for** loop is simple, whereas the iterator of the **while** loop starts with the value n and then decreases by half in each iteration until it reaches 1, inclusive. Let us assign an iterator variable, say i, to the **while** loop. In this case, the values of i are

$$i = n, \frac{n}{2}, \frac{n}{4}, \dots, \frac{n}{\frac{n}{2}} = 2, 1.$$

They can be rewritten as

$$i = 2^k, 2^{k-1}, 2^{k-2}, \dots, 2^1, 2^0.$$

Similar to what we did in Example 1.24, we introduce the exponent variable r, where $i = 2^r$ and $r = \log i$, and get the following value for *count*:

$$\sum_{r=0}^{k} \sum_{j=1}^{i} 1.$$

The above summation is exactly the same as the one in Example 1.24. Since the running time is proportional to *count*, we conclude that it is $\Theta(n)$.

Example 1.26   Consider Algorithm COUNT5, which consists of two nested loops and a variable *count* which counts the number of iterations performed by the **while** loop on input n that is of the form 2^{2^k} ($k = \log \log n$), for some positive integer k. In this case, the **for** loop is simple, whereas the **while** loop is not.

Algorithm 1.12 COUNT5
Input: $n = 2^{2^k}$, for some positive integer k.
Output: Number of times Step 6 is executed.

1. *count* ← 0
2. **for** $i \leftarrow 1$ **to** n
3. $j \leftarrow 2$
4.   **while** $j \leq n$
5. $j \leftarrow j^2$
6.   *count* ← *count* + 1
7.   **end while**
8. **end for**
9. **return** *count*

So, let us look at the values that are assumed by j.

$$j = 2, 2^2, 2^{2^2} = 2^4, 2^{4^2} = 2^8, \ldots, 2^{2^k},$$

which can be rewritten as

$$j = 2^{2^0}, 2^{2^1}, 2^{2^2}, 2^{2^3}, \ldots, 2^{2^{k-1}}, 2^{2^k}.$$

Let us introduce the index r such that $j = 2^{2^r}$, and equivalently, $r = \log \log j$. The value of *count* becomes equal to

$$\sum_{i=1}^{n} \sum_{r=0}^{k} 1 = \sum_{i=1}^{n} (k+1) = \sum_{i=1}^{n} (\log \log n + 1)$$

$$= (\log \log n + 1) \sum_{i=1}^{n} 1 = n(\log \log n + 1).$$

We conclude that the running time of the algorithm is $\Theta(n \log \log n)$.

1.11.2 *Counting the frequency of basic operations*

In some algorithms, it is cumbersome, or even impossible, to make use of the previous method in order to come up with a *tight* estimate of its running time. Unfortunately, at this point, we have not covered good examples of such algorithms. Good examples that will be covered in subsequent chapters include the single-source shortest path problem, Prim's algorithm for finding minimum spanning trees, depth-first search, computing convex hulls and others. However, Algorithm MERGE will serve as a reasonable candidate. Recall that the function of Algorithm MERGE is to merge two sorted arrays into one sorted array. In this algorithm, if we try to apply the previous method, the analysis becomes lengthy and awkward. Now, consider the following argument which we have alluded to in Sec. 1.4. Just prior to the execution of Step 16 of the algorithm, array B holds the final sorted list. Thus, for each element $x \in A$, the algorithm executes one element assignment operation that moves x from A to B. Similarly, in Step 16, the algorithm executes n element assignment operations in order to copy B back into A. This implies that the algorithm executes *exactly* $2n$ element assignments (Observation 1.2). On the other hand, there is no other operation that is executed more than $2n$ times. For example, *at most* one element comparison is needed to move each element from A to B (Observation 1.1).

In general, when analyzing the running time of an algorithm, we may be able to single out one elementary operation with the property that its frequency is at least as large as any other operation. Let us call such an operation a *basic operation*. We can relax this definition to include any operation whose frequency is *proportional* to the running time.

Definition 1.6 An elementary operation in an algorithm is called a *basic operation* if it is of highest frequency to within a constant factor among all other elementary operations.

Hence, according to this definition, the operation of element assignment is a basic operation in Algorithm MERGE and thus is indicative of its running time. By Observation 1.2, the number of element assignments needed to merge two arrays into one array of size n is exactly $2n$. Consequently, its running time is $\Theta(n)$. Note that the operation of element comparison is in general *not* a basic operation in Algorithm MERGE, as there may be only one element comparison throughout the execution of the algorithm. If, however, the algorithm is to merge two arrays of approximately the same size (e.g., $\lfloor (n/2) \rfloor$ and $\lceil (n/2) \rceil$), then we may safely say that it is basic *for that special instance*. This happens if, for example, the algorithm is invoked by Algorithm BOTTOMUPSORT in which case the two subarrays to be sorted are of approximately the same size.

In general, this method consists of identifying one basic operation and utilizing one of the asymptotic notations to find out the order of execution of this operation. This order will be the order of the running time of the algorithm. This is indeed the method of choice for a large class of problems. We list here some candidates of these basic operations:

- When analyzing searching and sorting algorithms, we may choose the element comparison operation *if it is an elementary operation*.
- In matrix multiplication algorithms, we select the operation of scalar multiplication.
- In traversing a linked list, we may select the "operation" of setting or updating a pointer.
- In graph traversals, we may choose the "action" of visiting a node and count the number of nodes visited.

Example 1.27 Using this method, we obtain an exact bound for Algorithm BOTTOMUPSORT as follows. First, note that the basic operations in this algorithm are inherited from Algorithm MERGE, as the latter is called by the former in each iteration of the **while** loop. By the above discussion, we may safely choose the elementary operation of element comparison as the basic operation. By Observation 1.5, the total number of element comparisons required by the algorithm when n is a power of 2 is between $(n \log n)/2$ and $n \log n - n + 1$. This means that the number of element comparisons when n is a power of 2 is $\Omega(n \log n)$ and $O(n \log n)$, i.e., $\Theta(n \log n)$. It can be shown that this holds even if n is not a power of 2. Since the operation of element comparison used by the algorithm is of maximum frequency to within a constant factor, we conclude that the running time of the algorithm is proportional to the number of comparisons. It follows that the algorithm runs in time $\Theta(n \log n)$.

One should be careful, however, when choosing a basic operation, as illustrated by the following example.

Example 1.28 Consider the following modification to Algorithm INSERTIONSORT. When trying to insert an element of the array in its proper position, we will not use linear search; instead, we will use a binary search technique similar to Algorithm BINARYSEARCH. Algorithm BINARYSEARCH can easily be modified so that it does *not* return 0 when x is not an entry of array A; instead, it returns the position of x relative to other entries of the sorted array A. For example, when Algorithm BINARYSEARCH is called with $A = \boxed{2 \mid 3 \mid 6 \mid 8 \mid 9}$ and $x = 7$, it returns 4. Incidentally, this shows that using binary search is not confined to testing for the membership of an element x in an array A; in many algorithms, it is used to find the *position* of an element x relative to other elements in a sorted list. Let Algorithm MODBINARYSEARCH be some implementation of this binary search technique. Thus, MODBINARYSEARCH($\{2, 3, 6, 8, 9\}, 7$) $= 4$. The modified sorting algorithm is given in Algorithm MODINSERTIONSORT.

The total number of element comparisons are those performed by Algorithm MODBINARYSEARCH. Since this algorithm is called $n - 1$ times, and since the maximum number of comparisons performed by the binary search algorithm on an array of size $i - 1$ is $\lfloor \log(i - 1) \rfloor + 1$ (Theorem 1.1), it follows that the total number of comparisons done by Algorithm MODINSERTIONSORT is *at most*

$$\sum_{i=2}^{n} (\lfloor \log(i - 1) \rfloor + 1) = n - 1 + \sum_{i=1}^{n-1} \lfloor \log i \rfloor \leq n - 1 + \sum_{i=1}^{n-1} \log i = O(n \log n).$$

Algorithm 1.13 MODINSERTIONSORT
Input: An array $A[1..n]$ of n elements.

Output: $A[1..n]$ sorted in nondecreasing order.

1. **for** $i \leftarrow 2$ **to** n
2. $x \leftarrow A[i]$
3. $k \leftarrow$ MODBINARYSEARCH $(A[1..i-1], x)$
4.   **for** $j \leftarrow i - 1$ **downto** k
5. $A[j+1] \leftarrow A[j]$
6.   **end for**
7. $A[k] \leftarrow x$
8. **end for**

The last equality follows from Example 1.12 and Eq. (A.18) on page 682. One may be tempted to conclude, based on the false assumption that the operation of element comparison is basic, that the overall running time is $O(n \log n)$. However, this is not the case, as the number of element assignments in Algorithm MODINSERTIONSORT is exactly that in Algorithm INSERTIONSORT when the two algorithms are run on the same input. This has been shown to be $O(n^2)$ (Observation 1.4). We conclude that this algorithm runs in time $O(n^2)$ and not $O(n \log n)$.

In some algorithms, all elementary operations are not basic. In these algorithms, it may be the case that the frequency of two or more operations combined together may turn out to be proportional to the running time of the algorithm. In this case, we express the running time as a function of the total number of times these operations are executed. For instance, if we cannot bound the number of either insertions or deletions, but can come up with a formula that bounds their total, then we may say something like: There are at most n insertions and deletions. This method is widely used in graph and network algorithms. Here, we give a simple example that involves only numbers and the two operations of addition and multiplication. There are better examples that involve graphs and complex data structures.

Example 1.29 Suppose we are given an array $A[1..n]$ of n integers and a positive integer $k, 1 \leq k \leq n$, and asked to multiply the first k integers in A and add the rest. An algorithm to do this is sketched below. Observe here that there are *no* basic operations, since the running time is proportional to the number of times *both* additions and multiplications are performed. Thus, we conclude that there are n elementary operations, multiplications *and* additions, which imply a bound of $\Theta(n)$. Note that in this example, we could have counted the number of iterations to obtain a precise measure of the running time as well. This is because in each iteration, the algorithm takes a constant amount of time. The total number of iterations is $k + (n - k) = n$.

```
1. prod ← 1;   sum ← 0
2. for j ← 1 to k
3.     prod ← prod × A[j]
4. end for
5. for j ← k + 1 to n
6.     sum ← sum + A[j]
7. end for
```

1.11.3 *Using recurrence relations*

In recursive algorithms, a formula bounding the running time is usually given in the form of a recurrence relation, that is, a function whose definition contains the function itself, e.g., $T(n) = 2T(n/2) + n$. Finding the solution of a recurrence relation has been studied well to the extent that the solution of a recurrence may be obtained mechanically (see Secs. 1.15 and A.8 for a discussion on recurrence relations). It may be possible to derive a recurrence that bounds the number of basic operations in a nonrecursive algorithm. For example, in Algorithm BINARYSEARCH, if we let $C(n)$ be the number of comparisons performed on an instance of size n in the worst case, we may express the number of comparisons done by the algorithm using the recurrence

$$C(n) \leq \begin{cases} 1 & \text{if } n = 1 \\ C(\lfloor n/2 \rfloor) + 1 & \text{if } n \geq 2. \end{cases}$$

The solution to this recurrence reduces to a summation as follows:

$$\begin{aligned} C(n) &\leq C(\lfloor n/2 \rfloor) + 1 \\ &\leq C(\lfloor \lfloor n/2 \rfloor /2 \rfloor) + 1 + 1 \\ &= C(\lfloor n/4 \rfloor) + 1 + 1 \quad \text{(Eq. (A.3), page 672)} \\ &\;\;\vdots \\ &\leq C[1] + \lfloor \log n \rfloor \\ &= \lfloor \log n \rfloor + 1. \end{aligned}$$

That is, $C(n) \leq \lfloor \log n \rfloor + 1$. It follows that $C(n) = O(\log n)$. Since the operation of element comparison is a basic operation in Algorithm BINARYSEARCH, we conclude that its time complexity is $O(\log n)$.

1.12 Worst Case and Average Case Analysis

Consider the problem of adding two $n \times n$ matrices A and B of integers. Clearly, the running time expressed in the number of scalar additions of an algorithm that computes $A + B$ is the same for any two arbitrary $n \times n$ matrices A and B. That is, the running time of the algorithm is insensitive to the input values; it is dependent only on its size measured in the number of entries. This is to be contrasted with an algorithm like INSERTIONSORT whose running time is highly dependent on the *input values* as well. By Observation 1.4, the number of element comparisons performed on an input array of size n lies between $n - 1$ and $n(n - 1)/2$ inclusive. This indicates that the performance of the algorithm is *not only a function of* n but also a function of the original order of the input elements. The dependence of the running time of an algorithm on the form of input data, not only its number, is characteristic of many problems. For example, the process of sorting is inherently dependent on the relative order of the data to be sorted. This does not mean that *all* sorting algorithms are sensitive to input data. For instance, the number of element comparisons performed by Algorithm SELECTIONSORT on an array of size n is the same regardless of the form or order of input values, as the number of comparisons done by the algorithm is a function of n only. More precisely, the time taken by a comparison-based algorithm to sort a set of n elements depends on their relative order. For instance, the number of steps required to sort the numbers 6, 3, 4, 5, 1, 7, 2 is the same as that for sorting the numbers 60, 30, 40, 50, 10, 70, 20. Obviously, it is impossible to come up with a function that describes the time complexity of an algorithm based on *both* input size and form; the latter, definitely, has to be suppressed.

Consider again Algorithm INSERTIONSORT. Let $A[1..n] = \{1, 2, \ldots, n\}$, and consider all $n!$ permutations of the elements in A. Each permutation corresponds to one possible input. The running time of the algorithm presumably differs from one permutation to another. Consider three permutations: a in which the elements in A are sorted in decreasing order, c in

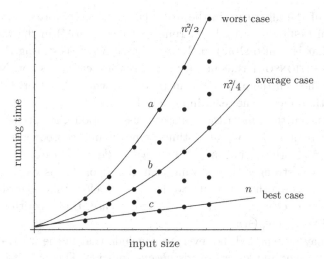

Fig. 1.6.   Performance of Algorithm INSERTIONSORT: worst, average and best cases.

which the elements in A are already sorted in increasing order and b in which the elements are ordered randomly (see Fig. 1.6). Thus, input a is a representative of the *worst case* of all inputs of size n, input c is a representative of the *best case* of all inputs of size n and input b is between the two. This gives rise to three methodologies for analyzing the running time of an algorithm: worst case analysis, average case analysis and best case analysis. The latter is not used in practice, as it does not give useful information about the behavior of an algorithm in general.

1.12.1   *Worst case analysis*

In worst case analysis of time complexity, we select the maximum cost among all possible inputs of size n. As stated above, for any positive integer n, Algorithm INSERTIONSORT requires $\Omega(n^2)$ to process some inputs of size n (e.g., input a in Fig. 1.6). For this reason, we say that the running time of this algorithm is $\Omega(n^2)$ *in the worst case*. Since the running time of the algorithm is $O(n^2)$, we also say that the running time of the algorithm is $O(n^2)$ *in the worst case*. Consequently, we may use the stronger Θ-notation and say that the running time of the algorithm is $\Theta(n^2)$ *in the worst case*. Clearly, using the Θ-notation is preferred, as it gives the exact behavior of the algorithm in the worst case. In other words, stating that Algorithm INSERTIONSORT has a running time of $\Theta(n^2)$ in the worst case implies that it is also $\Omega(n^2)$ in the worst case, whereas stating that Algorithm INSERTIONSORT runs in $O(n^2)$ in the worst case does not. Note that for any value of n there are input instances on which the algorithm spends no more than $O(n)$ time (e.g., input c in Fig. 1.6).

It turns out that under the worst case assumption, the notions of upper and lower bounds in many algorithms coincide and, consequently, we may say that an algorithm runs in time $\Theta(f(n))$ *in the worst case*. As explained above, this is stronger than stating that the algorithm is $O(f(n))$ *in the worst case*. As another example, we have seen before that Algorithm LINEARSEARCH is $O(n)$ and $\Omega(1)$. In the worst case, this algorithm is both $O(n)$ and $\Omega(n)$, i.e., $\Theta(n)$.

One may be tempted, however, to conclude that in the worst case, the notions of upper and lower bounds *always* coincide. This in fact is not the case. Consider for example an algorithm whose running time is known to be $O(n^2)$ in the worst case. However, it has not been proven that for all values of n greater than some threshold n_0 there exists an input of size n on which the algorithm spends $\Omega(n^2)$ time. In this case, we cannot claim that the algorithm's running time is $\Theta(n^2)$ *in the worst case*, even if we know that the algorithm takes $\Theta(n^2)$ time for *infinitely many* values of n. It follows that the algorithm's running time is not $\Theta(n^2)$ *in the worst case*. This is the case in many graph and network algorithms for which only an upper bound on the number of operations can be proven, and whether this upper bound is achievable is not clear. The next example gives a concrete instance of this case.

Example 1.30 Consider for example the algorithm shown below whose input is an element x and a sorted array A of n elements.

---
1. **if** n is odd **then** $k \leftarrow$ BINARYSEARCH(A, x)
2. **else** $k \leftarrow$ LINEARSEARCH(A, x)

This algorithm searches for x in A using binary search if n is odd and linear search if n is even. Obviously, the running time of this algorithm is $O(n)$, since when n is even, the running time is that of Algorithm LINEARSEARCH, which is $O(n)$. However, the algorithm is *not* $\Omega(n)$ in the worst case because there does not exist a threshold n_0 such that *for all* $n \geq n_0$, there exists some input of size n that causes the algorithm to take at least cn time for some constant c. We can only ascertain that the running time is $\Omega(\log n)$ in the worst case. Note that the running time being $\Omega(n)$ for infinitely many values of n does not mean that the algorithm's running time is $\Omega(n)$ in the worst case. It follows that, in the worst case, this algorithm is $O(n)$ and $\Omega(\log n)$, which implies that, in the worst case, it is not $\Theta(f(n))$ for any function $f(n)$.

1.12.2 *Average case analysis*

Another interpretation of an algorithm's time complexity is that of the average case. Here, the running time is taken to be the average time over all inputs of size n (see Fig. 1.6). In this method, it is necessary to know the probabilities of all input occurrences, i.e., it requires prior knowledge of the input distribution. However, even after relaxing some constraints including the assumption of a convenient input distribution, e.g., uniform distribution, the analysis is in many cases complex and lengthy.

Example 1.31 Consider Algorithm LINEARSEARCH. To simplify the analysis, let us assume that all elements of A are distinct and that x is in the array. Furthermore, and most importantly indeed, we will assume that each element y in A is equally likely to be in any position in the array. In other words, the probability that $y = A[j]$ is $1/n$, for all $y \in A$. The number of comparisons performed by the algorithm on average to find the position of x is

$$T(n) = \sum_{j=1}^{n} j \times \frac{1}{n} = \frac{1}{n} \sum_{j=1}^{n} j = \frac{1}{n} \frac{n(n+1)}{2} = \frac{n+1}{2}.$$

This shows that, on average, the algorithm performs $(n+1)/2$ element comparisons in order to locate x. Hence, the time complexity of Algorithm LINEARSEARCH is $\Theta(n)$ on average.

Example 1.32 Consider computing the average number of comparisons performed by Algorithm INSERTIONSORT. To simplify the analysis, let us assume that all elements of A are distinct. Furthermore, we will assume that all $n!$ permutations of the input elements are equally likely. Now, consider inserting element $A[i]$ in its proper position in $A[1..i]$. If its proper position is $j, 1 \leq j \leq i$, then the number of comparisons performed in order to insert $A[i]$ in its proper position is $i - j$ if $j = 1$ and $i - j + 1$ if $2 \leq j \leq i$. Since the probability that its proper position in $A[1..i]$ is $1/i$, the average number of comparisons needed to insert $A[i]$ in its proper position in $A[1..i]$ is

$$\frac{i-1}{i} + \sum_{j=2}^{i} \frac{i-j+1}{i} = \frac{i-1}{i} + \sum_{j=1}^{i-1} \frac{j}{i} = 1 - \frac{1}{i} + \frac{i-1}{2} = \frac{i}{2} - \frac{1}{i} + \frac{1}{2}.$$

Thus, the average number of comparisons performed by Algorithm INSERTIONSORT is

$$\sum_{i=2}^{n} \left(\frac{i}{2} - \frac{1}{i} + \frac{1}{2} \right) = \frac{n(n+1)}{4} - \frac{1}{2} - \sum_{i=2}^{n} \frac{1}{i} + \frac{n-1}{2} = \frac{n^2}{4} + \frac{3n}{4} - \sum_{i=1}^{n} \frac{1}{i}.$$

Since

$$\ln(n+1) \leq \sum_{i=1}^{n} \frac{1}{i} \leq \ln n + 1 \quad \text{(Eq. (A.16), page 681)},$$

it follows that the average number of comparisons performed by Algorithm INSERTIONSORT is approximately

$$\frac{n^2}{4} + \frac{3n}{4} - \ln n = \Theta(n^2).$$

Thus, on average, Algorithm INSERTIONSORT performs roughly half the number of operations performed in the worst case (see Fig. 1.6).

1.13　Amortized Analysis

In many algorithms, we may be unable to express the time complexity in terms of the Θ-notation to obtain an exact bound on the running time. Therefore, we will be content with the O-notation, which is sometimes pessimistic. If we use the O-notation to obtain an upper bound on the running time, the algorithm may be much faster than our estimate even in the worst case.

　　Consider an algorithm in which an operation is executed repeatedly with the property that its running time fluctuates throughout the execution of the algorithm. If this operation takes a large amount of time *occasionally* and runs much faster most of the time, then this is an indication that *amortized analysis* should be employed, assuming that obtaining an exact bound is too hard, if not impossible.

In amortized analysis, we average out the time taken by the operation throughout the execution of the algorithm and refer to this average as the *amortized running time* of that operation. Amortized analysis guarantees the average cost of the operation, and thus the algorithm, *in the worst case*. This is to be contrasted with the average time analysis in which the average is taken over all instances of the same size. Moreover, unlike the average case analysis, no assumptions about the probability distribution of the input are needed.

Amortized time analysis is generally harder than worst case analysis, but this hardness pays off when we derive a lower time complexity. A good example of this analysis will be presented in Sec. 3.3 when we study the union-find algorithms, which is responsible for maintaining a data structure for disjoint sets. It will be shown that this algorithm runs in time that is almost linear using amortized time analysis as opposed to a straightforward bound of $O(n \log n)$. In this section, we present two simple examples that convey the essence of amortization.

Example 1.33 Consider the following problem. We have a doubly linked list (see Sec. 2.2) that initially consists of one node which contains the integer 0. We have as input an array $A[1..n]$ of n positive integers that are to be processed in the following way. If the current integer x is odd, then append x to the list. If it is even, then first append x and then remove all odd elements before x in the list. A sketch of an algorithm for this problem is shown below and is illustrated in Fig. 1.7 on the input

$$\boxed{5 \mid 7 \mid 3 \mid 4 \mid 9 \mid 8 \mid 7 \mid 3}.$$

First, 5, 7 and 3 are appended to the list. When 4 is processed, it is inserted and then 5, 7 and 3 are deleted as shown in Fig. 1.7(f). Next, as shown in Fig. 1.7(i), after 9 and 8 have been inserted, 9 is deleted. Finally, the elements 7 and 3 are inserted but not deleted, as they do not precede any integer that is even.

```
1. for j ← 1 to n
2.     x ← A[j]
3.     append x to the list
4.     if x is even then
5.         while pred(x) is odd
6.             delete pred(x)
7.         end while
8.     end if
9. end for
```

Fig. 1.7.   Illustration of amortized time analysis.

Now, let us analyze the running time of this algorithm. If the input data contain no even integers, or if all the even integers are at the beginning, then no elements are deleted, and hence each iteration of the **for** loop takes constant time. On the other hand, if the input consists of $n - 1$ odd integers followed by one even integer, then the number of deletions is exactly $n - 1$, i.e., the number of iterations of the **while** loop is $n - 1$. This means that the **while** loop may cost $\Omega(n)$ time in some iterations. It follows that each iteration of the **for** loop takes $O(n)$ time, which results in an overall running time of $O(n^2)$.

Using amortization, however, we obtain a time complexity of $\Theta(n)$ as follows. The number of insertions is obviously n. As to the number of deletions, we note that no element is deleted more than once, and thus the number of deletions is between 0 and $n-1$. It follows that the total number of elementary operations of insertions and deletions altogether is between n and $2n-1$. This implies that the time complexity of the algorithm is indeed $\Theta(n)$. It should be emphasized, however, that in this case, we say that the **while** loop takes *constant amortized time in the worst case*. That is, the average time taken by the **while** loop is *guaranteed* to be $O(1)$ regardless of the input.

Example 1.34 Suppose we want to allocate storage for an unknown number of elements $x_1, x_2, \ldots$ in a stream of input. One technique to handle the allocation of memory is to first allocate an array A_0 of reasonable size, say m. When this array becomes full, then upon the arrival of the $(m+1)$st element, a new array A_1 of size $2m$ is allocated and all the elements stored in A_0 are moved from A_0 to A_1. Next, the $(m+1)$st element is stored in $A_1[m+1]$. We keep doubling the size of the newly allocated array whenever it becomes full and a new element is received, until all elements have been stored.

Suppose, for simplicity, that we start with an array of size 1, that is, A_0 consists of only one entry. First, upon arrival of x_1, we store x_1 in $A_0[1]$. When x_2 is received, we allocate a new array A_1 of size 2, set $A_1[1]$ to $A_0[1]$ and store x_2 in $A_1[2]$. Upon arrival of the third element x_3, we allocate a new array $A_2[1..4]$, move $A_1[1..2]$ to $A_2[1..2]$ and store x_3 in $A_2[3]$. The next element, x_4, will be stored directly in $A_2[4]$. Now, since A_2 is full, when x_5 is received, we allocate a new array $A_3[1..8]$, move $A_2[1..4]$ to $A_3[1..4]$ and store x_5 in $A_3[5]$. Next, we store x_6, x_7 and x_8 in the remaining free positions of A_3. We keep doubling the size of the newly allocated array upon arrival of a new element whenever the current array becomes full and move the contents of the current array to the newly allocated array.

We wish to count the number of element assignments. Suppose, for simplicity, that the total number of elements received, which is n, is a power of 2. Then, the arrays that have been allocated are $A_0, A_1, \ldots, A_k$, where $k = \log n$. Since x_1 has been moved k times, x_2 has been moved $k - 1$ times, etc., we may conclude that each element in $\{x_1, x_2, \ldots, x_n\}$ has been moved $O(k) = O(\log n)$ times. This implies that the total number of element assignments is $O(n \log n)$.

However, using amortized time analysis, we derive a much tighter bound as follows. Observe that every entry in each newly allocated array has been assigned to exactly once. Consequently, the total number of element assignments is equal to the sum of sizes of all arrays that have been allocated, which is equal to

$$\sum_{j=0}^{k} 2^j = 2^{k+1} - 1 = 2n - 1 = \Theta(n) \quad \text{(Eq. (A.10))}.$$

Thus, using amortization, it follows that the time needed to store and move each of the elements $x_1, x_2, \ldots, x_n$ is $\Theta(1)$ *amortized time.*

1.14   Input Size and Problem Instance

A measure of the performance of an algorithm is usually a function of its input: its size, order, distribution, etc. The most prominent of these, which is of interest to us here, is the input size. Using Turing machines as the model of computation, it is possible, and more convenient indeed, to measure the input to an algorithm in terms of the number of nonblank cells. This, of course, is impractical, given that we wish to investigate real-world problems that can be described in terms of numbers, vertices, line segments and other varieties of objects. For this reason, the notion of *input size* belongs to the practical part of algorithm analysis, and its interpretation has become a matter of convention. When discussing a problem, as opposed to an algorithm, we usually talk of a *problem instance*. Thus, a problem instance translates to input in the context of an algorithm that solves that problem. For example, we call an array A of n integers an instance of the problem of sorting numbers. At the same time, in the context of discussing Algorithm INSERTIONSORT, we refer to this array as an input to the algorithm.

The input size, as a quantity, is not a precise measure of the input, and its interpretation is subject to the problem for which the algorithm is, or is to be, designed. Some of the commonly used measures of input size are the following:

- In sorting and searching problems, we use the number of entries in the array or list as the input size.
- In graph algorithms, the input size usually refers to the number of vertices or edges in the graph, or both.
- In computational geometry, the size of input to an algorithm is usually expressed in terms of the number of points, vertices, edges, line segments, polygons, etc.
- In matrix operations, the input size is commonly taken to be the dimensions of the input matrices.
- In number theory algorithms and cryptography, the number of bits in the input is usually chosen to denote its length. The number of words used to represent a single number may also be chosen as well, as each word consists of a fixed number of bits.

These "heterogeneous" measures have brought about some inconsistencies when comparing the amount of time or space required by two algorithms. For example, an algorithm for adding two $n \times n$ matrices which performs n^2 additions sounds quadratic, while it is indeed linear in the input size.

Consider the brute-force algorithm for primality testing given in Example 1.16. Its time complexity was shown to be $O(\sqrt{n})$. Since this is a number problem, the time complexity of the algorithm is measured in terms of the number of bits in the binary representation of n. Since n can be represented using $k = \lceil \log(n+1) \rceil$ bits, the time complexity can be rewritten as $O(\sqrt{n}) = O(2^{k/2})$. Consequently, Algorithm BRUTE-FORCE PRIMALITYTEST is in fact an exponential algorithm.

Now, we will compare two algorithms for computing the sum $\sum_{j=1}^{n} j$. In the first algorithm, which we will call FIRST, the input is an array $A[1..n]$ with $A[j] = j$, for each $j, 1 \leq j \leq n$. The input to the second algorithm, call it SECOND, is just the number n. These two algorithms are shown as Algorithm FIRST and Algorithm SECOND.

Algorithm 1.14 FIRST
Input: A positive integer n and an array $A[1..n]$ with $A[j] = j, 1 \leq j \leq n$.
Output: $\sum_{j=1}^{n} A[j]$.

1. $sum \leftarrow 0$
2. **for** $j \leftarrow 1$ **to** n
3. $sum \leftarrow sum + A[j]$
4. **end for**
5. **return** sum

Algorithm 1.15 SECOND
Input: A positive integer n.
Output: $\sum_{j=1}^{n} j$.

1. $sum \leftarrow 0$
2. **for** $j \leftarrow 1$ **to** n
3. $sum \leftarrow sum + j$
4. **end for**
5. **return** sum

Obviously, both algorithms run in time $\Theta(n)$. Clearly, the time complexity of Algorithm FIRST is $\Theta(n)$. Algorithm SECOND is designed to solve a *number problem* and, as we have stated before, its input size is measured in terms of the number of bits in the binary representation of the integer n. Its input consists of $k = \lceil \log(n+1) \rceil$ bits. It follows that the time complexity of Algorithm SECOND is $\Theta(n) = \Theta(2^k)$. In other words, it is considered to be an *exponential* time algorithm. Notice that the number of elementary operations performed by both algorithms is the same.

1.15   Divide-and-Conquer Recurrences

The main objective of this section is to study some of the techniques specific to the solution of the most common divide-and-conquer recurrences that arise in the analysis of divide-and-conquer algorithms in one variable (see Chapter 5). These recurrences take the following form:

$$f(n) = \begin{cases} d & \text{if } n \leq n_0 \\ a_1 f(n/c_1) + a_2 f(n/c_2) + \cdots + a_p f(n/c_p) + g(n) & \text{if } n > n_0, \end{cases}$$

where $a_1, a_2, \ldots, a_p, c_1, c_2, \ldots, c_p$ and n_0 are nonnegative integers, d a nonnegative constant, $p \geq 1$ and $g(n)$ is a function from the set of nonnegative integers to the set of real numbers. We discuss here three of the most common techniques of solving divide-and-conquer recurrences. For general recurrences, see Appendix A (Sec. A.8).

1.15.1   *Expanding the recurrence*

Perhaps, the most natural approach to solve a recurrence is by expanding it repeatedly in the obvious way. This method is so mechanical and intuitive that it virtually does not need any explanation. However, one should keep in mind that, in some cases, it is time-consuming and, being mechanical, susceptible to calculation errors. This method is hard to apply on a recurrence in which the ratios in the definition of the function are not equal. An example of this is given later when we study the substitution method in Sec. 1.15.2.

Example 1.35   Consider the recurrence

$$f(n) = \begin{cases} d & \text{if } n = 1 \\ 2f(n/2) + bn \log n & \text{if } n \geq 2, \end{cases}$$

where b and d are nonnegative constants and n is a power of 2. We proceed to solve this recurrence as follows (here $k = \log n$):

$$
\begin{aligned}
f(n) &= 2f(n/2) + bn\log n \\
&= 2(2f(n/2^2) + b(n/2)\log(n/2)) + bn\log n \\
&= 2^2 f(n/2^2) + bn\log(n/2) + bn\log n \\
&= 2^2(2f(n/2^3) + b(n/2^2)\log(n/2^2)) + bn\log(n/2) + bn\log n \\
&= 2^3 f(n/2^3) + bn\log(n/2^2) + bn\log(n/2) + bn\log n \\
&\ \ \vdots \\
&= 2^k f(n/2^k) + bn(\log(n/2^{k-1}) + \log(n/2^{k-2}) + \ldots + \log(n/2^{k-k})) \\
&= dn + bn(\log 2^1 + \log 2^2 + \ldots + \log 2^k) \\
&= dn + bn \sum_{j=1}^{k} \log 2^j \\
&= dn + bn \sum_{j=1}^{k} j \\
&= dn + bn \frac{k(k+1)}{2} \\
&= dn + \frac{bn\log^2 n}{2} + \frac{bn\log n}{2}.
\end{aligned}
$$

Theorem 1.2 *Let b and d be nonnegative constants, and let n be a power of 2. Then, the solution to the recurrence*

$$
f(n) = \begin{cases} d & \text{if } n = 1 \\ 2f(n/2) + bn\log n & \text{if } n \geq 2 \end{cases}
$$

is

$$
f(n) = \Theta(n\log^2 n).
$$

Proof. The proof follows directly from Example 1.35. □

Lemma 1.1 *Let a and c be nonnegative integers, b, d and x nonnegative constants, and let $n = c^k$, for some nonnegative integer k. Then, the* *solution to the recurrence*

$$f(n) = \begin{cases} d & \text{if } n = 1 \\ af(n/c) + bn^x & \text{if } n \geq 2 \end{cases}$$

is

$$f(n) = bn^x \log_c n + dn^x \qquad \qquad \text{if } a = c^x,$$

$$f(n) = \left(d + \frac{bc^x}{a - c^x}\right) n^{\log_c a} - \left(\frac{bc^x}{a - c^x}\right) n^x \quad \text{if } a \neq c^x.$$

Proof. We proceed to solve this recurrence by expansion as follows:

$$\begin{aligned}
f(n) &= af(n/c) + bn^x \\
&= a(af(n/c^2) + b(n/c)^x) + bn^x \\
&= a^2 f(n/c^2) + (a/c^x)bn^x + bn^x \\
&\;\;\vdots \\
&= a^k f(n/c^k) + (a/c^x)^{k-1} bn^x + \cdots + (a/c^x)bn^x + bn^x \\
&= da^{\log_c n} + bn^x \sum_{j=0}^{k-1} (a/c^x)^j \\
&= dn^{\log_c a} + bn^x \sum_{j=0}^{k-1} (a/c^x)^j.
\end{aligned}$$

The last equality follows from Eq. (A.2) on page 671. We have two cases as follows:

(1) $a = c^x$. In this case,

$$\sum_{j=0}^{k-1} (a/c^x)^j = k = \log_c n.$$

Since $\log_c a = \log_c c^x = x$,

$$f(n) = bn^x \log_c n + dn^{\log_c a} = bn^x \log_c n + dn^x.$$

(2) $a \neq c^x$. In this case, by Eq. (A.9) on page 678,

$$bn^x \sum_{j=0}^{k-1} (a/c^x)^j = \frac{bn^x(a/c^x)^k - bn^x}{(a/c^x) - 1}$$

$$= \frac{ba^k - bn^x}{(a/c^x) - 1}$$

$$= \frac{bc^x a^k - bc^x n^x}{a - c^x}$$

$$= \frac{bc^x a^{\log_c n} - bc^x n^x}{a - c^x}$$

$$= \frac{bc^x n^{\log_c a} - bc^x n^x}{a - c^x}.$$

Hence,

$$f(n) = \left(d + \frac{bc^x}{a - c^x} \right) n^{\log_c a} - \left(\frac{bc^x}{a - c^x} \right) n^x. \qquad \square$$

Corollary 1.1 *Let a and c be nonnegative integers, b, d and x nonnegative constants, and let $n = c^k$, for some nonnegative integer k. Then, the solution to the recurrence*

$$f(n) = \begin{cases} d & \text{if } n = 1 \\ af(n/c) + bn^x & \text{if } n \geq 2 \end{cases}$$

satisfies

$$f(n) = bn^x \log_c n + dn^x \qquad \text{if } a = c^x,$$

$$f(n) \leq \left(\frac{bc^x}{c^x - a} \right) n^x \qquad \text{if } a < c^x,$$

$$f(n) \leq \left(d + \frac{bc^x}{a - c^x} \right) n^{\log_c a} \qquad \text{if } a > c^x.$$

Proof. If $a < c^x$, then $\log_c a < x$ or $n^{\log_c a} < n^x$. If $a > c^x$, then $\log_c a > x$ or $n^{\log_c a} > n^x$. The rest of the proof follows immediately from Lemma 1.1. $\qquad \square$

Corollary 1.2 *Let a and c be nonnegative integers, b and d nonnegative constants, and let $n = c^k$, for some nonnegative integer k. Then, the* *solution to the recurrence*

$$f(n) = \begin{cases} d & \text{if } n = 1 \\ af(n/c) + bn & \text{if } n \geq 2 \end{cases}$$

is

$$f(n) = bn \log_c n + dn \qquad\qquad\qquad \text{if } a = c,$$

$$f(n) = \left(d + \frac{bc}{a - c}\right) n^{\log_c a} - \left(\frac{bc}{a - c}\right) n \quad \text{if } a \neq c.$$

Proof.   Follows immediately from Lemma 1.1.   □

Theorem 1.3   *Let a and c be nonnegative integers, b, d and x nonnegative constants, and let $n = c^k$, for some nonnegative integer k. Then, the solution to the recurrence*

$$f(n) = \begin{cases} d & \text{if } n = 1 \\ af(n/c) + bn^x & \text{if } n \geq 2 \end{cases}$$

is

$$f(n) = \begin{cases} \Theta(n^x) & \text{if } a < c^x \\ \Theta(n^x \log n) & \text{if } a = c^x \\ \Theta(n^{\log_c a}) & \text{if } a > c^x. \end{cases}$$

In particular, if $x = 1$, then

$$f(n) = \begin{cases} \Theta(n) & \text{if } a < c \\ \Theta(n \log n) & \text{if } a = c \\ \Theta(n^{\log_c a}) & \text{if } a > c. \end{cases}$$

Proof.   Follows immediately from Lemma 1.1 and Corollary 1.1.   □

1.15.2   *Substitution*

This method is usually employed for proving upper and lower bounds. It can also be used to prove exact solutions. In this method, we guess a solution and try to prove it by appealing to mathematical induction (see Sec. A.2.5). Unlike what is commonly done in inductive proofs, here we first proceed to prove the inductive step with one or more unknown constants, and once the claim is established for $f(n)$, where n is arbitrary, we try to fine-tune the constant(s), if necessary, in order to make the solution apply to the boundary condition(s) as well. The difficulty in this method is in coming up with an intelligent guess that serves as a *tight* bound for the given recurrence. In many instances, however, the given recurrence resembles another one whose solution is known *a priori*. This helps in finding a starting guess that is reasonably good. The following examples illustrate this method.

Example 1.36 Consider the recurrence

$$f(n) = \begin{cases} d & \text{if } n = 1 \\ f(\lfloor n/2 \rfloor) + f(\lceil n/2 \rceil) + bn & \text{if } n \geq 2, \end{cases}$$

for some nonnegative constants b and d. When n is a power of 2, this recurrence reduces to

$$f(n) = 2f(n/2) + bn,$$

whose solution is, by Corollary 1.2, $bn \log n + dn$. Consequently, we will make the guess that $f(n) \leq cbn \log n + dn$ for some constant $c > 0$, whose value will be determined later. Assume that the claim is true for $\lfloor n/2 \rfloor$ and $\lceil n/2 \rceil$, where $n \geq 2$. Substituting for $f(n)$ in the recurrence, we obtain

$$\begin{aligned} f(n) &= f(\lfloor n/2 \rfloor) + f(\lceil n/2 \rceil) + bn \\ &\leq cb\lfloor n/2 \rfloor \log \lfloor n/2 \rfloor + d\lfloor n/2 \rfloor + cb\lceil n/2 \rceil \log \lceil n/2 \rceil + d\lceil n/2 \rceil + bn \\ &\leq cb\lfloor n/2 \rfloor \log \lceil n/2 \rceil + cb\lceil n/2 \rceil \log \lceil n/2 \rceil + dn + bn \\ &= cbn \log \lceil n/2 \rceil + dn + bn \\ &\leq cbn \log((n+1)/2) + dn + bn \\ &= cbn \log(n+1) - cbn + dn + bn. \end{aligned}$$

In order for $f(n)$ to be at most $cbn \log n + dn$, we must have $cbn \log(n+1) - cbn + bn \leq cbn \log n$ or $c \log(n+1) - c + 1 \leq c \log n$, which reduces to

$$c \geq \frac{1}{1 + \log n - \log(n+1)} = \frac{1}{1 + \log \frac{n}{n+1}}.$$

When $n \geq 2$,

$$\frac{1}{1 + \log \frac{n}{n+1}} \leq \frac{1}{1 + \log \frac{2}{3}} < 2.41,$$

and hence, we will set $c = 2.41$. When $n = 1$, we have $0 + d \le d$. It follows that

$$f(n) \le 2.41bn \log n + dn \quad \text{for all } n \ge 1.$$

Example 1.37   In this example, we show that the recurrence $f(n)$ defined in Example 1.36 is at least $cbn \log n + dn$. That is, we show that $cbn \log n + dn$ is a lower bound for the function $f(n)$, for some constant $c > 0$ that will be determined later. Assume that the claim is true for $\lfloor n/2 \rfloor$ and $\lceil n/2 \rceil$, where $n \ge 2$. Substituting for $f(n)$ in the recurrence, we obtain

$$
\begin{aligned}
f(n) &= f(\lfloor n/2 \rfloor) + f(\lceil n/2 \rceil) + bn \\
&\ge cb\lfloor n/2 \rfloor \log \lfloor n/2 \rfloor + d\lfloor n/2 \rfloor + cb\lceil n/2 \rceil \log \lceil n/2 \rceil + d\lceil n/2 \rceil + bn \\
&\ge cb\lfloor n/2 \rfloor \log \lfloor n/2 \rfloor + d\lfloor n/2 \rfloor + cb\lceil n/2 \rceil \log \lfloor n/2 \rfloor + d\lceil n/2 \rceil + bn \\
&= cbn \log \lfloor n/2 \rfloor + dn + bn \\
&\ge cbn \log(n/4) + dn + bn \\
&= cbn\log n - 2cbn + dn + bn \\
&= cbn\log n + dn + (bn - 2cbn).
\end{aligned}
$$

In order for $f(n)$ to be at least $cbn \log n + dn$, we must have $bn - 2cbn \ge 0$ or $c \le 1/2$. Consequently, $f(n) \ge bn \log n/2 + dn$. Since $f(n) \ge bn \log n/2 + dn$ holds when $n = 1$, it follows that

$$f(n) \ge \frac{bn \log n}{2} + dn \quad \text{for all } n \ge 1.$$

Theorem 1.4   *Let*

$$
f(n) = \begin{cases} d & \text{if } n = 1 \\ f(\lfloor n/2 \rfloor) + f(\lceil n/2 \rceil) + bn & \text{if } n \ge 2, \end{cases}
$$

for some nonnegative constants b and d. Then,

$$f(n) = \Theta(n \log n).$$

Proof.   The proof follows from Examples 1.36 and 1.37. $\square$

Example 1.38 Consider the recurrence

$$f(n) = \begin{cases} 0 & \text{if } n = 0 \\ b & \text{if } n = 1 \\ f(\lfloor c_1 n \rfloor) + f(\lfloor c_2 n \rfloor) + bn & \text{if } n \geq 2, \end{cases}$$

for some positive constants b, c_1 and c_2 such that $c_1 + c_2 = 1$. When $c_1 = c_2 = 1/2$, and n is a power of 2, this recurrence reduces to

$$f(n) = \begin{cases} b & \text{if } n = 1 \\ 2f(n/2) + bn & \text{if } n \geq 2, \end{cases}$$

whose solution is, by Corollary 1.2, $bn\log n + bn$. Consequently, we will make the guess that $f(n) \leq cbn \log n + bn$ for some constant $c > 0$, whose value will be determined later. Assume that the claim is true for $\lfloor c_1 n \rfloor$ and $\lfloor c_2 n \rfloor$, where $n \geq 2$. Substituting for $f(n)$ in the recurrence, we obtain

$$\begin{aligned} f(n) &= f(\lfloor c_1 n \rfloor) + f(\lfloor c_2 n \rfloor) + bn \\ &\leq cb\lfloor c_1 n \rfloor \log \lfloor c_1 n \rfloor + b\lfloor c_1 n \rfloor + cb\lfloor c_2 n \rfloor \log \lfloor c_2 n \rfloor + b\lfloor c_2 n \rfloor + bn \\ &\leq cbc_1 n \log c_1 n + bc_1 n + cbc_2 n \log c_2 n + bc_2 n + bn \\ &= cbn \log n + bn + cbn(c_1 \log c_1 + c_2 \log c_2) + bn \\ &= cbn \log n + bn + cben + bn, \end{aligned}$$

where $e = c_1 \log c_1 + c_2 \log c_2 < 0$. In order for $f(n)$ to be at most $cbn \log n + bn$, we must have $cben + bn \leq 0$ or $ce \leq -1$, or $c \geq -1/e$, a nonnegative constant. Consequently, $f(n) \leq -bn \log n/e + bn$. Clearly, this inequality holds for $n = 1$. It follows that

$$f(n) \leq \frac{-bn \log n}{c_1 \log c_1 + c_2 \log c_2} + bn \quad \text{for all } n \geq 1.$$

For example, if $c_1 = c_2 = 1/2$, $c_1 \log c_1 + c_2 \log c_2 = -1$, and hence $f(n) \leq bn \log n + bn$ for all $n \geq 1$. This conforms with Corollary 1.2 when n is a power of 2.

Example 1.39 In this example, we solve the recurrence defined in Example 1.38 when $c_1 + c_2 < 1$. When $c_1 = c_2 = 1/4$ and n is a power of 2, this recurrence reduces to the recurrence

$$f(n) = \begin{cases} b & \text{if } n = 1 \\ 2f(n/4) + bn & \text{if } n \geq 2, \end{cases}$$

whose solution is, by Corollary 1.2, $f(n) = 2bn - b\sqrt{n}$. Consequently, we will make the guess that $f(n) \leq cbn$ for some constant $c > 0$. That is, we show that cbn is an upper bound for the function $f(n)$ when $c_1 + c_2 < 1$, for some constant $c > 0$ that will be determined later. Assume that the claim is true for $\lfloor c_1 n \rfloor$ and $\lfloor c_2 n \rfloor$, where $n \geq 2$. Substituting for $f(n)$ in the recurrence, we obtain

$$\begin{aligned} f(n) &= f(\lfloor c_1 n \rfloor) + f(\lfloor c_2 n \rfloor) + bn \\ &\leq cb\lfloor c_1 n \rfloor + cb\lfloor c_2 n \rfloor + bn \\ &\leq cbc_1 n + cbc_2 n + bn \\ &= c(c_1 + c_2)bn + bn. \end{aligned}$$

In order for $f(n)$ to be at most cbn, we must have $c(c_1 + c_2)bn + bn \leq cbn$ or $c(c_1 + c_2) + 1 \leq c$, that is, $c(1 - c_1 - c_2) \geq 1$ or $c \geq 1/(1 - c_1 - c_2)$, a nonnegative constant. Clearly, $f(n) \leq bn/(1 - c_1 - c_2)$ holds for $n = 0$ and $n = 1$. It follows that

$$f(n) \leq \frac{bn}{1 - c_1 - c_2} \qquad \text{for all } n \geq 0.$$

For example, if $c_1 = c_2 = 1/4$, then we have $f(n) \leq 2bn$, and the exact solution is, as stated above, $f(n) = 2bn - b\sqrt{n}$.

Theorem 1.5 *Let b, c_1 and c_2 be nonnegative constants. Then, the solution to the recurrence*

$$f(n) = \begin{cases} 0 & \text{if } n = 0 \\ b & \text{if } n = 1 \\ f(\lfloor c_1 n \rfloor) + f(\lfloor c_2 n \rfloor) + bn & \text{if } n \geq 2 \end{cases}$$

is

$$f(n) = \begin{cases} O(n \log n) & \text{if } c_1 + c_2 = 1 \\ \Theta(n) & \text{if } c_1 + c_2 < 1. \end{cases}$$

Proof. By Example 1.38, $f(n) = O(n \log n)$ if $c_1 + c_2 = 1$. If $c_1 + c_2 < 1$, then by Example 1.39, $f(n) = O(n)$. Since $f(n) = \Omega(n)$, it follows that $f(n) = \Theta(n)$. □

1.15.3 *Change of variables*

In some recurrences, it is more convenient if we change the domain of the function and define a new recurrence in the new domain whose solution may be easier to obtain. In the following, we give two examples. The second example shows that this method is sometimes helpful, as it reduces the original recurrence to another much easier recurrence.

Example 1.40 Consider the recurrence

$$f(n) = \begin{cases} d & \text{if } n = 1 \\ 2f(n/2) + bn \log n & \text{if } n \geq 2, \end{cases}$$

which we have solved by expansion in Example 1.35. Here, n is a power of 2, so let $k = \log n$ and write $n = 2^k$. Then, the recurrence can be rewritten as

$$f(2^k) = \begin{cases} d & \text{if } k = 0 \\ 2f(2^{k-1}) + bk2^k & \text{if } k \geq 1. \end{cases}$$

Now, let $g(k) = f(2^k)$. Then, we have

$$g(k) = \begin{cases} d & \text{if } k = 0 \\ 2g(k-1) + bk2^k & \text{if } k \geq 1. \end{cases}$$

This recurrence is of the form of Eq. (A.23) on page 686. Hence, we follow the procedure outlined in Sec. A.8.2 to solve this recurrence. Let

$$2^k h(k) = g(k) \text{ with } h(0) = g(0) = d.$$

Then,

$$2^k h(k) = 2(2^{k-1} h(k-1)) + bk2^k,$$

or

$$h(k) = h(k-1) + bk.$$

The solution to this recurrence is

$$h(k) = h(0) + \sum_{j=1}^{k} bj = d + \frac{bk(k+1)}{2}.$$

Consequently,

$$g(k) = 2^k h(k) = d2^k + \frac{bk^2 2^k}{2} + \frac{bk2^k}{2} = dn + \frac{bn \log^2 n}{2} + \frac{bn \log n}{2},$$

which is the same solution obtained in Example 1.35.

Example 1.41   Consider the recurrence

$$f(n) = \begin{cases} 1 & \text{if } n = 2 \\ 1 & \text{if } n = 4 \\ f(n/2) + f(n/4) & \text{if } n > 4, \end{cases}$$

where n is assumed to be a power of 2. Let $g(k) = f(2^k)$, where $k = \log n$. Then, we have

$$g(k) = \begin{cases} 1 & \text{if } k = 1 \\ 1 & \text{if } k = 2 \\ g(k-1) + g(k-2) & \text{if } k > 2. \end{cases}$$

$g(k)$ is exactly the Fibonacci recurrence discussed in Example A.20, whose solution is

$$g(k) = \frac{1}{\sqrt{5}} \left(\frac{1+\sqrt{5}}{2} \right)^k - \frac{1}{\sqrt{5}} \left(\frac{1-\sqrt{5}}{2} \right)^k.$$

Consequently,

$$f(n) = \frac{1}{\sqrt{5}} \left(\frac{1+\sqrt{5}}{2} \right)^{\log n} - \frac{1}{\sqrt{5}} \left(\frac{1-\sqrt{5}}{2} \right)^{\log n}.$$

If we let $\phi = (1+\sqrt{5})/2 = 1.61803$, then

$$f(n) = \Theta(\phi^{\log n}) = \Theta(n^{\log \phi}).$$

Example 1.42 Let

$$f(n) = \begin{cases} d & \text{if } n = 2 \\ 2f(\sqrt{n}) + b\log n & \text{if } n > 2, \end{cases}$$

where $n = 2^{2^k}, k \geq 1$. $f(n)$ can be rewritten as

$$f(2^{2^k}) = \begin{cases} d & \text{if } k = 0 \\ 2f(2^{2^{k-1}}) + b2^k & \text{if } k > 0. \end{cases}$$

Let $g(k) = f(2^{2^k})$. Then,

$$g(k) = \begin{cases} d & \text{if } k = 0 \\ 2g(k-1) + b2^k & \text{if } k > 0. \end{cases}$$

This recurrence is of the form of Eq. (A.23) on page 686. Hence, we follow the procedure outlined in Sec. A.8.2 to solve this recurrence. If we let

$$2^k h(k) = g(k) \text{ with } h(0) = g(0) = d,$$

then we have

$$2^k h(k) = 2(2^{k-1}h(k-1)) + b2^k.$$

Dividing both sides by 2^k yields

$$h(k) = h(0) + \sum_{j=1}^{k} b = d + bk.$$

Hence,

$$g(k) = 2^k h(k) = d2^k + bk2^k.$$

Substituting $n = 2^{2^k}, \log n = 2^k$ and $\log \log n = k$ yields

$$f(n) = d\log n + b\log n \, \log\log n.$$

1.16　Practice Problems

1.1. How many element comparisons are executed by Algorithm SELECTIONSORT when the input size is $n = 10^9$? How many element comparisons are executed by Algorithm BOTTOMUPSORT for the same input size?

1.2. Which algorithm has a running time of $\Theta(n^2)$, SELECTIONSORT or INSERTIONSORT?

1.3. Let $t(n)$ be the running time of Algorithm INSERTIONSORT. Express $t(n)$ using the O, Ω and Θ notations whatever applies. Justify your answer.

1.4. Is Algorithm BOTTOMUPSORT $O(n \log n)$? Is it $\Omega(n \log n)$? Justify your answer.

1.5. Fill in the blanks with either *true* or *false*:

$f(n)$	$g(n)$	$f = O(g)$	$f = \Omega(g)$	$f = \Theta(g)$
$2n^3 + 3n$	$100n^2 + 2n + 100$			
$50n + \log n$	$10n + \log \log n$			
$50n \log n$	$10n \log \log n$			
$\log n$	$\log^2 n$			
$n!$	5^n			

1.6. Is $4^n = \Theta(2^{n^2})$? Prove your answer.

1.7. Show that $3^n \neq \Theta(2^{2n})$. *Hint*: $2^{2n} = 4^n$.

1.8. Let n be the input to Algorithm 1, where n is a power of 10.

Algorithm 1.16　Algorithm 1

Input: n.

Output: none

1. $m \leftarrow n$
2. **while** $m \geq 1$
3. 　　**for** $i \leftarrow 1$ **to** m
4. 　　　　$x \leftarrow 100$ 　⟸ Step 4
5. 　　**end for**
6. 　　$m \leftarrow \frac{m}{10}$
7. **end while**

(a) What is the number of times (expressed in n) is Step 4 executed? Give a brief justification.

(b) What is the time complexity of the algorithm expressed in the O-notation?

(c) Answer Part (b) if Step 6 is changed to $m \leftarrow \lfloor \frac{m}{100} \rfloor$.

(d) Answer Part (b) if Step 1 is changed to $m \leftarrow \lfloor \sqrt{n} \rfloor$.

1.9. Consider Algorithm 2 whose input is a positive integer n. Compute the number of times statement 5 is executed and express the running time using the O-notation.

Algorithm 1.17 Algorithm 2
Input: n.
Output: none.

1. $x \leftarrow \lfloor \sqrt{n} \rfloor$
2. **while** $x \geq 1$
3. $y \leftarrow x$
4.   **while** $y \geq 1$
5. $y \leftarrow y - 1$ ⟸ Step 5
6.   **end while**
7. $x \leftarrow \lfloor x/2 \rfloor$
8. **end while**

1.10. Which algorithm is optimal, insertion sort or bottomupsort?

1.11. Is $3^n = o(2^{2n})$? Prove your answer. See Problem 1.7.

1.12. Suppose that $f(n) = o(g(n))$. Does this imply that $f(n) = O(g(n))$? Explain.

1.13. Let $A[1..n]$ be an array of $2n$ elements with the property that both the odd-indexed elements $A[1], A[3], ...A[2n-1]$ and the even-indexed elements $A[2], A[4], ...A[2n]$ are sorted independently. Give an algorithm to sort all elements in A in $O(n)$ time.

1.14. Let A be an array of $2n$ elements, which contains an element x that is repeated $n+1$ times, and all other elements are distinct. Give an algorithm to find x using the least number of comparisons. Prove the correctness of your algorithm. *Hint*: Use the pigeonhole principle to show that there is a j such that $A[j] = A[j+1] = x$.

1.15. Consider the following recurrence:

$$f(n) = 2f(n/2) + n^2 \quad \text{for } n \geq 2; \ f(1) = 1,$$

where n is assumed to be a power of 2.

(a) Solve the recurrence by expansion.

(b) Solve the recurrence directly by applying Theorem 1.3.

1.17   Exercises

1.1. Let $A[1..60] = 11, 12, \ldots, 70$. How many comparisons are performed by Algorithm BINARYSEARCH when searching for the following values of x?

(a) 33.   (b) 7.   (c) 70.   (d) 77.

1.2. Let $A[1..2000] = 1, 2, \ldots, 2000$. How many comparisons are performed by Algorithm BINARYSEARCH when searching for the following values of x?

(a) −3.   (b) 1.   (c) 1000.   (d) 4000.

1.3. Draw the decision tree for the binary search algorithm with an input of

(a) 12 elements. (b) 17 elements. (c) 25 elements. (d) 35 elements.

1.4. Show that the height of the decision tree for binary search is $\lfloor \log n \rfloor$.

1.5. Illustrate the operation of Algorithm SELECTIONSORT on the array

$$\boxed{45\,|\,33\,|\,24\,|\,45\,|\,12\,|\,12\,|\,24\,|\,12}.$$

How many comparisons are performed by the algorithm?

1.6. Consider modifying Algorithm SELECTIONSORT as shown in Algorithm MODSELECTIONSORT.

(a) What is the minimum number of element assignments performed by Algorithm MODSELECTIONSORT? When is this minimum achieved?

(b) What is the maximum number of element assignments performed by Algorithm MODSELECTIONSORT? Note that each interchange is implemented using three element assignments. When is this maximum achieved?

Algorithm 1.18 MODSELECTIONSORT
Input: An array $A[1..n]$ of n elements.

Output: $A[1..n]$ sorted in nondecreasing order.

1. **for** $i \leftarrow 1$ **to** $n - 1$
2.   **for** $j \leftarrow i + 1$ **to** n
3.   **if** $A[j] < A[i]$ **then** interchange $A[i]$ and $A[j]$
4.   **end for**
5. **end for**

1.7. Illustrate the operation of Algorithm INSERTIONSORT on the array

$$\boxed{30\,|\,12\,|\,13\,|\,13\,|\,44\,|\,12\,|\,25\,|\,13}.$$

How many comparisons are performed by the algorithm?

1.8. How many comparisons are performed by Algorithm INSERTIONSORT when presented with the input

$$\boxed{4\,|\,3\,|\,12\,|\,5\,|\,6\,|\,7\,|\,2\,|\,9}\,?$$

1.9. Prove Observation 1.4.

1.10. Which algorithm is more efficient: Algorithm INSERTIONSORT or Algorithm SELECTIONSORT? What if the input array consists of very large records? Explain.

1.11. Illustrate the operation of Algorithm BOTTOMUPSORT on the array

$$A[1..16] = \boxed{11\,|\,12\,|\,1\,|\,5\,|\,15\,|\,3\,|\,4\,|\,10\,|\,7\,|\,2\,|\,16\,|\,9\,|\,8\,|\,14\,|\,13\,|\,6}.$$

How many comparisons are performed by the algorithm?

1.12. Illustrate the operation of Algorithm BOTTOMUPSORT on the array

$$A[1..11] = \boxed{2\,|\,17\,|\,19\,|\,5\,|\,13\,|\,11\,|\,4\,|\,8\,|\,15\,|\,12\,|\,7}.$$

How many comparisons are performed by the algorithm?

1.13. Give an array $A[1..8]$ of integers on which Algorithm BOTTOMUPSORT performs
(a) the minimum number of element comparisons.
(b) the maximum number of element comparisons.

1.14. Fill in the blanks with either *true* or *false*:

$f(n)$	$g(n)$	$f = O(g)$	$f = \Omega(g)$	$f = \Theta(g)$
$2n^3 + 3n$	$100n^2 + 2n + 100$			
$50n + \log n$	$10n + \log\log n$			
$50n \log n$	$10n \log\log n$			
$\log n$	$\log^2 n$			
$n!$	5^n			

1.15. Express the following functions in terms of the Θ-notation:
(a) $2n + 3\log^{100} n$.
(b) $7n^3 + 1000n \log n + 3n$.
(c) $3n^{1.5} + (\sqrt{n})^3 \log n$.
(d) $2^n + 100^n + n!$.

1.16. Express the following functions in terms of the Θ-notation:
(a) $18n^3 + \log n^8$.
(b) $(n^3 + n)/(n + 5)$.
(c) $\log^2 n + \sqrt{n} + \log\log n$.
(d) $n!/2^n + n^n$.

1.17. Consider the sorting algorithm shown below, which is called BUBBLESORT.

Algorithm 1.19 BUBBLESORT
Input: An array $A[1..n]$ of n elements.

Output: $A[1..n]$ sorted in nondecreasing order.

1. $i \leftarrow 1$;   *sorted* $\leftarrow$ *false*
2. **while** $i \leq n - 1$ **and not** *sorted*
3.   *sorted* $\leftarrow$ *true*
4.   **for** $j \leftarrow n$ **downto** $i + 1$
5.   **if** $A[j] < A[j - 1]$ **then**
6.   interchange $A[j]$ and $A[j - 1]$
7.   *sorted* $\leftarrow$ *false*
8.   **end if**
9.   **end for**
10. $i \leftarrow i + 1$
11. **end while**

(a) What is the minimum number of element comparisons performed by the algorithm? When is this minimum achieved?

(b) What is the maximum number of element comparisons performed by the algorithm? When is this maximum achieved?

(c) What is the minimum number of element assignments performed by the algorithm? When is this minimum achieved?

(d) What is the maximum number of element assignments performed by the algorithm? When is this maximum achieved?

(e) Express the running time of Algorithm BUBBLESORT in terms of the O and Ω notations.

(f) Can the running time of the algorithm be expressed in terms of the Θ-notation? Explain.

1.18. Find two monotonically increasing functions $f(n)$ and $g(n)$ such that $f(n) \neq O(g(n))$ and $g(n) \neq O(f(n))$.

1.19. Is $x = O(x \sin x)$? Use the definition of the O-notation to prove your answer.

1.20. Prove that $\sum_{j=1}^{n} j^k$ is $O(n^{k+1})$ and $\Omega(n^{k+1})$, where k is a positive integer. Conclude that it is $\Theta(n^{k+1})$.

1.21. Let $f(n) = \{1/n + 1/n^2 + 1/n^3 + \cdots\}$. Express $f(n)$ in terms of the Θ-notation. (*Hint:* Find a recursive definition of $f(n)$).

1.22. Show that $n^{100} = O(2^n)$, but $2^n \neq O(n^{100})$.

1.23. Show that 2^n is not $\Theta(3^n)$.

1.24. Is $n! = \Theta(n^n)$? Prove your answer.

1.25. Is $2^{n^2} = \Theta(2^{n^3})$? Prove your answer.

1.26. Carefully explain the difference between $O(1)$ and $\Theta(1)$.

1.27. Is the function $\lfloor \log n \rfloor!$ $O(n)$, $\Omega(n)$, $\Theta(n)$? Prove your answer.

1.28. Can we use the $\prec$ relation described in Sec. 1.8.6 to compare the order of growth of n^2 and $100n^2$? Explain.

1.29. Use the $\prec$ relation to order the following functions by growth rate: $n^{1/100}$, $\sqrt{n}$, $\log n^{100}$, $n \log n$, 5, $\log \log n$, $\log^2 n$, $(\sqrt{n})^n$, $(1/2)^n$, 2^{n^2}, $n!$.

1.30. Consider the following problem. Given an array $A[1..n]$ of integers, test each element a in A to see whether it is even or odd. If a is even, then leave it; otherwise, multiply it by 2.

(a) Which one of the O and Θ notations is more appropriate to measure the number of multiplications? Explain.

(b) Which one of the O and Θ notations is more appropriate to measure the number of element tests? Explain.

1.31. Give a more efficient algorithm than the one given in Example 1.22. What is the time complexity of your algorithm?

1.32. Consider Algorithm COUNT6 whose input is a positive integer n.

Algorithm 1.20 COUNT6

1. **comment:** *Exercise 1.32*
2. *count* $\leftarrow 0$
3. **for** $i \leftarrow 1$ **to** $\lfloor \log n \rfloor$
4.   **for** $j \leftarrow i$ **to** $i + 5$
5.   **for** $k \leftarrow 1$ **to** i^2
6.   *count* $\leftarrow$ *count* $+ 1$
7.   **end for**
8.   **end for**
9. **end for**

(a) How many times Step 6 is executed?

(b) Which one of the O and Θ notations is more appropriate to express the time complexity of the algorithm? Explain.

(c) What is the time complexity of the algorithm?

1.33. Consider Algorithm COUNT7 whose input is a positive integer n.

(a) What is the maximum number of times Step 6 is executed when n is a power of 2?

(b) What is the time complexity of the algorithm expressed in the O-notation?

(c) What is the time complexity of the algorithm expressed in the Ω-notation?

```
Algorithm 1.21 COUNT7
1. comment: Exercise 1.33
2. count ← 0
3. for i ← 1 to n
4.      j ← ⌊n/2⌋
5.      while j ≥ 1
6.          count ← count + 1
7.          if j is odd then j ← 0 else j ← j/2
8.      end while
9. end for
```

(d) Which one of the O and Θ notations is more appropriate to express the time complexity of the algorithm? Explain briefly.

1.34. Consider Algorithm COUNT8 whose input is a positive integer n.

```
Algorithm 1.22 COUNT8
1. comment: Exercise 1.34
2. count ← 0
3. for i ← 1 to n
4.      j ← ⌊n/3⌋
5.      while j ≥ 1
6.          for k ← 1 to i
7.              count ← count + 1
8.          end for
9.          if j is even then j ← 0 else j ← ⌊j/3⌋
10.     end while
11. end for
```

(a) What is the maximum number of times Step 7 is executed when n is a power of 2?

(b) What is the maximum number of times Step 7 is executed when n is a power of 3?

(c) What is the time complexity of the algorithm expressed in the O-notation?

(d) What is the time complexity of the algorithm expressed in the Ω-notation?

(e) Which one of the O and Θ notations is more appropriate to express the time complexity of the algorithm? Explain briefly.

1.35. Write an algorithm to find the maximum and minimum of a sequence of n integers stored in array $A[1..n]$ such that its time complexity is
(a) $O(n)$.
(b) $\Omega(n \log n)$.

1.36. Let $A[1..n]$ be an array of distinct integers, where $n > 2$. Give an $O(1)$ time algorithm to find an element in A that is neither the maximum nor the minimum.

1.37. Consider the element uniqueness problem: Given a set of integers, determine whether two of them are equal. Give an *efficient* algorithm to solve this problem. Assume that the integers are stored in array $A[1..n]$. What is the time complexity of your algorithm?

1.38. Give an algorithm that evaluates an input polynomial

$$a_n x^n + a_{n-1} x^{n-1} + \cdots + a_1 x + a_0$$

for a given value of x in time
(a) $\Omega(n^2)$.
(b) $O(n)$.

1.39. Let S be a set of n positive integers, where n is even. Give an efficient algorithm to partition S into two subsets S_1 and S_2 of $n/2$ elements each with the property that the difference between the sum of the elements in S_1 and the sum of the elements in S_2 is maximum. What is the time complexity of your algorithm?

1.40. Suppose we change the word "maximum" to "minimum" in Exercise 1.39. Give an algorithm to solve the modified problem. Compare the time complexity of your algorithm with that obtained in Exercise 1.39.

1.41. Let m and n be two positive integers. The *greatest common divisor* of m and n, denoted by $\gcd(m, n)$, is the largest integer that divides both m and n. For example $\gcd(12, 18) = 6$. Consider Algorithm EUCLID shown below, to compute $\gcd(m, n)$.
(a) Does it matter if in the first call $\gcd(m, n)$ it happens that $n < m$? Explain.

Algorithm 1.23 EUCLID
Input: Two positive integers m and n.
Output: $\gcd(m, n)$.

1. **comment:** *Exercise 1.41*
2. **repeat**
3. $r \leftarrow n \bmod m$
4. $n \leftarrow m$
5. $m \leftarrow r$
6. **until** $r = 0$
7. **return** n

(b) Prove the correctness of Algorithm EUCLID. (*Hint:* Make use of the following theorem: If r divides both m and n, then r divides $m - n$.)

(c) Show that the running time of Algorithm EUCLID is maximum if m and n are two consecutive numbers in the Fibonacci sequence defined by

$$f_1 = f_2 = 1; \quad f_n = f_{n-1} + f_{n-2} \quad \text{for } n > 2.$$

(d) Analyze the running time of Algorithm EUCLID *in terms of n*, assuming that $n \geq m$.

(e) Can the time complexity of Algorithm EUCLID be expressed using the Θ-notation? Explain.

1.42. Find the time complexity of Algorithm EUCLID discussed in Exercise 1.41 measured *in terms of the input size*. Is it logarithmic, linear, exponential? Explain.

1.43. Prove that for any constant $c > 0$, $(\log n)^c = o(n)$.

1.44. Show that any exponential function grows faster than any polynomial function by proving that for any constants c and d greater than 1,

$$n^c = o(d^n).$$

1.45. Consider the following recurrence:

$$f(n) = 4f(n/2) + n \quad \text{for } n \geq 2; \quad f(1) = 1,$$

where n is assumed to be a power of 2.
(a) Solve the recurrence by expansion.
(b) Solve the recurrence directly by applying Theorem 1.3.

1.46. Consider the following recurrence:

$$f(n) = 5f(n/3) + n \quad \text{for } n \geq 2; \quad f(1) = 1,$$

where n is assumed to be a power of 3.
(a) Solve the recurrence by expansion.
(b) Solve the recurrence directly by applying Theorem 1.3.

1.47. Consider the following recurrence:

$$f(n) = 9f(n/3) + n^2 \quad \text{for } n \geq 2; \quad f(1) = 1,$$

where n is assumed to be a power of 3.
(a) Solve the recurrence by expansion.
(b) Solve the recurrence directly by applying Theorem 1.3.

1.48. Consider the following recurrence:

$$f(n) = 2f(n/4) + \sqrt{n} \quad \text{for } n \geq 4; \quad f(n) = 1 \text{ if } n < 4,$$

where n is assumed to be of the form $2^{2^k}, k \geq 0$.
(a) Solve the recurrence by expansion.
(b) Solve the recurrence directly by applying Theorem 1.3.

1.49. Use the substitution method to find an upper bound for the recurrence

$$f(n) = f(\lfloor n/2 \rfloor) + f(\lfloor 3n/4 \rfloor) \quad \text{for } n \geq 4; \quad f(n) = 4 \text{ if } n < 4.$$

Express the solution using the O-notation.

1.50. Use the substitution method to find an upper bound for the recurrence

$$f(n) = f(\lfloor n/4 \rfloor) + f(\lfloor 3n/4 \rfloor) + n \quad \text{for } n \geq 4; \quad f(n) = 4 \text{ if } n < 4.$$

Express the solution using the O-notation.

1.51. Use the substitution method to find a lower bound for the recurrence in Exercise 1.49. Express the solution using the Ω-notation.

1.52. Use the substitution method to find a lower bound for the recurrence in Exercise 1.50. Express the solution using the Ω-notation.

1.53. Use the substitution method to solve the recurrence

$$f(n) = 2f(n/2) + n^2 \quad \text{for } n \geq 2; \quad f(1) = 1,$$

where n is assumed to be a power of 2. Express the solution using the Θ-notation.

1.54. Let

$$f(n) = f(n/2) + n \quad \text{for } n \geq 2; \quad f(1) = 1,$$

and

$$g(n) = 2g(n/2) + 1 \quad \text{for } n \geq 2; \quad g(1) = 1,$$

where n is a power of 2. Is $f(n) = g(n)$? Prove your answer.

1.55. Use the change of variable method to solve the recurrence

$$f(n) = f(n/2) + \sqrt{n} \quad \text{for } n \geq 4; \quad f(n) = 2 \text{ if } n < 4,$$

where n is assumed to be of the form 2^{2^k}. Find the asymptotic behavior of the function $f(n)$.

1.56. Use the change of variable method to solve the recurrence

$$f(n) = 2f(\sqrt{n}) + n \quad \text{for } n \geq 4; \quad f(n) = 1 \text{ if } n < 4,$$

where n is assumed to be of the form 2^{2^k}. Find the asymptotic behavior of the function $f(n)$.

1.57. Prove that the solution to the recurrence

$$f(n) = 2f(n/2) + g(n) \quad \text{for } n \geq 2; \quad f(1) = 1$$

is $f(n) = O(n)$ whenever $g(n) = o(n)$. For example, $f(n) = O(n)$ if $g(n) = n^{1-\epsilon}$, $0 < \epsilon < 1$.

1.18   Bibliographic Notes

There are several books on the design and analysis of algorithms. These include, in alphabetical order, Aho *et al.* (1974), Baase (1988), Brassard and Bratley (1988), Brassard and Bratley (1996), Cormen *et al.* (2009), Dromey (1982), Horowitz *et al.* (1978), Hu (1982), Knuth (1968, 1969, 1973), Manber (1989), Mehlhorn (1984a), Moret and Shapiro (1991), Purdom and Brown (1985), Reingold *et al.* (1977), Sedgewick (1988) and Wilf (1986). For a more popular account of algorithms, see Knuth (1977), Lewis and Papadimitriou (1978) and the two Turing Award Lectures of Karp (1986) and Tarjan (1987). Some of the more practical aspects of algorithm design are discussed in Bentley (1982) and Gonnet (1984). Knuth (1973) discusses in detail the sorting algorithms covered in this chapter. He gives step-counting analyses. The asymptotic notation was used in mathematics before the emergence of the field of algorithms. Knuth (1976) gives an account of its history. This article discusses the Ω and Θ notations and their proper usage and is an attempt to standardize these notations. Purdom and Brown (1985) presents a comprehensive treatment of advanced techniques for analyzing algorithms with numerous examples. The main mathematical aspects of the analysis of algorithms can be found in Greene and Knuth (1981). Weide (1977) provides a survey of both elementary and advanced analysis techniques. Hofri (1987) discusses the average case analysis of algorithms in detail.

Chapter 2

Data Structures

2.1 Introduction

The choice of a suitable data structure can influence the design of an efficient algorithm significantly. In this chapter, we briefly present some of the elementary data structures. Our presentation here is not self-contained, and many details have been omitted. More detailed treatment can be found in many books on data structures.

2.2 Linked Lists

A *linked list* consists of a finite sequence of elements or nodes that contain information plus (except possibly the last one) a link to another node. If node x points to node y, then x is called the *predecessor* of y and y the *successor* of x. There is a link to the first element called the *head* of the list. If there is a link from the last element to the first, the list is called *circular*. If in a linked list each node (except possibly the first one) points also to its predecessor, then the list is called a *doubly linked list*. If the first and last nodes of a doubly linked list are connected by a pair of links, then we have a *circular doubly linked list*. A linked list and its variations are diagrammed in Fig. 2.1.

The two primary operations on linked lists are insertion and deletion. Unlike arrays, it costs only a constant amount of time to insert or delete an element in a linked list. Imposing some restrictions on how a linked list is accessed results in two fundamental data structures: stacks and queues.

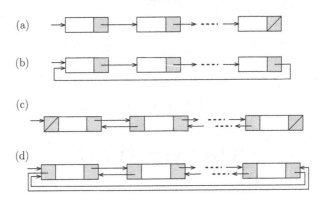

Fig. 2.1. Variations of linked lists: (a) Linked list. (b) Circular linked list. (c) Doubly linked list. (d) Circular doubly linked list.

2.2.1 Stacks and queues

A *stack* is a linked list in which insertions and deletions are permitted only at one end called the *top* of the stack. It may as well be implemented as an array. This data structure supports two basic operations: pushing an element into the stack and popping an element off the stack. If S is a stack, the operation $pop(S)$ returns the top of the stack and removes it permanently. If x is an element of the same type as the elements in S, then $push(S, x)$ adds x to S and updates the top of the stack so that it points to x.

A *queue* is a list in which insertions are permitted only at one end of the list called its *rear*, and all deletions are constrained to the other end called the *front* of the queue. As in the case of stacks, a queue may also be implemented as an array. The operations supported by queues are the same as those for the stack except that a push operation adds an element at the rear of the queue.

2.3 Graphs

A *graph* $G = (V, E)$ consists of a set of vertices $V = \{v_1, v_2, \ldots, v_n\}$ and a set of edges E. G is either *undirected* or *directed*. If G is undirected, then each edge in E is an *unordered* pair of vertices. If G is directed, then each edge in E is an *ordered* pair of vertices. Figure 2.2 shows an undirected

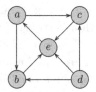

Fig. 2.2. An undirected and directed graphs.

graph (to the left) and a directed graph (to the right). For ease of reference, we will call the undirected and directed graphs in this figure G and D, respectively. Let (v_i, v_j) be an edge in E. If the graph is undirected, then v_i and v_j are *adjacent* to each other. If the graph is directed, then v_j is adjacent to v_i, but v_i is not adjacent to v_j unless (v_j, v_i) is an edge in E. For example, both a and c are adjacent to one another in G, whereas in D, c is adjacent to a but a is not adjacent to c. The *degree* of a vertex in an undirected graph is the number of vertices adjacent to it. The *indegree* and *outdegree* of a vertex v_i in a directed graph are the number of edges directed to v_i and out of v_i, respectively. For instance, the degree of e in G is 4, the indegree of c in D is 2 and its outdegree is 1. A *path* in a graph from vertex v_1 to vertex v_k is a sequence of vertices $v_1, v_2, \ldots, v_k$ such that $(v_i, v_{i+1}), 1 \le i \le k-1$, is an edge in the graph. The *length of a path* is the number of edges in the path. Thus, the length of the path $v_1, v_2, \ldots, v_k$ is $k-1$. The path is *simple* if all its vertices are distinct. The path is a *cycle* if $v_1 = v_k$. An *odd-length* cycle is one in which the number of edges is odd. An *even-length* cycle is defined similarly. For example, a, b, e, a is an odd-length cycle of length 3 in both G and D. A graph without cycles is called *acyclic*. A vertex v is said to be *reachable* from vertex u if there is a path that starts at u and ends at v. An undirected graph is *connected* if every vertex is reachable from every other vertex and *disconnected* otherwise. The *connected components* of a graph are the maximal connected subgraphs of the graph. Thus, if the graph is connected, then it consists of one connected component, the graph itself. Our example graph G is connected. In the case of directed graphs, a subgraph is called a *strongly connected component* if for every pair of vertices u and v in the subgraph, v is reachable from u and u is reachable from v. In our directed graph D, the subgraph consisting of the vertices $\{a, b, c, e\}$ is a strongly connected component.

An undirected graph is said to be *complete* if there is an edge between each pair of its vertices. A directed graph is said to be *complete* if there is an edge from each vertex to all other vertices. Let $G = (V, E)$ be a complete graph with n vertices. If G is directed, then $|E| = n(n - 1)$. If G is undirected, then $|E| = n(n - 1)/2$. The complete undirected graph with n vertices is denoted by K_n. An undirected graph $G = (V, E)$ is said to be *bipartite* if V can be partitioned into two disjoint subsets X and Y such that each edge in E has one end in X and the other end in Y. Let $m = |X|$ and $n = |Y|$. If there is an edge between each vertex $x \in X$ and each vertex $y \in Y$, then it is called a *complete* bipartite graph, and is denoted by $K_{m,n}$.

2.3.1 *Representation of graphs*

A graph $G = (V, E)$ can be conveniently represented by a boolean matrix M, called the *adjacency matrix* of G defined as $M[i, j] = 1$ if and only if (v_i, v_j) is an edge in G. Another representation of a graph is the *adjacency list* representation. In this scheme, the vertices adjacent to a vertex are represented by a linked list. Thus, there are $|V|$ such lists. Figure 2.3 shows the adjacency list representations of an undirected and directed graphs. Clearly, an adjacency matrix of a graph with n vertices has n^2 entries. In the case of adjacency lists, it costs $\Theta(m + n)$ space to represent a graph with n vertices and m edges.

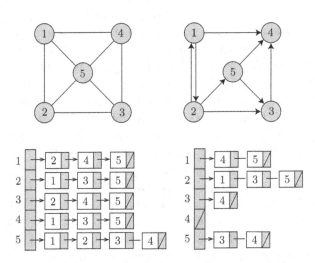

Fig. 2.3.   An example of adjacency list representation.

2.3.2 *Planar graphs*

A graph $G = (V, E)$ is planar if it can be embedded in the plane without edge crossings. Figure 2.4(a) shows an example of a planar graph. This graph is planar because it can be embedded in the plane as shown in Fig. 2.4(b).

The importance of planar graphs comes from the relationship between their number of vertices, number of edges and number of regions. Let n, m and r denote, respectively, the number of vertices, edges and regions in any embedding of a planar graph. Then, these three parameters are related by Euler's formula

$$n - m + r = 2$$

or

$$m = n + r - 2.$$

The proof of this formula can be found in Example A.12 on page 669. Moreover, there is a useful relationship between the number of vertices and the number of edges in a planar graph, that is,

$$m \leq 3n - 6 \quad n \geq 3.$$

The equality is attained if the graph is triangulated, i.e., each one of its regions (including the unbounded region) is triangular. The graph shown in Fig. 2.4(b) is triangulated and hence the relation $m = 3n - 6$ holds for this graph. The above relationships imply that in any planar graph, $m = O(n)$. Thus, the amount of space needed to store a planar graph is only $\Theta(n)$. This is to be contrasted with complete graphs, which require an amount of space in the order of $\Theta(n^2)$.

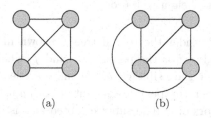

(a) (b)

Fig. 2.4. An example of a planar graph.

2.4   Trees

A *free tree* (or simply a *tree*) is a connected undirected graph that contains no cycles. A *forest* is a vertex-disjoint collection of trees, i.e., they do not have vertices in common.

Theorem 2.1   *If T is a tree with n vertices, then*

(a) *Any two vertices of T are connected by a* unique *path.*
(b) *T has* exactly *$n - 1$ edges.*
(c) *The addition of one more edge to T creates a cycle.*

Since the number of edges in a tree is $n - 1$, when analyzing the time or space complexity in the context of trees, the number of edges is insignificant.

2.5   Rooted Trees

A *rooted tree* T is a (free) tree with a distinguished vertex r called the *root* of T. This imposes an implicit direction on the path from the root to every other vertex. A vertex v_i is *the parent* of vertex v_j in T if v_i is on the path from the root to v_j and is adjacent to v_j. In this case, v_j is a *child* of v_i. The children of a vertex are called *siblings*. A *leaf* of a rooted tree is a vertex with no children; all other vertices are called *internal vertices*. A vertex u on the path from the root to a vertex v is an *ancestor* of v. If $u \neq v$, then u is a *proper* ancestor of v. A vertex w on the path from a vertex v to a leaf is a *descendant* of v. If $w \neq v$, then w is a *proper* descendant of v. The *subtree* rooted at a vertex v is the tree consisting of v and its proper descendants. The *depth* of a vertex v in a rooted tree is the length of the path from the root to v. Thus, the depth of the root is 0. The *height of a vertex v* is defined as the length of the longest path from v to a leaf. The *height of a tree* is the height of its root.

Example 2.1   Consider the rooted tree T shown in Fig. 2.5. Its root is the vertex labeled a. b is the parent of e and f, which in turn are the children of b. b, c and d are siblings. e, f, g and d are leaves; the others are internal vertices. e is a (proper) descendant of both a and b, which in turn are (proper) ancestors of e. The subtree rooted at b is the tree consisting of b and its children. The depth of g is 2; its height is 0. Since the distance

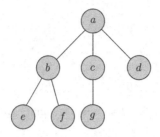

Fig. 2.5.   An example of a rooted tree.

from a to g is 2, and no other path from a to a leaf is longer than 2, the height of a is 2. It follows that the height of T is the height of its root, which is 2.

2.5.1   Tree traversals

There are several ways in which the vertices of a *rooted* tree can be systematically traversed or ordered. The three most important orderings are preorder, inorder and postorder. Let T be a tree with root r and subtrees $T_1, T_2, \ldots, T_n$.

- In a *preorder* traversal of the vertices of T, we visit the root r followed by visiting the vertices of T_1 in preorder, then the vertices of T_2 in preorder, and so on up to the vertices of T_n in preorder.
- In an *inorder* traversal of the vertices of T, we visit the vertices of T_1 in inorder, then the root r, followed by the vertices of T_2 in inorder, and so on up to the vertices of T_n in inorder.
- In a *postorder* traversal of the vertices of T, we visit the vertices of T_1 in postorder, then the vertices of T_2 in postorder, and so on up to the vertices of T_n in postorder, and finally we visit r.

2.6   Binary Trees

A *binary tree* is a finite set of vertices that is either empty or consists of a root r and two disjoint binary trees called the *left* and *right* subtrees. The roots of these subtrees are called the left and right *children* of r. Binary trees differ from rooted trees in two important ways. First, a binary tree may be empty while a rooted tree cannot be empty. Second, the distinction of left

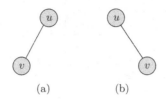

Fig. 2.6.   Two different binary trees.

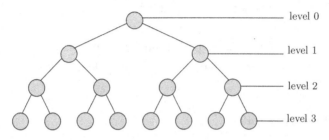

Fig. 2.7.   A complete binary tree.

and right subtrees causes the two binary trees shown in Figs. 2.6(a) and 2.6(b) to be different, and yet as rooted trees, they are indistinguishable.

All other definitions of rooted trees carry over to binary trees. A binary tree is said to be *full* if each internal vertex has exactly two children. A binary tree is called *complete* if it is full and all its leaves have the same depth, i.e., are on the same level. Figure 2.7 shows a complete binary tree. The set of vertices in a binary tree is partitioned into levels, with each level consisting of those vertices with the same depth (see Fig. 2.7).

Thus, level i consists of those vertices of depth i. We define a binary tree to be *almost complete* if it is complete except that *possibly* one or more leaves that occupy the rightmost positions may be missing. Hence, by definition, an almost-complete binary tree may be complete. Figure 2.8 shows an almost-complete binary tree. This tree is the same as the complete binary tree shown in Fig. 2.7 with the three rightmost leaves removed.

A complete (or almost-complete) binary tree with n vertices can be represented efficiently by an array $A[1..n]$ that lists its vertices according to the following simple relationship: The left and right children (if any) of a vertex stored in $A[j]$ are stored in $A[2j]$ and $A[2j + 1]$, respectively, and the parent of a vertex stored in $A[j]$ is stored in $A[\lfloor j/2 \rfloor]$.

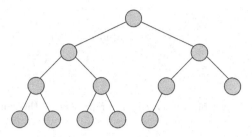

Fig. 2.8. An almost-complete binary tree.

2.6.1 *Some quantitative aspects of binary trees*

In the following observations, we list some useful relationships between the levels, number of vertices and height of a binary tree.

Observation 2.1   In a binary tree, the number of vertices at level j is at most 2^j.

Observation 2.2   Let n be the number of vertices in a binary tree T of height h. Then,

$$n \leq \sum_{j=0}^{h} 2^j = 2^{h+1} - 1.$$

The equality holds if T is complete. If T is almost complete, then we have

$$2^h \leq n \leq 2^{h+1} - 1.$$

Observation 2.3   The height of any binary tree with n vertices is at least $\lfloor \log n \rfloor$ and at most $n - 1$.

Observation 2.4   The height of a complete or almost-complete binary tree with n vertices is $\lfloor \log n \rfloor$.

Observation 2.5   In a full binary tree, the number of leaves is equal to the number of internal vertices plus one.

2.6.2 *Binary search trees*

A *binary search tree* is a binary tree in which the vertices are labeled with elements from a linearly ordered set in such a way that all elements stored

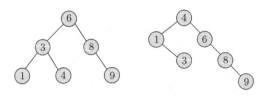

Fig. 2.9.   Two binary search trees representing the same set.

in the left subtree of a vertex v are less than the element stored at vertex v, and all elements stored in the right subtree of a vertex v are greater than the element stored at vertex v. This condition, which is called the *binary search tree property*, holds for every vertex of a binary search tree. The representation of a set by a binary search tree is not unique; in the worst case, it may be a degenerate tree, i.e., a tree in which each internal vertex has exactly one child. Figure 2.9 shows two binary search trees representing the same set.

The operations supported by this data structure are insertion, deletion, testing for membership and retrieving the minimum or maximum.

2.7   Practice Problems

2.1. Give an algorithm that traverses a circular list and reverses the direction of the links.

2.2. Consider representing a binary tree with n vertices by an array A that lists its vertices according to the following relationship: The left and right children (if any) of a vertex stored in $A[j]$ are stored in $A[2j]$ and $A[2j + 1]$, respectively, and the parent of a vertex stored in $A[j]$ is stored in $A[\lfloor j/2 \rfloor]$. What will be the size of A in the worst case? Explain.

2.3. Let $G = (V, E)$ be an undirected graph, and let $d(v)$ be the degree of vertex v. Show that

$$\sum_{v \in V} d(v) = 2|E|.$$

2.4. Let G be a planar graph with n vertices.

(a) What is the space complexity if the graph is stored using adjacency matrix?

(b) What is the space complexity if the graph is stored using adjacency lists? Give a brief justification for this part only.

2.5. Give an algorithm to count the number of leaf nodes in a binary tree. What is the running time of your algorithm?

2.6. Give an algorithm that traverses the nodes in a tree and outputs their labels in post order. What is the running time of your algorithm?

2.7. Prove that a complete binary tree with n leaves has $n - 1$ internal nodes.

2.8. Prove that a graph is bipartite if and only if it contains no odd-length cycles.

2.9. Show that any tree is a bipartite graph. (*Hint*: See Problem 2.8).

2.8 Exercises

2.1. Write an algorithm to delete an element x, if it exists, from a doubly linked list L. Assume that the variable *head* points to the first element in the list and the functions $pred(y)$ and $next(y)$ return the predecessor and successor of node y, respectively.

2.2. Give an algorithm to test whether a list has a repeated element.

2.3. Rewrite Algorithm INSERTIONSORT so that its input is a doubly linked list of n elements instead of an array. Will the time complexity change? Is the new algorithm more efficient?

2.4. A polynomial of the form $p(x) = a_1 x^{b_1} + a_2 x^{b_2} + \cdots + a_n x^{b_n}$, where $b_1 > b_2 > \cdots > b_n \geq 0$, can be represented by a linked list in which each record has three fields for a_i, b_i and the link to the next record. Give an algorithm to add two polynomials using this representation. What is the running time of your algorithm?

2.5. Give the adjacency matrix and adjacency list representations of the graph shown in Fig. 2.5.

2.6. Describe an algorithm to insert and delete edges in the adjacency list representation for
(a) a directed graph.
(b) an undirected graph.

2.7. Let S_1 be a stack containing n elements. Give an algorithm to sort the elements in S_1 so that the smallest element is on top of the stack after sorting. Assume you are allowed to use another stack S_2 as a temporary storage. What is the time complexity of your algorithm?

2.8. What if you are allowed to use two stacks S_2 and S_3 as a temporary storage in Exercise 2.7?

2.9. Let G be a directed graph with n vertices and m edges. When is it the case that the adjacency matrix representation is more efficient than the adjacency lists representation? Explain.

2.10. Prove that a graph is bipartite if and only if it has no odd-length cycles.

2.11. Draw *the* almost-complete binary tree with
(a) 10 nodes.
(b) 19 nodes.

2.12. Prove Observation 2.1.

2.13. Prove Observation 2.2.

2.14. Prove Observation 2.4.

2.15. Prove Observation 2.3.

2.16. Prove Observation 2.5.

2.17. Show how to list the elements stored in a binary tree in level order. For example, in Fig. 2.10, the output should be a, b, c, d, e, f, g. (*Hint:* Use a queue.)

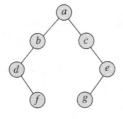

Fig. 2.10.   Exercise 2.17.

2.18. Is a tree a bipartite graph? Prove your answer (see Exercise 2.10).

2.19. Let T be a nonempty binary search tree. Give an algorithm to
(a)   return the minimum element stored in T.
(b)   return the maximum element stored in T.

2.20. Let T be a nonempty binary search tree. Give an algorithm to list all the elements in T in increasing order. What is the time complexity of your algorithm?

2.21. Let T be a nonempty binary search tree. Give an algorithm to delete an element x from T, if it exists. What is the time complexity of your algorithm?

2.22. Let T be a binary search tree. Give an algorithm to insert an element x in its proper position in T. What is the time complexity of your algorithm?

2.23. What is the time complexity of deletion and insertion in a binary search tree? Explain.

2.24. When discussing the time complexity of an operation in a binary search tree, which of the O and Θ notations is more appropriate? Explain.

2.9   Bibliographic Notes

This chapter outlines some of the basic data structures that are frequently used in the design and analysis of algorithms. More detailed treatment can be found in many books on data structures. These include, among others, Aho *et al.* (1983), Gonnet (1984), Knuth (1968, 1973), Reingold and Hansen (1983), Standish (1980), Tarjan (1983) and Wirth (1986). The definitions in this chapter conform with those in Tarjan (1983). The adjacency lists data structure was suggested by Tarjan and is described in Tarjan (1972) and Hopcroft and Tarjan (1973).

Chapter 3

Heaps and the Disjoint Sets Data Structures

3.1 Introduction

In this chapter, we investigate two major data structures that are more sophisticated than those in Chapter 2. They are fundamental in the design of efficient algorithms. Moreover, these data structures are interesting in their own right.

3.2 Heaps

In many algorithms, there is the need for a data structure that supports the following two operations: Insert an element and find the element of maximum (or minimum) value. A data structure that supports both of these operations is called a *priority queue*. If a regular queue is used, then finding the largest (or smallest) element is expensive, as this requires searching the entire queue. If a sorted array is used, then insertion is expensive, as it may require shifting a large portion of the elements. An efficient implementation of a priority queue is to use a simple data structure called *a heap*. Heaps are classified as either max-heaps or min-heaps. In this chapter, we will confine our attention to max-heaps, as the structure and operations associated with min-heaps are similar.

Definition 3.1   A (binary) *heap* is an *almost-complete* binary tree (see Sec. 2.6) with each node satisfying the *heap property*: If v and $p(v)$ are a node and its parent, respectively, then the key of the item stored in $p(v)$ is not less than the key of the item stored in v.

A heap data structure supports the following operations:

- *delete-max*$[H]$: Delete and return an item of maximum key from a nonempty heap H.
- *insert*$[H, x]$: Insert item x into heap H.
- *delete*$[H, i]$: Delete the ith item from heap H.

Thus, the heap property implies that the keys of the elements along every path from the root to a leaf are arranged in nonincreasing order. As described in Sec. 2.6, a heap T (being an almost-complete binary tree) with n nodes can be represented by an array $H[1..n]$ in the following way:

- The root of T is stored in $H[1]$.
- Suppose that a node x in T is stored in $H[j]$. If it has a left child, then this child is stored in $H[2j]$. If it (also) has a right child, then this child is stored in $H[2j + 1]$.
- The parent of element $H[j]$ that is not the root of the tree is stored in $H[\lfloor j/2 \rfloor]$.
- The leaves of T are stored at $H[\lfloor n/2 \rfloor + 1], H[\lfloor n/2 \rfloor + 2], \ldots, H[n]$.

Note that if a node in a heap has a right child, then it must also have a left child. This follows from the definition of an almost-complete binary tree. Consequently, a heap can be viewed as a binary tree, while it is in fact an array $H[1..n]$ with the property that for any index $j, 2 \leq j \leq n, key(H[\lfloor j/2 \rfloor]) \geq key(H[j])$. Figure 3.1 shows an example of a heap in both tree and array representations. To simplify this and subsequent figures, we will treat the keys of the items stored in a heap as if they themselves are the items. In Fig. 3.1, we note that if the tree nodes are numbered from 1 to n in a top-down and left-to-right manner, then each entry $H[i]$ is represented in the corresponding tree by the node numbered i. This numbering is indicated in the figure by the labels next to the tree nodes. Thus, using this method, given a heap as an array, we can easily construct its corresponding tree and vice versa.

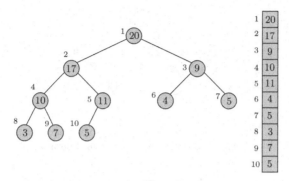

Fig. 3.1.   A heap and its array representation.

3.2.1   *Operations on heaps*

Before describing the main heap operations, we first present two secondary operations that are used as subroutines in the algorithms that implement heap operations.

3.2.1.1   *Sift-up*

Suppose that for some $i > 1$, $H[i]$ is changed to an element whose key is greater than the key of its parent. This violates the heap property and, consequently, the data structure is no longer a heap. To restore the heap property, an operation called *sift-up* is needed to move the new item up to its proper position in the binary tree so that the heap property is restored. The *sift-up* operation moves $H[i]$ up along the *unique* path from $H[i]$ to the root until its proper location along this path is found. At each step along the path, the key of $H[i]$ is compared with the key of its parent $H[\lfloor i/2 \rfloor]$. This is described more precisely in Algorithm SIFT-UP.

Algorithm SIFT-UP
Input: An array $H[1..n]$ and an index i between 1 and n.
Output: $H[i]$ is moved up, if necessary, so that it is not larger than its parent.

1. *done* ← **false**
2. **if** $i = 1$ **then exit**   {node i is the root}
3. **repeat**
4.   **if** $key(H[i]) > key(H[\lfloor i/2 \rfloor])$ **then** interchange $H[i]$ and $H[\lfloor i/2 \rfloor]$
5.   **else** *done* ← **true**
6. $i \leftarrow \lfloor i/2 \rfloor$
7. **until** $i = 1$ **or** *done*

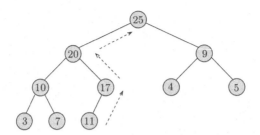

Fig. 3.2.   An example of the *sift-up* operation.

Example 3.1   Suppose the key stored in the 10th position of the heap shown in Fig. 3.1 is changed from 5 to 25. This will violate the heap property, as the new key 25 is now greater than the key stored in its parent node, namely 11. To restore the heap property, we apply the *sift-up* operation to the tree starting from that node in which 25 is stored. This action is depicted in Fig. 3.2. As shown in the figure, 25 is moved up to the root.

3.2.1.2 *Sift-down*

Suppose that $i \leq \lfloor n/2 \rfloor$ and the key of the element stored at $H[i]$ is changed to a value that is less than the key stored at $H[2i]$ or the maximum of the keys at $H[2i]$ and $H[2i+1]$ if $H[2i+1]$ exists. This violates the heap property and the tree is no longer a representation of a heap. To restore the heap property, an operation called *sift-down* is needed to "percolate" $H[i]$ down the binary tree until its proper location is found. At each step along the path, its key is compared with the maximum of the two keys stored in its children nodes (if any). This is described more formally in Algorithm SIFT-DOWN.

Example 3.2   Suppose we change the key 17 stored in the second position of the heap shown in Figs. 3.1 to 3.3. This will violate the heap property, as the new key 3 is now less than the maximum of the two keys stored in its children nodes, namely 11. To restore the heap property, we apply the *sift-down* operation starting from that node in which 3 is stored. This action is depicted in Fig. 3.3. As shown in the figure, 3 is percolated down until its proper position is found.

Now, using these two algorithms, it is fairly easy to write the algorithms for the main heap operations.

Algorithm SIFT-DOWN

Input: An array $H[1..n]$ and an index i between 1 and n.

Output: $H[i]$ is percolated down, if necessary, so that it is not smaller
than its children.

1. *done* ← **false**
2. **if** $2i > n$ **then exit**   {node i is a leaf}
3. **repeat**
4. $i \leftarrow 2i$
5.   **if** $i + 1 \leq n$ **and** $key(H[i+1]) > key(H[i])$ **then** $i \leftarrow i + 1$
6.   **if** $key(H[\lfloor i/2 \rfloor]) < key(H[i])$ **then** interchange $H[i]$ and $H[\lfloor i/2 \rfloor]$
7.   **else** *done* ← **true**
8.   **end if**
9. **until** $2i > n$ **or** *done*

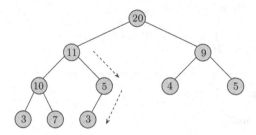

Fig. 3.3.   An example of the *sift-down* operation.

3.2.1.3 *Insert*

To insert an element x into a heap H, append x to the end of H after
its size has been increased by 1, and then sift x up, if necessary. This is
described in Algorithm INSERT. By Observation 2.4, if n is the size of the
new heap, then the height of the heap tree is $\lfloor \log n \rfloor$. It follows that the
time required to insert one element into a heap of size n is $O(\log n)$.

Algorithm 3.1 INSERT

Input: A heap $H[1..n]$ and a heap element x.

Output: A new heap $H[1..n+1]$ with x being one of its elements.

1. $n \leftarrow n + 1$ {increase the size of H}
2. $H[n] \leftarrow x$
3. SIFT-UP(H, n)

3.2.1.4 *Delete*

To delete an element $H[i]$ from a heap H of size n, replace $H[i]$ by $H[n]$, decrease the heap size by 1, and then sift $H[i]$ up or down, if necessary, depending on the value of its key relative to the keys stored in its parent and children nodes. This is described in Algorithm DELETE. Since, by Observation 2.4, the height of the heap tree is $\lfloor \log n \rfloor$, it follows that the time required to delete a node from a heap of size n is $O(\log n)$.

Algorithm 3.2 DELETE

Input: A nonempty heap $H[1..n]$ and an index i between 1 and n.

Output: A new heap $H[1..n-1]$ after $H[i]$ is removed.

1. $x \leftarrow H[i];$ $y \leftarrow H[n]$
2. $n \leftarrow n - 1$ {decrease the size of H}
3. **if** $i = n + 1$ **then exit**   {*done*}
4. $H[i] \leftarrow y$
5. **if** $key(y) \geq key(x)$ **then**   SIFT-UP(H, i)
6. **else** SIFT-DOWN(H, i)
7. **end if**

3.2.1.5 *Delete-max*

This operation deletes and returns an item of maximum key in a nonempty heap H. It costs $\Theta(1)$ time to return the element with maximum key in a heap, as it is the root of the tree. However, since deleting the root may destroy the heap, more work may be needed to restore the heap data structure. A straightforward implementation of this operation makes use of the delete operation: Simply return the element stored in the root and delete it from the heap. The method for this operation is given in Algorithm DELETEMAX. Obviously, its time complexity is that of the delete operation, i.e., $O(\log n)$.

Algorithm 3.3 DELETEMAX

Input: A heap $H[1..n]$.

Output: An element x of maximum key is returned and deleted from the heap.

1. $x \leftarrow H[1]$
2. DELETE$(H, 1)$
3. **return** x

3.2.2 Creating a heap

Given an array $A[1..n]$ of n elements, it is easy to construct a heap out of these elements by starting from an empty heap and successively inserting each element until A is transformed into a heap. Since inserting the jth key costs $O(\log j)$, the time complexity of creating a heap using this method is $O(n \log n)$ (see Example 1.12).

Interestingly, it turns out that a heap can be created from n elements in $\Theta(n)$ time. In what follows, we give the details of this method. Recall that the nodes of the tree corresponding to a heap $H[1..n]$ can conveniently be numbered from 1 to n in a top-down left-to-right manner. Given this numbering, we can transform an almost-complete binary tree with n nodes into a heap $H[1..n]$ as follows. Starting from the last internal node (the one numbered $\lfloor n/2 \rfloor$) to the root (node number 1), we scan all these nodes one by one, each time transforming, if necessary, the subtree rooted at the current node into a heap.

Example 3.3   Figure 3.4 provides an example of the linear time algorithm for transforming an array $A[1..n]$ into a heap. An input array and its tree representation are shown in Fig. 3.4(a). Each subtree consisting of only one leaf is already a heap, and hence the leaves are skipped. Next, as shown in Fig. 3.4(b), the two subtrees rooted at the 4th and 5th nodes are not heaps, and hence their roots are sifted down in order to transform them into heaps. At this point, all subtrees rooted at the second and third levels are heaps. Continuing this way, we adjust the two subtrees rooted at the third and second nodes in the first level, so that they conform to the heap property. This is shown in Figs. 3.4(c) and 3.4(d). Finally, we move up to the topmost level and percolate the element stored in the root node down to its proper position. The resulting tree, which is now a heap, and its array representation are shown in Fig. 3.4(e).

So far, we have shown how to work with trees. Performing the same procedure directly on the input array is fairly easy. Let $A[1..n]$ be the given array and T the almost-complete binary tree corresponding to A. First, we note that the elements

$$A[\lfloor n/2 \rfloor + 1], A[\lfloor n/2 \rfloor + 2], \ldots, A[n]$$

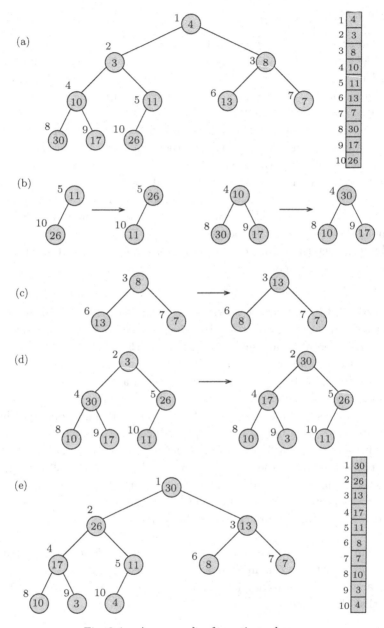

Fig. 3.4. An example of creating a heap.

correspond to the leaves of T, and therefore we start adjusting the array at $A[\lfloor n/2 \rfloor]$ and continue the adjustments at

$$A[\lfloor n/2 \rfloor - 1], A[\lfloor n/2 \rfloor - 2], \ldots, A[1].$$

Once the subtree rooted at $A[1]$, which is T itself, is adjusted, the resulting array is the desired heap. Algorithm MAKEHEAP constructs a heap whose items are the elements stored in an array $A[1..n]$.

Algorithm 3.4 MAKEHEAP
Input: An array $A[1..n]$ of n elements.

Output: $A[1..n]$ is transformed into a heap

1. **for** $i \leftarrow \lfloor n/2 \rfloor$ **downto** 1
2.   SIFT-DOWN(A, i)
3. **end for**

The running time of Algorithm MAKEHEAP is computed as follows. Let T be the almost-complete binary tree corresponding to the array $A[1..n]$, and assume $n \geq 2$. Then, by Observation 2.4, the height of T is $h = \lfloor \log n \rfloor$. Let $A[j]$ correspond to the jth node in level i of the tree. The number of iterations executed by Algorithm SIFT-DOWN when invoked by the statement SIFT-DOWN(A, j) is at most $h - i$. Since there are exactly 2^i nodes on level $i, 0 \leq i < h$, the total number of iterations is bounded above by

$$\sum_{i=0}^{h-1}(h - i)2^i = 2^0(h) + 2^1(h - 1) + 2^2(h - 2) + \cdots + 2^{h-1}(1)$$

$$= 1(2^{h-1}) + 2(2^{h-2}) + \cdots + h(2^{h-h})$$

$$= \sum_{i=1}^{h} i2^{(h-i)}$$

$$= 2^h \sum_{i=1}^{h} i/2^i$$

$$\leq n \sum_{i=1}^{h} i/2^i$$

$$< 2n.$$

The last inequality follows from Eq. (A.14) on page 678. The one before the last follows from the fact that the number of nodes n in a heap of height h is at least

$$2^0 + 2^1 + \cdots + 2^{h-1} + 1 = 2^h.$$

Since there are at most two element comparisons in each iteration of Algorithm SIFT-DOWN, the total number of element comparisons is bounded above by $4n$. Moreover, since there is at least one iteration in each call to Algorithm SIFT-DOWN for the first $\lfloor n/2 \rfloor$ nonleaf nodes, the minimum number of element comparisons is $2\lfloor n/2 \rfloor \geq n - 1$. Finally, it is obvious that the algorithm takes $\Theta(1)$ space to construct a heap out of n elements. Thus, we have the following theorem:

Theorem 3.1   *Let $C(n)$ be the number of element comparisons performed by Algorithm* MAKEHEAP *for the construction of a heap of n elements. Then, $n - 1 \leq C(n) < 4n$. Hence, the algorithm takes $\Theta(n)$ time and $\Theta(1)$ space to construct a heap out of n elements.*

3.2.3   Heapsort

We now turn our attention to the problem of sorting by making use of the heap data structure. Recall that Algorithm SELECTIONSORT sorts an array of n elements by finding the minimum in each of the $n - 1$ iterations. Thus, in each iteration, the algorithm searches for the minimum among the remaining elements using *linear search*. Since searching for the minimum using linear search costs $\Theta(n)$ time, the algorithm takes $\Theta(n^2)$ time. It turns out that by choosing the right data structure, Algorithm SELECTIONSORT can be improved substantially. Since we have at our disposal the heap data structure with the *delete-max* operation, we can exploit it to obtain an efficient algorithm. Given an array $A[1..n]$, we sort its elements in nondecreasing order *efficiently* as follows. First, we transform A into a heap with the property that the key of each element is the element itself, i.e., $key(A[i]) = A[i]$, $1 \leq i \leq n$. Next, since the maximum of the entries in A is now stored in $A[1]$, we may interchange $A[1]$ and $A[n]$ so that $A[n]$ is the maximum element in the array. Now, the element stored in $A[1]$ may be smaller than the element stored in one of its children. Therefore, we use Algorithm SIFT-DOWN to transform $A[1..n - 1]$ into a heap.

Next, we interchange $A[1]$ with $A[n-1]$ and adjust the array $A[1..n-2]$ into a heap. This process of exchanging elements and adjusting heaps is repeated until the heap size becomes 1, at which point $A[1]$ is minimum. The formal description is shown in Algorithm HEAPSORT.

Algorithm 3.5 HEAPSORT

Input: An array $A[1..n]$ of n elements.

Output: Array A sorted in nondecreasing order.

1. MAKEHEAP(A)
2. **for** $j \leftarrow n$ **downto** 2
3.   interchange $A[1]$ and $A[j]$
4.   SIFT-DOWN($A[1..j-1], 1$)
5. **end for**

An important advantage of this algorithm is that it sorts *in place*, i.e., it needs no auxiliary storage. In other words, the space complexity of Algorithm HEAPSORT is $\Theta(1)$. The running time of the algorithm is computed as follows. By Theorem 3.1, creating the heap costs $\Theta(n)$ time. The *sift-down* operation costs $O(\log n)$ time and is repeated $n-1$ times. It follows that the time required by the algorithm to sort n elements is $O(n \log n)$. This implies the following theorem:

Theorem 3.2 *Algorithm* HEAPSORT *sorts n elements in $O(n \log n)$ time and $\Theta(1)$ space.*

3.2.4 *Min and max heaps*

So far, we have viewed the heap as a data structure whose primary operation is retrieving the element with maximum key. The heap can trivially be modified so that the element with minimum key value is stored in the root instead. In this case, the heap property mandates that the key of the element stored in a node other than the root is greater than or equal to the key of the element stored in its parent. These two types of heaps are commonly referred to as max-heaps and min-heaps. The latter is not less important than the former, and they are both used quite often in optimization algorithms. It is customary to refer to either one of them as a "heap" and which one is meant is understood from the context in which it is used.

3.3   Disjoint Sets Data Structures

Suppose we are given a set S of n distinct elements. The elements are partitioned into disjoint sets. Initially, each element is assumed to be in a set by itself. A sequence σ of m *union* and *find* operations, which will be defined in the following, is to be executed so that after each *union* instruction, two *disjoint* subsets are combined into one subset. Observe that the number of *unions* is at most $n - 1$. In each subset, a distinguished element will serve as the *name of the set* or *set representative*. For example, if $S = \{1, 2, \ldots, 11\}$ and there are 4 subsets $\{1, 7, 10, 11\}$, $\{2, 3, 5, 6\}$, $\{4, 8\}$ and $\{9\}$, these subsets may be labeled as 1, 3, 8 and 9, in this order. The *find* operation returns the name of the set containing a particular element. For example, executing the operation *find*(11) returns 1, the name of the set containing 11. These two operations are defined more precisely as follows:

- FIND(x): Find and return the name of the set containing x.
- UNION(x, y): Replace the two sets *containing* x and y by their union. The name of the union set is either the name of the old set containing x or the name of the old set containing y; it will be determined later.

The goal is to design efficient algorithms for these two operations. To achieve this, we need a data structure that is both simple and at the same time allows for the efficient implementation of the *union* and *find* operations. A data structure that is both simple and leads to efficient implementation of these two operations is to represent each set as a rooted tree with data elements stored in its nodes. Each element x other than the root has a pointer to its parent $p(x)$ in the tree. The root has a *null* pointer, and it serves as the name or set representative of the set. This results in a forest in which each tree corresponds to one set.

For any element x, let $root(x)$ denote the root of the tree containing x. Thus, FIND(x) always returns $root(x)$. As the *union* operation must have as its arguments the roots of two trees, we will assume that for any two elements x and y, UNION(x, y) actually means UNION($root(x), root(y)$).

If we assume that the elements are the integers $1, 2, \ldots, n$, the forest can conveniently be represented by an array $A[1..n]$ such that $A[j]$ is the parent of element j, $1 \leq j \leq n$. The *null* parent can be represented by the number 0. Figure 3.5(a) shows four trees corresponding to the four sets $\{1, 7, 10, 11\}$, $\{2, 3, 5, 6\}$, $\{4, 8\}$ and $\{9\}$. Figure 3.5(b) shows their

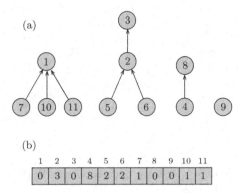

Fig. 3.5. An example of the representation of disjoint sets. (a) Tree representation. (b) Array representation when $S = \{1, 2, \ldots, n\}$.

array representation. Clearly, since the elements are consecutive integers, the array representation is preferable. However, in developing the algorithms for the *union* and *find* operations, we will assume the more general representation, that is, the tree representation.

Now, we focus our attention on the implementation of the *union* and *find* operations. A straightforward implementation is as follows. In the case of the operation FIND(x), simply follow the path from x until the root is reached, then return $root(x)$. In the case of the operation UNION(x, y), let the link of $root(x)$ point to $root(y)$, i.e., if $root(x)$ is u and $root(y)$ is v, then let v be the parent of u.

In order to improve on the running time, we present in the following two sections two heuristics: *union by rank* and *path compression*.

3.3.1 The union by rank heuristic

An obvious disadvantage of the straightforward implementation of the *union* operation stated above is that the height of a tree may become very large to the extent that a *find* operation may require $\Omega(n)$ time. In the extreme case, a tree may become degenerate. A simple example of this case is in order. Suppose we start with the singleton sets $\{1\}, \{2\}, \ldots, \{n\}$ and then execute the following sequence of *unions* and *finds* (see Fig. 3.6(a)):

$$\text{UNION}(1, 2), \text{UNION}(2, 3), \ldots, \text{UNION}(n - 1, n),$$

$$\text{FIND}(1), \text{FIND}(2), \ldots, \text{FIND}(n).$$

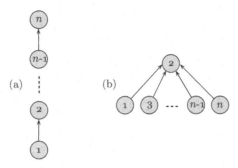

Fig. 3.6. The result of $n - 1$ *union* operations. (a) Without union by rank. (b) With union by rank.

In this case, the total cost of the n find operations is proportional to

$$n + (n - 1) + \cdots + 1 = \frac{n(n + 1)}{2} = \Theta(n^2).$$

In order to constrain the height of each tree, we adopt the *union by rank* heuristic: We store with each node a nonnegative number referred to as the *rank* of that node. The rank of a node is essentially its height (recall that the height of node v is the length of the longest path from v to a leaf node). Let x and y be two roots of two different trees in the current forest. Initially, each node has rank 0. When performing the operation UNION(x, y), we compare $rank(x)$ and $rank(y)$. If $rank(x) < rank(y)$, we make y the parent of x. If $rank(x) > rank(y)$, we make x the parent of y. Otherwise, if $rank(x) = rank(y)$, we make y the parent of x and increase $rank(y)$ by one. Applying this rule to the sequence of operations above yields the tree shown in Fig. 3.6(b). Note that the total cost of the n find operations is now reduced to $\Theta(n)$. This, however, is not always the case. As will be shown later, using this rule, the time required to process n finds is $O(n \log n)$.

Let x be any node and $p(x)$ the parent of x. The following two observations are fundamental.

Observation 3.1 $rank(p(x)) \geq rank(x) + 1$.

Observation 3.2   The value of $rank(x)$ is initially zero and increases in subsequent union operations until x is no longer a root. Once x becomes a child of another node, its rank never changes.

Lemma 3.1 *The number of nodes in a tree with root x is at least $2^{rank(x)}$.*

Proof. By induction on the number of union operations. Initially, x is a tree by itself and its rank is zero. Let x and y be two roots, and consider the operation UNION(x, y). Assume that the lemma holds before this operation. If $rank(x) < rank(y)$, then the formed tree rooted at y has more nodes than the old tree with root y and its rank is unchanged. If $rank(x) > rank(y)$, then the formed tree rooted at x has more nodes than the old tree with root x and its rank is unchanged. Thus, if $rank(x) \neq rank(y)$, then the lemma holds after the operation. If, however, $rank(x) = rank(y)$, then in this case, by induction, the formed tree with root y has at least $2^{rank(x)} + 2^{rank(y)} = 2^{rank(y)+1}$ nodes. Since $rank(y)$ will be increased by one, the lemma holds after the operation. □

Clearly, if x is the root of tree T, then the height of T is exactly the rank of x. By Lemma 3.1, if the number of nodes in the tree rooted at x is k, then the height of that tree is at most $\lfloor \log k \rfloor$. It follows that the cost of each find operation is $O(\log n)$. The time required by the operation UNION(x, y) is $O(1)$ if both arguments are roots. If not both x and y are roots, then the running time reduces to that of the *find* operation. Consequently, the time complexity of a *union* operation is that of the *find* operation, which is $O(\log n)$. It follows that, using the union by rank heuristic, the time complexity of a sequence of m interspersed *union* and *find* instructions is $O(m \log n)$.

3.3.2 Path compression

To enhance the performance of the *find* operation further, another heuristic known as *path compression* is *also* employed. In a FIND(x) operation, after the root y is found, we traverse the path from x to y one more time and change the parent pointers of all nodes along the path to point directly to y. The action of path compression is illustrated in Fig. 3.7. During the execution of the operation FIND(4), the name of the set is found to be 1. Therefore, the parent pointer of each node on the path from 4 to 1 is reset so that it points to 1. It is true that path compression increases the amount of work required to perform a *find* operation. However, this process will pay off in subsequent *find* operations, as we will be traversing shorter paths.

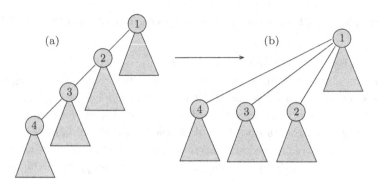

Fig. 3.7. The effect of executing the *find* operation FIND(4) with path compression.

Note that when path compression is used, the rank of a node may be greater than its height, so it serves as an upper bound on the height of that node.

3.3.3   The union-find algorithms

Algorithms FIND and UNION describe the final versions of the *find* and *union* operations, respectively, using the two heuristics stated above.

Algorithm 3.6 FIND
Input: A node x.
Output: $root(x)$, the root of the tree containing x.

1. $y \leftarrow x$
2. **while** $p(y) \neq null$ {Find the root of the tree containing x}
3. $y \leftarrow p(y)$
4. **end while**
5. $root \leftarrow y;$ $y \leftarrow x$
6. **while** $p(y) \neq null$ {Do path compression}
7. $w \leftarrow p(y)$
8. $p(y) \leftarrow root$
9. $y \leftarrow w$
10. **end while**
11. **return** $root$

Algorithm 3.7 UNION

Input: Two elements x and y.

Output: The union of the two trees containing x and y. The original trees are destroyed.

1. $u \leftarrow$ FIND(x); $v \leftarrow$ FIND(y)
2. **if** $rank(u) \leq rank(v)$ **then**
3. $p(u) \leftarrow v$
4.   **if** $rank(u) = rank(v)$ **then** $rank(v) \leftarrow rank(v) + 1$
5. **else** $p(v) \leftarrow u$
6. **end if**

Example 3.4   Let $S = \{1, 2, \ldots, 9\}$ and consider applying the following sequence of *unions* and *finds*: UNION$(1, 2)$, UNION$(3, 4)$, UNION$(5, 6)$, UNION$(7, 8)$, UNION$(2, 4)$, UNION$(8, 9)$, UNION$(6, 8)$, FIND(5), UNION$(4, 8)$, FIND(1). Figure 3.8(a) shows the initial configuration. Figure 3.8(b) shows the data structure after the first four *union* operations. The result of the next three *union* operations is shown in Fig. 3.8(c). Figure 3.8(d) shows the effect of executing the operation FIND(5). The results of the operations UNION$(4, 8)$ and FIND(1) are shown in Figs. 3.8(e) and 3.8(f), respectively.

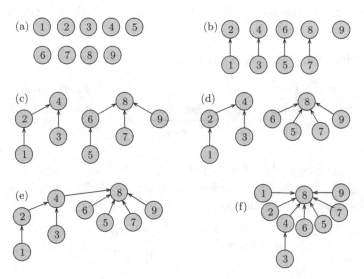

Fig. 3.8.   An example of the union-find algorithms.

3.3.4 *Analysis of the union-find algorithms*

We have shown before that the running time required to process an interspersed sequence σ of m union and find operations using union by rank is $O(m \log n)$. Now, we show that if path compression is *also* employed, then using amortized time analysis (see Sec. 1.13), it is possible to prove that the bound is *almost* $O(m)$.

Lemma 3.2   *For any integer $r \geq 0$, the number of nodes of rank r is at most $n/2^r$.*

Proof.   Fix a particular value of r. When a node x is assigned a rank of r, label by x all the nodes contained in the tree rooted at x. By Lemma 3.1, the number of labeled nodes is at least 2^r. If the root of that tree changes, then the rank of the root of the new tree is at least $r + 1$. This means that those nodes labeled with x will never be labeled again. Since the maximum number of nodes labeled is n, and since each root of rank r has at least 2^r nodes, it follows that there are at most $n/2^r$ nodes with rank r.   □

Corollary 3.1   *The rank of any node is at most $\lfloor \log n \rfloor$.*

Proof.   If for some node x, $rank(x) = r \geq \lfloor \log n \rfloor + 1$, then by Lemma 3.2, there are at most $n/2^{\lfloor \log n \rfloor + 1} < 1$ nodes of rank r.   □

Definition 3.2   For any positive integer $n, \log^* n$ is defined as

$$\log^* n = \begin{cases} 0 & \text{if } n = 0 \text{ or } 1 \\ \min\{i \geq 0 \mid \underbrace{\log \log \ldots \log}_{i \text{ times}} n \leq 1\} & \text{if } n \geq 2. \end{cases}$$

For example, $\log^* 2 = 1$, $\log^* 4 = 2$, $\log^* 16 = 3$, $\log^* 65536 = 4$ and $\log^* 2^{65536} = 5$. For the amortized time complexity analysis, we will introduce the following function:

$$F(j) = \begin{cases} 1 & \text{if } j = 0 \\ 2^{F(j-1)} & \text{if } j \geq 1. \end{cases}$$

The most important property of $F(j)$ is its explosive growth. For example, $F(1) = 2$, $F(2) = 4$, $F(3) = 16$, $F(4) = 65536$ and $F(5) = 2^{65536}$.

Let σ be a sequence of m union and find instructions. We partition the ranks into *groups*. We put rank r in group $\log^* r$. For example, ranks 0 and 1 are in group 0, rank 2 is in group 1, ranks 3 and 4 are in group 2, ranks 5 through 16 are in group 3 and ranks 17 through 65536 are in group 4. Since the largest possible rank is $\lfloor \log n \rfloor$, the largest group number is at most $\log^* \log n = \log^* n - 1$.

We assess the charges of a find instruction $\text{FIND}(u)$ as follows. Let v be a node on the path from node u to the root of the tree containing u, and let x be that root. If v is the root, a child of the root, or if the parent of v is in a different rank group from v, then charge one time unit to the find instruction itself. If $v \neq x$, and both v and its parent are in the same rank group, then charge one time unit to *node v*. Note that the nodes on the path from u to x are monotonically increasing in rank, and since there are at most $\log^* n$ different rank groups, no find instruction is charged more than $O(\log^* n)$ time units. It follows that the total number of time units charged to all the find instructions in the sequence σ is $O(m \log^* n)$.

After x is found to be the root of the tree containing u, by applying path compression, x will be the parent of both u and v. If later on, x becomes a child of another node, and v and x are in different groups, no more node costs will be charged to v in subsequent find instructions. An important observation is that if node v is in rank group $g > 0$, then v can be moved and charged at most $F(g) - F(g-1)$ times before it acquires a parent in a higher group. If node v is in rank group 0, it will be moved at most once before having a parent in a higher group.

Now, we derive an upper bound on the total charges made to the nodes. By Lemma 3.2, the number of nodes of rank r is at most $n/2^r$. If we define $F(-1) = 0$, then the number of nodes in group g is at most

$$\sum_{r=F(g-1)+1}^{F(g)} \frac{n}{2^r} \leq \frac{n}{2^{F(g-1)+1}} \sum_{r=0}^{\infty} \frac{1}{2^r}$$

$$= \frac{n}{2^{F(g-1)}}$$

$$= \frac{n}{F(g)}.$$

Since the maximum number of node charges assigned to a node in group g is equal to $F(g) - F(g-1)$, the number of node charges assigned to all nodes in group g is at most

$$\frac{n}{F(g)} \left(F(g) - F(g-1)\right) \leq n.$$

Since there are at most $\log^* n$ groups $(0, 1, \ldots, \log^* n - 1)$, it follows that the number of node charges assigned to all nodes is $O(n \log^* n)$. Combining this with the $O(m \log^* n)$ charges to the find instructions yields the following theorem:

Theorem 3.3 *Let $T(m)$ denote the running time required to process an interspersed sequence σ of $m \geq n$ union and* find *operations using union by rank and path compression. Then, $T(m) = O(m \log^* n)$.*

Note that for almost all practical purposes, $\log^* n \leq 5$. This means that the running time is $O(m)$ for virtually all practical applications.

3.4　Practice Problems

3.1. Which of the following two statements is correct?

　(a)　A priority queue is a heap.
　(b)　A heap is a priority queue.

3.2. Explain how to implement a priority queue using a linked list.

3.3. What are the running times of insertion and deletion in the linked list representation of priority queue in Problem 3.2?

3.4. Use the $O(n)$ time algorithm for making a heap to transform the array $\boxed{3\ |\ 2\ |\ 5\ |\ 4\ |\ 6\ |\ 7}$ into a heap. Show your work.

3.5. Let $H[1..n]$ be a heap (max heap) of size n. Where is the second largest element located?

3.6. Use the heap data structure to design an algorithm to find the second largest element in an array $A[1..n]$ in $\Theta(n)$ time. *Hint*: Make use of Problem 3.5.

3.7. Give an algorithm that finds the minimum element in a heap $H[1..n]$ using no more than $\frac{n}{2}$ comparisons. Assume that n is even.

3.8. Let A be an array of numbers. Design an algorithm to test whether A is a heap.

3.9. Use algorithm HEAPSORT to sort the array $\boxed{6\ |\ 5\ |\ 4\ |\ 3\ |\ 2\ |\ 1}$.

3.10. Is the running time of Algorithm HEAPSORT $\Theta(n \log n)$? Justify your answer

3.11. Compare the space complexity of Algorithm HEAPSORT to that of BOTTOMUPSORT.

3.12. Let $\{1\}, \{2\}, \{3\}, \ldots, \{8\}$ be n singleton sets, each represented by a tree with exactly one node. Use the union-find algorithms with union by rank and path compression to find the tree representation of the set resulting from each of the following *unions* and *finds*: UNION(1, 2), UNION(3, 4), UNION(5, 6), UNION(7, 8), UNION(1, 3), UNION(5, 7), FIND(1), UNION(1, 5), FIND(1).

3.13. Solve Problem 3.12 using *the weight-balancing rule and path compression* (see Exercise 3.28).

3.5 Exercises

3.1. What are the merits and demerits of implementing a priority queue using an ordered list?

3.2. What are the costs of *insert* and *delete-max* operations of a priority queue that is implemented as a regular queue.

3.3. Which of the following arrays are heaps?
(a) | 8 | 6 | 4 | 3 | 2 |.   (b) | 7 |.   (c) | 9 | 7 | 5 | 6 | 3 |.
(d) | 9 | 4 | 8 | 3 | 2 | 5 | 7 |.   (e) | 9 | 4 | 7 | 2 | 1 | 6 | 5 | 3 |.

3.4. Where do the following element keys reside in a heap?
(a) Second largest key.   (b) Third largest key.   (c) Minimum key.

3.5. Give an efficient algorithm to test whether a given array $A[1..n]$ is a heap. What is the time complexity of your algorithm?

3.6. Which heap operation is more costly: insertion or deletion? Justify your answer. Recall that both operations have the same time complexity, that is, $O(\log n)$.

3.7. Let H be the heap shown in Fig. 3.1. Show the heap that results from
(a) deleting the element with key 17.
(b) inserting an element with key 19.

3.8. Show the heap (in both tree and array representations) that results from deleting the maximum key in the heap shown in Fig. 3.4(e).

3.9. How fast is it possible to find the *minimum* key in a max-heap of n elements?

3.10. Prove or disprove the following claim. Let x and y be two elements in a heap whose keys are positive integers, and let T be the tree representing that heap. Let h_x and h_y be the heights of x and y in T, respectively. Then, if x is greater than y, h_x cannot be less than h_y (see Sec. 2.5 for the definition of node height).

3.11. Illustrate the operation of Algorithm MAKEHEAP on the array

$$\boxed{3\mid 7\mid 2\mid 1\mid 9\mid 8\mid 6\mid 4}.$$

3.12. Show the steps of transforming the following array into a heap:

$$\boxed{1\mid 4\mid 3\mid 2\mid 5\mid 7\mid 6\mid 8}.$$

3.13. Let $A[1..19]$ be an array of 19 integers, and suppose we apply Algorithm MAKEHEAP on this array.
 (a) How many calls to Algorithm SIFT-DOWN will there be? Explain.
 (b) What is the maximum number of element interchanges in this case? Explain.
 (c) Give an array of 19 elements that requires the above maximum number of element interchanges.

3.14. Show how to use Algorithm HEAPSORT to arrange in increasing order the integers in the array

$$\boxed{4\mid 5\mid 2\mid 9\mid 8\mid 7\mid 1\mid 3}.$$

3.15. Given an array $A[1..n]$ of integers, we can create a heap $B[1..n]$ from A as follows. Starting from the empty heap, repeatedly insert the elements of A into B, each time adjusting the current heap, until B contains all the elements in A. Show that the running time of this algorithm is $\Theta(n \log n)$ in the worst case.

3.16. Illustrate the operation of the algorithm in Exercise 3.15 on the array

$$\boxed{6 \mid 9 \mid 2 \mid 7 \mid 1 \mid 8 \mid 4 \mid 3}.$$

3.17. Explain the behavior of Algorithm HEAPSORT when the input array is already sorted in
(a) increasing order.
(b) decreasing order.

3.18. Give an example of a binary search tree with the heap property.

3.19. Give an algorithm to merge two heaps of the same size into one heap. What is the time complexity of your algorithm?

3.20. Compute the minimum and maximum number of element comparisons performed by Algorithm HEAPSORT.

3.21. A d-heap is a generalization of the binary heap discussed in this chapter. It is represented by an almost-complete d-ary rooted tree for some $d \geq 2$. Rewrite Algorithm SIFT-UP for the case of d-heaps. What is its time complexity?

3.22. Rewrite Algorithm SIFT-DOWN for the case of d-heaps (see Exercise 3.21). What is its time complexity measured in terms of d and n?

3.23. Give a sequence of n union and find operations that results in a tree of height $\Theta(\log n)$ using only the heuristic of union by rank. Assume the set of elements is $\{1, 2, \ldots, n\}$.

3.24. Give a sequence of n union and find operations that requires $\Theta(n \log n)$ time using only the heuristic of union by rank. Assume the set of elements is $\{1, 2, \ldots, n\}$.

3.25. What are the ranks of nodes 3, 4 and 8 in Fig. 3.8(f)?

3.26. Let T be a tree resulting from a sequence of unions and finds using both the heuristics of union by rank and path compression, and let x be a node in T. Prove that $rank(x)$ is an upper bound on the height of x.

3.27. Let σ be a sequence of *union* and *find* instructions in which all the *unions* occur before the *finds*. Show that the running time is linear if both the heuristics of union by rank and path compression are used.

3.28. Another heuristic that is similar to union by rank is the *weight-balancing rule*. In this heuristic, the action of the operation UNION(x, y) is to let the root of the tree with fewer nodes point to the root of the tree with a larger number of nodes. If both trees have the same number of nodes, then let y be the parent of x. Compare this heuristic with the union by rank heuristic.

3.29. Prove that the weight-balancing rule described in Exercise 3.28 guarantees that the resulting tree is of height $O(\log n)$.

3.30. Let T be a tree resulting from a sequence of *unions* and *finds* using the heuristics of union by rank and path compression. Let x be the root of T and y a leaf node in T. Prove that the ranks of the nodes on the path from y to x form a *strictly* increasing sequence.

3.31. Prove the observation that if node v is in rank group $g > 0$, then v can be moved and charged at most $F(g) - F(g - 1)$ times before it acquires a parent in a higher group.

3.32. Another possibility for the representation of disjoint sets is by using linked lists. Each set is represented by a linked list, where the set representative is the first element in the list. Each element in the list has a pointer to the set representative. Initially, one list is created for each element. The union of two sets is implemented by merging the two sets. Suppose two sets S_1 represented by list L_1 and S_2 represented by list L_2 are to be merged. If the first element in L_1 is to be used as the name of the resulting set, then the pointer to the set name at each element in L_2 must be changed so that it points to the first element in L_1.

(a) Explain how to improve this representation so that each *find* operation takes $O(1)$ time.

(b) Show that the total cost of performing $n - 1$ *unions* is $\Theta(n^2)$ in the worst case.

3.33. (Refer to Exercise 3.32). Show that if when performing the union of two sets, the first element in the list with a larger number of elements is always chosen as the name of the new set, then the total cost of performing $n - 1$ *unions* becomes $O(n \log n)$.

3.6 Bibliographic Notes

Heaps and the data structures for disjoint sets appear in several books on algorithms and data structures (see the Bibliographic Notes of Chapters 1 and 2). They are covered in greater depth in Tarjan (1983). Heaps were first introduced as part of heapsort by Williams (1964). The linear time algorithm for building a heap is due to Floyd (1964). A number of variants of heaps can be found in Cormen *et al.* (2009), e.g., binomial heaps, Fibonacci heaps. A comparative study of many data structures for priority queues can be found in Jones (1986). The disjoint sets data structure was first studied by Galler and Fischer (1964) and Fischer (1972). A more detailed analysis was carried out by Hopcroft and Ullman (1973) and then a more exact analysis by Tarjan (1975). In this paper, a lower bound that is *not* linear was established when both union by rank and path compression are used.

PART 2
Techniques Based on Recursion

Recursive algorithms. This part of the book is concerned with a particular class of algorithms, called *recursive algorithms.* These algorithms turn out to be of fundamental importance and indispensable in virtually every area in the field of computer science. The use of recursion makes it possible to solve complex problems using algorithms that are concise, easy to comprehend and efficient (from an algorithmic point of view). In its simplest form, recursion is the process of dividing the problem into one or more *subproblems,* which are identical in structure to the original problem and then combining the solutions to these subproblems to obtain the solution to the original problem. We identify three special cases of this general design technique: (1) Induction or tail-recursion; (2) Nonoverlapping subproblems; (3) Overlapping subproblems with redundant invocations to subproblems, allowing trading space for time. The higher numbered cases subsume the lower numbered ones. The first two cases will not require additional space for the maintenance of solutions for continued reuse. The third class, however, renders the possibility of efficient solutions for many problems that at first glance appear to be time-consuming to solve.

Chapter 4 is devoted to the study of induction as a technique for the development of algorithms. In other words, the idea of induction in mathematical proofs is carried over to the design of efficient algorithms. In this chapter, several examples are presented to show how to use induction to solve increasingly sophisticated problems.

Chapter 5 provides a general overview of one of the most important algorithm design techniques, namely divide and conquer. First, we derive divide-and-conquer algorithms for the search problem and sorting by merging. In particular, Algorithm MERGESORT is compared with Algorithm BOTTOMUPSORT presented in Chapter 1, which is an iterative version of the former. This comparison reveals the most appealing merits of divide-and-conquer algorithms: conciseness, ease of comprehension and implementation, and most importantly, the simple inductive proofs for the correctness of divide-and-conquer algorithms. Next, some useful algorithms like Algorithm QUICKSORT and Algorithm SELECT for finding the kth smallest element are discussed in detail.

Chapter 6 provides some examples of the use of dynamic programming to solve problems for which recursion results in many redundant calls. In this design technique, recursion is first used to model the solution of the problem. This recursive model is then converted into an efficient iterative algorithm. By trading space for time, this is achieved by saving results of subproblems as they get solved and using a kind of table lookup for future reference to those solved subproblems. In this chapter, dynamic programming is applied to solve the longest common subsequence problem, matrix chain multiplication, the all-pairs shortest path problem and the knapsack problem.

Chapter 4

Induction

4.1 Introduction

Consider a problem with parameter n, which normally represents the number of objects in an instance of the problem. When searching for a solution to such a problem, sometimes it is easier to start with a solution to the problem with a smaller parameter, say $n-1$, $n/2$, etc., and extend the solution to include all the n objects. This approach is based on the well-known proof technique of mathematical induction. Basically, given a problem with parameter n, designing an algorithm by induction is based on the fact that if we know how to solve the problem when presented with a parameter less than n, called *the induction hypothesis*, then our task reduces to extending that solution to include those instances with parameter n.

This method can be generalized to encompass all recursive algorithm design techniques including divide and conquer and dynamic programming. However, since these two have distinct marking characteristics, we will confine our attention in this chapter to those strategies that use tail recursion and devote Chapters 5 and 6 to the study of divide and conquer and dynamic programming, respectively. The algorithms that we will cover in this chapter are usually recursive with only one recursive call, commonly called *tail recursion*. Thus, in most cases, they can conveniently be converted into iterative algorithms.

An advantage of this design technique (and all recursive algorithms in general) is that the proof of correctness of the designed algorithm is naturally embedded in its description, and a simple inductive proof can easily be constructed if desired.

4.2 Finding the Majority Element

Let $A[1..n]$ be a sequence of integers. An integer a in A is called the *majority* if it appears more than $\lfloor n/2 \rfloor$ times in A. For example, 3 is the majority in the sequence 1, 3, 2, 3, 3, 4, 3 since it appears four times and the number of elements is seven. There are several ways to solve this problem. The brute-force method is to compare each element with every other element and produce a count for each element. If the count of some element is more than $\lfloor n/2 \rfloor$, then it is declared as the majority; otherwise, there is no majority in the list. But the number of comparisons here is $n(n-1)/2 = \Theta(n^2)$, which makes this method too costly. A more efficient algorithm is to sort the elements and count how many times each element appears in the sequence. This costs $\Theta(n \log n)$ in the worst case, as the sorting step requires $\Omega(n \log n)$ comparisons in the worst case (Theorem 11.2). Another alternative is to find the median, i.e., the $\lceil n/2 \rceil$th element. Since the majority must be the median, we can scan the sequence to test if the median is indeed the majority. This method takes $\Theta(n)$ time, as the median can be found in $\Theta(n)$ time. As we will see in Sec. 5.5, the hidden constant in the time complexity of the median finding algorithm is too large, and the algorithm is fairly complex.

It turns out that there is an elegant solution that uses much fewer comparisons. We derive this algorithm using induction. The essence of the algorithm is based on the following observation:

Observation 4.1   If two *different* elements in the original sequence are removed, then the majority in the original sequence remains the majority in the new sequence.

This observation suggests the following algorithm for finding an element that is a *candidate* for being the majority. Set a counter to zero and let $x = A[1]$. Starting from $A[2]$, scan the elements one by one increasing the counter by one if the current element is equal to x and decreasing the counter by one if the current element is not equal to x. If all the elements have been scanned and the counter is greater than zero, then return x as the candidate. If the counter becomes zero when comparing x with $A[j]$,

$1 < j < n$, then call Algorithm *candidate* recursively on the elements $A[j + 1..n]$. Notice that decrementing the counter implements the idea of throwing two different elements as stated in Observation 4.1. This method is described more precisely in Algorithm MAJORITY. Converting this recursive algorithm into an iterative one is straightforward and is left as an exercise. Clearly, the running time of Algorithm MAJORITY is $\Theta(n)$.

Algorithm 4.1 MAJORITY
Input: An array $A[1..n]$ of n elements.

Output: The majority element if it exists; otherwise, *none*.

  1. $c \leftarrow candidate(1)$
  2. $count \leftarrow 0$
  3. **for** $j \leftarrow 1$ **to** n
  4.   **if** $A[j] = c$ **then** $count \leftarrow count + 1$
  5. **end for**
  6. **if** $count > \lfloor n/2 \rfloor$ **then return** c
  7. **else return** *none*

Algorithm *candidate(m)*
  1. $j \leftarrow m$; $c \leftarrow A[m]$; $count \leftarrow 1$
  2. **while** $j < n$ **and** $count > 0$
  3. $j \leftarrow j + 1$
  4.   **if** $A[j] = c$ **then** $count \leftarrow count + 1$
  5.   **else** $count \leftarrow count - 1$
  6. **end while**
  7. **if** $j = n$ **then return** c {See Exercises 4.7 and 4.8}
  8. **else return** $candidate(j + 1)$

4.3 Integer Exponentiation

In this section, we develop an efficient algorithm for raising a real number x to the nth power, where n is a nonnegative integer. The straightforward method is to iteratively multiply x by itself n times. This method is very inefficient, as it requires $\Theta(n)$ multiplications, which is exponential in the input size (see Sec. 1.14). An efficient method can be deduced as follows. Let $m = \lfloor n/2 \rfloor$, and suppose we know how to compute x^m. Then, we have two cases: If n is even, then $x^n = (x^m)^2$; otherwise, $x^n = x(x^m)^2$. This idea immediately yields the recursive algorithm shown as Algorithm EXPREC.

    Algorithm EXPREC can be rendered iterative using repeated squaring as follows. Let the binary digits of n be $d_k, d_{k-1}, \ldots, d_0$. Starting from $y = 1$,

---

Algorithm 4.2 EXPREC
Input: A real number x and a nonnegative integer n.
Output: x^n.

1. $power(x, n)$

Algorithm $power(x, m)$ {Compute x^m}
1. **if** $m = 0$ **then** $y \leftarrow 1$
2. **else**
3. $y \leftarrow power(x, \lfloor m/2 \rfloor)$
4. $y \leftarrow y^2$
5.   **if** m is odd **then** $y \leftarrow xy$
6. **end if**
7. **return** y

---

we scan the binary digits from left to right. If the current binary digit is 0, we simply square y, and if it is 1, we square y and multiply it by x. This yields Algorithm EXP.

Algorithm 4.3 EXP
Input: A real number x and a nonnegative integer n.
Output: x^n.

1. $y \leftarrow 1$
2. Let n be $d_k d_{k-1} \ldots d_0$ in binary notation.
3. **for** $j \leftarrow k$ **downto** 0
4. $y \leftarrow y^2$
5.   **if** $d_j = 1$ **then** $y \leftarrow xy$
6. **end for**
7. **return** y

Assuming that each multiplication takes constant time, the running time of both versions of the algorithm is $\Theta(\log n)$, which is linear in the input size.

4.4 Evaluating Polynomials (Horner's Rule)

Suppose we have a sequence of $n + 1$ real numbers $a_0, a_1, \ldots, a_n$ and a real number x, and we want to evaluate the polynomial

$$P_n(x) = a_n x^n + a_{n-1} x^{n-1} + \cdots + a_1 x + a_0.$$

The straightforward approach would be to evaluate each term separately. This approach is very inefficient since it requires $n + n - 1 \cdots + 1 = n(n+1)/2$ multiplications. A much faster method can be derived by induction as follows. We observe that

$$P_n(x) = a_n x^n + a_{n-1} x^{n-1} + \cdots + a_1 x + a_0$$
$$= ((\ldots(((a_n x + a_{n-1})x + a_{n-2})x + a_{n-3})\ldots)x + a_1)x + a_0.$$

This evaluation scheme is known as *Horner's rule*. Using this scheme leads to the following more efficient method. Suppose we know how to evaluate

$$P_{n-1}(x) = a_n x^{n-1} + a_{n-1} x^{n-2} + \cdots + a_2 x + a_1.$$

Then, using one more multiplication and one more addition, we have

$$P_n(x) = x P_{n-1}(x) + a_0.$$

This implies Algorithm HORNER.

Algorithm 4.4 HORNER
Input: A sequence of $n + 1$ real numbers $a_0, a_1, \ldots, a_n$ and a real number x.
Output: $P_n(x) = a_n x^n + a_{n-1} x^{n-1} + \ldots + a_1 x + a_0$.

1. $p \leftarrow a_n$
2. **for** $j \leftarrow 1$ **to** n
3. $p \leftarrow xp + a_{n-j}$
4. **end for**
5. **return** p

It is easy to see that Algorithm HORNER costs n multiplications and n additions. This is a remarkable achievement, which is attributed to the judicious choice of the induction hypothesis.

4.5 Radix Sort

In this section, we study a sorting algorithm that runs in linear time for almost all practical purposes. Let $L = \{a_1, a_2, \ldots, a_n\}$ be a list of n numbers each consisting of exactly k digits. That is, each number is of the form $d_k d_{k-1} \ldots d_1$, where each d_i is a digit between 0 and 9. In this problem, instead of applying induction on n, the number of objects, we use induction on k, the number of digits. One way to sort the numbers in L is to distribute them into 10 lists $L_0, L_1, \ldots, L_9$ by their *most significant* digit, so that those numbers with $d_k = 0$ constitute list L_0, those with $d_k = 1$ constitute list L_1 and so on. At the end of this step, for each $i, 0 \le i \le 9$, L_i contains those numbers whose most significant digit is i. We have two choices now. The first choice is to sort each list using another sorting algorithm and then concatenate the resulting lists into one sorted list. Observe that in the worst case, all numbers may have the same most significant digit, which means that they will all end up in one list and the other nine lists will be empty. Hence, if the sorting algorithm used runs in $\Theta(n \log n)$ time, the running time of this method will be $\Theta(n \log n)$. Another possibility is to recursively sort each list on digit d_{k-1}. But this approach will result in the addition of more and more lists, which is undesirable.

Surprisingly, It turns out that if the numbers are first distributed into the lists by their *least significant* digit, then a very efficient algorithm results. This algorithm is commonly known as *radix sort*. It is straightforward to derive the algorithm using induction on k. Suppose that the numbers are sorted lexicographically according to their least $k - 1$ digits, i.e., digits $d_{k-1}, d_{k-2}, \ldots, d_1$. Then, after sorting them on their kth digits, they will eventually be sorted. The implementation of the algorithm does not require any other sorting algorithm. Nor does it require recursion. The algorithm works as follows. First, distribute the numbers into 10 lists $L_0, L_1, \ldots, L_9$ according to digit d_1, so that those numbers with $d_1 = 0$ constitute list L_0, those with $d_1 = 1$ constitute list L_1 and so on. Next, the lists are coalesced in the order $L_0, L_1, \ldots, L_9$. Then, they are distributed into 10 lists according to digit d_2, coalesced in order, and so on. After distributing them according to d_k and collecting them in order, all numbers will be sorted. The following example illustrates the idea.

Example 4.1   Figure 4.1 shows an example of radix sort. The left column in the figure shows the input numbers. Successive columns show the results after sorting by the 1st, 2nd, 3rd and 4th digits.

The method is described more precisely in Algorithm RADIXSORT. There are k passes, and each pass costs $\Theta(n)$ time. Thus, the running time of the algorithm is $\Theta(kn)$. If k is constant, the running time is simply $\Theta(n)$. The algorithm uses $\Theta(n)$ space, as there are 10 lists needed and the overall size of the lists is $\Theta(n)$.

7467	6792	9134	9134	1239
1247	9134	1239	9187	1247
3275	3275	1247	1239	3275
6792	4675	7467	1247	4675
9187	7467	3275	3275	6792
9134	1247	4675	7467	7467
4675	9187	9187	4675	9134
1239	1239	6792	6792	9187

Fig. 4.1. Example of radix sort.

Algorithm 4.5 RADIXSORT
Input: A linked list of numbers $L = \{a_1, a_2, \ldots, a_n\}$ and k, the number of digits.
Output: L sorted in nondecreasing order.

1. **for** $j \leftarrow 1$ **to** k
2.   Prepare 10 empty lists $L_0, L_1, \ldots, L_9$.
3.   **while** L is not empty
4. $a \leftarrow$ next element in L. Delete a from L.
5. $i \leftarrow j$th digit in a. Append a to list L_i.
6.   **end while**
7. $L \leftarrow L_0$
8.   **for** $i \leftarrow 1$ **to** 9
9. $L \leftarrow L, L_i$ {append list L_i to L}
10.   **end for**
11. **end for**
12. **return** L

It should be noted that the algorithm can be generalized to any radix, not just radix 10 as in the algorithm. For example, we can treat each four bits as one digit and work on radix 16. The number of lists will always be equal to the radix. More generally, we can use Algorithm RADIXSORT to sort whole records on each field. If, for example, we have a file of dates each consisting of year, month and day, we can sort the whole file by sorting first by day, then by month and finally by year.

4.6   Generating Subsets of a Set

In this section, we study the problem of generating all 2^n subsets of the set of numbers $S_n = \{1, 2, \ldots, n\}$. One simple method would be to generate all subsets of $S_{n-1} = \{1, 2, \ldots, n-1\}$ and then setting the subsets of S_n as

$$W_n = \{s \mid s \in W_{n-1}\} \cup \{s \cup \{n\} \mid s \in W_{n-1}\}.$$

This, however, results in space complexity of $\Theta(2^n)$, which is undesirable. In what follows, we present two recursive and one iterative algorithms that use only $\Theta(n)$ of space. All algorithms are simple and efficient.

4.6.1 *The first algorithm*

Using induction, it is fairly easy to derive several algorithms more efficiently. In this section, we present a simple algorithm that has only $\Theta(n)$ space complexity. The algorithm is based on the assumption that we can generate all the subsets of $n - 1$ numbers. Suppose we can generate all subsets of $n - 1$ numbers. Then, we can extend our method to generate the subsets of the numbers $1, 2, \ldots, n$ as follows: (1) The algorithm first generates $\{\}$ and then all subsets of the numbers $2, 3, \ldots, n$. (2) It then generates $\{1\}$ and then prepends 1 to all subsets of the numbers $2, 3, \ldots, n$. This method is described in Algorithm SUBSETS1 below. The algorithm maintains a vector v of n binary digits such that the kth digit is 1 if and only if k is included in the current subset. For example, $v = \{0, 1, 1\}$ corresponds to the subset $\{2, 3\}$ for the case $n = 3$.

Algorithm 4.6 SUBSETS1
Input: A positive integer n.

Output: All subsets of the numbers $1, 2, \ldots, n$.

  1. **for** $j \leftarrow 1$ **to** n
  2. $v[j] \leftarrow 0$
  3. **end for**
  4. $sub1(1)$

Algorithm $sub1(k)$
  1. **if** $k \leq n$ **then**
  2.   **for** $j \leftarrow 0$ **to** 1
  3. $v[k] \leftarrow j$
  4. $sub1(k + 1)$
  5.   **if** $k = n$ **then**
  6.   **for** $i \leftarrow 1$ **to** n **if** $v[i] = 1$ **then output** i
  7.   **end for**
  8. **end if**

Example 4.2 Consider running the algorithm on inputs $n = 2$ and $n = 3$. If we trace the output for $n = 2$, we obtain the following subsets in their order of generation:

$$\{\}, \{2\}, \{1\}, \{1, 2\}.$$

For input $n = 3$, the output of the algorithm will consist of the following subsets in their order of generation:

$$\{\}, \{3\}, \{2\}, \{2, 3\}, \{1\}, \{1, 3\}, \{1, 2\}, \{1, 2, 3\}.$$

We analyze the running time of the algorithm as follows. First, we count the number of iterations of the **for** loop. The **for** loop is executed 2 times plus the number of times it is executed in the recursive call $sub1(k + 1)$. Since when $n = 0$, the number of iterations is zero, the number of iterations $f(n)$ can be expressed by the recurrence

$$f(n) = \begin{cases} 0 & \text{if } n = 0 \\ 2f(n-1) + 2 & \text{if } n \geq 1. \end{cases}$$

We proceed to solve this recurrence as follows:

$$\begin{aligned} f(n) &= 2f(n-1) + 2 \\ &= 2(2f(n-1) + 2) + 2 \\ &= 2^2 f(n-1) + 2^2 + 2 \\ &\vdots \\ &= 2^n f(0) + \sum_{j=1}^{n} 2^j \\ &= 0 + 2^{n+1} - 2 = 2^{n+1} - 2. \end{aligned}$$

Since the output statement takes $\Theta(n)$ steps and is executed 2^n times, it follows that the running time of the entire algorithm is $\Theta(n2^n)$, which is optimal. Clearly, the space needed by the algorithm is $\Theta(n)$.

4.6.2 *The second algorithm*

Using induction, we derive another efficient algorithm for generating the subsets of the set of numbers $\{1, 2, \ldots, n\}$. The algorithm to be presented also has $\Theta(n)$ space complexity. It is based on the assumption that we can generate all the subsets of $n - 1$ numbers. Suppose we can generate all subsets of $n - 1$ numbers. Then, we can extend our method to generate the subsets of the numbers $1, 2, \ldots, n$ as follows: (1) The algorithm first generates $\{\}$ and then all subsets of the numbers $2, 3, \ldots, n$. (2) It then generates $\{1\}$ and then prepends 1 to all subsets of the numbers $2, 3, \ldots, n$. This method is described in Algorithm SUBSETS2.

Algorithm 4.7 SUBSETS2
Input: A positive integer n.
Output: All subsets of the numbers $1, 2, \ldots, n$.

1. $i \leftarrow 0$
2. $sub2(1)$

Algorithm $sub2(k)$
1. **if** $k \leq n$ **then**
2. $sub2(k + 1)$
3.   **if** $k = n$ **then for** $j \leftarrow 1$ **to** i **output** $A[j]$
4. $i \leftarrow i + 1$
5. $A[i] \leftarrow k$
6. $sub2(k + 1)$
7.   **if** $k = n$ **then for** $j \leftarrow 1$ **to** i **output** $A[j]$
8. $i \leftarrow i - 1$
9. **end if**

Example 4.3   If we run the algorithm on inputs $n = 2$ and $n = 3$, we get the same output as that of the first algorithm. Namely, the output for $n = 2$, in order of generation of the subsets is

$$\{\}, \{2\}, \{1\}, \{1, 2\},$$

and the output for $n = 3$, in order of generation of the subsets is

$$\{\}, \{3\}, \{2\}, \{2, 3\}, \{1\}, \{1, 3\}, \{1, 2\}, \{1, 2, 3\}.$$

The analysis of the algorithm is very similar to that of the first algorithm. In particular, the number of iterations is $2^{n+1} - 2$, and the overall running time of the algorithm is $O(n2^n)$. Clearly, the space needed by the algorithm is $\Theta(n)$.

4.6.3 *Iterative algorithm*

In this section, we derive an iterative algorithm for generating the subsets of the set of numbers $S = \{1, 2, \ldots, n\}$. The algorithm to be presented is based on the assumption that if we can generate a subset, then we can generate the next subset in lexicographic order. It is shown below as Algorithm SUBSETS3. It uses Algorithm NEXTSUBSET to generate each and every subset. Note that A and k are global in the algorithm, that is, they are common to both Algorithm SUBSETS3 and Algorithm NEXTSUBSET.

The subsets are generated as $S_j, 0 \leq j \leq 2^n - 1$, where each subset is represented by a vector of 0s and 1s. A vector representing a subset S_j occupies the first k locations of the array A and is the reverse of the binary number j. For example, the subset $\{1, 2, 5\}$ is represented by the vector $A[1..5] = \langle 1, 1, 0, 0, 1 \rangle$, which is the reverse of the binary number 10011. In this case, the next subset has the vector representation $A[1..5] = \langle 0, 0, 1, 0, 1 \rangle$, which is the reverse of the binary number 10100. This vector is the representation of the subset $\{3, 5\}$.

In the main algorithm, the **for** loop is iterated 2^n times, once for each subset to be generated. The **while** loop in Algorithm NEXTSUBSET is iterated as many times as there are consecutive 1s in the beginning of

---

Algorithm NEXTSUBSET
Input: An array $A[1..k]$ of binary digits representing a subset of $\{1, 2, \ldots, n\}$.
Output: The next subset in lexicographic order.

```
 1. if k = 0 then
 2.      k ← k+1
 3.      A[k] = 0
 4.      exit
 5. end if
 6. i ← 1
 7. while A[i] = 1 and i < k
 8.      A[i] = 0
 9.      i ← i + 1
10. end while
11. if A[i] = 1 and i = k then
12.      A[i] = 0
13.      k ← k + 1
14.      A[k] = 1
15. else A[i] = 1
```

Algorithm 4.8 SUBSETS3
Input: A positive integer n.
Output: All subsets of the set $\{1, 2, \ldots, n\}$.

1. $k \leftarrow 0$;
2. **for** $j \leftarrow 1$ **to** 2^n
3.   NEXTSUBSET()
4.   **for** $l \leftarrow 1$ **to** k **if** $A[l] = 1$ **then output** l
5. **end for**

---

the subset representation. In each iteration, a 1 is flipped to 0. If all bits in $A[1..k]$ are 1s, they are all changed to 0s and a 1 is appended at position $k + 1$; this is done in Steps 11–14. Finally, the leftmost 0, if any, is changed to 1.

Example 4.4   Consider computing the next vector of $\langle 1, 1, 1, 0, 1 \rangle$ corresponding to subset $\{1, 2, 3, 5\}$. Here, $k = 5$. The **while** loop is executed three times, once for each 1 in the beginning of the vector. Thus, these 1s are flipped to 0s. Next, the first 0 from the left is flipped to 1. The resulting vector is $\langle 0, 0, 0, 1, 1 \rangle$, which corresponds to the subset $\{4, 5\}$. On the other hand, the next vector of $\langle 1, 1, 1, 1, 1 \rangle$ is $\langle 0, 0, 0, 0, 0, 1 \rangle$ corresponding to subsets $\{1, 2, 3, 4, 5\}$ and $\{6\}$, respectively.

Example 4.5   If we run the main algorithm SUBSETS3 on input $n = 3$, it will generate the binary vectors
$\langle 0 \rangle, \langle 1 \rangle, \langle 0, 1 \rangle, \langle 1, 1 \rangle, \langle 0, 0, 1 \rangle, \langle 1, 0, 1 \rangle, \langle 0, 1, 1 \rangle, \langle 1, 1, 1 \rangle$,
and output the corresponding subsets
$\{\}, \{1\}, \{2\}, \{1, 2\}, \{3\}, \{1, 3\}, \{2, 3\}, \{1, 2, 3\}$.
If we run the algorithm on input $n = 4$, it will output the subsets
$\{\}, \{1\}, \{2\}, \{1, 2\}, \{3\}, \{1, 3\}, \{2, 3\}, \{1, 2, 3\}, \{4\}, \{1, 4\}, \{2, 4\}, \{1, 2, 4\},$
$\{3, 4\}, \{1, 3, 4\}, \{2, 3, 4\}, \{1, 2, 3, 4\}$.

We analyze the running time of the algorithm as follows. First we count the number of iterations in the **while** loop of Algorithm NEXTSUBSET. This loop is iterated at most $k - 1$ times for each subset, which is $O(n)$ for a total of $O(n2^n)$. It can be shown, however, that the total number of iterations is $\Theta(2^n)$. To see this, we count the total number of flips (flipping a 0 to 1 and a 1 to 0). $A[1]$ is flipped in every call to Algorithm NEXTSUBSET for a total of 2^n flips, $A[2]$ is flipped in every other call for a total of $2^n/2$ flips and $A[3]$ is flipped in every fourth call for a total of $2^n/4$ flips. In general, $A[i]$ is flipped in every (2^{i-1})th call for a total of $2^n/2^{i-1}$ flips. Hence, the total number of flips is

$$2^n + 2^{n-1} + \cdots + 2^1 = 2^{n+1} - 2 = \Theta(2^n).$$

It is not hard to see that the total number of iterations in the **while** loop is equal to the number of flips minus two if all bits are 1s and is equal to the number of flips minus one otherwise. Hence, the number of iterations in the **while** loop is $\Theta(2^n)$. Finally, the **for** loop in the output statement is iterated k times for each subset, which is $O(n)$. It follows that the overall running time of the algorithm is $O(n2^n)$. Since the working space required by the algorithm is that for storing the array A and local variables, the space complexity of the algorithm is $\Theta(n)$.

4.7 Generating Permutations

In this section, we study the problem of generating all permutations of the numbers $1, 2, \ldots, n$. We will use an array $P[1..n]$ to hold each permutation. Using induction, it is fairly easy to derive several algorithms. In this section, we will present two of them that are based on the assumption that we can generate all the permutations of $n - 1$ numbers.

4.7.1 *The first algorithm*

Suppose we can generate all permutations of $n - 1$ numbers. Then, we can extend our method to generate the permutations of the numbers $1, 2, \ldots, n$ as follows. Generate all the permutations of the numbers $2, 3, \ldots, n$ and add the number 1 to the beginning of each permutation. Next, generate all permutations of the numbers $1, 3, 4, \ldots, n$ and add the number 2 to the beginning of each permutation. Repeat this procedure until finally the permutations of $1, 2, \ldots, n - 1$ are generated and the number n is added at the beginning of each permutation. This method is described in Algorithm PERMUTATIONS1. Note that when $P[j]$ and $P[m]$ are interchanged before the recursive call, they must be interchanged back after the recursive call.

In the algorithm, the call to Algorithm $perm1(m)$ finds the permutations of $m, m + 1, \ldots, n$.

Algorithm 4.9 PERMUTATIONS1
Input: A positive integer n.
Output: All permutations of the numbers $1, 2, \ldots, n$.

1. **for** $j \leftarrow 1$ **to** n
2. $\quad P[j] \leftarrow j$
3. **end for**
4. $perm1(1)$

Algorithm $perm1(m)$
1. **if** $m = n$ **then output** $P[1..n]$
2. **else**
3. $\quad$ **for** $j \leftarrow m$ **to** n
4. $\quad\quad$ interchange $P[j]$ and $P[m]$
5. $\quad\quad$ $perm1(m + 1)$
6. $\quad\quad$ interchange $P[j]$ and $P[m]$
7. $\quad\quad$ **comment:** *At this point* $P[m..n] = m, m+1, \ldots, n$.
8. $\quad$ **end for**
9. **end if**

We analyze the running time of the algorithm as follows. Since there are $n!$ permutations, Step 1 of Algorithm $perm1$ takes $\Theta(nn!)$ time to output all permutations. Now, we count the number of iterations of the **for** loop. In the first call to Algorithm $perm1$, $m = 1$. Hence, the **for** loop is executed n times plus the number of times it is executed in the recursive call $perm1(2)$. Since when $n = 1$, the number of iterations is zero, the number of iterations $f(n)$ can be expressed by the recurrence

$$f(n) = \begin{cases} 0 & \text{if } n = 1 \\ nf(n-1) + n & \text{if } n \geq 2. \end{cases}$$

Following the technique outlined in Sec. A.8.2, we proceed to solve this recurrence as follows. Let $n!h(n) = f(n)$ (note that $h(1) = 0$). Then,

$$n!h(n) = n(n-1)!h(n-1) + n,$$

or

$$h(n) = h(n-1) + \frac{n}{n!} = h(n-1) + \frac{1}{(n-1)!}.$$

The solution to this recurrence is

$$h(n) = h(1) + \sum_{j=2}^{n} \frac{1}{(j-1)!} = \sum_{j=1}^{n-1} \frac{1}{j!} < \sum_{j=1}^{\infty} \frac{1}{j!} = (e-1),$$

where $e = 2.7182818\ldots$ (Eq. (A.1)). Hence,

$$f(n) = n!h(n) < n!(e-1).$$

Since the running time of the output statement is $\Theta(nn!)$, it follows that the running time of the entire algorithm is $\Theta(nn!)$.

4.7.2 *The second algorithm*

In this section, we describe another algorithm for enumerating all the permutations of the numbers $1, 2, \ldots, n$. At the beginning, all n entries of the array $P[1..n]$ are free, and each free entry will be denoted by 0. For the induction hypothesis, let us assume that we have a method that generates all permutations of the numbers $1, 2, \ldots, n - 1$. Then, we can extend our method to generate all the permutations of the n numbers as follows. First, we put n in $P[1]$ and generate all the permutations of the first $n - 1$ numbers using the subarray $P[2..n]$. Next, we put n in $P[2]$ and generate all the permutations of the first $n - 1$ numbers using the subarrays $P[1]$ and $P[3..n]$. Then, we put n in $P[3]$ and generate all the permutations of the first $n - 1$ numbers using the subarrays $P[1..2]$ and $P[4..n]$. This continues until finally we put n in $P[n]$ and generate all the permutations of the first $n - 1$ numbers using the subarray $P[1..n - 1]$. Initially, all n entries of $P[1..n]$ contain 0's. The method is described more precisely in Algorithm PERMUTATIONS2.

Algorithm PERMUTATIONS2 works as follows. If the value of m is equal to 0, then this is an indication that Algorithm *perm2* has been called for all consecutive values $n, n - 1, \ldots, 1$. In this case, array $P[1..n]$ has no free entries and contains a permutation of the numbers $1, 2, \ldots, n$. If, on the other hand, $m > 0$, then we know that $m + 1, m + 2, \ldots, n$ have already been assigned to some entries of the array $P[1..n]$. Thus, we search for a free entry $P[j]$ in the array and set $P[j]$ to m, and then we call Algorithm *perm2* recursively with parameter $m - 1$. After the recursive call, we *must* set $P[j]$ to 0 indicating that it is now free and can be used in subsequent calls.

Algorithm 4.10 PERMUTATIONS2
Input: A positive integer n.
Output: All permutations of the numbers $1, 2, \ldots, n$.

1. **for** $j \leftarrow 1$ **to** n
2. $\quad P[j] \leftarrow 0$
3. **end for**
4. $perm2(n)$

Algorithm $perm2(m)$
1. **if** $m = 0$ **then output** $P[1..n]$
2. **else**
3. $\quad$ **for** $j \leftarrow 1$ **to** n
4. $\quad\quad$ **if** $P[j] = 0$ **then**
5. $\quad\quad\quad P[j] \leftarrow m$
6. $\quad\quad\quad perm2(m-1)$
7. $\quad\quad\quad P[j] \leftarrow 0$
8. $\quad\quad$ **end if**
9. $\quad$ **end for**
10. **end if**

We analyze the running time of the algorithm as follows. Since there are $n!$ permutations, Step 1 of Algorithm $perm2$ takes $\Theta(nn!)$ time to output all permutations. Now, we count the number of iterations of the **for** loop. The **for** loop is executed n times in *every* call $perm2(m)$ plus the number of times it is executed in the recursive call $perm2(m-1)$. When Algorithm $perm2$ is invoked by the call $perm2(m)$ with $m > 0$, the array P contains *exactly* m zeros, and hence the recursive call $perm2(m-1)$ will be executed *exactly* m times. Since when $m = 0$, the number of iterations is zero, the number of iterations can be expressed by the recurrence

$$f(m) = \begin{cases} 0 & \text{if } m = 0 \\ mf(m-1) + n & \text{if } m \geq 1. \end{cases}$$

Following the technique outlined in Sec. A.8.2, we proceed to solve this recurrence as follows. Let $m!h(m) = f(m)$ (note that $h(0) = 0$). Then,

$$m!h(m) = m(m-1)!h(m-1) + n,$$

or

$$h(m) = h(m-1) + \frac{n}{m!}.$$

Initially, $m = n$, so we set $m = n$, and we have as a result

$$h(n) = h(n-1) + \frac{n}{n!} = h(n-1) + \frac{1}{(n-1)!}.$$

The solution to this recurrence is

$$h(n) = h(1) + \sum_{j=1}^{n} \frac{1}{(j-1)!} = \sum_{j=0}^{n-1} \frac{1}{j!} < \sum_{j=0}^{\infty} \frac{1}{j!} = e,$$

where $e = 2.7182818\ldots$ (Eq. (A.1)). Hence,

$$f(n) = n! \sum_{j=0}^{n-1} \frac{1}{j!} < en!.$$

Since the running time of the output statement is $\Theta(nn!)$, it follows that the running time of the entire algorithm is $\Theta(nn!)$.

4.7.3 *Iterative algorithm*

In this section, we describe an iterative algorithm for generating the permutations of the numbers $1, 2, \ldots, n$. The algorithm to be presented is based on the assumption that if we can generate a permutation, then we can generate the next permutation in lexicographic order. Thus, the algorithm is straightforward; it first generates the first permutation, which is $1, 2, \ldots, n$, and then loops $n! - 1$ times, each time finding the next permutation in lexicographic order. An outline of the algorithm that generates the next permutation given the current one is shown below. Here, P is the input permutation and n is its length. The details are given in Algorithm NEXTPERM. Note that when the rightmost index i is 0, then this is an indication that the current permutation is the last one in lexicographic order.

Example 4.6 As an example, consider running Algorithm NEXTPERM on input $P = 2, 1, 4, 3$. Here, $n = 4$. First, the algorithm finds the rightmost index i such that $P[i]$ is less than $P[i+1]$, which is 2. Next, the algorithm finds the highest index j to the right of index $i = 2$ such that $P[j] > P[2]$, which is 4. It then interchanges $P[2] = 1$ with $P[4] = 3$, which gives $2, 3, 4, 1$. Finally, it reverses $P[3..4] = 4, 1$. The resulting next permutation is $P = 2, 3, 1, 4$.

---

1. Find the rightmost index i such that $P[i]$ is less than $P[i + 1]$.
2. Find the highest index j to the right of index i such that $P[j] > P[i]$ ($P[i + 1..n]$ is sorted in decreasing order).
3. Interchange $P[i]$ and $P[j]$.
4. Reverse the elements in $P[i + 1..n]$.
5. **return** P.

Algorithm 4.11 NEXTPERM
Input: A permutation P of the numbers $1, 2, \ldots, n$.
Output: The next permutation in lexicographic order.

1. $i \leftarrow n - 1$
2. **while** $P[i] > P[i + 1]$
3. $\quad i = i - 1$
4. **if** i = 0 **then return** (0)
5. $j \leftarrow n$;
6. **while** $j > i$ **and** $P[j] < P[i]$
7. $\quad j \leftarrow j - 1$
8. Interchange $P[i]$ and $P[j]$
9. $P[i + 1..n] \leftarrow reverse(P[i+1..n])$
10. **return** P.

Example 4.7   As another example, let $P = 5, 1, 4, 2, 7, 6, 3$. Then, the algorithm first finds the rightmost index i such that $P[i]$ is less than $P[i+1]$, which is 4. Next, the algorithm finds the highest index j to the right of index $i = 4$ such that $P[j] > P[4]$, which is 7. It then interchanges $P[4] = 2$ with $P[7] = 3$, which gives $5, 1, 4, 3, 7, 6, 2$. Finally, it reverses $P[5..7] = 7, 6, 2$. The resulting next permutation is $P = 5, 1, 4, 3, 2, 6, 7$.

Hence, to generate all permutations of $1, 2, \ldots, n$, we only need to invoke Algorithm NEXTPERM $n! - 1$ times, as shown in Algorithm PERMUTATIONS3 below.

Algorithm 4.12 PERMUTATIONS3
Input: A positive integer n.
Output: All permutations of the numbers $1, 2, \ldots, n$.

1. $P[1..n] \leftarrow 1, 2, \ldots, n$
2. **for** $k \leftarrow 1$ **to** n **output** $P[k]$
3. **for** $i \leftarrow 1$ **to** $n! - 1$
4. $\quad P = $ NEXTPERM(P)
5. $\quad$ **for** $k \leftarrow 1$ **to** n **output** $P[k]$
6. **end for**

Clearly, the running time of Algorithm NEXTPERM is $O(n)$, and hence the running time of Algorithm PERMUTATIONS3 is dominated by the output step, which costs $\Theta(nn!)$. The space complexity of the algorithm is $\Theta(n)$.

4.8 Practice Problems

4.1. Show that no more than one majority element may exist in an array.

4.2. Let A be a sorted array of n elements, which is known to have a majority element. Explain how to find the majority element in $O(1)$ time.

4.3. Illustrate the operation of Algorithm MAJORITY on the arrays

   (a) | 5 | 7 | 5 | 4 | 5 |.

   (b) | 5 | 7 | 5 | 4 | 8 |.

   (c) | 2 | 4 | 1 | 4 | 4 | 4 | 6 | 4 |.

4.4. Use induction to develop a recursive algorithm for finding the maximum element in a given sequence $A[1..n]$ of n elements.

4.5. Use induction to develop a recursive algorithm for finding the average of n real numbers $A[1..n]$.

4.6. Use induction to develop a recursive algorithm that searches for an element x in a given sequence $A[1..n]$ of n elements.

4.7. Use Algorithm EXPREC to compute 2^{12}.

4.8. Use Algorithm EXP to compute 2^{12}.

4.9. Use Horner's rule described in Sec. 4.4 to evaluate the following polynomials at the point $x = 2$:

   (a) $3x^5 + 2x^4 + 4x^3 + x^2 + 2x + 5$.

   (b) $2x^7 + 3x^5 + 2x^3 + 5x^2 + 3x + 7$.

4.10. Illustrate the operation of Algorithm RADIXSORT on the following sequence of eight numbers:

   (a) 4567, 2463, 6523, 7461, 4251, 3241, 6492, 7563.

   (b) 16543, 25895, 18674, 98256, 91428, 73234, 16597, 73195.

4.11. Consider Algorithm NEXTSUBSET in Sec. 4.6.3. What is the next subset of $\{2, 4, 5\}$ generated by the algorithm? Here, $k = 5$.

4.12. Consider Algorithm NEXTPERM in Sec. 4.7.3. What is the next permutation of $5, 1, 4, 3, 2, 6, 7$ generated by the algorithm?

4.9 Exercises

4.1. Give a recursive algorithm that computes the nth Fibonacci number f_n defined by

$$f_1 = f_2 = 1; \quad f_n = f_{n-1} + f_{n-2} \text{ for } n \geq 3.$$

4.2. Give a recursive version of Algorithm SELECTIONSORT.

4.3. Give a recursive version of Algorithm INSERTIONSORT.

4.4. Give a recursive version of Algorithm BUBBLESORT given in Exercise 1.17.

4.5. Derive a linear time and iterative version of Algorithm MAJORITY. Do not compute the median.

4.6. Prove Observation 4.1.

4.7. Prove or disprove the following claim. If in Step 7 of Algorithm *candidate* in Algorithm MAJORITY $j = n$ but *count* $= 0$, then c is the majority element.

4.8. Prove or disprove the following claim. If in Step 7 of Algorithm *candidate* in Algorithm MAJORITY $j = n$ and *count* > 0, then c is the majority element.

4.9. Use Algorithm EXPREC to compute
(a) 2^5.   (b) 2^7.   (c) 3^5.   (d) 5^7.

4.10. Solve Exercise 4.9 using Algorithm EXP instead of Algorithm EXPREC.

4.11. Let A be a square matrix. Explain how to compute A^n efficiently, where n is a positive integer. How many matrix multiplications did you use?

4.12. Let A be a square matrix. Explain how to compute $A + A^2 + \ldots + A^n$ efficiently, where n is a positive integer. Use the Θ-notation to express the number of matrix multiplications.

(a) Using integer exponentiation. Assume each power is evaluated separately.

(b) Using Horner's rule.

4.13. Express the time complexity of Algorithm RADIXSORT in terms of n when the input consists of n positive integers in the interval
  (a) $[1..n]$.
  (b) $[1..n^2]$.
  (c) $[1..2^n]$.

4.14. Let $A[1..n]$ be an array of positive integers in the interval $[1..n!]$. Which sorting algorithm do you think is faster: BOTTOMUPSORT or RADIXSORT? (see Sec. 1.7).

4.15. What is the time complexity of Algorithm RADIXSORT if arrays are used instead of linked lists? Explain.

4.16. A sorting method known as *bucket sort* works as follows. Let $A[1..n]$ be a sequence of n numbers within a reasonable range, say all numbers are between 1 and m, where m is not too large compared to n. The numbers are distributed into k buckets, with the first bucket containing those numbers between 1 and $\lfloor m/k \rfloor$, the second bucket containing those numbers between $\lfloor m/k \rfloor + 1$ to $\lfloor 2m/k \rfloor$ and so on. The numbers in each bucket are then sorted using another sorting algorithm, say Algorithm INSERTIONSORT. Analyze the running time of the algorithm.

4.17. Instead of using another sorting algorithm in Exercise 4.16, design a recursive version of bucket sort that recursively sorts the numbers in each bucket. What is the major disadvantage of this recursive version?

4.18. A sorting algorithm is called *stable* if the order of equal elements is preserved after sorting. Which of the following sorting algorithms are stable?
  (a) SELECTIONSORT   (b) INSERTIONSORT   (c) BUBBLESORT
  (d) BOTTOMUPSORT   (e) HEAPSORT   (f) RADIXSORT.

4.19. Let $f(x) = a_0 + a_1x + a_2x^2 + \cdots + a_{n-1}x^{n-1}$ be a polynomial of degree $n - 1$, where n is a power of 2. Design a recursive algorithm to implement Horner's rule to evaluate $f(x)$ at the point $x = b$. What is the time complexity of your algorithm?

4.20. Modify Algorithm SUBSETS1 in Sec. 4.6 for generating the subsets of numbers so that it outputs only m-subsets, that is, subsets of size m.

4.21. Modify Algorithm SUBSETS1 in Sec. 4.6 for generating the subsets of numbers so that it outputs all subsets containing 1 before all subsets without 1.

4.22. Do Exercise 4.20 for Algorithm SUBSETS2.

4.23. Do Exercise 4.21 for Algorithm SUBSETS2.

4.24. Explain why in Algorithm SUBSETS2 in Sec. 4.6, the statement $i \leftarrow i - 1$ is necessary.

4.25. Carefully explain why in Algorithm PERMUTATIONS1 when $P[j]$ and $P[m]$ are interchanged before the recursive call, they must be interchanged back after the recursive call.

4.26. Carefully explain why in Algorithm PERMUTATIONS2 $P[j]$ must be reset to 0 after the recursive call.

4.27. Carefully explain why in Algorithm PERMUTATIONS2, when Procedure *perm2* is invoked by the call *perm2(m)* with $m > 0$, the array P contains *exactly* m zeros, and hence the recursive call *perm2(m − 1)* will be executed *exactly* m times.

4.28. Modify Algorithm PERMUTATIONS2 so that the permutations of the numbers $1, 2, \ldots, n$ are generated in a reverse order to that produced by Algorithm PERMUTATIONS2.

4.29. Let $A[1..n]$ be a sorted array of n integers and x an integer. Design a recursive $O(n)$ time algorithm to determine whether there are two elements in A, if any, whose sum is exactly x.

4.30. Convert the algorithm in Exercise 4.29 into an iterative algorithm.

4.31. Let a and b be two positive integers. The greatest common divisor of a and b, denoted by $\gcd(a, b)$, is the largest integer that divides both a and b. Derive a recursive algorithm to compute $\gcd(a, b)$. *Hint*: If c divides a and b, then c divides their difference.

4.32. Derive the running time of the algorithm in Exercise 4.31. Note that the running time is in terms of the size of the input, which is the number of digits in $\max\{a, b\}$.

4.33. Convert the algorithm in Exercise 4.31 into an iterative algorithm. An efficient iterative algorithm for computing the gcd of two numbers was given in Exercise 1.41.

4.34. Use induction to solve Exercise 2.7.

4.35. Use induction to solve Exercise 2.8.

4.10 Bibliographic Notes

The use of induction as a mathematical technique for proving the correctness of algorithms was first developed by Floyd (1967). Recursion has been studied extensively in algorithm design. See for example the books of Burge (1975) and Paull (1988). The use of induction as a design technique appears in Manber (1988). Manber (1989) is a whole book that is mostly devoted to the induction design technique. Unlike this chapter, induction in that book encompasses a wide variety of problems and is used in its broad sense to cover other design techniques like divide and conquer and dynamic programming. The problem of finding the majority was studied for example by Misra and Gries (1982). Fischer and Salzberg (1982) show that using more sophisticated data structures, the number of comparisons can be reduced to $3n/2 + 1$ in the worst case, and this bound is optimal. Horner's rule for polynomial evaluation is named after the English mathematician W. G. Horner. Radix sort is used by card-sorting machines. In old machines, the machine did the distribution step and the operator collected the piles after each pass and combined them into one for the next pass. Algorithm PERMUTATIONS2 appears in Banachowski *et al.* (1991).

Chapter 5

Divide and Conquer

5.1 Introduction

The name "divide and conquer" has been given to a powerful algorithm design technique that is used to solve a variety of problems. In its simplest form, a divide-and-conquer algorithm divides the problem instance into a number of subinstances (in most cases, two), *recursively* solves each subinstance separately, and then combines the solutions to the subinstances to obtain the solution to the original problem instance. To illustrate this approach, consider the problem of finding both the minimum and maximum in an array of integers $A[1..n]$ and assume for simplicity that n is a power of 2. A straightforward algorithm might look like the one below. It returns a pair (x, y), where x is the minimum and y is the maximum.

---
1. $x \leftarrow A[1]$; $y \leftarrow A[1]$
2. **for** $i \leftarrow 2$ **to** n
3.   **if** $A[i] < x$ **then** $x \leftarrow A[i]$
4.   **if** $A[i] > y$ **then** $y \leftarrow A[i]$
5. **end for**
6. **return** (x, y)

Clearly, the number of *element* comparisons performed by this method is $2n - 2$. However, using the divide-and-conquer strategy, we can find both the minimum and maximum in only $(3n/2) - 2$ element comparisons. The idea is very simple: Divide the input array into two halves $A[1..n/2]$ and $A[(n/2) + 1..n]$, find the minimum and maximum in each half and return

145

the minimum of the two minima and the maximum of the two maxima. The divide-and-conquer algorithm is given in Algorithm MINMAX.

Algorithm 5.1 MINMAX
Input: An array $A[1..n]$ of n integers, where n is a power of 2.

Output: (x, y): the minimum and maximum integers in A.

  1. $minmax(1, n)$

Algorithm $minmax(low, high)$
  1. **if** $high - low = 1$ **then**
  2.   **if** $A[low] < A[high]$ **then return** $(A[low], A[high])$
  3.   **else return** $(A[high], A[low])$
  4.   **end if**
  5. **else**
  6. $mid \leftarrow \lfloor (low + high)/2 \rfloor$
  7. $(x_1, y_1) \leftarrow minmax(low, mid)$
  8. $(x_2, y_2) \leftarrow minmax(mid + 1, high)$
  9. $x \leftarrow \min\{x_1, x_2\}$
 10. $y \leftarrow \max\{y_1, y_2\}$
 11.   **return** (x, y)
 12. **end if**

Let $C(n)$ denote the number of comparisons performed by the algorithm on an array of n elements, where n is a power of 2. Note that the element comparisons are performed only in steps 2, 9 and 10. Also note that the number of comparisons performed by steps 7 and 8 as a result of the recursive calls is $C(n/2)$. This gives rise to the following recurrence relation for the number of comparisons done by the algorithm:

$$C(n) = \begin{cases} 1 & \text{if } n = 2 \\ 2C(n/2) + 2 & \text{if } n > 2. \end{cases}$$

We proceed to solve this recurrence by expansion as follows ($k = \log n$):

$$C(n) = 2C(n/2) + 2$$
$$= 2(2C(n/4) + 2) + 2$$
$$= 4C(n/4) + 4 + 2$$
$$= 4(2C(n/8) + 2) + 4 + 2$$

$$= 8C(n/8) + 8 + 4 + 2$$

$$\vdots$$

$$= 2^{k-1}C(n/2^{k-1}) + 2^{k-1} + 2^{k-2} + \cdots + 2^2 + 2$$

$$= 2^{k-1}C(2) + \sum_{j=1}^{k-1} 2^j$$

$$= (n/2) + 2^k - 2 \quad \text{(Eq. (A.10), page 678)}$$

$$= (3n/2) - 2.$$

This result deserves to be called a theorem.

Theorem 5.1 *Given an array $A[1..n]$ of n elements, where n is a power of 2, it is possible to find both the minimum and maximum of the elements in A using only $(3n/2) - 2$ element comparisons.*

5.2 Binary Search

Recall that in binary search, we test a given element x against the middle element in a *sorted* array $A[low..high]$. If $x < A[mid]$, where $mid = \lfloor (low + high)/2 \rfloor$, then we discard $A[mid..high]$ and the same procedure is repeated on $A[low..mid - 1]$. Similarly, if $x > A[mid]$, then we discard $A[low..mid]$ and repeat the same procedure on $A[mid + 1..high]$. This suggests the recursive Algorithm BINARYSEARCHREC as another alternative to implement this search method.

5.2.1 *Analysis of the recursive binary search algorithm*

To find the running time of the algorithm, we compute the number of element comparisons, since this is a basic operation, i.e., the running time of the algorithm is proportional to the number of element comparisons performed (see Sec. 1.11.2). We will assume that each three-way comparison counts as one comparison. First, note that if $n = 0$, i.e., the array is empty, then the algorithm does not perform any element comparisons. If $n = 1$, the else part will be executed and, in case $x \neq A[mid]$, the algorithm will recurse on an empty array. It follows that if $n = 1$, then exactly one comparison is

---

Algorithm 5.2 BINARYSEARCHREC
Input: An array $A[1..n]$ of n elements sorted in nondecreasing order and
      an element x.
Output: j if $x = A[j], 1 \leq j \leq n$, and 0 otherwise.

1. $binarysearch(1, n)$

Algorithm $binarysearch(low, high)$
1. **if** $low > high$ **then return** 0
2. **else**
3. $mid \leftarrow \lfloor (low + high)/2 \rfloor$
4.   **if** $x = A[mid]$ **then return** mid
5.   **else if** $x < A[mid]$ **then return** $binarysearch(low, mid - 1)$
6.   **else return** $binarysearch(mid + 1, high)$
7. **end if**

---

performed. If $n > 1$, then there are two possibilities: If $x = A[mid]$, then
only one comparison is performed; otherwise, the number of comparisons
required by the algorithm is one plus the number of comparisons done by
the recursive call on either the first or second half of the array. If we let
$C(n)$ denote the number of comparisons performed by Algorithm BINA-
RYSEARCHREC in the worst case on an array of size n, then $C(n)$ can be
expressed by the recurrence

$$C(n) \leq \begin{cases} 1 & \text{if } n = 1 \\ 1 + C(\lfloor n/2 \rfloor) & \text{if } n \geq 2. \end{cases}$$

Let k be such that $2^{k-1} \leq n < 2^k$, for some integer $k \geq 2$. If we expand the
above recurrence, we obtain

$$C(n) \leq 1 + C(\lfloor n/2 \rfloor)$$
$$\leq 2 + C(\lfloor n/4 \rfloor)$$
$$\vdots$$
$$\leq (k - 1) + C(\lfloor n/2^{k-1} \rfloor)$$
$$= (k - 1) + 1$$
$$= k,$$

since $\lfloor \lfloor n/2 \rfloor /2 \rfloor = \lfloor n/4 \rfloor$, etc. (see Eq. (A.3), page 672) and $\lfloor n/2^{k-1} \rfloor = 1$ (since $2^{k-1} \leq n < 2^k$). Taking the logarithms of the inequalities

$$2^{k-1} \leq n < 2^k$$

and adding 1 to both sides yields

$$k \leq \log n + 1 < k + 1,$$

or

$$k = \lfloor \log n \rfloor + 1,$$

since k is integer. It follows that

$$C(n) \leq \lfloor \log n \rfloor + 1.$$

We have, in effect, proved the following theorem.

Theorem 5.2 *The number of element comparisons performed by Algorithm* BINARYSEARCHREC *to search for an element in an array of n elements is at most* $\lfloor \log n \rfloor + 1$. *Thus, the time complexity of Algorithm* BINARYSEARCHREC *is* $O(\log n)$.

We close this section by noting that the recursion depth is $O(\log n)$, and since in each recursion level $\Theta(1)$ of space is needed, the total amount of space needed by the algorithm is $O(\log n)$. Contrast this recursive algorithm with the iterative version which needs only $\Theta(1)$ space (see Sec. 1.3).

5.3 Mergesort

In this section, we consider an example of a simple divide-and-conquer algorithm that reveals the essence of this algorithm design technique. We give here more detailed description of how a generic divide-and-conquer algorithm works in order to solve a problem instance in a top-down manner. Consider the example of BOTTOMUPSORT shown in Fig. 1.3. We have seen how the elements were sorted by an *implicit* traversal of the associated sorting tree level by level. In each level, we have pairs of sequences that *have already been sorted* and are to be merged to obtain larger sorted sequences. We continue ascending the tree level by level until we reach the root at which the final sequence has been sorted.

Now, let us consider doing the reverse, i.e., top-down instead of bottom-up. In the beginning, we have the input array

$$A[1..8] = \boxed{9\;|\;4\;|\;5\;|\;2\;|\;1\;|\;7\;|\;4\;|\;6}.$$

We divide this array into the two 4-element arrays

$$\boxed{9\;|\;4\;|\;5\;|\;2} \text{ and } \boxed{1\;|\;7\;|\;4\;|\;6}.$$

Next, we sort these two arrays *individually* and then simply merge them to obtain the desired sorted array. Call this algorithm SORT. As for the sorting method used for each half, we are free to make use of any sorting algorithm to sort the two subarrays. In particular, we may use Algorithm SORT itself. If we do so, then we have indeed arrived at the well-known MERGESORT algorithm. A precise description of this algorithm is given in Algorithm MERGESORT.

Algorithm 5.3 MERGESORT
Input: An array $A[1..n]$ of n elements.
Output: $A[1..n]$ sorted in nondecreasing order.

1. $mergesort(A, 1, n)$

Algorithm $mergesort(A, low, high)$
1. **if** $low < high$ **then**
2. $\quad mid \leftarrow \lfloor (low + high)/2 \rfloor$
3. $\quad mergesort(A, low, mid)$
4. $\quad mergesort(A, mid + 1, high)$
5. $\quad$ MERGE $(A, low, mid, high)$
6. **end if**

A simple proof by induction establishes the correctness of the algorithm.

5.3.1 *How the algorithm works*

Consider Fig. 5.1, which illustrates the behavior of Algorithm MERGESORT on the input array

$$A[1..8] = \boxed{9\;|\;4\;|\;5\;|\;2\;|\;1\;|\;7\;|\;4\;|\;6}.$$

As shown in the figure, the main call $mergesort(A, 1, 8)$ induces a series of recursive calls represented by an *implicit* binary tree. Each node of the

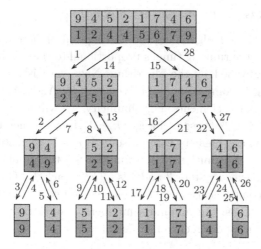

Fig. 5.1. The behavior of Algorithm MERGESORT.

tree consists of two arrays. The top array is the input to the call represented by that node, whereas the bottom array is its output. Each edge of the tree is replaced with two antidirectional edges indicating the flow of control. The main call causes the call $mergesort(A, 1, 4)$ to take effect, which, in turn, produces the call $mergesort(A, 1, 2)$, and so on. Edge labels indicate the order in which these recursive calls take place. This chain of calls corresponds to a *preorder* traversal of the tree: Visit the root, the left subtree and then the right subtree (see Sec. 2.5.1). The computation, however, corresponds to a *postorder* traversal of the tree: Visit the left subtree, the right subtree and then the root. To implement this traversal, a stack is used to hold the local data of each active call.

As indicated in the figure, the process of sorting the original array reduces to that used in Algorithm BOTTOMUPSORT when n is a power of 2. Each pair of numbers are merged to produce 2-element sorted sequences. These sorted 2-element sequences are then merged to obtain 4-element sorted sequences and so on. Compare Fig. 5.1 with Fig. 1.3. The only difference between the two algorithms is in the *order* of merges: In Algorithm BOTTOMUPSORT, merges are carried out level by level, while in Algorithm MERGESORT, the merges are performed in postorder. This justifies the remark stated in Observation 5.1 that the number of comparisons performed by MERGESORT is identical to that of Algorithm BOTTOMUPSORT when n is a power of 2.

5.3.2 *Analysis of the mergesort algorithm*

As in the binary search algorithm, the basic operation here is element comparison. That is, the running time is proportional to the number of element comparisons performed by the algorithm. Now, we wish to compute the number of element comparisons $C(n)$ required by Algorithm MERGESORT to sort an array of n elements. For simplicity, we will assume that n is a power of 2, i.e., $n = 2^k$ for some integer $k \geq 0$. If $n = 1$, then the algorithm does not perform any element comparisons. If $n > 1$, then steps 2 through 5 are executed. By definition of the function C, the number of comparisons required to execute steps 3 and 4 is $C(n/2)$ each. By Observation 1.1, the number of comparisons needed to merge the two subarrays is between $n/2$ and $n - 1$. Thus, the minimum number of comparisons done by the algorithm is given by the recurrence

$$C(n) = \begin{cases} 0 & \text{if } n = 1 \\ 2C(n/2) + n/2 & \text{if } n \geq 2. \end{cases}$$

Letting $d = 0, a = c = 2$ and $b = 1/2$ in Corollary 1.2, we obtain

$$C(n) = \frac{n \log n}{2}.$$

The maximum number of comparisons done by the algorithm is given by the recurrence

$$C(n) = \begin{cases} 0 & \text{if } n = 1 \\ 2C(n/2) + n - 1 & \text{if } n \geq 2. \end{cases}$$

We proceed to solve this recurrence by expansion as follows:

$$\begin{aligned} C(n) &= 2C(n/2) + n - 1 \\ &= 2(2C(n/2^2) + n/2 - 1) + n - 1 \\ &= 2^2 C(n/2^2) + n - 2 + n - 1 \\ &= 2^2 C(n/2^2) + 2n - 2 - 1 \\ &\ \vdots \\ &= 2^k C(n/2^k) + kn - 2^{k-1} - 2^{k-2} - \ldots - 2 - 1 \end{aligned}$$

$$= 2^k C(1) + kn - \sum_{j=0}^{k-1} 2^j$$

$$= 2^k \times 0 + kn - (2^k - 1) \quad \text{(Eq. (A.10), page 678)}$$

$$= kn - 2^k + 1$$

$$= n \log n - n + 1.$$

As a result, we have the following observation:

Observation 5.1   The total number of element comparisons performed by Algorithm MERGESORT to sort an array of size n, *where n is a power of* 2, is between $(n \log n)/2$ and $n \log n - n + 1$. These are exactly the numbers stated in Observation 1.5 for Algorithm BOTTOMUPSORT.

As described before, this is no coincidence, as Algorithm BOTTOMUP-SORT performs the same element comparisons as Algorithm MERGESORT *when n is a power of* 2. Section 5.6.4 shows empirical results in which the number of comparisons performed by the two algorithms are close to each other when n is not a power of 2.

If n is any arbitrary positive integer (not necessarily a power of 2), the recurrence relation for $C(n)$, the number of element comparisons performed by Algorithm MERGESORT, becomes

$$C(n) = \begin{cases} 0 & \text{if } n = 1 \\ C(\lfloor n/2 \rfloor) + C(\lceil n/2 \rceil) + bn & \text{if } n \geq 2 \end{cases}$$

for some nonnegative constant b. By Theorem 1.4, the solution to this recurrence is $C(n) = \Theta(n \log n)$.

Since the operation of element comparison is a basic operation in the algorithm, it follows that the running time of Algorithm MERGESORT is $T(n) = \Theta(n \log n)$. By Theorem 11.2, the running time of any algorithm for sorting by comparisons is $\Omega(n \log n)$. It follows that Algorithm MERGESORT is optimal.

Clearly, as in Algorithm BOTTOMUPSORT, the algorithm needs $\Theta(n)$ of space for carrying out the merges. It is not hard to see that the space needed for the recursive calls is $\Theta(n)$ (Problem 5.7). It follows that the space complexity of the algorithm is $\Theta(n)$. The following theorem summarizes the main results of this section.

Theorem 5.3 *Algorithm* MERGESORT *sorts an array of n elements in time* $\Theta(n \log n)$ *and space* $\Theta(n)$.

5.4 The Divide-and-Conquer Paradigm

Now, since we have at our disposal Algorithm BOTTOMUPSORT, why resort to a recursive algorithm such as MERGESORT, especially if we take into account the amount of extra space needed for the stack and the extra time brought about by the overhead inherent in handling recursive calls? From a practical point of view, there does not seem to be any reason to favor a recursive algorithm on its equivalent iterative version. However, from a theoretical point of view, recursive algorithms share the merits of being easy to state, grasp and analyze. To see this, compare the pseudocode of Algorithm MERGESORT with that of BOTTOMUPSORT. It takes much more time to debug the latter or even to comprehend the idea behind it. This suggests that a designer of an algorithm might be better off starting with an outline of a recursive description, if possible, which may afterwards be refined and converted into an iterative algorithm. Note that this is always possible, as every recursive algorithm can be converted into an iterative algorithm which functions in exactly the same way on every instance of the problem. In general, the divide-and-conquer paradigm consists of the following steps:

(a) The *divide* step. In this step of the algorithm, the input is partitioned into $p \geq 1$ parts, each of size *strictly* less than n, the size of the original instance. The most common value of p is 2, although other small constants greater than 2 are not uncommon. We have already seen an example of the case when $p = 2$, i.e., Algorithm MERGESORT. If $p = 1$ as in Algorithm BINARYSEARCHREC, then part of the input is discarded and the algorithm recurses on the remaining part. This case is equivalent to saying that the input data is divided into two parts, where one part is discarded; note that some work must be done in order to discard some of the elements. p may also be as high as $\log n$, or even n^ϵ, where ϵ is some constant, $0 < \epsilon < 1$.

(b) The *conquer* step. This step consists of performing p recursive call(s) if the problem size is greater than some predefined threshold n_0. This threshold is derived by mathematical analysis of the algorithm. Once it is found, it can be increased by *any constant* amount without affecting the time complexity of the algorithm. In Algorithm MERGESORT, although $n_0 = 1$, it can be set to *any* positive constant without affecting the $\Theta(n \log n)$ time complexity. This is because the time complexity, by definition, is concerned with the behavior of the algorithm when n approaches infinity. For example, we can modify MERGESORT so that when $n \leq 16$, the algorithm uses a straightforward (iterative) sorting algorithm, e.g., INSERTIONSORT. We can increase it to a much larger value, say 1000. However, after some point, the behavior of the algorithm starts to degrade. An (approximation to the) optimal threshold may be found empirically by fine tuning its value until the desired constant is found. It should be emphasized, however, that in some algorithms, the threshold may not be as low as 1, that is, it must be greater than some constant that is usually found by a careful analysis of the algorithm. An example of this is the median finding algorithm which will be introduced in Sec. 5.5. It will be shown that the threshold for that particular algorithm must be relatively high in order to guarantee linear running time.

(c) The *combine* step.[a] In this step, the solutions to the p recursive call(s) are combined to obtain the desired output. In Algorithm MERGESORT, this step consists of merging the two sorted sequences obtained by the two recursive calls using Algorithm MERGE. The combine step in a divide-and-conquer algorithm may consist of merging, sorting, searching, finding the maximum or minimum, matrix addition, etc.

The combine step is very crucial to the performance of virtually all divide-and-conquer algorithms, as the efficiency of the algorithm is largely dependent on how judiciously this step is implemented. To see this, suppose that Algorithm MERGESORT uses an algorithm that merges two sorted arrays of size $n/2$ each in time $\Theta(n \log n)$. Then, the recurrence relation that describes the behavior of this modified sorting algorithm becomes

$$T(n) = \begin{cases} 0 & \text{if } n = 1 \\ 2C(n/2) + bn \log n & \text{if } n \geq 2, \end{cases}$$

---

[a]Sometimes, this step is referred to as the *merge* step; this has nothing to do with the process of merging two sorted sequences as in Algorithm MERGESORT.

for some nonnegative constant b. By Theorem 1.2, the solution to this recurrence is $T(n) = \Theta(n \log^2 n)$, which is asymptotically larger than the time complexity of Algorithm MERGESORT by a factor of $\log n$.

On the other hand, the divide step is invariant in *almost* all divide-and-conquer algorithms: Partition the input data into p parts and proceed to the conquer step. In many divide-and-conquer algorithms, it takes $O(n)$ time or even only $O(1)$ time. For example, the time taken by Algorithm MERGESORT to divide the input into two halves is constant; it is the time needed to compute *mid*. In QUICKSORT algorithm, which will be introduced in Sec. 5.6, it is the other way around: The divide step requires $\Theta(n)$ time, whereas the combine step is nonexistent.

In general, a divide-and-conquer algorithm has the following format:

(1) If the size of the instance I is "small", then solve the problem using a straightforward method and return the answer. Otherwise, continue to the next step.
(2) Divide the instance I into p subinstances $I_1, I_2, \ldots, I_p$ of approximately the same size.
(3) Recursively call the algorithm on each subinstance $I_j, 1 \leq j \leq p$, to obtain p partial solutions.
(4) Combine the results of the p partial solutions to obtain the solution to the original instance I. Return the solution of instance I.

The overall performance of a divide-and-conquer algorithm is very sensitive to changes in these steps. In the first step, the threshold should be chosen carefully. As discussed before, it may need to be fine tuned until a reasonable value is found and no more adjustment is needed. In the second step, the number of partitions should be selected appropriately so as to achieve the asymptotically minimum running time. Finally, the combine step should be as efficient as possible.

5.5   Selection: Finding the Median and the kth Smallest Element

The median of a sequence of n sorted numbers $A[1..n]$ is the "middle" element. If n is odd, then the middle element is the $(n+1)/2$th element in the sequence. If n is even, then there are two middle elements occurring at positions $n/2$ and $n/2 + 1$. In this case, we will choose the $n/2$th smallest element. Thus, in both cases, the median is the $\lceil n/2 \rceil$th smallest element.

A straightforward method of finding the median is to sort all elements and pick the middle one. This takes $\Omega(n \log n)$ time, as any comparison-based sort process must spend at least this much in the worst case (Theorem 11.2).

It turns out that the median, or in general the kth smallest element, in a set of n elements can be found in optimal linear time. This problem is also known as the *selection problem*. The basic idea is as follows. Suppose after the divide step of *every* recursive call in a recursive algorithm, we discard a *constant* fraction of the elements and recurse on the remaining elements. Then, the size of the problem decreases *geometrically*. That is, in each call, the size of the problem is reduced by a *constant factor*. For concreteness, let us assume that an algorithm discards $1/3$ of whatever objects it is processing and recurses on the remaining $2/3$. Then, the number of elements becomes $2n/3$ in the second call, $4n/9$ in the third call, $8n/27$ in the fourth call and so on. Now, suppose that in each call, the algorithm does not spend more than a constant time for each element. Then, the overall time spent on processing all elements gives rise to the geometric series

$$cn + (2/3)cn + (2/3)^2 cn + \cdots + (2/3)^j cn + \cdots ,$$

where c is some appropriately chosen constant. By Eq. (A.12), this quantity is less than

$$\sum_{j=0}^{\infty} cn(2/3)^j = 3cn = \Theta(n).$$

This is exactly what is done in the selection algorithm. Algorithm SELECT shown below for finding the kth smallest element behaves in the same way. First, if the number of elements is less than 44, a predefined threshold, then the algorithm uses a straightforward method to compute the kth smallest element. The choice of this threshold will be apparent later when we analyze the algorithm. The next step partitions the elements into $\lfloor n/5 \rfloor$ groups of five elements each. If n is not a multiple of 5, the remaining elements are excluded, and this should not affect the performance of the algorithm. Each group is sorted and its median, the third element, is extracted. Next, the median of these medians, denoted by mm, is computed recursively. Step 6 of the algorithm partitions the elements in A into three arrays: A_1, A_2 and A_3, which, respectively, contain those elements less than, equal to and greater than mm. Finally, in Step 7, it is determined in which of the three arrays the kth smallest element occurs, and depending on the outcome of this test, the algorithm either returns the kth smallest element or recurses on either A_1 or A_3.

Algorithm 5.4 SELECT
Input: An array $A[1..n]$ of n elements and an integer k, $1 \leq k \leq n$.
Output: The kth smallest element in A.

1. $select(A, k)$

Algorithm $select(A, k)$
1. $n \leftarrow |A|$
2. **if** $n < 44$ **then** sort A and **return** $(A[k])$
3. Let $q = \lfloor n/5 \rfloor$. Divide A into q groups of 5 elements each. If 5 does not divide p, then discard the remaining elements.
4. Sort each of the q groups individually and extract its median. Let the set of medians be M.
5. $mm \leftarrow select(M, \lceil q/2 \rceil)$ {mm is the median of medians}
6. Partition A into three arrays:
   $A_1 = \{a \mid a < mm\}$
   $A_2 = \{a \mid a = mm\}$
   $A_3 = \{a \mid a > mm\}$
7. **case**
   $|A_1| \geq k$: **return** $select(A_1, k)$
   $|A_1| + |A_2| \geq k$: **return** mm
   $|A_1| + |A_2| < k$: **return** $select(A_3, k - |A_1| - |A_2|)$
8. **end case**

Example 5.1 For the sake of this example, let us temporarily change the threshold in the algorithm from 44 to a smaller number, say 6. Suppose we want to find the median of the following 25 numbers: 8, 33, 17, 51, 57, 49, 35, 11, 25, 37, 14, 3, 2, 13, 52, 12, 6, 29, 32, 54, 5, 16, 22, 23, 7. Let $A[1..25]$ be this sequence of numbers and $k = \lceil 25/2 \rceil = 13$. We find the 13th smallest element in A as follows.

First, we divide the set of numbers into 5 groups of 5 elements each: (8, 33, 17, 51, 57), (49, 35, 11, 25, 37), (14, 3, 2, 13, 52), (12, 6, 29, 32, 54), (5, 16, 22, 23, 7). Next, we sort each group in increasing order: (8, 17, 33, 51, 57), (11, 25, 35, 37, 49), (2, 3, 13, 14, 52), (6, 12, 29, 32, 54), (5, 7, 16, 22, 23).

Now, we extract the median of each group and form the set of medians: $M = \{33, 35, 13, 29, 16\}$. Next, we use the algorithm recursively to find the median of medians in M: $mm = 29$. Now, we partition A into three sequences: $A_1 = \{8, 17, 11, 25, 14, 3, 2, 13, 12, 6, 5, 16, 22, 23, 7\}$, $A_2 = \{29\}$ and $A_3 = \{33, 51, 57, 49, 35, 37, 52, 32, 54\}$. Since $13 \leq 15 = |A_1|$, the elements in A_2 and A_3 are discarded, and the 13th element must be in A_1. We repeat the same procedure above, so we set $A = A_1$. We divide the elements into 3 groups of 5 elements each: $(8,17,11,25,14),(3,2,13,12,6),(5,16,22,23,7)$. After sorting each group, we find the new set of medians: $M = \{14, 6, 16\}$. Thus, the new median of medians mm is 14. Next, we partition A into three sequences: $A_1 = \{8, 11, 3, 2, 13, 12, 6, 5, 7\}$, $A_2 = \{14\}$ and $A_3 = \{17, 25, 16, 22, 23\}$. Since $13 > 10 = |A_1| + |A_2|$, we set $A = A_3$ and find the 3rd element in A ($3 = 13 - 10$). The algorithm will return $A[3] = 22$. Thus, the median of the numbers in the given sequence is 22.

5.5.1 *Analysis of the selection algorithm*

It is not hard to see that Algorithm SELECT correctly computes the kth smallest element. Now, we analyze the running time of the algorithm. Consider Fig. 5.2 in which a number of elements have been divided into 5-element groups with the elements in each group ordered from bottom to top in increasing order.

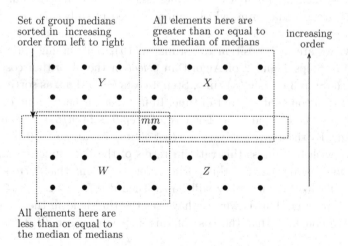

Fig. 5.2.   Analysis of Algorithm SELECT.

Furthermore, these groups have been aligned in such a way that their medians are in increasing order from left to right. It is clear from the figure that all elements enclosed within the rectangle labeled W are less than or equal to mm, and all elements enclosed within the rectangle labeled X are greater than or equal to mm. Let A_1' denote the set of elements that are less than or equal to mm and A_3' the set of elements that are greater than or equal to mm. In the algorithm, A_1 is the set of elements that are strictly less than mm and A_3 is the set of elements that are strictly greater than mm. Since A_1' is at least as large as W (see Fig. 5.2), we have

$$|A_1'| \geq 3\lceil \lfloor n/5 \rfloor / 2 \rceil \geq \frac{3}{2} \lfloor n/5 \rfloor.$$

Hence,

$$|A_3| \leq n - \frac{3}{2} \lfloor n/5 \rfloor \leq n - \frac{3}{2} \left(\frac{n-4}{5} \right) = n - 0.3n + 1.2 = 0.7n + 1.2.$$

By a symmetrical argument, we see that

$$|A_3'| \geq \frac{3}{2} \lfloor n/5 \rfloor \quad \text{and} \quad |A_1| \leq 0.7n + 1.2.$$

Thus, we have established upper bounds on the number of elements in A_1 and A_3, i.e., the number of elements less than mm and the number of elements greater than mm, which cannot exceed roughly $0.7n$, *a constant fraction* of n.

Now, we are in a position to estimate $T(n)$, the running time of the algorithm. Steps 1 and 2 of Algorithm *select* in the algorithm cost $\Theta(1)$ time each. Step 3 costs $\Theta(n)$ time. Step 4 costs $\Theta(n)$ time, as sorting each group costs a constant amount of time. In fact, sorting each group costs no more than seven comparisons. The cost of Step 5 is $T(\lfloor n/5 \rfloor)$. Step 6 takes $\Theta(n)$ time. By the above analysis, the cost of Step 7 is at most $T(0.7n+1.2)$. Now, we wish to express this ratio in terms of the floor function and get rid of the constant 1.2. For this purpose, let us assume that $0.7n + 1.2 \leq \lfloor 0.75n \rfloor$. Then, this inequality will be satisfied if $0.7n + 1.2 \leq 0.75n - 1$, that is, if $n \geq 44$. This is why we have set the threshold in the algorithm to 44. We conclude that the cost of this step is at most $T(\lfloor 0.75n \rfloor)$ for

$n \geq 44$. This analysis implies the following recurrence for the running time of Algorithm SELECT:

$$T(n) \leq \begin{cases} c & \text{if } n < 44 \\ T(\lfloor n/5 \rfloor) + T(\lfloor 3n/4 \rfloor) + cn & \text{if } n \geq 44, \end{cases}$$

for some constant c that is sufficiently large. Since $(1/5) + (3/4) < 1$, it follows by Theorem 1.5 that the solution to this recurrence is $T(n) = \Theta(n)$. In fact, by Example 1.39,

$$T(n) \leq \frac{cn}{1 - 1/5 - 3/4} = 20cn.$$

Note that each ratio $> 0.7n$ results in a different threshold. For instance, choosing $0.7n + 1.2 \leq \lfloor 0.71n \rfloor$ results in a threshold of about 220. The following theorem summarizes the main result of this section.

Theorem 5.4 *The kth smallest element in a set of n elements drawn from a linearly ordered set can be found in $\Theta(n)$ time. In particular, the median of n elements can be found in $\Theta(n)$ time.*

It should be emphasized, however, that the multiplicative constant in the time complexity of the algorithm is too large. In Sec. 13.5, we will present a simple randomized selection algorithm with $\Theta(n)$ expected running time and a small multiplicative constant. Also, Algorithm SELECT can be rewritten without the need for the auxiliary arrays A_1, A_2 and A_3 (Exercise 5.22).

5.6 Quicksort

In this section, we describe a very popular and efficient sorting algorithm: QUICKSORT. This sorting algorithm has an average running time of $\Theta(n \log n)$. One advantage of this algorithm over Algorithm MERGESORT is that it sorts the elements in place, i.e., it does not need auxiliary storage *for the elements to be sorted*. Before we describe the sorting algorithm, we need the following partitioning algorithm, which is the basis for Algorithm QUICKSORT.

5.6.1 *A partitioning algorithm*

Let $A[low..high]$ be an array of n numbers and $x = A[low]$. We consider the problem of rearranging the elements in A so that all elements less than or equal to x precede x which in turn precedes all elements greater than x. After permuting the elements in the array, x will be $A[w]$ for some w, $low \leq w \leq high$. For example, if $A = \boxed{5\,|\,3\,|\,9\,|\,2\,|\,7\,|\,1\,|\,8}$, and $low = 1$ and $high = 7$, then after rearranging the elements, we will have $A = \boxed{1\,|\,3\,|\,2\,|\,5\,|\,7\,|\,9\,|\,8}$. Thus, after the elements have been rearranged, $w = 4$. The action of rearrangement is also called *splitting* or *partitioning* around x, which is called the *pivot* or *splitting element*.

Definition 5.1   We say that an element $A[j]$ is in its *proper position* or *correct position* if it is neither smaller than the elements in $A[low..j-1]$ nor larger than the elements in $A[j+1..high]$.

An important observation is the following:

Observation 5.2   After partitioning an array A using $x \in A$ as a pivot, x will be in its correct position.

In other words, if we sort the elements in A in nondecreasing order after they have been rearranged, then we will still have $A[w] = x$. Note that it is fairly simple to partition a given array $A[low..high]$ if we are allowed to use another array $B[low..high]$ as an auxiliary storage. What we are interested in is carrying out the partitioning *without* an auxiliary array. In other words, we are interested in rearranging the elements of A *in place*. There are several ways to achieve this from which we choose the method described formally in Algorithm SPLIT.

Throughout the execution of the algorithm, we maintain two pointers i and j that are initially set to low and $low + 1$, respectively. These two pointers move from left to right so that after each iteration of the **for** loop, we have (see Fig. 5.3(a)):

(1) $A[low] = x$.
(2) $A[k] \leq x$ for all k, $low \leq k \leq i$.
(3) $A[k] > x$ for all k, $i < k \leq j$.

After the algorithm scans all elements, it interchanges the pivot with $A[i]$, so that all elements smaller than or equal to the pivot are to its left

---

Algorithm 5.5 SPLIT

Input: An array of elements $A[low..high]$.

Output: (1) A with its elements rearranged, if necessary, as described above.
(2) w, the new position of the splitting element A[low].

1. $i \leftarrow low$
2. $x \leftarrow A[low]$
3. **for** $j \leftarrow low + 1$ **to** $high$
4.   **if** $A[j] \leq x$ **then**
5. $i \leftarrow i + 1$
6.   **if** $i \neq j$ **then** interchange $A[i]$ and $A[j]$
7.   **end if**
8. **end for**
9. interchange $A[low]$ and $A[i]$
10. $w \leftarrow i$
11. **return** A and w

(a) After each iteration of the for loop.

(b) After the algorithm terminates.

Fig. 5.3. The behavior of Algorithm SPLIT.

and all elements larger than the pivot are to its right (see Fig. 5.3(b)). Finally, the algorithm sets w, the position of the pivot, to i.

Example 5.2 To aid in the understanding of the algorithm, we apply it to the input array $\boxed{5\,|\,7\,|\,1\,|\,6\,|\,4\,|\,8\,|\,3\,|\,2}$. The working of the algorithm on this input is illustrated in Fig. 5.4. Figure 5.4.(a) shows the input array. Here, $low = 1$ and $high = 8$, and the pivot is $x = 5 = A[1]$. Initially, i and j point to elements $A[1]$ and $A[2]$, respectively (see Fig. 5.4(a)). To start the partitioning, j is moved to the right, and since $A[3] = 1 \leq 5 = x$, i is incremented and then $A[i]$ and $A[j]$ are interchanged, as shown in Fig. 5.4(b). Similarly, j is incremented twice and then $A[3]$ and $A[5]$ are interchanged, as shown in Fig. 5.4(c). Next, j is moved to the right where an

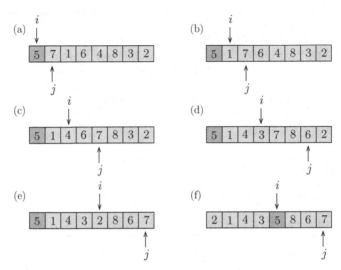

Fig. 5.4.   Example of partitioning a sequence of numbers using Algorithm SPLIT.

element that is less than x, namely $A[7] = 3$ is found. Again, i is incremented and $A[4]$ and $A[7]$ are interchanged, as shown in Fig. 5.4(d). Once more j is incremented and since $A[8] = 2$ is less than the pivot, i is incremented and then $A[5]$ and $A[8]$ are interchanged (see Fig. 5.4(e)). Finally, before the algorithm ends, the pivot is moved to its *proper* position by interchanging $A[i]$ with $A[1]$, as shown in Fig. 5.4(f).

The following observation is easy to verify:

Observation 5.3   The number of element comparisons performed by Algorithm SPLIT is exactly $n - 1$. Thus, its time complexity is $\Theta(n)$.

Finally, we note that the only extra space used by the algorithm is that needed to hold its local variables. Therefore, the space complexity of the algorithm is $\Theta(1)$.

5.6.2   *The sorting algorithm*

In its simplest form, Algorithm QUICKSORT can be summarized as follows. The elements $A[low..high]$ to be sorted are rearranged using Algorithm SPLIT so that the pivot element, which is always $A[low]$, occupies its correct position $A[w]$, and all elements that are less than or equal to $A[w]$ occupy the positions $A[low..w-1]$, while all elements that are greater than $A[w]$ occupy the positions $A[w+1..high]$. The subarrays $A[low..w-1]$ and $A[w+1..high]$ are then recursively sorted to produce the entire sorted array. The formal algorithm is shown as Algorithm QUICKSORT.

Algorithm 5.6 QUICKSORT
Input: An array $A[1..n]$ of n elements.
Output: The elements in A sorted in nondecreasing order.

1. $quicksort(A, 1, n)$

Algorithm $quicksort(A, low, high)$
1. **if** $low < high$ **then**
2.   SPLIT($A[low..high], w$)   {w is the new position of $A[low]$}
3. $quicksort(A, low, w-1)$
4. $quicksort(A, w+1, high)$
5. **end if**

The relationship of Algorithm SPLIT to Algorithm QUICKSORT is similar to the relationship of Algorithm MERGE to Algorithm MERGESORT; both sorting algorithms consist of a series of calls to one of these two basic algorithms, namely MERGE and SPLIT. However, there is a subtle difference between the two from the algorithmic point of view: In Algorithm MERGE-SORT, merging the sorted sequences belongs to the combine step, whereas splitting in Algorithm QUICKSORT belongs to the divide step. Indeed, the combine step in Algorithm QUICKSORT is nonexistent.

Example 5.3   Suppose we want to sort the array $\boxed{4}\ \boxed{6}\ \boxed{3}\ \boxed{1}$ $\boxed{8}\ \boxed{7}\ \boxed{2}\ \boxed{5}$. The sequence of splitting the array and its subarrays is illustrated in Fig. 5.5. Each pair of arrays in the figure corresponds to an input to and output of Algorithm SPLIT. Darkened boxes are used for the pivots. For example, in the first call, Algorithm SPLIT was presented with the above 8-element array. By Observation 5.2, after splitting the array, 4 will occupy its proper position, namely position 4. Consequently, the problem now reduces to sorting the two subarrays $\boxed{2}\ \boxed{3}\ \boxed{1}$ and $\boxed{8}\ \boxed{7}\ \boxed{6}\ \boxed{5}$. Since calls are implemented in a preorder fashion, the second call induces the third call on input $\boxed{1}$. Another call on only one element, namely $\boxed{3}$ is executed. At this point, the flow of control backs up to the first call and another call on the subarray $\boxed{8}\ \boxed{7}\ \boxed{6}\ \boxed{5}$ is initiated. Continuing this way, the array is finally sorted after eight calls to Algorithm QUICKSORT.

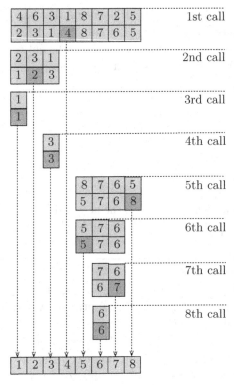

Fig. 5.5. Example of the execution of Algorithm QUICKSORT.

5.6.3 Analysis of the quicksort algorithm

In this section, we analyze the running time of Algorithm QUICKSORT. We will show that although it exhibits a running time of $\Theta(n^2)$ in the worst case, its average time complexity is indeed $\Theta(n \log n)$. This together with the fact that it sorts in place makes it very popular and comparable to HEAPSORT in practice. Although no auxiliary storage is required by the algorithm to store the array elements, the space required by the algorithm is $O(n)$. This is because in every recursive call, the left and right indices of the right part of the array to be sorted next, namely $w + 1$ and $high$, must be stored. It will be left as an exercise to show that the work space needed by the algorithm varies between $\Theta(\log n)$ and $\Theta(n)$ (Exercise 5.31).

5.6.3.1 *The worst case behavior*

To find the running time of Algorithm QUICKSORT in the worst case, we only need to find one situation in which the algorithm exhibits the longest running time for each value of n. Suppose that in *every* call to Algorithm QUICKSORT, it happens that the pivot, which is $A[low]$, is the smallest number in the array. This means that Algorithm SPLIT will return $w = low$ and, consequently, there will be only one nontrivial recursive call, the other call being a call on an empty array. Thus, if Algorithm QUICKSORT is initiated by the call QUICKSORT$(A, 1, n)$, the next two recursive calls will be QUICKSORT$(A, 1, 0)$ and QUICKSORT$(A, 2, n)$, with the first being a trivial call. It follows that the worst case happens if the input array is already sorted in nondecreasing order! In this case the smallest element will *always* be chosen as the pivot, and as a result, the following n calls to Algorithm QUICKSORT will take place:

$$quicksort(A, 1, n), quicksort(A, 2, n), \ldots, quicksort(A, n, n).$$

These, in turn, initiate the following nontrivial calls to Algorithm SPLIT.

$$\text{SPLIT}(A[1..n], w), \text{SPLIT}(A[2..n], w), \ldots, \text{SPLIT}(A[n..n], w).$$

Since the number of comparisons done by the splitting algorithm on input of size j is $j - 1$ (Observation 5.3), it follows that the total number of comparisons performed by Algorithm QUICKSORT in the worst case is

$$(n - 1) + (n - 2) + \cdots + 1 + 0 = \frac{n(n - 1)}{2} = \Theta(n^2).$$

It should be emphasized, however, that this extreme case is not the only case that leads to a quadratic running time. If, for instance, the algorithm always selects one of the smallest (or largest) k elements, for any *constant* k that is sufficiently small relative to n, then the algorithm's running time is also quadratic.

The worst case running time can be improved to $\Theta(n \log n)$ by always selecting the median as the pivot in linear time, as shown in Sec. 5.5. This is because the splitting of elements is highly balanced; in this case, the two recursive calls have approximately the same number of elements. This results in the following recurrence for counting the number of comparisons:

$$C(n) = \begin{cases} 0 & \text{if } n = 1 \\ 2C(n/2) + \Theta(n) & \text{if } n > 1, \end{cases}$$

whose solution is $C(n) = \Theta(n \log n)$. However, the hidden constant in the time complexity of the median finding algorithm is too high to be used in conjunction with Algorithm QUICKSORT. Thus, we have the following theorem:

Theorem 5.5 *The running time of Algorithm* QUICKSORT *is $\Theta(n^2)$ in the worst case. If, however, the median is always chosen as the pivot, then its time complexity is $\Theta(n \log n)$.*

It turns out, however, that Algorithm QUICKSORT as originally stated, is a fast sorting algorithm in practice (given that the elements to be sorted are in random order); this is supported by its average time analysis, which is discussed below. If the elements to be sorted are not in random order, then choosing the pivot randomly, instead of always using $A[low]$, results in a very efficient algorithm. This version of Algorithm QUICKSORT will be presented in Sec. 13.4.

5.6.3.2 *The average case behavior*

It is important to note that the above extreme cases are *practically* rare, and in practice, the running time of Algorithm QUICKSORT is fast. This motivates the investigation of its performance *on average*. It turns out that, on average, its time complexity is $\Theta(n \log n)$, and not only that, but also the multiplicative constant is fairly small. For simplicity, we will assume that the input elements are distinct. Note that the behavior of the algorithm is independent of the input *values*; what matters is their relative order. For this reason, we may assume without loss of generality, that the elements to be sorted are the first n positive integers $1, 2, \ldots, n$. When analyzing the average behavior of an algorithm, it is important to assume some probability distribution on the input. In order to simplify the analysis further, we will assume that each permutation of the elements is equally likely. That is, we will assume that each of the $n!$ permutations of the numbers $1, 2, \ldots, n$ is equally likely. This ensures that each number in the array is equally likely to be the first element and thus chosen as the pivot, i.e., the probability that any element of A will be picked as the pivot is $1/n$. Let $C(n)$ denote the number of comparisons done by the algorithm on average on an input of size n. From the assumptions stated (all elements are distinct and have the same probability of being picked as the pivot), the average cost is computed as follows. By Observation 5.3, Step 2 costs exactly $n - 1$ comparisons. Steps 3 and 4 cost $C(w-1)$ and $C(n-w)$ comparisons, respectively. Hence, the total number of comparisons is

$$C(n) = (n - 1) + \frac{1}{n} \sum_{w=1}^{n} (C(w - 1) + C(n - w)). \tag{5.1}$$

Since

$$\sum_{w=1}^{n} C(n - w) = C(n - 1) + C(n - 2) + \cdots + C(0) = \sum_{w=1}^{n} C(w - 1),$$

Eq. (5.1) can be simplified to

$$C(n) = (n - 1) + \frac{2}{n} \sum_{w=1}^{n} C(w - 1). \tag{5.2}$$

This recurrence seems to be complicated when compared with the recurrences we are used to, as the value of $C(n)$ depends on *all* its history: $C(n - 1), C(n - 2), \ldots, C(0)$. However, we can remove this dependence as follows. First, we multiply Eq. (5.2) by n:

$$nC(n) = n(n - 1) + 2 \sum_{w=1}^{n} C(w - 1). \tag{5.3}$$

If we replace n by $n - 1$ in Eq. (5.3), we obtain

$$(n - 1)C(n - 1) = (n - 1)(n - 2) + 2 \sum_{w=1}^{n-1} C(w - 1). \tag{5.4}$$

Subtracting Eq. (5.4) from Eq. (5.3) and rearranging terms yields

$$\frac{C(n)}{n + 1} = \frac{C(n - 1)}{n} + \frac{2(n - 1)}{n(n + 1)}. \tag{5.5}$$

Now, we change to a new variable D by letting

$$D(n) = \frac{C(n)}{n + 1}.$$

In terms of the new variable D, Eq. (5.5) can be rewritten as

$$D(n) = D(n-1) + \frac{2(n-1)}{n(n+1)}, \quad D(1) = 0. \tag{5.6}$$

Clearly, the solution of Eq. (5.6) is

$$D(n) = 2\sum_{j=1}^{n} \frac{j-1}{j(j+1)}.$$

We simplify this expression as follows:

$$2\sum_{j=1}^{n} \frac{j-1}{j(j+1)} = 2\sum_{j=1}^{n} \frac{2}{(j+1)} - 2\sum_{j=1}^{n} \frac{1}{j}$$

$$= 4\sum_{j=2}^{n+1} \frac{1}{j} - 2\sum_{j=1}^{n} \frac{1}{j}$$

$$= 2\sum_{j=1}^{n} \frac{1}{j} - \frac{4n}{n+1}$$

$$= 2\ln n - \Theta(1) \quad (\text{Eq. (A.16)})$$

$$= \frac{2}{\log e} \log n - \Theta(1)$$

$$\approx 1.44\log n.$$

Consequently,

$$C(n) = (n+1)D(n) \approx 1.44n\log n.$$

We have, in effect, proven the following theorem.

Theorem 5.6 *The average number of comparisons performed by Algorithm* QUICKSORT *to sort an array of n elements is* $\Theta(n\log n)$.

5.6.4 *Comparison of sorting algorithms*

Table 5.1 gives the output of a sorting experiment for the average number of comparisons of five sorting algorithms using values of n between 500 and 5000.

The numbers under each sorting algorithm are the counts of the number of comparisons performed by the respective algorithm. From the table, we

Table 5.1. Comparison of sorting algorithms.

n	SELECTIONSORT	INSERTIONSORT	BOTTOMUPSORT	MERGESORT	QUICKSORT
500	124750	62747	3852	3852	6291
1000	499500	261260	8682	8704	15693
1500	1124250	566627	14085	13984	28172
2000	1999000	1000488	19393	19426	34020
2500	3123750	1564522	25951	25111	52513
3000	4498500	2251112	31241	30930	55397
3500	6123250	3088971	37102	36762	67131
4000	7998000	4042842	42882	42859	79432
4500	10122750	5103513	51615	49071	98635
5000	12497500	6180358	56888	55280	106178

can see that the average number of comparisons performed by Algorithm QUICKSORT is almost double that of MERGESORT and BOTTOMUPSORT.

5.7 Quickselect

Consider Algorithm SELECT, which was presented in Sec. 5.5. We have shown that the algorithm's running time is $\Theta(n)$ with a large multiplicative constant that makes the algorithm impractical, especially for small and moderate values of n. In this section, we present a simple and fast algorithm for selection. Its running time is $\Theta(n)$ on average with a small multiplicative constant, although it exhibits an $O(n^2)$ behavior in the worst case. The algorithm behaves like the binary search algorithm in the sense that it keeps discarding portions of the input until the desired kth smallest element is found. A precise description of the algorithm is given in Algorithm QUICKSELECT.

To improve the performance of the algorithm, instead of selecting the pivot as $A[1]$, a sample of the input elements is chosen and their median is computed. In the median-of-three heuristic, the median of three elements (e.g., the first, middle and last elements; see Exercise 5.27) is found and set as the pivot. If the size of the sample grows with n and is $o(n)$, then the average number of comparisons to select an item of random rank is $2n + o(n)$. By analyzing the lower-order terms, it can be shown that the optimal sample size is $\Theta(\sqrt{n})$. This analysis pertaining to selecting the pivot also applies to Algorithm QUICKSORT.

Algorithm 5.7 QUICKSELECT
Input: An array $A[1..n]$ of n elements and an integer k, $1 \le k \le n$.
Output: The kth smallest element in A.

1. $qselect(A, k)$

Algorithm $qselect(A, k)$
1. $v \leftarrow A[1]$
2. Partition A into three arrays:
   $A_1 = \{a \mid a < v\}$
   $A_2 = \{a \mid a = v\}$
   $A_3 = \{a \mid a > v\}$
3. **case**
   $|A_1| \ge k$: **return** $qselect(A_1, k)$
   $|A_1| + |A_2| \ge k$: **return** v
   $|A_1| + |A_2| < k$: **return** $qselect(A_3, k - |A_1| - |A_2|)$
4. **end case**

5.8 Multiselection

Let $A[1..n]$ be an array of n elements drawn from a linearly ordered set, and let $K[1..r]$, $1 \le r \le n$, be a *sorted* array of r positive integers between 1 and n, that is an array of ranks. The *multiselection* problem is to select the $K[i]$th smallest element in A for all values of i, $1 \le i \le r$. For simplicity, we will assume that the elements in A are distinct. To make the presentation simple, we will assume that the elements are represented by the sequence $A = \langle a_1, a_2, \ldots, a_n \rangle$ and the ranks are represented by the sorted sequence $K = \langle k_1, k_2, \ldots, k_r \rangle$. If $r = 1$, then we have the selection problem. On the other hand, if $r = n$, then the problem is tantamount to the problem of sorting.

The algorithm for multiselection, which we will refer to as MULTI-SELECT, is straightforward. Let the middle rank be $k = k_{\lceil r/2 \rceil}$. Use Algorithm SELECT to find and output the kth smallest element a. Next, partition A into two subsequences A_1 and A_2 of elements, respectively, smaller than and larger than a. Let $K_1 = \langle k_1, k_2, \ldots, k_{\lceil r/2 \rceil - 1} \rangle$ and $K_2 = \langle k_{\lceil r/2 \rceil + 1} - k, k_{\lceil r/2 \rceil + 2} - k, \ldots, k_r - k \rangle$. Finally, make two recursive calls: One with A_1 and K_1 and another with A_2 and K_2. A less informal description of the algorithm is shown below.

In Step 4, SELECT is the $\Theta(n)$ time algorithm for selection presented in Sec. 5.5. Obviously, Algorithm MULTISELECT solves the

---

Algorithm 5.8 MULTISELECT
Input: A sequence $A = \langle a_1, a_2, \ldots, a_n \rangle$ of n elements and a sorted sequence of r ranks $K = \langle k_1, k_2, \ldots, k_r \rangle$.
Output: The k_ith smallest element in A, $1 \le i \le r$.

1. $multiselect(A, K)$

Algorithm $multiselect(A, K)$
1. $r \leftarrow |K|$
2. If $r > 0$ **then**
3.   Set $k = k_{\lceil r/2 \rceil}$.
4.   Use Algorithm SELECT to find a, the kth smallest element in A.
5.   Output a.
6.   Let $A_1 = \langle a_i \mid a_i < a \rangle$ and $A_2 = \langle a_i \mid a_i > a \rangle$.
7.   Let $K_1 = \langle k_1, k_2, \ldots, k_{\lceil r/2 \rceil - 1} \rangle$ and
      $K_2 = \langle k_{\lceil r/2 \rceil + 1} - k, k_{\lceil r/2 \rceil + 2} - k, \ldots, k_r - k \rangle$.
8.   MULTISELECT(A_1, K_1).
9.   MULTISELECT(A_2, K_2).
10. **end if**

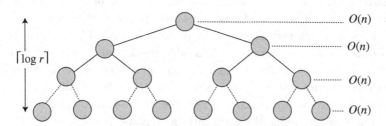

Fig. 5.6. Recursion tree for multiselection.

multiselection problem. We now analyze its time complexity. Consider the recursion tree depicted in Fig. 5.6. The root of the tree corresponds to the main call, and its two children correspond to the first two recursive calls. The rest of the nodes correspond to the remaining recursive calls. In particular, the leaves represent calls in which there is only one rank. The bulk of the work done in the root node is that for executing Algorithm SELECT on an input of size n, partitioning the elements into A_1 and A_2 and dividing K into K_1 and K_2. Obviously, this takes $O(n)$ time, as Algorithm SELECT runs in time $O(n)$. Similarly, the next two recursive calls execute Algorithm SELECT on inputs of sizes n_1 and n_2, where $n_1 + n_2 = n - 1$. These two recursive calls plus partitioning A and K require

$O(n_1) + O(n_2) = O(n)$ time. In each subsequent level of the tree, Algorithm SELECT is called a number of times using a total of less than n elements, for a total time of $O(n)$. The total time needed for partitioning in each level is $O(n)$. Hence, the time needed in each level of the tree is $O(n)$. But the number of levels in the recursion tree is equal to $\lceil \log r \rceil$, assuming that $r > 1$. It follows that the overall running time of Algorithm MULTISELECT is $O(n \log r)$.

As to the lower bound for multiselection, suppose that it is $o(n \log r)$. Then, by letting $r = n$, we would be able to sort n elements in $o(n \log n)$ time, contradicting the $\Omega(n \log n)$ lower bound for comparison-based sorting (see Sec. 11.3.2 and Theorem 11.2). It follows that the multiselection problem is $\Omega(n \log r)$, and hence the algorithm given above runs in time $\Theta(n \log r)$ and is optimal.

5.9 Multiplication of Large Integers

We have assumed in the beginning that multiplication of integers whose size is *fixed* costs a unit amount of time. This is no longer valid when multiplying two integers of arbitrary length. As explained in Sec. 1.14, the input to an algorithm dealing with numbers of variable size is usually measured in the number of bits or, equivalently, digits. Let u and v be two n-bit integers. The traditional multiplication algorithm requires $\Theta(n^2)$ digit multiplications to compute the product of u and v. Using the divide-and-conquer technique, this bound can be reduced significantly as follows. For simplicity, assume that n is a power of 2.

Each integer is divided into two parts of $n/2$ bits each. Then, u and v can be rewritten as $u = w2^{n/2} + x$ and $v = y2^{n/2} + z$ (see Fig. 5.7).

The product of u and v can be computed as

$$ uv = (w2^{n/2} + x)(y2^{n/2} + z) = wy2^n + (wz + xy)2^{n/2} + xz. \qquad (5.7) $$

$$ u = w2^{n/2} + x : \quad \boxed{\begin{array}{c|c} w & x \end{array}} $$

$$ v = y2^{n/2} + z : \quad \boxed{\begin{array}{c|c} y & z \end{array}} $$

Fig. 5.7. Multiplication of two large integers.

Note that multiplying by 2^n amounts to simply shifting by n bits to the left, which takes $\Theta(n)$ time. Thus, in this formula, there are four multiplications and three additions. This implies the following recurrence:

$$T(n) = \begin{cases} d & \text{if } n = 1 \\ 4T(n/2) + bn & \text{if } n > 1, \end{cases}$$

for some constants b and $d > 0$. The solution to this recurrence is, by Theorem 1.3, $T(n) = \Theta(n^2)$.

Now, consider computing $wz + xy$ using the identity

$$wz + xy = (w + x)(y + z) - wy - xz. \tag{5.8}$$

Since wy and xz need not be computed twice (they are computed in Eq. (5.7)), combining Eqs. (5.7) and (5.8) results in only three multiplications, namely

$$uv = wy2^n + ((w + x)(y + z) - wy - xz)2^{n/2} + xz.$$

Thus, multiplying u and v reduces to three multiplications of integers of size $n/2$ and six additions and subtractions. These additions cost $\Theta(n)$ time. This method yields the following recurrence:

$$T(n) = \begin{cases} d & \text{if } n = 1 \\ 3T(n/2) + bn & \text{if } n > 1, \end{cases}$$

for some appropriately chosen constants b and $d > 0$. Again, by Theorem 1.3,

$$T(n) = \Theta(n^{\log 3}) = O(n^{1.59}),$$

a remarkable improvement on the traditional method.

5.10 Matrix Multiplication

Let A and B be two $n \times n$ matrices. We wish to compute their product $C = AB$. In this section, we show how to apply the divide-and-conquer strategy to this problem to obtain an efficient algorithm.

5.10.1 *The traditional algorithm*

In the traditional method, C is computed using the formula

$$C(i,j) = \sum_{k=1}^{n} A(i,k)B(k,j).$$

It can be easily shown that this algorithm requires n^3 multiplications and $n^3 - n^2$ additions (Problem 5.17). This results in a time complexity of $\Theta(n^3)$.

5.10.2 *Strassen's algorithm*

This algorithm has a $o(n^3)$ time complexity, i.e., its running time is asymptotically less than n^3. This is a remarkable improvement on the traditional algorithm. The idea behind this algorithm consists in reducing the number of multiplications at the expense of increasing the number of additions and subtractions. In short, this algorithm uses seven multiplications and 18 additions of $n/2 \times n/2$ matrices.

Let

$$A = \begin{pmatrix} a_{11} & a_{12} \\ a_{21} & a_{22} \end{pmatrix} \quad \text{and} \quad B = \begin{pmatrix} b_{11} & b_{12} \\ b_{21} & b_{22} \end{pmatrix}$$

be two 2×2 matrices. To compute the matrix product

$$C = \begin{pmatrix} c_{11} & c_{12} \\ c_{21} & c_{22} \end{pmatrix} = \begin{pmatrix} a_{11} & a_{12} \\ a_{21} & a_{22} \end{pmatrix} \begin{pmatrix} b_{11} & b_{12} \\ b_{21} & b_{22} \end{pmatrix},$$

we first compute the following products:

$$d_1 = (a_{11} + a_{22})(b_{11} + b_{22}),$$
$$d_2 = (a_{21} + a_{22})b_{11},$$
$$d_3 = a_{11}(b_{12} - b_{22}),$$
$$d_4 = a_{22}(b_{21} - b_{11}),$$
$$d_5 = (a_{11} + a_{12})b_{22},$$
$$d_6 = (a_{21} - a_{11})(b_{11} + b_{12}),$$
$$d_7 = (a_{12} - a_{22})(b_{21} + b_{22}).$$

Next, we compute C from the equation

$$C = \begin{pmatrix} d_1 + d_4 - d_5 + d_7 & d_3 + d_5 \\ d_2 + d_4 & d_1 + d_3 - d_2 + d_6 \end{pmatrix}.$$

Since commutativity of scalar products is not used here, the above formula holds for matrices as well. So, the d_i's are in general $n/2 \times n/2$ matrices.

5.10.2.1 *Time complexity*

The number of additions used is 18 and the number of multiplications is seven. In order to count the number of scalar operations, let a and m denote the costs of scalar addition and multiplication, respectively. If $n = 1$, the total cost is just m since we have only one scalar multiplication. Thus, the total cost of multiplying two $n \times n$ matrices is governed by the recurrence

$$T(n) = \begin{cases} m & \text{if } n = 1 \\ 7T(n/2) + 18(n/2)^2 a & \text{if } n \geq 2, \end{cases}$$

or

$$T(n) = \begin{cases} m & \text{if } n = 1 \\ 7T(n/2) + (9a/2)n^2 & \text{if } n \geq 2. \end{cases}$$

Assuming that n is a power of 2, then by Lemma 1.1,

$$T(n) = \left(m + \frac{(9a/2)2^2}{7 - 2^2} \right) n^{\log 7} - \left(\frac{(9a/2)2^2}{7 - 2^2} \right) n^2$$

$$= mn^{\log 7} + 6an^{\log 7} - 6an^2.$$

That is, the running time is $\Theta(n^{\log 7}) = O(n^{2.81})$.

5.10.3 *Comparison of the two algorithms*

In the above derivations, the coefficient of a is the number of additions and the coefficient of m is the number of multiplications. Strassen's algorithm significantly reduces the total number of multiplications, which are more costly than additions. Table 5.2 compares the number of arithmetic operations performed by the two algorithms.

Table 5.3 compares Strassen's algorithm with the traditional algorithm for some values of n.

Table 5.2.   The number of arithmetic operations done by the two algorithms.

	Multiplications	Additions	Complexity
Traditional alg.	n^3	$n^3 - n^2$	$\Theta(n^3)$
Strassen's alg.	$n^{\log 7}$	$6n^{\log 7} - 6n^2$	$\Theta(n^{\log 7})$

Table 5.3.   Comparison between Strassen's algorithm and the traditional algorithm.

	n	Multiplications	Additions
Traditional alg.	100	1,000,000	990,000
Strassen's alg.	100	411,822	2,470,334
Traditional alg.	1000	1,000,000,000	999,000,000
Strassen's alg.	1000	264,280,285	1,579,681,709
Traditional alg.	10,000	10^{12}	9.99×10^{12}
Strassen's alg.	10,000	0.169×10^{12}	10^{12}

5.11   The Closest Pair Problem

Let S be a set of n points in a plane. In this section, we consider the problem of finding a pair of points p and q in S whose mutual distance is minimum. In other words, we want to find two points $p_1 = (x_1, y_1)$ and $p_2 = (x_2, y_2)$ in S with the property that the distance between them defined by

$$d(p_1, p_2) = \sqrt{(x_1 - x_2)^2 + (y_1 - y_2)^2}$$

is minimum among all pairs of points in S. Here, $d(p_1, p_2)$ is referred to as the *Euclidean distance* between p_1 and p_2. The brute-force algorithm simply examines all the possible $n(n-1)/2$ distances and returns that pair with the smallest separation. In this section, we describe a $\Theta(n \log n)$ time algorithm to solve the closest pair problem using the divide-and-conquer design technique. Instead of finding that pair which realizes the minimum distance, the algorithm to be developed will only return the distance between them. Modifying the algorithm to return that pair as well is easy.

The general outline of the algorithm can be summarized as follows. The first step in the algorithm is to sort the points in S by increasing

x-coordinate. This sorting step is done only once throughout the execution of the algorithm. Next, the point set S is divided about a vertical line L into two subsets S_l and S_r such that $|S_l| = \lfloor |S|/2 \rfloor$ and $|S_r| = \lceil |S|/2 \rceil$. Let L be the vertical line passing by the x-coordinate of $S[\lfloor n/2 \rfloor]$. Thus, all points in S_l are on or to the left of L, and all points in S_r are on or to the right of L. Now, recursively, the minimum separations δ_l and δ_r of the two subsets S_l and S_r, respectively, are computed. For the combine step, the smallest separation δ' between a point in S_l and a point in S_r is also computed. Finally, the desired solution is the minimum of δ_l, δ_r and δ'.

As in most divide-and-conquer algorithms, most of the work comes from the combine step. At this point, it is not obvious how to implement this step. The crux of this step is in computing δ'. The naïve method which computes the distance between each point in S_l and each point in S_r requires $\Omega(n^2)$ in the worst case, and hence an efficient approach to implement this step must be found.

Let $\delta = \min\{\delta_l, \delta_r\}$. If the closest pair consists of some point p_l in S_l and some point p_r in S_r, then p_l and p_r must be within distance δ of the dividing line L. Thus, if we let S_l' and S_r' denote, respectively, the points in S_l and in S_r within distance δ of L, then p_l must be in S_l' and p_r must be in S_r' (see Fig. 5.8).

Again, comparing each point in S_l' with each point in S_r' requires $\Omega(n^2)$ in the worst case, since we may have $S_l' = S_l$ and $S_r' = S_r$. The crucial observation is that not all these $O(n^2)$ comparisons are indeed necessary; we only need to compare each point p in S_l, say, with those within distance δ. A close inspection of Fig. 5.8 reveals that the points lying within the two

Fig. 5.8.   Illustration of the combine step.

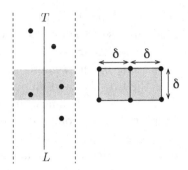

Fig. 5.9.   Further illustration of the combine step.

strips of width δ around L have a special structure. Suppose that $\delta' \leq \delta$. Then, there exist two points $p_l \in S_l'$ and $p_r \in S_r'$ such that $d(p_l, p_r) = \delta'$. It follows that the vertical distance between p_l and p_r is at most δ. Furthermore, since $p_l \in S_l'$ and $p_r \in S_r'$, these two points are inside or on the boundary of a $\delta \times 2\delta$ rectangle centered around the vertical line L (see Fig. 5.9).

Let T be the set of points within the two vertical strips. Referring again to Fig. 5.9, if the distance between any two points in the $\delta \times 2\delta$ rectangle must be at most δ, then the rectangle can accommodate at most eight points: at most four points from S_l and at most four points from S_r. The maximum number is attained when one point from S_l coincides with one point from S_r at the intersection of L with the top of the rectangle, and one point from S_l coincides with one point from S_r at the intersection of L with the bottom of the rectangle. This implies the following important observation.

Observation 5.4   Each point in T needs to be compared with at most seven points in T.

The above observation gives only an upper bound on the number of points to be compared with each point p in T but does not give any information as to which points are to be compared with p. A moment of reflection shows that p must be compared with its *neighbors* in T. To find such neighbors, we resort to sorting the points in T by increasing y-coordinate. After that, it is not hard to see that we only need to compare each point

p in T with those seven points following p in increasing order of their y-coordinates.

5.11.1 *Time complexity*

Let us analyze the running time of the algorithm developed so far. Sorting the points in S requires $O(n \log n)$ time. Dividing the points into S_l and S_r takes $\Theta(1)$ time, as the points are sorted. As to the combine step, we see that it consists of sorting the points in T and comparing each point with at most seven other points. Sorting costs $|T| \log |T| = O(n \log n)$, and there are at most $7|T|$ comparisons. Thus, the combine step takes $\Theta(n \log n)$ time in the worst case, and hence the recurrence relation for the performance of the algorithm becomes

$$T(n) = \begin{cases} c & \text{if } n \leq 3 \\ 2T(n/2) + O(n \log n) & \text{if } n > 3, \end{cases}$$

for some nonnegative constant c since if the number of points is 2 or 3, the minimum separation can be calculated in a straightforward method. By Theorem 1.2, the solution to the above recurrence is $T(n) = O(n \log^2 n)$, which is not the desired bound.

We observe that if we reduce the time taken by the combine step to $\Theta(n)$, then the time complexity of the algorithm will be $\Theta(n \log n)$. This can be achieved by embedding Algorithm MERGESORT in the algorithm for finding the closest pair for sorting the points by their y-coordinates. After dividing the points into the two halves S_l and S_r, these two subsets are sorted recursively and stored in Y_l and Y_r, which are merged to obtain Y. This approach reduces the time required by the combine step to $\Theta(n)$, as sorting in every recursive invocation is now replaced by merging, which costs only $\Theta(|Y|)$ time. Thus, the recurrence relation reduces to

$$T(n) = \begin{cases} c & \text{if } n \leq 3 \\ 2T(n/2) + \Theta(n) & \text{if } n > 3, \end{cases}$$

for some nonnegative constant c. The solution to this familiar recurrence is the desired $\Theta(n \log n)$ bound. The above discussion implies Algorithm CLOSESTPAIR. In the algorithm, for a point p, $x(p)$ denotes the x-coordinate of point p. Also, $S_l = S[low..mid]$ and $S_r = S[mid + 1..high]$.

Algorithm 5.9 CLOSESTPAIR

Input: A set S of n points in the plane.

Output: The minimum separation realized by two points in S.

1. Sort the points in S in nondecreasing order of their x-coordinates.
2. $(\delta, Y) \leftarrow cp(1, n)$
3. **return** δ

Algorithm $cp(low, high)$

1. **if** $high - low + 1 \leq 3$ **then**
2.   compute δ by a straightforward method.
3.   Let Y contain the points in nondecreasing order of y-coordinates.
4. **else**
5. $mid \leftarrow \lfloor (low + high)/2 \rfloor$
6. $x_0 \leftarrow x(S[mid])$
7. $(\delta_l, Y_l) \leftarrow cp(low, mid)$
8. $(\delta_r, Y_r) \leftarrow cp(mid + 1, high)$
9. $\delta \leftarrow \min\{\delta_l, \delta_r\}$
10. $Y \leftarrow$ Merge Y_l with Y_r in nondecreasing order of y-coordinates.
11. $k \leftarrow 0$
12.   **for** $i \leftarrow 1$ **to** $|Y|$ {Extract T from Y}
13.   **if** $|x(Y[i]) - x_0| \leq \delta$ **then**
14. $k \leftarrow k + 1$
15. $T[k] \leftarrow Y[i]$
16.   **end if**
17.   **end for**   {k is the size of T}
18. $\delta' \leftarrow 2\delta$ {Initialize δ' to any number greater than δ}
19.   **for** $i \leftarrow 1$ **to** $k - 1$ {Compute δ'}
20.   **for** $j \leftarrow i + 1$ **to** $\min\{i + 7, k\}$
21.   **if** $d(T[i], T[j]) < \delta'$ **then** $\delta' \leftarrow d(T[i], T[j])$
22.   **end for**
23.   **end for**
24. $\delta \leftarrow \min\{\delta, \delta'\}$
25. **end if**
26. **return** (δ, Y)

The following theorem summarizes the main result. Its proof is embedded in the description of the algorithm and the analysis of its running time.

Theorem 5.7 *Given a set S of n points in the plane, Algorithm* CLOSESTPAIR *finds the minimum separation between the pairs of points in S in* $\Theta(n \log n)$ *time.*

5.12   A Dominance Problem

Let S be a set of n points in the plane. A point $p \in S$ is dominated by another point $q \in S$, denoted by $p \prec q$, if $x(p) < x(q)$ and $y(p) < y(q)$. In this section, we consider the problem of finding for each point $p \in S$ the number of points in S dominated by p.

Assume that no two points have the same x-coordinate (see Exercise 5.42). Let $count(p)$ denote the number of points dominated by p. The first step in the algorithm is to sort the points in S by increasing x-coordinate. This sorting step is done only once throughout the execution of the algorithm. Next, the point set S is divided about a vertical line L into two subsets S_l and S_r such that $|S_l| = \lceil |S|/2 \rceil$ and $|S_r| = \lfloor |S|/2 \rfloor$. All points in S_l are on or to the left of L, and all points in S_r are to the right of L. Now, recursively, solve the problem for the two halves S_l and S_r. For the combine step, assume the points in S_l and S_r are sorted by y-coordinates. Initialize $d \leftarrow 0$. Sweep a horizontal line from the bottom to the top, stopping at every point $p \in S_l \cup S_r$. If $p \in S_l$, then increment $d \leftarrow d + 1$, else assign $count(p) = count(p) + d$.

To keep the points sorted by y-coordinate, we merge the points in S_l and S_r, assuming that they are both sorted by y-coordinate. This can be achieved by embedding Algorithm MERGESORT in the algorithm for sorting the points by their y-coordinates. After dividing the points into the two halves S_l and S_r, these two subsets are sorted recursively and stored in Y_l and Y_r, which are merged to obtain Y. This approach reduces the time required by the combine step to $\Theta(n)$, as sorting in every recursive invocation is now replaced by merging, which costs only $\Theta(|Y|)$ time. Thus, the recurrence relation is

$$T(n) = \begin{cases} c & \text{if } n = 1 \\ 2T(n/2) + \Theta(n) & \text{if } n > 1, \end{cases}$$

for some nonnegative constant c. The solution to this familiar recurrence is the desired $\Theta(n \log n)$ bound. The above discussion implies Algorithm DOMINANCE.

Algorithm 5.10 DOMINANCE

Input: A set S of n points in the plane.

Output: The number of points in S dominated by each point p.

1. Sort the points in S in nondecreasing order of their x-coordinates.
2. $dom(S)$
3. **return** $count(p)$ for all points $p \in S$

Algorithm $dom(S)$

1. **if** S consists of one point p **then** $count(p) \leftarrow 0$
2. **else**
3.   Let L be the vertical line passing by the median point.
4.   Divide S into two parts S_l and S_r such that the points
       in S_l are on or to the left of L, and all points in S_r are to the
       right of L.
5. $dom(S_l)$; $dom(S_r)$
6. $d \leftarrow 0$
7.   Sweep a horizontal line bottom-up starting from the point
       in S with lowest y-coordinate:
8.   **for** each point $p \in S$
9.   **if** $p \in S_l$ **then** $d \leftarrow d + 1$
10.   **else** $count(p) = count(p) + d$
11.   **end if**
12. **end if**

5.13   Practice Problems

5.1. Give a divide-and-conquer version of Algorithm LINEARSEARCH given
   in Sec. 1.3. The algorithm should start by dividing the input elements
   into approximately two halves. How much work space is required by
   the algorithm?

5.2. Give a divide-and-conquer algorithm to find the sum of all numbers
   in an array $A[1..n]$ of integers. The algorithm should start by dividing
   the input elements into approximately two halves. How much work
   space is required by the algorithm?

5.3. Give a divide-and-conquer algorithm to find the average of all numbers in an array $A[1..n]$ of integers, where n is a power of 2. The algorithm should start by dividing the input elements into two halves.
   How much work space is required by the algorithm?

5.4. Let $A[1..n]$ be an array of n integers and x an integer. Derive a
   divide-and-conquer algorithm to find the frequency of x in A, i.e., the

number of times x appears in A. What is the time complexity of your algorithm?

5.5. Consider Algorithm SLOWMINMAX which is obtained from Algorithm MINMAX by replacing the test

$$\textbf{if } high - low = 1$$

by the test

$$\textbf{if } high = low$$

and making some other changes in the algorithm accordingly. Thus, in Algorithm SLOWMINMAX, the recursion is halted when the size of the input array is 1. Count the number of comparisons required by this algorithm to find the minimum and maximum of an array $A[1..n]$, where n is a power of 2. Explain why the number of comparisons in this algorithm is greater than that in Algorithm MINMAX. (*Hint*: In this case, the initial condition is $C(1) = 0$).

5.6. Use Algorithm MERGESORT to sort the array

   (a) | 32 | 15 | 14 | 15 | 11 | 17 | 25 | 51 | .

   (b) | 12 | 25 | 17 | 19 | 51 | 32 | 45 | 18 | 22 | 37 | 15 | .

5.7. Show that the space complexity of Algorithm MERGESORT is $\Theta(n)$.

5.8. Carry out Algorithm SELECT on the array below to return the 18th smallest element in the array. Assume that if the number of elements in the array is less than six elements, then you can sort and return the sought element.

8, 36, 17, 51, 54, 40, 35, 11, 9, 37, 12, 3, 2, 13, 15, 12, 6, 5, 8, 13, 5, 34, 37, 36, 7, 4, 10, 14, 16

5.9. Repeat Problem 5.8 using Algorithm QUICKSELECT in Sec. 5.7.

5.10. Repeat Problem 5.9 using the median-of-three heuristic stated in Sec. 5.7.

5.11. Repeat Problem 5.9 using the median of the sample consisting of the first $\lfloor \sqrt{n} \rfloor$ elements as the pivot.

5.12. Apply Algorithm SPLIT on the array | 27 | 13 | 31 | 18 | 45 | 16 | 17 | 53 | .

5.13. Use Algorithm QUICKSORT to sort the array

   (a) | 24 | 33 | 24 | 45 | 12 | 12 | 24 | 12 | .

   (b) | 3 | 4 | 5 | 6 | 7 | .

   (c) | 23 | 32 | 27 | 18 | 45 | 11 | 63 | 12 | 19 | 16 | 25 | 52 | 14 | .

5.14. Explain the behavior of Algorithm QUICKSORT when the input is already sorted in decreasing order. You may assume that the input elements are all distinct.

5.15. Repeat Problem 5.14 for Algorithm QUICKSELECT.

5.16. Write out an algorithm for the traditional algorithm for matrix multiplication described in Sec. 5.10.

5.17. Show that the traditional algorithm for matrix multiplication described in Sec. 5.10 requires n^3 multiplications and $n^3 - n^2$ additions (see Problem 5.16).

5.14   Exercises

5.1. Give a divide-and-conquer algorithm that returns a pair (x, y), where x is the largest number and y is the second largest number in an array of n numbers. Derive the time complexity of your algorithm.

5.2. Repeat Exercise 5.1 for finding the largest and second largest elements using $n - 2 + \log n$ comparisons. (*Hint*: See Sec. 11.3.4.2).

5.3. Modify Algorithm MINMAX so that it works when n is not a power of 2. Is the number of comparisons performed by the new algorithm $\lfloor 3n/2 - 2 \rfloor$ even if n is not a power of 2? Prove your answer.

5.4. Derive an iterative minimax algorithm that finds both the minimum and maximum in a set of n elements using only $3n/2 - 2$ comparisons, where n is a power of 2.

5.5. Modify Algorithm BINARYSEARCHREC so that it searches for two keys. In other words, given an array $A[1..n]$ of n elements and two elements x_1 and x_2, the algorithm should return two integers k_1 and k_2 representing the positions of x_1 and x_2, respectively, in A.

5.6. Design a search algorithm that divides a sorted array into one third and two thirds instead of two halves as in Algorithm BINARYSEARCHREC. Analyze the time complexity of the algorithm.

5.7. Modify Algorithm BINARYSEARCHREC so that it divides the sorted array into three equal parts instead of two as in Algorithm BINARYSEARCHREC. In each iteration, the algorithm should test the element x to be searched for against two entries in the array. Analyze the time complexity of the algorithm.

5.8. Use mathematical induction to prove the correctness of Algorithm MERGESORT. Assume that Algorithm MERGE works correctly.

5.9. It was shown in Sec. 5.3 that algorithms BOTTOMUPSORT and MERGESORT are very similar. Give an example of an array of numbers in which

(a) Algorithm BOTTOMUPSORT and Algorithm MERGESORT perform the same number of element comparisons.

(b) Algorithm BOTTOMUPSORT performs more element comparisons than Algorithm MERGESORT.

(c) Algorithm BOTTOMUPSORT performs fewer element comparisons than Algorithm MERGESORT.

5.10. Consider the following modification of Algorithm MERGESORT. The algorithm first divides the input array $A[low..high]$ into four parts A_1, A_2, A_3 and A_4 instead of two. It then sorts each part recursively and finally merges the four sorted parts to obtain the original array in sorted order. Assume for simplicity that n is a power of 4.

(a) Write out the modified algorithm.

(b) Analyze its running time.

5.11. What will be the running time of the modified algorithm in Exercise 5.10 if the input array is divided into k parts instead of 4? Here, k is a *fixed* positive integer greater than 1.

5.12. Consider the following modification to Algorithm MERGESORT. We apply the algorithm on the input array $A[1..n]$ and continue the recursive calls until the size of a subinstance becomes relatively small, say m or less. At this point, we switch to Algorithm INSERTIONSORT and apply it on the small instance. So, the first test of the modified algorithm will look like the following:

if $high - low + 1 \leq m$ **then** INSERTIONSORT($A[low..high]$).

What is the largest value of m in terms of n such that the running time of the modified algorithm will still be $\Theta(n \log n)$? You may assume for simplicity that n is a power of 2.

5.13. Use Algorithm SELECT to find the kth smallest element in the list of numbers given in Example 5.1, where

(a) $k = 1$.   (b) $k = 9$.   (c) $k = 17$.   (d) $k = 22$.   (e) $k = 25$.

5.14. What will happen if in Algorithm SELECT the true median of the elements is chosen as the pivot instead of the median of medians? Explain.

5.15. Let $A[1..105]$ be a sorted array of 105 integers. Suppose we run Algorithm SELECT to find the 17th element in A. How many recursive calls to Algorithm *select* in Algorithm SELECT will there be? Explain your answer clearly.

5.16. Explain the behavior of Algorithm SELECT if the input array is already sorted in nondecreasing order. Compare that to the behavior of Algorithm BINARYSEARCHREC.

5.17. In Algorithm SELECT, groups of size 5 are sorted in each invocation of the algorithm. This means that finding an algorithm that sorts a group of size 5 that uses the fewest number of comparisons is important. Show that it is possible to sort five elements using only seven comparisons.

5.18. One reason that Algorithm SELECT is inefficient is that it does not make full use of the comparisons that it makes: After it discards one portion of the elements, it starts on the subproblem from scratch. Give a precise count of the number of comparisons the algorithm performs when presented with n elements. Note that it is possible to sort five elements using only seven comparisons (see Exercise 5.17).

5.19. Based on the number of comparisons counted in Exercise 5.18, determine for what values of n one should use a straightforward sorting method and extract the kth element directly.

5.20. Let g denote the size of each group in Algorithm SELECT for some positive integer $g \geq 3$. Derive the running time of the algorithm in terms of g. What happens when g is too large compared to the value used in the algorithm, namely 5?

5.21. Which of the following group sizes 3, 4, 5, 7, 9, 11 guarantees $\Theta(n)$ worst case performance for Algorithm SELECT? Prove your answer (see Exercise 5.20).

5.22. Rewrite Algorithm SELECT using Algorithm SPLIT to partition the input array. Assume for simplicity that all input elements are distinct. What is the advantage of the modified algorithm?

5.23. Let $A[1..n]$ and $B[1..n]$ be two arrays of distinct integers sorted in increasing order. Give an efficient algorithm to find the median of the $2n$ elements in both A and B. What is the running time of your algorithm?

5.24. Make use of the algorithm obtained in Exercise 5.23 to device a divide-and-conquer algorithm for finding the median in an array $A[1..n]$. What is the time complexity of your algorithm? (*Hint*: Make use of Algorithm MERGESORT).

5.25. Consider the problem of finding *all* the first k smallest elements in an array $A[1..n]$ of n *distinct* elements. Here, k is *not* constant, i.e., it is part of the input. We can solve this problem easily by sorting the elements and returning $A[1..k]$. This, however, costs $O(n \log n)$ time. Give a $\Theta(n)$ time algorithm for this problem. Note that running Algorithm SELECT k times costs $\Theta(kn) = O(n^2)$ time, as k is not constant.

5.26. Let $f(n)$ be the number of element interchanges that Algorithm SPLIT makes when presented with the input array $A[1..n]$ excluding interchanging $A[low]$ with $A[i]$.
  (a) For what input arrays $A[1..n]$ is $f(n) = 0$?
  (b) What is the maximum value of $f(n)$? Explain when this maximum is achieved?

5.27. Modify Algorithm SPLIT so that it partitions the elements in $A[low..high]$ around x, where x is the median of $\{A[low], A[\lfloor (low + high)/2 \rfloor], A[high]\}$. Will this improve the running time of Algorithm QUICKSORT? Explain.

5.28. Algorithm SPLIT is used to partition an array $A[low..high]$ around $A[low]$. Another algorithm to achieve the same result works as follows. The algorithm has two pointers i and j. Initially, $i = low$ and

$j = high$. Let the pivot be $x = A[low]$. The pointers i and j move from left to right and from right to left, respectively, until it is found that $A[i] > x$ and $A[j] \leq x$. At this point, $A[i]$ and $A[j]$ are interchanged. This process continues until $i \geq j$. Write out the complete algorithm. What is the number of comparisons performed by the algorithm?

5.29. Let $A[1..n]$ be a sequence of integers. Give an algorithm to reorder the elements in A so that all negative integers are positioned to the left of all nonnegative integers. Your algorithm should run in time $\Theta(n)$.

5.30. Convert Algorithm QUICKSELECT into an iterative algorithm.

5.31. Show that the work space needed by Algorithm QUICKSORT varies between $\Theta(\log n)$ and $\Theta(n)$. What is its average space complexity?

5.32. Explain the behavior of Algorithm QUICKSORT when the input array $A[1..n]$ consists of n identical elements.

5.33. Give an iterative version of Algorithm QUICKSORT.

5.34. Which of the following sorting algorithms are stable (see Exercise 4.18)?
(a) HEAPSORT   (b) MERGESORT   (c) QUICKSORT

5.35. A sorting algorithm is called *adaptive* if its running time depends not only on the number of elements n but also on their order. Which of the following sorting algorithms are adaptive?
(a) SELECTIONSORT   (b) INSERTIONSORT   (c) BUBBLESORT
(d) HEAPSORT   (e) BOTTOMUPSORT   (f) MERGESORT
(g) QUICKSORT   (h) RADIXSORT

5.36. Let $x = a + bi$ and $y = c + di$ be two complex numbers. The product xy can easily be calculated using four multiplications, that is, $xy = (ac - bd) + (ad + bc)i$. Devise a method for computing the product xy using only three multiplications.

5.37. Explain how to modify Strassen's algorithm for matrix multiplication so that it can also be used with matrices whose size is not necessarily a power of 2.

5.38. Let $f(x) = a_0 + a_1 x + a_2 x^2 + \cdots + a_{n-1} x^{n-1}$ be a polynomial of degree $n - 1$, where n is a power of 2. Design a divide and conquer algorithm to implement Horner's rule to evaluate $f(x)$ at the point $x = b$. What is the time complexity of your algorithm?

5.39. Give a divide-and-conquer algorithm to solve the one-dimensional closest pair problem: Given a set of n points on the x-axis, determine the two points that are closest to each other. Your algorithm should run in $O(n \log n)$ time.

5.40. Suppose we modify the algorithm for the closest pair problem so that not each point in T is compared with seven points in T. Instead, every point to the left of the vertical line L is compared with a number of points to its right.
  (a) What are the necessary modifications to the algorithm?
  (b) How many points to the right of L have to be compared with every point to its left? Explain.

5.41. Rewrite the algorithm for the closest pair problem without making use of Algorithm MERGESORT. Instead, use a presorting step in which the input is sorted by y-coordinates at the start of the algorithm once and for all. The time complexity of your algorithm should be $\Theta(n \log n)$.

5.42. Modify Algorithm DOMINANCE in Sec. 5.12 to solve the more general case, in which some points may lie on the same vertical line.

5.43. Give a divide-and-conquer algorithm for the dominance problem in Sec. 5.12, which starts by dividing the input into four parts instead of two (see Fig 5.10).

5.44. Design a divide-and-conquer algorithm to determine whether two given binary trees T_1 and T_2 are identical.

5.45. Design a divide-and-conquer algorithm that computes the height of a binary tree.

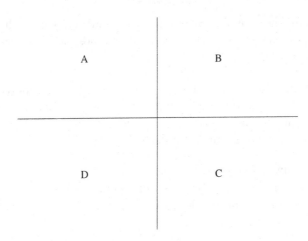

Fig. 5.10.   Problem 5.43.

5.15   Bibliographic Notes

Algorithms MERGESORT and QUICKSORT are discussed in detail in Knuth (1973). Algorithm QUICKSORT is due to Hoare (1962). The linear time algorithm for selection is due to Blum *et al.* (1973). Algorithm QUICKSELECT is a variant of Algorithm Find due to Hoare (1961). The $\sqrt{n}$ bound for the number of comparisons in Algorithm QUICKSELECT is due to Martinez *et al.* (2001). The algorithm for integer multiplication is due to Karatsuba and Ofman (1962). Strassen's algorithm for matrix multiplication is due to Strassen (1969). While Strassen's algorithm uses a fast method to multiply 2×2 matrices as the base case, similar algorithms have since been developed that use more complex base cases. For example, Pan (1978) proposed a method based on an efficient scheme for multiplying 70×70 matrices. The exponent in the time complexity has been steadily reduced. This is only of theoretical interest, as Strassen's algorithm remains the only one of practical interest. The algorithm for the closest pair problem is due to Shamos and can be found in virtually any book on computational geometry.

Chapter 6

Dynamic Programming

6.1 Introduction

In this chapter, we study a powerful algorithm design technique that is widely used to solve combinatorial optimization problems. An algorithm that employs this technique is not recursive by itself, but the underlying solution of the problem is usually stated in the form of a recursive function. Unlike the case in divide-and-conquer algorithms, immediate implementation of the recurrence results in identical recursive calls that are executed more than once. For this reason, this technique resorts to evaluating the recurrence in a bottom-up manner, saving intermediate results that are used later on to compute the desired solution. This technique applies to many combinatorial optimization problems to derive efficient algorithms. It is also used to improve the time complexity of the brute-force methods to solve some of the NP-hard problems (see Chapter 9). For example, the traveling salesman problem can be solved in time $O(n^2 2^n)$ using dynamic programming, which is superior to the $\Theta(n!)$ bound of the obvious algorithm that enumerates all possible tours. The two simple examples that follow illustrate the essence of this design technique.

Example 6.1 One of the most popular examples used to introduce recursion and induction is the problem of computing the Fibonacci sequence:

$$f_1 = 1, f_2 = 1, f_3 = 2, f_4 = 3, f_5 = 5, f_6 = 8, f_7 = 13, \ldots.$$

Each number in the sequence $2, 3, 5, 8, 13, \ldots$ is the sum of the two preceding numbers. Consider the inductive definition of this sequence:

$$f(n) = \begin{cases} 1 & \text{if } n = 1 \text{ or } n = 2 \\ f(n-1) + f(n-2) & \text{if } n \geq 3. \end{cases}$$

This definition suggests a recursive algorithm that looks like the following (assuming that the input is always positive).

---

1. **algorithm** $f(n)$
2. **if** $(n = 1)$ **or** $(n = 2)$ **then return** 1
3. **else return** $f(n-1) + f(n-2)$

This recursive version has the advantages of being concise, easy to write and debug and, most of all, its abstraction. It turns out that there is a rich class of recursive algorithms and, in many instances, a complex algorithm can be written succinctly using recursion. We have already encountered in the previous chapters a number of efficient algorithms that possess the merits of recursion. It should not be thought, however, that the recursive algorithm given above for computing the Fibonacci sequence is an efficient one. On the contrary, it is far from being efficient, as there are many duplicate recursive calls to the algorithm. To see this, just expand the recurrence a few times:

$$\begin{aligned} f(n) &= f(n-1) + f(n-2) \\ &= 2f(n-2) + f(n-3) \\ &= 3f(n-3) + 2f(n-4) \\ &= 5f(n-4) + 3f(n-5). \end{aligned}$$

This leads to a huge number of identical calls. If we assume that computing $f(1)$ or $f(2)$ requires a unit amount of time, then the time complexity of this algorithm can be stated as

$$T(n) = \begin{cases} 1 & \text{if } n = 1 \text{ or } n = 2 \\ T(n-1) + T(n-2) & \text{if } n \geq 3. \end{cases}$$

Clearly, the solution to this recurrence is $T(n) = f(n)$, i.e., the time required to compute $f(n)$ is $f(n)$ itself. It is well known that $f(n) = O(\phi^n)$ for large n, where $\phi = (1 + \sqrt{5})/2 \approx 1.61803$ is the golden ratio (see Example A.20). In other words, the running time required to compute $f(n)$ is exponential *in the value of n*. An obvious approach that reduces the time complexity drastically is to enumerate the sequence *bottom-up* starting from f_1 until f_n is reached. This takes $\Theta(n)$ time and $\Theta(1)$ space, a substantial improvement.

Example 6.2   As a similar example, consider computing the binomial coefficient $\binom{n}{k}$ defined recursively as

$$\binom{n}{k} = \begin{cases} 1 & \text{if } k = 0 \text{ or } k = n \\ \binom{n-1}{k-1} + \binom{n-1}{k} & \text{if } 0 < k < n. \end{cases}$$

Using the same argument as in Example 6.1, it can be shown that the time complexity of computing $\binom{n}{k}$ using the above formula is proportional to $\binom{n}{k}$ itself. The function

$$\binom{n}{k} = \frac{n!}{k!(n-k)!}$$

grows rapidly. For example, by Stirling's formula (Eq. (A.4) on page 673), we have (assuming n is even)

$$\binom{n}{n/2} = \frac{n!}{((n/2)!)^2} \approx \frac{\sqrt{2\pi n}\, n^n/e^n}{\pi n (n/2)^n/e^n} \geq \frac{2^n}{\sqrt{\pi n}}.$$

An efficient computation of $\binom{n}{k}$ may proceed by constructing the Pascal triangle row by row (see Fig. A.1) and stopping as soon as the value of $\binom{n}{k}$ has been computed. The details will be left as an exercise (Exercise 6.2).

6.2   The Longest Common Subsequence Problem

A simple problem that illustrates the principle of dynamic programming is the following. Given two strings A and B of lengths n and m, respectively, over an alphabet Σ, determine the *length of the longest subsequence that is common to both A and B*. Here, a subsequence of $A = a_1 a_2, \ldots a_n$ is a string of the form $a_{i_1} a_{i_2}, \ldots a_{i_k}$, where each i_j is between 1 and n and $1 \leq i_1 < i_2 < \cdots < i_k \leq n$. For example, if $\Sigma = \{x, y, z\}$, $A = zxyxyz$ and $B = xyyzx$, then xyy is a subsequence of length 3 of both A and B. However, it is not the *longest* common subsequence of A and B since the string $xyyz$ is also a common subsequence of length 4 of both A and B. Since these two strings do not have a common subsequence of length greater than 4, the length of the longest common subsequence of A and B is 4.

One way to solve this problem is to use the brute-force method: enumerate all the 2^n subsequences of A, and for each subsequence, determine if it is also a subsequence of B in $\Theta(m)$ time. Clearly, the running time of this algorithm is $\Theta(m 2^n)$, which is exponential.

In order to make use of the dynamic programming technique, we first find a recursive formula for the length of the longest common subsequence. Let $A = a_1 a_2, \ldots a_n$ and $B = b_1 b_2, \ldots b_m$. Let $L[i, j]$ denote the length of a *longest* common subsequence of $a_1 a_2, \ldots a_i$ and $b_1 b_2, \ldots b_j$. Note that i or j may be zero, in which case one or both of $a_1 a_2, \ldots a_i$ and $b_1 b_2, \ldots b_j$ may be the empty string. Naturally, if $i = 0$ or $j = 0$, then $L[i, j] = 0$. The following observation is easy to prove:

Observation 6.1 Suppose that both i and j are greater than 0. Then,

- If $a_i = b_j$, $L[i, j] = L[i - 1, j - 1] + 1$.
- If $a_i \neq b_j$, $L[i, j] = \max\{L[i, j - 1], L[i - 1, j]\}$.

The following recurrence for computing the length of the longest common subsequence of A and B follows immediately from Observation 6.1:

$$L[i, j] = \begin{cases} 0 & \text{if } i = 0 \text{ or } j = 0 \\ L[i - 1, j - 1] + 1 & \text{if } i > 0, j > 0 \text{ and } a_i = b_j \\ \max\{L[i, j - 1], L[i - 1, j]\} & \text{if } i > 0, j > 0 \text{ and } a_i \neq b_j. \end{cases}$$

6.2.1 *The algorithm*

Using the technique of dynamic programming to solve the longest common subsequence problem is now straightforward. We use an $(n + 1) \times (m + 1)$ table to compute the values of $L[i, j]$ for each pair of values of i and j,

$0 \leq i \leq n$ and $0 \leq j \leq m$. We only need to fill the table $L[0..n, 0..m]$ row by row using the above formula. The method is formally described in Algorithm LCS.

Algorithm 6.1 LCS
Input: Two strings A and B of lengths n and m, respectively, over an alphabet Σ.
Output: The length of the longest common subsequence of A and B.

1. **for** $i \leftarrow 0$ **to** n
2. $\quad L[i, 0] \leftarrow 0$
3. **end for**
4. **for** $j \leftarrow 0$ **to** m
5. $\quad L[0, j] \leftarrow 0$
6. **end for**
7. **for** $i \leftarrow 1$ **to** n
8. $\quad$ **for** $j \leftarrow 1$ **to** m
9. $\quad\quad$ **if** $a_i = b_j$ **then** $L[i, j] \leftarrow L[i - 1, j - 1] + 1$
10. $\quad\quad$ **else** $L[i, j] \leftarrow \max\{L[i, j - 1], L[i - 1, j]\}$
11. $\quad\quad$ **end if**
12. $\quad$ **end for**
13. **end for**
14. **return** $L[n, m]$

Algorithm LCS can easily be modified so that it outputs the longest common subsequence. Clearly, the time complexity of the algorithm is exactly the size of the table, $\Theta(nm)$, as filling each entry requires $\Theta(1)$ time. The algorithm can easily be modified so that it requires only $\Theta(\min\{m, n\})$ space (Exercise 6.3). This implies the following theorem.

Theorem 6.1 *An optimal solution to the longest common subsequence problem can be found in $\Theta(nm)$ time and $\Theta(\min\{m, n\})$ space.*

Example 6.3 Figure 6.1 shows the result of applying Algorithm LCS on the instance $A =$ "xyxxzxyzxy" and $B =$ "zxzyyzxxyxxz".

First, row 0 and column 0 are initialized to 0. Next, the entries are filled row by row by executing Steps 9 and 10 exactly mn times. This generates the rest of the table. As shown in the table, the length of a longest common subsequence is 6. One possible common subsequence is the string "xyxxxz" of length 6, which can be constructed from the entries in the table in bold face.

	0	1	2	3	4	5	6	7	8	9	10	11	12
0	0	0	0	0	0	0	0	0	0	0	0	0	0
1	0	0	1	1	1	1	1	1	1	1	1	1	1
2	0	0	1	1	2	**2**	2	2	2	2	2	2	2
3	0	0	1	1	2	2	2	**3**	3	3	3	3	3
4	0	0	1	1	2	2	2	3	**4**	4	4	4	4
5	0	1	1	2	2	2	3	3	4	4	4	4	5
6	0	1	2	2	2	2	3	4	4	4	**5**	5	5
7	0	1	2	2	3	3	3	4	4	5	5	5	5
8	0	1	2	3	3	3	4	4	4	5	5	5	**6**
9	0	1	2	3	3	3	4	5	5	5	6	6	6
10	0	1	2	3	4	4	4	5	5	6	6	6	6

Fig. 6.1.   An example of the longest common subsequence problem.

6.3   Matrix Chain Multiplication

In this section, we study in detail another simple problem that reveals the
essence of dynamic programming. Suppose we want to compute the product
$M_1 M_2 M_3$ of three matrices M_1, M_2 and M_3 of dimensions $2 \times 10, 10 \times 2$ and
2×10, respectively, using the standard method of matrix multiplication. If
we multiply M_1 and M_2 and then multiply the result by M_3, the number
of scalar multiplications will be $2 \times 10 \times 2 + 2 \times 2 \times 10 = 80$. If, instead, we
multiply M_1 by the result of multiplying M_2 and M_3, then the number of
scalar multiplications becomes $10 \times 2 \times 10 + 2 \times 10 \times 10 = 400$. Thus, carrying out the multiplication $M_1(M_2 M_3)$ costs five times the multiplication
$(M_1 M_2) M_3$.

In general, the cost of multiplying a chain of n matrices $M_1 M_2 \ldots M_n$
depends on the order in which the $n-1$ multiplications are carried out. That
order which minimizes the number of scalar multiplications can be found
in many ways. Consider for example the brute-force method that tries to
compute the number of scalar multiplications of every possible order. For
instance, if we have four matrices M_1, M_2, M_3 and M_4, the algorithm will
try all the following five orderings:

$$(M_1(M_2(M_3 M_4))),$$
$$(M_1((M_2 M_3) M_4)),$$
$$((M_1 M_2)(M_3 M_4)),$$
$$((M_1 M_2) M_3) M_4)),$$
$$((M_1(M_2 M_3)) M_4).$$

In general, the number of orderings is equal to the number of ways to place parentheses to multiply the n matrices in every possible way. Let $f(n)$ be the number of ways to fully parenthesize a product of n matrices. Suppose we want to perform the multiplication

$$(M_1 M_2 \ldots M_k) \times (M_{k+1} M_{k+2} \ldots M_n).$$

Then, there are $f(k)$ ways to parenthesize the first k matrices. For each one of the $f(k)$ ways, there are $f(n-k)$ ways to parenthesize the remaining $n-k$ matrices, for a total of $f(k)f(n-k)$ ways. Since k can assume any value between 1 and $n-1$, the overall number of ways to parenthesize the n matrices is given by the summation

$$f(n) = \sum_{k=1}^{n-1} f(k)f(n-k).$$

Observe that there is only one way to multiply two matrices and two ways to multiply three matrices. That is, $f(2) = 1$ and $f(3) = 2$. In order for the recurrence to make sense, we let $f(1) = 1$. It can be shown that

$$f(n) = \frac{1}{n}\binom{2n-2}{n-1}.$$

This recurrence generates the so-called *Catalan numbers* defined by

$$C_n = f(n+1),$$

the first 10 terms of which are

$$1, 1, 2, 5, 14, 42, 132, 429, 1430, 4862, 16796, \ldots.$$

Thus, for example, there are 4862 ways to multiply 10 matrices. By Stirling's formula (Eq. (A.4) on page 673),

$$n! \approx \sqrt{2\pi n}\,(n/e)^n, \quad \text{where } e = 2.71828\ldots,$$

we have

$$f(n) = \frac{1}{n}\binom{2n-2}{n-1} = \frac{(2n-2)!}{n((n-1)!)^2} \approx \frac{4^n}{4\sqrt{\pi}\,n^{1.5}}.$$

Thus,

$$f(n) = \Omega\left(\frac{4^n}{n^{1.5}}\right).$$

Since for each parenthesized expression, finding the number of scalar multiplications costs $\Theta(n)$, it follows that the running time of the brute-force method to find the optimal way to multiply the n matrices is $\Omega(4^n/\sqrt{n})$, which is impractical even for values of n of moderate size.

In the rest of this section, we derive a recurrence relation for the least number of scalar multiplications and then apply the dynamic programming technique to find an efficient algorithm for evaluating that recurrence. Extending the algorithm to find the *order* of matrix multiplications is easy (Exercise 6.7). Since for each $i, 1 \leq i < n$, the number of columns of matrix M_i must be equal to the number of rows of matrix M_{i+1}, it suffices to specify the number of rows of each matrix and the number of columns of the rightmost matrix M_n. Thus, we will assume that we are given $n + 1$ dimensions $r_1, r_2, \ldots, r_{n+1}$, where r_i and r_{i+1} are, respectively, the number of rows and columns in matrix M_i, $1 \leq i \leq n$. Henceforth, we will write $M_{i,j}$ to denote the product of $M_i M_{i+1} \ldots M_j$. We will also assume that the cost of multiplying the chain $M_{i,j}$, denoted by $C[i,j]$, is measured in terms of the number of scalar multiplications. For a given pair of indices i and j with $1 \leq i < j \leq n$, $M_{i,j}$ can be computed as follows. Let k be an index between $i+1$ and j. Compute the two matrices $M_{i,k-1} = M_i M_{i+1} \ldots M_{k-1}$ and $M_{k,j} = M_k M_{k+1} \ldots M_j$. Then, $M_{i,j} = M_{i,k-1} M_{k,j}$. Clearly, the total cost of computing $M_{i,j}$ in this way is the cost of computing $M_{i,k-1}$ plus the cost of computing $M_{k,j}$ plus the cost of multiplying $M_{i,k-1}$ and $M_{k,j}$, which is $r_i r_k r_{j+1}$. This leads to the following formula for finding that value of k which minimizes the number of scalar multiplications required to perform the matrix multiplication $M_i M_{i+1} \ldots M_j$:

$$C[i,j] = \min_{i<k\leq j} \{C[i, k-1] + C[k,j] + r_i r_k r_{j+1}\}. \qquad (6.1)$$

It follows that in order to find the minimum number of scalar multiplications required to perform the matrix multiplication $M_1 M_2 \ldots M_n$, we only need to solve the recurrence

$$C[1,n] = \min_{1<k\leq n} \{C[1, k-1] + C[k,n] + r_1 r_k r_{n+1}\}.$$

However, as noted in Examples 6.1 and 6.2, this will lead to a huge number of overlapping recursive calls and hence solving the recurrence directly in a top-down fashion will not result in an efficient algorithm.

6.3.1 *The dynamic programming algorithm*

In what follows, we describe how the technique of dynamic programming can be used to efficiently evaluate the above recurrence in time $\Theta(n^3)$. Consider Fig. 6.2, which illustrates the method on an instance consisting of $n = 6$ matrices. In this figure, diagonal d is filled with the *minimum* costs of multiplying various chains of $d + 1$ consecutive matrices. In particular, diagonal 5 consists of exactly one entry which represents the minimum cost of multiplying the six matrices, which is the desired result. In diagonal 0, each chain consists of one matrix only, and hence this diagonal is filled with 0's. We fill this triangular table with costs of multiplication diagonalwise, starting at diagonal 0 and ending at diagonal 5. First, diagonal 0 is filled with 0's, as there are no scalar multiplications involved. Next, diagonal 1 is filled with the costs of multiplying two consecutive matrices. The rest of the diagonals are filled using the formula stated above and the values previously stored in the table. Specifically, to fill diagonal d, we make use of the values stored in diagonals $0, 1, 2, \ldots, d - 1$.

As an example, the computation of $C[2, 5]$ is the minimum of the following three costs (see Fig. 6.2):

(1) The cost of computing $M_{2,2}$ (which is 0) plus the cost of computing $M_{3,5}$ plus the cost of multiplying $M_{2,2}$ by $M_{3,5}$.

Fig. 6.2. Illustration of matrix chain multiplication.

(2) The cost of computing $M_{2,3}$ plus the cost of computing $M_{4,5}$ plus the cost of multiplying $M_{2,3}$ by $M_{4,5}$.

(3) The cost of computing $M_{2,4}$ plus the cost of computing $M_{5,5}$ (which is 0) plus the cost of multiplying $M_{2,4}$ by $M_{5,5}$.

To compute any other entry $C[i,j]$ in the table other than the main diagonal, we do the following. First, we draw two directed vectors: one from $C[i,i]$ to $C[i,j-1]$ and one from $C[i+1,j]$ to $C[j,j]$ (see Fig. 6.2). Next, we compute the cost of multiplying each pair of matrices as we follow the two arrows starting from the pair $C[i,i]$ and $C[i+1,j]$ to the pair $C[i,j-1]$ and $C[j,j]$. Finally, we select the minimum cost and store it in $C[i,j]$.

In general, multiplying a chain of n matrices gives rise to a triangular table of n rows and n columns similar to the one shown in Fig. 6.2. The formal algorithm that produces such a table is given as Algorithm MATCHAIN.

Algorithm 6.2 MATCHAIN

Input: An array $r[1..n+1]$ of positive integers corresponding to the dimensions of a chain of n matrices, where $r[1..n]$ are the number of rows in the n matrices and $r[n+1]$ is the number of columns in M_n.

Output: The least number of scalar multiplications required to multiply the n matrices.

1. **for** $i \leftarrow 1$ **to** n {*Fill in diagonal d_0*}
2. $C[i,i] \leftarrow 0$
3. **end for**
4. **for** $d \leftarrow 1$ **to** $n-1$ {*Fill in diagonals d_1 to d_{n-1}*}
5.   **for** $i \leftarrow 1$ **to** $n-d$ {*Fill in entries in diagonal d_i*}
6. $j \leftarrow i+d$
7.   **comment:** *The next three lines compute $C[i,j]$*
8. $C[i,j] \leftarrow \infty$
9.   **for** $k \leftarrow i+1$ **to** j
10. $C[i,j] \leftarrow \min\{C[i,j],\ C[i,k-1]+C[k,j]+r[i]r[k]r[j+1]\}$
11.   **end for**
12.   **end for**
13. **end for**
14. **return** $C[1,n]$

Step 1 fills diagonal 0 with 0's. The execution of each iteration of the **for** loop in Step 2 advances to the next diagonal. Each iteration of the **for** loop in Step 3 advances to a new entry in that diagonal (each diagonal

$C[1,1] = 0$	$C[1,2] = 200$	$C[1,3] = 320$	$C[1,4] = 620$	$C[1,5] = 348$
	$C[2,2] = 0$	$C[2,3] = 240$	$C[2,4] = 640$	$C[2,5] = 248$
		$C[3,3] = 0$	$C[3,4] = 240$	$C[3,5] = 168$
			$C[4,4] = 0$	$C[4,5] = 120$
				$C[5,5] = 0$

Fig. 6.3. An example of the matrix chain multiplication algorithm.

contains $n - d$ entries). Steps 8–11 compute entry $C[i, j]$ using Eq. (6.1). First, it is initialized to a very large value. Next, its value is chosen as the minimum of d quantities corresponding to d multiplications of subchains, as explained for the case of the instance $C[2, 5]$ described above and shown in Fig. 6.2.

Example 6.4 Figure 6.3 shows the result of applying Algorithm MATCHAIN to find the minimum number of scalar multiplication required to compute the product of the following five matrices:

$$M_1 : 5 \times 10, \quad M_2 : 10 \times 4, \quad M_3 : 4 \times 6, \quad M_4 : 6 \times 10, \quad M_5 : 10 \times 2.$$

Each entry $C[i, j]$ of the upper triangular table is labeled with the minimum number of scalar multiplications required to multiply the matrices $M_i \times M_{i+1} \times \cdots M_j$ for $1 \leq i \leq j \leq 5$. The final solution is $C[1, 5] = 348$.

Finding the time and space complexities of Algorithm MATCHAIN is straightforward. For some constant $c > 0$, the running time of the algorithm is proportional to

$$\sum_{d=1}^{n-1} \sum_{i=1}^{n-d} \sum_{k=1}^{d} c = \frac{cn^3 - cn}{6}.$$

Hence, the time complexity of the algorithm is $\Theta(n^3)$. Clearly, the work space needed by the algorithm is dominated by that needed for the triangular array, i.e., $\Theta(n^2)$. So far, we have demonstrated an algorithm that computes the minimum cost of multiplying a chain of matrices. The following theorem summarizes the main result.

Theorem 6.2 *The minimum number of scalar multiplications required to multiply a chain of n matrices can be found in $\Theta(n^3)$ time and $\Theta(n^2)$ space.*

Finally, we close this section by noting that, surprisingly, this problem can be solved in time $O(n \log n)$ (see the Bibliographic Notes).

6.4   The Dynamic Programming Paradigm

Examples 6.1 and 6.2 and Secs. 6.2 and 6.3 provide an overview of the dynamic programming algorithm design technique and its underlying principle. The idea of saving solutions to subproblems in order to avoid their recomputation is the basis of this powerful method. This is usually the case in many combinatorial optimization problems in which the solution can be expressed in the form of a recurrence whose direct solution causes subinstances to be computed more than once.

An important observation about the working of dynamic programming is that the algorithm computes an optimal solution to *every* subinstance of the original instance *considered by the algorithm*. In other words, all the table entries generated by the algorithm represent *optimal* solutions to the subinstances considered by the algorithm. For example, in Fig. 6.1, each entry $L[i, j]$ is the length of a longest common subsequence for the subinstance obtained by taking the first i letters from the first string and the first j letters from the second string. Also, in Fig. 6.2, each entry $C[i, j]$ is the minimum number of scalar multiplications needed to perform the product $M_i M_{i+1} \ldots M_j$. Thus, for example, the algorithm that generates Fig. 6.2 not only computes the minimum number of scalar multiplication for obtaining the product of the n matrices but also computes the minimum number of scalar multiplication of the product of any sequence of consecutive matrices in $M_1 M_2 \ldots M_n$.

The above argument illustrates an important principle in algorithm design called the *principle of optimality*: Given an optimal sequence of decisions, each subsequence must be an optimal sequence of decisions by itself. We have already seen that the problems of finding the length of a longest common subsequence and the problem of matrix chain multiplication can be formulated in such a way that the principle of optimality applies. As another example, let $G = (V, E)$ be a directed graph and let π be a *shortest* path from vertex s to vertex t, where s and t are two vertices in V. Suppose that another vertex, say $x \in V$, is on this path. Then, it follows that the portion of π from s to x must be a path of shortest length, and so is the portion of π from x to t. This can trivially be proven by contradiction. On the other hand, let π' be a *simple* path of *longest* length from s to t.

If vertex $y \in V$ is on π', then this does not mean, for example, that the portion of π' from s to y is a longest simple path from s to y. This suggests that dynamic programming may be used to find a shortest path, but it is not obvious if it can be used to find a longest simple path. In the case of directed acyclic graphs, dynamic programming may be used to find the longest path between two given vertices (Exercise 6.24). Note that in this case, all paths are simple.

6.5 The All-Pairs Shortest Path Problem

Let $G = (V, E)$ be a directed graph in which each edge (i, j) has a non-negative length $l[i, j]$. If there is no edge from vertex i to vertex j, then $l[i, j] = \infty$. The problem is to find the *distance* from each vertex to all other vertices, where the distance from vertex x to vertex y is the length of a shortest path from x to y. For simplicity, we will assume that $V = \{1, 2, \ldots, n\}$. Let i and j be two different vertices in V. Define $d_{i,j}^k$ to be the length of a shortest path from i to j that does *not* pass through any vertex in $\{k + 1, k + 2, \ldots, n\}$. Thus, for example, $d_{i,j}^0 = l[i, j]$, $d_{i,j}^1$ is the length of a shortest path from i to j that does not pass through any vertex except *possibly* vertex 1, $d_{i,j}^2$ is the length of a shortest path from i to j that does not pass through any vertex except *possibly* vertex 1 or vertex 2 or both, and so on. Then, by definition, $d_{i,j}^n$ is the length of a shortest path from i to j, i.e., the distance from i to j. Given this definition, we can compute $d_{i,j}^k$ recursively as follows:

$$d_{i,j}^k = \begin{cases} l[i, j] & \text{if } k = 0 \\ \min\{d_{i,j}^{k-1}, d_{i,k}^{k-1} + d_{k,j}^{k-1}\} & \text{if } 1 \leq k \leq n. \end{cases}$$

6.5.1 *The algorithm*

The following algorithm, which is due to Floyd, proceeds by solving the above recurrence in a bottom-up fashion. It uses $n + 1$ matrices $D_0, D_1, \ldots, D_n$ of dimension $n \times n$ to compute the lengths of the shortest constrained paths.

Initially, we set $D_0[i, i] = 0$, $D_0[i, j] = l[i, j]$ if $i \neq j$ and (i, j) is an edge in G; otherwise, $D_0[i, j] = \infty$. We then make n iterations such that after the kth iteration, $D_k[i, j]$ contains the value of a shortest length path from vertex i to vertex j that does not pass through any vertex numbered higher

Fig. 6.4.   An instance of the all-pairs shortest path problem.

than k. Thus, in the kth iteration, we compute $D_k[i,j]$ using the formula

$$D_k[i,j] = \min\{D_{k-1}[i,j], D_{k-1}[i,k] + D_{k-1}[k,j]\}.$$

Example 6.5   Consider the directed graph shown in Fig. 6.4.
The matrices D_0, D_1, D_2 and D_3 are

$$D_0 = \begin{bmatrix} 0 & 2 & 9 \\ 8 & 0 & 6 \\ 1 & \infty & 0 \end{bmatrix}, \quad D_1 = \begin{bmatrix} 0 & 2 & 9 \\ 8 & 0 & 6 \\ 1 & 3 & 0 \end{bmatrix},$$

$$D_2 = \begin{bmatrix} 0 & 2 & 8 \\ 8 & 0 & 6 \\ 1 & 3 & 0 \end{bmatrix}, \quad D_3 = \begin{bmatrix} 0 & 2 & 8 \\ 7 & 0 & 6 \\ 1 & 3 & 0 \end{bmatrix}.$$

The final computed matrix D_3 holds the desired distances.

An important observation is that in the kth iteration, both the kth row and kth column are not changed. Therefore, we can perform the computation with only one copy of the D matrix. An algorithm to perform this computation using only one $n \times n$ matrix is given as Algorithm FLOYD.

Algorithm 6.3 FLOYD
Input: An $n \times n$ matrix $l[1..n, 1..n]$ such that $l[i,j]$ is the length of the edge
    (i,j) in a directed graph $G = (\{1, 2, \ldots, n\}, E)$.
Output: A matrix D with $D[i,j]$ = the distance from i to j.

1. $D \leftarrow l$ {*copy the input matrix l into D*}
2. **for** $k \leftarrow 1$ **to** n
3.   **for** $i \leftarrow 1$ **to** n
4.   **for** $j \leftarrow 1$ **to** n
5. $D[i,j] = \min\{D[i,j], D[i,k] + D[k,j]\}$
6.   **end for**
7.   **end for**
8. **end for**

Clearly, the running time of the algorithm is $\Theta(n^3)$ and its space complexity is $\Theta(n^2)$.

6.6 The Knapsack Problem

The knapsack problem can be defined as follows. Let $U = \{u_1, u_2, \ldots, u_n\}$ be a set of n items to be packed in a knapsack of size C. For $1 \leq j \leq n$, let s_j and v_j be the size and value of the jth item, respectively. Here C and $s_j, v_j, 1 \leq j \leq n$, are all *positive integers*. The objective is to fill the knapsack with some items from U whose total size is at most C and such that their total value is maximum. Assume without loss of generality that the size of each item does not exceed C. More formally, given U of n items, we want to find a subset $S \subseteq U$ such that

$$\sum_{u_i \in S} v_i$$

is maximized subject to the constraint

$$\sum_{u_i \in S} s_i \leq C.$$

This version of the knapsack problem is sometimes referred to in the literature as the 0/1 knapsack problem. This is because the knapsack cannot contain more than one item of the same type. Another version of the problem in which the knapsack may contain more than one item of the same type is discussed in Exercise 6.17.

We derive a recursive formula for filling the knapsack as follows. Let $V[i, j]$ denote the value obtained by filling a knapsack of size j with items taken from the first i items $\{u_1, u_2, \ldots, u_i\}$ in an optimal way. Here, the range of i is from 0 to n and the range of j is from 0 to C. Thus, what we seek is the value $V[n, C]$. Obviously, $V[0, j]$ is 0 for all values of j, as there is nothing in the knapsack. On the other hand, $V[i, 0]$ is 0 for all values of i since nothing can be put in a knapsack of size 0. For the general case, when both i and j are greater than 0, we have the following observation, which is easy to prove:

Observation 6.2 $V[i, j]$ is the maximum of the following two quantities:

- $V[i - 1, j]$: The maximum value obtained by filling a knapsack of size j with items taken from $\{u_1, u_2, \ldots, u_{i-1}\}$ only *in an optimal way*.

- $V[i-1, j-s_i] + v_i$: The maximum value obtained by filling a knapsack of size $j - s_i$ with items taken from $\{u_1, u_2, \ldots, u_{i-1}\}$ *in an optimal way* plus the value of item u_i. This case applies only if $j \geq s_i$ and it amounts to adding item u_i to the knapsack.

Observation 6.2 implies the following recurrence for finding the *value* in an optimal packing:

$$V[i,j] = \begin{cases} 0 & \text{if } i = 0 \text{ or } j = 0 \\ V[i-1, j] & \text{if } j < s_i \\ \max\{V[i-1, j], V[i-1, j-s_i] + v_i\} & \text{if } i > 0 \text{ and } j \geq s_i. \end{cases}$$

6.6.1   The algorithm

Using dynamic programming to solve this integer programming problem is now straightforward. We use an $(n+1) \times (C+1)$ table to evaluate the values of $V[i,j]$. We only need to fill the table $V[0..n, 0..C]$ row by row using the above formula. The method is formally described in Algorithm KNAPSACK.

Algorithm 6.4 KNAPSACK
Input: A set of items $U = \{u_1, u_2, \ldots, u_n\}$ with sizes $s_1, s_2, \ldots, s_n$ and
      values $v_1, v_2, \ldots, v_n$ and a knapsack capacity C.
Output: The maximum value of the function $\sum_{u_i \in S} v_i$ subject to
      $\sum_{u_i \in S} s_i \leq C$ for some subset of items $S \subseteq U$.

1. **for** $i \leftarrow 0$ **to** n
2. $V[i, 0] \leftarrow 0$
3. **end for**
4. **for** $j \leftarrow 0$ **to** C
5. $V[0, j] \leftarrow 0$
6. **end for**
7. **for** $i \leftarrow 1$ **to** n
8.   **for** $j \leftarrow 1$ **to** C
9. $V[i, j] \leftarrow V[i-1, j]$
10.   **if** $s_i \leq j$ **then** $V[i, j] \leftarrow \max\{V[i, j], V[i-1, j-s_i] + v_i\}$
11.   **end for**
12. **end for**
13. **return** $V[n, C]$

Clearly, the time complexity of the algorithm is exactly the size of the table, $\Theta(nC)$, as filling each entry requires $\Theta(1)$ time. Algorithm KNAPSACK can easily be modified so that it outputs the items packed in the knapsack as well. It can also be easily modified so that it requires only $\Theta(C)$ of space, as only the last computed row is needed for filling the current row. This implies the following theorem:

Theorem 6.3 *An optimal solution to the Knapsack problem can be found in* $\Theta(nC)$ *time and* $\Theta(C)$ *space.*

Note that the time bound, as stated in the above theorem, is not polynomial in the input size. Therefore, the algorithm is considered to be exponential in the input size. For this reason, it is referred to as a *pseudopolynomial time* algorithm, as the running time is polynomial in the input value.

Example 6.6 Suppose that we have a knapsack of capacity 9, which we want to pack with items of four different sizes 2, 3, 4 and 5 and values 3, 4, 5 and 7, respectively. Our goal is to pack the knapsack with as many items as possible in a way that maximizes the total value without exceeding the knapsack capacity. We proceed to solve this problem as follows. First, we prepare an empty rectangular table with five rows numbered 0 to 4 and 10 columns labeled 0 through 9. Next, we initialize the entries in column 0 and row 0 with the value 0. Filling row 1 is straightforward: $V[1, j] = 3$, the value of the first item, if and only if $j \geq 2$, the size of the first item. Each entry $V[2, j]$ in the second column has two possibilities. The first possibility is to set $V[2, j] = V[1, j]$, which amounts to putting the first item in the knapsack. The second possibility is to set $V[2, j] = V[1, j - 3] + 4$, which amounts to adding the second item so that it either contains the second item only or both the first and second items. Of course, adding the second item is possible only if $j \geq 3$. Continuing this way, rows 3 and 4 are filled to obtain the table shown in Fig. 6.5.

The ith entry of column 9, that is, $V[i, 9]$ contains the maximum value we can get by filling the knapsack using the first i items. Thus, an optimal

	0	1	2	3	4	5	6	7	8	9
0	0	0	0	0	0	0	0	0	0	0
1	0	0	3	3	3	3	3	3	3	3
2	0	0	3	4	4	7	7	7	7	7
3	0	0	3	4	5	7	8	9	9	12
4	0	0	3	4	5	7	8	10	11	12

Fig. 6.5. An example of the algorithm for the knapsack problem.

packing is found in the last entry of the last column and is achieved by packing items 3 and 4. There is also another optimal solution, which is packing items 1, 2 and 3. This packing corresponds to entry $V[3,9]$ in the table, which is the optimal packing before the fourth item was considered.

6.7   Practice Problems

6.1. Give an efficient algorithm to compute $f(n)$, the nth number in the Fibonacci sequence (see Example 6.1). What is the time complexity of your algorithm? Is it a polynomial time algorithm? Explain.

6.2. Give an efficient algorithm to compute the binomial coefficient $\binom{n}{k}$ (see Example 6.2). What is the time complexity of your algorithm? Is it a polynomial time algorithm? Explain.

6.3. Use Algorithm LCS to find the length of a longest common subsequence of the two strings $A = $ "xzyzzyx" and $B = $ "zxyyzxz". Give one longest common subsequence.

6.4. Consider using Algorithm MATCHAIN to multiply the following five matrices:

$$M_1 : 4 \times 5, \qquad M_2 : 5 \times 3, \qquad M_3 : 3 \times 6, \qquad M_4 : 6 \times 4, \qquad M_5 : 4 \times 5.$$

Assume the intermediate results shown in Fig. 6.6 for obtaining the multiplication $M_1 \times M_2 \times M_3 \times M_4 \times M_5$, where $C[i,j]$ is the minimum number of scalar multiplications needed to carry out the multiplication $M_i \times \cdots \times M_j, 1 \leq i \leq j \leq 5$. Also shown in the figure parenthesized expressions showing the optimal sequence for carrying out the multiplication $M_i \times \cdots \times M_j$. Find $C[1,5]$ and the optimal parenthesized expressions for carrying out the multiplication $M_1 \times \cdots \times M_5$.

$C[1,1] = 0$ M_1	$C[1,2] = 60$ $M_1 M_2$	$C[1,3] = 132$ $(M_1 M_2) M_3$	$C[1,4] = 180$ $(M_1 M_2)(M_3 M_4)$	
	$C[2,2] = 0$ M_2	$C[2,3] = 90$ $M_2 M_3$	$C[2,4] = 132$ $M_2(M_3 M_4)$	$C[2,5] = 207$ $M_2((M_3 M_4) M_5)$
		$C[3,3] = 0$ M_3	$C[3,4] = 72$ $M_3 M_4$	$C[3,5] = 132$ $(M_3 M_4) M_5$
			$C[4,4] = 0$ M_4	$C[4,5] = 120$ $M_4 M_5$
				$C[5,5] = 0$ M_5

Fig. 6.6.   An incomplete table for the matrix chain multiplication problem.

Fig. 6.7. An instance of the all-pairs shortest path problem.

6.5. Let $G = (V, E)$ be a weighted directed graph, and let $s, t \in V$. Assume that there is at least one path from s to t.

(a) Let π be a path of shortest length from s to t that passes by another vertex x. Show that the portion of the path from s to x is a shortest path from s to x.

(b) Let π' be a longest simple path from s to t that passes by another vertex y. Show that the portion of the path from s to y is not necessarily a longest path from s to y.

6.6. Run the all-pairs shortest path algorithm on the weighted directed graph shown in Fig. 6.7.

6.7. Use the all-pairs shortest path algorithm to compute the distance matrix for the directed graph with the lengths of the edges between all pairs of vertices are as given by the matrix

$$
\text{(a)} \begin{bmatrix} 0 & 1 & \infty & 2 \\ 2 & 0 & \infty & 2 \\ \infty & 9 & 0 & 4 \\ 8 & 2 & 3 & 0 \end{bmatrix} \qquad \text{(b)} \begin{bmatrix} 0 & 2 & 4 & 6 \\ 2 & 0 & 1 & 2 \\ 5 & 9 & 0 & 1 \\ 9 & \infty & 2 & 0 \end{bmatrix}.
$$

6.8. Solve the following instance of the knapsack problem. There are four items of sizes 2, 3, 5 and 6 and values 3, 4, 5 and 7, and the knapsack capacity is 11.

6.8 Exercises

6.1. Prove Observation 6.1.

6.2. Show how to modify Algorithm LCS so that it outputs a longest common subsequence as well.

6.3. Show how to modify Algorithm LCS so that it requires only $\Theta(\min\{m, n\})$ space.

6.4. Give a parenthesized expression for the optimal order of multiplying the five matrices in Example 6.4.

6.5. Consider applying Algorithm MATCHAIN on the following five matrices:

$$M_1 : 2 \times 3, \quad M_2 : 3 \times 6, \quad M_3 : 6 \times 4, \quad M_4 : 4 \times 2, \quad M_5 : 2 \times 7.$$

   (a) Find the minimum number of scalar multiplications needed to multiply the five matrices, (that is $C[1, 5]$).
   (b) Give a parenthesized expression for the order in which this optimal number of multiplications is achieved.

6.6. Give an example of three matrices in which one order of their multiplication costs at least 100 times the other order.

6.7. Show how to modify the matrix chain multiplication algorithm so that it also produces the order of multiplications as well.

6.8. Give an example of a directed graph that contains some edges with negative costs and yet the all-pairs shortest path algorithm gives the correct distances.

6.9. Give an example of a directed graph that contains some edges with negative costs such that the all-pairs shortest path algorithm fails to give the correct distances.

6.10. Show how to modify the all-pairs shortest path algorithm so that it detects negative-weight cycles (A negative-weight cycle is a cycle whose total length is negative).

6.11. Prove Observation 6.2.

6.12. Solve the following instance of the knapsack problem. There are five items of sizes 3, 5, 7, 8 and 9 and values 4, 6, 7, 9 and 10, and the knapsack capacity is 22.

6.13. Explain what would happen when running the knapsack algorithm on an input in which one item has negative size.

6.14. Show how to modify Algorithm KNAPSACK so that it requires only $\Theta(C)$ space, where C is the knapsack capacity.

6.15. Show how to modify Algorithm KNAPSACK so that it outputs the items packed in the knapsack as well.

6.16. In order to lower the prohibitive running time of the knapsack problem, which is $\Theta(nC)$, we may divide C and all the s_i's by a large number K and take the floor. That is, we may transform the given instance into a new instance with capacity $\lfloor C/K \rfloor$ and item sizes $\lfloor s_i/K \rfloor, 1 \leq i \leq n$. Now, we apply the algorithm for the knapsack discussed in Sec. 6.6. This technique is called *scaling and rounding* (see Sec. 14.6). What will be the running time of the algorithm when applied to the new instance? Give a counterexample to show that scaling and rounding does not always result in an optimal solution to the *original* instance.

6.17. Another version of the knapsack problem is to let the set U contain a set of *types* of items, and the objective is to fill the knapsack with any number of items of each type in order to maximize the total value without exceeding the knapsack capacity. Assume that there is an unlimited number of items of each type. More formally, let $T = \{t_1, t_2, \ldots, t_n\}$ be a set of n *types* of items and C the knapsack capacity. For $1 \leq j \leq n$, let s_j and v_j be, respectively, the size and value of the items of type j. Find a set of nonnegative integers $x_1, x_2, \ldots, x_n$ such that

$$\sum_{i=1}^{n} x_i v_i$$

is maximized subject to the constraint

$$\sum_{i=1}^{n} x_i s_i \leq C.$$

$x_1, x_2, \ldots, x_n$ are nonnegative integers.

Note that $x_j = 0$ means that no item of the jth type is packed in the knapsack. Rewrite the dynamic programming algorithm for this version of the knapsack problem.

6.18. Solve the following instance of the version of the knapsack problem described in Exercise 6.17. There are four types of items with sizes 2, 3, 5 and 6 and values 4, 7, 9 and 11, and the knapsack capacity is 8.

6.19. Show how to modify the knapsack algorithm discussed in Exercise 6.17 so that it computes the number of items packed from each type.

6.20. Consider the *money change* problem. We have a currency system that has n coins with values $v_1, v_2, \ldots, v_n$, where $v_1 = 1$, and we want to pay change of value y in such a way that the total number of coins is minimized. More formally, we want to minimize the quantity

$$\sum_{i=1}^{n} x_i$$

subject to the constraint

$$\sum_{i=1}^{n} x_i v_i = y.$$

Here, $x_1, x_2, \ldots, x_n$ are nonnegative integers (so x_i may be zero).
(a) Give a dynamic programming algorithm to solve this problem.
(b) What are the time and space complexities of your algorithm?
(c) Can you see the resemblance of this problem to the version of the knapsack problem discussed in Exercise 6.17? Explain.

6.21. Apply the algorithm in Exercise 6.20 to the instance $v_1 = 1$, $v_2 = 5, v_3 = 7, v_4 = 11$ and $y = 20$.

6.22. Let $G = (V, E)$ be a directed graph with n vertices. G induces a relation R on the set of vertices V defined by: $u \, R \, v$ if and only if there is a directed edge from u to v, i.e., if and only if $(u, v) \in E$. Let M_R be the adjacency matrix of G, i.e., M_R is an $n \times n$ matrix satisfying $M_R[u, v] = 1$ if $(u, v) \in E$ and 0 otherwise. The *reflexive and transitive closure* of M_R, denoted by M_R^*, is defined as follows. For $u, v \in$

V, if $u = v$ or there is a path in G from u to v, then $M_R^*[u, v] = 1$ and 0 otherwise. Give a dynamic programming algorithm to compute M_R^* for a given directed graph. (*Hint:* You only need a slight modification of Floyd's algorithm for the all-pairs shortest path problem).

6.23. Let $G = (V, E)$ be a directed graph with n vertices. Define the $n \times n$ distance matrix D as follows. For $u, v \in V$, $D[u, v] = d$ if and only if the length of the shortest path from u to v measured in the number of edges is exactly d. For example, for any $v \in V$, $D[v, v] = 0$ and for any $u, v \in V$ $D[u, v] = 1$ if and only if $(u, v) \in E$. Give a dynamic programming algorithm to compute the distance matrix D for a given directed graph. (*Hint:* Again, you only need a slight modification of Floyd's algorithm for the all-pairs shortest path problem).

6.24. Let $G = (V, E)$ be a directed acyclic graph (dag) with n vertices. Let s and t be two vertices in V such that the indegree of s is 0 and the outdegree of t is 0. Give a dynamic programming algorithm to compute a longest path in G from s to t. What is the time complexity of your algorithm?

6.9 Bibliographic Notes

Dynamic programming was first popularized in the book by Bellman (1957). Other books in this area include Bellman and Dreyfus (1962), Dreyfus (1977) and Nemhauser (1966). Two general survey papers by Brown (1979a) and Held and Karp (1967) are highly recommended. The all-pairs shortest paths algorithm is due to Floyd (1962). Matrix chain multiplication is described in Godbole (1973). An $O(n \log n)$ algorithm to solve this problem can be found in Hu and Shing (1980, 1982, 1984). The one- and two-dimensional knapsack problems have been studied extensively; see for example Gilmore (1977), Gilmore and Gomory (1966) and Hu (1969).

PART 3

First-Cut Techniques

When a solution to a problem is sought, perhaps the first strategy that comes to one's mind is the greedy method. If the problem involves graphs, then one might consider traversing the graph, visiting its vertices and performing some actions depending on a decision made at that point. The technique used to solve that problem is usually specific to the problem itself. A common characteristic of both greedy algorithms and graph traversal is that they are fast, as they involve making local decisions.

A graph traversal algorithm might be viewed as a greedy algorithm and vice versa. In graph traversal techniques, the choice of the next vertex to be examined is restricted to the set of neighbors of the current node. This is in contrast to examining a bigger neighborhood, clearly a simple greedy strategy. On the other hand, a greedy algorithm can also be viewed as a graph traversal of a particular graph. For any greedy algorithm, there is an implicit directed acyclic graph (dag) each of whose nodes stands for a state in that greedy computation. An intermediate state represents some decisions that were already taken in a greedy fashion, while others remain to be determined. In that dag, an edge from vertex u to vertex v exists only if in the greedy method, the algorithm's state represented by v is arrived at from that represented by vertex u as a consequence of one decision by the greedy algorithm.

Although these techniques tend to be applied as initial solutions, they rarely remain as the providers of optimal solutions. Their contribution consequently is one of providing an initial solution that sets the stage for careful examination of the specific properties of the problem.

In Chapter 7, we study in detail some algorithms that give optimal solutions to well-known problems in computer science and engineering. The two famous problems of the single-source shortest path and finding a minimum cost spanning tree in an undirected graph are representative of those problems for which the greedy strategy results in an optimal solution. Other problems, like Huffman code, will also be covered in this chapter.

Chapter 8 is devoted to graph traversals (depth-first search and breadth-first search) that are useful in solving many problems, especially graph and geometric problems.

Chapter 7

The Greedy Approach

7.1 Introduction

As in the case of dynamic programming algorithms, greedy algorithms are usually designed to solve optimization problems in which a quantity is to be minimized or maximized. However, unlike dynamic programming algorithms, greedy algorithms typically consist of an iterative procedure that tries to find a *local* optimal solution. In some instances, these local optimal solutions translate to global optimal solutions. In others, they fail to give optimal solutions. A greedy algorithm makes a correct guess on the basis of little calculation without worrying about the future. Thus, it builds a solution step by step. Each step increases the size of the partial solution and is based on local optimization. The choice made is that which produces the largest immediate gain while maintaining feasibility. Since each step consists of little work based on a small amount of information, the resulting algorithms are typically efficient. The hard part in the design of a greedy algorithm is proving that the algorithm does indeed solve the problem it is designed for. This is to be contrasted with recursive algorithms that usually have very simple inductive proofs. In this chapter, we will study some of the most prominent problems for which the greedy strategy works, i.e., gives an optimal solution: the single-source shortest path problem, minimum cost spanning trees (Prim's and Kruskal's algorithms) and Huffman codes. We will postpone those greedy algorithms that give suboptimal solutions to Chapter 14. The exercises contain some problems for which the greedy strategy works (e.g., Exercises 7.1, 7.5 and 7.23) and

219

others for which the greedy method fails to give the optimal solution on some instances (e.g., Exercises 7.2–7.4 and 7.7). The following is a simple example of a problem for which the greedy strategy works.

Example 7.1 Consider the *money change problem*: Given a set of coins $C = \{c_1, c_2, \ldots, c_n\}$ of values $v_1, v_2, \ldots, v_n$, where $1 = v_1 < v_2 < \cdots < v_n$, and a value x, it is required to give a change of x using the least number of coins from the set C. This problem was stated in Exercise 6.20. For instance, C could consist of the following coins: dollar (100 cents), quarter (25 cents), dime (10 cents), nickel (5 cents) and 1-cent coins. (A unit-value coin is always required). A greedy algorithm to solve this problem consists in giving as many as possible of c_n, then as many as possible of c_{n-1}, and so on. In the case of the example above, the algorithm gives as many dollars as possible, then as many quarters as possible, etc. Using this strategy, a value $x = 236 = 2 \times 100 + 3 \times 10 + 1 \times 5 + 1 \times 1$, for a total of 7 coins. This strategy always works by giving an optimal solution for this particular coinage system. However, for some sets of denominations, it may not work (see Problem 7.1).

Example 7.2 Consider the *fractional knapsack problem* defined as follows. Given n items of sizes $s_1, s_2, \ldots, s_n$, and values $v_1, v_2, \ldots, v_n$ and size C, the knapsack capacity, the objective is to find nonnegative *real numbers* $x_1, x_2, \ldots, x_n, 0 \le x_i \le 1$, that maximize the sum

$$\sum_{i=1}^{n} x_i v_i$$

subject to the constraint

$$\sum_{i=1}^{n} x_i s_i \le C.$$

This problem can easily be solved using the following greedy strategy. For each item, compute $y_i = v_i/s_i$, the ratio of its value to its size. Sort the items by decreasing ratio and fill the knapsack with as much as possible from the first item, then the second, and so forth. This problem reveals many of the characteristics of a greedy algorithm discussed above: The algorithm consists of a simple iterative procedure that selects that item which produces the largest immediate gain while maintaining feasibility.

7.2   The Shortest Path Problem

Let $G = (V, E)$ be a directed graph in which each edge has a nonnegative
length, and there is a distinguished vertex s called the *source*. The single-
source shortest path problem, or simply the shortest path problem, is to
determine the *distance* from s to every other vertex in V, where the distance
from vertex s to vertex x is defined as the length of a shortest path from
s to x. For simplicity, we will assume that $V = \{1, 2, \ldots, n\}$ and $s = 1$.
This problem can be solved using a greedy technique known as *Dijkstra's
algorithm*. Initially, the set of vertices is partitioned into two sets $X = \{1\}$
and $Y = \{2, 3, \ldots, n\}$. The intention is that X contains the set of vertices
whose distance from the source has already been determined. At each step,
we select a vertex $y \in Y$ whose distance from the source vertex has already
been found and move it to X. Associated with each vertex y in Y is a label
$\lambda[y]$, which is the length of a shortest path that passes only through vertices
in X. Once a vertex $y \in Y$ is moved to X, the label of each vertex $w \in Y$
that is adjacent to y is updated indicating that a shorter path to w via y
has been discovered. Throughout this section, for any vertex $v \in V$, $\delta[v]$
will denote the distance from the source vertex to v. As will be shown later,
at the end of the algorithm, $\delta[v] = \lambda[v]$ for each vertex $v \in V$. A sketch of
the algorithm is given below.

---

1. $X \leftarrow \{1\}$; $Y \leftarrow V - \{1\}$
2. For each vertex $v \in Y$ if there is an edge from 1 to v, then let $\lambda[v]$
    (the label of v) be the length of that edge; otherwise, let $\lambda[v] = \infty$. Let
    $\lambda[1] = 0$.
3. **while** $Y \neq \{\}$
4.   Let $y \in Y$ be such that $\lambda[y]$ is minimum.
5.   move y from Y to X.
6.   update the labels of those vertices in Y that are adjacent to y.
7. **end while**

Example 7.3   To see how the algorithm works, consider the directed
graph shown in Fig. 7.1(a). The first step is to label each vertex v with
$\lambda[v] = length[1, v]$. As shown in the figure, vertex 1 is labeled with 0,
and vertices 2 and 3 are labeled with 1 and 12 since $length[1, 2] = 1$ and
$length[1, 3] = 12$. All other vertices are labeled with ∞ since there are
no edges from the source vertex to these vertices. Initially, $X = \{1\}$ and

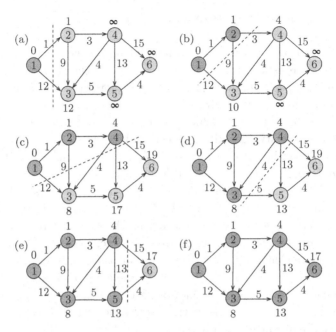

Fig. 7.1.   An example of Dijkstra's algorithm.

$Y = \{2, 3, 4, 5, 6\}$. In the figure, those vertices to the left of the dashed line belong to X and the others belong to Y. In Fig. 7.1(a), we note that $\lambda[2]$ is the smallest among all vertices' labels in Y, and hence it is moved to X indicating that the distance to vertex 2 has been found. To finish processing vertex 2, the labels of its neighbors 3 and 4 are inspected to see if there are paths that pass through 2 and are shorter than their old paths. In this case, we say that we *update* the labels of the vertices adjacent to 2. As shown in the figure, the path from 1 to 2 to 3 is shorter than the path from 1 to 3, and thus $\lambda[3]$ is changed to 10, which is the length of the path that passes through 2. Similarly, $\lambda[4]$ is changed to 4 since now there is a finite path of length 4 from 1 to 4 that passes through vertex 2. These updates are shown in Fig. 7.1(b). The next step is to move that vertex with minimum label, namely 4, to X and update the labels of its neighbors in Y as shown in Fig. 7.1(c). In this figure we notice that the labels of vertices 5 and 6 became finite and $\lambda[3]$ is lowered to 8. Now, vertex 3 has a minimum label, so it is moved to X and $\lambda[5]$ is updated accordingly as shown in Fig. 7.1(d).

Continuing in this way, the distance to vertex 5 is found and thus it is moved to X as shown in Fig. 7.1(e). As shown in Fig. 7.1(f), vertex 6 is the only vertex remaining in Y and hence its label coincides with the length of its distance from 1. In Fig. 7.1(f), the label of each vertex represents its distance from the source vertex.

7.2.1 *Implementation of the shortest path algorithm*

A more detailed description of the algorithm is given in Algorithm DIJKSTRA.

Algorithm 7.1 DIJKSTRA
Input: A weighted directed graph $G = (V, E)$, where $V = \{1, 2, \ldots, n\}$.
Output: The distance from vertex 1 to every other vertex in G.

1. $X = \{1\}$; $Y \leftarrow V - \{1\}$; $\lambda[1] \leftarrow 0$
2. **for** $y \leftarrow 2$ **to** n
3.   **if** y is adjacent to 1 **then** $\lambda[y] \leftarrow length[1, y]$
4.   **else** $\lambda[y] \leftarrow \infty$
5.   **end if**
6. **end for**
7. **for** $j \leftarrow 1$ **to** $n - 1$
8.   Let $y \in Y$ be such that $\lambda[y]$ is minimum
9. $X \leftarrow X \cup \{y\}$ {add vertex y to X}
10. $Y \leftarrow Y - \{y\}$ {delete vertex y from Y}
11.   **for** each edge (y, w)
12.   **if** $w \in Y$ **and** $\lambda[y] + length[y, w] < \lambda[w]$ **then**
13. $\lambda[w] \leftarrow \lambda[y] + length[y, w]$
14.   **end for**
15. **end for**

We will assume that the input graph is represented by adjacency lists, and the length of edge (x, y) is stored in the vertex for y in the adjacency list for x. For instance, the directed graph shown in Fig. 7.1 is represented as shown in Fig. 7.2. We will also assume that the length of each edge in E is *nonnegative*. The two sets X and Y will be implemented as boolean vectors $X[1..n]$ and $Y[1..n]$. Initially, $X[1] = 1$ and $Y[1] = 0$, and for all $i, 2 \leq i \leq n$, $X[i] = 0$ and $Y[i] = 1$. Thus, the operation $X \leftarrow X \cup \{y\}$ is implemented by setting $X[y]$ to 1, and the operation $Y \leftarrow Y - \{y\}$ is implemented by setting $Y[y]$ to 0.

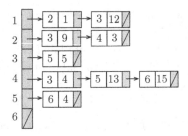

Fig. 7.2.   Directed graph representation for the shortest path algorithm.

7.2.2   *Correctness*

Lemma 7.1   *In Algorithm* DIJKSTRA, *when a vertex y is chosen in Step 8, if its label $\lambda[y]$ is finite, then $\lambda[y] = \delta[y]$.*

Proof.   By induction on the order in which vertices leave the set Y and enter X. The first vertex to leave is 1, and we have $\lambda[1] = \delta[1] = 0$. Assume that the statement is true for all vertices which left Y before y. Since $\lambda[y]$ is finite, there must exists a path from 1 to y whose length is $\lambda[y]$. Now, we show that $\lambda[y] \leq \delta[y]$. Let $\pi = 1, \ldots, x, w, \ldots, y$ be a shortest path from 1 to y, where x is the rightmost vertex to leave Y before y (see Fig. 7.3). We have

$$
\begin{aligned}
\lambda[y] &\leq \lambda[w] \quad \text{since } y \text{ left } Y \text{ before } w \\
&\leq \lambda[x] + length(x, w) \quad \text{by the algorithm} \\
&= \delta[x] + length(x, w) \quad \text{by induction} \\
&= \delta[w] \quad \text{since } \pi \text{ is a path of shortest length} \\
&\leq \delta[y] \quad \text{since } \pi \text{ is a path of shortest length.} \qquad \square
\end{aligned}
$$

It will be left as an exercise to show that the above proof is based on the assumption that all edge lengths are nonnegative (Exercise 7.11).

7.2.3   *Time complexity*

The time complexity of the algorithm is computed as follows. Step 1 costs $\Theta(n)$ time. The **for** loop in step 2 costs $\Theta(n)$ time. The time taken by Step 8 to search for the vertex with minimum label is $\Theta(n)$. This is because the algorithm has to inspect each entry in the vector representing the set Y.

Fig. 7.3.   Proof of correctness of Algorithm DIJKSTRA.

Since it is executed $n - 1$ times, the overall time required by Step 8 is $\Theta(n^2)$. Steps 9 and 10 cost $\Theta(1)$ time per iteration for a total of $\Theta(n)$ time. The **for** loop in Step 11 is executed m times throughout the algorithm, where $m = |E|$. This is because each edge (y, w) is inspected exactly once by the algorithm. It follows that the time complexity of the algorithm is $\Theta(m + n^2) = \Theta(n^2)$.

Theorem 7.1   *Given a directed graph G with nonnegative weights on its edges and a source vertex s, Algorithm* DIJKSTRA *finds the length of the distance from s to every other vertex in $\Theta(n^2)$ time.*

Proof.   Lemma 7.1 establishes the correctness of the algorithm and the time complexity follows from the above discussion.   □

7.2.4   *Improving the time bound*

Now, we are ready to make a major improvement to Algorithm DIJKSTRA in order to lower its $\Theta(n^2)$ time complexity to $O(m \log n)$ for graphs in which $m = o(n^2)$. We will also improve it further, so that in the case of dense graphs it runs in time linear in the number of edges.

The basic idea is to use the min-heap data structure (see Sec. 3.2) to maintain the vertices in the set Y so that the vertex y in Y closest to a vertex in $V - Y$ can be extracted in $O(\log n)$ time. The key associated with each vertex v is its label $\lambda[v]$. The final algorithm is shown as Algorithm SHORTESTPATH.

Each vertex $y \in Y$ is assigned a key which is the cost of the edge connecting 1 to y if it exists; otherwise, that key is set to ∞. The heap H initially contains all vertices adjacent to vertex 1. Each iteration of the

---

Algorithm 7.2 SHORTESTPATH
Input: A weighted directed graph $G = (V, E)$, where $V = \{1, 2, \ldots, n\}$.
Output: The distance from vertex 1 to every other vertex in G.
      Assume that we have an empty heap H at the beginning.

  1. $Y \leftarrow V - \{1\};$ $\lambda[1] \leftarrow 0;$ $key(1) \leftarrow \lambda[1]$
  2. **for** $y \leftarrow 2$ **to** n
  3.   **if** y is adjacent to 1 **then**
  4. $\lambda[y] \leftarrow length[1, y]$
  5. $key(y) \leftarrow \lambda[y]$
  6.   INSERT(H, y)
  7.   **else**
  8. $\lambda[y] \leftarrow \infty$
  9. $key(y) \leftarrow \lambda[y]$
10.   **end if**
11. **end for**
12. **for** $j \leftarrow 1$ **to** $n - 1$
13. $y \leftarrow$ DELETEMIN(H)
14. $Y \leftarrow Y - \{y\}$ {delete vertex y from Y}
15.   **for** each vertex $w \in Y$ that is adjacent to y
16.   **if** $\lambda[y] + length[y, w] < \lambda[w]$ **then**
17. $\lambda[w] \leftarrow \lambda[y] + length[y, w]$
18. $key(w) \leftarrow \lambda[w]$
19.   **end if**
20.   **if** $w \notin H$ **then** INSERT(H, w)
21.   **else** SIFTUP$(H, H^{-1}(w))$
22.   **end if**
23.   **end for**
24. **end for**

---

for loop in Step 12 starts by extracting that vertex y with minimum key. The key of each vertex w in Y adjacent to y is then updated. Next, if w is not in the heap, then it is inserted; otherwise, it is sifted up, if necessary. The function $H^{-1}(w)$ returns the position of w in H. This can be implemented by simply having an array that has for its jth entry the position of vertex j in the heap (recall that the heap is implemented as an array $H[1..n]$). The running time is dominated by the heap operations. There are $n - 1$ DELETEMIN operations, $n - 1$ INSERT operations and at most $m - n + 1$ SIFTUP operations. Each heap operation takes $O(\log n)$ time, which results in $O(m \log n)$ time in total. It should be emphasized that the input to the algorithm is the adjacency lists of the graph.

    A d-heap is essentially a generalization of a binary heap in which each internal node in the tree has at most d children instead of 2, where d is a number that can be arbitrarily large (see Exercise 3.21). If we use a d-heap, the running time is improved as follows. Each DELETEMIN operation takes $O(d \log_d n)$ time, and each INSERT or SIFTUP operation requires $O(\log_d n)$ time. Thus, the total running time is $O(nd \log_d n + m \log_d n)$. If we choose $d = \lceil 2 + m/n \rceil$, the time bound is $O(m \log_{\lceil 2+m/n \rceil} n)$. If $m \geq n^{1+\epsilon}$ for some $\epsilon > 0$ that is not too small, i.e., the graph is dense, then the running time is

$$O(m \log_{\lceil 2+m/n \rceil} n) = O(m \log_{\lceil 2+n^\epsilon \rceil} n)$$

$$= O\left(m \frac{\log n}{\log n^\epsilon}\right)$$

$$= O\left(m \frac{\log n}{\epsilon \log n}\right)$$

$$= O\left(\frac{m}{\epsilon}\right).$$

This implies the following theorem:

Theorem 7.2 *Given a graph G with nonnegative weights on its edges and a source vertex s, Algorithm* SHORTESTPATH *finds the distance from s to every other vertex in $O(m \log n)$ time. If the graph is dense, i.e., if $m \geq n^{1+\epsilon}$ for some $\epsilon > 0$, then it can be further improved to run in time $O(m/\epsilon)$.*

7.3 Minimum Cost Spanning Trees (Kruskal's Algorithm)

Definition 7.1 Let $G = (V, E)$ be a connected undirected graph with weights on its edges. A *spanning tree* (V, T) of G is a subgraph of G that is a tree. If G is weighted and the sum of the weights of the edges in T is minimum, then (V, T) is called a *minimum cost spanning tree* or simply a *minimum spanning tree*.

We will assume throughout this section that G is connected. If G is not connected, then the algorithm can be applied to each connected component of G. Kruskal's algorithm works by maintaining a forest consisting of several spanning trees that are gradually merged until finally the forest consists of exactly one tree: a minimum cost spanning tree. The algorithm starts by sorting the edges in nondecreasing order by weight. Next, starting from the forest (V, T) consisting of the vertices of the graph and none of its edges, the following step is repeated until (V, T) is transformed into a tree: Let (V, T) be the forest constructed so far, and let $e \in E - T$ be the current edge being considered. If adding e to T does not create a cycle, then include e in T; otherwise, discard e. This process will terminate after adding *exactly* $n - 1$ edges. The algorithm is summarized below.

---

1. Sort the edges in G by nondecreasing weight.
2. For each edge in the sorted list, include that edge in the spanning tree T if it does not form a cycle with the edges currently included in T; otherwise, discard it.

Example 7.4   Consider the *weighted* graph shown in Fig. 7.4(a). As shown in Fig. 7.4(b), the first edge that is added is $(1, 2)$ since it is of minimum cost. Next, as shown in Figs. 7.4(c)–7.4(e), edges $(1, 3)$, $(4, 6)$ and then $(5, 6)$ are included in T in this order. Next, as shown in Fig. 7.4(f), the edge $(2, 3)$ creates a cycle and hence is discarded. For the same reason, as shown in Fig. 7.4(g), edge $(4, 5)$ is also discarded. Finally, edge $(3, 4)$

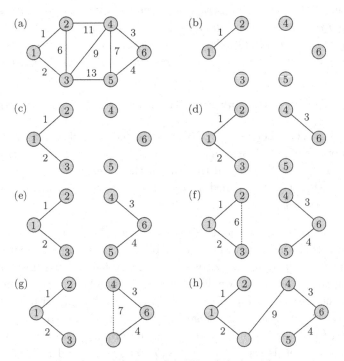

Fig. 7.4.   An example of Kruskal algorithm.

is included, which results in the minimum spanning tree (V, T) shown in Fig. 7.4(h).

7.3.1 Implementation of Kruskal's algorithm

To implement the algorithm efficiently, we need some mechanism for testing whether including an edge creates a cycle. For this purpose, we need to specify a data structure that represents the forest at each instant of the algorithm and detects cycles dynamically as edges are added to T. A suitable choice of such data structure is the disjoint sets representation discussed in Sec. 3.3. In the beginning, each vertex of the graph is represented by a tree consisting of one vertex. During the execution of the algorithm, each connected component of the forest is represented by a tree. This method is described more formally in Algorithm KRUSKAL. First, the set of edges is sorted in nondecreasing order by weight. Next, n singleton sets are created, one for each vertex, and the set of spanning tree edges is initially empty. The while loop is executed until the minimum cost spanning tree is constructed.

Algorithm 7.3 KRUSKAL
Input: A weighted connected undirected graph $G = (V, E)$ with n vertices.
Output: The set of edges T of a minimum cost spanning tree for G.

1. Sort the edges in E by nondecreasing weight.
2. **for** each vertex $v \in V$
3.   MAKESET($\{v\}$)
4. **end for**
5. $T = \{\}$
6. **while** $|T| < n - 1$
7.   Let (x, y) be the next edge in E.
8.   **if** FIND(x) $\neq$ FIND(y) **then**
9.   Add (x, y) to T
10.   UNION(x, y)
11.   **end if**
12. **end while**

7.3.2 Correctness

Lemma 7.2 *Algorithm* KRUSKAL *correctly finds a minimum cost spanning tree in a weighted undirected graph.*

Proof. We prove by induction on the size of T that T is a subset of the set of edges in a minimum cost spanning tree. Initially, $T = \{\}$ and the statement is trivially true. For the induction step, assume before adding the edge $e = (x, y)$ in Step 9 of the algorithm that $T \subset T^*$, where T^* is the set of edges in a minimum cost spanning tree $G^* = (V, T^*)$. Let X be the set of vertices in the subtree containing x. Let $T' = T \cup \{e\}$. We will show that T' is also a subset of the set of edges in a minimum cost spanning tree. By the induction hypothesis, $T \subset T^*$. If T^* contains e, then there is nothing to prove. Otherwise, by Theorem 2.1(c), $T^* \cup \{e\}$ contains exactly one cycle with e being one of its edges. Since $e = (x, y)$ connects one vertex in X to another vertex in $V - X$, T^* must also contain another edge $e' = (w, z)$ such that $w \in X$ and $z \in V - X$. We observe that $cost(e') \geq cost(e)$; for otherwise, e' would have been added before since it does not create a cycle with the edges of T^* which contains the edges of T. If we now construct $T^{**} = T^* - \{e'\} \cup \{e\}$, we notice that $T' \subset T^{**}$. Moreover, T^{**} is the set of edges in a minimum cost spanning tree since e is of minimum cost among all edges connecting the vertices in X with those in $V - X$. $\square$

7.3.3 *Time complexity*

We analyze the time complexity of the algorithm as follows. Step 1 costs $O(m \log m)$, where $m = |E|$. The **for** loop in Step 2 costs $\Theta(n)$. Step 7 costs $\Theta(1)$, and since it is executed $O(m)$ times, its total cost is $O(m)$. Step 9 is executed exactly $n - 1$ times for a total of $\Theta(n)$ time. The *union* operation is executed $n-1$ times, and the *find* operation at most $2m$ times. By Theorem 3.3, the overall cost of these two operations is $O(m \log^* n)$. Thus, the overall running time of the algorithm is dominated by the sorting step, i.e., $O(m \log m) = O(m \log n)$.

Theorem 7.3 *Algorithm* KRUSKAL *finds a minimum cost spanning tree in a weighted undirected graph with m edges in $O(m \log n)$ time.*

Proof. Lemma 7.2 establishes the correctness of the algorithm and the time complexity follows from the above discussion. $\square$

Since m can be as large as $n(n - 1)/2 = \Theta(n^2)$, the time complexity expressed in terms of n is $O(n^2 \log n)$. If the graph is planar, then $m = O(n)$ (see Sec. 2.3.2) and hence the running time of the algorithm becomes $O(n \log n)$.

7.4　Minimum Cost Spanning Trees (Prim's Algorithm)

As in the previous section, we will assume throughout this section that G is connected. If G is not connected, then the algorithm can be applied to each connected component of G.

This is another algorithm for finding a minimum cost spanning tree in a weighted undirected graph that has a totally different approach from that of Algorithm KRUSKAL. Prim's algorithm for finding a minimum spanning tree for an undirected graph is very similar to Dijkstra's algorithm for the shortest path problem. The algorithm grows the spanning tree starting from an arbitrary vertex. Let $G = (V, E)$, where for simplicity V is taken to be the set of integers $\{1, 2, \ldots, n\}$. The algorithm begins by creating two sets of vertices: $X = \{1\}$ and $Y = \{2, 3, \ldots, n\}$. It then grows a spanning tree, one edge at a time. At each step, it finds an edge (x, y) of minimum weight, where $x \in X$ and $y \in Y$ and moves y from Y to X. This edge is added to the current minimum spanning tree edges in T. This step is repeated until Y becomes empty. The algorithm is outlined below. It finds the set of edges T of a minimum cost spanning tree.

---

1. $T \leftarrow \{\}$;　　$X \leftarrow \{1\}$;　　$Y \leftarrow V - \{1\}$
2. **while** $Y \neq \{\}$
3. 　　Let (x, y) be of minimum weight such that $x \in X$ and $y \in Y$.
4. 　　$X \leftarrow X \cup \{y\}$
5. 　　$Y \leftarrow Y - \{y\}$
6. 　　$T \leftarrow T \cup \{(x, y)\}$
7. **end while**

Example 7.5　Consider the graph shown in Fig. 7.5(a). The vertices to the left of the dashed line belong to X and those to its right belong to Y. First, as shown in Fig. 7.5(a), $X = \{1\}$ and $Y = \{2, 3, \ldots, 6\}$. In Fig. 7.5(b), vertex 2 is moved from Y to X since edge $(1, 2)$ has the least cost among all the edges incident to vertex 1. This is indicated by moving the dashed line so that 1 and 2 are now to its left. As shown in Fig. 7.5(b), the candidate vertices to be moved from Y to X are 3 and 4. Since edge $(1, 3)$ is of least cost among all edges with one end in X and one end in Y, 3 is moved from Y to X. Next, from the two candidate vertices 4 and 5 in Fig. 7.5(c), 4 is moved since the edge $(3, 4)$ has the least cost. Finally, vertices 6 and then

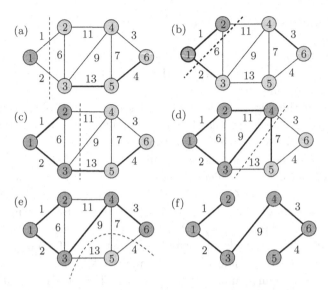

Fig. 7.5. An example of Prim's algorithm.

5 are moved from Y to X, as shown in Fig. 7.5(e). Each time a vertex y is moved from Y to X, its corresponding edge is included in T, the set of edges of the minimum spanning tree. The resulting minimum spanning tree is shown in Fig. 7.5(f).

7.4.1 *Implementation of Prim's algorithm*

We will assume that the input is represented by adjacency lists. The cost (i.e., weight) of an edge (x, y), denoted by $c[x, y]$, is stored at the node for y in the adjacency list corresponding to x. This is exactly the input representation for Dijkstra's algorithm shown in Fig. 7.2 (except that here we are dealing with undirected graphs). The two sets X and Y will be implemented as boolean vectors $X[1..n]$ and $Y[1..n]$, respectively. Initially, $X[1] = 1$ and $Y[1] = 0$, and for all $i, 2 \leq i \leq n$, $X[i] = 0$ and $Y[i] = 1$. Thus, the operation $X \leftarrow X \cup \{y\}$ is implemented by setting $X[y]$ to 1, and the operation $Y \leftarrow Y - \{y\}$ is implemented by setting $Y[y]$ to 0. The set of tree edges T will be implemented as a linked list, and thus the operation $T \leftarrow T \cup \{(x, y)\}$ simply appends edge (x, y) to T. It is easy to build the adjacency list representation of the resulting minimum cost spanning tree from this linked list.

If (x, y) is an edge such that $x \in X$ and $y \in Y$, we will call y a *bordering vertex*. Bordering vertices are candidates for being moved from Y to X. Let y be a bordering vertex. Then, there is at least one vertex $x \in X$ that is adjacent to y. We define the *neighbor* of y, denoted by $N[y]$, to be that vertex x in X with the property that $c[x, y]$ is minimum among all vertices adjacent to y in X. We also define $C[y] = c[y, N[y]]$. Thus, $N[y]$ is the nearest neighbor to y in X, and $C[y]$ is the cost of the edge connecting y and $N[y]$. A detailed description of the algorithm is given as Algorithm PRIM.

Initially, we set $N[y]$ to 1 and $C[y] = c[1, y]$ for each vertex y adjacent to 1. For each vertex y that is not adjacent to 1, we set $C[y]$ to ∞. In each iteration, that vertex y with minimum $C[y]$ is moved from Y to X. After it has been moved, $N[w]$ and $C[w]$ are updated for each vertex w in Y that is adjacent to y.

Algorithm 7.4 PRIM

Input: A weighted connected undirected graph $G = (V, E)$, where
$\qquad V = \{1, 2, \ldots, n\}$.

Output: The set of edges T of a minimum cost spanning tree for G.

```
1.  T ← {};   X ← {1};   Y ← V − {1}
2.  for y ← 2 to n
3.      if y adjacent to 1 then
4.          N[y] ← 1
5.          C[y] ← c[1, y]
6.      else C[y] ← ∞
7.      end if
8.  end for
9.  for j ← 1 to n − 1      {find n − 1 edges}
10.     Let y ∈ Y be such that C[y] is minimum
11.     T ← T ∪ {(y, N[y])}      {add edge (y, N[y]) to T}
12.     X ← X ∪ {y}      {add vertex y to X}
13.     Y ← Y − {y}      {delete vertex y from Y}
14.     for each vertex w ∈ Y that is adjacent to y
15.         if c[y, w] < C[w] then
16.             N[w] ← y
17.             C[w] ← c[y, w]
18.         end if
19.     end for
20. end for
```

7.4.2 Correctness

Lemma 7.3 *Algorithm* PRIM *correctly finds a minimum cost spanning tree in a connected undirected graph.*

Proof. We prove by induction on the size of T that (X, T) is a subtree of a minimum cost spanning tree. Initially, $T = \{\}$ and the statement is trivially true. Assume the statement is true before adding edge $e = (x, y)$, where $x \in X$ and $y \in Y$. Let $X' = X \cup \{y\}$ and $T' = T \cup \{e\}$. We will show that $G' = (X', T')$ is also a subset of some minimum cost spanning tree. First, we show that G' is a tree. Since e is connected to exactly one vertex in X, namely x, and since by the induction hypothesis (X, T) is a tree, G' is connected and has no cycles, i.e., a tree. We now show that G' is a subtree of a minimum cost spanning tree. By the induction hypothesis, $T \subset T^*$, where T^* is the set of edges in a minimum spanning tree $G^* = (V, T^*)$. If T^* contains e, then there is nothing to prove. Otherwise, by Theorem 2.1(c), $T^* \cup \{e\}$ contains exactly one cycle with e being one of its edges. Since $e = (x, y)$ connects one vertex in X to another vertex in Y, T^* must also contain another edge $e' = (w, z)$ such that $w \in X$ and $z \in Y$. If we now construct $T^{**} = T^* - \{e'\} \cup \{e\}$, we notice that $T' \subseteq T^{**}$. Moreover, T^{**} is the set of edges in a minimum cost spanning tree since e is of minimum cost among all edges connecting the vertices in X with those in Y. $\square$

7.4.3 Time complexity

The time complexity of the algorithm is computed as follows. Step 1 costs $\Theta(n)$ time. The **for** loop in Step 2 requires $\Theta(n)$ time. The time taken by Step 10 to search for a vertex y closest to X is $\Theta(n)$ per iteration. This is because the algorithm inspects each entry in the vector representing the set Y. Since this step is executed $n - 1$ times, the overall time taken by Step 10 is $\Theta(n^2)$. Steps 11–13 cost $\Theta(1)$ time per iteration for a total of $\Theta(n)$ time. The **for** loop in Step 14 is executed $2m$ times, where $m = |E|$. This is because each edge (y, w) is inspected twice: once when y is moved to X and the other when w is moved to X. Hence, the overall time required by the **for** loop is $\Theta(m)$. It follows that the time complexity of the algorithm is $\Theta(m + n^2) = \Theta(n^2)$.

Theorem 7.4 *Algorithm* PRIM *finds a minimum cost spanning tree in a weighted undirected graph with n vertices in $\Theta(n^2)$ time.*

Proof. Lemma 7.3 establishes the correctness of the algorithm and the rest follows from the above discussion. $\qquad\square$

7.4.4 Improving the time bound

Now, we improve on Algorithm PRIM as we did to Algorithm DIJKSTRA in order to lower its $\Theta(n^2)$ time complexity to $O(m \log n)$ for graphs in which $m = o(n^2)$. We will also improve it further, so that in the case of dense graphs it runs in time linear in the number of edges.

As in Algorithm SHORTESTPATH, the basic idea is to use the min-heap data structure (see Sec. 3.2) to maintain the set of bordering vertices so that the vertex y in Y incident to an edge of lowest cost that is connected to a vertex in $V - Y$ can be extracted in $O(\log n)$ time. The modified algorithm is given as Algorithm MST.

Algorithm 7.5 MST

Input: A weighted connected undirected graph $G = (V, E)$, where
$\qquad V = \{1, 2, \ldots, n\}$.

Output: The set of edges T of a minimum cost spanning tree for G.
$\qquad$ Assume that we have an empty heap H at the beginning.

1. $T \leftarrow \{\}$; $\quad Y \leftarrow V - \{1\}$
2. **for** $y \leftarrow 2$ **to** n
3. $\quad$ **if** y is adjacent to 1 **then**
4. $\qquad$ $N[y] \leftarrow 1$
5. $\qquad$ $key(y) \leftarrow c[1, y]$
6. $\qquad$ INSERT(H, y)
7. $\quad$ **else** $key(y) \leftarrow \infty$
8. $\quad$ **end if**
9. **end for**
10. **for** $j \leftarrow 1$ **to** $n - 1$ $\quad$ {find $n - 1$ edges}
11. $\quad$ $y \leftarrow$ DELETEMIN(H)
12. $\quad$ $T \leftarrow T \cup \{(y, N[y])\}$ $\qquad$ {add edge $(y, N[y])$ to T}
13. $\quad$ $Y \leftarrow Y - \{y\}$ $\qquad$ {delete vertex y from Y}
14. $\quad$ **for** each vertex $w \in Y$ that is adjacent to y
15. $\qquad$ **if** $c[y, w] < key(w)$ **then**
16. $\qquad\quad$ $N[w] \leftarrow y$
17. $\qquad\quad$ $key(w) \leftarrow c[y, w]$
18. $\qquad$ **end if**
19. $\qquad$ **if** $w \notin H$ **then** INSERT(H, w)
20. $\qquad$ **else** SIFTUP$(H, H^{-1}(w))$
21. $\quad$ **end for**
22. **end for**

The heap H initially contains all vertices adjacent to vertex 1. Each vertex $y \in Y$ is assigned a key which is the cost of the edge connecting y to 1 if it exists; otherwise, that key is set to ∞. Each iteration of the **for** loop starts by extracting that vertex y with minimum key. The key of each vertex w in Y adjacent to y is then updated. Next, if w is not in the heap, then it is inserted; otherwise, it is sifted up, if necessary. The function $H^{-1}(w)$ returns the position of w in H. This can be implemented by simply having an array that has for its jth entry the position of vertex j in the heap. As in Algorithm SHORTESTPATH, the running time is dominated by the heap operations. There are $n-1$ DELETEMIN operations, $n-1$ INSERT operations and at most $m - n + 1$ SIFTUP operations. Each one of these operations takes $O(\log n)$ time using binary heaps which results in $O(m \log n)$ time in total.

A d-heap is essentially a generalization of a binary heap in which each internal node in the tree has at most d children instead of 2, where d is a number that can be arbitrarily large (see Exercise 3.21). If we use a d-heap, the running time is improved as follows. Each DELETEMIN takes $O(d \log_d n)$ time, and each INSERT or SIFTUP operation requires $O(\log_d n)$ time. Thus, the total running time is $O(nd \log_d n + m \log_d n)$. If we choose $d = \lceil 2 + m/n \rceil$, the time bound becomes $O(m \log_{\lceil 2+m/n \rceil} n)$. If $m \geq n^{1+\epsilon}$ for some $\epsilon > 0$ that is not too small, i.e., the graph is dense, then the running time is

$$O(m \log_{\lceil 2+m/n \rceil} n) = O(m \log_{\lceil 2+n^\epsilon \rceil} n)$$

$$= O\left(m \frac{\log n}{\log(2 + n^\epsilon)}\right)$$

$$= O\left(m \frac{\log n}{\log n^\epsilon}\right)$$

$$= O\left(\frac{m}{\epsilon}\right).$$

This implies the following theorem:

Theorem 7.5   *Given a weighted undirected graph G, Algorithm* MST *finds a minimum cost spanning tree in $O(m \log n)$ time. If the graph is dense, i.e., if $m \geq n^{1+\epsilon}$ for some $\epsilon > 0$, then it can be improved further to run in time $O(m/\epsilon)$.*

7.5   File Compression

Suppose we are given a file, which is a string of characters. We wish to compress the file as much as possible in such a way that the original file can easily be reconstructed. Let the set of characters in the file be $C = \{c_1, c_2, \ldots, c_n\}$. Let also $f(c_i), 1 \leq i \leq n$, be the frequency of character c_i in the file, i.e., the number of times c_i appears in the file. Using a fixed number of bits to represent each character, called the *encoding* of the character, the size of the file depends only on the number of characters in the file. However, since the frequency of some characters may be much larger than others, it is reasonable to use *variable* length encodings. Intuitively, those characters with large frequencies should be assigned short encodings, whereas long encodings may be assigned to those characters with small frequencies. When the encodings vary in length, we stipulate that the encoding of one character must not be the prefix of the encoding of another character; such codes are called *prefix codes*. For instance, if we assign the encodings 10 and 101 to the letters "a" and "b", there will be an ambiguity as to whether 10 is the encoding of "a" or is the prefix of the encoding of the letter "b".

Once the prefix constraint is satisfied, the decoding becomes unambiguous; the sequence of bits is scanned until an encoding of some character is found. One way to "parse" a given sequence of bits is to use a full binary tree, in which each internal node has exactly two branches labeled by 0 and 1. The leaves in this tree correspond to the characters. Each sequence of 0's and 1's on a path from the root to a leaf corresponds to a character encoding. In what follows, we describe how to construct a full binary tree that minimizes the size of the compressed file.

The algorithm presented is due to Huffman. The code constructed by the algorithm satisfies the prefix constraint and minimizes the size of the compressed file. The algorithm consists of repeating the following procedure until C consists of only one character. Let c_i and c_j be two characters with minimum frequencies. Create a new node c whose frequency is the sum of the frequencies of c_i and c_j, and make c_i and c_j the children of c. Let $C = C - \{c_i, c_j\} \cup \{c\}$.

Example 7.6   Consider finding a prefix code for a file that consists of the letters a, b, c, d and e. See Fig. 7.6. Suppose that these letters appear in

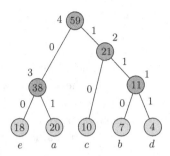

Fig. 7.6. An example of a Huffman tree.

the file with the following frequencies.

$$f(a) = 20, f(b) = 7, f(c) = 10, f(d) = 4 \text{ and } f(e) = 18.$$

Each leaf node is labeled with its corresponding character and its frequency of occurrence in the file. Each internal node is labeled with the sum of the weights of the leaves in its subtree and the order of its creation. For instance, the first internal node created has a sum of 11 and it is labeled with 1. From the binary tree, the encodings for a, b, c, d and e are, respectively, 01, 110, 10, 111 and 00. Suppose each character was represented by three binary digits before compression. Then, the original size of the file is $3(20 + 7 + 10 + 4 + 18) = 177$ bits. The size of the compressed file using the above code becomes $2 \times 20 + 3 \times 7 + 2 \times 10 + 3 \times 4 + 2 \times 18 = 129$ bits, a saving of about 27%.

7.5.1 The algorithm

Since the main operations required to construct a Huffman tree are insertion and deletion of characters with minimum frequency, a min-heap is a good candidate data structure that supports these operations. The algorithm builds a tree by adding $n - 1$ internal vertices one at a time; its leaves correspond to the input characters. Initially and during its execution, the algorithm maintains a forest of trees. After adding $n - 1$ internal nodes, the forest is transformed into a tree: the Huffman tree. Algorithm HUFFMAN below gives a more precise description of the construction of a full binary tree corresponding to a Huffman code of an input string of characters together with their frequencies.

Algorithm 7.6 HUFFMAN
Input: A set $C = \{c_1, c_2, \ldots, c_n\}$ of n characters and their frequencies
$\{f(c_1), f(c_2), \ldots, f(c_n)\}$.
Output: A Huffman tree (V, T) for C.

1. Insert all characters into a min-heap H according to their frequencies.
2. $V \leftarrow C$; $T = \{\}$
3. **for** $j \leftarrow 1$ **to** $n - 1$
4. $c \leftarrow$ DELETEMIN(H)
5. $c' \leftarrow$ DELETEMIN(H)
6. $f(v) \leftarrow f(c) + f(c')$ {v is a new node}
7.   INSERT(H, v)
8. $V = V \cup \{v\}$ {Add v to V}
9. $T = T \cup \{(v, c), (v, c')\}$ {Make c and c' children of v in T}
10. **end while**

7.5.2 *Time complexity*

The time complexity of the algorithm is computed as follows. The time needed to insert all characters into the heap is $\Theta(n)$ (Theorem 3.1). The time required to delete two elements from the heap and add a new element is $O(\log n)$. Since this is repeated $n - 1$ times, the overall time taken by the **for** loop is $O(n \log n)$. It follows that the time complexity of the algorithm is $O(n \log n)$.

7.6 Practice Problems

7.1. Give a counterexample to show that the greedy algorithm obtained in Example 7.1 for the money change problem does not always work if we instead use coins of values 1 cent, 5 cents, 7 cents and 11 cents. Note that in this case dynamic programming can be used to find the minimum number of coins (see Exercises 6.20 and 6.21).

7.2. Apply Algorithm DIJKSTRA on the directed graph shown in Fig. 7.7. Assume that vertex 1 is the start vertex.

Fig. 7.7. Directed graph.

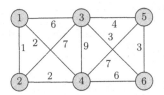

Fig. 7.8.   An undirected graph.

7.3. Is Algorithm DIJKSTRA optimal? Explain.

7.4. What are the merits and demerits of using the adjacency matrix representation instead of the adjacency lists in the input to Algorithm DIJKSTRA?

7.5. Give an example of a directed graph to show that Algorithm DIJKSTRA does not always work if some of the edges have negative weights.

7.6. Show the result of applying Algorithm KRUSKAL to find a minimum cost spanning tree for the undirected graph shown in Fig. 7.8.

7.7. Show the result of applying Algorithm PRIM to find a minimum cost spanning tree for the undirected graph shown in Fig. 7.8.

7.8. Use Algorithm HUFFMAN to find an optimal code for the characters a, b, c, d, e and f whose frequencies in a given text are, respectively, 7, 5, 3, 2, 12 and 9.

7.7   Exercises

7.1. Suppose in the money change problem of Example 7.1, the coin values are: $1, 2, 4, 8, 16, \ldots, 2^k$, for some positive integer k. Give an $O(\log n)$ algorithm to solve the problem if the value to be paid is $y < 2^{k+1}$.

7.2. Let $G = (V, E)$ be an undirected graph. A vertex cover for G is a subset $S \subseteq V$ such that every edge in E is incident to at least one vertex in S. Consider the following algorithm for finding a vertex cover for G. First, order the vertices in V by decreasing order of degree. Next, execute the following step until all edges are covered. Pick a vertex of highest degree that is incident to at least one edge in the remaining graph, add it to the cover, and delete all edges incident to that vertex. Show that this greedy approach does not always result in a vertex cover of minimum size.

7.3. Let $G = (V, E)$ be an undirected graph. A clique C in G is a subgraph of G that is a complete graph by itself. A clique C is maximum if there is no other clique C' in G such that the size of C' is greater than the size of C. Consider the following method that attempts to find a maximum clique in G. Initially, let $C = G$. Repeat the following step until C is a clique. Delete from C a vertex that is not connected to every other vertex in C. Show that this greedy approach does not always result in a maximum clique.

7.4. Let $G = (V, E)$ be an undirected graph. A coloring of G is an assignment of colors to the vertices in V such that no two adjacent vertices have the same color. The coloring problem is to determine the minimum number of colors needed to color G. Consider the following greedy method that attempts to solve the coloring problem. Let the colors be $1, 2, 3, \ldots$. First, color as many vertices as possible using color 1. Next, color as many vertices as possible using color 2, and so on. Show that this greedy approach does not always color the graph using the minimum number of colors.

7.5. Let $A_1, A_2, \ldots, A_m$ be m arrays of integers each sorted in nondecreasing order. Each array A_j is of size n_j. Suppose we want to merge all arrays into one array A using an algorithm similar to Algorithm MERGE described in Sec. 1.4. Give a greedy strategy for the order in which these arrays should be merged so that the overall number of comparisons is minimized. For example, if $m = 3$, we may merge A_1 with A_2 to obtain A_4 and then merge A_3 with A_4 to obtain A. Another alternative is to merge A_2 with A_3 to obtain A_4 and then merge A_1 with A_4 to obtain A. Yet another alternative is to merge A_1 with A_3 to obtain A_4 and then merge A_2 with A_4 to obtain A. (*Hint*: Give an algorithm similar to Algorithm HUFFMAN.)

7.6. Analyze the time complexity of the algorithm in Exercise 7.5. (*Hint*: If we merge the two smallest arrays, then the next two smallest arrays, etc., then each time we merge, the resulting array size is at least double the smaller array size.)

7.7. Consider the following greedy algorithm which attempts to find the distance from vertex s to vertex t in a directed graph G with positive lengths on its edges. Starting from vertex s, go to the nearest vertex, say x. From vertex x, go to the nearest vertex, say y. Continue in this manner until you arrive at vertex t. Give a graph with the fewest number of vertices to show that this heuristic does not always produce the distance from s to t. (Recall that the distance from vertex u to vertex v is the length of a shortest path from u to v.)

7.8. Modify Algorithm DIJKSTRA so that it finds the shortest paths in addition to their lengths. (*Hint*: Use an array P such that $P[v]$ stores the parent of the new vertex v.)

7.9. Prove that the subgraph defined by the paths obtained from the modified shortest path algorithm as described in Exercise 7.8 is a tree. This tree is called the *shortest path tree*.

7.10. Can a directed graph have two distinct shortest path trees (see Exercise 7.9)? Prove your answer.

7.11. Show that the proof of correctness of Algorithm DIJKSTRA (Lemma 7.1) does not work if some of the edges in the input graph have negative weights.

7.12. Let $G = (V, E)$ be a directed graph such that removing the directions from its edges results in a planar graph. What is the running time of Algorithm SHORTESTPATH when applied to G? Compare that to the running time when using Algorithm DIJKSTRA.

7.13. Let $G = (V, E)$ be a directed graph such that $m = O(n^{1.2})$, where $n = |V|$ and $m = |E|$. What changes should be made to Algorithm SHORTESTPATH so that it will run in time $O(m)$?

7.14. Let $G = (V, E)$ be an undirected graph such that $m = O(n^{1.99})$, where $n = |V|$ and $m = |E|$. Suppose you want to find a minimum cost spanning tree for G. Which algorithm would you choose: Algorithm PRIM or Algorithm KRUSKAL? Explain.

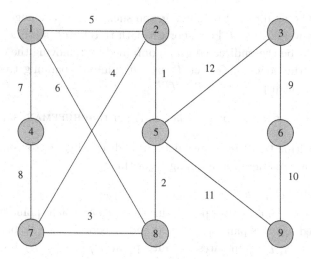

Fig. 7.9.   Undirected graph.

7.15. Refer to Fig. 7.9.

  (a) Run Prim's algorithm starting from vertex 3 in order to find a minimum spanning tree of the graph. Make sure you indicate the order in which each edge is added to the minimum spanning tree.

  (b) Can this graph have more than one minimum spanning trees? Justify your answer.

7.16. Let e be an edge of minimum weight in an undirected graph G. Show that e belongs to some minimum cost spanning tree of G.

7.17. Does Algorithm PRIM work correctly if the graph has negative weights? Prove your answer.

7.18. Let G be an undirected weighted graph such that no two edges have the same weight. Prove that G has a unique minimum cost spanning tree.

7.19. What is the number of spanning trees of a *complete* undirected graph G with n vertices? For example, the number of spanning trees of K_3, the complete graph on three vertices, is 3.

7.20. Let G be a directed weighted graph such that no two edges have the same weight. Let T be a shortest path tree for G (see Exercise 7.9). Let G' be the undirected graph obtained by removing the directions from the edges of G. Let T' be a minimum spanning tree for G'. Prove or disprove that $T = T'$.

7.21. Prove that the graph obtained in Algorithm HUFFMAN is a tree.

7.22. Algorithm HUFFMAN constructs the code tree in a bottom-up fashion. Is it a dynamic programming algorithm?

7.23. Let $B = \{b_1, b_2, \ldots, b_n\}$ and $W = \{w_1, w_2, \ldots, w_n\}$ be two sets of black and white points in the plane. Each point is represented by the pair (x, y) of x and y coordinates. A black point $b_i = (x_i, y_i)$ dominates a white point $w_j = (x_j, y_j)$ if and only if $x_i \geq x_j$ and $y_i \geq y_j$. A *matching* between a black point b_i and a white point w_j is possible if b_i dominates w_j. A matching $M = \{(b_{i_1}, w_{j_1}), (b_{i_2}, w_{j_2}), \ldots, (b_{i_k}, w_{j_k})\}$ between the black and white points is maximum if k, the number of matched pairs in M, is maximum. Design a greedy algorithm to find a maximum matching in $O(n \log n)$ time. (*Hint*: Sort the black points in increasing x-coordinates and use a heap for the white points.)

7.8 Bibliographic Notes

The greedy graph algorithms are discussed in most books on algorithms (see the Bibliographic Notes of Chapter 1).

Algorithm DIJKSTRA for the single source shortest path problem is from Dijkstra (1959). The implementation using a heap is due to Johnson (1977); see also Tarjan (1983). The best known asymptotic running time for this problem is $O(m + n \log n)$, which is due to Fredman and Tarjan (1987).

Graham and Hell (1985) discuss the long history of the minimum cost spanning tree problem, which has been extensively studied. Algorithm KRUSKAL comes from Kruskal (1956). Algorithm PRIM is due to Prim (1957). The improvement using heaps can be found in Johnson (1975). More sophisticated algorithms can be found in Yao (1975), Cheriton and Tarjan (1976) and Tarjan (1983). Algorithm HUFFMAN for file compression is due to Huffman (1952) (see also Knuth, 1968).

Chapter 8

Graph Traversal

8.1 Introduction

In some graph algorithms such as those for finding shortest paths or minimum spanning trees, the vertices and edges are visited in an order that is imposed by their respective algorithms. However, in some other algorithms, the order of visiting the vertices is unimportant; what is important is that the vertices are visited in a *systematic* order, regardless of the input graph. In this chapter, we discuss two methods of graph traversal: depth-first search and breadth-first search.

8.2 Depth-First Search

Depth-first search is a powerful traversal method that aids in the solution of many problems involving graphs. It is essentially a generalization of the preorder traversal of rooted trees (see Sec. 2.5.1). Let $G = (V, E)$ be a directed or undirected graph. A depth-first search traversal of G works as follows. First, all vertices are marked *unvisited*. Next, a starting vertex is selected, say $v \in V$, and marked *visited*. Let w be any vertex that is adjacent to v. We mark w as *visited* and advance to another vertex, say x, that is adjacent to w and is marked *unvisited*. Again, we mark x as *visited* and advance to another vertex that is adjacent to x and is marked *unvisited*. This process of selecting an unvisited vertex adjacent to the current vertex continues as deep as possible until we find a vertex y whose adjacent vertices

245

have all been marked *visited*. At this point, we *back up* to the most recently visited vertex, say z, and visit an unvisited vertex that is adjacent to z, if any. Continuing this way, we finally return back to the starting vertex v. This method of traversal has been given the name *depth-first search*, as it continues the search in the forward (deeper) direction. The algorithm for such a traversal can be written using recursion, as shown in Algorithm DFS or a stack (see Exercise 8.1).

Algorithm 8.1 DFS
Input: A (directed or undirected) graph $G = (V, E)$.
Output: Preordering and postordering of the vertices in the corresponding depth-first search tree.

1. *predfn* ← 0;   *postdfn* ← 0
2. **for** each vertex $v \in V$
3.   mark v *unvisited*
4. **end for**
5. **for** each vertex $v \in V$
6.   **if** v is marked *unvisited* **then** *dfs*(v)
7. **end for**

Algorithm *dfs*(v)
1. mark v *visited*
2. *predfn* ← *predfn* + 1
3. **for** each edge $(v, w) \in E$
4.   **if** w is marked *unvisited* **then** *dfs*(w)
5. **end for**
6. *postdfn* ← *postdfn* + 1

The algorithm starts by marking all vertices *unvisited*. It also initializes two counters *predfn* and *postdfn* to zero. These two counters *are not part of the traversal*; their importance will be apparent when we later make use of depth-first search to solve some problems. The algorithm then calls Algorithm *dfs* for each unvisited vertex in V. This is because not all the vertices may be reachable from the start vertex. Starting from some vertex $v \in V$, Algorithm *dfs* performs the search on G by visiting v, marking v *visited* and then recursively visiting its adjacent vertices. When the search is complete, if all vertices are reachable from the start vertex, a spanning tree called the *depth-first search spanning tree* is constructed whose edges are those inspected in the forward direction, i.e., when exploring unvisited vertices. In other words, let (v, w) be an edge such that w is marked *unvisited* and suppose the algorithm was invoked by the call *dfs(v)*. Then, in this case, that edge will be part of the depth-first search spanning tree. If not all the vertices are reachable from the start vertex, then the search results in a *forest* of spanning trees instead.

After the search is complete, each vertex is labeled with *predfn* and *postdfn* numbers. These two labels impose preorder and postorder numbering on the vertices in the spanning tree (or forest) generated by the depth-first search traversal. They give the order in which visiting a vertex starts and ends. In the following, we say that edge (v, w) is being *explored* to mean that within the call *dfs(v)*, the algorithm is inspecting the edge (v, w) to test whether w has been visited before or not. The edges of the graph are classified differently according to whether the graph is directed or undirected.

8.2.1 *The case of undirected graphs*

Let $G = (V, E)$ be an undirected graph. As a result of the traversal, the edges of G are classified into the following two types:

(1) **Tree edges:** Edges in the depth-first search tree. An edge (v, w) is a tree edge if w was first visited when exploring the edge (v, w).
(2) **Back edges:** All other edges.

Example 8.1 Figure 8.1(b) illustrates the action of depth-first search traversal on the undirected graph shown in Fig. 8.1(a). Vertex a has been selected as the start vertex. The depth-first search tree is shown in Fig. 8.1(b) with solid lines. Dotted lines represent back edges. Each vertex in the depth-first search tree is labeled with two numbers: *predfn* and *postdfn*. Note that since vertex e has *postdfn* = 1, it is the first vertex whose depth-first search is complete. Note also that since the graph is connected, the start vertex is labeled with *predfn* = 1 and *postdfn* = 10, the number of vertices in the graph.

8.2.2 *The case of directed graphs*

Depth-first search in directed graphs results in one or more (directed) spanning trees whose number *depends on the start vertex*. If v is the start vertex, depth-first search generates a tree consisting of all vertices reachable from v. If not all vertices are included in that tree, the search resumes from another

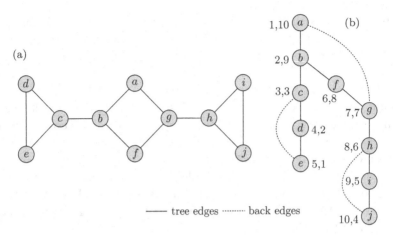

Fig. 8.1. An example of depth-first search traversal of an undirected graph.

unvisited vertex, say w, and a tree consisting of all unvisited vertices that are reachable from w is constructed. This process continues until all vertices have been visited. In depth-first search traversal of directed graphs, however, the edges of G are classified into four types:

(1) **Tree edges:** Edges in the depth-first search tree. An edge (v, w) is a tree edge if w was first visited when exploring the edge (v, w).
(2) **Back edges:** Edges of the form (v, w) such that w is an *ancestor* of v in the depth-first search tree (constructed so far) and vertex w was marked *visited* when (v, w) was explored.
(3) **Forward edges:** Edges of the form (v, w) such that w is a *descendant* of v in the depth-first search tree (constructed so far) and vertex w was marked *visited* when (v, w) was explored.
(4) **Cross edges:** All other edges.

Example 8.2   Figure 8.2(b) illustrates the action of depth-first search traversal on the directed graph shown in Fig. 8.2(a). Starting at vertex a, the vertices a, b, e and f are visited in this order. When Algorithm *dfs* is initiated again at vertex c, vertex d is visited and the traversal is complete after b is visited from c. We notice that the edge (e, a) is a back edge since e is a descendant of a in the depth-first search tree, and (e, a) is not a tree edge. On the other hand, edge (a, f) is a forward edge since a is an ancestor of f in the depth-first search tree, and (a, f) is not a tree edge. Since neither

Fig. 8.2. An example of depth-first search traversal of a directed graph.

e nor f is an ancestor of the other in the depth-first search tree, edge (f, e) is a cross edge. The two edges (c, b) and (d, e) are, obviously, cross edges; each edge connects two vertices in two different trees. Note that had we chosen to visit vertex f immediately after a instead of visiting vertex b, both edges (a, b) and (a, f) would have been tree edges. In this case, the result of the depth-first search traversal is shown in Fig. 8.2(c). Thus, the type of an edge depends on the order in which the vertices are visited.

8.2.3 *Time complexity of depth-first search*

Now, we analyze the time complexity of Algorithm DFS when applied to a graph G with n vertices and m edges. The **for** loop of the algorithm in lines 2–4 costs $\Theta(n)$ time. The **for** loop of the algorithm in lines 5–7 costs $\Theta(n)$ time. The number of algorithm calls is exactly n since once the algorithm is invoked on vertex v, it will be marked *visited* and hence no more calls on v will take place. The cost of an algorithm call if we exclude the **for** loop in Algorithm *dfs* is $\Theta(1)$. It follows that the overall cost of algorithm calls excluding the **for** loop is $\Theta(n)$. Now, it remains to find the cost of the **for** loop in Algorithm *dfs*. The number of times this step is executed to test whether a vertex w is marked *unvisited* is equal to the number of vertices adjacent to vertex v. Hence, the total number of times this step is executed is equal to the number of edges in the case of directed graphs and twice the number of edges in the case of undirected graphs. Consequently, the cost of this step is $\Theta(m)$ in both directed and undirected graphs. It follows that the running time of the algorithm is $\Theta(m + n)$. If the graph is connected or $m \geq n$, then the running time is simply $\Theta(m)$. It should be emphasized, however, that the graph is assumed to be represented by adjacency lists. The time complexity of Algorithm DFS when the graph is represented by an adjacency matrix is left as an exercise (Exercise 8.2).

8.3　Applications of Depth-First Search

Depth-first search is used quite often in graph and geometric algorithms. It is a powerful tool and has numerous applications. In this section, we list some of its important applications.

8.3.1　*Graph acyclicity*

Let $G = (V, E)$ be a directed or undirected graph with n vertices and m edges. To test whether G has at least one cycle, we apply depth-first search on G. If a back edge is detected during the search, then G is cyclic; otherwise, G is acyclic.

8.3.2　*Topological sorting*

Given a directed acyclic graph (dag for short) $G = (V, E)$, the problem of *topological sorting* is to find a linear ordering of its vertices in such a way that if $(v, w) \in E$, then v appears before w in the ordering. For example, one possible topological sorting of the vertices in the dag shown in Fig. 8.3(a) is a, b, d, c, e, f, g. We will assume that the dag has only one vertex, say s, of indegree 0. If not, we may simply add a new vertex s and edges from s to all vertices of indegree 0 (see Fig. 8.3(b)).

　　　Next, we simply carry out a depth-first search on G starting at vertex s. When the traversal is complete, the values of the counter *postdfn* define a *reverse* topological ordering of the vertices in the dag. Thus, to obtain

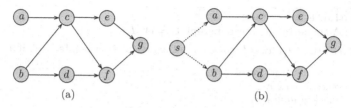

Fig. 8.3.   Illustration of topological sorting.

the ordering, we may add an output step to Algorithm DFS just after the counter *postdfn* is incremented. The resulting output is reversed to obtain the desired topological ordering.

8.3.3   *Finding articulation points in a graph*

A vertex v in an undirected graph G with more than two vertices is called an *articulation point* if there exist two vertices u and w different from v such that any path between u and w must pass through v. Thus, if G is connected, the removal of v and its incident edges will result in a disconnected subgraph of G. A graph is called *biconnected* if it is connected and has no articulation points. To find the set of articulation points, we perform a depth-first search traversal on G. During the traversal, we maintain two labels with each vertex $v \in V$: $\alpha[v]$ and $\beta[v]$. $\alpha[v]$ is simply *predfn* in the depth-first search algorithm, which is incremented at each call to the depth-first search algorithm. $\beta[v]$ is initialized to $\alpha[v]$, but may change later on during the traversal. For each vertex v visited, we let $\beta[v]$ be the minimum of the following:

- $\alpha[v]$.
- $\alpha[u]$ for each vertex u such that (v, u) is a back edge.
- $\beta[w]$ for each edge (v, w) in the depth-first search tree.

The articulation points are determined as follows:

- The root is an articulation point if and only if it has two or more children in the depth-first search tree.
- A vertex v other than the root is an articulation point if and only if v has a child w with $\beta[w] \geq \alpha[v]$.

The formal algorithm for finding the articulation points is given as Algorithm ARTICPOINTS.

Algorithm 8.2 ARTICPOINTS
Input: A connected undirected graph $G = (V, E)$.

Output: Array $A[1..count]$ containing the articulation points of G, if any.

1. Let s be the start vertex.
2. **for** each vertex $v \in V$
3.   mark v *unvisited*
4. **end for**
5. $predfn \leftarrow 0$; $count \leftarrow 0$; $rootdegree \leftarrow 0$
6. $dfs(s)$

Algorithm $dfs(v)$
1. mark v *visited*; $artpoint \leftarrow$ **false** ; $predfn \leftarrow predfn + 1$
2. $\alpha[v] \leftarrow predfn$; $\beta[v] \leftarrow predfn$ {*Initialize $\alpha[v]$ and $\beta[v]$*}
3. **for** each edge $(v, w) \in E$
4.   **if** (v, w) is a tree edge **then**
5. $dfs(w)$
6.   **if** $v = s$ **then**
7. $rootdegree \leftarrow rootdegree + 1$
8.   **if** $rootdegree = 2$ **then** $artpoint \leftarrow$ **true**
9.   **else**
10. $\beta[v] \leftarrow \min\{\beta[v], \beta[w]\}$
11.   **if** $\beta[w] \geq \alpha[v]$ **then** $artpoint \leftarrow$ **true**
12.   **end if**
13.   **else if** (v, w) is a back edge **then** $\beta[v] \leftarrow \min\{\beta[v], \alpha[w]\}$
14.   **else** do nothing   {*w is the parent of v*}
15.   **end if**
16. **end for**
17. **if** $artpoint$ **then**
18. $count \leftarrow count + 1$
19. $A[count] \leftarrow v$
20. **end if**

First, the algorithm performs the necessary initializations. In particular, *count* is the number of articulation points and *rootdegree* is the degree of the root of the depth-first search tree. This is needed to decide later whether the root is an articulation point as mentioned above. Next, the depth-first search commences starting at the root. For each vertex v visited, $\alpha[v]$ and $\beta[v]$ are initialized to *predfn*. When the search backs up from some vertex w to v, two actions take place. First, $\beta[v]$ is set to $\beta[w]$ if $\beta[w]$ is found to be smaller then $\beta[v]$. Second, if $\beta[w] \geq \alpha[v]$, then this is an indication that v is an articulation point. This is because any path from w to an ancestor of v

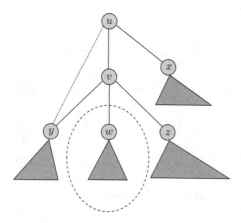

Fig. 8.4. Illustration of the algorithm for finding the articulation points.

must pass through v. This is illustrated in Fig. 8.4 in which any path from the subtree rooted at w to u must include v, and hence v is an articulation point. The subtree rooted at w contains one or more connected components. In this figure, the root u is an articulation point since its degree is greater than 1.

Example 8.3 We illustrate the action of Algorithm ARTICPOINTS by finding the articulation points of the graph shown in Fig. 8.1(a). See Fig. 8.5. Each vertex v in the depth-first search tree is labeled with $\alpha[v]$ and $\beta[v]$. The depth-first search starts at vertex a and proceeds to vertex e. A back edge (e, c) is discovered, and hence $\beta[e]$ is assigned the value $\alpha[c] = 3$. Now, when the search backs up to vertex d, $\beta[d]$ is assigned $\beta[e] = 3$. Similarly, when the search backs up to vertex c, its label $\beta[c]$ is assigned the value $\beta[d] = 3$. Now, since $\beta[d] \geq \alpha[c]$, vertex c is marked as an articulation point. When the search backs up to b, it is also found that $\beta[c] \geq \alpha[b]$, and hence b is also marked as an articulation point. At vertex b, the search branches to a new vertex f and proceeds, as illustrated in the figure, until it reaches vertex j. The back edge (j, h) is detected, and hence $\beta[j]$ is set to $\alpha[h] = 8$. Now, as described before, the search backs up to i and then h and sets $\beta[i]$ and $\beta[h]$ to $\beta[j] = 8$. Again, since $\beta[i] \geq \alpha[h]$, vertex h is marked as an articulation point. For the same reason, vertex g is marked as an articulation point. At vertex g, the back edge (g, a) is detected, and

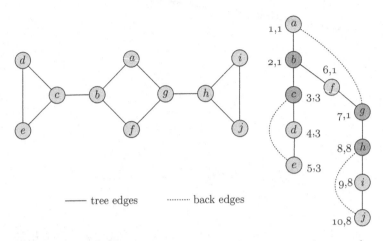

Fig. 8.5. An example of finding the articulation points in a graph.

hence $\beta[g]$ is set to $\alpha[a] = 1$. Finally, $\beta[f]$ and then $\beta[b]$ are set to 1 and the search terminates at the start vertex. The root a is not an articulation point since it has only one child in the depth-first search tree.

8.3.4 *Strongly connected components*

Given a directed graph $G = (V, E)$, a *strongly connected component* in G is a *maximal* set of vertices in which there is a path between each pair of vertices. Algorithm STRONGCONNECTCOMP below uses depth-first search in order to identify all the strongly connected components in a directed graph.

Algorithm 8.3 STRONGCONNECTCOMP
Input: A directed graph $G = (V, E)$.

Output: The strongly connected components in G.

1. Perform a depth-first search on G and assign each vertex its corresponding *postdfn* number.
2. Construct a new graph G' by reversing the direction of edges in G.
3. Perform a depth-first search on G' starting from the vertex with highest *postdfn* number. If the depth-first search does not reach all vertices, start the next depth-first search from the vertex with highest *postdfn* number among the remaining vertices.
4. Each tree in the resulting forest corresponds to a strongly connected component.

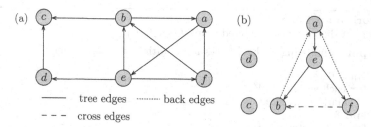

Fig. 8.6. Finding strongly connected components.

Example 8.4 Consider the directed graph G shown in Fig. 8.2(a). Applying depth-first search on this directed graph results in the forest shown in Fig. 8.2(b). Also shown in the figure is the postordering of the vertices, which is e, f, b, a, d, c. If we reverse the direction of the edges in G, we obtain G', which is shown in Fig. 8.6(a). Starting from vertex c in G', a depth-first search traversal yields the tree consisting of vertex c only. Similarly, applying depth-first search on the remaining vertices starting at vertex d results in the tree consisting of only vertex d. Finally, applying depth-first search on the remaining vertices starting at vertex a yields the tree whose vertices are a, b, e and f. The resulting forest is shown in Fig. 8.6(b). Each tree in the forest corresponds to a strongly connected component. Thus, G contains three strongly connected components.

8.4 Breadth-First Search

Unlike depth-first search, in breadth-first search, when we visit a vertex v, we next visit all vertices adjacent to v. The resulting tree is called a *breadth-first search tree*. This method of traversal can be implemented by a queue to store unexamined vertices. Algorithm BFS for breadth-first search can be applied to directed and undirected graphs. Initially, all vertices are marked *unvisited*. The counter *bfn*, which is initialized to zero, represents the order in which the vertices are removed from the queue. In the case of undirected graphs, an edge is either a tree edge or a cross edge. If the graph is directed, an edge is either a tree edge, a back edge or a cross edge; there are no forward edges.

Algorithm 8.4 BFS
Input: A directed or undirected graph $G = (V, E)$.

Output: Numbering of the vertices in breadth-first search order.

1. $bfn \leftarrow 0$
2. **for** each vertex $v \in V$
3.   mark v *unvisited*
4. **end for**
5. **for** each vertex $v \in V$
6.   **if** v is marked *unvisited* **then** bfs(v)
7. **end for**

Algorithm bfs(v)

1. $Q \leftarrow \{v\}$
2. mark v *visited*
3. **while** $Q \neq \{\}$
4. $v \leftarrow Pop(Q)$
5. $bfn \leftarrow bfn + 1$
6.   **for** each edge $(v, w) \in E$
7.   **if** w is marked *unvisited* **then**
8.   Push(w, Q)
9.   mark w *visited*
10.   **end if**
11.   **end for**
12. **end while**

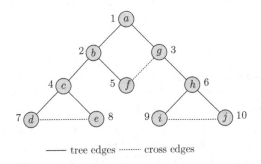

tree edges   cross edges

Fig. 8.7. An example of breadth-first search traversal of an undirected graph.

Example 8.5 Figure 8.7 illustrates the action of breadth-first search traversal when applied to the graph shown in Fig. 8.1(a) starting from vertex a. After popping off vertex a, vertices b and g are pushed into the queue and marked *visited*. Next, vertex b is removed from the queue, and its adjacent vertices that have not yet been visited, namely c and f, are pushed into the queue and marked *visited*. This process of pushing vertices into the queue and removing them later on is continued until vertex j is finally removed from the queue. At this point, the queue becomes empty and the breadth-first search traversal is complete. In the figure, each vertex is labeled with its bfn number, the order in which that vertex was removed from the queue. Notice that the edges in the figure are either tree edges or cross edges.

8.4.1 *Time complexity*

The time complexity of breadth-first search when applied to a graph (directed or undirected) with n vertices and m edges is the same as that of depth-first search, i.e., $\Theta(n + m)$. If the graph is connected or $m \geq n$, then the time complexity is simply $\Theta(m)$.

8.5 Applications of Breadth-First Search

We close this chapter with an application of breadth-first search that is important in graph and network algorithms. Let $G = (V, E)$ be a connected undirected graph and s a vertex in V. When Algorithm BFS is applied to G starting at s, the resulting breadth-first search tree is such that the path from s to any other vertex has the least number of edges. Thus, suppose we want to find the distance from s to every other vertex, where the distance from s to a vertex v is defined to be the least number of edges in any path from s to v. This can easily be done by labeling each vertex with its distance *prior* to pushing it into the queue. Thus, the start vertex will be labeled 0, its adjacent vertices with 1, and so on. Clearly, the label of each vertex is its shortest distance from the start vertex. For instance, in Fig. 8.7, vertex a will be labeled 0, vertices b and g will be labeled 1, vertices c, f and h will be labeled 2, and finally vertices d, e, i and j will be labeled 3. Note that this vertex numbering is *not* the same as the breadth-first numbering in the algorithm. The minor changes to the breadth-first search algorithm are left as an exercise (Exercise 8.16). In this case, the resulting search tree is the shortest path tree.

8.6   Practice Problems

8.1. Show the result of running depth-first search on the undirected graph
shown in Fig. 8.8(a) starting at vertex a. Give the classification of
edges as tree edges or back edges.

8.2. Show the result of running depth-first search on the directed graph
shown in Fig. 8.8(b) starting at vertex a. Give the classification of
edges as tree edge, back edges, forward edges or cross edges.

8.3. Show the result of running depth-first search on the undirected graph
of Fig. 8.9 starting at vertex f. Give the classification of edges.

8.4. Show the result of running depth-first search on the directed graph
of Fig. 8.10 starting at vertex e. Give the classification of edges.

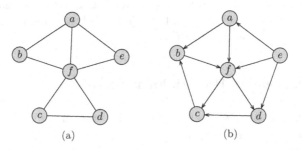

Fig. 8.8.   Undirected and directed graphs.

Fig. 8.9.   An undirected graph.

Fig. 8.10.   A directed graph.

8.5. Apply the articulation points algorithm to obtain the articulation points of the undirected graph shown in Fig. 8.9.

8.6. Show that in the strongly connected components algorithm, any choice of the first vertex to carry out the depth-first search traversal leads to the same solution.

8.7. Apply the strongly connected components algorithm on the directed graph shown in Fig. 8.10.

8.8. Show the result of running breadth-first search on the undirected graph shown in Fig. 8.8(a) starting at vertex a.

8.9. Show the result of running breadth-first search on the directed graph shown in Fig. 8.8(b) starting at vertex a.

8.7 Exercises

8.1. Give an iterative version of Algorithm DFS that uses a stack to store unvisited vertices.

8.2. What will be the time complexity of the depth-first search algorithm if the input graph is represented by an adjacency matrix (see Sec. 2.3.1 for graph representation).

8.3. Show that when depth-first search is applied to an undirected graph G, the edges of G will be classified as either tree edges or back edges. That is, there are no forward edges or cross edges.

8.4. Suppose that Algorithm DFS is applied to an undirected graph G. Give an algorithm that classifies the edges of G as either tree edges or back edges.

8.5. Suppose that Algorithm DFS is applied to a directed graph G. Give an algorithm that classifies the edges of G as either tree edges, back edges, forward edges or cross edges.

8.6. Give an algorithm that counts the number of connected components in an undirected graph using depth-first search or breadth-first search.

8.7. Given an undirected graph G, design an algorithm to list the vertices in each connected component of G separately.

8.8. Give an $O(n)$ time algorithm to determine whether a connected undirected graph with n vertices contains a cycle.

8.9. Let T be the depth-first search tree resulting from a depth-first search traversal on a connected undirected graph. Show that the root of T is an articulation point if and only if it has two or more children (see Sec. 8.3.3).

8.10. Let T be the depth-first search tree resulting from a depth-first search traversal on a connected undirected graph. Show that a vertex v other than the root is an articulation point if and only if v has a child w with $\beta[w] \geq \alpha[v]$ (see Sec. 8.3.3).

8.11. An edge of a connected undirected graph G is called a *bridge* if its deletion disconnects G. Modify the algorithm for finding articulation points so that it detects bridges instead of articulation points.

8.12. Show the result of running breadth-first search on the undirected graph of Fig. 8.9 starting at vertex f.

8.13. Show the result of running breadth-first search on the directed graph of Fig. 8.10 starting at vertex e.

8.14. Show that when breadth-first search is applied to an undirected graph G, the edges of G will be classified as either tree edges or cross edges. That is, there are no back edges or forward edges.

8.15. Show that when breadth-first search is applied to a directed graph G, the edges of G will be classified as tree edges, back edges or cross edges. That is, unlike the case of depth-first search, the search does not result in forward edges.

8.16. Let G be a graph (directed or undirected), and let s be a vertex in G. Modify Algorithm BFS so that it outputs the shortest path measured in the number of edges from s to every other vertex.

8.17. Use depth-first search to find a spanning tree for the complete bipartite graph $K_{3,3}$ (see Sec. 2.3 for the definition of $K_{3,3}$).

8.18. Use breadth-first search to find a spanning tree for the complete bipartite graph $K_{3,3}$. Compare this tree with the tree obtained in Exercise 8.17.

8.19. Suppose that Algorithm BFS is applied to an undirected graph G. Give an algorithm that classifies the edges of G as either tree edges or cross edges.

8.20. Suppose that Algorithm BFS is applied to a directed graph G. Give an algorithm that classifies the edges of G as either tree edges, back edges or cross edges.

8.21. Show that the time complexity of breadth-first search when applied on a graph with n vertices and m edges is $\Theta(n + m)$.

8.22. Design an efficient algorithm to determine whether a given graph is bipartite (see Sec. 2.3 for the definition of a bipartite graph).

8.23. Design an algorithm to find a cycle of shortest length in a directed graph. Here, the length of a cycle is measured in terms of its number of edges.

8.24. Let G be a connected undirected graph and T the spanning tree resulting from applying breadth-first search on G starting at vertex r. Prove or disprove that the height of T is minimum among all spanning trees with root r.

8.8 Bibliographic Notes

Graph traversals are discussed in several books on algorithms, either separately or intermixed with other graph algorithms (see the Bibliographic Notes of Chapter 1). Hopcroft and Tarjan (1973a) were the first to recognize the algorithmic importance of depth-first search. Several applications of depth-first search can be found in this paper and in Tarjan (1972). Algorithm STRONGCONNECTCOMP for the strongly connected components is similar to the one by Sharir (1981). Tarjan (1972) contains an algorithm for finding the strongly connected components that needs only one depth-first search traversal. Breadth-first search was discovered independently by Moore (1959) and Lee (1961).

PART 4
Complexity of Problems

In this part of the book, we turn our attention to the study of the computational complexity of a problem as opposed to the cost of a particular algorithm to solve that problem. We define the computational complexity of a problem to be the computational complexity of the most efficient algorithm to solve that problem.

In Chapter 9, we study a class of problems known as NP-complete problems. This class of problems encompasses numerous problems drawn from many problem domains. These problems share the property that if any one problem in the class is solvable in polynomial time, then all other problems in the class are solvable in polynomial time. We have chosen to cover this topic informally, in the sense that no specific model of computation is assumed. Instead, only the abstract notion of algorithm is used. This makes it easy to the novice reader to comprehend the ideas behind NP-completeness without missing out on the details of a formal model (e.g., the Turing machine). The most important point stressed in this chapter is to study the standard technique of proving that a problem is NP-complete. This is illustrated using several examples of NP-complete problems.

A more formal treatment of NP-completeness, as a special case of completeness in general, is postponed to Chapter 10. This chapter is somewhat advanced and relies heavily on more than one variant of the Turing machine model of computation. This chapter is concerned with the classification of problems based on the amount of time and space needed to solve a particular problem. First, the two variants of Turing machines, one for measuring time and the other for space, are introduced. Next, the most prominent time and space classes are defined, and the relationships among them are studied. This is followed by defining the technique of transformation or reduction in the context of Turing machines. The notion of completeness in general is then addressed with the help of some examples. Finally, the chapter closes with a preview of the polynomial time hierarchy.

Chapter 11 is concerned with establishing lower bounds for various problems. In this chapter, two models of computations are used for that purpose. First, the decision tree model is used to establish lower bounds for comparison-based problems like searching and sorting. Next, the more powerful algebraic decision tree model is used to establish lower bounds for some other problems. Some of these problems belong to the field of computational geometry, namely the convex hull problem, the closest pair problem and the Euclidean minimum spanning tree problem.

Chapter 9

NP-Complete Problems

9.1 Introduction

In the previous chapters, we have been working mostly with the design and analysis of those algorithms for which the running time can be expressed in terms of a polynomial of *low* degree, say 3. In this chapter, we turn our attention to a class of problems for which no efficient algorithms have been found. Moreover, it is unlikely that an efficient algorithm will someday be discovered for any one of these problems. Let Π be any problem. We say that there exists a polynomial time algorithm to solve problem Π if there exists an algorithm for Π whose time complexity is $O(n^k)$, where n is the input size and k is a nonnegative integer. It turns out that many of the interesting real-world problems do not fall into this category, as their solution requires an amount of time that is measured in terms of exponential and hyperexponential functions, e.g., 2^n and $n!$. It has been agreed upon in the computer science community to refer to those problems for which there exist polynomial time algorithms as *tractable* and those for which it is unlikely that there exist polynomial time algorithms as *intractable*.

In this chapter, we will study a *subclass* of intractable problems, commonly referred to as the class of NP-complete problems. This class contains, among many others, hundreds of well-known problems having the common property that if one of them is solvable in polynomial time, then all the others are solvable in polynomial time. Interestingly, many of these are natural problems in the sense that they arise in real-world applications. Moreover, the running times of the existing algorithms to solve these problems are invariably measured in terms of hundreds or thousands of years for inputs of moderate size (see Table 1.1 on page 22).

When studying the theory of NP-completeness, it is easier to restate a problem so that its solution has only two outcomes: *yes* or *no*. In this case, the problem is called a *decision problem*. In contrast, an *optimization problem* is a problem that is concerned with the minimization or maximization of a certain quantity. In the previous chapters, we have encountered numerous optimization problems, like finding the minimum or maximum in a list of elements, finding the shortest path in a directed graph and computing a minimum cost spanning tree of an undirected graph. In the following, we give three examples of how to formulate a problem as a decision problem and an optimization problem.

Example 9.1 Let S be a sequence of real numbers. The ELEMENT UNIQUENESS problem asks whether all the numbers in S are distinct. Rephrased as a decision problem, we have

Decision problem: ELEMENT UNIQUENESS.
Input: A sequence S of integers.
Question: Are there two elements in S that are equal?
Stated as an optimization problem, we are interested in finding an element in S of highest frequency. For instance, if $S = 1, 5, 4, 5, 6, 5, 4$, then 5 is of highest frequency since it appears in the sequence 3 times, which is maximum. Let us call this optimization version ELEMENT COUNT. This version can be stated as follows.

Optimization problem: ELEMENT COUNT.
Input: A sequence S of integers.
Output: An element in S of highest frequency.
This problem can be solved in optimal $O(n \log n)$ time in the obvious way, which means it is tractable.

Example 9.2 Given an undirected graph $G = (V, E)$, a coloring of G using k colors is an assignment of one of k colors to each vertex in V in such a way that no two adjacent vertices have the same color. The coloring problem asks whether it is possible to color an undirected graph using a specified number of colors. Formulated as a decision problem, we have

Decision problem: COLORING.
Input: An undirected graph $G = (V, E)$ and a positive integer $k \geq 1$.
Question: Is G k-colorable?, i.e., can G be colored using *at most* k colors?
This problem is intractable. If k is restricted to 3, the problem reduces to the well-known 3-COLORING problem, which is also intractable even when the graph is planar.

An optimization version of this problem asks for the *minimum* number of colors needed to color a graph in such a way that no two adjacent vertices have the same color. This number, denoted by $\chi(G)$, is called the *chromatic number* of G.

Optimization problem: CHROMATIC NUMBER.
Input: An undirected graph $G = (V, E)$.
Output: The chromatic number of G.

Example 9.3 Given an undirected graph $G = (V, E)$, a *clique* of size k in G, for some positive integer k, is a complete subgraph of G with k vertices. The clique problem asks whether an undirected graph contains a clique of a specified size. Rephrased as a decision problem, we have

Decision problem: CLIQUE.
Input: An undirected graph $G = (V, E)$ and a positive integer k.
Question: Does G have a clique of size k?
The optimization version of this problem asks for the *maximum* number k such that G contains a clique of size k but no clique of size $k + 1$. We will call this problem MAX-CLIQUE.

Optimization problem: MAX-CLIQUE.
Input: An undirected graph $G = (V, E)$.
Output: A positive integer k, which is the maximum clique size in G.

If we have an efficient algorithm that solves a decision problem, then it can easily be modified to solve its corresponding optimization problem. For instance, if we have an algorithm A that solves the decision problem for graph coloring, we can find the chromatic number of a graph G using binary search and Algorithm A as a subroutine. Clearly, $1 \leq \chi(G) \leq n$, where n is the number of vertices in G. Hence, the chromatic number of G can be found using only $O(\log n)$ calls to algorithm A. Because of this reason, in the study of NP-complete problems, and computational complexity or even computability in general, it is easier to restrict one's attention to decision problems.

It is customary in the study of NP-completeness, or computational complexity in general, to adopt a formal model of computation, such as the Turing machine model of computation, as it makes the topic more formal and the proofs more rigorous. In this chapter, however, we will work with the abstract notion of "algorithm", and will not attempt to formalize it by associating it with any model of computation. A more formal treatment that uses the Turing machine as a model of computation can be found in Chapter 10.

9.2 The Class P

Definition 9.1 Let A be an algorithm to solve a problem Π. We say that A is *deterministic* if, when presented with an instance of the problem Π, it has only one choice in each step throughout its execution. Thus, if A is run again and again on the same input instance, its output never changes.

All algorithms we have covered in the previous chapters are deterministic. The modifier "deterministic" will mostly be dropped if it is understood from the context.

Definition 9.2 The *class* of decision problems P consists of those decision problems whose *yes/no* solution can be obtained using a *deterministic algorithm* that runs in polynomial number of steps, i.e., in $O(n^k)$ steps, for some nonnegative integer k, where n is the input size.

We have encountered numerous such problems in the previous chapters. Since in this chapter, we are dealing with decision problems, we list here some of the decision problems in the class P. The solutions to these problems should be fairly easy.

SORTING: Given a list of n integers, are they sorted in nondecreasing order?
SET DISJOINTNESS: Given two sets of integers, is their intersection empty?
SHORTEST PATH: Given a directed graph $G = (V, E)$ with positive weights on its edges, two distinguished vertices $s, t \in V$ and a positive integer k, is there a path from s to t whose length is at most k?

2-COLORING: Given an undirected graph G, is it 2-colorable?, i.e., can its vertices be colored using only 2 colors such that no two adjacent vertices are assigned the same color? Note that G is 2-colorable if and only if it is bipartite, that is, if and only if it does not contain cycles of odd length (see Sec. 2.3).

2-SAT: Given a boolean expression f in conjunctive normal form (CNF), where each clause consists of exactly two literals, is f satisfiable? (see Sec. 9.4.1).

We say that a class of problems C is *closed under complementation* if for any problem $\Pi \in C$, the complement of Π is also in C. For instance, the complement of the 2-COLORING problem can be stated as follows. Given a graph G, is it *not* 2-colorable? Let us call this problem NOT-2-COLOR. We can show that it is in P as follows. Since 2-COLORING is in P, there is a deterministic algorithm A which when presented with a 2-colorable graph halts and answers *yes* and when presented with a graph that is not 2-colorable halts and answers *no*. We can simply design a deterministic algorithm for the problem NOT-2-COLOR by simply interchanging the *yes* and *no* answers in Algorithm A. This, informally, proves the following fundamental theorem:

Theorem 9.1 *The class* P *is closed under complementation.*

9.3 The Class NP

The class NP consists of those problems Π for which there exists a *deterministic* algorithm A which, when presented with a claimed solution to an instance of Π, will be able to verify its correctness *in polynomial time*. That is, if the claimed solution leads to a *yes* answer, there is a way to *verify* this solution in polynomial time.

In order to define this class less informally, we must first define the concept of a *nondeterministic algorithm*. On input x, a nondeterministic algorithm consists of two phases:

(1) The *guessing phase*: In this phase, an arbitrary string of characters y is generated. It may correspond to a solution to the input instance or not. In fact, it may not even be in the proper format of the desired solution. It may differ from one run to another of the nondeterministic algorithm.

It is only required that this string be generated in a polynomial number of steps, i.e., in $O(n^i)$ time, where $n = |x|$ and i is a nonnegative integer. In many problems, this phase can be accomplished in linear time.

(2) The *verification phase*: In this phase, a *deterministic* algorithm verifies two things. First, it checks whether the generated solution string y is in the proper format. If it is not, then the algorithm halts with the answer *no*. If, on the other hand, y is in the proper format, then the algorithm continues to check whether it is a solution to the instance x of the problem. If it is indeed a solution to the instance x, then it halts and answers *yes*; otherwise, it halts and answers no. It is also required that this phase be completed in a polynomial number of steps, i.e., in $O(n^j)$ time, where j is a nonnegative integer.

Let A be a nondeterministic algorithm for a problem Π. We say that A *accepts* an instance I of Π if and only if on input I there is a guess that leads to a *yes* answer. In other words, A accepts I if and only if it is possible on some run of the algorithm that its verification phase will answer *yes*. It should be emphasized that if the algorithm answers *no*, then this does not mean that A does *not* accept its input, as the algorithm might have guessed an incorrect solution.

As to the running time of a (nondeterministic) algorithm, it is simply the sum of the two running times: the one for the guessing phase and that for the verification phase. So, it is $O(n^i) + O(n^j) = O(n^k)$, for some nonnegative integer k.

Definition 9.3   The *class* of decision problems NP consists of those decision problems for which there exists a nondeterministic algorithm that runs in polynomial time.

Example 9.4   Consider the problem COLORING. We show that this problem belongs to the class NP in two ways.

(1) The first method is as follows. Let I be an instance of the problem COLORING. Let s be a claimed solution to I. It is easy to construct a *deterministic* algorithm that tests whether s is indeed a solution to I. It follows by our *informal* definition of the class NP that the problem COLORING belongs to the class NP.

(2) The second method is to construct a nondeterministic algorithm for this problem. An algorithm A can easily be constructed that does the following when presented with an encoding of a graph G. First, A "guesses" a solution by generating an arbitrary assignment of the colors to the set of vertices. Next, A verifies that the guess is a valid assignment. If it is a valid assignment, then A halts and answers *yes*; otherwise, it halts and answers *no*. First, note that according to the definition of a nondeterministic algorithm, A answers *yes* only if the answer to the instance of the problem is *yes*. Second, regarding the operation time needed, A spends no more than polynomial time in both the guessing and verification phases.

We have the following distinction between the two important classes P and NP:

- P is the class of decision problems that we can *decide* or *solve* using a deterministic algorithm that runs in polynomial time.
- NP is the class of decision problems that we can *check* or *verify* their solution using a deterministic algorithm that runs in polynomial time. Equivalently, NP is the class of decision problems solvable by nondeterministic polynomial time algorithms.

9.4 NP-Complete Problems

The term "NP-complete" denotes the subclass of decision problems in NP that are hardest in the sense that if one of them is proven to be solvable by a polynomial time deterministic algorithm, then all problems in NP are solvable by a polynomial time deterministic algorithm, i.e., NP = P. For proving that a problem is NP-complete, we need the following definition.

Definition 9.4   Let Π and Π' be two decision problems. We say that Π *reduces to Π' in polynomial time*, symbolized as $\Pi \propto_{poly} \Pi'$, if there exists a *deterministic* algorithm A that behaves as follows. When A is presented with an instance I of problem Π, it transforms it into an instance I' of problem Π' such that the answer to I is *yes* if and only if the answer to I' is *yes*. Moreover, this transformation must be achieved in polynomial time.

Definition 9.5   A decision problem Π is said to be NP hard if for every problem Π' in NP, $\Pi' \propto_{poly} \Pi$.

Definition 9.6   A decision problem Π is said to be NP-complete if

(1) Π is in NP, and
(2) for every problem Π' in NP, $\Pi' \propto_{poly} \Pi$.

Thus, the difference between an NP-complete problem Π and an NP-hard problem Π' is that Π must be in the class NP whereas Π' may not be in NP.

9.4.1   *The satisfiability problem*

Given a boolean formula f, we say that it is in conjunctive normal form (CNF) if it is the conjunction of clauses. A clause is the disjunction of literals, where a literal is a boolean variable or its negation. An example of such a formula is

$$f = (x_1 \vee x_2) \wedge (\overline{x_1} \vee x_3 \vee x_4 \vee \overline{x_5}) \wedge (x_1 \vee \overline{x_3} \vee x_4).$$

A formula is said to be *satisfiable* if there is a truth assignment to its variables that makes it *true*. For example, the above formula is satisfiable, since it evaluates to *true* under any assignment in which both x_1 and x_3 are set to *true*.

Decision problem: SATISFIABILITY.
Input: A CNF boolean formula f.
Question: Is f satisfiable?

The satisfiability problem was the first problem proven to be NP-complete. Being the first NP-complete problem, there was no other NP-complete problem that reduces to it. Therefore, the proof was to show that *all* problems in the class NP can be reduced to it in polynomial time. In other words, the essence of the proof is to show that any problem in NP can be solved by a polynomial time algorithm that uses the satisfiability problem as a subroutine that is invoked by the algorithm *exactly once*. The proof consists of constructing a boolean formula f in conjunctive normal form for an instance I of Π such that there is a truth assignment that satisfies f if and only if a nondeterministic algorithm A for the problem Π accepts the instance I. f is constructed so that it "simulates" the computation of A on instance I. This, informally, implies the following fundamental theorem.

Theorem 9.2   SATISFIABILITY *is NP-complete.*

9.4.2   *Proving NP-completeness*

The following theorem states that the reducibility relation $\propto_P$ is transitive. This is necessary to show that other problems are NP-complete as well. We explain this as follows. Suppose that for some problem Π in NP we can prove that SATISFIABILITY reduces to Π in polynomial time. By the above theorem, all problems in NP reduce to SATISFIABILITY in polynomial time. Consequently, if the reducibility relation $\propto_P$ is transitive, then this implies that *all* problems in NP reduce to Π in polynomial time.

Theorem 9.3   *Let* Π, Π' *and* Π'' *be three decision problems such that* $\Pi \propto_{poly} \Pi'$ *and* $\Pi' \propto_{poly} \Pi''$. *Then,* $\Pi \propto_{poly} \Pi''$.

Proof.   Let A be an algorithm that realizes the reduction $\Pi \propto_{poly} \Pi'$ in $p(n)$ steps for some polynomial p. Let B be an algorithm that realizes the reduction $\Pi' \propto_{poly} \Pi''$ in $q(n)$ steps for some polynomial q. Let x be an input to A of size n. Clearly, the size of the output of algorithm A when presented with input x cannot exceed $cp(n)$, as the algorithm can output at most c symbols in each step of its execution for some positive integer $c > 0$. If algorithm B is presented with an input of size $p(n)$ or less, its running time is, by definition, $O(q(cp(n))) = O(r(n))$ for some polynomial r. It follows that the reduction from Π to Π' followed by the reduction from Π' to Π'' is a polynomial time reduction from Π to Π''. $\square$

Corollary 9.1   *If* Π *and* Π' *are two problems in* NP *such that* $\Pi' \propto_{poly} \Pi$, *and* Π' *is NP-complete, then* Π *is NP-complete.*

Proof.   Since Π' is NP-complete, every problem in NP reduces to Π' in polynomial time. Since $\Pi' \propto_{poly} \Pi$, then by Theorem 9.3, every problem in NP reduces to Π in polynomial time. It follows that Π is NP-complete. $\square$

By the above corollary, to prove that a problem Π is NP-complete, we only need to show that

(1) $\Pi \in$ NP, and
(2) there is an NP-complete problem Π' such that $\Pi' \propto_{poly} \Pi$.

Example 9.5   Consider the following two problems.

(1) **The problem** HAMILTONIAN CYCLE: Given an undirected graph
    $G = (V, E)$, does it have a Hamiltonian cycle, i.e., a cycle that visits
    each vertex exactly once?
(2) **The problem** TRAVELING SALESMAN: Given a set of n cities with
    their intercity distances, and an integer k, does there exist a *tour* of
    length at most k? Here, a tour is a cycle that visits each city *exactly*
    once.

It is well known that the problem HAMILTONIAN CYCLE is NP-complete.
We will use this fact to show that the problem TRAVELING SALESMAN is
also NP-complete.

The first step in the proof is to show that TRAVELING SALESMAN is in
NP. This is very simple, since a nondeterministic algorithm can start by
guessing a sequence of cities, and then verifies that this sequence is a tour.
If this is the case, it then continues to see if the length of the tour is at
most k, the given bound.

The second step is to show that HAMILTONIAN CYCLE can be reduced
to TRAVELING SALESMAN in polynomial time, i.e.,

$$\text{HAMILTONIAN CYCLE} \propto_{poly} \text{TRAVELING SALESMAN}.$$

Let G be any arbitrary instance of HAMILTONIAN CYCLE. We construct a
weighted graph G' and a bound k such that G has a Hamiltonian cycle if
and only if G' has a tour of total length at most k. Let $G = (V, E)$. We let
$G' = (V, E')$ be the complete graph on the set of vertices V, i.e.,

$$E' = \{(u, v) \mid u, v \in V\}.$$

Next, we assign a length to each edge in E' as follows:

$$l(e) = \begin{cases} 1 & \text{if } e \in E \\ n & \text{if } e \notin E, \end{cases}$$

where $n = |V|$. Finally, we assign $k = n$. It is easy to see from the construc-
tion that G has a Hamiltonian cycle if and only if G' has a tour of length
exactly n. It should be emphasized that the assignment $k = n$ is *part of the
reduction*.

9.4.3 3-*Satisfiability*

The problem 3-SAT is defined as follows. Given a boolean formula f in conjunctive normal form such that each clause consists of exactly three literals, is f satisfiable? 3-SAT is very useful as it is much easier to prove many problems to be NP-complete by reducing from 3-SAT rather than from SATISFIABILITY.

Theorem 9.4 3-SAT *is NP-complete.*

Proof. It is straightforward to prove that 3-SAT is in NP. We prove that SATISFIABILITY $\propto_{poly}$ 3-SAT. Given an instance of SATISFIABILITY $f = C_1 \wedge C_2 \wedge \cdots \wedge C_m$ with m clauses and n boolean variables $x_1, x_2, \ldots, x_n$, we construct an instance of 3-SAT $f' = C_1' \wedge C_2' \wedge \cdots \wedge C_{m'}'$ of 3-literal clauses with the property that f is satisfiable if and only if f' is satisfiable. Moreover, $m' = O(p(m))$ for some polynomial p. We convert each clause C_j, $1 \le j \le m$, into one or more 3-literal clauses as follows. For this purpose, we introduce new literals $y_1^j, y_2^j, \ldots$. Let C_j be $(x_1, x_2, \ldots, x_k)$. We have four cases depending on the value of k.

$k = 1$. $C_j = (x_1)$ is converted to four clauses:

$$(x_1 \vee y_1^j \vee y_2^j)(x_1 \vee y_1^j \vee \overline{y_2^j})(x_1 \vee \overline{y_1^j} \vee y_2^j)(x_1 \vee \overline{y_1^j} \vee \overline{y_2^j}).$$

$k = 2$. $C_j = (x_1, x_2)$ is converted to two clauses:

$$(x_1 \vee x_1 \vee y_1^j)(x_1 \vee x_1 \vee \overline{y_1^j}).$$

$k = 3$. $C_j' = C_j$.
$k = 4$. $C_j = (x_1, x_2, x_3, x_4)$ is converted to the two clauses:

$$(x_1 \vee x_2 \vee y_1^j)(\overline{y_1^j} \vee x_3 \vee x_4).$$

$k > 4$. $C_j = (x_1, x_2, \ldots, x_k)$ is converted to the clauses:

$$(x_1 \vee x_2 \vee y_1^j)(\overline{y_1^j} \vee x_3 \vee y_2^j)(\overline{y_2^j} \vee x_3 \vee y_3^j) \ldots (\overline{y_{k-2}^j} \vee x_{k-2} \vee y_{k-3}^j)(\overline{y_{k-3}^j} \vee x_{k-1} \vee x_k).$$

$\square$

9.4.4 *Vertex cover, independent set and clique problems*

In this section, we prove the NP-completeness of three famous problems in graph theory.

CLIQUE: Given an undirected graph $G = (V, E)$ and a positive integer k, does G contain a clique of size k? (recall that a clique in G of size k is a complete subgraph of G on k vertices).

VERTEX COVER: Given an undirected graph $G = (V, E)$ and a positive integer k, is there a subset $C \subseteq V$ of size k such that each edge in E is incident to at least one vertex in C?

INDEPENDENT SET: Given an undirected graph $G = (V, E)$ and a positive integer k, does there exist a subset $S \subseteq V$ of k vertices such that for each pair of vertices $u, w \in S, (u, w) \notin E$?

It is easy to show that all these three problems are indeed in NP. In what follows, we give reductions that establish their NP-completeness.

SATISFIABILITY $\propto_{poly}$ CLIQUE

Given an instance of SATISFIABILITY $f = C_1 \wedge C_2 \wedge \cdots \wedge C_m$ with m clauses and n boolean variables $x_1, x_2, \ldots, x_n$, we construct a graph $G = (V, E)$, where V is the set of all *occurrences* of the $2n$ literals (recall that a literal is a boolean variable or its negation), and

$$E = \{(x_i, x_j) \mid x_i \quad \text{and} \quad x_j \text{ are in two different clauses and } x_i \neq \overline{x_j}\}.$$

It is easy to see that the above construction can be accomplished in polynomial time.

Example 9.6   An example of the reduction is provided in Fig. 9.1. Here, the instance of SATISFIABILITY is

$$f = (x \vee \overline{y} \vee z) \wedge (\overline{x} \vee y) \wedge (\overline{x} \vee \overline{y} \vee z).$$

Lemma 9.1   *f is satisfiable if and only if G has a clique of size m.*

Proof.   A clique of size m corresponds to an assignment of *true* to m literals in m different clauses. An edge between two literals a and b means that there is no contradiction when both a and b are assigned the value *true*. It follows that f is satisfiable if and only if there is a noncontradictory assignment of *true* to m literals in m different clauses if and only if G has a clique of size m. $\qquad \Box$

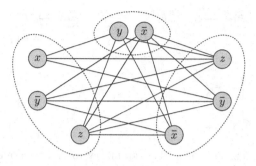

Fig. 9.1. Reducing SATISFIABILITY to CLIQUE.

SATISFIABILITY $\propto_{poly}$ VERTEX COVER

Given an instance I of SATISFIABILITY, we transform it into an instance I' of VERTEX COVER. Let I be the formula $f = C_1 \wedge C_2 \wedge \cdots \wedge C_m$ with m clauses and n boolean variables $x_1, x_2, \ldots, x_n$. We construct I' as follows:

(1) For each boolean variable x_i in f, G contains a pair of vertices x_i and $\overline{x_i}$ joined by an edge.
(2) For each clause C_j containing n_j literals, G contains a clique C_j of size n_j.
(3) For each vertex w in C_j, there is an edge connecting w to its corresponding literal in the vertex pairs $(x_i, \overline{x_i})$ constructed in part (1). Call these edges *connection edges*.
(4) Let $k = n + \sum_{j=1}^{m}(n_j - 1)$.

It is easy to see that the above construction can be accomplished in polynomial time.

Example 9.7   An example of the reduction is provided in Fig. 9.2. Here, the instance I is the formula

$$f = (x \vee \overline{y} \vee \overline{z}) \wedge (\overline{x} \vee y).$$

It should be emphasized that the instance I' is not only the figure shown; it also includes the integer $k = 3 + 2 + 1 = 6$. A boolean assignment of $x = true, y = true$ and $z = false$ satisfies f. This assignment corresponds to the 6 covering vertices shown shaded in the figure.

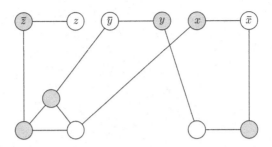

Fig. 9.2.   Reducing SATISFIABILITY to VERTEX COVER.

Lemma 9.2 f *is satisfiable if and only if the constructed graph has a vertex cover of size* k.

Proof. $\Rightarrow$: If x_i is assigned *true*, add vertex x_i to the vertex cover; otherwise, add $\overline{x_i}$ to the vertex cover. Since f is satisfiable, in each clique C_j there is a vertex u whose corresponding literal v has been assigned the value *true*, and thus the connection edge (u, v) is covered. Therefore, add the other $n_j - 1$ vertices in each clique C_j to the vertex cover. Clearly, the size of the vertex cover is $k = n + \sum_{j=1}^{m}(n_j - 1)$.

$\Leftarrow$: Suppose that the graph can be covered with k vertices. At least one vertex of each edge $(x_i, \overline{x_i})$ must be in the cover. We are left with $k - n = \sum_{j=1}^{m}(n_j - 1)$ vertices. It is not hard to see that any cover of a clique of size n_j must have at least $n_j - 1$ vertices. So, in each clique, the cover must include all its vertices except the one that is incident to a connection edge that is covered by a vertex in some vertex pair $(x_i, \overline{x_i})$. To see that f is satisfiable, for each vertex x_i, if it is in the cover, then let $x_i = true$; otherwise, (if $\overline{x_i}$ is in the cover), let $x_i = false$. Thus, in each clique, there must be one vertex which is connected to a vertex x_i or $\overline{x_i}$, which is assigned the value *true* since it is in the cover. It follows that each clause has at least one literal whose value is *true*, i.e., f is satisfiable. $\Box$

VERTEX COVER $\propto_{poly}$ INDEPENDENT SET

The transformation from VERTEX COVER to INDEPENDENT SET is straightforward. The following lemma provides the reduction:

Lemma 9.3   *Let* $G = (V, E)$ *be a connected undirected graph. Then,* $S \subseteq V$ *is an independent set if and only if* $V - S$ *is a vertex cover in* G.

Proof. Let $e = (u, v)$ be any edge in G. S is an independent set if and only if at least one of u or v is in $V - S$, i.e., $V - S$ is a vertex cover in G. □

A simple reduction from VERTEX COVER to CLIQUE is left as an exercise (Exercise 9.6). A reduction from INDEPENDENT SET to CLIQUE is straightforward since a clique in a graph G is an independent set in $\overline{G}$, the complement of G. Thus, we have the following theorem:

Theorem 9.5 *The problems* VERTEX COVER, INDEPENDENT SET *and* CLIQUE *are NP-complete.*

Proof. It is fairly easy to show that these problems are in the class NP. The above reductions whose proofs are given in Lemmas 9.1–9.3 complete the proof. □

9.4.5 *More NP-complete problems*

The following is a list of additional NP-complete problems.

(1) 3-COLORING: Given an undirected graph $G = (V, E)$, can G be colored using three colors? This problem is a special case of the more general problem COLORING stated on page 267, which is known to be NP-complete.

(2) Three-dimensional matching: Let X, Y and Z be pairwise disjoint sets of size k each. Let W be the set of triples $\{(x, y, z) \mid x \in X, y \in Y, z \in Z\}$. Does there exist a *perfect matching* M of W? That is, does there exist a subset $M \subseteq W$ of size k such that no two triplets in M agree in any coordinate? The corresponding two-dimensional matching problem is the regular perfect bipartite matching problem (see Chapter 16).

(3) HAMILTONIAN PATH: Given an undirected graph $G = (V, E)$, does it contain a simple open path that visits each vertex exactly once?

(4) PARTITION: Given a set S of n integers, is it possible to partition S into two subsets S_1 and S_2 so that the sum of the integers in S_1 is equal to the sum of the integers in S_2?

(5) KNAPSACK: Given n items with sizes $s_1, s_2, \ldots, s_n$ and values $v_1, v_2, \ldots, v_n$, a knapsack capacity C and a constant integer k, is it possible to fill the knapsack with some of these items whose total size is at most C and whose total value is at least k? This problem can be

solved in time $\Theta(nC)$ using dynamic programming (Theorem 6.3). This is polynomial in the input value but exponential in the input size.

(6) BIN PACKING: Given n items with sizes $s_1, s_2, \ldots, s_n$, a bin capacity C and a positive integer k, is it possible to pack the n items using at most k bins?

(7) SET COVER: Given a set X, a family $\mathcal{F}$ of subsets of X and an integer k between 1 and $|\mathcal{F}|$, do there exist k subsets in $\mathcal{F}$ whose union is X?

(8) MULTIPROCESSOR SCHEDULING: Given n jobs $J_1, J_2, \ldots, J_n$ each having a run time t_i, a positive integer m (number of processors) and a finishing time T, can these jobs be scheduled on m identical processors so that their finishing time is at most T? The finishing time is defined to be the maximum execution time among all the m processors.

(9) LONGEST PATH: Given a weighted graph $G = (V, E)$, two distinguished vertices $s, t \in V$ and a positive integer c, is there a *simple* path in G from s to t of length c or more?

9.5 The Class co-NP

The class co-NP consists of those problems whose complements are in NP. One might suspect that the class co-NP is comparable in hardness to the class NP. It turns out, however, that this is highly unlikely, which supports the conjecture that co-NP $\neq$ NP. Consider, for example, the complement of TRAVELING SALESMAN: Given n cities with their intercity distances, is it the case that there does *not* exist any tour of length k or less? It seems that there is no *nondeterministic* algorithm that solves this problem without exhausting all the $(n-1)!$ possibilities. As another example, consider the complement of SATISFIABILITY: Given a formula f, is it the case that there is *no* assignment of truth values to its boolean variables that satisfies f? In other words, is f unsatisfiable? There does not seem to be a nondeterministic algorithm that solves this problem without inspecting all the 2^n assignments, where n is the number of boolean variables in f.

Definition 9.7 A problem Π is complete for the class co-NP if

(1) Π is in co-NP, and
(2) for every problem Π' in co-NP, $\Pi' \propto_{poly} \Pi$.

Let some deterministic algorithm A realize a reduction from one problem Π' to another problem Π, both in NP. Recall that, by definition of reduction, A is *deterministic* and runs in polynomial time. Therefore, by Theorem 9.1, A is also a reduction from $\overline{\Pi'}$ to $\overline{\Pi}$, where $\overline{\Pi}$ and $\overline{\Pi'}$ are the complements of Π and Π', respectively. This implies the following theorem:

Theorem 9.6 *A problem Π is NP-complete if and only if its complement, $\overline{\Pi}$, is complete for the class co-NP.*

In particular, since SATISFIABILITY is NP-complete, the complement of SATISFIABILITY is complete for the class co-NP. It is not known whether the class co-NP is closed under complementation. It follows, however, that the complement of SATISFIABILITY is in NP if and only if NP is closed under complementation.

A CNF formula f is unsatisfiable if and only if its negation is a tautology (A formula f is called a *tautology* if f is *true* under all truth assignments to its boolean variables). The negation of a CNF formula $C_1 \wedge C_2 \wedge \cdots \wedge C_k$, where $C_i = (x_1 \vee x_2 \vee \cdots \vee x_{m_i})$, for all $i, 1 \le i \le k$, can be converted into a disjunctive normal form (DNF) formula $C_1' \vee C_2' \vee \cdots \vee C_k'$, where $C_i' = (y_1 \wedge y_2 \wedge \cdots \wedge y_{m_i})$, for all $i, 1 \le i \le k$, using the identities

$$\overline{(C_1 \wedge C_2 \wedge \cdots \wedge C_k)} = (\overline{C_1} \vee \overline{C_2} \vee \cdots \vee \overline{C_k})$$

and

$$\overline{(x_1 \vee x_2 \vee \cdots \vee x_{m_i})} = (\overline{x_1} \wedge \overline{x_2} \wedge \cdots \wedge \overline{x_{m_i}}).$$

The resulting DNF formula is a tautology if and only if the negation of the CNF formula is a tautology. Therefore, we have the following theorem:

Theorem 9.7 *The problem* TAUTOLOGY: *Given a formula f in DNF, is it a tautology? is it complete for the class co-NP.*

It follows that

- TAUTOLOGY is in P if and only if co-NP = P, and
- TAUTOLOGY is in NP if and only if co-NP = NP.

The following theorem is fundamental. Its simple proof is left as an exercise (Exercise 9.19).

Theorem 9.8   *If a problem* Π *and its complement* $\overline{\Pi}$ *are NP-complete, then co-NP = NP.*

In other words, If both a problem Π and its complement are NP-complete, then the class NP is closed under complementation. As discussed before, this is highly unlikely, and it is an open question. In fact, it is stronger than the NP ≠ P question. The reason is that if we can prove that co-NP ≠ NP, then it follows immediately that NP ≠ P. For suppose it has been proven that co-NP ≠ NP, and assume for the sake of contradiction that NP = P. Then, substituting P for NP in the proven result, we obtain co-P ≠ P. But this contradicts the fact that P is closed under complementation (Theorem 9.1). This contradiction implies that NP ≠ P.

9.6   The Relationships between the Three Classes

Figure 9.3 shows the relationships between the three classes we have discussed in this chapter. From the figure, it is clear that P lies in the intersection of NP and co-NP, assuming that NP ≠ co-NP.

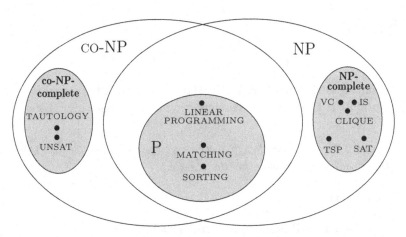

Fig. 9.3.   The relationships between the three complexity classes.

9.7 Practice Problems

9.1. Give an efficient algorithm to solve the decision version of the problem SORTING stated on page 268. What is the time complexity of your algorithm?

9.2. Give an efficient algorithm to solve the problem SET DISJOINTNESS stated on page 268. What is the time complexity of your algorithm?

9.3. Design a polynomial time algorithm for the problem 2-COLORING defined on page 269. (*Hint:* Color the first vertex white, all adjacent vertices black, etc.)

9.4. Let I be an instance of the problem COLORING, and let s be a claimed solution to I. Describe a deterministic algorithm to test whether s is a solution to I.

9.5. Design a nondeterministic algorithm to solve the problem SATISFIABILITY.

9.6. Design a nondeterministic algorithm to solve the problem TRAVELING SALESMAN.

9.7. Convert the following instance of SATISFIABILITY into an instance of 3-SAT:

(a) $(x_1 \vee x_2 \vee \overline{x_3}) \wedge (\overline{x_1} \vee x_3)$

(b) $(x_1 \vee \overline{x_2}) \wedge (\overline{x_1} \vee \overline{x_2})$

(c) $(x_1) \wedge (\overline{x_2} \vee \overline{x_3}) \wedge (\overline{x_1} \vee x_2 \vee x_3 \vee x_4 \vee \overline{x_5})$

9.8. Consider the following instance of SATISFIABILITY:

$$(x_1 \vee x_2 \vee \overline{x_3}) \wedge (\overline{x_1} \vee x_3) \wedge (\overline{x_2} \vee x_3) \wedge (\overline{x_1} \vee \overline{x_2})$$

(a) Following the reduction method from SATISFIABILITY to CLIQUE, transform the above formula into an instance of CLIQUE for which the answer is *yes* if and only if the above formula is satisfiable.

(b) Find a clique of size 4 in your graph and convert it into a satisfying assignment for the formula given above.

9.9. Consider the formula f given in Problem 9.8.

(a) Following the reduction method from SATISFIABILITY to VERTEX COVER, transform f into an instance of VERTEX COVER for which the answer is *yes* if and only if f is satisfiable.

(b) Find a vertex cover in your graph and convert it into a satisfying assignment for f.

9.8 Exercises

9.1. Let Π_1 and Π_2 be two problems such that $\Pi_1 \propto_{poly} \Pi_2$. Suppose that problem Π_2 can be solved in $O(n^k)$ time and the reduction can be done in $O(n^j)$ time. Show that problem Π_1 can be solved in $O(n^{jk})$ time.

9.2. Given that the Hamiltonian cycle problem for undirected graphs is NP-complete, show that the Hamiltonian cycle problem for directed graphs is also NP-complete.

9.3. Show that the problem BIN PACKING is NP-complete, assuming that the problem PARTITION is NP-complete.

9.4. Let Π_1 and Π_2 be two NP-complete problems. Prove or disprove that $\Pi_1 \propto_{poly} \Pi_2$.

9.5. Give a polynomial time algorithm to find a clique of size k in a given undirected graph $G = (V, E)$ with n vertices. Here, k is a *fixed* positive integer. Does this contradict the fact that the problem CLIQUE is NP-complete? Explain.

9.6. The NP-completeness of the problem CLIQUE was shown by reducing SATISFIABILITY to it. Give a simpler reduction from VERTEX COVER to CLIQUE.

9.7. Show that any cover of a clique of size n must have exactly $n - 1$ vertices.

9.8. Show that if one can devise a polynomial time algorithm for the problem SATISFIABILITY, then NP = P (see Exercise 9.1).

9.9. In Chapter 6, it was shown that the problem KNAPSACK can be solved in time $\Theta(nC)$, where n is the number of items and C is the knapsack capacity. However, it was mentioned in this chapter that it is NP-complete. Is there any contradiction? Explain.

9.10. When showing that an optimization problem is not harder than its decision problem version, it was justified by using binary search and

an algorithm for the decision problem in order to solve the optimization version. Will the justification still be valid if linear search is
used instead of binary search? Explain. (*Hint*: Consider the problem
TRAVELING SALESMAN.)

9.11. Prove that if an NP-complete problem Π is shown to be solvable in
polynomial time, then NP = P (see Exercises 9.1 and 9.8).

9.12. Prove that NP = P if and only if for some NP-complete problem Π,
Π ∈ P.

9.13. Is the problem LONGEST PATH NP-complete when the path is not
restricted to be simple? Prove your answer.

9.14. Is the problem LONGEST PATH NP-complete when restricted to
directed acyclic graphs? Prove your answer (see Exercises 9.13
and 6.24).

9.15. Show that the problem of finding a shortest *simple* path between two
vertices s and t in a directed or undirected graph is NP-complete if
the weights are allowed to be negative.

9.16. Show that the problem SET COVER is NP-complete by reducing the
problem VERTEX COVER to it.

9.17. Simplify the reduction from the problem SATISFIABILITY to VERTEX
COVER by using 3-SAT instead of SATISFIABILITY.

9.18. Compare the difficulty of the problem TAUTOLOGY to SATISFIABIL-
ITY. What does this imply about the difficulty of the class co-NP.

9.19. Prove Theorem 9.8.

9.9 Bibliographic Notes

The study of NP-completeness started with two papers. The first was the
seminal paper of Cook (1971) in which the problem SATISFIABILITY was
the first problem shown to be NP-complete. The second was Karp (1972)
in which a list of 24 problems were shown to be NP-complete. Both Stephen

Cook and Richard Karp have won the ACM Turing awards and their Turing award lectures were published in Cook (1983) and Karp (1986). Garey and Johnson (1979) provides comprehensive coverage of the theory of NP-completeness and covers the four basic complexity classes introduced in this chapter. Their book contains the proof that SATISFIABILITY is NP-complete and a list of several hundred NP-complete problems. One of the most famous of the open problems to be resolved is LINEAR PROGRAMMING. This problem has been proven to be solvable in polynomial time using the ellipsoid method (Khachiyan, 1979). It has received much attention, although its practical significance is yet to be determined. An introduction to the theory of NP-completeness can also be found in Aho *et al.* (1974) and Hopcroft and Ullman (1979).

Chapter 10

Introduction to Computational Complexity

10.1 Introduction

Computational complexity is concerned with the classification of problems based on the amount of time, space or any other resource needed to solve a problem, such as the number of processors and communication cost. In this chapter, we review some of the basic concepts in this field and confine our attention to the two classical resource measures: time and space.

10.2 Model of Computation: The Turing Machine

When studying computational complexity, a universal computing device is required for the classification of computational problems. It turns out that most, if not all, of the results are robust and are invariant under different models of computations. In this chapter, we will choose the *Turing machine* as our model of computation. In order to measure the amount of time and space needed to solve a problem, it will be much easier to consider those problems whose solution output is either *yes* or *no*. A problem of this type is called a *decision problem* (see Sec. 9.1). The set of instances of a decision problem is partitioned into two sets: those instances for which the answer is *yes* and those for which the answer is *no*. We can encode such problems as languages. An *alphabet* Σ is a finite set of symbols. A language L is simply a subset of the set of all finite length strings of symbols chosen from Σ, denoted by Σ^*. For example, a graph $G = (V, E)$, where $V = \{1, 2, \ldots, n\}$ can be encoded by the string $w(G) = (x_{11}, x_{12}, \ldots, x_{1n})(x_{21}, x_{22}, \ldots, x_{2n}) \cdots (x_{n1}, x_{n2}, \ldots, x_{nn})$, where $x_{ij} = 1$ if $(i, j) \in E$ and 0 otherwise. Thus, the encoded graph $w(G)$ is a string of symbols over the finite alphabet $\{0, 1, (,)\}$.

The standard Turing machine has only one worktape, which is divided into separate cells. Each cell of the worktape contains one symbol from some finite alphabet Σ. The Turing machine has the ability to read and rewrite the symbol contained in the cell of the worktape currently scanned by its worktape head. The worktape head moves either one cell to the left, one cell to the right, or it remains on the current cell at each step. The actions of the Turing machine are specified by its *finite state control*. A Turing machine at any moment of time is in some *state*. For the current state and for the current scanned symbol on the worktape, the finite state control specifies which actions are possible: It specifies which one of the states to enter next, which symbol to print on the scanned cell of the worktape, and in what way to move the worktape head.

10.3 k-Tape Turing Machines and Time Complexity

Since the standard Turing machine as described in the previous section can move its worktape head one cell per step, it clearly needs n steps to move the head n cells. In order to make an appropriate model of Turing machine adequately measure the amount of time used by an algorithm, we need to allow for more than one worktape. A k-*tape Turing machine*, for some $k \geq 1$, is just the natural extension of the one-tape Turing machine. It has k worktapes instead of just one, and it has k worktape heads. Each worktape head is associated with one of the worktapes and the heads can move independently from one another.

Definition 10.1 A (nondeterministic) k-tape Turing machine is a 6-tuple $M = (S, \Sigma, \Gamma, \delta, p_0, p_f)$, where

(1) S is a finite *set of states*,
(2) Γ is a finite *set of tape symbols* which includes the special symbol B (the blank symbol),
(3) $\Sigma \subseteq \Gamma - \{B\}$, the *set of input symbols*,

(4) δ, the *transition function*, is a function that maps elements of $S \times \Gamma^k$ into finite subsets of $S \times ((\Gamma - \{B\}) \times \{L, P, R\})^k$,

(5) $p_0 \in S$, the *initial* state, and

(6) $p_f \in S$, the *final* or *accepting* state.

Note that we have assumed without loss of generality that there is only one final state. A k-tape Turing machine $M = (S, \Sigma, \Gamma, \delta, p_0, p_f)$ is *deterministic* if for every $p \in S$ and for every $a_1, a_2, \ldots, a_k \in \Gamma$, the set $\delta(p, a_1, a_2, \ldots, a_k)$ contains *at most* one element.

Definition 10.2   Let $M = (S, \Sigma, \Gamma, \delta, p_0, p_f)$ be a k-tape Turing machine. A *configuration* of M is a $(k + 1)$-tuple

$$K = (p, w_{11}\uparrow w_{12}, w_{21}\uparrow w_{22}, \ldots, w_{k1}\uparrow w_{k2}),$$

where $p \in S$ and $w_{j1}\uparrow w_{j2}$ is the content of the jth tape of M, $1 \le j \le k$.

Here, the head of the jth tape is pointing to the first symbol in the string w_{j2}. If w_{j1} is empty, then the head is pointing to the first nonblank symbol on the tape. If w_{j2} is empty, then the head is pointing to the first blank symbol after the string w_{j1}. Both w_{j1} and w_{j2} may be empty, indicating that the tape is empty. This is the case in the beginning of the computation, where all tapes except possibly the input tape are empty. Thus, the *initial configuration* is denoted by

$$(p_0, \uparrow x, \uparrow B, \ldots, \uparrow B),$$

where x is the initial input. The set of *final or accepting configurations* is the set of all configurations

$$(p_f, w_{11}\uparrow w_{12}, w_{21}\uparrow w_{22}, \ldots, w_{k1}\uparrow w_{k2}).$$

Definition 10.3   A *computation* by a Turing machine M on input x is a sequence of configurations $K_1, K_2, \ldots, K_t$, for some $t \ge 1$, where K_1 is the initial configuration, and for all $i, 2 \le i \le t$, K_i results from K_{i-1} in one move of M. Here, t is referred to as the *length of the computation*. If K_t is a final configuration, then the computation is called an *accepting computation*.

Definition 10.4 The *time taken by a Turing machine M on input x*, denoted by $T_M(x)$, is defined as follows:

(1) If there is an accepting computation of M on input x, then $T_M(x)$ is the length of the shortest accepting computation, and
(2) If there is no accepting computation of M on input x, then $T_M(x) = \infty$.

Let L be a language and f a function from the set of nonnegative integers to the set of nonnegative integers. We say that L is in DTIME(f) (resp., NTIME(f)) if there exists a deterministic (resp., nondeterministic) Turing machine M that behaves as follows. On input x, if $x \in L$, then $T_M(x) \leq f(|x|)$; otherwise, $T_M(x) = \infty$. Similarly, we may define DTIME(n^k), NTIME(n^k) for any $k \geq 1$. The two classes P and NP discussed in Chapter 9 can now be defined formally as follows:

$$\text{P} = \text{DTIME}(n) \cup \text{DTIME}(n^2) \cup \text{DTIME}(n^3) \cup$$
$$\cdots \cup \text{DTIME}(n^k) \cup \cdots,$$

and

$$\text{NP} = \text{NTIME}(n) \cup \text{NTIME}(n^2) \cup \text{NTIME}(n^3) \cup$$
$$\cdots \cup \text{NTIME}(n^k) \cup \cdots.$$

In other words, P is the set of all languages recognizable in polynomial time using a deterministic Turing machine, and NP is the set of all languages recognizable in polynomial time using a nondeterministic Turing machine. We have seen many examples of problems in the class P in earlier chapters. We have also encountered several problems that belong to the class NP in Chapter 9. There are also other important time complexity classes; two of them are

$$\text{DEXT} = \bigcup_{c \geq 0} \text{DTIME}(2^{cn}), \quad \text{NEXT} = \bigcup_{c \geq 0} \text{NTIME}(2^{cn}),$$

$$\text{EXPTIME} = \bigcup_{c \geq 0} \text{DTIME}(2^{n^c}) \quad \text{NEXPTIME} = \bigcup_{c \geq 0} \text{NTIME}(2^{n^c}).$$

Example 10.1 Consider the following 1-tape Turing machine M that recognizes the language $L = \{a^n b^n \mid n \geq 1\}$. Initially, its tape contains the string $a^n b^n$. M repeats the following step until all symbols on the tape have been marked or M cannot move its tape head. M marks the leftmost unmarked symbol if it is an a and then moves its head all the way to the right and marks the rightmost unmarked symbol if it is a b. If the number of a's is equal to the number of b's, then all symbols on the tape will eventually be marked, and hence M will enter the accepting state. Otherwise, either the number of a's is less than or greater than the number of b's. If the number of a's is less than the number of b's, then after all the a's have been marked, and after marking the last b, the leftmost symbol is a b, and hence M will not be able to move its tape head. This will also be the case if the number of a's is greater than the number of b's. It is easy to see that if the input string is accepted, then the number of moves of the tape head is less than or equal to cn^2 for some constant $c > 0$. It follows that L is in DTIME(n^2).

10.4 Off-line Turing Machines and Space Complexity

For an appropriate measure of space, we need to separate the space used to store computed information. For example, to say that a Turing machine uses only $\lfloor \log n \rfloor$ of its worktape cells is possible only if we separate the input string and we do not count the n cells used to store the input string of length n. For this reason, our model of a Turing machine that will be used to measure space complexity will have a separate read-only input tape. The Turing machine is not permitted to rewrite the symbols that it scans on the input tape. This version of Turing machines is commonly referred to as an *off-line* Turing machine. The difference between a k-tape Turing machine and an off-line Turing machine is that an off-line Turing machine has exactly two tapes: a read-only *input* tape and a read-write *worktape*.

Definition 10.5 A (nondeterministic) *off-line* Turing machine is a 6-tuple $M = (S, \Sigma, \Gamma, \delta, p_0, p_f)$, where

(1) S is a finite *set of states,*
(2) Γ is a finite *set of tape symbols,* which includes the special symbol B (the blank symbol),
(3) $\Sigma \subseteq \Gamma - \{B\}$ is the *set of input symbols;* it contains two special symbols # and \$ (the *left endmarker* and the *right endmarker*, respectively),
(4) δ, the *transition function,* is a function that maps elements of $S \times \Sigma \times \Gamma$ into finite subsets of $S \times \{L, P, R\} \times (\Gamma - \{B\}) \times \{L, P, R\}$,
(5) $p_0 \in S$ is the *initial state,* and
(6) $p_f \in S$ is the *final* or *accepting* state.

Note that we have assumed without loss of generality that there is only one final state. The input is presented to an off-line Turing machine in its read-only tape enclosed by the endmarkers, $ and #, and it is never changed. In the case of off-line Turing machines, a configuration is defined by the 3-tuple

$$K = (p, i, w_1 \uparrow w_2),$$

where p is the current state, i is the cell number in the input tape pointed to by the input head and $w_1 \uparrow w_2$ is the contents of the worktape. Here, the head of the worktape is pointing to the first symbol of w_2.

Definition 10.6 The *space used by an off-line Turing machine M on input x*, denoted by $S_M(x)$, is defined as follows:

(1) If there is an accepting computation of M on input x, then $S_M(x)$ is the number of worktape cells used in an accepting computation that uses the *least* number of worktape cells, and

(2) If there is no accepting computation of M on input x, then $S_M(x) = \infty$.

Example 10.2 Consider the following Turing machine M that recognizes the language $L = \{a^n b^n \mid n \geq 1\}$. M scans its input tape from left to right and counts the number of a's representing the value of this count in binary notation on its worktape. It does this by incrementing a counter in its worktape. M then verifies that the number of occurrences of the symbol b is the same by subtracting 1 from the counter for each b scanned. If n is the length of the input string x, then M uses $\lceil \log(n/2) + 1 \rceil$ worktape cells in order to accept x.

Let L be a language and f a function from the set of nonnegative integers to the set of nonnegative integers. We say that L is in DSPACE(f) (resp., NSPACE(f)) if there exists a deterministic (resp., nondeterministic) off-line Turing machine M that behaves as follows. On input x, if $x \in L$, then $S_M(x) \leq f(|x|)$; otherwise, $S_M(x) = \infty$. For example, $L(M) = \{a^n b^n \mid n \geq 1\}$ in Example 10.2 is in DSPACE($\log n$) since M is deterministic and for any string x, if $x \in L$, M uses at most $\lceil \log(n/2) + 1 \rceil$ worktape cells in order to accept x, where $n = |x|$. Similarly, we may define DSPACE(n^k),

NSPACE(n^k) for any $k \geq 1$. We now define two important space complexity classes PSPACE and NSPACE as follows.

$$\text{PSPACE} = \text{DSPACE}(n) \cup \text{DSPACE}(n^2) \cup \text{DSPACE}(n^3) \cup$$
$$\cdots \cup \text{DSPACE}(n^k) \cup \cdots \text{NSPACE}$$
$$= \text{NSPACE}(n) \cup \text{NSPACE}(n^2) \cup \text{NSPACE}(n^3) \cup$$
$$\cdots \cup \text{NSPACE}(n^k) \cup \cdots .$$

In other words, PSPACE is the set of all languages recognizable in polynomial space using a deterministic off-line Turing machine, and NSPACE is the set of all languages recognizable in polynomial space using a nondeterministic off-line Turing machine. There are also two fundamental complexity classes:

LOGSPACE = DSPACE $(\log n)$ and NLOGSPACE = NSPACE $(\log n)$,

which define the two classes of languages recognizable in logarithmic space using a deterministic and nondeterministic off-line Turing machine, respectively. In the following example, we describe a problem that belongs to the class NLOGSPACE.

Example 10.3   GRAPH ACCESSIBILITY PROBLEM (GAP): Given a finite directed graph $G = (V, E)$, where $V = \{1, 2, \ldots, n\}$, is there a path from vertex 1 to vertex n? Here, 1 is the start vertex and n is the goal vertex. We construct a nondeterministic Turing machine M that determines whether there is a path from vertex 1 to vertex n. M performs this task by first beginning with the path of length zero from vertex 1 to itself, and extending the path at each later step by *nondeterministically* choosing a next vertex, which is a successor of the last vertex in the current path. It records in its worktape only the last vertex in this path; it does not record the entire list of vertices in the path. Since the last vertex can be represented by writing its number in binary notation on the worktape, M uses at most $\lceil \log(n + 1) \rceil$ worktape cells. Since M chooses a path nondeterministically, if a path from vertex 1 to vertex n exists, then M will be able to make a correct sequence of choices and construct such a path. It will answer *yes* when it detects that the last vertex in the path chosen is n. On the other hand, M is not forced to make the right sequence of choices, even when an appropriate path exists. For example, M may loop, by choosing an endless sequence of vertices in G that form a cycle or M may terminate without indicating that an appropriate path exists by making an incorrect choice for the successor of the last vertex in the path. Since M needs to store in its worktape only the binary representation of the current vertex whose length is $\lceil \log(n+1) \rceil$, it follows that GAP is in NLOGSPACE.

10.5　Tape Compression and Linear Speed-up

Since the tape alphabet can be arbitrarily large, several tape symbols can be encoded into one. This results in tape compression by a constant factor, i.e., the amount of space used is reduced by some constant $c > 1$. Similarly, one can speed up the computation by a constant factor. Thus, in computational complexity, the constant factors may be ignored; only the rate of growth is important in classifying problems. In the following, we state without proof two theorems on tape compression and linear speed-up.

Theorem 10.1　*If a language L is accepted by an $S(n)$ space-bounded off-line Turing machine M, then for any constant $c, 0 < c < 1$, L is accepted by a $cS(n)$ space-bounded off-line Turing machine M'.*

Theorem 10.2　*If a language L is accepted by a $T(n)$ time-bounded Turing machine M with $k > 1$ tapes such that $n = o(T(n))$, then for any constant $c, 0 < c < 1$, L is accepted by a $cT(n)$ time-bounded Turing machine M'.*

Example 10.4　Let $L = \{ww^R \mid w \in \{a,b\}^+\}$, i.e., L consists of the set of palindromes over the alphabet $\{a,b\}$. A 2-tape Turing machine M can be constructed to accept L as follows. The input string is initially in the first tape. The second tape is used to mark the input symbols in the following way. Scan the first symbol and mark it. Go to the rightmost symbol, scan it and mark it. Continue this process until the input string is consumed, in which case it is accepted, or until a mismatch is found, in which case the input string is rejected. Another 2-tape Turing machine M' that recognizes the language L works as follows. Scan *simultaneously* the two leftmost symbols, mark them and go to the right to scan and mark the two rightmost symbols, etc. Clearly, the time required by M' is almost half the time required by M.

10.6 Relationships between Complexity Classes

Definition 10.7   A total function T from the set of nonnegative integers to the set of nonnegative integers is said to be *time constructible* if and only if there is a Turing machine which on *every* input of length n halts in exactly $T(n)$ steps. A total function S from the set of nonnegative integers to the set of nonnegative integers is said to be *space constructible* if and only if there is a Turing machine which on *every* input of length n halts in a configuration in which exactly $S(n)$ tape cells of its work space are nonblank, and no other work space has been used during the computation. Almost all known functions are time and space constructible, e.g., $n^k, c^n, n!$.

Theorem 10.3

(a) $\text{DTIME}(f(n)) \subseteq \text{NTIME}(f(n))$ *and* $\text{DSPACE}(f(n)) \subseteq \text{NSPACE}(f(n))$.

(b) $\text{DTIME}(f(n)) \subseteq \text{DSPACE}(f(n))$ *and* $\text{NTIME}(f(n)) \subseteq \text{NSPACE}(f(n))$.

(c) *If S is a space constructible function and $S(n) \geq \log n$, then* $\text{NSPACE}(S(n)) \subseteq \text{DTIME}(c^{S(n)})$, $c \geq 2$.

(d) *If S is a space constructible function and $S(n) \geq \log n$, then*

$$\text{DSPACE}(S(n)) \subseteq \text{DTIME}(c^{S(n)}), \quad c \geq 2.$$

(e) *If T is a time constructible function, then*

$$\text{NTIME}(T(n)) \subseteq \text{DTIME}(c^{T(n)}), \quad c \geq 2.$$

Proof.

(a) By definition, every deterministic Turing machine is nondeterministic.

(b) In n steps, at most $n + 1$ tape cells can be scanned by the tape heads.

(c) Let M be a nondeterministic off-line Turing machine such that on all inputs of length n, M uses a work space bounded above by $S(n) \geq \log n$. Let s and t be the number of states and worktape symbols of M, respectively. Since M is $S(n)$ space-bounded and $S(n)$ is space constructible, the maximum number of distinct configurations that M can possibly enter on input x of length n is $s(n+2)S(n)t^{S(n)}$. This is the product of the number of states, number of input tape head positions, number of worktape head positions and number of possible worktape contents. Since $S(n) \geq \log n$, this expression is bounded above by $d^{S(n)}$ for some constant $d \geq 2$. Therefore,

M cannot make more than $d^{S(n)}$ moves, for otherwise one configuration will be repeated and the machine will never halt. Without loss of generality, we may assume that if M accepts, it erases both of its tapes and brings the tape heads to the first cell before entering the accepting state. Consider a deterministic Turing machine M' that, on input x of length n, generates a graph having all the configurations of M as its vertices, and setting a directed edge between two configurations if and only if the second one is reachable from the first in one step according to the transition function of M. The number of configurations is computed using the space constructibility of S. M' then checks whether there is a directed path in the graph joining the initial and the *unique* accepting configuration, and accepts if and only if this is the case. This can be done in time $O(d^{2S(n)}) = O(c^{S(n)})$ for some constant $c \geq 2$ (a shortest path in a directed graph with n vertices can be found in $O(n^2)$ time). Obviously, M' accepts the same language as M does, and therefore this language is in DTIME($c^{S(n)}$) for some constant $c \geq 2$.

(d) The proof follows immediately from parts (a) and (c).

(e) The proof follows immediately from parts (b) and (c).   □

Corollary 10.1   LOGSPACE $\subseteq$ NLOGSPACE $\subseteq$ P.

Theorem 10.4   *If S is a space constructible function and $S(n) \geq \log n$, then* NSPACE($S(n)$) $\subseteq$ DSPACE($S^2(n)$).

Proof.   Let M be an $S(n)$ nondeterministic off-line Turing machine that halts on all inputs. We will construct an $S^2(n)$ deterministic off-line Turing machine M' such that $L(M') = L(M)$. The strategy is that M' can simulate M using divide and conquer. Let s and t be the number of states and worktape symbols of M, respectively. Since M is $S(n)$ space-bounded and $S(n)$ is space constructible, the maximum number of distinct configurations that M can possibly enter on input x of length n is $s(n+2)S(n)t^{S(n)}$. This is the product of the number of states, number of input tape head positions, number of worktape head positions and number of possible worktape contents. Since $S(n) \geq \log n$, this expression is bounded above by $2^{cS(n)}$ for some constant $c \geq 1$. Therefore, M cannot make more than $2^{cS(n)}$ moves, for otherwise one configuration will be repeated and the machine will never halt. Let the initial configuration on input x be C_i and the final configuration C_f. M will accept x if and only if x causes the machine to go from C_i to C_f. Suppose that this takes M j moves. Then, there must exist a configuration C such that x causes M to go into configuration C of size $O(S(n))$ in at most $j/2$ steps and then from C to C_f in at most $j/2$ steps. M' will check for *all* possible configurations C using the divide-and-conquer function REACHABLE shown below. The first call to this function is REACHABLE$(C_i, C_f, 2^{cS(n)})$.

The function REACHABLE decides whether there is a partial computation of length at most j between two configurations. It does so by looking for the middle configuration C and checking recursively that it is indeed the middle configuration. This checking amounts to verifying the existence of two partial computations of length at most $j/2$ each.

```
1.  Function REACHABLE(C₁, C₂, j)
2.     if j = 1 then
3.        if C₁ = C₂ or C₂ is reachable from C₁ in one step
4.           then return true
5.           else return false
6.        end if
7.     else for each possible configuration C of size ≤ S(n)
8.        if REACHABLE (C₁, C, j/2) and REACHABLE (C, C₂, j/2)
9.           then return true
10.          else return false
11.       end if
12.    end if
13. end REACHABLE.
```

It is immediately clear that M' accepts its input if and only if M does. Let us show the space bound for M'. To simulate the recursive calls, M' uses its worktape as a stack, storing in it the information corresponding to successive calls of the function. Each call decreases the value of j by a factor of 2. Therefore, the depth of recursion is $cS(n)$, and hence no more than $cS(n)$ calls are active simultaneously. For each call, M' stores the current values of C_1, C_2 and C, of size $O(S(n))$ each. Therefore, $O(S^2(n))$ space suffices to hold the whole stack. It follows that M' is an $S^2(n)$ deterministic off-line Turing machine with $L(M') = L(M)$. □

Corollary 10.2 *For any $k \geq 1$,*

NSPACE$(n^k) \subseteq$ DSPACE(n^{2k}) and NSPACE$(\log^k n) \subseteq$ DSPACE$(\log^{2k} n)$.

Moreover, NSPACE $=$ PSPACE.

Corollary 10.3   *There is a* deterministic *algorithm to solve the problem* GAP *using* $O(\log^2 n)$ *space.*

Proof.   Immediate from Theorem 10.4 and the fact that GAP has a non-deterministic algorithm that uses $O(\log n)$ space (see Example 10.3).   □

10.6.1   *Space and time hierarchy theorems*

Now we present two hierarchy theorems which are concerned with the relationships between classes when the same resource on the same model is bounded by different functions. Specifically, we will present some sufficient conditions for the strict inclusion between deterministic time and space classes. These theorems are known as the *space hierarchy* and *time hierarchy* theorems. Let M be a 1-tape Turing machine. We encode M as a string of 0's and 1's corresponding to a binary number as follows. Assume without loss of generality that the input alphabet of M is $\{0, 1\}$, and the blank is the only additional tape symbol. For convenience, call the symbols 0, 1 and the blank X_1, X_2 and X_3, respectively, and denote by D_1, D_2 and D_3 the directions L, R and P, respectively. Then, a move $\delta(q_i, X_j) = (q_k, X_l, D_m)$ is encoded by the binary string $0^i 10^j 10^k 10^l 10^m$. Thus, the binary code for M is $111C_1 11C_2 11 \ldots 11C_r 111$, where each C_i is the code for one move as shown above. Each Turing machine may have many encodings, as the encodings of moves can be listed in any order. On the other hand, there are binary numbers that do not correspond to any encodings of Turing machines. These binary numbers may collectively be taken as the encodings of the null Turing machine, i.e., the Turing machine with no moves. It follows that we may talk of the nth Turing machine and so on. In a similar manner, we can encode k-tape Turing machines for all $k \geq 1$ and off-line Turing machines.

Theorem 10.5   *Let $S(n)$ and $S'(n)$ be two space constructible space bounds, and assume that $S'(n)$ is $o(S(n))$. Then, $\text{DSPACE}(S(n))$ contains a language that is not in $\text{DSPACE}(S'(n))$.*

Proof.   The proof is by diagonalization. Without loss of generality, we may consider only off-line Turing machines with input alphabet $\{0, 1\}$. We may also assume that a prefix of any number of 1's is permitted in any encoding of a Turing machine, so that each Turing machine has infinitely many encodings. We construct a Turing machine M with space bound $S(n)$

that disagrees on at least one input with any Turing machine with space bound $S'(n)$. M treats its input x as an encoding of an off-line Turing machine. Let x be an input to M of length n. First, to ensure that M does not use more than $S(n)$ space, it first marks exactly $S(n)$ cells of its worktape. Since $S(n)$ is space constructible, this can be done by simulating a Turing machine that uses exactly $S(n)$ space on each input of length n. From now on, M aborts its operation whenever the computation attempts to use a cell beyond the marked cells. Thus, M is indeed an $S(n)$ bounded Turing machine, that is, $L(M)$ is in DSPACE($S(n)$). Next, M simulates M_x on input x, where M_x is the Turing machine whose encoding is the input x. M accepts x if and only if it completes the simulation using $S(n)$ space and M_x halts and rejects x. If M_x is $S'(n)$ space bounded and uses t tape symbols, then the simulation requires $\lceil \log t \rceil S'(n)$.

It should be noted that $L(M)$ may be accepted by a Turing machine other than M. We now show that if a Turing machine M' accepts $L(M)$, then M' cannot be $S'(n)$ space bounded. For suppose that there exists an $S'(n)$ space bounded Turing machine M' that accepts $L(M)$, and assume without loss of generality that M' halts on all inputs. Since $S'(n)$ is $o(S(n))$, and since any off-line Turing machine can have an encoding with arbitrarily many 1's, there exists an encoding x' of M' such that $\lceil \log t \rceil S'(n') < S(n')$, where $n' = |x'|$. Clearly, on input x', M has sufficient space to simulate M'. But then, on input x', M will accept if and only if M' halts and rejects. It follows that $L(M') \neq L(M)$, and hence $L(M)$ is in DSPACE($S(n)$) and not in DSPACE($S'(n)$). $\qquad\square$

For the time hierarchy theorem, we need the following lemma whose proof is omitted:

Lemma 10.1 *If L is accepted by a k-tape Turing machine in time $T(n)$, then L is accepted by a 2-tape Turing machine in time $T(n) \log T(n)$.*

Theorem 10.6 *Let $T(n)$ and $T'(n)$ be two time bounds such that $T(n)$ is time constructible and $T'(n) \log T'(n)$ is $o(T(n))$. Then, DTIME($T(n)$) contains a language which is not in DTIME($T'(n)$).*

Proof. The proof is similar to that of Theorem 10.5. Therefore, we will only state here the necessary modifications. On input x of length n, M shuts itself off after executing exactly $T(n)$ steps. This can be done by simulating a $T(n)$ time bounded Turing machine on extra tapes (note that this is possible since $T(n)$ is time constructible). It should be noted that M has only a fixed number of tapes, and it is supposed to simulate Turing machines with arbitrarily many tapes. By Lemma 10.1, this results in a slowdown by a factor of $\log T'(n)$. Also, as in the proof of Theorem 10.5, M' may have many tape symbols, which slows down the simulation by a factor of $c = \lceil \log t \rceil$, where t is the number of tape symbols used by M'. Thus, the encoding x' of M' of length n' must satisfy the inequality $cT'(n') \log T'(n') \leq T(n')$. Since M accepts x' only if M' halts and rejects x', it follows that $L(M') \neq L(M)$, and hence $L(M)$ is in DTIME($T(n)$) and not in DTIME($T'(n)$).   □

10.6.2   Padding arguments

Suppose we are given any particular problem Π. Then, we can create a version of Π that has lower complexity by *padding* each instance of Π with a long sequence of extra symbols. This technique is called *padding*. We illustrate the idea behind this concept in connection with an example. Let $L \subseteq \Sigma^*$ be a language, where Σ is an alphabet that does not contain the symbol 0. Suppose that L is in DTIME(n^2). Define the language

$$L' = \{x0^k \mid x \in L \text{ and } k = |x|^2 - |x|\}.$$

L' is called a *padded* version of L. Now, we show that L' is in DTIME(n). Let M be a Turing machine that accepts L. We construct another Turing machine M' that recognizes L' as follows. M' first checks that the input string x' is of the form $x0^k$, where $x \in \Sigma^*$ and $k = |x|^2 - |x|$. This can be done in an amount of time bounded by $|x'|$. Next, if x' is of the form $x0^k$, then M' simulates on input $x' = x0^k$ the computation of M on input x. If M accepts x, then M' accepts; otherwise, M' rejects. Since M requires at most $|x|^2$ steps to decide if x is in the language L, M' needs at most $|x'| = |x|^2$ steps to decide if x' is in the language L'. Therefore, L' is in DTIME(n). In more general terms, if L is in DTIME($f(n^2)$), then L' is in DTIME($f(n)$). For example, if L is in DTIME(n^4), then L' is in DTIME(n^2), and if L is in DTIME(2^{n^2}), then L' is in DTIME(2^n).

We now present two theorems that are based on padding arguments.

Theorem 10.7   *If* DSPACE(n) $\subseteq$ P, *then* PSPACE $=$ P.

Proof.   Assume that DSPACE(n) $\subseteq$ P. Let $L \subseteq \Sigma^*$ be a set in PSPACE, where Σ is an alphabet that does not contain the symbol 0. Let M be a Turing machine that accepts L in space $p(n)$ for some polynomial p. Consider the set

$$L' = \{x0^k \mid x \in L \text{ and } k = p(|x|) - |x|\}.$$

Then, as in the discussion above, there is a Turing machine M' that recognizes L' in linear space. That is, L' is in DSPACE(n). By hypothesis, L' is in P. Hence, there is a Turing machine M'' that accepts L' in polynomial time. Clearly, another Turing machine, which on input x appends to it 0^k, where $k = p(|x|) - |x|$, and then simulates M'', can easily be constructed. Obviously, this machine accepts L in polynomial time. It follows that PSPACE $\subseteq$ P. Since P $\subseteq$ PSPACE, it follows that PSPACE $=$ P. $\square$

Corollary 10.4 P $\neq$ DSPACE(n).

Proof. If P $=$ DSPACE(n), then by the above theorem, PSPACE $=$ P. Consequently, PSPACE $=$ DSPACE(n). But this violates the space hierarchy theorem (Theorem 10.5). It follows that P $\neq$ DSPACE(n). $\square$

Theorem 10.8 *If* NTIME(n) $\subseteq$ P, *then* NEXT $=$ DEXT.

Proof. Assume that NTIME(n) $\subseteq$ P. Let $L \subseteq \Sigma^*$ be a set in NTIME(2^{cn}), where Σ is an alphabet that does not contain the symbol 0. Let M be a nondeterministic Turing machine that accepts L in time 2^{cn} for some constant $c > 0$. Consider the set

$$L' = \{x0^k \mid x \in L \text{ and } k = 2^{cn} - |x|\}.$$

Then, there is a nondeterministic Turing machine M' that recognizes L' in linear time, that is, L' is in NTIME(n). By hypothesis, L' is in P. Hence, there is a deterministic Turing machine M'' that accepts L' in polynomial time. Clearly, another deterministic Turing machine, which on input x appends to it 0^k, where $k = 2^{cn} - |x|$, and then simulates M'', can easily be constructed. Obviously, this machine accepts L in time 2^{cn}. It follows that NTIME(2^{cn}) $\subseteq$ DTIME(2^{cn}). Since DTIME(2^{cn}) $\subseteq$ NTIME(2^{cn}), we have as a result NTIME(2^{cn}) $=$ DTIME(2^{cn}). Since c is arbitrary, it follows that NEXT $=$ DEXT. $\square$

In other words, the above theorem says that if NEXT $\neq$ DEXT, then there is a language L that is recognizable in linear time by a nondeterministic Turing machine but not recognizable by any polynomial time deterministic Turing machine.

Corollary 10.5   *If* NP = P, *then* NEXT = DEXT.

10.7 Reductions

In this section, we develop methods for comparing complexity classes of computational problems. Such comparisons will be made by describing transformations from one problem to another. A *transformation* is simply a function that maps instances of one problem into instances of another problem. Let $A \in \Sigma^*$ and $B \in \Delta^*$ be two arbitrary problems, which are encoded as sets of strings over the alphabets Σ and Δ, respectively. A function f which maps strings over the alphabet Σ into strings over the alphabet Δ is a transformation of A into B, if the following property is satisfied:

$$\forall x \in \Sigma^* \ x \in A \text{ if and only if } f(x) \in B.$$

A transformation f from A to B is useful since it implies a transformation also from any algorithm to solve B into an algorithm to solve A. That is, one may construct the following algorithm to solve the problem A, given as input an arbitrary string $x \in \Sigma^*$:

(1) Transform x into $f(x)$.
(2) Decide whether $f(x) \in B$ or not.
(3) If $f(x) \in B$, then answer *yes*; otherwise, answer *no*.

The complexity of this algorithm to solve A depends upon two factors: the complexity of transforming x into $f(x)$, and the complexity of deciding whether a given string is in B or not. However, it is clear that an efficient algorithm for B will be transformed into an efficient algorithm for A by the above process if the transformation is not too complex.

Definition 10.8   If there is a transformation f from a problem A to a problem B, then we say that A is *reducible to* B, denoted by $A \propto B$.

Definition 10.9   Let $A \subseteq \Sigma^*$ and $B \subseteq \Delta^*$ be sets of strings. Suppose that there is a transformation $f : \Sigma^* \to \Delta^*$. Then,

- *A is polynomial time reducible to B*, denoted by $A \propto_{poly} B$, if $f(x)$ can be computed in polynomial time.
- *A is log space reducible to B*, denoted by $A \propto_{log} B$, if $f(x)$ can be computed using $O(\log |x|)$ space.

Definition 10.10   Let $\propto$ be a reducibility relation. Let $\mathcal{L}$ be a family of languages. Define the *closure of $\mathcal{L}$ under the reducibility relation* $\propto$ by

$$closure_{\propto}(\mathcal{L}) = \{L \mid \exists L' \in \mathcal{L} \ (L \propto L')\}.$$

Then, $\mathcal{L}$ is *closed under the reducibility relation* $\propto$ if and only if

$$closure_{\propto}(\mathcal{L}) \subseteq \mathcal{L}.$$

If $\mathcal{L}$ consists of one language L, then we will write $closure_{\propto}(L)$ instead of $closure_{\propto}(\{L\})$.

For example, $closure_{\propto_{poly}}(\mathrm{P})$ is the set of all languages that are reducible to P in polynomial time, and $closure_{\propto_{log}}(\mathrm{P})$ is the set of all languages that are reducible to P in log space. We will show later that P is closed under both the reducibility relations $\propto_{poly}$ and $\propto_{log}$ by showing that $closure_{\propto_{poly}}(\mathrm{P}) \subseteq \mathrm{P}$ and $closure_{\propto_{log}}(\mathrm{P}) \subseteq \mathrm{P}$.

Now, we establish the relationship between the two important forms of reducibility: polynomial time and log space reducibilities.

Lemma 10.2   *The number of distinct configurations that a log space bounded off-line Turing machine M can enter with an input of length n is bounded above by a polynomial in n.*

Proof.   Let s and t be the number of states and worktape symbols of M, respectively. The number of distinct configurations that M can possibly enter on an input of length n is given by the product of the following quantities: s (the number of states of M), $n + 2$ (the number of distinct input head positions of M on an input of length n plus the left and right markers), $\log n$ (the number of distinct worktape head positions) and $t^{\log n}$ (the number of distinct strings that can be written within the $\log n$ worktape cells). Thus, the number of distinct configurations of M on an input of length n is

$$s(n+2)(\log n)t^{\log n} = s(n+2)(\log n)n^{\log t} \le n^c, \quad c > 1,$$

for all but finitely many n. It follows that the number of configurations is bounded by a polynomial in n. □

Theorem 10.9 *For any two languages A and B,*

$$\text{if } A \propto_{log} B, \text{ then } A \propto_{poly} B.$$

Proof. Immediate from Lemma 10.2 (also Corollary 10.1). □

Consequently, any log space reduction is a polynomial time reduction. It follows that for any family $\mathcal{L}$ of languages, if $\mathcal{L}$ is closed under polynomial time reductions, then it is also closed under log space reductions.

Lemma 10.3 P *is closed under polynomial time reductions.*

Proof. Let $L \subseteq \Sigma^*$, for some finite alphabet Σ, be any language such that $L \propto_{poly} L'$ for some language $L' \in P$. By definition, there is a function f computable in polynomial time, such that

$$\forall x \in \Sigma^* \ x \in L \text{ if and only if } f(x) \in L'.$$

Since $L' \in P$, there exists a deterministic Turing machine M' that accepts L' and operates in time n^k, for some $k \ge 1$. Since f is computable in polynomial time, there exists a deterministic Turing machine M'' that computes f and operates in time n^l, for some $l \ge 1$. We construct a Turing machine M that accepts the set L. M performs the following steps on input x over the alphabet Σ:

(1) Transform x into $f(x)$ using Turing machine M''.
(2) Determine whether $f(x) \in L'$ or not using the Turing machine M'.
(3) If M' decides that $f(x) \in L'$, then accept; otherwise, do not accept.

The time complexity of this algorithm for the Turing machine M is simply the sum of the amounts of time spent doing Steps (1), (2) and (3). Let x be a string of length n and let $f(x)$ be a string of length m. Then, the amount of time used by this algorithm on input x is bounded by $n^l + m^k + 1$, since Step (1) takes at most n^l steps, Step (2) at most m^k steps, and Step (3) one step. We observe that $f(x)$ cannot be longer than n^l, since M'' operates in

n^l steps and at most one symbol is printed by M'' on the output tape per step. In other words, $m \leq n^l$. Therefore, $n^l + m^k + 1 \leq n^l + n^{kl} + 1$, for all but finitely many n. We have demonstrated thereby that a deterministic Turing machine exists that recognizes the set L in polynomial time. Thus, if $L \propto_{poly} L'$ then $L \in$ P. $\square$

The proof of the following lemma is similar to the proof of Lemma 10.3:

Lemma 10.4 NP *and* PSPACE *are closed under polynomial time reductions.*

Corollary 10.6 P, NP *and* PSPACE *are closed under log space reductions.*

Lemma 10.5 LOGSPACE *is closed under log space reductions.*

Proof. Let $L \subseteq \Sigma^*$, for some finite alphabet Σ, be any language such that $L \propto_{log} L'$ for some language $L' \in$ LOGSPACE. By definition, there is a function f computable in log space such that

$$\forall x \in \Sigma^* \ x \in L \text{ if and only if } f(x) \in L'.$$

Since $L' \in$ LOGSPACE, there exists a deterministic Turing machine M' that accepts L' in space $\log n$. Since f is computable in log space, there exists a deterministic Turing machine M'' that computes f using at most $\log n$ worktape cells on input of size n. We construct a deterministic Turing machine M that accepts the set L. M performs the following steps on input x over the alphabet Σ:

(1) Set i to 1.
(2) If $1 \leq i \leq |f(x)|$, then compute the ith symbol of $f(x)$ using the Turing machine M''. Call this symbol σ. If $i = 0$, then let σ be the left endmarker symbol #. If $i = |f(x)| + 1$, then let σ be the right endmarker symbol \$.
(3) Simulate the actions of the Turing machine M' on the symbol σ until the input head of M' moves right or left. If the input head moves to the right, then add one to i and go to Step (2). If the input head of M' moves to the left, then subtract one from i and go to Step (2). If M' enters a final state before moving its input head either right or left, thereby accepting $f(x)$, then accept the input string x.

It should be noted that M does indeed recognize the set L. It accepts a string x if and only if M' accepts the string $f(x)$. Step (2) requires at most $\log n$ worktape space, since M'' works in $\log n$ space. The worktape contents of the simulated Turing machine M' are stored in the worktape space of M. This needs at most $\log |f(x)|$ space, since M' is a log space Turing machine and it is being simulated on input $f(x)$. As we have seen in Lemma 10.2, M'' is polynomially time bounded, since M'' operates in space $\log n$ and eventually terminates with the value of the function f. Therefore, $|f(x)| \leq |x|^c$, for some $c > 0$. Thus, the worktape space needed for representing the contents of the worktape of M' is bounded by

$$\log |f(x)| \leq \log |x|^c = c \log |x|, \ c > 0.$$

Also, the value i, $0 \leq i \leq |f(x)| + 1$, that records the position of the input head of M' can be stored on the worktape of M using binary notation within space $\log |f(x)| \leq \log |x|^c = c \log |x|$ worktape cells. Therefore, the algorithm described for the Turing machine M requires at most $d \log n$ worktape cells, for some $d > 0$, to recognize the set L. It follows that L is in LOGSPACE and hence $closure_{\propto_{log}}(\text{LOGSPACE}) \subseteq \text{LOGSPACE}$. □

The following lemma is proven in the same manner as Lemma 10.5.

Lemma 10.6   NLOGSPACE *is closed under log space reductions.*

10.8 Completeness

Definition 10.11   Let $\propto$ be a reducibility relation, and $\mathcal{L}$ a family of languages. A language L is complete for $\mathcal{L}$ with respect to the reducibility relation $\propto$ if L is in the class $\mathcal{L}$ and every language in $\mathcal{L}$ is reducible to the language L by the relation $\propto$, that is, $\mathcal{L} \subseteq closure_{\propto}(L)$.

We have presented in Chapter 9 some problems that are complete for the class NP with respect to polynomial time reductions. In fact, most of the reductions in the proofs of NP-completeness found in the literature are log space reductions.

We observe that every set $S \in$ LOGSPACE is log space reducible to a set with just one element. That is, given a set $S \subseteq \Sigma^*$ in LOGSPACE, we define the function f_S by

$$f_S(x) = \begin{cases} 1 & \text{if } x \in S \\ 0 & \text{otherwise.} \end{cases}$$

It follows, trivially, that the set $\{1\}$ is LOGSPACE-complete with respect to log space reduction. In fact, every problem in LOGSPACE is LOGSPACE-complete with respect to log space reduction. This is because log space reductions are too powerful to distinguish between sets in LOGSPACE.

10.8.1 *NLOGSPACE-complete problems*

In the following theorem, we prove that the problem GAP is complete for the class NLOGSPACE.

Theorem 10.10   GAP *is log space complete for the class* NLOGSPACE.

Proof.   We have shown in Example 10.3 that GAP is in the class NLOGSPACE. It remains to show that any problem in that class reduces to GAP using log space reduction. Let L be in NLOGSPACE. We show that $L \propto_{log}$ GAP. Since L is in NLOGSPACE, there is a nondeterministic off-line Turing machine M that accepts L, and for every x in L, there is an accepting computation by M that visits at most $\log n$ worktape cells, where $n = |x|$. We construct a log space reduction which transforms each input string x into an instance of the problem GAP consisting of a directed graph $G = (V, E)$. The set of vertices V consists of the set of all configurations $K = (p, i, w_1 \uparrow w_2)$ of M on input x such that $|w_1 w_2| \leq \log n$. The set of edges consists of the set of pairs (K_1, K_2) such that M can move *in one step* on input x from the configuration K_1 to the configuration K_2. Furthermore, the start vertex s is chosen to be the initial configuration K_i of M on input x. If we assume that when M enters the final state q_f, it erases all symbols in its worktape and positions its input head on the first cell, then the goal vertex t is chosen to be the final configuration $K_f = (p_f, 1, \uparrow B)$. It is not hard to see that M accepts x within $\log n$ worktape space if and only if G has a path from its start vertex s to its goal vertex t. To finish the proof, note that G can be constructed using only $O(\log n)$ space. $\qquad\square$

Corollary 10.7   GAP *is in* LOGSPACE *if and only if*

$$\text{NLOGSPACE} = \text{LOGSPACE}.$$

Proof. If NLOGSPACE = LOGSPACE, then clearly GAP is in LOGSPACE. On the other hand, assume that GAP is in LOGSPACE. Then,

$$closure_{\propto_{log}}(\text{GAP}) \subseteq closure_{\propto_{log}}(\text{LOGSPACE}) \subseteq \text{LOGSPACE},$$

since LOGSPACE is closed under $\propto_{log}$. Since GAP is complete for the class NLOGSPACE, we have

$$\text{NLOGSPACE} \subseteq closure_{\propto_{log}}(\text{GAP}).$$

Thus, NLOGSPACE $\subseteq$ LOGSPACE. Since LOGSPACE $\subseteq$ NLOGSPACE, it follows that NLOGSPACE = LOGSPACE. $\square$

The proof of the following theorem is left as an exercise (Exercise 10.15).

Theorem 10.11   2-SAT *is log space complete for the class* NLOGSPACE.

10.8.2   *PSPACE-complete problems*

Definition 10.12   A problem Π is PSPACE-complete if it is in PSPACE and all problems in PSPACE can be reduced to Π using polynomial time reduction.

The relationship of the following problem to PSPACE is similar to the relationship of the problem SATISFIABILITY to NP.

QUANTIFIED BOOLEAN FORMULAS (QBF): Given a boolean expression E on n variables $x_1, x_2, \ldots, x_n$, is the boolean formula

$$F = (Q_1 x_1)(Q_2 x_2) \cdots (Q_n x_n) E$$

true? Here, each Q_i is either $\exists$ or $\forall$.

Theorem 10.12   QUANTIFIED BOOLEAN FORMULA *is* PSPACE-*complete.*

That QUANTIFIED BOOLEAN FORMULA is in PSPACE follows from the fact that we can check whether F is true by trying all the possible truth assignments for the variables $x_1, x_2, \ldots, x_n$ and evaluating E for each. It is not hard to see that no more than polynomial space is needed, even though exponential time will be required to examine all 2^n truth assignments. The proof that each language $L \in$ PSPACE can be transformed to QUANTIFIED BOOLEAN FORMULA is similar to the proof that the problem SATISFIABILITY is NP-complete.

An interesting PSPACE-complete problem is the following:

CSG RECOGNITION: Given a context-sensitive grammar G and a string x, is $x \in L(G)$? Here, $L(G)$ is the language generated by G.
It is well known that the class NSPACE(n) is precisely the set of languages generated by context-sensitive grammars. This problem can be rephrased in terms of Turing machines as follows. A *linear bounded automaton* is a restricted type of Turing machine in which the worktape space consists of $n + 2$ cells, where n is the input length. Thus, equivalently, the following problem is PSPACE-complete:
LBA ACCEPTANCE: Given a nondeterministic linear bounded automaton M and a string x, does M accept x?
This problem remains PSPACE-complete even if the Turing machine is deterministic. Thus, all problems that are solvable in polynomial space can be reduced in polynomial time to a problem that requires only linear space.

In addition to the above problems, the set of PSPACE-complete problems includes many interesting problems in widely different areas, especially in game theory. Several two-person games involving a natural alternation of turns for the two players which correspond to an alternation of quantifiers in QUANTIFIED BOOLEAN FORMULA are known to be PSPACE-complete. For example, generalized versions of the games HEX, GEOGRAPHY and KAYLES are PSPACE-complete. Also, generalized versions of the more familiar games CHECKERS and GO are known to be PSPACE-complete under certain drawing restrictions.

10.8.3   *P-complete problems*

Although the class P contains all problems for which there exists an efficient algorithm, there are problems in P that are *practically* intractable. The following example reveals the hardness of a practical problem in this class.

Example 10.5   Consider the problem k-CLIQUE defined as follows. Given an undirected graph $G = (V, E)$ with n vertices, determine whether G contains a clique of size k, where k is *fixed*. The only known algorithm to solve this problem is by considering all the k subsets of V. This results in $\Omega(n^k/k!)$ time complexity. Thus, even for moderate values of k, the problem is *practically* intractable.

Definition 10.13   A problem Π is P-complete if it is in P and all problems in P can be reduced to Π using log space reduction.

It is widely conjectured that there are problems in P for which any algorithm must use an amount of space that is more than logarithmic in the input size, that is, the set P — LOGSPACE is not empty.

The class of P-complete problems is not empty, and it does contain several problems that are solvable in polynomial time of low degree such as depth-first search, which is solvable in linear time, and the max-flow problem, which is solvable in $O(n^3)$ time. These problems are important in the field of parallel algorithms, as they contain those problems which are hard to parallelize efficiently; they usually admit sequential algorithms that are greedy in nature and thus inherently sequential.

Definition 10.14   The class NC consists of those problems that can be solved in polylogarithmic time, that is $O(\log^k n)$ time, using a polynomial number of processors.

This class remains invariant under different models of parallel computation. It encompasses those problems that are well-parallelizable in the sense that increasing the number of processors results in significant speedup. Observe that NC $\subseteq$ P, as the total number of steps performed by a parallel algorithm is the product of the running time and the number of processors, which is polynomial in the case of NC algorithms. In other words, such a parallel algorithm can be transformed into a polynomial time sequential algorithm.

However, there is a general belief that NC $\neq$ P. Interestingly, if a problem is P-complete, then every other problem in P can be reduced to it in polylogarithmic time using a polynomial number of processors. This type of transformation is called *NC-reduction*. It can be shown that NC is closed under NC-reduction. This motivates the next alternative definition of P-complete problems.

Definition 10.15   A problem Π is P-complete if it is in P and all problems in P can be reduced to Π using NC-reduction.

This definition yields the following theorem:

Theorem 10.13   *If a problem Π is P-complete and Π is in NC, then* P = NC.

In other words, if P $\neq$ NC, then all P-complete problems must belong to P $-$ NC. Thus, although P-complete problems are not likely to be solvable in logarithmic space, they also do not seem to admit efficient parallel algorithms.

The following is a sample of some P-complete problems.

(1) CIRCUIT VALUE problem (CVP): Given a boolean circuit C consisting of m gates $\{g_1, g_2, \ldots, g_m\}$, and a specified set of input values $\{x_1, x_2, \ldots, x_n\}$, determine whether the output of the circuit is equal to 1. Here, a gate is $\vee, \wedge$ or $\neg$.

(2) ORDERED DEPTH-FIRST SEARCH: Given a directed graph $G = (V, E)$ and three vertices $s, u, v \in V$, determine whether u is visited before v in a depth-first search traversal of G starting at s.

(3) LINEAR PROGRAMMING: Given an $n \times m$ matrix A of integers, a vector b of n integers, a vector c of m integers and an integer k, determine whether there exists a vector x of m nonnegative rational numbers such that $Ax \leq b$ and $cx \geq k$.

(4) MAX-FLOW: Given a weighted directed graph $G = (V, E)$ with two distinguished vertices s and t, determine whether the maximum flow from s to t is odd.

10.8.4   *Some conclusions of completeness*

Theorem 10.14   *Let Π be an NP-complete problem with respect to polynomial time reductions. Then,* NP = P *if and only if* $\Pi \in P$.

Proof.   The theorem is easily established using the definition of completeness. Suppose that NP = P. Since Π is complete for NP, $\Pi \in$ NP, and hence $\Pi \in$ P. On the other hand, suppose that $\Pi \in$ P. Since Π is NP-complete,

NP $\subseteq$ *closure* $\propto_{poly}(\Pi)$. Thus,

$$\text{NP} \subseteq closure \propto_{poly}(\Pi) \subseteq closure \propto_{poly}(\text{P}) \subseteq \text{P},$$

as P is closed under $\propto_{poly}$. Since P $\subseteq$ NP, it follows that NP = P. $\square$

Theorem 10.14 is also true when the problem Π is complete for NP with respect to log space reductions. This results in the following stronger theorem, whose proof is similar to the proof of Theorem 10.14.

Theorem 10.15 *Let Π be a problem that is complete for* NP *with respect to log space reductions. Then,*

(1) NP = P *if and only if* $\Pi \in$ P.
(2) NP = NLOGSPACE *if and only if* $\Pi \in$ NLOGSPACE.
(3) NP = LOGSPACE *if and only if* $\Pi \in$ LOGSPACE.

In comparing Theorem 10.14 with Theorem 10.15, the number of conclusions that can be drawn from knowing that a problem Π is log space complete for the class NP is more than the number of conclusions that can be drawn from knowing that Π is complete for NP with respect to polynomial time reductions. In fact, most, if not all, polynomial time reductions between natural NP-complete problems described in the literature are also log space reductions. Also, log space reductions can distinguish between the complexity of sets in P and polynomial time reductions cannot. The proofs of the following theorems are similar to the proof of Theorems 10.14.

Theorem 10.16 *Let Π be a problem that is complete for the class* PSPACE *with respect to log space reductions. Then,*

(1) PSPACE = NP *if and only if* $\Pi \in$ NP.
(2) PSPACE = P *if and only if* $\Pi \in$ P.

Theorem 10.17 *If a problem Π is P-complete, then*

(1) P = LOGSPACE *if and only if* Π *is in* LOGSPACE.
(2) P = NLOGSPACE *if and only if* Π *is in* NLOGSPACE.

The following theorem is a generalization of Corollary 10.7.

Theorem 10.18   *Let* Π *be a problem that is complete for* NLOGSPACE *with respect to log space reductions. Then,*

NLOGSPACE $=$ LOGSPACE *if and only if* $\Pi \in$ LOGSPACE.

10.9   The Polynomial Time Hierarchy

An *oracle Turing machine* is a k-tape Turing machine with an additional tape called the *oracle tape* and a special state called the *query state*. The purpose of the oracle is to answer questions about the membership of an element in an arbitrary set. Let M be a Turing machine for an arbitrary set A with an oracle for another arbitrary set B. Whenever M wants to know whether an element x is in the set B, it writes x on its oracle tape, and then enters its query state. The oracle answers this question *in one step*: It erases the oracle tape and then prints *yes* on the oracle tape if the string x is in the set B and *no* if the string x is not in the set B. M can consult the oracle more than once. Thus, it may ask during the course of a computation whether each of the strings $x_1, x_2, \ldots, x_k$ are in the set B.

Let A and B be arbitrary sets. A is said to be *recognizable deterministically (nondeterministically) in polynomial time using an oracle for B* if there is a deterministic (nondeterministic) oracle Turing machine which accepts the set A using an oracle for B and, for some fixed $k \geq 1$, takes at most $|x|^k$ steps on any input string x.

Definition 10.16   If a language A is accepted by a deterministic oracle Turing machine in polynomial time using an oracle for the language B, then A is said to be *polynomial time Turing reducible* to B.

Let P^B denote the family of all languages recognizable deterministically in polynomial time using an oracle for the set B, and let NP^B denote the family of all languages recognizable nondeterministically in polynomial time using an oracle for the set B. Let $\mathcal{F}$ be a family of languages. The family co-$\mathcal{F}$ denotes the family of complements of sets in $\mathcal{F}$. That is, co-$\mathcal{F} = \{$co-$S \mid S \in \mathcal{F}\}$.

Definition 10.17 The *polynomial time hierarchy* consists of the families of sets $\Delta_i^p, \Sigma_i^p, \Pi_i^p$, for all integers $i \geq 0$, defined by

$$\Delta_0^p = \Sigma_0^p = \Pi_0^p = P,$$

and for all $i \geq 0$

$$\begin{cases} \Delta_{i+1}^p = \bigcup_{B \in \Sigma_i^p} P^B \\[2mm] \Sigma_{i+1}^p = \bigcup_{B \in \Sigma_i^p} NP^B \\[2mm] \Pi_{i+1}^p = \text{co-}\Sigma_{i+1}^p. \end{cases}$$

The following theorems summarize some of the properties of the classes in the polynomial time hierarchy. In these theorems, we will use the more general concept of algorithm in place of Turing machines.

Theorem 10.19 $\Delta_1^p = P, \Sigma_1^p = NP$ *and* $\Pi_1^p = \text{co-NP}$.

Proof. We show that, for any set B in P, every set A in P^B is again in P. Let the oracle set B be recognized in polynomial time by a deterministic algorithm T_B that runs in cn^k steps, for some $c > 0$. Let T_A be an algorithm that accepts the set A in polynomial time using oracle B and runs in dn^l steps, for some $d > 0$. One can replace each request for an answer from the oracle in T_A by the execution of the algorithm T_B, which decides the membership in the set B. Since the algorithm T_A runs in dn^l steps, the maximum length of any question, i.e., string, to the oracle is dn^l. In replacing each one of these requests by an execution of the algorithm T_B, we make each such step of T_A take at most $c(dn^l)^k$ steps. So, the new algorithm recognizes A without the use of an oracle in at most $dn^l(cd^k n^{kl})$ steps. Since $dn^l cd^k n^{kl} \leq c'n^{kl+l}$, for some constant $c' > 0$, it follows that there is a polynomial time algorithm for A. Thus, for every set $B \in \Sigma_0^p = P, P^B \subseteq P$. It follows that $\Delta_1^p = \bigcup_{B \in \Sigma_0^p} P^B \subseteq P$. To finish the proof, note that $P = P^\phi$ and the empty set ϕ is in Σ_0^p, that is, $P \subseteq \Delta_1^p$. The proof that $\Sigma_1^p = NP$ is similar. It follows, by definition, that $\Pi_1^p = \text{co-NP}$. $\square$

Theorem 10.20 *For all $i \geq 0, \Sigma_i^p \cup \Pi_i^p \subseteq \Delta_{i+1}^p$.*

Proof. By definition, $\Delta_{i+1}^p = \bigcup_{B \in \Sigma_i^p} P^B$. Since a polynomial time algorithm can easily be constructed to accept B using the set B as an oracle, it follows that $\Sigma_i^p \subseteq \Delta_{i+1}^p$. Also, as we have seen, a polynomial time algorithm can easily be constructed to accept co-B using an oracle for B. Therefore, $\Pi_i^p = \text{co-}\Sigma_i^p \subseteq \Delta_{i+1}^p$. □

Theorem 10.21 *For all $i \geq 1, \Delta_i^p \subseteq \Sigma_i^p \cap \Pi_i^p$.*

Proof. First, $\Delta_i^p = \bigcup_{B \in \Sigma_{i-1}^p} P^B \subseteq \bigcup_{B \in \Sigma_{i-1}^p} NP^B = \Sigma_i^p$, since a nondeterministic algorithm is a generalization of a deterministic algorithm. To show that $\Delta_i^p \subseteq \Pi_i^p$, for all $i \geq 1$, it is sufficient to show that co-$\Delta_i^p = \Delta_i^p$. That is, since $\Delta_i^p \subseteq \Sigma_i^p$, we have also that co-$\Delta_i^p \subseteq$ co-$\Sigma_i^p = \Pi_i^p$. Thus, if $\Delta_i^p = $ co-Δ_i^p, then $\Delta_i^p \subseteq \Pi_i^p$. So, we must show that co-$\Delta_i^p = \Delta_i^p$. Let A be a set in $\Delta_i^p = \bigcup_{B \in \Sigma_{i-1}^p} P^B$. Then, there is a deterministic polynomial time algorithm M_A for accepting A which uses an oracle for a set B in the family Σ_{i-1}^p. An algorithm M_A' for co-A can be constructed which uses an oracle for B. M_A' simply stops and accepts if M_A does not accept, and stops and rejects if M_A does stop and accept. It follows that co-$\Delta_i^p = \Delta_i^p$. □

The known relationships between the classes in the polynomial time hierarchy are shown in Fig. 10.1.

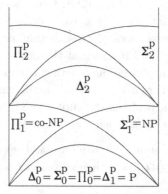

Fig. 10.1. Inclusion relations among complexity classes in the polynomial time hierarchy.

Theorem 10.22   *If $\Sigma_i^p = \Sigma_{i+1}^p$ for some $i \geq 0$, then $\Sigma_{i+j}^p = \Sigma_i^p$ for all $j \geq 1$.*

Proof.   We prove this by induction on j. Assume $\Sigma_{i+j}^p = \Sigma_i^p$, for some $j \geq 1$. Then,

$$\Sigma_{i+j+1}^p = \bigcup_{B \in \Sigma_{i+j}^p} NP^B = \bigcup_{B \in \Sigma_i^p} NP^B = \Sigma_{i+1}^p = \Sigma_i^p.$$

So, $\Sigma_{i+j+1}^p = \Sigma_i^p$, and hence $\Sigma_{i+j}^p = \Sigma_i^p$ for all $j \geq 1$. $\square$

Corollary 10.8   *If NP = P, then the polynomial time hierarchy collapses, that is, each family in the polynomial time hierarchy coincides with P.*

In fact, the converse implication is also true. If, for any $i \geq 1$, it were true that $\Sigma_i^p = P$, then since $NP \subseteq \Sigma_1^p \subseteq \Sigma_i^p$, it would follow that $NP = P$. Thus, any set A that is complete for the class Σ_i^p, for any $i \geq 1$, satisfies the property that it is in P if and only if NP = P.

Many problems which are not known to be in NP are in the polynomial time hierarchy. Several of these problems are related to NP-complete problems but are concerned with finding a maximum or a minimum. The following are two examples of problems in P^{NP} and NP^{NP}.

Example 10.6   CHROMATIC NUMBER. Given an undirected graph $G = (V, E)$ and a positive integer k, is k the *smallest* number of colors that can be assigned to the vertices of G such that no two adjacent vertices are assigned the same color? Recall that the problem COLORING stated on page 267 is the problem of deciding whether it is possible to color a given graph using k colors, where k is a positive number that is part of the input. It is well known that the problem COLORING is NP-complete. An algorithm to accept CHROMATIC NUMBER using an oracle for COLORING is as follows:

(1) If (G, k) is *not* in COLORING, then stop and reject, otherwise continue.
(2) If $(G, k - 1)$ is in COLORING, then stop and reject, otherwise continue.
(3) Stop and accept.

We observe that checking whether (G, k) is in COLORING is implemented by asking the oracle COLORING and is answered in one step, by assumption. So, the algorithm presented above is clearly polynomial time bounded, since it needs at most two steps to either accept or reject. It follows that CHRO-MATIC NUMBER is in $\Delta_2^p = \text{P}^{\text{NP}}$.

Example 10.7 MINIMUM EQUIVALENT EXPRESSION. Given a well-formed boolean expression E and a nonnegative integer k, is there a well-formed boolean expression E' that contains k or fewer occurrences of literals such that E' is equivalent to E (i.e., E' if and only if E)?

MINIMUM EQUIVALENT EXPRESSION does not appear to be in Δ_2^p. It is not obvious whether an oracle for a problem in NP can be used to solve MINIMUM EQUIVALENT EXPRESSION in *deterministic* polynomial time. However, this problem can be solved in *nondeterministic* polynomial time using an oracle for SATISFIABILITY. The algorithm is as follows:

(1) Guess a boolean expression E' containing k or fewer occurrences of literals.
(2) Use SATISFIABILITY to determine whether $\neg((E' \to E) \wedge (E \to E'))$ is satisfiable.
(3) If it is *not* satisfiable, then stop and accept, otherwise stop and reject.

The correctness of the above algorithm follows from the fact that a well-formed formula E is *not* satisfiable if and only if its negation is a tautology. Thus, since we want $(E'$ if and only if $E)$ to be a tautology, we only need to check whether

$$\neg((E' \to E) \wedge (E \to E'))$$

is *not* satisfiable. As to the time needed, Step 1, generating E', can easily be accomplished in polynomial time using a nondeterministic algorithm. Step 2, querying the SATISFIABILITY oracle, is done in one step. It follows that MINIMUM EQUIVALENT EXPRESSION is in $\Sigma_2^p = \text{NP}^{\text{NP}}$.

10.10 Practice Problems

10.1. Show that the language in Example 10.1 is in DTIME(n). (*Hint*: Use a 2-tape Turing machine.)
10.2. Show that the language $L = \{ww \mid w \in \{a,b\}^+\}$ is in LOGSPACE by constructing a log space bounded off-line Turing machine that

recognizes L. Here, $\{a, b\}^+$ denotes all nonempty strings over the alphabet $\{a, b\}$.

10.3. Consider the following decision problem of sorting: Given a sequence of n distinct positive integers between 1 and n, are they sorted in increasing order? Show that this problem is in

   (a) DTIME($n \log n$).

   (b) LOGSPACE.

10.4. Give an algorithm to solve the problem k-CLIQUE defined in Example 10.5. Use the O-notation to express the time complexity of your algorithm.

10.5. Show that the problem k-CLIQUE defined in Example 10.5 is in LOGSPACE. Recall that k is fixed.

10.6. Consider the following decision problem of the selection problem. Given an array $A[1..n]$ of integers, an integer x and an integer $k, 1 \leq k \leq n$, is the kth smallest element in A equal to x? Show that this problem is in LOGSPACE.

10.7. Let A be an $n \times n$ matrix. Show that computing A^2 is in LOGSPACE. How about computing A^k for an arbitrary $k \geq 3$, where k is part of the input?

10.8. Show that all finite sets are in LOGSPACE.

10.9. Show that the family of sets accepted by finite state automata is a *proper* subset of LOGSPACE. (*Hint*: The language $\{a^n b^n \mid n \geq 1\}$ is not accepted by any finite state automaton, but it is in LOGSPACE).

10.11 Exercises

10.1. Show that the problem 2-SAT described in Sec. 9.2 on page 268 is in NLOGSPACE. Conclude that it is in P.

10.2. Show that if T_1 and T_2 are two time-constructible functions, then so are $T_1 + T_2$, $T_1 T_2$ and 2^{T_1}.

10.3. Show that if NSPACE(n) $\subseteq$ NP, then NP = NSPACE. Conclude that NSPACE(n) $\neq$ NP.

10.4. Show that if LOGSPACE = NLOGSPACE, then for every space constructible function $S(n) \geq \log n$, DSPACE($S(n)$) = NSPACE($S(n)$).

10.5. Describe a log space reduction from the set $L = \{www \mid w \in \{a,b\}^+\}$ to the set $L' = \{ww \mid w \in \{a,b\}^+\}$. That is, show that $L \propto_{log} L'$.

10.6. Show that the relation $\propto_{poly}$ is transitive. That is, if $\Pi \propto_{poly} \Pi'$ and $\Pi' \propto_{poly} \Pi''$, then $\Pi \propto_{poly} \Pi''$.

10.7. Show that the relation $\propto_{log}$ is transitive. That is, if $\Pi \propto_{log} \Pi'$ and $\Pi' \propto_{log} \Pi''$, then $\Pi \propto_{log} \Pi''$.

10.8. The problems 2-COLORING and 2-SAT were defined in Sec. 9.2. Show that 2-COLORING is log space reducible to 2-SAT. (*Hint:* Let $G = (V, E)$. Let the boolean variable x_v correspond to vertex v for each vertex $v \in V$, and for each edge $(u, v) \in E$, construct the two clauses $(x_u \vee x_v)$ and $(\neg x_u \vee \neg x_v)$.)

10.9. Show that for any $k \geq 1$, DTIME(n^k) is not closed under polynomial time reductions.

10.10. Show that, for any $k \geq 1$, the class DSPACE($\log^k n$) is closed under log space reductions.

10.11. A set S is *linear time reducible* to a set T, denoted by $S \propto_n T$, if there exists a function f that can be computed in linear time (that is, $f(x)$ can be computed in $c|x|$ steps, for all input strings x, where c is some constant > 0) such that

$$\forall x \; x \in S \text{ if and only if } f(x) \in T.$$

Show that if $S \propto_n T$ and T is in DTIME(n^k), then S is in DTIME(n^k). That is, DTIME(n^k) ($k \geq 1$) is closed under linear time reducibility.

10.12. Suppose that k in Problem 10.5 (see also Example 10.5) is not fixed, that is, k is part of the input. Will the problem still be in LOGSPACE? Explain.

10.13. Show that the class NLOGSPACE is closed under complementation. Conclude that the complement of the problem GAP is NLOGSPACE-complete.

10.14. Show that the problem GAP remains NLOGSPACE-complete even if the graph is acyclic.

10.15. Show that the problem 2-SAT described in Sec. 9.2 on page 268 is complete for the class NLOGSPACE under log space reduction (see Exercise 10.1). (*Hint*: Reduce the complement of the problem GAP to it. Let $G = (V, E)$ be a directed acyclic graph. GAP is NLOGSPACE-complete even if the graph is acyclic (Exercise 10.14). By Exercise 10.13, the complement of the problem GAP is NLOGSPACE-complete. Associate with each vertex v in V a boolean variable x_v. Associate with each edge $(u, v) \in E$ the clause $(\neg x_u \vee x_v)$, and add the clauses (x_s) for the start vertex and $(\neg x_t)$ for the goal vertex t. Prove that 2-SAT is satisfiable if and only if there is no path from s to t).

10.16. Define the class

$$\text{POLYLOGSPACE} = \bigcup_{k \geq 1} \text{DSPACE}(\log^k n).$$

Show that there is no set that is complete for the class POLY-LOGSPACE. (*Hint*: The class DSPACE($\log^k n$) is closed under log space reduction.)

10.17. Prove that PSPACE $\subseteq$ P if and only if PSPACE $\subseteq$ PSPACE(n). (*Hint*: Use padding argument.)

10.18. Does there exist a problem that is complete for the class DTIME(n) under log space reduction? Prove your answer.

10.19. Let $\mathcal{L}$ be a class that is closed under complementation and let the set L (that is not necessarily in $\mathcal{L}$) be such that

$$\forall L' \in \mathcal{L} \ L' \propto L.$$

Show that

$$\forall L'' \in \text{co-}\mathcal{L} \ L'' \propto \overline{L}.$$

10.20. Show that for any class of languages $\mathcal{L}$, if L is complete for the class $\mathcal{L}$, then $\overline{L}$ is complete for the class co-$\mathcal{L}$.

10.21. Show that NLOGSPACE is strictly contained in PSPACE.

10.22. Show that DEXT $\neq$ PSPACE. (*Hint*: Show that DEXT is not closed under $\propto_{poly}$.)

10.23. Show that polynomial time Turing reduction as defined on page 313 implies polynomial time transformation as defined in Sec. 10.7. Is the converse true? Explain.

10.24. Consider the MAX-CLIQUE problem defined as follows. Given a graph $G = (V, E)$ and a positive integer k, decide whether the maximal complete subgraph of G is of size k. Show that MAX-CLIQUE is in Δ_2^p.

10.25. Show that $\Sigma_1^p = $ NP.

10.26. Show that if $\Sigma_k^p \subseteq \Pi_k^p$, then $\Sigma_k^p = \Pi_k^p$.

10.12 Bibliographic Notes

Some references to computational complexity include Balcazar *et al.* (1988, 1990), Bovet and Crescenzi (1994), Garey and Johnson (1979), Hopcroft and Ullman (1979) and Papadimitriou (1994). The book by Bovet and Crescenzi (1994) provides a good introduction to the field of computational complexity. The first attempt to make a systematic approach to computational complexity was made by Rabin (1960). The study of time and space complexity can be said to begin with Hartmanis and Stearns (1965), Stearns *et al.* (1965) and Lewis *et al.* (1965). This work contains most of the basic theorems of complexity classes and time and space hierarchy. Theorem 10.4 is due to Savitch (1970). Extensive research in this field emerged and enormous number of papers have been published since then. For comments about NP-complete problems, see the Bibliographic Notes of Chapter 9. PSPACE-complete problems were first studied in Karp (1972) including CSG RECOGNITION and LBA ACCEPTANCE. QUANTIFIED BOOLEAN FORMULAS was shown to be PSPACE-complete in Stockmeyer and Meyer (1973) and Stockmeyer (1974). The *linear bounded automata problem*, which predates the NP = P question, is the problem of deciding whether nondeterministic LBAs are equivalent to deterministic LBAs, that is whether NSPACE(n) = DSPACE(n).

NLOGSPACE-complete problems were studied by Savitch (1970), Sudborough (1975a, 1975b), Springsteel (1976), Jones (1975) and Jones *et al.* (1976). The NLOGSPACE-completeness of the GRAPH ACCISSIBILITY problem (GAP) was proven in Jones (1975).

P-complete problems under log space reductions were considered by Cook (1973, 1974), Cook and Sethi (1976), Jones (1975). Jones and Lasser (1976) contains a collection of P-complete problems. In Lander (1975), the CIRCUIT VALUE problem was proven to be P-complete with respect to log space reduction. The P-completeness of the MAX-FLOW problem with respect to log space reduction is due to Goldschlager *et al.* (1982). The problem ORDERED DEPTH-FIRST SEARCH was presented in Reif (1985). LINEAR PROGRAMMING is proved to be P-complete under log space reduction in Dobkin *et al.* (1979). The definition of P-complete problems in terms of NC-reductions is due to Cook (1985).

The polynomial hierarchy was first studied in Stockmeyer (1976). See also Wrathall (1976) for complete problems.

Very detailed bibliographic notes, as well as more recent topics in the field of computational complexity, including the study of probabilistic algorithms, parallel algorithms and interactive proof systems, can be found in recent books on computational complexity cited above. See the book by Greenlaw *et al.* (1995) for a thorough exposition of the theory of P-completeness, including an extensive list of P-complete problems.

Chapter 11

Lower Bounds

11.1 Introduction

When we described algorithms in the previous chapters, we analyzed their time complexities, mostly in the worst case. We have occasionally characterized a particular algorithm as being "efficient" in the sense that it has the lowest possible time complexity. In Chapter 1, we have denoted by an optimal algorithm an algorithm for which both the upper bound of the *algorithm* and the lower bound of the *problem* are asymptotically equivalent. For virtually all algorithms we have encountered, we have been able to find an upper bound on the amount of computation the algorithm requires. But the problem of finding a lower bound of a particular problem is much harder, and indeed there are numerous problems whose lower bound is unknown. This is due to the fact that when considering the lower bound of a problem, we have to establish a lower bound on *all* algorithms that solve that problem. This is by no means an easy task compared with computing the worst case running time of a given algorithm. It turns out, however, that most of the known lower bounds are either *trivial* or derived using a model of computation that is severely constrained, in the sense that it is not capable of performing some elementary operations, e.g., multiplication.

11.2 Trivial Lower Bounds

In this section, we consider those lower bounds that can be deduced using intuitive argument without resorting to any model of computation or doing sophisticated mathematics. We will give two examples of establishing trivial lower bounds.

Example 11.1   Consider the problem of finding the sum in a list of n numbers. Clearly, every element in the list must be inspected. This means that we must spend at least $\Omega(1)$ time corresponding to one addition for each element. It follows that any algorithm to find the sum of n numbers must spend $\Omega(n)$ time.

Example 11.2   Consider the problem of matrix multiplication. Any algorithm to multiply two $n \times n$ matrices must compute exactly n^2 values. Since at least $\Omega(1)$ time must be spent in each evaluation, the time complexity of any algorithm for multiplying two $n \times n$ matrices is $\Omega(n^2)$.

11.3   The Decision Tree Model

There are certain problems where it is realistic to consider the branching instruction as the basic operation (see Definition 1.6 on page 40). Thus, in this case, the number of comparisons becomes the primary measure of complexity. In the case of sorting, for example, the output is identical to the input except for order. Therefore, it becomes reasonable to consider a model of computation in which all steps are two-way branches, based on a comparison between two quantities. The usual representation of an algorithm consisting solely of branches is a binary tree called a *decision tree*.

Let Π be a problem for which a lower bound is sought, and let the size of an instance of Π be represented by a positive integer n. Then, *for each pair of algorithm and value of n*, there is a corresponding decision tree that "solves" instances of the problem of size n. As an example, Fig. 1.2 shows two decision trees corresponding to Algorithm BINARYSEARCH on instances of sizes 10 and 14, respectively.

11.3.1   *The search problem*

In this section, we derive a lower bound on the search problem: Given an array $A[1..n]$ of n elements, determine whether a given element x is in the array. In Chapter 1, we have presented Algorithm LINEARSEARCH to solve this problem. We have also presented Algorithm BINARYSEARCH for the case when the list is sorted.

In the case of searching, each node of the decision tree corresponds to a decision. The test represented by the root is made first and control passes to one of its children depending on the outcome. If the element x being searched for is less than the element corresponding to an internal node, control passes to its left child. If it is greater, then control passes to its right child. The search ceases if x is equal to the element corresponding to a node or if the node is a leaf.

Consider first the case when the list is not sorted. It is easy to see that n comparisons are both necessary and sufficient in the worst case. It follows that the problem of searching an arbitrary list requires at least $\Omega(n)$ time in the worst case, and hence Algorithm LINEARSEARCH is optimal.

As regards the case when the list is sorted, we argue as follows. Let A be an algorithm for searching a sorted list with n elements, and consider the decision tree T associated with A and n. Let the number of nodes in T be m. We observe that $m \geq n$. We also observe that the number of comparisons performed in the worst case must correspond to the longest path from the root of T to a leaf plus one. This is exactly the height of T plus one. By Observation 2.3, the height of T is at least $\lfloor \log n \rfloor$. It follows that the number of comparisons performed in the worst case is $\lfloor \log n \rfloor + 1$. This implies the following theorem:

Theorem 11.1 *Any algorithm that searches a sorted sequence of n elements must perform at least $\lfloor \log n \rfloor + 1$ comparisons in the worst case.*

By the above theorem and Theorem 1.1, we conclude that Algorithm BINARYSEARCH is optimal.

11.3.2 *The sorting problem*

In this section, we derive a lower bound on the problem of *sorting by comparisons*. All sorting problems that are not comparison-based, e.g., radix sort and bucket sort are excluded. In the case of sorting, each internal vertex of the tree represents a decision, and each leaf corresponds to an output. The test represented by the root is made first and control passes to one of its children depending on the outcome. The desired output is available at the leaf reached. With each pair of sorting algorithm and value of n representing

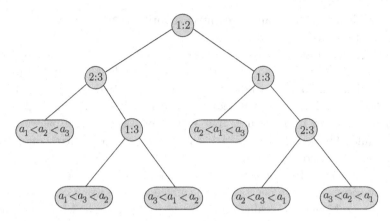

Fig. 11.1.   A decision tree for sorting three elements.

the number of elements to be sorted, we associate a decision tree. Thus, for a fixed value of n, the decision tree corresponding to MERGESORT, for example, is different from that of HEAPSORT or INSERTIONSORT. If the elements to be sorted are $a_1, a_2, \ldots, a_n$, then the outcome is a permutation of these elements. It follows that any decision tree for the SORTING problem must have at least $n!$ leaves. Figure 11.1 shows an example of a decision tree for an algorithm that sorts three distinct elements.

Clearly, the time complexity in the worst case is the length of a longest path from the root to a leaf, which is the height of the decision tree.

Lemma 11.1   *Let T be a binary tree with at least $n!$ leaves. Then, the height of T is at least $n \log n - 1.5n = \Omega(n \log n)$.*

Proof.   Let l be the number of leaves in T, and let h be its height. By Observation 2.1, the number of vertices at level h, which are leaves, is at most 2^h. Since $l \geq n!$, we have

$$n! \leq l \leq 2^h.$$

Consequently, $h \geq \log n!$. By Eq. (A.18) (page 682),

$$h \geq \log n! = \sum_{j=1}^{n} \log j \geq n \log n - n \log e + \log e \geq n \log n - 1.5n. \quad \square$$

Lemma 11.1 implies the following important theorem.

Theorem 11.2   *Any comparison-based algorithm that sorts n elements must perform $\Omega(n \log n)$ element comparisons in the worst case.*

In Chapter 5, we have shown that if n is a power of 2, then Algorithm MERGESORT performs $n \log n - n + 1$ comparisons in the worst case, which is very close to the lower bound in Lemma 11.1. In other words, the lower bound we have obtained is almost achievable by Algorithm MERGESORT.

11.3.3   *Finding the maximum*

Any decision tree for finding the maximum of n elements must have at least 2^{n-1} leaves since each path from the root to one of the leaves must contain at least $n - 1$ internal nodes. It follows that any comparison-based algorithm for finding the maximum must perform at least $\log 2^{n-1} = n - 1$ comparisons.

11.3.4   *Finding the largest and second largest elements*

In this section, we derive a lower bound on the problem of finding the largest and second largest in a set of n elements and outline an algorithm to find them using the least number of comparisons.

11.3.4.1   *Lower bound*

Theorem 11.3   *Any comparison-based algorithm for computing the largest and second largest elements in a set of n elements must do at least $n - 2 + \log n$ comparisons in the worst case.*

Proof.   Partition the set of all possible inputs into equivalence classes $C_i, 1 \le i \le n$, such that two inputs are in the same equivalence class if their maximum appears in position i. The set of all leaves of the decision tree are also partitioned into equivalence classes L_i, where L_i corresponds to C_i. For all leaves of the decision tree in L_i, the position of the largest element, which is i, is identical, and hence, in the subtree that defines L_i, all comparisons are made on the positions of the $n - 1$ smallest elements since the second largest element is to be determined. Therefore, this subtree can be viewed as a comparison tree for determining the largest element in a set of $n - 1$ elements, and thus it has at least 2^{n-2} leaves (see Sec. 11.3.3). Since there are n classes, the original tree contains at least $n 2^{n-2}$ leaves.

It follows that the number of comparisons, which is the height of the tree, is at least $\log(n2^{n-2}) = n - 2 + \log n$. □

11.3.4.2 *Optimal algorithm*

We now describe a simple algorithm for finding the largest and second largest elements in a sequence of n elements that uses $n - 2 + \log n$ comparisons. This means that the bound in Theorem 11.3 is achievable, and thus the algorithm is optimal. Assume without loss of generality that n is a power of 2. The method used is called the *tournament method*, which derives its name from the fact that it performs its comparisons in the same way that tournaments are played. In the first round, pairs of elements are compared. In succeeding rounds, the winners from the preceding round are compared, and so on until there is only one element left. At this point, the largest element has been found at the root of the tree using $n - 1$ comparisons, which is the number of internal nodes. Next, to compute the second largest element, we do a second pass bottom-up and compare the maximum element with elements that lost to the maximum; their number is equal to $\log n - 1$. It follows that the total number of comparisons is $n - 1 + \log n - 1 = n - 2 + \log n$.

Example 11.3 Figure 11.2 depicts the complete binary tree for the tournament of finding the largest and second largest elements in the sequence of 8 numbers $\langle 6, 1, 5, 3, 8, 7, 4, 2 \rangle$. In the first pass, the maximum is found at the root. In the second pass, the largest element 8 is compared with $7, 4$ and 6, and the second largest element 7 is found. These elements are shown in bold in the figure.

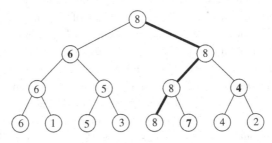

Fig. 11.2.   A tournament for finding the largest and second largest elements.

Using a simple adversary argument, it can be shown that in order to find the second largest element, the maximum must also be determined. This implies the following corollary.

Corollary 11.1 *Any comparison-based algorithm for computing the second largest element in a set of n elements must do at least $n - 2 + \log n$ comparisons in the worst case.*

11.4 The Algebraic Decision Tree Model

The decision tree model as described in Sec. 11.3 is severely restricted, as it only allows a comparison between two elements as the primary operation. If the decision at each internal vertex is a comparison of a polynomial of the input variables with the number 0, then the resulting decision tree is called an *algebraic decision tree*. This model of computation is far more powerful than the decision tree model and in fact attains the power of the RAM model of computation. When establishing lower bounds for decision problems using this model, we usually ignore all arithmetic operations and confine our attention to the number of branching instructions. Thus, this model is similar to the decision tree model in the sense that it is best suited for combinatorial algorithms that deal with rearrangements of elements. We define this model of computation more formally as follows.

An *algebraic decision tree* on a set of n variables $x_1, x_2, \ldots, x_n$ is a binary tree with the property that each vertex is labeled with a statement in the following way. Associated with every internal vertex is a statement that is essentially a test of the form: If $f(x_1, x_2, \ldots, x_n) : 0$, then branch to the left child, else branch to the right child. Here, "$:$" stands for any comparison relation from the set $\{=, <, \leq\}$. On the other hand, one of the answers *yes* or *no* is associated with each leaf vertex.

An algebraic decision tree is of order d, for some integer $d \geq 1$, if all polynomials associated with the internal nodes of the tree have degree at most d. If $d = 1$, i.e., if all polynomials at the internal vertices of an algebraic decision tree are linear, then it is called a *linear algebraic decision tree* (or simply *linear decision tree*). Let Π be a decision problem whose input is a set of n real numbers $x_1, x_2, \ldots, x_n$. Then, associated with Π is a subset W of the n-dimensional space E^n such that a point $(x_1, x_2, \ldots, x_n)$ is in W if and only if the answer to the problem Π when presented with the input

$x_1, x_2, \ldots, x_n$ is yes. We say that an algebraic decision tree T decides the membership in W if whenever the computation starts at the root of T with some point $p = (x_1, x_2, \ldots, x_n)$, control eventually reaches a *yes* leaf if and only if $(x_1, x_2, \ldots, x_n) \in W$.

As in the decision tree model, to derive a lower bound on the worst case time complexity of a problem Π, it suffices to derive a lower bound on the height of the algebraic decision tree that solves Π. Now, let W be the subset of the n-dimensional space E^n that is associated with the problem Π. Suppose that in some way the number $\#W$ of the *connected components* of the set W is known. We want to derive a lower bound on the height of the algebraic decision tree for Π in terms of $\#W$. We now establish this relation for the case of linear decision trees.

Let T be a linear decision tree. Then, every path from the root to a leaf in T corresponds to a sequence of conditions having one of the following forms:

$$f(x_1, x_2, \ldots, x_n) = 0, \ g(x_1, x_2, \ldots, x_n) < 0, \quad \text{and} \quad h(x_1, x_2, \ldots, x_n) \leq 0.$$

Note that each of these functions is linear since we have assumed that T is a linear decision tree. Thus, when the root of T is presented with a point $(x_1, x_2, \ldots, x_n)$, control eventually reaches a leaf l if and only if all conditions on the path from the root to l are satisfied. By the linearity of these conditions, the leaf l corresponds to an intersection of hyperplanes, open halfspaces and closed halfspaces, i.e., it corresponds to a convex set. Since this set is convex, it is necessarily connected, i.e., it consists of exactly one component. Thus, each *yes*-leaf corresponds to exactly one connected component. It follows that the number of leaves of T is at least $\#W$. By an argument similar to that in the proof of Lemma 11.1, the height of the tree is at least $\lceil \log(\#W) \rceil$. This implies the following theorem.

Theorem 11.4 *Let W be a subset of E^n, and let T be a linear decision tree of n variables that accepts the set W. Then, the height of T is at least $\lceil \log(\#W) \rceil$.*

The linear decision tree model is certainly very restricted. Therefore, it is desirable to extend it to the more general algebraic decision tree model. It turns out, however, that in this model, the above argument no longer applies; a *yes*-leaf may have associated with it many connected components.

In this case, more complex mathematical analysis leads to the following theorem.

Theorem 11.5 *Let W be a subset of E^n, and let d be a fixed positive integer. Then, the height of any order d algebraic decision tree T that accepts W is $\Omega(\log \#W - n)$.*

One of the most important combinatorial problems is that of sorting a set of n real numbers using only the operation of comparisons. We have shown that under the decision tree model, this problem requires $\Omega(n \log n)$ comparisons in the worst case. It can be shown that this bound is still valid under many computational models, and in particular the algebraic decision tree model of computation. We state this fact as a theorem.

Theorem 11.6 *In the algebraic decision tree model of computation, sorting n real numbers requires $\Omega(n \log n)$ element comparisons in the worst case.*

11.4.1 *The element uniqueness problem*

The problem ELEMENT UNIQUENESS is stated as follows. Given a set of n real numbers, decide whether two of them are equal. We will now obtain a lower bound on the time complexity of this problem using the algebraic decision tree model of computation. A set of n real numbers $\{x_1, x_2, \ldots, x_n\}$ can be viewed as a point $(x_1, x_2, \ldots, x_n)$ in the n-dimensional space E^n. Let $W \subseteq E^n$ be the membership set of the problem ELEMENT UNIQUE-NESS on $\{x_1, x_2, \ldots, x_n\}$. In other words, W consists of the set of points $\{x_1, x_2, \ldots, x_n\}$ with the property that no two coordinates of which are equal. It is not hard to see that W contains $n!$ disjoint connected components. Specifically, each permutation π of $\{1, 2, \ldots, n\}$ corresponds to the set of points in E^n

$$W_\pi = \{(x_1, x_2, \ldots, x_n) \mid x_{\pi(1)} < x_{\pi(2)} < \cdots < x_{\pi(n)}\}.$$

Clearly,

$$W = W_1 \cup W_2 \cup \cdots \cup W_{n!}.$$

Moreover, these subsets are connected and disjoint. Thus, $\#W = n!$, and it follows from Theorem 11.5. that in the algebraic decision tree model of computation, any algorithm that solves the ELEMENT UNIQUENESS problem requires $\Omega(\log n!) = \Omega(n \log n)$ element comparisons in the worst case.

11.4.2 The set equality problem

The problem SET EQUALITY is stated as follows. Given two sets $A = \{x_1, x_2, \ldots, x_n\}$ and $B = \{y_1, y_2, \ldots, y_n\}$ of n real numbers each, decide whether $A = B$. Assume without loss of generality that $B = \{1, 2, \ldots, n\}$. Let $W \subseteq E^n$ be the membership set of the problem SET EQUALITY on A and B. Then,

$$W = \{\pi(1), \pi(2), \ldots, \pi(n) \mid \pi \text{ is a permutation of } \{1, 2, \ldots, n\}\}.$$

In other words, W consists of the set of points $\{x_1, x_2, \ldots, x_n\}$ that are permutations of $\{1, 2, \ldots, n\}$. It is not hard to see that W consists of $n!$ disjoint connected components. Thus, $\#W = n!$, and it follows from Theorem 11.5. that in the algebraic decision tree model of computation, any algorithm that solves the SET EQUALITY problem requires $\Omega(\log n!) = \Omega(n \log n)$ element comparisons in the worst case.

11.4.3 The set inclusion problem

The problem SET INCLUSION is stated as follows. Given two sets $A = \{x_1, x_2, \ldots, x_n\}$ and $B = \{y_1, y_2, \ldots, y_n\}$ of n real numbers each, decide whether $A \subseteq B$. Assume without loss of generality that $B = \{1, 2, \ldots, n\}$. Let $W \subseteq E^n$ be the membership set of the problem SET INCLUSION on A and B. Then,

$$W = \{\{x_1, x_2, \ldots, x_n\} \mid \{x_1, x_2, \ldots, x_n\} \subseteq \{1, 2, \ldots, n\}\}.$$

In other words, W consists of the set of points $\{x_1, x_2, \ldots, x_n\}$ that are subsets of $\{1, 2, \ldots, n\}$. It is not hard to see that W contains n^n disjoint connected components, as there are n possibilities for each element of A. Thus, $\#W = n^n$, and it follows from Theorem 11.5. that in the algebraic decision tree model of computation, any algorithm that solves the SET INCLUSION problem requires $\Omega(\log n^n) = \Omega(n \log n)$ element comparisons in the worst case.

11.4.4 *The set disjointness problem*

The problem SET DISJOINTNESS is stated as follows. Given two sets $A = \{x_1, x_2, \ldots, x_n\}$ and $B = \{y_1, y_2, \ldots, y_n\}$ of n real numbers each, decide whether $A \cap B = \phi$. A set of $2n$ real numbers $\{x_1, x_2, \ldots, x_n, y_1, y_2, \ldots, y_n\}$ can be viewed as a point in the $2n$-dimensional space E^{2n}. Let $W \subseteq E^{2n}$ be the membership set of the problem SET DISJOINTNESS on A and B. Then,

$$W = \{\{x_1, x_2, \ldots, x_n, y_1, y_2, \ldots, y_n\} \mid x_i \neq y_j\}.$$

In other words, W consists of the set of points $\{x_1, x_2, \ldots, x_n, y_1, y_2, \ldots, y_n\}$ having the property that

$$\{x_1, x_2, \ldots, x_n\} \cap \{y_1, y_2, \ldots, y_n\} = \phi.$$

It is not hard to see that W contains $(n!)^2$ disjoint connected components, as there are $n! \times n!$ possible permutations for A and B. Thus, $\#W = (n!)^2$, and it follows from Theorem 11.5. that in the algebraic decision tree model of computation, any algorithm that solves the SET DISJOINTNESS problem requires $\Omega(\log(n!)^2) = \Omega(2 \log n!) = \Omega(n \log n)$ element comparisons in the worst case.

11.5 Linear Time Reductions

For the problem ELEMENT UNIQUENESS, we were able to obtain a lower bound using the algebraic decision tree model of computation directly by investigating the problem and applying Theorem 11.5. Another approach for establishing lower bounds is by making use of reductions. Let A be a problem whose lower bound is known to be $\Omega(f(n))$, where $n = o(f(n))$, e.g., $f(n) = n \log n$. Let B be a problem for which we wish to establish a lower bound of $\Omega(f(n))$. We establish this lower bound for problem B as follows:

(1) Convert the input to A into a suitable input to problem B.
(2) Solve problem B.
(3) Convert the output into a correct solution to problem A.

In order to achieve a linear time reduction, Steps 1 and 3 above must be performed in time $O(n)$. In this case, we say that the problem A has been reduced to the problem B in linear time, and we denote this by writing

$$A \propto_n B.$$

Now, we give examples of establishing an $\Omega(n \log n)$ lower bound for three problems using the linear time reduction technique.

11.5.1 *The convex hull problem*

Let $\{x_1, x_2, \ldots, x_n\}$ be a set of positive real numbers. We show that we can use *any* algorithm for the CONVEX HULL problem to sort these numbers using additional $O(n)$ time for converting the input and output. Since the SORTING problem is $\Omega(n \log n)$, it follows that the CONVEX HULL problem is $\Omega(n \log n)$ as well; otherwise, we would be able to sort in $o(n \log n)$ time, contradicting Theorem 11.6.

With each real number x_j, we associate a point (x_j, x_j^2) in the two-dimensional plane. Thus, all the n constructed points lie on the parabola $y = x^2$ (see Fig. 11.3).

If we use any algorithm for the CONVEX HULL problem to solve the constructed instance, the output will be a list of the constructed points sorted by their x-coordinates. To obtain the sorted numbers, first we find the point with minimum x-coordinate p_0. Next, starting from p_0, we traverse the list and read off the first coordinate of each point. The result is the original set of numbers in sorted order. Thus, we have shown that

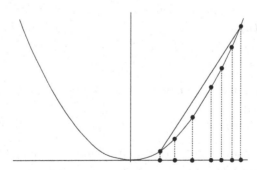

Fig. 11.3.   Reducing sorting to the CONVEX HULL problem.

$$\text{SORTING} \propto_n \text{CONVEX HULL},$$

which proves the following theorem.

Theorem 11.7   *In the algebraic decision tree model of computation, any algorithm that solves the* CONVEX HULL *problem requires* $\Omega(n \log n)$ *operations in the worst case.*

11.5.2   *The closest pair problem*

Given a set S of n points in the plane, the CLOSEST PAIR problem calls for identifying a pair of points in S with minimum separation (see Sec. 5.11). We show here that this problem requires $\Omega(n \log n)$ operations in the worst case by reducing the problem ELEMENT UNIQUENESS to it.

Let $\{x_1, x_2, \ldots, x_n\}$ be a set of positive real numbers. We show that we can use an algorithm for the CLOSEST PAIR problem to decide whether there are two numbers that are equal. Corresponding to each number x_j, we construct a point $p_j = (x_j, 0)$. Thus, the constructed set of points are all on the line $y = 0$. Let A be any algorithm that solves the CLOSEST PAIR problem. Let $(x_i, 0)$ and $(x_j, 0)$ be the output of algorithm A when presented with the set of constructed points. Clearly, there are two equal numbers in the original instance of the problem ELEMENT UNIQUENESS if and only if the distance between x_i and x_j is equal to zero. Thus, we have shown that

$$\text{ELEMENT UNIQUENESS} \propto_n \text{CLOSEST PAIR}.$$

This proves the following theorem.

Theorem 11.8   *In the algebraic decision tree model of computation, any algorithm that solves the* CLOSEST PAIR *problem requires* $\Omega(n \log n)$ *operations in the worst case.*

11.5.3   *The Euclidean minimum spanning tree problem*

Let S be a set of n points in the plane. The EUCLIDEAN MINIMUM SPANNING TREE problem (EMST) is to construct a tree of minimum total length whose vertices are the given points in S. We show that this problem requires $\Omega(n \log n)$ operations in the worst case by reducing the SORTING problem to it.

Let $\{x_1, x_2, \ldots, x_n\}$ be a set of positive real numbers to be sorted. Corresponding to each number x_j, we construct a point $p_j = (x_j, 0)$. Thus, the constructed set of points are all on the line $y = 0$. Let A be any algorithm that solves the EUCLIDEAN MINIMUM SPANNING TREE problem. If we feed algorithm A with the constructed set of points, the resulting minimum spanning tree will consist of $n - 1$ line segments $l_1, l_2, \ldots, l_{n-1}$ on the line $y = 0$, with the property that for each $j, 1 \leq j \leq n-2$, the right endpoint of l_j is the left endpoint of l_{j+1}. We can obtain the numbers $\{x_1, x_2, \ldots, x_n\}$ in sorted order by traversing the tree starting from the leftmost point and reading off the first component of each point. Thus, we have shown that

$$\text{SORTING } \propto_n \text{ EUCLIDEAN MINIMUM SPANNING TREE.}$$

It follows that in the algebraic decision tree model of computation, any algorithm that solves the EUCLIDEAN MINIMUM SPANNING TREE problem requires $\Omega(n \log n)$ operations in the worst case.

11.5.4 The diameter of a point set

Let S be a set of n points in the plane. The diameter of S, denoted by $Diam(S)$, is the maximum distance realized by two points in S. We show that finding $Diam(S)$ requires $\Omega(n \log n)$ operations in the worst case.

We reduce the problem SET DISJOINTNESS to DIAMETER. Let the two sets input to SET DISJOINTNESS be $A = \{a_1, a_2, \ldots, a_n\}$ and $B = \{b_1, b_2, \ldots, b_n\}$. Map the elements of A into the first quadrant of the unit circle and the elements of B into the third quadrant of the same circle in counterclockwise order. Then, the diameter of the mapped elements is equal to 2 if and only if the two sets have at least one element in common. See Fig. 11.4, in which $A = \{1, 3, 5, 7\}$ and $B = \{2, 4, 5, 8\}$.

Fig. 11.4. Reducing SET DISJOINTNESS to DIAMETER.

11.6 Practice Problems

11.1. Give a trivial lower bound for finding the inverse of an $n \times n$ matrix.

11.2. Give a trivial lower bound on the number of comparisons needed for deciding whether a given array $A[1..n]$ of n elements is sorted.

11.3. Give a trivial lower bound on the number of comparisons needed to compute the median of n elements using a comparison-based algorithm.

11.4. Draw the decision tree for Algorithm LINEARSEARCH on four elements.

11.5. Draw the decision tree for Algorithm INSERTIONSORT on three elements.

11.6. Draw the decision tree for Algorithm MERGESORT on three elements.

11.7. Apply the algorithm in Sec. 11.3.4.2 to find the largest and second largest in the set of numbers $\{4, 9, 1, 10, 3, 11, 8, 2\}$.

11.8. Let A and B be two unordered lists of n elements each. Consider the problem of deciding whether the elements in A are identical to those in B, i.e., the elements in A are a permutation of the elements in B. Use the Ω-notation to express the number of comparisons required to solve this problem.

11.7 Exercises

11.1. What is the minimum number of comparisons needed to test whether an array $A[1..n]$ is a heap? Explain.

11.2. Let S be a list of n unsorted elements. Show that constructing a binary search tree from the elements in S requires $\Omega(n \log n)$ in the decision tree model (see Sec. 2.6.2 for the definition of a binary search tree).

11.3. Let $S = \{x_1, x_2, \ldots, x_n\}$ be a set of n distinct positive integers. We want to find an element x that is in the upper half when S is sorted, or in other words, an element that is greater than the median. Use the Ω-notation to express the minimum number of element comparisons required to solve this problem.

11.4. Prove Corollary 11.1.

11.5. Show that any algorithm to merge two sorted lists of size n each by comparisons does at least $2n - 1$ such comparisons in the worst case.

11.6. Let A and B be two sets of points in the plane each containing n elements. Show that the problem of finding two closest points, one in A and the other in B requires $\Omega(n \log n)$ operations in the worst case.

11.7. Consider the TRIANGULATION problem: Given n points in the plane, join them by nonintersecting straight line segments so that every region internal to their convex hull is a triangle. Prove that this problem requires $\Omega(n \log n)$ operations in the worst case. (*Hint*: Reduce the SORTING problem to the special case of the TRIANGU-LATION problem when exactly $n - 1$ points are collinear and one point is not on the same line.)

11.8. Consider the NEAREST POINT problem: Given a set S of n points in the plane and a query point p, find a point in S that is closest to p. Show that any algorithm to solve this problem requires $\Omega(\log n)$ operations in the worst case. (*Hint*: Reduce binary search to the special case where all points lie on the same line.)

11.9. The CLOSEST PAIR problem is defined as follows. Given a set S of n points in the plane, find two points in S that are closest to each other. Show that this problem requires $\Omega(n \log n)$ operations in the worst case.

11.10. The ALL NEAREST POINTS problem is defined as follows. Given n points in the plane, find a nearest neighbor of each. Show that this problem requires $\Omega(n \log n)$ operations in the worst case. (*Hint*: Reduce the CLOSEST PAIR problem to it.)

11.11. Consider the problem of partitioning a planar point set S into two subsets S_1 and S_2 such that the maximum of $Diam(S_1)$ and $Diam(S_2)$ is minimum. Show that this problem requires $\Omega(n \log n)$ operations in the worst case. (*Hint*: Reduce the problem of finding the diameter of a point set S to this problem; see Sec. 11.5.4.)

11.8   Bibliographic Notes

For a detailed account of lower bounds for sorting, merging and selection, see Knuth (1973). This book provides an in-depth analysis. A sorting algorithm that requires the fewest known number of comparisons was originally presented in Ford and Johnson (1959). A merging algorithm with the minimum number of comparisons was presented by Hwang and Lin (1972). A lower bound on selection can be found in Hyafil (1976). Other relevant papers containing lower bound results include Fussenegger and Gabow (1976), Reingold (1971, 1972) and Friedman (1972). Theorem 11.4 is due to Dobkin and Lipton (1979). Theorem 11.5, and the lower bounds on set equality, set inclusion and set disjointness are due to Ben-Or (1983).

PART 5

Coping with Hardness

In the previous part of the book, we have seen that many practical problems have no efficient algorithms, and the known ones for these problems require an amount of time measured in years or centuries even for instances of moderate size.

There are three useful methodologies that could be used to cope with this difficulty. The first methodology is suitable for those problems that exhibit good average time complexity but for which the worst case polynomial time solution is elusive. This methodology is based on a methodic examination of the implicit state space induced by the problem instance under study. In the process of exploring the state space of the instance, some pruning takes place.

The second methodology in this part is based on the probabilistic notion of accuracy. At the heart of these solutions is a simple decision maker or test that can accurately perform one task (either passing or failing the alternative) and not say much about the complementary option. An iteration through this test will enable the construction of the solution or the increase in the confidence level in the solution to the desired degree.

341

The final methodology is useful for incremental solutions where one is willing to compromise on the quality of solution in return for faster (polynomial time) solutions. Only some classes of hard problems admit such polynomial time approximations. Still fewer of those provide a spectrum of polynomial time solutions where the degree of the polynomial is a function of accuracy.

In Chapter 12, we study two solution space search techniques that work for some problems, especially those in which the solution space is large. These techniques are backtracking and branch-and-bound. In these techniques, a solution to the problem can be obtained by exhaustively searching through a large but finite number of possibilities. It turns out that for many hard problems, backtracking and branch-and-bound are the only known techniques to solve these problems. After all, for some problems like the traveling salesman problem, even the problem of finding an approximate solution is NP-hard. In this chapter, a well-known branch-and-bound algorithm for the traveling salesman problem is presented. Other examples that are solved using the backtracking technique in this chapter include 3-coloring and the 8-queens problems.

Randomized algorithms are the subject of Chapter 13. In this chapter, we first show that randomization improves the performance of algorithm QUICKSORT significantly and results in a randomized selection algorithm that is considerably simpler and (almost always) much faster than Algorithm SELECT discussed in Chapter 5. Next, we present randomized algorithms for multiselection, min-cut, pattern matching and sampling problems. Finally, we apply randomization to a problem in number theory: primality testing. We will describe an efficient algorithm for this problem that almost all the time decides correctly whether a given positive integer is prime or not.

Chapter 14 discusses another avenue for dealing with hard problems: Instead of obtaining an optimal solution, we may be content with an approximate solution. In this chapter, we study some approximation algorithms for some NP-hard problems, including the bin packing problem, the Euclidean traveling salesman problem, the knapsack problem and the vertex cover problem. These problems share the common feature that the ratio of the optimal solution to the approximate solution is bounded by a small (and reasonable) constant. For the knapsack problem, we show a polynomial approximation scheme, that is, an algorithm that receives as input the desired approximation ratio and delivers an output whose relative ratio to the optimal solution is within the input ratio. This kind of polynomial approximation scheme is not polynomial in the reciprocal of the desired ratio. For this reason, we extend this scheme to the fully polynomial time approximation scheme that is also polynomial in the reciprocal of the desired ratio. As an example of this technique, we present an approximation algorithm for the subset sum problem.

Chapter 12

Backtracking

12.1 Introduction

In many real-world problems, as in most of the NP-hard problems, a solution can be obtained by exhaustively searching through a large but finite number of possibilities. Moreover, for virtually all these problems, there does not exist an algorithm that uses a method other than exhaustive search. Hence, the need arose for developing systematic techniques of searching, with the hope of cutting down the search space to possibly a much smaller space. In this chapter, we present a general technique for organizing the search known as *backtracking*. This algorithm design technique can be described as an organized exhaustive search which often avoids searching all possibilities. It is generally suitable for solving problems where a potentially large but finite number of solutions have to be inspected.

12.2 The 3-Coloring Problem

Consider the problem 3-COLORING: Given an undirected graph $G = (V, E)$, it is required to color each vertex in V with one of three colors, say 1, 2 and 3, such that no two adjacent vertices have the same color. We call such a coloring legal; otherwise, if two adjacent vertices have the same color, it is illegal. A coloring can be represented by an n-tuple $(c_1, c_2, \ldots, c_n)$ such that $c_i \in \{1, 2, 3\}, 1 \le i \le n$. For example, (1, 2, 2, 3, 1) denotes a coloring of a graph with five vertices. There are 3^n possible colorings (legal and illegal) to color a graph with n vertices. The set of all possible colorings can be

345

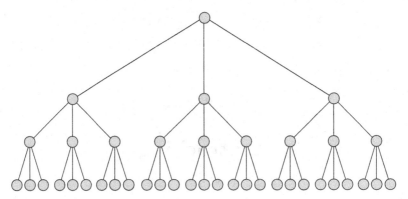

Fig. 12.1. The search tree for all possible three-colorings for a graph with three vertices.

represented by a complete ternary tree called the *search tree*. In this tree, each path from the root to a leaf node represents one coloring assignment. Figure 12.1 shows such a tree for the case of a graph with three vertices.

Let us call an incomplete coloring of a graph *partial* if no two adjacent colored vertices have the same color. Backtracking works by generating the underlying tree one node at a time. If the path from the root to the current node corresponds to a legal coloring, the process is terminated (unless more than one coloring is desired). If the length of this path is less than n and the corresponding coloring is partial, then one child of the current node is generated and is marked as the current node. If, on the other hand, the corresponding path is not partial, then the current node is marked as a dead node and a new node corresponding to another color is generated. If, however, all three colors have been tried with no success, the search *backtracks* to the parent node whose color is changed and so on.

Example 12.1 Consider the graph shown in Fig. 12.2(a), where we are interested in coloring its vertices using the colors $\{1, 2, 3\}$. Figure 12.2(b) shows part of the search tree generated during the process of searching for a legal coloring. First, after generating the third node, it is discovered that the coloring $(1, 1)$ is not partial, and hence that node is marked as a dead node by marking it with $\times$ in the figure. Next, b is assigned the color 2, and it is seen that the coloring $(1, 2)$ is partial. Hence, a new child node corresponding to vertex c is generated with an initial color assignment of 1. Repeating the above procedure of ignoring dead nodes and expanding those

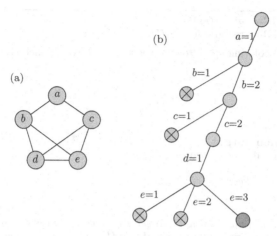

Fig. 12.2. An example of using backtracking to solve the problem 3-COLORING.

corresponding to partial colorings, we finally arrive at the legal coloring $(1, 2, 2, 1, 3)$.

It is interesting to note that we have arrived at the solution after generating only 10 nodes out of the 364 nodes comprising the search tree.

There are two important observations to be noted in Example 12.1, which generalize to all backtracking algorithms. First, the nodes are generated in a depth-first-search manner. Second, there is no need to store the whole search tree; we only need to store the path from the root to the current active node. In fact, no *physical* nodes are generated at all; the whole tree is *implicit*. In our example above, we only need to keep track of the color assignment.

12.2.1 *The algorithm*

Now we proceed to give two algorithms that use backtracking to solve the 3-COLORING problem, one is recursive and the other is iterative. In both algorithms, we assume for simplicity that the set of vertices is $\{1, 2, \ldots, n\}$. The recursive algorithm is shown as Algorithm 3-COLORREC.

Initially, no vertex is colored, and this is indicated by setting all colors to 0 in Step 1. The call *graphcolor*(1) causes the first vertex to be colored with 1. Clearly, (1) is a partial coloring, and hence the algorithm is then recursively called with $k = 2$. The assignment statement causes the second

---

Algorithm 12.1 3-COLORREC
Input: An undirected graph $G = (V, E)$.
Output: A 3-coloring $c[1..n]$ of the vertices of G, where each $c[j]$ is 1,2 or 3.

1. **for** $k \leftarrow 1$ **to** n
2. $c[k] \leftarrow 0$
3. **end for**
4. *flag* $\leftarrow$ **false**
5. *graphcolor*(1)
6. **if** *flag* **then output** c
7. **else output** "no solution"

Algorithm *graphcolor*(k)
1. **for** *color* $= 1$ **to** 3
2. $c[k] \leftarrow$ *color*
3.   **if** c is a legal coloring **then** set *flag* $\leftarrow$ **true** and **exit**
4.   **else if** c is partial **then** *graphcolor*($k + 1$)
5. **end for**

---

vertex to be colored with 1 as well. The resulting coloring is $(1, 1)$. If vertices 1 and 2 are not connected by an edge, then this coloring is partial. Otherwise, the coloring is not partial, and hence the second vertex will be colored with 2 and the resulting coloring is $(1, 2)$. After the second vertex has been colored, i.e., if the current coloring is partial, the algorithm is again invoked with $k = 3$, and so on. Suppose that the algorithm fails to color vertex j for some vertex $j \geq 3$. This happens if the **for** loop is executed three times without finding a legal or partial coloring. In this case, the previous recursive call is activated and another color for vertex $j - 1$ is tried. If again none of the three colors result in a partial coloring, the one before the last recursive call is activated. This is where backtracking takes place. The process of advancing and backtracking is continued until the graph is either colored or all possibilities have been exhausted without finding a legal coloring. Checking whether a coloring is partial can be done incrementally: If the coloring vector c contains m nonzero numbers and $c[m]$ does not result in a conflict with any other color, then it is partial; otherwise, it is not partial. Checking whether a coloring is legal amounts to checking whether the coloring vector consists of noncontradictory n colors.

The iterative backtracking algorithm is given as Algorithm 3-COLORITER. The main part of this algorithm consists of two nested **while** loops. The inner **while** loop implements advances (generating new nodes), whereas the outer **while** loop implements backtracking (to previously generated nodes). The working of this algorithm is similar to that of the recursive version.

Algorithm 12.2 3-COLORITER
Input: An undirected graph $G = (V, E)$.
Output: A 3-coloring $c[1..n]$ of the vertices of G, where each $c[j]$ is 1,2 or 3.

1. **for** $k \leftarrow 1$ **to** n
2. $c[k] \leftarrow 0$
3. **end for**
4. *flag* $\leftarrow$ **false**
5. $k \leftarrow 1$
6. **while** $k \geq 1$
7.   **while** $c[k] \leq 2$
8. $c[k] \leftarrow c[k] + 1$
9.   **if** c is a legal coloring **then** set *flag* $\leftarrow$ **true** and **exit** from the two while loops.
10.   **else if** c is partial **then** $k \leftarrow k + 1$ {*advance*}
11.   **end while**
12. $c[k] \leftarrow 0$
13. $k \leftarrow k - 1$ {*backtrack*}
14. **end while**
15. **if** *flag* **then output** c
16. **else output** "no solution"

As to the time complexity of these two algorithms, we note that $O(3^n)$ nodes are generated in the worst case. For each generated node, $O(n)$ work is required to check if the current coloring is legal, partial or neither. Hence, the overall running time is $O(n3^n)$ in the worst case.

12.3 The 8-Queens Problem

The classical 8-QUEENS can be stated as follows. How can we arrange eight queens on an 8×8 chessboard so that no two queens can attack each other? Two queens can attack each other if they are in the same row, column or diagonal. The n-queens problem is defined similarly, where in this case we have n queens and an $n \times n$ chessboard for an arbitrary value of $n \geq 1$. To simplify the discussion, we will study the 4-queens problem, and the generalization to any arbitrary n is straightforward.

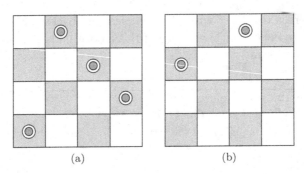

Fig. 12.3.   Two configurations of the 4-queens problem.

Consider a chessboard of size 4×4. Since no two queens can be put in the same row, each queen is in a different row. Since there are four positions in each row, there are 4^4 possible configurations. Each possible configuration can be described by a vector with four components $x = (x_1, x_2, x_3, x_4)$. For example, the vector $(2, 3, 4, 1)$ corresponds to the configuration shown in Fig. 12.3(a). A component is zero (and hence not included explicitly in the vector) if there is no queen placed in its corresponding row. For example, the partial vector $(3, 1)$ corresponds to the configuration shown in Fig. 12.3(b). In fact, since no two queens can be placed in the same column, a legal placement corresponds to a permutation of the numbers 1, 2, 3 and 4. This reduces the search space from 4^4 to $4!$. Modifying the algorithm accordingly will be left as an exercise.

12.3.1   *The algorithm*

To solve the 4-QUEENS problem using backtracking, the algorithm tries to generate and search a complete 4-ary rooted tree in a depth-first manner. The root of the tree corresponds to the placement of no queens. The nodes on the first level correspond to the possible placements of the queen in the first row, those on the second level correspond to the possible placements of the queen in the second row and so on. The backtracking algorithm to solve this problem is given as Algorithm 4-QUEENS. In the algorithm, we used the term *legal* to mean a placement of 4 queens that do not attack each other, and the term *partial* to mean a placement of less than 4 queens that do not attack each other. Clearly, two queens placed at positions x_i and x_j are in the same column if and only if $x_i = x_j$. It is not hard to see that two queens are in the same diagonal if and only if

$$x_i - x_j = i - j \text{ or } x_i - x_j = j - i.$$

Algorithm 12.3 4-QUEENS
Input: none.
Output: Vector $x[1..4]$ corresponding to the solution of the 4-queens problem.

1. **for** $k \leftarrow 1$ to 4
2. $x[k] \leftarrow 0$ {*no queens are placed on the chessboard* }
3. **end for**
4. *flag* $\leftarrow$ **false**
5. $k \leftarrow 1$
6. **while** $k \geq 1$
7.   **while** $x[k] \leq 3$
8. $x[k] \leftarrow x[k] + 1$
9.   **if** x is a legal placement **then** set *flag* $\leftarrow$ **true**
           and **exit** from the two while loops.
10.   **else if** x is partial **then** $k \leftarrow k + 1$ {*advance*}
11.   **end while**
12. $x[k] \leftarrow 0$
13. $k \leftarrow k - 1$ {*backtrack*}
14. **end while**
15. **if** *flag* **then output** x
16. **else output** "no solution"

Example 12.2   Applying the algorithm produces the solution shown in Fig. 12.4. In the figure, deadend nodes are marked with $\times$. First, x_1 is set to 1 and x_2 is set to 1. This results in a deadend, as the two queens are in the same column. The same result happens if x_2 is set to 2 since in this case, the two queens are on the same diagonal. Setting x_2 to 3 results in the partial vector $(1, 3)$ and the search advances to find a value for x_3. As shown in the figure, no matter what value x_3 assumes, no partial vector results with $x_1 = 1$, $x_2 = 3$ and $x_3 > 0$. Hence, the search backtracks to the second level and x_2 is reassigned a new value, namely 4. As shown in the figure, this results in the partial vector $(1, 4, 2)$. Again, this vector cannot be extended and consequently, after generating a few nodes, the search backs up to the first level. Now, x_1 is incremented to 2 and, in the same manner, the partial vector $(2, 4, 1)$ is found. As shown in the figure, this vector is extended to the legal vector $(2, 4, 1, 3)$, which corresponds to a legal placement.

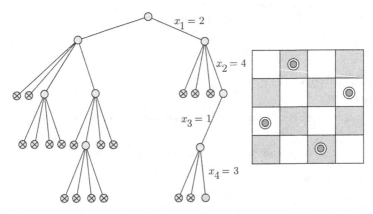

Fig. 12.4.   An example of using backtracking to solve the 4-queens problem.

Now, consider a brute-force method to solve the general n-queens problem. As mentioned before, since no two queens can be placed in the same column, the solution vector must be a permutation of the numbers $1, 2, \ldots, n$. Thus, the brute-force method can be improved to test $n!$ configurations instead of n^n. However, the following argument shows that backtracking drastically cuts the number of tests. Consider the $(n-2)!$ vectors corresponding to those configurations in which the first two queens are placed in the first column. The brute-force method blindly tests all these vectors, whereas in backtracking these tests can be avoided using $O(1)$ tests. Although the backtracking method to solve the n-queens problem costs $O(n^n)$ in the worst case, it empirically far exceeds the $O(n!)$ brute-force method in efficiency, as its expected running time is generally much faster. For example, the algorithm discovered the solution shown in Fig. 12.4 after generating 27 nodes out of a total of 341 possible nodes.

12.4   The General Backtracking Method

In this section, we describe the general backtracking algorithm as a systematic search method that can be applied to a class of search problems whose solution consists of a vector $(x_1, x_2, \ldots, x_i)$ satisfying some predefined constraints. Here, i is some integer between 0 and n, where n is a constant that is dependent on the problem formulation. In the two algorithms we have covered, 3-COLORING and the 8-QUEENS problems, i was fixed. However, in some problems, i may vary from one solution to another, as the following example illustrates.

Example 12.3   Consider a variant of the PARTITION problem defined as follows. Given a set of n integers $X = \{x_1, x_2, \ldots, x_n\}$ and an integer y, find a subset Y of X whose sum is equal to y. For instance if

$$X = \{10, 20, 30, 40, 50, 60\}$$

and $y = 60$, then there are three solutions of different lengths, namely

$$\{10, 20, 30\}, \{20, 40\} \text{ and } \{60\}.$$

It is not hard to devise a backtracking algorithm to solve this problem. Note that this problem can be formulated in another way so that the solution is a boolean vector of length n in the obvious way. Thus, the above three solutions may be expressed by the boolean vectors

$$\{1, 1, 1, 0, 0, 0, \}, \{0, 1, 0, 1, 0, 0\} \text{ and } \{0, 0, 0, 0, 0, 1\}.$$

In backtracking, each x_i in the solution vector belongs to a *finite* linearly ordered set X_i. Thus, the backtracking algorithm considers the elements of the Cartesian product $X_1 \times X_2 \times \cdots \times X_n$ in lexicographic order. Initially, the algorithm starts with the empty vector. It then chooses the *least* element of X_1 as x_1. If (x_1) is a partial solution, the algorithm proceeds by choosing the least element of X_2 as x_2. If (x_1, x_2) is a partial solution, then the least element of X_3 is included; otherwise, x_2 is set to the next element in X_2. In general, suppose that the algorithm has detected the partial solution $(x_1, x_2, \ldots, x_j)$. It then considers the vector $v = (x_1, x_2, \ldots, x_j, x_{j+1})$. We have the following cases:

(1) If v represents a final solution to the problem, the algorithm records it as a solution and either terminates in case only one solution is desired or continues to find other solutions.
(2) (The advance step). If v represents a partial solution, the algorithm advances by choosing the least element in the set X_{j+2}.
(3) If v is neither a final nor a partial solution, we have two subcases:
    (a) If there are still more elements to choose from in the set X_{j+1}, the algorithm sets x_{j+1} to the next member of X_{j+1}.

(b) (The backtrack step). If there are no more elements to choose from in the set X_{j+1}, the algorithm backtracks by setting x_j to the next member of X_j. If again there are no more elements to choose from in the set X_j, the algorithm backtracks by setting x_{j-1} to the next member of X_{j-1}, and so on.

Now, we describe the general backtracking algorithm formally using two algorithms: one recursive (BACKTRACKREC) and the other iterative (BACKTRACKITER). We will assume that the solution is one vector.

Algorithm 12.4 BACKTRACKREC
Input: Explicit or implicit description of the sets $X_1, X_2, \ldots, X_n$.
Output: A solution vector $v = (x_1, x_2, \ldots, x_i), 0 \leq i \leq n$.

1. $v \leftarrow (\ )$
2. $flag \leftarrow$ **false**
3. $advance(1)$
4. **if** $flag$ **then** output v
5. **else output** "no solution"

Algorithm $advance(k)$
1. **for each** $x \in X_k$
2. $x_k \leftarrow x$; append x_k to v
3.   **if** v is a final solution **then** set $flag \leftarrow$ **true** and **exit**
4.   **else if** v is partial **then** $advance(k+1)$
5. **end for**

These two algorithms very much resemble those backtracking algorithms described in Secs. 12.2 and 12.3. In general, to search for a solution to a problem using backtracking, one of these two prototype algorithms may be utilized as a framework around which an algorithm specially tailored to the problem at hand can be designed.

12.5   Branch and Bound

Branch-and-bound design technique is similar to backtracking in the sense that it generates a search tree and looks for one or more solutions. However, while backtracking searches for a solution or a set of solutions that satisfy certain properties (including maximization or minimization), branch-and-bound algorithms are typically concerned with only maximization or

---

Algorithm 12.5 BACKTRACKITER
Input: Explicit or implicit description of the sets $X_1, X_2, \ldots, X_n$.
Output: A solution vector $v = (x_1, x_2, \ldots, x_i), 0 \leq i \leq n$.

1. $v \leftarrow (\ )$
2. *flag* $\leftarrow$ **false**
3. $k \leftarrow 1$
4. **while** $k \geq 1$
5.   **while** X_k is not exhausted
6. $x_k \leftarrow$ next element in X_k; append x_k to v
7.   **if** v is a final solution **then** set *flag* $\leftarrow$ **true**
        and **exit** from the two while loops.
8.   **else if** v is partial **then** $k \leftarrow k + 1$ {*advance*}
9.   **end while**
10.   Reset X_k so that the next element is the first.
11. $k \leftarrow k - 1$ {*backtrack*}
12. **end while**
13. **if** *flag* **then** output v
14. **else output** "no solution"

---

minimization of a given function. Moreover, in branch-and-bound algorithms, a bound is calculated at each node x on the possible value of any solution given by nodes that may later be generated in the subtree rooted at x. If the bound calculated is worse than a previous bound, the subtree rooted at x is blocked, i.e., none of its children are generated.

Henceforth, we will assume that the algorithm is to minimize a given cost function; the case of maximization is similar. In order for branch and bound to be applicable, the cost function must satisfy the following property. For all partial solutions $(x_1, x_2, \ldots, x_{k-1})$ and their extensions $(x_1, x_2, \ldots, x_k)$, we must have

$$cost(x_1, x_2, \ldots, x_{k-1}) \leq cost(x_1, x_2, \ldots, x_k).$$

Given this property, a partial solution $(x_1, x_2, \ldots, x_k)$ can be discarded once it is generated if its cost is greater than or equal to a previously computed solution. Thus, if the algorithm finds a solution whose cost is c, and there is a partial solution whose cost is at least c, no more extensions of this partial solution are generated.

The TRAVELING SALESMAN problem will serve as a good example for the branch and bound method. This problem is defined as follows. Given a set of cities and a cost function that is defined on each pair of cities, find

	1	2	3	4	5
1	∞	17	7	35	18
2	9	∞	5	14	19
3	29	24	∞	30	12
4	27	21	25	∞	48
5	15	16	28	18	∞

A

	1	2	3	4	5	
1	∞	10	0	25	11	-7
2	4	∞	0	6	14	-5
3	17	12	∞	15	0	-12
4	6	0	4	∞	27	-21
5	0	1	13	0	∞	-15

B   -3

Fig. 12.5.   An instance matrix of the TRAVELING SALESMAN and its reduction.

a tour of minimum cost. Here, a tour is a closed path that visits each city exactly once. The cost function may be the distance, travel time, air fare, etc. An instance of the TRAVELING SALESMAN is given by its cost matrix whose entries are assumed to be nonnegative. The matrix A in Fig. 12.5 is an example of such an instance. With each partial solution $(x_1, x_2, \ldots, x_k)$, we associate a *lower bound* y which is interpreted as follows. The cost of any complete tour that visits the cities $x_1, x_2, \ldots, x_k$ *in this order* must be at least y.

We observe that each complete tour must contain exactly one edge and its associated cost from each row and each column of the cost matrix. We also observe that if a constant r is subtracted from every entry in any row or column of the cost matrix A, the cost of any tour under the new matrix is exactly r less than the cost of the same tour under A. This motivates the idea of *reducing* the cost matrix so that each row or column contains at least one entry that is equal to 0. We will refer to such a matrix as the *reduction* of the original matrix. In Fig. 12.5, matrix B is the reduction of matrix A.

Matrix B in the figure results from subtracting the shown amounts from each row and from column 4. The total amount subtracted is 63. It is not hard to see that the cost of any tour is at least 63. In general, let $(r_1, r_2, \ldots, r_n)$ and $(c_1, c_2, \ldots, c_n)$ be the amounts subtracted from rows 1 to n and columns 1 to n, respectively, in an $n \times n$ cost matrix A. Then,

$$y = \sum_{i=1}^{n} r_i + \sum_{i=1}^{n} c_i$$

is a lower bound on the cost of any complete tour.

Now, we proceed to describe a branch-and-bound algorithm to solve the traveling salesman problem through an example. Our example is to find an optimal tour for the instance given in Fig. 12.5. The search tree, which is a binary tree, is depicted in Fig. 12.6.

The root of the tree is represented by the reduction matrix B and is labeled with the lower bound computed above, namely 63. This node is split into two nodes corresponding to the left and right subtrees. The right subtree contains all solutions that exclude the edge $(3, 5)$ and thus the entry $D_{3,5}$ is set to ∞. We will justify the choice of the edge $(3, 5)$ later. Since there are no zeros in row 3 of matrix D, it can be reduced further by 12. This is accompanied by increasing the lower bound by 12 to become 75. The left subtree will contain all solutions that include the edge $(3, 5)$ and thus both the third row and fifth column of matrix C are removed, since we can never go from 3 to any other city nor arrive at 5 from any other city. Furthermore, since all solutions in this subtree use the edge $(3, 5)$, the edge $(5, 3)$ will not be used any more, and hence its corresponding entry $C_{5,3}$ is set to ∞. As each row and column of this matrix contains a zero, it cannot be reduced further and hence the lower bound of this node is the same as its parent's lower bound.

Now, as the lower bound of the node containing matrix C is less than that of the node containing matrix D, the next split is performed on the node containing matrix C. We use edge $(2, 3)$ to split this node.

The right subtree will contain all solutions that exclude the edge $(2, 3)$ and thus the entry $F_{2,3}$ is set to ∞. Since there are no zeros in row 2 of matrix F, it can be reduced further by 4. This increases the lower bound from 63 to 67. The left subtree will contain all solutions that include the edge $(2, 3)$, and hence both the second row and third column of matrix E are removed. Now, following the same procedure above, we would change $E_{3,2}$ to ∞. However, this entry does not exist in matrix E. If we follow the path from the root to the node containing this matrix, we see that the two edges $(3, 5)$ and $(2, 3)$, i.e., the subpath $2,3,5$ must be in any tour in the subtree whose root contains matrix E. This implies that the entry $E_{5,2}$ must be set to ∞. In general, if the edge included is (u_i, v_1) and the path from the root contains the two paths $u_1, u_2, \ldots, u_i$ and $v_1, v_2, \ldots, v_j$, then M_{v_j, u_1} is set to ∞, where M is the matrix at the current node. To finish processing matrix E, we subtract 10 from the first row, which increases the lower bound from 63 to 73.

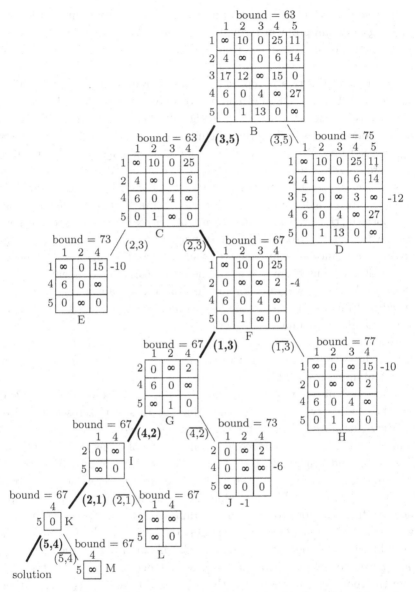

Fig. 12.6. Solution of the TRAVELING SALESMAN using branch and bound.

Following the above procedure, the matrices G, H, I, J, K, L, M are computed in this order. The optimal tour can be traced from the root by following the lines shown in bold face, that is, $1, 3, 5, 4, 2, 1$. Its total cost is $7 + 12 + 18 + 21 + 9 = 67$.

At the beginning of this example, we chose to split using the edge $(3, 5)$ because it caused the greatest increase in the lower bound of the right subtree. This heuristic is useful because it is faster to find the solution by following the left edges, which reduce the dimension as opposed to the right edges which merely add a new ∞ and probably more zeros. However, we did not use this heuristic when splitting at the node containing matrix C. It is left as an exercise to find the optimal solution with fewer node splittings.

From the above example, it seems that the heap is an ideal data structure to use in order to expand the node with the least cost (or maximum cost in case of maximization). Although branch-and-bound algorithms are generally complicated and hard to program, they proved to be efficient in practice.

12.6   Practice Problems

12.1. Apply the algorithm for 3-COLORING presented in Sec. 12.2 on the graph shown in Fig. 12.7.

12.2. Consider the algorithm for 3-COLORING presented in Sec. 12.2. Give an efficient algorithm to test whether a vector corresponding to a 3-coloring of a graph is legal.

12.3. Consider the algorithm for 3-COLORING presented in Sec. 12.2. Explain how to efficiently test whether the current vector is partial throughout the execution of the algorithm.

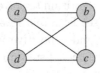

Fig. 12.7.   An undirected graph.

12.4. Give a recursive algorithm for the 4-COLORING problem. What is the running time of your algorithm?

12.5. Give an iterative algorithm for the 4-COLORING problem. What is the running time of your algorithm?

12.6. Apply the algorithm developed in Problem 12.4 or 12.5 on the graph in Fig. 12.2(a).

12.7. Show that two queens placed at positions x_i and x_j are in the same diagonal if and only if

$$x_i - x_j = i - j \text{ or } x_i - x_j = j - i.$$

12.8. Give a recursive algorithm for the 8-QUEENS problem.

12.9. Does the n-queens problem have a solution for every value of $n \geq 4$? Prove your answer.

12.7   Exercises

12.1. Modify Algorithm 4-QUEENS so that it reduces the search space from 4^4 to 4! as described in Sec. 12.3.

12.2. Design a backtracking algorithm to generate all permutations of the numbers $1, 2, \ldots, n$.

12.3. Design a backtracking algorithm to generate all 2^n subsets of the numbers $1, 2, \ldots, n$.

12.4. Write a backtracking algorithm to solve the *knight tour problem*: Given an 8×8 chessboard, decide if it is possible for a knight placed at a certain position of the board to visit every square of the board exactly once and return to its start position.

12.5. Write a backtracking algorithm to solve the following variant of the PARTITION problem (see Example 12.3): Given n positive integers $X = \{x_1, x_2, \ldots, x_n\}$ and a positive integer y, does there exist a subset $Y \subseteq X$ whose elements sum up to y?

12.6. Give a backtracking algorithm to solve the HAMILTONIAN CYCLE problem: Given an undirected graph $G = (V, E)$, determine whether it contains a simple cycle that visits each vertex exactly once.

12.7. Consider the KNAPSACK problem defined in Sec. 6.6. It was shown that using dynamic programming, the problem can be solved in time $\Theta(nC)$, where n is the number of items and C is the knapsack capacity.

    (a) Give a backtracking algorithm to solve the knapsack problem.

    (b) Which technique is more efficient to solve the knapsack problem: backtracking or dynamic programming? Explain.

12.8. Give a backtracking algorithm to solve the money change problem defined in Problem 6.20.

12.9. Apply the algorithm in Exercise 12.8 for the money change problem on the instance in Exercise 6.21.

12.10. Give a backtracking algorithm to solve the *assignment problem* defined as follows. Given n employees to be assigned to n jobs such that the cost of assigning the ith person to the jth job is $c_{i,j}$, find an assignment that minimizes the total cost. Assume that the cost is nonnegative, that is, $c_{i,j} \geq 0$ for $1 \leq i, j \leq n$.

12.11. Modify the solution of the instance of the TRAVELING SALESMAN problem given in Sec. 12.5 so that it results in fewer node splittings.

12.12. Apply the branch-and-bound algorithm for the TRAVELING SALES-MAN problem discussed in Sec. 12.5 on the instance

$$\begin{bmatrix} \infty & 5 & 2 & 10 \\ 2 & \infty & 5 & 12 \\ 3 & 7 & \infty & 5 \\ 8 & 2 & 4 & \infty \end{bmatrix}.$$

12.13. Consider again the KNAPSACK problem defined in Sec. 6.6. Use branch and bound and a suitable lower bound to solve the instance of this problem in Example 6.6.

12.14. Carry out a branch-and-bound algorithm to solve the following instance of the assignment problem defined in Exercise 12.10. There are four employees and four jobs. The cost function is represented by the matrix below. In this matrix, row i corresponds to the ith employee, and column j corresponds to the jth job.

$$\begin{bmatrix} 3 & 5 & 2 & 4 \\ 6 & 7 & 5 & 3 \\ 3 & 7 & 4 & 5 \\ 8 & 5 & 4 & 6 \end{bmatrix}.$$

12.8 Bibliographic Notes

There are several books that cover backtracking in some detail. These include Brassard and Bratley (1988), Horowitz *et al.* (1978), Reingold *et al.* (1977). It is also described in Golomb and Brumert (1965). Techniques for analyzing its efficiency are given in Knuth (1975). The recursive form of backtracking was used by Tarjan (1972) in various graph algorithms. Branch-and-bound techniques have been successfully used in optimization problems since the late 1950s. Many of the diverse applications are outlined in the survey paper by Lawler and Wood (1966). The approach to solve the TRAVELING SALESMAN problem in this chapter is due to Little *et al.* (1963). Another technique to solve the TRAVELING SALESMAN problem is described in the survey paper by Bellmore and Nemhauser (1968).

Chapter 13

Randomized Algorithms

13.1 Introduction

In this chapter, we discuss one form of algorithm design in which we relax the condition that an algorithm must solve the problem correctly *for all* possible inputs, and demand that its possible incorrectness is something that can safely be ignored due, say, to its very low likelihood of occurrence. Also, we will not demand that the output of an algorithm must be the same in every run on a particular input. We will be concerned with those algorithms that in the course of their execution can toss a fair coin, yielding truly random outcomes. The consequences of adding this element of randomness turn out to be surprising. Rather than producing unpredictable results, the randomness introduced will be shown to be extremely useful and capable of yielding fast solutions to problems that have only very inefficient deterministic algorithms.

A *randomized algorithm* can be defined as one that receives, in addition to its input, a stream of random bits that it can use in the course of its action for the purpose of making random choices. A randomized algorithm may give different results when applied to the same input in different runs. It follows that the execution time of a randomized algorithm may vary from one run to another when applied to the same input. By now, it is recognized that, in a wide range of applications, randomization is an extremely important tool for the construction of algorithms. There are two main advantages that randomized algorithms often have. First, often the execution time or space requirement of a randomized algorithm is smaller than that of the

363

best deterministic algorithm that we know of for the same problem. Second, if we look at the various randomized algorithms that have been invented so far, we find that invariably they are extremely simple to comprehend and implement. The following is a simple example of a randomized algorithm.

Example 13.1   Suppose we have a polynomial expression in n variables, say $f(x_1, x_2, \ldots, x_n)$, and we wish to check whether or not f is identically zero. To do this analytically could be a horrendous job. Suppose, instead, we generate a random n-vector $(r_1, r_2, \ldots, r_n)$ of real numbers and evaluate $f(r_1, r_2, \ldots, r_n)$. If $f(r_1, r_2, \ldots, r_n) \neq 0$, we know that $f \neq 0$. If $f(r_1, r_2, \ldots, r_n) = 0$, then either f is identically zero or we have been extremely lucky in our choice of $(r_1, r_2, \ldots, r_n)$. If we repeat this several times and keep on getting $f = 0$, then we conclude that f is identically zero. The probability that we have made an error is negligible.

In some deterministic algorithms, especially those that exhibit good average running time, the mere introduction of randomization suffices to convert a simple and naïve algorithm with bad worst case behavior into a randomized algorithm that performs well with high probability on every possible input. This will be apparent when we study randomized algorithms for sorting and selection in Secs. 13.4 and 13.5.

13.2   Las Vegas and Monte Carlo Algorithms

Randomized algorithms can be classified into two categories. The first category is referred to as *Las Vegas* algorithms. It constitutes those randomized algorithms that always give a *correct* answer or do not give an answer at all. This is to be contrasted with the other category of randomized algorithms, which is referred to as *Monte Carlo* algorithms. A Monte Carlo algorithm always gives an answer but may *occasionally* produce an answer that is incorrect. However, the probability of producing an incorrect answer can be made arbitrarily small by running the algorithm repeatedly with independent random choices in each run.

To be able to generally discuss the computational complexity of a randomized algorithm, it is useful to first introduce some criteria for evaluating the performance of algorithms. Let A be an algorithm. If A is deterministic, then one measure of the time complexity of the algorithm is its average running time: The average time taken by A when for each value of n, each input of size n is considered equally likely. That is, a uniform distribution on all its inputs is assumed (see Sec. 1.12.2). This may be misleading, as the input distribution may not be uniform. If A is a randomized algorithm, then its running time on a *fixed* instance I of size n may vary from one execution to another. Therefore, a more natural measure of performance is the *expected running time of A on a fixed instance I*. This is the mean time taken by algorithm A to solve the instance I over and over.

13.3   Two Simple Examples

Let $A[1..n]$ be an array of n elements. By *sampling* one element from A, we mean picking an index j unformly at random from the set $\{1, 2, \ldots, n\}$ and returning $A[j]$.

13.3.1   *A Monte Carlo algorithm*

Let $A[1..n]$ be an array of n distinct numbers, where n is even. We wish to select one number x that is larger than the median. Consider the following algorithm, which we will refer to as Algorithm MC.

Algorithm 13.1

1. Let $x \leftarrow -\infty$.
2. Repeat Steps 3 to 4 k times.
3. Sample one element y from A.
4. If $y > x$ then $x \leftarrow y$.
5. Return x.

Let $\mathbf{Pr}[\text{Success}]$ be the probability that the sampled element is $>$ the median, and let $\mathbf{Pr}[\text{Failure}]$ be the probability that the sampled element is $\leq$ the median. Obviously, $\mathbf{Pr}[\text{Failure}]$ in the first iteration is $1/2$. Consequently, $\mathbf{Pr}[\text{Failure}]$ in all k iterations is $1/2^k$. Hence, $\mathbf{Pr}[\text{Success}]$ within the first k iterations is $1 - 1/2^k$.

An algorithm runs with high probability of success if its probability of success is of the form $1 - 1/n^c$ for some constant $c > 0$, where n is the input size. So, setting $k = \log n$, we have that the algorithm uses $\log n$ iterations and returns the correct result with probability $1 - 1/n$.

13.3.2   A Las Vegas algorithm

Let $A[1..n]$ be an array of n elements, where n is even. A contains $(n/2)+1$ copies of the same element x and $(n/2)-1$ distinct elements that are different from x. We wish to find this repeated element x. Consider the following algorithm, which we will refer to as Algorithm LV.

Algorithm 13.2
1. Repeat Steps 2 to 3 indefinitely.
2. Sample two indices i and j from $\{1, 2, \ldots, n\}$.
3. If $i \neq j$ and $A[i] = A[j]$ then set $x \leftarrow A[i]$ and exit.

If we let $\mathbf{Pr}[\text{Success}]$ denote the probability that $i \neq j$ and $A[i] = A[j]$ in one iteration, then

$$\mathbf{Pr}[\text{Success}] = \frac{(n/2)+1}{n} \times \frac{n/2}{n} > \frac{n/2}{n} \times \frac{n/2}{n} = \frac{1}{4}.$$

This is because there are $(n/2)+1$ possibilities for the first drawing and $n/2$ possibilities for the second drawing. Hence, $\mathbf{Pr}[\text{Failure}] \leq 3/4$ in one iteration. It follows that the probability of failure in all k iterations is less than or equal to $(3/4)^k$. Consequently, the probability of success within the first k iterations is greater than $1 - (3/4)^k$. Since we wish to have the probability of success to be of the form $1 - 1/n^c$, setting $(3/4)^k = 1/n^c$ and solving for k yields $k = c\log_{(4/3)} n$. If, for example, we set $c = 4$, then Algorithm LV always returns the correct result in time $O(\log n)$ with probability $1 - 1/n^4$.

It should be emphasized that in Algorithm MC, the probability is with respect to its correctness while the running time is fixed. In the case of Algorithm LV, the probability is with respect to its running time while its result is always correct.

13.4   Randomized Quicksort

This is, perhaps, one of the most popular randomized algorithms. Consider Algorithm QUICKSORT which was presented in Sec. 5.6. We have shown that the algorithm's running time is $\Theta(n \log n)$ on average, provided that all permutations of the input elements are equally likely. This, however, is not the case in many practical applications. We have also shown that if the input is already sorted, then its running time is $\Theta(n^2)$. This is also the case if the input is *almost* sorted. Consider, for instance, an application that updates a large *sorted* file by appending a small number of elements to the original sorted file and then using Algorithm QUICKSORT to sort it afresh. In this case, the smaller the number of added elements the closer the running time to $\Theta(n^2)$.

One approach to circumvent this problem and guarantee an expected running time of $O(n \log n)$ is to introduce a preprocessing step whose sole purpose is to permute the elements to be sorted *randomly*. This preprocessing step can be performed in $\Theta(n)$ time (Exercise 13.3). Another simpler approach which leads to the same effect is to introduce an element of randomness into the algorithm. This can be done by selecting the pivot on which to split the elements *randomly*. The result of choosing the pivot randomly is to relax the assumption that all permutations of the input elements are equally likely. Modifying the original Algorithm QUICKSORT by introducing this step results in Algorithm RANDOMIZEDQUICKSORT shown below. The new algorithm simply chooses uniformly at random an index v in the interval $[low..high]$ and interchanges $A[v]$ with $A[low]$. This is because Algorithm SPLIT uses $A[low]$ as the pivot (see Sec. 5.6.1). The algorithm then continues as in the original QUICKSORT algorithm. Here, the function $random(low, high)$ returns a random number between low and $high$. It is important to note that any number between low and $high$ is generated with equal probability of $1/(high - low + 1)$.

Algorithm 13.3 RANDOMIZEDQUICKSORT
Input: An array $A[1..n]$ of n elements.

Output: The elements in A sorted in nondecreasing order.

1. $rquicksort(1, n)$

Algorithm $rquicksort(low, high)$
1. **if** $low < high$ **then**
2. $v \leftarrow random(low, high)$
3.   interchange $A[low]$ and $A[v]$
4.   SPLIT$(A[low..high], w)$ {w is the new position of the pivot}
5. $rquicksort(low, w - 1)$
6. $rquicksort(w + 1, high)$
7. **end if**

13.4.1   *Expected running time of randomized quicksort*

Assume without loss of generality that the elements in the array A are distinct. Let $a_1, a_2, \ldots, a_n$ be the elements in array A sorted in increasing order, that is, $a_1 < a_2 < \cdots < a_n$. Let p_{ij} be the probability that a_i and a_j will ever be compared throughout the execution of the algorithm. In the beginning, an element a_v is chosen uniformly at random. All other elements are compared to a_v resulting in two lists: $A_1 = \{a_j \mid a_j < a_v\}$ and $A_2 = \{a_j \mid a_j > a_v\}$. Notice that after this splitting around the pivot a_v, none of the elements in A_1 will be compared with elements in A_2.

Consider the elements in the set $S = \{a_k \mid a_i \leq a_k \leq a_j\}$. Suppose that during the execution of the algorithm, $a_k \in S$ is chosen as the pivot. Then, if $a_k \in \{a_i, a_j\}$, a_i and a_j will be compared; otherwise (if $a_k \notin \{a_i, a_j\}$), they will never be compared. In other words, a_i and a_j will be compared if and only if either a_i or a_j is *first* selected as the pivot among all the elements in S. Consequently, the probability that a_i and a_j will ever be compared throughout the execution of the algorithm is

$$p_{ij} = \frac{2}{|S|} = \frac{2}{j - i + 1}.$$

Now, we bound the total number of comparisons. Towards this end, define the indicator random variable X_{ij} to be 1 if a_i and a_j are ever compared and 0 otherwise. Then,

$$\mathbf{Pr}[X_{ij} = 1] = p_{ij},$$

and the total number of comparisons X performed by the algorithm satisfies

$$X = \sum_{i=1}^{n-1} \sum_{j=i+1}^{n} X_{ij}.$$

Hence, the expected number of comparisons is

$$\mathbf{E}\left[\sum_{i=1}^{n-1} \sum_{j=i+1}^{n} X_{ij}\right] = \sum_{i=1}^{n-1} \sum_{j=i+1}^{n} \mathbf{E}[X_{ij}],$$

where the equality follows from the linearity of expectation (see Sec. B.3).

Substituting for $\mathbf{E}[X_{ij}] = p_{ij} = 2/(j - i + 1)$ yields

$$\mathbf{E}[X] = \sum_{i=1}^{n-1} \sum_{j=i+1}^{n} \frac{2}{j - i + 1}$$

$$= 2 \sum_{i=1}^{n-1} \sum_{j=2}^{n-i+1} \frac{1}{j}$$

$$< 2 \sum_{i=1}^{n} \sum_{j=1}^{n} \frac{1}{j}$$

$$= 2nH_n$$

$$\approx 2n \ln n,$$

where H_n is the harmonic series. Since $H_n = \ln n + O(1)$, it follows that the expected running time of Algorithm RANDOMIZEDQUICKSORT is $O(n \log n)$.

Thus, we have the following theorem:

Theorem 13.1 *The expected number of element comparisons performed by Algorithm* RANDOMIZEDQUICKSORT *on input of size n is $O(n \log n)$.*

13.5 Randomized Quickselect

Consider Algorithm SELECT, which was presented in Sec. 5.5. We have shown that the algorithm's running time is $\Theta(n)$ with a large multiplicative constant that makes the algorithm impractical, especially for small and moderate values of n. On the other hand, Algorithm QUICKSELECT, presented in Sec. 5.7, is fast and simple with an average time complexity of $\Theta(n)$. In this section, we present a randomized Las Vegas version of Algorithm QUICKSELECT. Its expected running time is $\Theta(n)$ with a small multiplicative constant. A precise description of the algorithm is given in Algorithm RQUICKSELECT.

13.5.1 *Expected running time of randomized quickselect*

In what follows we investigate the running time of Algorithm RQUICKSE-LECT. Assume without loss of generality that the elements in A are distinct. We prove by induction that the expected number of element comparisons

---

Algorithm 13.4 RQUICKSELECT
Input: An array $A[1..n]$ of n elements and an integer k, $1 \leq k \leq n$.
Output: The kth smallest element in A.

1. $rqselect(A, k)$

Algorithm $rqselect(A, k)$
1. $v \leftarrow random(1, |A|)$
2. $x \leftarrow A[v]$
3. Partition A into three arrays:
   $A_1 = \{a \mid a < x\}$
   $A_2 = \{a \mid a = x\}$
   $A_3 = \{a \mid a > x\}$
4. **case**
   $|A_1| \geq k$: **return** $rqselect(A_1, k)$
   $|A_1| + |A_2| \geq k$: **return** x
   $|A_1| + |A_2| < k$: **return** $rqselect(A_3, k - |A_1| - |A_2|)$
5. **end case**

---

done by the algorithm is less than $4n$. Let $C(n)$ be the expected number of element comparisons performed by the algorithm on a sequence of n elements. Since v, which is chosen randomly, may assume any of the integers $1, 2, \ldots, n$ with equal probability, we have two cases to consider according to whether $v < k$ or $v > k$. If $v < k$, the number of remaining elements is $n - v$, and if $v > k$, the number of remaining elements is $v - 1$. Thus, the expected number of element comparisons performed by the algorithm is

$$
C(n) = n + \frac{1}{n} \left[\sum_{j=1}^{k-1} C(n-j) + \sum_{j=k+1}^{n} C(j-1) \right]
$$

$$
= n + \frac{1}{n} \left[\sum_{j=n-k+1}^{n-1} C(j) + \sum_{j=k}^{n-1} C(j) \right].
$$

Maximizing over k yields the following inequality:

$$
C(n) \leq n + \max_{k} \left[\frac{1}{n} \left[\sum_{j=n-k+1}^{n-1} C(j) + \sum_{j=k}^{n-1} C(j) \right] \right]
$$

$$
= n + \frac{1}{n} \left[\max_{k} \left[\sum_{j=n-k+1}^{n-1} C(j) + \sum_{j=k}^{n-1} C(j) \right] \right].
$$

Since $C(n)$ is a nondecreasing function of n, the quantity

$$\sum_{j=n-k+1}^{n-1} C(j) + \sum_{j=k}^{n-1} C(j), \tag{13.1}$$

is maximum when $k = \lceil n/2 \rceil$ (Exercise 13.2). Therefore, by induction

$$C(n) \le n + \frac{1}{n}\left[\sum_{j=n-\lceil n/2\rceil+1}^{n-1} 4j + \sum_{j=\lceil n/2\rceil}^{n-1} 4j\right]$$

$$= n + \frac{4}{n}\left[\sum_{j=\lfloor n/2\rfloor+1}^{n-1} j + \sum_{j=\lceil n/2\rceil}^{n-1} j\right]$$

$$\le n + \frac{4}{n}\left[\sum_{j=\lceil n/2\rceil}^{n-1} j + \sum_{j=\lceil n/2\rceil}^{n-1} j\right]$$

$$= n + \frac{8}{n}\sum_{j=\lceil n/2\rceil}^{n-1} j$$

$$= n + \frac{8}{n}\left[\sum_{j=1}^{n-1} j - \sum_{j=1}^{\lceil n/2\rceil-1} j\right]$$

$$= n + \frac{8}{n}\left[\frac{n(n-1)}{2} - \frac{\lceil n/2\rceil(\lceil n/2\rceil-1)}{2}\right]$$

$$\le n + \frac{8}{n}\left[\frac{n(n-1)}{2} - \frac{(n/2)(n/2-1)}{2}\right]$$

$$= 4n - 2$$

$$< 4n.$$

Thus, we have the following theorem:

Theorem 13.2 *The expected number of element comparisons performed by Algorithm* RQUICKSELECT *on input of size n is less than $4n$.*

13.5.2   The dice problem

Suppose we roll an n-sided die, $n > 1$. If the outcome is k, $1 < k \leq n$, then we roll a k-sided die. We continue the process of throwing dice until the number 1 comes up. Compute the expected number of die flips until we get 1.

Let X_n be the number of rolls when the die shows n until 1 comes up. If we flip and k shows up, then

$$X_n = 1 + X_k; \quad X_1 = 0,$$

where $1 \leq k \leq n$. Taking expected values, we have

$$\mathbf{E}[X_n] = \sum_{k=1}^{n} (1 + \mathbf{E}[X_k]) \frac{1}{n} = \frac{1}{n} \sum_{k=1}^{n} (1 + \mathbf{E}[X_k]),$$

where the equality follows from the linearity of expectation (see Sec. B.3). Multiplying both sides by n, we have

$$n\mathbf{E}[X_n] = \sum_{k=1}^{n} (1 + \mathbf{E}[X_k]). \tag{13.2}$$

For an $(n-1)$-sided die, we have

$$(n-1)\mathbf{E}[X_{n-1}] = \sum_{k=1}^{n-1} (1 + \mathbf{E}[X_k]). \tag{13.3}$$

Subtracting (13.3) from (13.2) yields

$$n\mathbf{E}[X_n] - (n-1)\mathbf{E}[X_{n-1}] = 1 + \mathbf{E}[X_n].$$

Hence,

$$\mathbf{E}[X_n] = \mathbf{E}[X_{n-1}] + \frac{1}{n-1}$$

$$= E[x_{n-2}] + \frac{1}{n-2} + \frac{1}{n-1}$$

$$= E[X_1] + \frac{1}{n-1} + \frac{1}{n-2} + \cdots + 1$$

$$= 0 + \sum_{j=1}^{n-1} \frac{1}{j}$$

$$= H_{n-1},$$

where H_n is the harmonic series and $H_n = \ln n + O(1)$. It follows that the total number of rolls before 1 appears is approximately $\ln(n-1)$.

Now, we investigate the problem of finding the total of all numbers that appear on the dice faces from the beginning of the experiment to the end. Starting from an n-sided die, let this total be Y_n. In this experiment, n is excluded from the set of possible outcomes. That is, when rolling an n-sided die, the set of possible outcomes is $\{1, 2, \ldots, n-1\}$. Thus, If we flip the n-sided die and k shows up, $1 \le k < n$, then

$$Y_n = n + Y_k; \quad Y_1 = 1.$$

Taking expected values, we have

$$E[Y_n] = n + \sum_{k=1}^{n-1} E[Y_k] \frac{1}{n} = n + \frac{1}{n} \sum_{k=1}^{n-1} E[Y_k],$$

where the equality follows from the linearity of expectation (see Sec. B.3). Multiplying both sides by n, we have

$$nE[Y_n] = n^2 + \sum_{k=1}^{n-1} E[Y_k]. \tag{13.4}$$

For an $(n-1)$-sided die, we have

$$(n-1)E[Y_{n-1}] = (n-1)^2 + \sum_{k=1}^{n-2} E[Y_k]. \tag{13.5}$$

Subtracting (13.5) from (13.4) yields

$$nE[Y_n] - (n-1)E[Y_{n-1}] = 2n - 1 + E[Y_{n-1}],$$

or

$$E[Y_n] = E[Y_{n-1}] + \frac{2n-1}{n} = E[Y_{n-1}] + 2 - \frac{1}{n}.$$

Hence,

$$E[Y_n] = E[Y_{n-1}] + 2 - \frac{1}{n}$$

$$= E[Y_{n-2}] + 4 - \frac{1}{n} - \frac{1}{n-1}$$

$$= E[Y_1] + 2(n-1) - \sum_{j=2}^{n-1} \frac{1}{j}$$

$$= 1 + 2(n-1) - \sum_{j=2}^{n-1} \frac{1}{j}$$

$$= 2 + 2(n-1) - \sum_{j=1}^{n-1} \frac{1}{j}$$

$$= 2n - H_n,$$

where H_n is the harmonic series, and $H_n = \ln n + O(1)$. It follows that the total numbers on faces before 1 appears is approximately $\ln(n-1)$.

13.5.3 *Application of the dice problem: Quickselect*

Intuitively, when running Algorithm RQUICKSELECT (randomized quickselect), the number of element comparisons is much less when k is small compared to larger values, especially in the middle, e.g., the median. Now, we investigate the very special case when $k = 1$, and show that in this case, the number of comparisons is low. Consider running Algorithm RQUICKSELECT to find the smallest element on an input of size n, that is, the input $k = 1$ in the algorithm. Assume without loss of generality that the elements in A are distinct. v, which is chosen randomly, may assume any of the integers $1, 2, \ldots, n$ with equal probability, and the number of remaining elements is always $v - 1$. Thus, the number of remaining elements is between 1 and $n - 1$ with equal probability. Let r be the number of remaining elements. Then, r corresponds to the outcome of rolling a fair n-sided die, and then rolling j-sided dice repeatedly until 1 shows up as described above. It follows that the total number of iterations in Algorithm RQUICKSELECT to find the smallest element in the worst case is equal to the number of times the dice are rolled, which is $H_{n-1} \approx \ln(n-1)$, as shown above. Likewise, the total number of comparisons in the worst case corresponds to the total numbers shown on the faces of the rolled dice, which, as shown above, is $2n - H_n \approx 2n - \ln n$.

13.6 Occupancy Problems

Given m identical balls and n identical boxes, we want to place each ball in a bin independently and uniformly at random. This process has a vast number of applications. Some typical questions related to it include: What is the expected number of bins with k balls? What is the maximum number of balls in any bin? How many ball throwings are needed to fill all bins? What is the probability that one bin contains at least 2 balls? These are some of the problems referred to as *occupancy problems*.

Approximations related to e. We will make use of the following approximations:

$$\left(1 + \frac{x}{n}\right)^n \approx e^x \text{ and, in particular, } \left(1 - \frac{1}{n}\right)^n \approx e^{-1}$$

and

$$1 - x \le e^{-x} \quad \left(\text{since } e^{-x} = 1 - x + \frac{x^2}{2!} - \dots\right).$$

13.6.1 *Number of balls in each bin*

We consider the number of balls in each bin when throwing m balls into n bins. For any $i, 1 \le i \le n$, define the indicator random variable (see Sec. B.3) X_{ij} for ball j landing in bin i as

$$X_{ij} = \begin{cases} 1 & \text{if ball } j \text{ lands into bin } i \\ 0 & \text{otherwise.} \end{cases}$$

Then, X_{ij} represents a Bernoulli trial (see Sec. B.4.2) with probability

$$\mathbf{Pr}[X_{ij} = 1] = p = \frac{1}{n}.$$

Let $X_i = \sum_{j=1}^m X_{ij}$. Then, X_i is the number of balls in bin i, and it has the binomial distribution (see Sec. B.4.3) with probability

$$\mathbf{Pr}[X_i = k] = \binom{m}{k} p^k (1 - p)^{m-k}.$$

$\mathbf{E}[X_i] = pm = m/n$. This should be intuitive. So, if $m = n$, $\mathbf{E}[X_i] = 1$.

Number of fixed points. As an example for the case when $m = n$, consider a random permutation $\pi = \pi_1, \pi_2, \ldots, \pi_n$ of the numbers $1, 2, \ldots, n$. The expected number of elements with $\pi_i = i$ is 1.

The Poisson approximation. The probability of the number of balls in bin X_i can be written as

$$\mathbf{Pr}[X_i = k] = \binom{m}{k} p^k (1-p)^{m-k} = \binom{m}{k} \left(\frac{1}{n}\right)^k \left(1 - \frac{1}{n}\right)^{m-k}.$$

If m and n are both large compared to k, $\mathbf{Pr}[X_i = k]$ can be approximated by

$$\mathbf{Pr}[X_i = k] \approx \frac{m^k}{k!} \left(\frac{1}{n}\right)^k \left(\left(1 - \frac{1}{n}\right)^n\right)^{m/n} \approx \frac{(m/n)^k}{k!} e^{-m/n}.$$

Thus, if we let $\lambda = m/n$, then $\mathbf{Pr}[X_i = k]$ can be written as

$$\mathbf{Pr}[X_i = k] \approx \frac{\lambda^k e^{-\lambda}}{k!}.$$

This is the Poisson distribution with parameter $\lambda = m/n$ (see Sec. B.4.5).

13.6.2 *Number of empty bins*

Define the random variable X_i to be 1 if bin i is empty and 0 otherwise. Clearly, a ball goes into a bin different from i with probability $(n-1)/n$. Hence,

$$\mathbf{Pr}[X_i = 1] = \left(\frac{n-1}{n}\right)^m = \left(1 - \frac{1}{n}\right)^m = \left(\left(1 - \frac{1}{n}\right)^n\right)^{m/n} \approx e^{-m/n}.$$

Since X_i is an indicator random variable (see Sec. B.3),

$$\mathbf{E}[X_i] = \mathbf{Pr}[X_i = 1] \approx e^{-m/n}.$$

If X is the number of empty bins, then it follows by linearity of expectations (see Sec. B.3) that the expected number of empty bins $\mathbf{E}[X]$ is

$$\mathbf{E}[X] = \mathbf{E}\left[\sum_{i=1}^{n} X_i\right] = \sum_{i=1}^{n} \mathbf{E}[X_i] = n e^{-m/n}.$$

Thus, if $m = n$, then the number of empty bins is n/e.

13.6.3 *Balls falling into the same bin*

Assume $m \le n$, that is, the number of balls is no larger than the number of bins. For $1 \le j \le m$, let $\mathcal{E}_j$ be the event that ball j will go into a nonempty bin. So, we want to compute

$$\mathbf{Pr}[\mathcal{E}_1 \cup \mathcal{E}_2 \cup \cdots \cup \mathcal{E}_m].$$

It is easier to solve the complement: No ball will go into a nonempty bin. That is, we will compute

$$\mathbf{Pr}[\overline{\mathcal{E}_1} \cap \overline{\mathcal{E}_2} \cap \cdots \cap \overline{\mathcal{E}_m}].$$

Clearly, the first ball will fall into an empty bin with probability 1, the second with probability $(n-1)/n$, and so on. Hence,

$$
\begin{aligned}
\mathbf{Pr}\left[\bigcap_{j=1}^{m} \overline{\mathcal{E}_j}\right] &= 1 \times \frac{n-1}{n} \times \frac{n-2}{n} \times \cdots \times \frac{n-m+1}{n} \\
&= 1 \times \left(1 - \frac{1}{n}\right) \times \left(1 - \frac{2}{n}\right) \times \cdots \times \left(1 - \frac{m-1}{n}\right) \\
&\le e^0 \times e^{\frac{-1}{n}} \times e^{\frac{-2}{n}} \times \cdots \times e^{\frac{-(m-1)}{n}} \\
&= e^{-(1+2+\cdots+(m-1))/n} \\
&= e^{-m(m-1)/2n} \\
&\approx e^{-m^2/2n}.
\end{aligned}
$$

Consequently, if $m \approx \lceil \sqrt{2n} \rceil$, all balls will fall into distinct bins with probability e^{-1}. It follows that

$$
\begin{aligned}
\mathbf{Pr}[\text{at least one bin contains at least two balls}] &\ge 1 - e^{-m(m-1)/2n} \\
&\approx 1 - e^{-m^2/2n}.
\end{aligned}
$$

Sampling. The importance of of the above derivation becomes clear if we consider the problem of sampling m elements from a universe of size n. It shows that we should have n large enough to reduce the likelihood of collisions. For example, if we generate m random numbers between 1 and n, we should make certain that n is large enough.

The Birthday Paradox. We have essentially proven the following famous result. We compute the probability that there are two people in a group of

m people who happen to have the same birthday. If we let the size of the group $m = 23$ and $n = 365$, then the probability is

$$1 - e^{-23(23-1)/(2 \times 365)} = 1 - e^{-0.69315} = 0.50000.$$

If the group size is 50, the probability is about 0.97.

13.6.4   *Filling all bins*

Suppose we want to fill all n bins so that each bin has at least one ball using an unlimited supply of balls. When we throw the first ball, it will go directly into an empty bin. When we throw the second, it will go to an empty bin with high probability. After several throws, there may be collisions, i.e., balls falling into nonempty bins. Intuitively, the more nonempty bins the more balls we need to hit an empty bin. Call the experiment of throwing a ball at random a trial. We will call a trial success if the ball lands in an empty bin and let p_i, $1 \leq i \leq n$, be the probability of success. Let X_i count the number of trials until the ith success. Then, X_i has the geometric distribution (see Sec. B.4.4), and hence $\mathbf{E}[X_i] = 1/p_i$. Clearly, $p_1 = 1, p_2 = (n-1)/n$, and in general,

$$p_i = \frac{n - i + 1}{n} \quad \text{and} \quad \mathbf{E}[X_i] = \frac{n}{n - i + 1}.$$

Let X be the random variable that counts the total number of trials. Then, $X = \sum_{i=1}^{n} X_i$, and

$$\mathbf{E}[X] = \mathbf{E}\left[\sum_{i=1}^{n} X_i\right]$$

$$= \sum_{i=1}^{n} \mathbf{E}[X_i]$$

$$= \sum_{i=1}^{n} \frac{n}{n - i + 1}$$

$$= n \sum_{i=1}^{n} \frac{1}{i}$$

$$= n H_n,$$

where H_n is the harmonic series. Since $H_n = \ln n + O(1)$, $\mathbf{E}[X] = n \ln n + O(n) = \Theta(n \log n)$.

13.7 Tail Bounds

One of the major tools in the analysis of randomized algorithms is to investigate the probability of their failure and the deviation from their expected running time. Instead of stating that an algorithm runs in $O(f(n))$ expected time, it is desirable to show that it does not deviate "much" from this time bound, or in other words, it runs in time $O(f(n))$ with high probability. To estimate such a probability, a number of "tail" inequalities are customarily used to establish such high bounds.

13.7.1 *Markov inequality*

Markov inequality does not require knowledge of the probability distribution; only the expected value is needed (see Sec. B.3).

Theorem 13.3 *Let X be a nonnegative random variable, and t a positive number. Then,*

$$\mathbf{Pr}[X \geq t] \leq \frac{\mathbf{E}[X]}{t}.$$

Proof. Since X is nonnegative and t is positive, we have

$$\mathbf{E}[X] = \sum_x x\mathbf{Pr}[X = x]$$

$$= \sum_{x<t} x\mathbf{Pr}[X = x] + \sum_{x\geq t} x\mathbf{Pr}[X = x]$$

$$\geq \sum_{x\geq t} x\mathbf{Pr}[X = x] \quad \text{since } x \text{ is nonnegative}$$

$$\geq t \sum_{x\geq t} \mathbf{Pr}[X = x]$$

$$= t\mathbf{Pr}[X \geq t].$$

$\square$

Example 13.2   Consider a sequence of n flips of a fair coin. We use Markov inequality to obtain an upper bound on the probability that the number of heads is at least $2n/3$. Let X denote the total number of heads. Clearly, X has the binomial distribution with parameters $(n, 1/2)$. Hence, $\mathbf{E}[X] = np = n/2$. Applying Markov inequality,

$$\mathbf{Pr}\left[X \geq \frac{2n}{3}\right] \leq \frac{\mathbf{E}[X]}{2n/3} = \frac{n/2}{2n/3} = \frac{3}{4}.$$

13.7.2   *Chebyshev inequality*

Chebyshev bound is more useful than Markov inequality. However, it requires the knowledge of the expected value $\mathbf{E}[X]$ and variance of the random variable $\mathbf{var}[X]$ (see Sec. B.3). The variance is defined by

$$\mathbf{var}[X] = \mathbf{E}[(X - \mathbf{E}[X])^2].$$

Theorem 13.4   *Let t be a positive number. Then,*

$$\mathbf{Pr}[|X - \mathbf{E}[X]| \geq t] \leq \frac{\mathbf{var}[X]}{t^2}.$$

Proof.   Let $Y = (X - \mathbf{E}[X])^2$. Then,

$$\mathbf{Pr}[Y \geq t^2] = \mathbf{Pr}[(X - \mathbf{E}[X])^2 \geq t^2] = \mathbf{Pr}[|X - \mathbf{E}[X]| \geq t].$$

Applying Markov inequality yields

$$\mathbf{Pr}[|X - \mathbf{E}[X]| \geq t] = \mathbf{Pr}[Y \geq t^2] \leq \frac{\mathbf{E}[Y]}{t^2} = \frac{\mathbf{var}[X]}{t^2}$$

since $\mathbf{E}[Y] = \mathbf{var}[X]$. $\square$

A similar proof results in the following variant of Chebyshev Inequality:

$$\mathbf{Pr}[|X - \mathbf{E}[X]| \geq t\sigma_X] \leq \frac{1}{t^2},$$

where $\sigma_X = \sqrt{\mathbf{var}[X]}$ is the standard deviation of X.

Example 13.3   We apply Chebyshev inequality instead of Markov's in Example 13.2. Since X has the binomial distribution with parameters $(n, 1/2)$, $\mathbf{E}[X] = np = n/2$ and $\mathbf{var}[X] = np(1-p) = n/4$.

$$
\begin{aligned}
\mathbf{Pr}\left[X \geq \frac{2n}{3}\right] &= \mathbf{Pr}\left[X - \mathbf{E}[X] \geq \frac{2n}{3} - \frac{n}{2}\right] \\
&= \mathbf{Pr}\left[X - \mathbf{E}[X] \geq \frac{n}{6}\right] \\
&\leq \mathbf{Pr}\left[|X - \mathbf{E}[X]| \geq \frac{n}{6}\right] \\
&\leq \frac{\mathbf{var}[X]}{(n/6)^2} \\
&= \frac{n/4}{(n/6)^2} \\
&= \frac{9}{n}.
\end{aligned}
$$

So, there is a significant improvement; the bound is not constant as in Example 13.2.

13.7.3   *Chernoff bounds*

Let $X_1, X_2, \ldots, X_n$ be a collection of n independent indicator random variables representing Bernoulli trials such that each X_i has probability $\mathbf{Pr}[X_i = 1] = p_i$. We are interested in bounding the probability that their sum $X = \sum_{i=1}^{n} X_i$ will deviate from the mean $\mu = \mathbf{E}[X]$ by a multiple of μ.

13.7.3.1   *Lower tail*

Theorem 13.5   *Let δ be some constant in the interval $(0, 1)$. Then,*

$$
\mathbf{Pr}[X < (1 - \delta)\mu] < \left(\frac{e^{-\delta}}{(1 - \delta)^{(1-\delta)}}\right)^{\mu},
$$

which can be simplified to

$$
\mathbf{Pr}[X < (1 - \delta)\mu] < e^{-\mu\delta^2/2}.
$$

Proof.   First we state $\mathbf{Pr}[X < (1 - \delta)\mu]$ in terms of exponentials.

$$\mathbf{Pr}[X < (1 - \delta)\mu] = \mathbf{Pr}[-X > -(1 - \delta)\mu] = \mathbf{Pr}[e^{-tX} > e^{-t(1-\delta)\mu}],$$

where t is a positive real number to be determined later. Applying Markov inequality to the right-hand side yields

$$\mathbf{Pr}[X < (1 - \delta)\mu] < \frac{\mathbf{E}[e^{-tX}]}{e^{-t(1-\delta)\mu}}.$$

Since $X = \sum_{i=1}^{n} X_i$,

$$e^{-tX} = \prod_{i=1}^{n} e^{-tX_i}.$$

Substituting in the above inequality yields

$$\mathbf{Pr}[X < (1 - \delta)\mu] < \frac{\mathbf{E}\left[\prod_{i=1}^{n} e^{-tX_i}\right]}{e^{-t(1-\delta)\mu}} = \frac{\prod_{i=1}^{n} \mathbf{E}[e^{-tX_i}]}{e^{-t(1-\delta)\mu}}.$$

Now,

$$\mathbf{E}[e^{-tX_i}] = p_i e^{-t \times 1} + (1 - p_i)e^{-t \times 0} = p_i e^{-t} + (1 - p_i) = 1 - p_i(1 - e^{-t}).$$

Using the inequality $1 - x < e^{-x}$ with $x = p_i(1 - e^{-t})$, we have

$$\mathbf{E}[e^{-tX_i}] < e^{p_i(e^{-t} - 1)}.$$

Since $\mu = \sum_{i=1}^{n} p_i$, simplifying we obtain

$$\prod_{i=1}^{n} \mathbf{E}[e^{-tX_i}] < \prod_{i=1}^{n} e^{p_i(e^{-t}-1)} = e^{\left(\sum_{i=1}^{n} p_i(e^{-t}-1)\right)} = e^{\mu(e^{-t}-1)}.$$

Substituting in the formula for the bound gives

$$\mathbf{Pr}[X < (1 - \delta)\mu] < \frac{e^{\mu(e^{-t}-1)}}{e^{-t(1-\delta)\mu}} = e^{\mu(e^{-t}+t-t\delta-1)}.$$

Now, we choose t so as to minimize the quantity $\mu(e^{-t} + t - t\delta - 1)$. Setting its derivative to 0 yields

$$-e^{-t} + 1 - \delta = 0,$$

which solves for $t = \ln(1/(1-\delta))$. Substituting for t in the above inequality, we obtain

$$\mathbf{Pr}[X < (1-\delta)\mu] < e^{\mu((1-\delta)+(1-\delta)\ln(1/(1-\delta))-1)},$$

which simplifies to

$$\mathbf{Pr}[X < (1-\delta)\mu] < \left(\frac{e^{-\delta}}{(1-\delta)^{(1-\delta)}}\right)^{\mu}.$$

This proves the first part of the theorem. Now, we simplify this expression. The log of the denominator is $(1-\delta)\ln(1-\delta)$. The expansion of the natural log of $1-\delta$ is

$$\ln(1-\delta) = -\delta - \frac{\delta^2}{2} - \frac{\delta^3}{3} - \frac{\delta^4}{4}\cdots.$$

Multiplying by $(1-\delta)$ yields

$$(1-\delta)\ln(1-\delta) = -\delta + \left(\frac{\delta^2}{1} - \frac{\delta^2}{2}\right) + \left(\frac{\delta^3}{2} - \frac{\delta^3}{3}\right) + \left(\frac{\delta^4}{3} - \frac{\delta^4}{4}\right) + \cdots$$

$$= -\delta + \frac{\delta^2}{2} + \sum_{j=3}^{\infty} \frac{\delta^j}{j(j-1)}$$

$$> -\delta + \frac{\delta^2}{2}.$$

Hence,

$$(1-\delta)^{(1-\delta)} = e^{(1-\delta)\ln(1-\delta)} > e^{-\delta+\delta^2/2}.$$

Substituting this inequality into the above bound yields

$$\mathbf{Pr}[X < (1-\delta)\mu] < \left(\frac{e^{-\delta}}{(1-\delta)^{(1-\delta)}}\right)^{\mu} < \left(\frac{e^{-\delta}}{e^{-\delta+\delta^2/2}}\right)^{\mu} = e^{-\mu\delta^2/2},$$

which proves the simplified bound. $\qquad\square$

13.7.3.2 *Upper tail*

The proof of the following theorem for the upper tail is similar to the proof of Theorem 13.5 and is omitted.

Theorem 13.6   *Let $\delta > 0$. Then,*

$$\mathbf{Pr}[X > (1+\delta)\mu] < \left(\frac{e^{\delta}}{(1+\delta)^{(1+\delta)}}\right)^{\mu},$$

which can be simplified to

$$\mathbf{Pr}[X > (1+\delta)\mu] < e^{-\mu\delta^2/4} \quad \text{if } \delta < 2e - 1,$$

and

$$\mathbf{Pr}[X > (1+\delta)\mu] < 2^{-\delta\mu} \quad \text{if } \delta > 2e - 1.$$

Example 13.4   We refer to Examples 13.2 and 13.3, where we seek the probability that the number of heads in a sequence of n flips of a fair coin is at least $2n/3$.

Let $\mu = \mathbf{E}[X] = n/2$. Solving for δ,

$$(1+\delta)\mu = \frac{2n}{3}$$

gives $\delta = \frac{1}{3}$. We apply Chernoff bound of Theorem 13.6. Since $\delta < 2e - 1$, we have

$$\mathbf{Pr}\left[X \geq \frac{2n}{3}\right] < e^{-\mu\delta^2/4}$$

$$= e^{-(n/2)(1/9)/4}$$

$$= e^{-n/72}.$$

So, compared to the bounds obtained in Examples 13.2 and 13.3, we see that there is an exponential fall off.

13.8   Application of Chernoff Bounds: Multiselection

In this section, we propose a simple and efficient algorithm for the problem of multiselection (see Sec. 5.8), and show how to use Chernoff bound in its analysis. Let $A = \langle a_1, a_2, \ldots, a_n \rangle$ be a sequence of n elements drawn from a linearly ordered set, and let $K = \langle k_1, k_2, \ldots, k_r \rangle$ be a *sorted* sequence of r positive integers between 1 and n, that is a sequence of ranks. The *multiselection* problem is to select the k_ith smallest element in A for all values of $i, 1 \leq i \leq r$.

Randomized QUICKSORT is a very powerful algorithm, and as it turns out, a slight modification of the algorithm solves the multiselection problem efficiently. The idea is very simple and straightforward. Call the elements sought by the multiselection problem *targets*. For example, if $j \in K$, then the jth smallest element in A is a target. Pick an element $a \in A$ uniformly at random and partition the elements in A around a into small and large elements. If both small and large elements contain targets, let QUICKSORT continue normally. Otherwise, if only the small (large) elements contain targets, then discard the large (small) elements and recurse on the small (large) elements only. So, the algorithm is a hybrid of both QUICKSORT and QUICKSELECT algorithms. Note that by QUICKSORT, we mean the randomized version of the algorithm presented in Sec. 13.4.

In the algorithm to be presented, we will use the following notation to repeatedly partition A into smaller subsequences. Let $a \in A$ with rank $k_i \in K$. Partition A into two subsequences

$$A_1 = \langle a_j \in A \mid a_j \le a \rangle$$

and

$$A_2 = \langle a_j \in A \mid a_j > a \rangle.$$

This partitioning of A induces the following partitioning of K:

$$K_1 = \langle k \in K \mid k \le k_i \rangle$$

and

$$K_2 = \langle k - k_i \mid k \in K \quad \text{and} \quad k > k_i \rangle.$$

In the pair (A, K), A will be called *active* if $|K| > 0$; otherwise, it will be called *inactive*.

A more formal description of the algorithm is shown as Algorithm QUICKMULTISELECT. Figure 13.1 shows an example of the execution of the algorithm. In this example, the input to the algorithm is shown in the root node. Also shown is a, which is the randomly chosen pivot. The rest of the recursion tree is self explanatory.

Clearly, in Step 3 of the algorithm, recursion should be halted when the input size becomes sufficiently small. That is, if the size of A is small, then sort A and return the elements whose ranks are in K. It was stated this

---

Algorithm 13.5 QUICKMULTISELECT
Input: A sequence $A = \langle a_1, a_2, \ldots, a_n \rangle$ of n elements and a sorted sequence of r ranks $K = \langle k_1, k_2, \ldots, k_r \rangle$.
Output: The k_ith smallest element in A, $1 \leq i \leq r$.

  1. $qmultiselect(A, K)$

Algorithm $qmultiselect(A, K)$
  1. $r \leftarrow |K|$
  2. **If** $r > 0$ **then**
  3.   If $|A| = 1$ and $|K| = 1$ then output a and exit.
  4.   Let a be an an element chosen from A uniformly at random.
  5.   By comparing a with the elements in A, determine the two subsequences A_1 and A_2 of elements $\leq a$ and $> a$, respectively. At the same time, compute $r(a)$, the rank of a in A.
  6.   Partition K into $K_1 = \langle k \in K \mid k \leq r(a) \rangle$ and
       $K_2 = \langle k - r(a) \mid k \in K$ and $k > r(a) \rangle$
  7. $qmultiselect\ (A_1, K_1)$.
  8. $qmultiselect\ (A_2, K_2)$.
  9. **end if**

Fig. 13.1.   Example of the execution of Algorithm QUICKMULTISELECT.

way only for the sake of simplifying its analysis and to make it more general (so that it will degenerate to QUICKSORT when $r = n$).

For the analysis of the algorithm, we need Boole's inequality for a finite number of events:

Boole's inequality: For any finite sequence of events $\mathcal{E}_1, \mathcal{E}_2, \ldots, \mathcal{E}_n$,

$$\mathbf{Pr}[\mathcal{E}_1 \cup \mathcal{E}_2 \cup \ldots \cup \mathcal{E}_n] \leq \mathbf{Pr}[\mathcal{E}_1] + \mathbf{Pr}[\mathcal{E}_2] + \cdots + \mathbf{Pr}[\mathcal{E}_n]. \tag{13.6}$$

13.8.1 Analysis of the algorithm

In this section, the sequence A as well as the subsequences A_1 and A_2 will be called intervals. Fix a target element $t \in A$, and let the intervals containing t throughout the execution of the algorithm be $I_0^t, I_1^t, I_2^t, \ldots$ of sizes $n = n_0^t, n_1^t, n_2^t, \ldots$. Thus, in the algorithm, $I_0^t = A$, $I_1^t = A_1$ if $t \in A_1$ and $I_1^t = A_2$ if $t \in A_2$, and so on. For example, there are two targets in Fig. 13.1, namely 20 and 50. The intervals containing target 20 are: $I_0^{20} = \langle 70, 30, 10, 40, 20, 60, 50 \rangle$, $I_1^{20} = \langle 30, 10, 40, 20 \rangle$, $I_2^{20} = \langle 30, 10, 20 \rangle$, $I_3^{20} = \langle 10, 20 \rangle$ and $I_4^{20} = \langle 20 \rangle$. Henceforth, we will drop the superscript t and refer to I_j^t as I_j and refer to n_j^t as n_j.

In the jth partitioning step, a pivot a chosen randomly partitions the interval I_j into two intervals, one of which is of size at least $3n/4$ if and only if the rank of a in I_j is $\leq n_j/4$ or the rank of a in I_j is $\geq 3n_j/4$. The probability that a random element is among the smallest or largest $n_j/4$ elements of I_j is $\leq 1/2$. It follows that for any $j \geq 0$,

$$\mathbf{Pr}[n_{j+1} \geq 3n_j/4] \leq \frac{1}{2}. \tag{13.7}$$

Now, we show that the recursion depth is $O(\log n)$ with high probability. Next, we will show that the algorithm's running time is $O(n \log r)$ with high probability too.

Let $d = 16 \ln(4/3) + 4$. For clarity, we will write $\lg x$ in place of $\log_{4/3} x$.

Lemma 13.1 *For the sequence of intervals $I_0, I_1, I_2, \ldots$, after dm partitioning steps, $|I_{dm}| < (3/4)^m n$ with probability $1 - O((4/3)^{-2m})$. Consequently, the algorithm will terminate after $d \lg n$ partitioning steps with probability $1 - O(n^{-1})$.*

Proof. Call the jth partitioning step successful if $n_{j+1} < 3n_j/4$, $j \geq 0$. Thus, the number of successful splittings needed to reduce the size of I_0

to at most $(3/4)^m n$ is at most m. Therefore, it suffices to show that the number of failures exceeds $dm - m$ with probability $O((4/3)^{-2m})$. Define the indicator random variable X_j, $0 \le j < dm$, to be 1 if $n_{j+1} \ge 3n_j/4$ and 0 if $n_{j+1} < 3n_j/4$. Let

$$X = \sum_{j=0}^{dm-1} X_j.$$

So, X counts the number of failures. Clearly, the X_j's are independent with $\mathbf{Pr}[X_j = 1] \le 1/2$ (Eq. 13.7), and hence X is the sum of indicator random variables of a collection of individual Bernoulli trials, where $X_j = 1$ if the jth partitioning step leads to failure. The expected value of X is

$$\mu = \mathbf{E}[X] = \sum_{j=0}^{dm-1} \mathbf{E}[X_j] = \sum_{j=0}^{dm-1} \mathbf{Pr}[X_j = 1] \le \frac{dm}{2}.$$

Given the above, we can apply Chernoff bound of Theorem 13.6:

$$\mathbf{Pr}[X \ge (1 + \delta)\mu] \le \exp\left(\frac{-\mu\delta^2}{4}\right); \ 0 < \delta < 2e - 1$$

to derive an upper bound on the number of failures. Specifically, we will bound the probability

$$\mathbf{Pr}[X \ge dm - m].$$

$$\mathbf{Pr}[X \ge dm - m] = \mathbf{Pr}[X \ge (2 - 2/d)(dm/2)]$$

$$= \mathbf{Pr}[X \ge (1 + (1 - 2/d))(dm/2)]$$

$$\le \exp\left(\frac{-(dm/2)(1 - 2/d)^2}{4}\right)$$

$$= \exp\left(\frac{-m(d - 4 + 4/d)}{8}\right)$$

$$\le \exp\left(\frac{-m(d - 4)}{8}\right)$$

$$= \exp\left(\frac{-m(16\ln(4/3))}{8}\right)$$

$$= e^{-2m\ln(4/3)}$$

$$= (4/3)^{-2m}.$$

Consequently,

$$\mathbf{Pr}[\ |I_{dm}| \le (3/4)^m n] \ge \mathbf{Pr}[X < dm - m] \ge 1 - (4/3)^{-2m}.$$

Since the algorithm will terminate when the sizes of all active intervals become 1, setting $m = \lg n$, we have

$$\mathbf{Pr}[\ |I_{d\lg n}| \le 1] = \mathbf{Pr}[\ |I_{d\lg n}| \le (3/4)^{\lg n} n]$$
$$\ge \mathbf{Pr}[X < d\lg n - \lg n]$$
$$\ge 1 - (4/3)^{-2\lg n}$$
$$= 1 - n^{-2}.$$

What we have computed so far is $\mathbf{Pr}[\ |I_{d\lg n}^t| \le 1]$ for target t. Since the number of targets can be as large as $O(n)$, using Boole's inequality (Eq. 13.6), it follows that the algorithm will terminate after $d\lg n$ partitioning steps with probability at least

$$1 - O(n) \times n^{-2} = 1 - O(n^{-1}). \qquad \square$$

Theorem 13.7 *The running time of the algorithm is $O(n \log r)$ with probability $1 - O(n^{-1})$.*

Proof. Assume without loss of generality that $r > 1$ and is a power of 2. The algorithm will go through two phases: The first phase consists of the first $\log r$ iterations, and the remaining iterations constitute the second phase. An iteration here consists of all recursive invocations of the algorithm on the same level of the recursion tree. The first phase consists of "mostly" the first $\log r$ iterations of Algorithm QUICKSORT, while the second phase is "mostly" an execution of Algorithm QUICKSELECT. At the end of the first phase, the number of active intervals will be at most r. Throughout the second phase, the number of active intervals will also be at most r, as the number of unprocessed ranks is at most r. In each iteration, including those in the first phase, an active interval I is split into two intervals. If both intervals are active, then they will be retained; otherwise, one will be discarded. So, for $c \ge 2$, after $c \log r$ iterations, $O(r^c)$ intervals will have been discarded, and at most r will have been retained.

Clearly, the time needed for partitioning set A in the first phase of the algorithm is $O(n \log r)$, as the recursion depth is $\log r$. As to partitioning the set K of ranks, which is sorted, binary search can be employed after each partitioning of A. Since $|K| = r$, binary search will be applied at most r times for a total of $O(r \log r)$ extra steps.

Now, we use Lemma 13.1 to bound the number of comparisons performed by the second phase. In this phase, with probability $1 - O(n^{-1})$, there are at most $d \lg n - \log r$ iterations with at most r intervals, whose total number of elements is $\leq n$ at the beginning of the second phase. Call these intervals $I_{\log r}^1, I_{\log r}^2, \ldots$ at the beginning of the second phase. The number of comparisons needed to partition interval I_j^t is $|I_j^t|$. By Lemma 13.1, it follows that, with probability $1 - O(n^{-1})$, the number of comparisons needed to partition the sequence of intervals $I_{\log r}^t, I_{\log r+1}^t, I_{\log r+2}^t, \ldots$ is the total of their lengths, which is at most

$$\sum_{j=0}^{d \lg n - \log r} \left(\frac{3}{4}\right)^j |I_{\log r}^t|.$$

It follows that, with probability $1 - O(n^{-1})$, the number of comparisons in the second phase is upperbounded by

$$\sum_{t \geq 1} \sum_{j=0}^{d \lg n - \log r} \left(\frac{3}{4}\right)^j |I_{\log r}^t| = \sum_{t \geq 1} |I_{\log r}^t| \sum_{j=0}^{d \lg n - \log r} \left(\frac{3}{4}\right)^j \leq n \sum_{j=0}^{\infty} \left(\frac{3}{4}\right)^j = 4n.$$

Thus, the running time for the first phase is $O(n \log r)$, and for the second, it is $O(n)$. It follows that the running time of the algorithm is $O(n \log r)$ with probability $1 - O(n^{-1})$. $\qquad\square$

13.9   Random Sampling

Consider the problem of selecting a sample of m elements randomly from a set of n elements, where $m < n$. For simplicity, we will assume that the elements are positive integers between 1 and n. In this section, we present a simple Las Vegas algorithm for this problem.

Consider the following selection method. First mark all the n elements as *unselected*. Next, repeat the following step until exactly m elements have been selected. Generate a random number r between 1 and n. If r is marked *unselected*, then mark it *selected* and add it to the sample. This method is described more precisely in Algorithm RANDOMSAMPLING. A disadvantage of this algorithm is that its space complexity is $\Theta(n)$, as it uses an array of size n to mark all integers between 1 and n. If n is too large compared to m (e.g., $n > m^2$), the algorithm can easily be modified to eliminate the need for this array.

Algorithm 13.6 RANDOMSAMPLING
Input: Two positive integers m, n with $m < n$.

Output: An array $A[1..m]$ of m distinct positive integers selected randomly from the set $\{1, 2, \ldots, n\}$.

1. **comment:** $S[1..n]$ *is a boolean array indicating whether an integer has been selected.*
2. **for** $i \leftarrow 1$ **to** n
3. $S[i] \leftarrow$ **false**
4. **end for**
5. $k \leftarrow 0$
6. **while** $k < m$
7. $r \leftarrow random(1, n)$
8.   **if not** $S[r]$ **then**
9. $k \leftarrow k + 1$
10. $A[k] \leftarrow r$
11. $S[r] \leftarrow$ **true**
12.   **end if**
13. **end while**

Clearly, the smaller the difference between m and n, the larger the running time. For example, if $n = 1000$ and $m = 990$, then the algorithm will spend too much time in order to generate the last integers in the sample, e.g., the 990th integer. To circumvent this problem, we may select 10 integers randomly, discard them and keep the remaining 990 integers as the desired sample. Therefore, we will assume that $m \leq n/2$, since otherwise we may select $n - m$ integers randomly, discard them and keep the remaining integers as our sample.

The analysis is similar to that of filling all bins with balls discussed in Sec. 13.6.4. Let p_k be the probability of generating an unselected integer given that $k - 1$ numbers have already been selected, where $1 \leq k \leq m$. Clearly,

$$p_k = \frac{n - k + 1}{n}.$$

If $X_k, 1 \leq k \leq m$, is the random variable denoting the number of integers generated in order to select the kth integer, then X_k has the geometric distribution (see Sec. B.4.4) with expected value

$$\mathbf{E}(X_k) = \frac{1}{p_k} = \frac{n}{n-k+1}.$$

Let Y be the random variable denoting the total number of integers generated in order to select m out of n integers. By *linearity of expectation* (see Sec. B.3), we have

$$\mathbf{E}(Y) = \mathbf{E}(X_1) + \mathbf{E}(X_2) + \cdots + \mathbf{E}(X_m).$$

Hence,

$$\mathbf{E}(Y) = \sum_{k=1}^{m} \mathbf{E}(X_k)$$

$$= \sum_{k=1}^{m} \frac{n}{n-k+1}$$

$$= n \sum_{k=1}^{n} \frac{1}{n-k+1} - n \sum_{k=m+1}^{n} \frac{1}{n-k+1}$$

$$= n \sum_{k=1}^{n} \frac{1}{k} - n \sum_{k=1}^{n-m} \frac{1}{k}.$$

By Eq. (A.16) on page 681,

$$\sum_{j=1}^{n} \frac{1}{k} \leq \ln n + 1 \quad \text{and} \quad \sum_{k=1}^{n-m} \frac{1}{k} \geq \ln(n-m+1).$$

Hence,

$$\mathbf{E}(Y) \leq n \left(\ln n + 1 - \ln(n - m + 1) \right)$$

$$\approx n \left(\ln n + 1 - \ln(n - m) \right)$$

$$\leq n \left(\ln n + 1 - \ln(n/2) \right) \quad \text{since } m \leq n/2$$

$$= n \left(\ln 2 + 1 \right)$$

$$= n \ln 2e$$

$$\approx 1.69 \, n.$$

Hence, $T(n)$, the expected running time of the algorithm, is $O(n)$.

13.10   The Min-Cut Problem

Let $G = (V, E)$ be an undirected graph on n vertices. An *edge cut*, or simply a *cut*, in G is a subset C of the set of edges E whose removal disconnects G into two or more components. We will present a randomized algorithm to find a minimum cut, that is, a cut of minimum cardinality. Let (u, v) be an edge in G. (u, v) is said to be *contracted* if its two ends u and v are merged into one vertex, all edges connecting u and v are deleted, and all other edges are retained. Note that contraction of an edge may result in multiple edges, but no self loops, so G may become a multigraph (with no self loops).

The algorithm is very simple. It consists of $n - 2$ iterations. In the ith iteration, where $1 \leq i \leq n - 2$, select an edge uniformly at random and contract it. After each edge contraction, the number of vertices will decrease by 1. See Fig. 13.2 for an example of the algorithm. In this example, the resulting cut shown in Fig. 13.2(e) is of size 4, which is not minimum.

Now, we show that this simple algorithm results in a minimum cut with probability at least $2/n(n - 1)$. Let k be the size of a minimum cut in G, and fix a cut C of size k. We will compute the probability that no edge in the cut C is selected (and hence deleted) throughout the execution of the

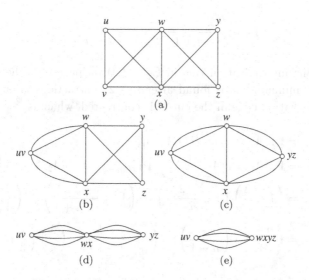

Fig. 13.2.   Example of successive contractions.

algorithm. For iteration i, $1 \leq i \leq n - 2$, let A_i denote the event that the ith edge selected by the algorithm is not in C, and let $B_i = A_1 \cap A_2 \cdots \cap A_i$. That is, B_i is the event that all of the first i chosen edges are not in the cut C. Since the size of a minimum cut is k, the minimum vertex degree is k, which means that the total number of edges is at least $kn/2$. Hence, the probability of the first event $B_1 = A_1$ is at least

$$1 - \frac{k}{kn/2} = 1 - \frac{2}{n}.$$

Now, assume that the selected edge in the first iteration is not in C. Then, since the vertex degrees do not decrease, the probability of the second event $B_2 = A_1 \cap A_2$ is at least

$$1 - \frac{k}{k(n-1)/2} = 1 - \frac{2}{n-1}.$$

Similarly, in the ith iteration, the probability of the ith event

$$B_i = A_1 \cap A_2 \cap \cdots \cap A_i$$

is at least

$$1 - \frac{k}{k(n-i+1)/2} = 1 - \frac{2}{n-i+1}.$$

Applying the multiplication rule in Eq. (B.3) on page 693, the probability that a minimum cut is found after $n - 2$ contractions is at least the probability that no edge in the cut C is contracted, which is

$$\begin{aligned}
\mathbf{Pr}[B_{n-2}] &= \mathbf{Pr}[A_1 \cap A_2 \cap \cdots \cap A_{n-2}] \\
&= \mathbf{Pr}[A_1]\,\mathbf{Pr}[A_2 \mid A_1]\ \cdots \mathbf{Pr}[A_{n-2} \mid A_1 \cap A_2 \cap \cdots \cap A_{n-3}] \\
&= \left(1 - \frac{2}{n}\right)\left(1 - \frac{2}{n-1}\right) \cdots \left(1 - \frac{2}{n-i+1}\right) \cdots \left(\frac{2}{4}\right)\left(\frac{1}{3}\right) \\
&= \left(\frac{n-2}{n}\right)\left(\frac{n-3}{n-1}\right) \cdots \left(\frac{n-i-1}{n-i+1}\right) \cdots \left(\frac{2}{4}\right)\left(\frac{1}{3}\right) \\
&= \frac{2}{n(n-1)}.
\end{aligned}$$

It follows that the algorithm will fail to find a minimum cut with probability at most

$$1 - \frac{2}{n(n-1)} \leq 1 - \frac{2}{n^2}.$$

Hence, repeating the algorithm $n^2/2$ times and selecting the minimum cut, the probability that the minimum cut is not found in any of the $n^2/2$ repetitions is at most

$$\left(1 - \frac{2}{n^2}\right)^{n^2/2} < \frac{1}{e}.$$

Hence, repeating the algorithm $n^2/2$ times and selecting the minimum cut, the probability of finding a cut of minimum cardinality is at least

$$1 - \frac{1}{e}.$$

Now, we analyze the running time of the algorithm. Each contraction costs $O(n)$ time, and this is repeated $n-2$ times for each run of the algorithm for a total of $O(n^2)$ time. Since the algorithm is repeated $n^2/2$ times, the overall running time of the algorithm is $O(n^4)$. Repeating the algorithm further will result in better probability of success on the expense of increasing the running time.

The best known deterministic algorithm for finding a minimum cut runs in time $O(n^3)$. It can be shown that the running time of the randomized algorithm can be substantially improved to $O(n^2 \log n)$ with probability of success $\Omega(1/\log n)$. Consequently, in order to have constant probability of finding a minimum cut it is sufficient to repeat this algorithm $O(\log n)$ times. The time complexity becomes $O(n^2 \log^2 n)$.

13.11   Testing String Equality

In this section, we outline an example of how randomization can be employed to cut down drastically on the communication cost. Suppose that two parties A and B can communicate over a communication channel, which we will assume to be very reliable. A has a very long string x and B has a very long string y, and they want to determine whether $x = y$. Obviously, A can send x to B, who in turn can immediately test whether $x = y$. But this method would be extremely expensive, in view of the cost of using the channel. Another alternative would be for A to derive from x a much shorter string that could serve as a "fingerprint" of x and send it to B. B then would use the same derivation to obtain a fingerprint for y and then compare the two fingerprints. If they are equal, then B would assume that $x = y$; otherwise, B would conclude that $x \neq y$. B then notifies A of the outcome of the test. This method requires the transmission of a much shorter string across the channel. For a string w, let $I(w)$ be the integer represented by the bit string w. One method of fingerprinting is to choose a prime number p and then use the fingerprint function

$$I_p(x) = I(x) \pmod{p}.$$

If p is not too large, then the fingerprint $I_p(x)$ can be sent as a short string. The number of bits to be transmitted is thus $O(\log p)$. If $I_p(x) \neq I_p(y)$, then obviously $x \neq y$. However, the converse is not true. That is, if $I_p(x) = I_p(y)$, then it is not necessarily the case that $x = y$. We refer to this phenomenon as a *false match*. In general, a false match occurs if $x \neq y$, but $I_p(x) = I_p(y)$, i.e., p divides $I(x) - I(y)$. We will later bound the probability of a false match.

The weakness of this method is that, for fixed p, there are certain pairs of strings x and y on which the method will always fail. We get around the problem of the existence of these pairs x and y by choosing p at random every time the equality of two strings is to be checked, rather than agreeing on p in advance. Moreover, choosing p at random allows for resending another fingerprint and thus increasing the confidence in the case $x = y$. This method is described in Algorithm STRINGEQUALITYTEST (the value of M will be determined later).

Algorithm 13.7 STRINGEQUALITYTEST

1. A chooses p at random from the set of primes less than M.
2. A sends p and $I_p(x)$ to B.
3. B checks whether $I_p(x) = I_p(y)$ and confirms the equality or inequality of the two strings x and y.

Now, we compute the probability of a false match. Let n be the number of bits in the binary representation of x. Of course, n is also equal to the number of bits in the binary representation of y; otherwise, the problem is trivial. Let $\pi(n)$ be the number of distinct primes less than n. It is well known that $\pi(n)$ is asymptotic to $n/\ln n$. It is also known that if $k < 2^n$, then, except when n is very small, the number of distinct primes that divide k is less than $\pi(n)$. Since failure can occur only in the case of a false match, i.e., $x \neq y$ but $I_p(x) = I_p(y)$, this is only possible if p divides $I(x) - I(y)$. Hence, the probability of failure for two n-bit strings x and y is

$$\frac{|\{p \mid p \text{ is a prime } < 2^n \text{ and } p \text{ divides } I(x) - I(y)\}|}{\pi(M)} \leq \frac{\pi(n)}{\pi(M)}.$$

If we choose $M = 2n^2$, we obtain

$$\mathbf{Pr}\,[\text{failure}] \leq \frac{\pi(n)}{\pi(M)} \approx \frac{n/\ln n}{2n^2/\ln n^2} = \frac{1}{n}.$$

Furthermore, if we repeat the algorithm k times, each time selecting a prime number less than M at random, then the probability becomes at most $(1/n)^k$. If, for example, we set $k = \lceil \log\log n \rceil$, then the probability of failure becomes

$$\mathbf{Pr}\,[\text{failure}] \leq \frac{1}{n^{\lceil \log\log n \rceil}}.$$

Example 13.5 Suppose that x and y are one million bits each, i.e., $n = 1,000,000$. Then, $M = 2 \times 10^{12} = 2^{40.8631}$. In this case, the number of bits required to transmit p is at most $\lfloor \log M \rfloor + 1 = 40 + 1 = 41$. The number of bits required to transmit the fingerprint of x is at most $\lfloor \log(p-1) \rfloor + 1 \leq \lfloor \log M \rfloor + 1 = 41$. Thus, the total number of bits transmitted is at most 82. The probability of failure in one transmission is at most $1/n = 1/1,000,000$. Since $\lceil \log\log n \rceil = 5$, repeating the algorithm five times reduces the probability of false match to $n^{-\lceil \log\log n \rceil} = (10^6)^{-5} = 10^{-30}$, which is negligible.

13.12 Pattern Matching

Now, we apply the same idea of fingerprinting described in Sec. 13.11 to a classical problem in computer science: pattern matching. Given a string of text $X = x_1 x_2 \ldots x_n$ and a pattern $Y = y_1 y_2 \ldots y_m$, where $m \leq n$, determine whether or not the pattern appears in the text. Without loss of generality, we will assume that the text alphabet is $\Sigma = \{0, 1\}$. The most straightforward method for solving this problem is simply to move the pattern across the entire text, and in every position, compare the pattern with the portion of the text of length m. This brute-force method leads to an $O(mn)$ running time. There are, however, more complicated deterministic algorithms whose running time is $O(n + m)$.

Here, we will present a simple and efficient Monte Carlo algorithm that also achieves a running time of $O(n + m)$. We will convert it later into a Las Vegas algorithm having the same time complexity. The algorithm follows the same brute-force algorithm of sliding the pattern Y across the text X, but instead of comparing the pattern with each block $X(j) = x_j x_{j+1} \ldots x_{j+m-1}$, we will compare the fingerprint $I_p(Y)$ of the pattern with the fingerprints $I_p(X(j))$ of the blocks of text. The $O(n)$ fingerprints of the text are fortunately easy to compute. The key observation is that when we shift from one block of text to the next, the fingerprint of the new block $X(j + 1)$ can easily be computed from the fingerprint of $X(j)$. Specifically,

$$I_p(X(j + 1)) = (2I_p(X(j)) - 2^m x_j + x_{j+m}) \pmod{p}.$$

If we let $W_p = 2^m \pmod{p}$, then we have the recurrence

$$I_p(X(j + 1)) = (2I_p(X(j)) - W_p x_j + x_{j+m}) \pmod{p}. \tag{13.8}$$

The pattern matching algorithm is shown as Algorithm PATTERN-MATCHING (the value of M will be determined later).

Algorithm 13.8 PATTERNMATCHING
Input: A string of text X and a pattern Y of length n and m, respectively.
Output: The first position of Y in X if Y occurs in X; otherwise, 0.

1. Choose p at random from the set of primes less than M.
2. $j \leftarrow 1$
3. Compute $W_p = 2^m \pmod{p}$, $I_p(Y)$ and $I_p(X_j)$
4. **while** $j \leq n - m + 1$
5.   **if** $I_p(X_j) = I_p(Y)$ **then return** j {A match is found (probably)}
6. $j \leftarrow j + 1$
7.   Compute $I_p(X_j)$ using Eq. 13.8.
8. **end while**
9. **return** 0   {Y does not occur in X (definitely)}

The computation of each of W_p, $I_p(Y)$ and $I_p(X(1))$ costs $O(m)$ time. When implementing the computation of $I_p(X(j + 1))$ from $I_p(X(j))$, we do not need to use the more expensive operations of multiplication and division; only a constant number of additions and subtractions is needed. Thus, the computation of each $I_p(X(j))$, for $2 \leq j \leq n - m + 1$, costs only $O(1)$ time for a total of $O(n)$ time. Hence, the running time is $O(n+m)$. The above analysis is valid under the uniform-cost RAM model of computation. If we use the more realistic logarithmic-cost RAM model of computation, then the time complexity is increased by a factor of $\log p$.

Now, we analyze the frequency with which this algorithm will fail. A false match will occur only if for some j, we have

$$Y \neq X(j) \text{ but } I_p(Y) = I_p(X(j)).$$

This is only possible if the chosen prime number p divides

$$\prod_{\{j \mid Y \neq X(j)\}} |I(Y) - I(X(j))|.$$

This product cannot exceed $(2^m)^n = 2^{mn}$, and hence the number of primes that divide it cannot exceed $\pi(mn)$. If we choose $M = 2mn^2$, then the probability of a false match cannot exceed

$$\frac{\pi(mn)}{\pi(M)} \approx \frac{mn/\ln(mn)}{2mn^2/\ln(mn^2)} = \frac{\ln(mn^2)}{2n\ln(mn)} < \frac{\ln(mn)^2}{2n\ln(mn)} = \frac{1}{n}.$$

It is interesting to note that, according to the above derivation, the probability of failure depends only on the length of the text, and the length of the pattern has no effect on this probability. Note also that in the case when $m = n$, the problem reduces to that of testing the equality of two strings of equal length discussed in Sec. 13.11, and that the probability of failure is identical to the one derived for that problem.

To convert the algorithm into a Las Vegas algorithm is easy. Whenever the two fingerprints $I_p(Y)$ and $I_p(X(j))$ match, the two strings are tested for equality. The expected time complexity of this Las Vegas algorithm becomes

$$O(n + m)\left(1 - \frac{1}{n}\right) + mn\left(\frac{1}{n}\right) = O(n + m).$$

Thus, we have an efficient pattern matching algorithm that always gives the correct result.

13.13 Primality Testing

In this section, we study a well-known Monte Carlo algorithm for testing whether a given positive integer n is prime. The obvious method of repeatedly dividing by the numbers from 2 to $\lfloor\sqrt{n}\rfloor$ is extremely inefficient, as it leads to exponential time complexity in the input size (see Example 1.16). This method is appropriate only for small numbers, and its only advantage is that it outputs a divisor of n if it is composite. It turns out that factoring an integer is a much harder problem than merely testing whether it is prime or composite.

In primality tests, we use the idea of finding a "witness", which is a proof that a number is composite. Obviously, finding a divisor of n is a proof that it is composite. However, such witnesses are very rare. Indeed, if we take a number n that is fairly large, the number of its prime divisors is very small compared to the number of integers between 1 and n. It is well known that if $n < 2^k$, then except when k is very small, the number of distinct primes that divide n is less than $\pi(k) \approx k/\ln k$.

This motivates the search for another type of witness. Before discussing the alternate witness, we will dispose of an algorithm for an operation that will be used throughout this section. Let a, m and n be positive integers with $m \leq n$. We need the operation of raising a to the mth power and reducing the result modulo n. Algorithm EXPMOD below computes $a^m \pmod{n}$. It is similar to the exponentiation algorithm presented in Sec. 4.3. Notice that we reduce modulo n after each squaring or multiplication rather than first computing a^m and reducing modulo n once at the end. A call to this algorithm is of the form EXPMOD(a, m, n).

Algorithm 13.9 EXPMOD
Input: Positive integers a, m and n with $m \leq n$.
Output: $a^m \pmod{n}$.

1. Let the binary digits of m be $b_k = 1, b_{k-1}, \ldots, b_0$.
2. $c \leftarrow 1$
3. **for** $j \leftarrow k$ **downto** 0
4. $c \leftarrow c^2 \pmod{n}$
5.   **if** $b_j = 1$ **then** $c \leftarrow ac \pmod{n}$
6. **end for**
7. **return** c

It is easy to see that the running time of Algorithm EXPMOD is $\Theta(\log m) = O(\log n)$, if we want to charge one unit of time per one multiplication. However, since we are dealing here with arbitrarily large integers, we will count the exact number of bit multiplications performed by the algorithm. If we use the obvious way of multiplying two integers, then each multiplication costs $O(\log^2 n)$. Thus, the overall running time of Algorithm EXPMOD is $O(\log^3 n)$.

Now, we present a series of primality tests all of which are based on Fermat's theorem:

Theorem 13.8   *If n is prime, then for all $a \not\equiv 0 \pmod{n}$, we have*

$$a^{n-1} \equiv 1 \pmod{n}.$$

Consider Algorithm PTEST1. By Fermat's theorem, if Algorithm PTEST1 returns *composite*, then we are sure that n is composite. The ancient Chinese conjectured that a natural number n must be prime if it satisfies the congruence $2^n \equiv 2 \pmod{n}$. The question remained open until 1819, when Sarrus showed that $2^{340} \equiv 1 \pmod{341}$, and yet $341 = 11 \times 31$ is composite. Some other composite numbers that satisfy the congruence $2^{n-1} \equiv 1 \pmod{n}$ are 561, 645, 1105, 1387, 1729 and 1905. Thus, if Algorithm PTEST1 returns *prime*, then n may or may not be prime.

Algorithm 13.10 PTEST1
Input: A positive odd integer $n \geq 5$.
Output: *prime* if n is prime; otherwise, *composite*.

1. **if** EXPMOD$(2, n-1, n) \equiv 1 \pmod{n}$ **then return** *prime* {probably}
2. **else return** *composite*   {definitely}

Surprisingly, this simple test gives an erroneous result very rarely. For example, for all composite numbers between 4 and 2000, the algorithm returns *prime* only for the numbers 341, 561, 645, 1105, 1387, 1729 and 1905. Moreover, there are only 78 values of n less than 100,000 for which the test errs, the largest of which is $93961 = 7 \times 31 \times 433$.

It turns out, however, that for many composite numbers n, there exist integers a for which $a^{n-1} \equiv 1 \pmod{n}$. In other words, the converse of Fermat's theorem is not true (we have already proven this for $a = 2$).

Indeed, there are composite integers n known as *Carmichael numbers* that satisfy Fermat's theorem *for all positive integers a that are relatively prime to n*. The smallest Carmichael numbers are $561 = 3 \times 11 \times 17$, $1105 = 5 \times 13 \times 17$, $1729 = 7 \times 13 \times 19$ and $2465 = 5 \times 17 \times 29$. Carmichael numbers are very rare; there are, for example, only 255 of them less than 10^8. When a composite number n satisfies Fermat's theorem relative to base a, n is called a *base-a pseudoprime*. Thus, Algorithm PTEST1 returns *prime* whenever n is prime or base-2 pseudoprime. One way to improve on the performance of Algorithm PTEST1 is to choose the base *randomly* between 2 and $n - 2$. This yields Algorithm PTEST2. As in Algorithm PTEST1, Algorithm PTEST2 errs only if n is a base-a pseudoprime. For example, $91 = 7 \times 13$ is base-3 pseudoprime since $3^{90} \equiv 1 \pmod{91}$.

Algorithm 13.11 PTEST2
Input: A positive odd integer $n \geq 5$.
Output: *prime* if n is prime; otherwise, *composite*.

1. $a \leftarrow random(2, n - 2)$
2. **if** EXPMOD$(a, n - 1, n) \equiv 1 \pmod{n}$ **then return** *prime* {probably}
3. **else return** *composite* {definitely}

Let Z_n^* be the set of positive integers less than n that are relatively prime to n. It is well known that Z_n^* forms a group under the operation of multiplication modulo n. Define

$$F_n = \{a \in Z_n^* \mid a^{n-1} \equiv 1 \pmod{n}\}.$$

If n is prime or a Carmichael number, then $F_n = Z_n^*$. So, suppose n is not a Carmichael number or a prime number. Then, $F_n \neq Z_n^*$. It is easy to verify that F_n under the operation of multiplication modulo n forms a group that is a proper subgroup of Z_n^*. Consequently, the order of F_n divides the order of Z_n^*, that is, $|F_n|$ divides $|Z_n^*|$. It follows that the number of elements in F_n is at most half the number of elements in Z_n^*. This proves the following lemma.

Lemma 13.2 *If n is not a Carmichael number, then Algorithm PTEST2 will detect the compositeness of n with probability at least $1/2$.*

Unfortunately, it has recently been shown that there are, in fact, infinitely many Carmichael numbers. In the remainder of this section, we describe a more powerful randomized primality test algorithm that circumvents the difficulty that arises as a result of the existence of infinitely many Carmichael numbers. The algorithm has the property that if n is composite, then the probability that this is discovered is at least $\frac{1}{2}$. In other words, the probability that it will err is at most $\frac{1}{2}$. Thus, by repeating the test k times, the probability that it will err is at most 2^{-k}. The algorithm, which we will call PTEST3, is based on the following reasoning. Let $n \geq 5$ be an odd prime. Write $n - 1 = 2^q m$ ($q \geq 1$ since $n - 1$ is even). Then, by Fermat's theorem, the sequence

$$a^m \pmod{n}, a^{2m} \pmod{n}, a^{4m} \pmod{n}, \ldots, a^{2^q m} \pmod{n}$$

must end with 1, and the value just preceding the first appearance of 1 will be $n - 1$. This is because the only solutions to $x^2 \equiv 1 \pmod{n}$ are $x = \pm 1$ when n is prime. This reasoning leads to Algorithm PTEST3.

Algorithm 13.12 PTEST3
Input: A positive odd integer $n \geq 5$.
Output: *prime* if n is prime; otherwise, *composite*.

1. $q \leftarrow 0$; $\quad m \leftarrow n - 1$
2. **repeat** {find q and m}
3. $\quad\quad m \leftarrow m/2$
4. $\quad\quad q \leftarrow q + 1$
5. **until** m is odd
6. $a \leftarrow random(2, n - 2)$
7. $x \leftarrow$ EXPMOD(a, m, n)
8. **if** $x = 1$ **then return** *prime* {probably}
9. **for** $j \leftarrow 0$ **to** $q - 1$
10. $\quad\quad$ **if** $x \equiv -1 \pmod{n}$ **then return** *prime* {probably}
11. $\quad\quad x \leftarrow x^2 \pmod{n}$
12. **end for**
13. **return** *composite* {definitely}

Theorem 13.9 *If Algorithm* PTEST3 *returns "composite", then n is composite.*

Proof. Suppose that Algorithm PTEST3 returns "*composite*", but n is an odd prime. We claim that $a^{2^j m} \equiv 1 \pmod{n}$ for $j = q, q - 1, \ldots, 0$. If so, then setting $j = 0$ yields $a^m \equiv 1 \pmod{n}$, which means that the algorithm must have returned *prime* by Step 8, a contradiction to the outcome of the algorithm. This contradiction establishes the theorem. Now, we prove our claim. By Fermat's theorem, since n is prime, the statement is true for $j = q$. Suppose it is true for some j, $1 \leq j \leq q$. Then, it is also true for $j - 1$ also because

$$(a^{2^{j-1}m})^2 = a^{2^j m} \equiv 1 \pmod{n}$$

implies that the quantity being squared is ± 1. Indeed, the equation $x^2 = 1$ in Z_n^* has only the solution $x = \pm 1$. But -1 is ruled out by the outcome of the algorithm since it must have executed Step 13. Consequently,

$$a^{2^{j-1}m} \equiv 1 \pmod{n}.$$

This completes the proof of the claim. $\qquad\qquad\qquad\qquad\qquad\square$

Note that the contrapositive statement of the above theorem is: If n is prime, then Algorithm PTEST3 returns *prime*, which means that the algorithm will never err if n is prime.

Obviously, Algorithm PTEST3 is as good as Algorithm PTEST2 in dealing with non-Carmichael numbers. It can be shown, although we will not pursue it here, that the probability that Algorithm PTEST3 errs when presented with a Carmichael number is at most $1/2$. So, the probability that it will err on any composite number is at most $1/2$. Thus, by repeating the test k times, the probability that it will err is at most 2^{-k}. If we set $k = \lceil \log n \rceil$, the probability of failure becomes $2^{-\lceil \log n \rceil} \leq 1/n$. In other words, the algorithm will give the correct answer with probability at least $1 - 1/n$, which is negligible when n is sufficiently large. This results in our final algorithm, which we will call PRIMALITYTEST.

We compute the running time of Algorithm PRIMALITYTEST as follows (assuming that a random integer can be generated in $O(1)$ time). The value of q computed in Step 4 is $O(\log n)$. So, the **repeat** loop costs $O(q) = O(\log n)$ time. We have shown before that the cost of Step 8 is $\Theta(\log^3 n)$. It is repeated at most $k = \lceil \log n \rceil$ times for a total of $O(\log^4 n)$. The cost of the inner **for** loop is equal to the cost of each squaring, $O(\log^2 n)$, times $O(q) = O(\log n)$ times $O(k) = O(\log n)$ for a total of $O(kq \log^2 n) = O(\log^4 n)$. Thus, the time complexity of the algorithm is $O(\log^4 n)$. The following theorem summarizes the main result.

Algorithm 13.13 PRIMALITYTEST
Input: A positive odd integer $n \geq 5$.
Output: *prime* if n is prime; otherwise, *composite*.

1. $q \leftarrow 0$; $m \leftarrow n - 1$; $k \leftarrow \lceil \log n \rceil$
2. **repeat**   {find q and m}
3. $m \leftarrow m/2$
4. $q \leftarrow q + 1$
5. **until** m is odd
6. **for** $i \leftarrow 1$ **to** k
7. $a \leftarrow random(2, n - 2)$
8. $x \leftarrow$ EXPMOD(a, m, n)
9.   **if** $x = 1$ **then return** *prime*   {probably}
10.   **for** $j \leftarrow 0$ **to** $q - 1$
11.   **if** $x \equiv -1 \pmod{n}$ **then return** *prime*   {probably}
12. $x \leftarrow x^2 \pmod{n}$
13.   **end for**
14. **end for**
15. **return** *composite*   {definitely}

Theorem 13.10   *In time* $O(\log^4 n)$, *Algorithm* PRIMALITYTEST *behaves as follows when presented with an odd integer* $n \geq 5$:

(1) *If n is prime, then it outputs* prime.
(2) *If n is composite, then it outputs* composite *with probability at least* $1 - 1/n$.

13.14 Practice Problems

13.1. Let p_1, p_2 and p_3 be three polynomials of degrees n, n and $2n$, respectively. Give a randomized algorithm to test whether $p_3(x) = p_1(x) \times p_2(x)$.

13.2. Consider the following modification of Algorithm BINARYSEARCH (see Sec. 1.3). Instead of halving the search interval in each iteration, select one of the remaining positions at random. Assume that every position between *low* and *high* is equally likely to be chosen by the algorithm. Compare the performance of this algorithm with that of Algorithm BINARYSEARCH.

13.3. In the discussion of Algorithm RANDOMIZEDQUICKSORT, it was stated that one possibility to obtain a $\Theta(n \log n)$ expected time for

Algorithm QUICKSORT is by permuting the input elements so that their order becomes random. Describe an $O(n)$ time algorithm to randomly permute the input array before processing it by Algorithm QUICKSORT.

13.4. A fair die is tossed 1000 times. Give a Markov bound for the probability that the sum is greater than 5000.

13.5. Apply Markov inequality to find the probability that in the dice problem discussed in Sec. 13.5.2, there will be more than 20 rolls using a 100-sided die.

13.6. Apply Markov inequality to find the probability that in the problem of finding the minimum using RQUICKSELECT, the number of comparisons is more than $3n$. See Sec. 13.5.3.

13.7. A fair die is tossed 1000 times. Give a Chebyshev bound for the probability that the sum is greater than 5000.

13.8. Suppose there are n items to be stored in a hash table of size k, where the location of each item in the hash table is chosen uniformly at random. A collision happens if two items are assigned to the same location. How large should k be in order to have a probability at least a half for a collision? (*Hint*: This is similar to the birthday paradox.)

13.15　Exercises

13.1. Let n be a positive integer. Design an efficient randomized algorithm that generates a random permutation of the integers $1, 2, \ldots, n$. Assume that you have access to a fair coin. Analyze the time complexity of your algorithm.

13.2. Show that Eq. (13.1) is maximum when $k = \lceil n/2 \rceil$.

13.3. Consider randomized binary search discussed in Problem 13.2. Apply the result in the dice problem discussed in Sec. 13.5.2 to find the expected number of comparisons when searching for an element x that is not in the searched array $A[1..n]$ and less than or greater than all elements in A. Compare your answer with that obtained in Problem 13.2.

13.4. Suppose that a Monte Carlo algorithm gives the correct solution with probability at least $1 - \epsilon_1$, regardless of the input. How many executions of the same algorithm are necessary in order to raise the probability to at least $1 - \epsilon_2$, where $0 < \epsilon_2 < \epsilon_1 < 1$.

13.5. Let A be a Monte Carlo algorithm whose expected running time is at most $T(n)$ and gives a correct solution with probability $p(n)$. Suppose the correctness of any solution of the algorithm can always be verified in time $T'(n)$. Show that A can be converted into a Las Vegas algorithm A' for the same problem that runs in expected time at most $(T(n) + T'(n))/p(n)$.

13.6. Let $L = x_1, x_2, \ldots, x_n$ be a sequence of elements that contains exactly k occurrences of the element x $(1 \leq k \leq n)$. We want to find one j such that $x_j = x$. Consider repeating the following procedure until x is found. Generate a random number i between 1 and n and check whether $x_i = x$. Which method is faster, on the average, this method or linear search? Explain.

13.7. Let L be a list of n elements that contains a majority element (see Sec. 4.2). Give a randomized algorithm that finds the majority element. Is randomization suitable for this problem in view of the fact that there is an $O(n)$ time algorithm to solve it?

13.8. Let A, B and C be three $n \times n$ matrices. Give a $\Theta(n^2)$ time algorithm to test whether $AB = C$. The algorithm is such that if $AB = C$, then it returns *true*. What is the probability that it returns *true* when $AB \neq C$? (*Hint*: Let x be a vector of n random entries. Perform the test $A(BX) = CX$.)

13.9. Let A and B be two $n \times n$ matrices. Give a $\Theta(n^2)$ time algorithm to test whether $A = B^{-1}$. See Exercise 13.8.

13.10. An instructor collects the homeworks of his n students and later distributes them back randomly. That is, he gives each homework to a random student. What is the expected number of students who will receive their own homeworks? (*Hint*: Define the random variables $X_i = 1$ if student i gets his own homework, and $X_i = 0$ otherwise. Then, $\mathbf{E}[X_i] = \mathbf{Pr}[X_i = 1] = 1/n$. Apply linearity of expectations (see Sec. B.3).)

13.11. If m balls are randomly thrown into n bins, compute the probability that
(a) bins 1 and 2 are empty.
(b) two bins are empty.

13.12. If m balls are randomly thrown into two bins, compute the probability that bin 1 contains m_1 balls and bin 2 contains m_2 balls, where $m_1 + m_2 = m$.

13.13. If m balls are randomly thrown into three bins, compute the probability that bin 1 contains m_1 balls, bin 2 contains m_2 balls and bin 3 contains m_3 balls, where $m_1 + m_2 + m_3 = m$. See Exercise 13.12.

13.14. (The coupon collector's problem) There are n types of coupons, and at each trial, a coupon is chosen randomly. Each chosen coupon is equally likely to be of any of the n types. Compute the expected number of trials needed to collect at least one coupon from each of the n types. (*Hint*: This is similar to filling all bins with balls discussed in Sec. 13.6.4.)

13.15. (Random linear search) Consider performing linear search on an array A of n elements to search for an element x in a random fashion. In each iteration, the algorithm compares x with a random element of A and reports the outcome. Show that this method performs $\Theta(n \log n)$ comparisons in the worst case. (*Hint*: This is similar to filling all bins with balls discussed in Sec. 13.6.4.)

13.16. A fair coin is tossed 1000 times. Give a Chernoff bound for the probability that the number of heads is less than 5000.

13.17. Consider the sampling problem in Sec. 13.9. Suppose we perform one pass over the n integers and choose each one with probability m/n. Show that the size of the resulting sample has a large variance, and hence its size may be much smaller or larger than m.

13.18. Modify Algorithm RANDOMSAMPLING in Sec. 13.9 to eliminate the need for the boolean array $S[1..n]$. Assume that n is too large compared to m, say $n > m^2$. What is the new time and space complexities of the modified algorithm?

13.19. A multigraph is a graph in which multiple edges are allowed between pairs of vertices. Show that the number of distinct minimum cuts in a multigraph with n vertices is at most $n(n-1)/2$ (see Sec. 13.10).

13.20. Consider the algorithm for finding a minimum cut discussed in Sec. 13.10. Suppose the algorithm is repeated $n(n-1)\ln n$ times instead of $n^2/2$. Compute the probability of success and the running time of the algorithm. (*Hint*: You may make use of the inequality $1 - \frac{2}{n(n-1)} \leq e^{-\frac{2}{n(n-1)}}$.)

13.21. Consider the algorithm for finding a minimum cut discussed in Sec. 13.10. Suppose we stop the contractions when the number of remaining vertices is $\sqrt{n}$ and find the minimum cut in the resulting graph using a deterministic $O(n^3)$ time algorithm. Show that the probability of success is $\Omega(1/n)$. Give probabilistic and timing analyses of the algorithm that results from repeating this modified algorithm n times.

13.22. Suppose A and B can communicate through a communication channel. A has n strings $x_1, x_2, \ldots, x_n$, $x_i \in \{0,1\}^n$, and B has n strings $y_1, y_2, \ldots, y_n$, $y_i \in \{0,1\}^n$. The problem is to determine whether there is a $j \in \{1, 2, \ldots, n\}$ such that $x_j = y_j$. Describe a randomized algorithm to solve this problem. Give its probabilistic and timing analyses.

13.23. Consider F_n as defined on page 402. Suppose that n is neither a Carmichael number nor a prime. Show that F_n under the operation of multiplication modulo n forms a group that is a proper subgroup of Z_n^*.

13.16 Bibliographic Notes

The real start of randomized algorithms was with the publication of Rabin's paper "Probabilistic algorithms" (Rabin, 1976). In this paper, two efficient randomized algorithms were presented: one for the closest pair problem and the other for primality testing. The probabilistic algorithm of Solovay and Strassen (1977, 1978), also for primality testing, is another celebrated result. Hromkovic (2005), Motwani and Raghavan (1995), and Mitzenmacher and

Upfal (2005) are comprehensive books on randomized algorithms. Some good surveys in this field include Karp (1991), Welsh (1983) and Gupta *et al.* (1994). Randomized quicksort is based on Hoare (1962). The randomized selection algorithm is due to Hoare (1961). The randomized algorithm for multiselection is due to Alsuwaiyel (2006).

Chapter 14

Approximation Algorithms

14.1 Introduction

There are many hard combinatorial optimization problems that cannot be solved *efficiently* using backtracking or randomization. An alternative in this case for tackling *some* of these problems is to devise an *approximation algorithm*, given that we will be content with a "reasonable" solution that approximates an optimal solution. Associated with each approximation algorithm, there is a performance bound that guarantees that the solution to a given instance will not be far away from the neighborhood of the exact solution. A marking characteristic of (most of) approximation algorithms is that they are fast, as they are mostly greedy heuristics. As stated in Chapter 7, the proof of correctness of a greedy algorithm may be complex. In general, the better the performance bound, the harder it becomes to prove the correctness of an approximation algorithm. This will be evident when we study some approximation algorithms. One should not be optimistic, however, about finding an efficient approximation algorithm, as there are hard problems for which even the existence of a "reasonable" approximation algorithm is unlikely unless NP = P.

14.2 Basic Definitions

A *combinatorial optimization problem* Π is either a *minimization problem* or a *maximization problem*. It consists of three components:

(1) A set D_Π of *instances*.
(2) For each instance $I \in D_\Pi$, there is a finite set $S_\Pi(I)$ of *candidate solutions* for I.
(3) Associated with each solution $\sigma \in S_\Pi(I)$ to an instance I in D_Π, there is a value $f_\Pi(\sigma)$ called the *solution value* for σ.

If Π is a minimization problem, then an *optimal solution* σ^* for an instance $I \in D_\Pi$ has the property that for all $\sigma \in S_\Pi(I)$, $f_\Pi(\sigma^*) \leq f_\Pi(\sigma)$. An optimal solution for a maximization problem is defined similarly. Throughout this chapter, we will denote by $OPT(I)$ the value $f_\Pi(\sigma^*)$.

An *approximation algorithm* A for an optimization problem Π is a (polynomial time) algorithm such that given an instance $I \in D_\Pi$, it outputs some solution $\sigma \in S_\Pi(I)$. We will denote by $A(I)$ the value $f_\Pi(\sigma)$.

Example 14.1   In this example, we illustrate the above definitions. Consider the problem BIN PACKING: Given a collection of items of sizes between 0 and 1, it is required to pack these items into the minimum number of bins of unit capacity. Obviously, this is a minimization problem. The set of instances D_Π consists of all sets $I = \{s_1, s_2, \ldots, s_n\}$, such that for all $j, 1 \leq j \leq n, s_j$ is between 0 and 1. The set of solutions S_Π consists of a set of subsets $\sigma = \{B_1, B_2, \ldots, B_k\}$ which is a disjoint partition of I such that for all $j, 1 \leq j \leq k$,

$$\sum_{s \in B_j} s \leq 1.$$

Given a solution σ, its value $f(\sigma)$ is simply $|\sigma| = k$. An optimal solution for this problem is that solution σ having the least cardinality. Let A be (the trivial) algorithm that assigns one bin for each item. Then, by definition, A is an approximation algorithm. Clearly, this is not a good approximation algorithm.

Throughout this chapter, we will be interested in optimization problems as opposed to decision problems. For example, the decision problem version of the BIN PACKING problem has also as input a bound K, and the solution is either *yes* if all items can be packed using at most K bins and *no* otherwise. Clearly, if a decision problem is NP-hard, then the optimization version of that problem is also NP-hard.

14.3 Difference Bounds

Perhaps, the most we can hope from an approximation algorithm is that the difference between the value of the optimal solution and the value of the solution obtained by the approximation algorithm is always constant. In other words, for all instances I of the problem, the most desirable solution that can be obtained by an approximation algorithm A is such that $|A(I) - OPT(I)| \leq K$, for some constant K. There are very few NP-hard optimization problems for which approximation algorithms with difference bounds are known. One of them is the following problem.

14.3.1 *Planar graph coloring*

Let $G = (V, E)$ be a planar graph. By the Four Color Theorem, every planar graph is 4-colorable. It is fairly easy to determine whether a graph is 2-colorable or not (Exercise 9.3). On the other hand, to determine whether it is 3-colorable is NP-complete. Given an instance I of G, an approximation algorithm A may proceed as follows. Assume G is nontrivial, i.e., it has at least one edge. Determine if the graph is 2-colorable. If it is, then output 2; otherwise, output 4. If G is 2-colorable, then $|A(I) - OPT(I)| = 0$. If it is not 2-colorable, then $|A(I) - OPT(I)| \leq 1$. This is because in the latter case, G is either 3-colorable or 4-colorable.

14.3.2 *Hardness result: The knapsack problem*

The problem KNAPSACK is defined as follows (see Sec. 6.6). Given n items $\{u_1, u_2, \ldots, u_n\}$ with *integer* sizes $s_1, s_2, \ldots, s_n$ and *integer* values $v_1, v_2, \ldots, v_n$, and a knapsack capacity C that is a positive integer, the problem is to fill the knapsack with some of these items whose total size is at most C and whose total value is maximum. In other words, find a subset $S \subseteq U$ such that

$$\sum_{u_j \in S} s_j \leq C \quad \text{and} \quad \sum_{u_j \in S} v_j \text{ is maximum.}$$

We will show that there is no approximation algorithm with difference bound that solves the knapsack problem. Suppose there is an approximation algorithm A to solve the knapsack problem with difference bound K, i.e., for all instances I of the problem, $|A(I) - OPT(I)| \leq K$, where

K is a positive integer. Given an instance I, we can use algorithm A to output an optimal solution as follows. Construct a new instance I' such that for all $j, 1 \leq j \leq n$, $s'_j = s_j$ and $v'_j = (K + 1)v_j$. It is easy to see that any solution to I' is a solution to I and vice versa. The only difference is that the value of the solution for I' is $(K+1)$ times the value of the solution for I. Since $A(I') = (K + 1)A(I)$, $|A(I') - OPT(I')| \leq K$ implies

$$|A(I) - OPT(I)| \leq \left\lfloor \frac{K}{K + 1} \right\rfloor = 0.$$

This means that A always gives the optimal solution, i.e., it solves the knapsack problem. Since the knapsack problem is known to be NP-complete, it is highly unlikely that the approximation algorithm A exists unless NP = P. (Recall that, by definition, an approximation algorithm runs in polynomial time).

14.4   Relative Performance Bounds

Clearly, a difference bound is the best bound guaranteed by an approximation algorithm. However, it turns out that very few hard problems possess such a bound, as exemplified by the knapsack problem for which we have shown that the problem of finding an approximation algorithm with a difference bound is impossible unless NP = P. In this section, we will discuss another performance guarantee, namely the *relative performance* guarantee.

Let Π be a minimization problem and I an instance of Π. Let A be an approximation algorithm to solve Π. We define the *approximation ratio* $R_A(I)$ to be

$$R_A(I) = \frac{A(I)}{OPT(I)}.$$

If Π is a maximization problem, then we define $R_A(I)$ to be

$$R_A(I) = \frac{OPT(I)}{A(I)}.$$

Thus, the approximation ratio is always greater than or equal to one. This has been done so that we will have a uniform measure for the quality of the solution produced by A.

The *absolute performance ratio* R_A for the approximation algorithm A is defined by

$$R_A = \inf\{r \mid R_A(I) \leq r \text{ for all instances } I \in D_\Pi\}.$$

The *asymptotic performance ratio* R_A^∞ for the approximation algorithm A is defined by

$$R_A^\infty = \inf\left\{r \geq 1 \,\middle|\, \begin{array}{l} \text{for some integer } N, R_A(I) \leq r \text{ for all} \\ \text{instances } I \in D_\Pi \text{ with } OPT(I) \geq N \end{array}\right\}.$$

It turns out that quite a few problems possess approximation algorithms with relative performance ratios. For some problems, the asymptotic ratio is more appropriate than the absolute performance ratio. For some others, both ratios are identical. In the following sections, we will consider some problems for which an approximation algorithm with *constant* relative performance ratio exists.

14.4.1   *The bin packing problem*

The optimization version of the BIN PACKING problem can be stated as follows. Given a collection of items $u_1, u_2, \ldots, u_n$ of sizes $s_1, s_2, \ldots, s_n$, where each s_j is between 0 and 1, we are required to pack these items into the minimum number of bins of unit capacity. We list here four heuristics for the BIN PACKING problem.

- **First Fit (*FF*):** In this method, the bins are indexed as 1,2, ... All bins are initially empty. The items are considered for packing in the order $u_1, u_2, \ldots, u_n$. To pack item u_i, find the least index j such that bin j contains at most $1 - s_i$, and add item u_i to the items packed in bin j.
- **Best Fit (*BF*):** This method is the same as the *FF* method except that when item u_i is to be packed, we look for that bin, which is filled to level $l \leq 1 - s_i$ and l is as large as possible.
- **First Fit Decreasing (*FFD*):** In this method, the items are first ordered by decreasing order of size, and then packed using the *FF* method.
- **Best Fit Decreasing (*BFD*):** In this method, the items are first ordered by decreasing order of size, and then packed using the *BF* method.

It is easy to prove that $R_{FF} < 2$, where R_{FF} is the absolute performance ratio of the *FF* heuristic. Let $FF(I)$ denote the number of bins used by the

FF heuristic to pack the items in instance I, and let $OPT(I)$ be the number of bins in an optimal packing. First, we note that if $FF(I) > 1$, then

$$FF(I) < \left\lceil 2\sum_{i=1}^{n} s_i \right\rceil. \tag{14.1}$$

To see this, note that no two bins can be half empty. Suppose for the sake of contradiction that there are two bins B_i and B_j that are half empty, where $i < j$. Then, the *first* item u_k put into bin B_j is of size 0.5 or less. But this means that the *FF* algorithm would have had put u_k in B_i instead of starting a new bin. To see that this bound is achievable, consider the case when for all $i, 1 \leq i \leq n, s_i = 0.5 + \epsilon$, where $\epsilon < 1/(2n)$ is arbitrarily small. Then, in this case, the number of bins needed is exactly n, which is less than $\lceil n + 2n\epsilon \rceil = n + 1$.

On the other hand, it is easy to see that the minimum number of bins required in an optimal packing is at least the sum of the sizes of all items. That is,

$$OPT(I) \geq \left\lceil \sum_{i=1}^{n} s_i \right\rceil. \tag{14.2}$$

Dividing inequality (14.1) by inequality (14.2), we have that

$$R_{FF}(I) = \frac{FF(I)}{OPT(I)} < 2.$$

In the BIN PACKING problem, it is more appropriate to use the asymptotic performance ratio, as it is more indicative of the performance of the algorithm for large values of n. A better bound for the *FF* heuristic is given by the following theorem whose proof is lengthy and complex.

Theorem 14.1   *For all instances I of the* BIN PACKING *problem,*

$$FF(I) \leq \frac{17}{10} OPT(I) + 2.$$

It can be shown that the *BF* heuristic also has a performance ratio of $17/10$. The *FFD* algorithm has a better performance ratio, which is given by the following theorem.

Theorem 14.2 *For all instances I of the* BIN PACKING *problem,*

$$FFD(I) \leq \frac{11}{9} OPT(I) + 4.$$

Again, it can be shown that the *BFD* heuristic also has a performance ratio of 11/9.

14.4.2 *The Euclidean traveling salesman problem*

In this section, we consider the following problem. Given a set S of n points in the plane, find a tour τ on these points of shortest length. Here, a tour is a circular path that visits every point exactly once. This problem is a special case of the traveling salesman problem and is commonly referred to as the EUCLIDEAN TRAVELING SALESMAN PROBLEM (ETSP), which is known to be NP-complete.

Let p_1 be an arbitrary starting point. An intuitive method would proceed in a greedy manner, visiting first that point closest to p_1, say p_2, and then that point which is closest to p_2, and so on. This method is referred to as the *nearest neighbor* (*NN*) heuristic, and it can be shown that it does not result in a bounded performance ratio, i.e., $R_{NN} = \infty$. Indeed, it can be shown that this method results in the performance ratio

$$R_{NN}(I) = \frac{NN(I)}{OPT(I)} = O(\log n).$$

An alternative approximation algorithm satisfying $R_A = 2$ can be summarized as follows. First, a minimum cost spanning tree T is constructed. Next, a multigraph T' is constructed from T by making two copies of each edge in T. Next, an Eulerian tour τ_e is found (an Eulerian tour is a cycle that visits every edge exactly once). Once τ_e is found, it can easily be converted into the desired Hamiltonian tour τ by tracing the Eulerian tour τ_e and deleting those vertices that have already been visited. Figure 14.1 illustrates the method. A minimum spanning tree of the input graph shown in Fig. 14.1(a) is converted into an Eulerian multigraph in Fig. 14.1(b). Figure 14.1(c) shows the resulting tour after bypassing those points that have already been visited.

Call this method the *MST* (minimum spanning tree) heuristic. We now show that $R_{MST} < 2$. Let τ^* denote an optimal tour. Then, the length of the

Fig. 14.1. An illustration of the approximation algorithm for the EUCLIDEAN
TRAVELING SALESMAN PROBLEM.

constructed minimum spanning tree T is strictly less than the length of τ^*.
This is because deleting an edge from τ^* results in a spanning tree. Thus,
the length of T' is strictly less than twice the length of τ^*. By the *triangle
inequality*, bypassing those vertices that have already been visited in τ_e
does not increase the length of the tour (recall that the triangle inequality
states that the sum of the lengths of any two sides in a triangle is greater
than or equal to the length of the third side). It follows that the length
of τ is strictly less than twice the length of τ^*. This establishes the bound
$R_{MST} < 2$.

The idea behind the MST approximation algorithm can be improved to
obtain a better performance ratio for this problem. To make T Eulerian,
we do not double its edges. Instead, we first identify the set X of vertices
of odd degree. The cardinality of X is always even (Exercise 14.2). Next,
we find a minimum weight matching M on the members of X. Finally, we
set $T' = T \cup M$. Clearly, each vertex in T' has an even degree, and thus T'
is Eulerian. Continuing as before, we proceed to find τ. Let us refer to this
method as the minimum matching (MM) heuristic. It is described more
precisely in Algorithm ETSPAPPROX.

Now, we show that the performance ratio of this algorithm is $3/2$. Let τ^*
be an optimal tour. First, observe that $length(T) < length(\tau^*)$. Next, note
that $length(M) \le (1/2)length(\tau^*)$. To see this, let τ' be τ^* with all vertices
not in X removed. Then, τ', which is a cycle, consists of two matchings
M_1 and M_2 on the set of points in X. In other words, if we let the edges
in τ' be numbered as $e_1, e_2, e_3, \ldots$, then $M_1 = \{e_1, e_3, e_5, \ldots\}$ and $M_2 =
\{e_2, e_4, e_6, \ldots\}$. Since M is a minimum weight matching, its total weight is

---

Algorithm 14.1 ETSPAPPROX
Input: An instance I of EUCLIDEAN TRAVELING SALESMAN PROBLEM.
Output: A tour τ for instance I.

1. Find a minimum spanning tree T of S.
2. Identify the set X of odd degree in T.
3. Find a minimum weight matching M on X.
4. Find an Eulerian tour τ_e in $T \cup M$.
5. Traverse τ_e edge by edge and bypass each previously visited vertex. Let τ be the resulting tour.

---

less than or equal to either one of M_1 or M_2. It follows that

$$length(\tau) \leq length(\tau_e)$$
$$= length(T) + length(M)$$
$$< length(\tau^*) + \frac{1}{2} length(\tau^*)$$
$$= \frac{3}{2} length(\tau^*).$$

Thus, for any instance of EUCLIDEAN TRAVELING SALESMAN PROBLEM,

$$R_{MM}(I) = \frac{MM(I)}{OPT(I)} < \frac{3}{2}.$$

We remark that the above two approximation algorithms apply to any instance of the general traveling salesman problem in which the triangle inequality is respected. Since Algorithm ETSPAPPROX involves finding a minimum weight matching, its time complexity is $O(n^3)$.

14.4.3 *The vertex cover problem*

Recall that a vertex cover C in a graph $G = (V, E)$ is a set of vertices such that each edge in E is incident to at least one vertex in C. We have shown in Sec. 9.4.4 that the problem of deciding whether a graph contains a vertex cover of size k, where k is a positive integer, is NP-complete.

Perhaps, the most intuitive heuristic that comes to mind is as follows. Repeat the following step until E becomes empty. Pick an edge e arbitrarily and add one of its endpoints, say v, to the vertex cover. Next, delete e and all other edges incident to v. Surely, this is an approximation algorithm that outputs a vertex cover. However, it can be shown that the performance ratio of this algorithm is unbounded. Surprisingly, if when considering an edge e, we add both of its endpoints to the vertex cover, then the performance ratio becomes 2. The process of picking an edge, adding its endpoints to the cover and deleting all edges incident to these endpoints is equivalent to finding a *maximal* matching in G. Note that this matching need not be of maximum cardinality. This approximation algorithm is outlined in Algorithm VCOVERAPPROX.

Algorithm 14.2 VCOVERAPPROX
Input: An undirected graph $G = (V, E)$.
Output: A vertex cover C for G.

  1. $C \leftarrow \{\}$
  2. **while** $E \neq \{\}$
  3.   Let $e = (u, v)$ be any edge in E.
  4. $C \leftarrow C \cup \{u, v\}$
  5.   Remove e and all edges incident to u or v from E.
  6. **end while**

Algorithm VCOVERAPPROX clearly outputs a vertex cover. We now show that $R_{VC} = 2$. It is not hard to see that the edges picked in Step 3 of the algorithm correspond to a *maximal* matching M, that is, a matching on the set of edges that cannot be extended. To cover the edges in M, we need at least $|M|$ vertices. This implies that the size of an optimal vertex cover is at least $|M|$. However, the size of the cover obtained by the algorithm is exactly $2|M|$. It follows that $R_{VC} = 2$. To see that this ratio is achievable, consider the graph

$$G = (\{v_1, v_2\}, \{(v_1, v_2)\}).$$

For this graph, an optimal cover is $\{v_1\}$, while the cover obtained by the algorithm is $\{v_1, v_2\}$.

14.4.4   *Hardness result: The traveling salesman problem*

In the last sections, we have presented approximation algorithms with reasonable performance ratios. It turns out, however, that there are many problems that do not admit bounded performance ratios. For example, the problems COLORING, CLIQUE, INDEPENDENT SET and the *general* TRAVELING SALESMAN problem (see Chapter 9) have no known approximation algorithms with bounded ratios. Let $G = (V, E)$ be an undirected graph. By Lemma 9.3, a subset $S \subseteq V$ is an independent set of vertices if and only if $V - S$ is a vertex cover. Moreover, it can be shown that if S is of maximum cardinality, then $V - S$ is of minimum cardinality (Exercise 14.6). One may be tempted to conclude from this that an approximation algorithm for VERTEX COVER will help in finding an approximation algorithm for INDEPENDENT SET. This, however, is not the case. To see why, suppose that G has a minimum vertex cover of size $(n/2) - 1$. The approximation algorithm VCOVERAPPROX above for the vertex cover problem will find one of size at most $n - 2$. But the complement of this cover is an independent set of size 2, while the size of a maximum independent set is, by Exercise 14.6, exactly $n - ((n/2) - 1) = (n/2) + 1$.

Now, we turn our attention to the general traveling salesman problem. The following theorem shows that it is impossible to find an approximation algorithm with bounded ratio for the traveling salesman problem unless NP = P.

Theorem 14.3 *There is no approximation algorithm A for the problem* TRAVELING SALESMAN *with $R_A < \infty$ unless* NP = P.

Proof. Suppose, to the contrary, that there is an approximation algorithm A for the problem TRAVELING SALESMAN with $R_A \leq K$, for some positive integer K. We will show that this can be used to derive a polynomial time algorithm for the problem HAMILTONIAN CYCLE, which is known to be NP-complete (see Chapter 9). Let $G = (V, E)$ be an undirected graph with n vertices. We construct an instance I of the traveling salesman problem as follows. Let V correspond to the set of cities and define a distance function $d(u, v)$ for all pairs of cities u and v by

$$d(u, v) = \begin{cases} 1 & \text{if } (u, v) \in E \\ Kn & \text{if } (u, v) \notin E. \end{cases}$$

Clearly, if G has a Hamiltonian cycle, then $OPT(I) = n$; otherwise, $OPT(I) > Kn$. Therefore, since $R_A \leq K$, we will have $A(I) \leq Kn$ if and only if G has a Hamiltonian cycle. This implies that there exists a polynomial time algorithm for the problem HAMILTONIAN CYCLE. But this implies that NP = P, which is highly unlikely. To finish the proof, note that the construction of instance I of the traveling salesman problem can easily be achieved in polynomial time.   □

14.5   Polynomial Approximation Schemes

So far we have seen that for some NP-complete problems there exist approximation algorithms with bounded approximation ratio. On the other hand, for some problems, it is impossible to devise an approximation algorithm with bounded ratio unless NP = P. On the other extreme, it turns out that there are problems for which there exists a series of approximation algorithms whose performance ratio converges to 1. Examples of these problems include the problems KNAPSACK, SUBSET-SUM and MULTIPROCESSOR SCHEDULING.

Definition 14.1   An *approximation scheme* for an optimization problem is a family of algorithms $\{A_\epsilon \mid \epsilon > 0\}$ such that $R_{A_\epsilon} \leq 1 + \epsilon$.

Thus, an approximation scheme can be viewed as an approximation algorithm A whose input is an instance I of the problem and a bound error ϵ such that $R_A(I, \epsilon) \leq 1 + \epsilon$.

Definition 14.2   A *polynomial approximation scheme* (PAS) is an approximation scheme $\{A_\epsilon\}$, where each algorithm A_ϵ runs in time that is polynomial in the length of the input instance I.

Note that in this definition, A_ϵ may not be polynomial in $1/\epsilon$. In the next section, we will strengthen the definition of an approximation scheme so that the algorithms run in time that is also polynomial in $1/\epsilon$. In this section, we will investigate a polynomial approximation scheme for the knapsack problem.

14.5.1   *The knapsack problem*

Let $U = \{u_1, u_2, \ldots, u_n\}$ be a set of items to be packed in a knapsack of size C. For $1 \leq j \leq n$, let s_j and v_j be the size and value of the jth item, respectively. Recall that the objective is to fill the knapsack with some items in U whose total size is at most C and such that their total value is maximum (see Sec. 6.6). Assume without loss of generality that the size of each item is not larger than C.

Consider the greedy algorithm that first orders the items by decreasing value to size ratio (v_j/s_j) and then considers the items one by one for packing. If the current item fits in the available space, then it is included; otherwise, the next item is considered. The algorithm terminates as soon as all items have been considered or no more items can be included in the knapsack. This greedy algorithm does not result in a bounded ratio as is evident from the following instance. Let $U = \{u_1, u_2\}, s_1 = 1, v_1 = 2, s_2 = v_2 = C > 2$. In this case, the algorithm will pack only item u_1, while in the optimal packing, item u_2 is selected instead. Since C can be arbitrarily large, the performance ratio of this greedy algorithm is unbounded.

Surprisingly, a simple modification of the above algorithm results in a performance ratio of 2. The modification is to also test the packing consisting of the item of largest value only, and then the better of the two packings is chosen as the output. Call this approximation algorithm KNAPSACKGREEDY. This approximation algorithm is outlined in Algorithm KNAPSACKGREEDY. It will be left as an exercise to show that $R_{\text{KNAPSACKGREEDY}} = 2$ (Exercise 14.3).

Algorithm 14.3 KNAPSACKGREEDY

Input: $2n + 1$ positive integers corresponding to item sizes $\{s_1, s_2, \ldots, s_n\}$, item values $\{v_1, v_2, \ldots, v_n\}$ and the knapsack capacity C.

Output: A subset Z of the items whose total size is at most C.

1. Renumber the items so that $v_1/s_1 \geq v_2/s_2 \geq \ldots \geq v_n/s_n$.
2. $j \leftarrow 0$; $K \leftarrow 0$; $V \leftarrow 0$; $Z \leftarrow \{\}$
3. **while** $j < n$ and $K < C$
4.   j $\leftarrow$ j+1
5.   **if** $s_j \leq C - K$ **then**
6. $Z \leftarrow Z \cup \{u_j\}$
7. $K \leftarrow K + s_j$
8. $V \leftarrow V + v_j$
9.   **end if**
10. **end while**
11. Let $Z' = \{u_s\}$, where u_s is an item of maximum value.
12. **if** $V \geq v_s$ **then return** Z
13. **else return** Z'.

Now, we describe a polynomial approximation scheme for the knapsack problem. The idea is quite simple. Let $\epsilon = 1/k$ for some positive integer k.

Algorithm A_ϵ consists of two steps. The first step is to choose a subset of *at most* k items and put them in the knapsack. The second step is to run Algorithm KNAPSACKGREEDY on the remaining items in order to complete the packing. These two steps are repeated $\sum_{j=0}^{k} \binom{n}{j}$ times, once for each subset of size $j, 0 \leq j \leq k$. In the following theorem, we bound both the running time and performance ratio of Algorithm A_ϵ, for all $k \geq 1$.

Theorem 14.4   *Let $\epsilon = 1/k$ for some integer $k \geq 1$. Then, the running time of Algorithm A_ϵ is $O(kn^{k+1})$, and its performance ratio is $1 + \epsilon$.*

Proof.   Since $\sum_{j=0}^{k} \binom{n}{j} = O(kn^k)$ (see Exercise 14.4), the number of subsets of size at most k is $O(kn^k)$. The amount of work done in each iteration is $O(n)$, and hence the time complexity of the algorithm is $O(kn^{k+1})$.

Now, we bound the performance ratio of the algorithm. Let I be an instance of the knapsack problem with items $U = \{u_1, u_2, \ldots, u_n\}$ and C being the knapsack capacity. Let X be the set of items corresponding to an optimal solution. If $|X| \leq k$, then there is nothing to prove, as the algorithm will try all possible k-subsets. So, suppose that $|X| > k$. Let $Y = \{u_1, u_2, \ldots, u_k\}$ be the set of k items of largest value in X, and let $Z = \{u_{k+1}, u_{k+2}, \ldots, u_r\}$ denote the set of remaining items in X, assuming $v_j/s_j \geq v_{j+1}/s_{j+1}$ for all $j, k+1 \leq j \leq r-1$. Since the elements in Y are of largest value, we must have

$$v_j \leq \frac{OPT(I)}{k+1} \quad \text{for} \quad j = k+1, k+2, \ldots, r. \tag{14.3}$$

Consider now the iteration in which the algorithm tries the set Y as the initial k-subset, and let u_m be the first item of Z not included in the knapsack by the algorithm. If no such item exists, then the output of the algorithm is optimal. So, assume that u_m exists. The optimal solution can be written as

$$OPT(I) = \sum_{j=1}^{k} v_j + \sum_{j=k+1}^{m-1} v_j + \sum_{j=m}^{r} v_j. \tag{14.4}$$

Let W denote the set of items packed by the algorithm, but not in $\{u_1, u_2, \ldots, u_m\}$, that were considered by the algorithm before u_m. In other words, if $u_j \in W$, then $u_j \notin \{u_1, u_2, \ldots, u_m\}$ and $v_j/s_j \geq v_m/s_m$.

Now, $A(I)$ can be written as

$$A(I) \geq \sum_{j=1}^{k} v_j + \sum_{j=k+1}^{m-1} v_j + \sum_{j \in W} v_j. \qquad (14.5)$$

Let

$$C' = C - \sum_{j=1}^{k} s_j - \sum_{j=k+1}^{m-1} s_j, \quad \text{and} \quad C'' = C' - \sum_{j \in W} s_j$$

be the residual capacities available, respectively, in the optimal and approximate solutions for the items of $U - Y$ following u_{m-1}. From 14.4,

$$OPT(I) \leq \sum_{j=1}^{k} v_j + \sum_{j=k+1}^{m-1} v_j + C' \frac{v_m}{s_m}.$$

By definition of m, we have $C'' < s_m$ and $v_j/s_j \geq v_m/s_m$ for every item $u_j \in W$. Since

$$C' = \sum_{u_j \in W} s_j + C'', \quad \text{and} \quad C'' < s_m,$$

we must have

$$OPT(I) < \sum_{j=1}^{k} v_j + \sum_{j=k+1}^{m-1} v_j + \sum_{j \in W} v_j + v_m.$$

Hence, from 14.5, $OPT(I) < A(I) + v_m$, and from 14.3,

$$OPT(I) < A(I) + \frac{OPT(I)}{k+1},$$

that is,

$$\frac{OPT(I)}{A(I)} \left(1 - \frac{1}{k+1} \right) = \frac{OPT(I)}{A(I)} \left(\frac{k}{k+1} \right) < 1.$$

Consequently,

$$R_k = \frac{OPT(I)}{A(I)} < 1 + \frac{1}{k} = 1 + \epsilon. \qquad \square$$

14.6   Fully Polynomial Approximation Schemes

The polynomial approximation scheme described in Sec. 14.5 runs in time that is exponential in $1/\epsilon$, the reciprocal of the desired error bound. In this section, we demonstrate an approximation scheme in which the approximation algorithm runs in time that is also polynomial in $1/\epsilon$. This can be achieved for some NP-hard problems using a constrained approximation scheme which we define below.

Definition 14.3   A *fully polynomial approximation scheme* (FPAS) is an approximation scheme $\{A_\epsilon\}$, where each algorithm A_ϵ runs in time that is polynomial in *both* the length of the input instance and $1/\epsilon$.

Definition 14.4   A *pseudopolynomial time* algorithm is an algorithm that runs in time that is polynomial in the *value of* L, where L is the largest number in the input instance.

Notice that if an algorithm runs in time that is polynomial in $\log L$, then it is a polynomial time algorithm. Here, $\log L$ is commonly referred to as the *size* of L. In Chapter 6, we have seen an example of a pseudopolynomial time algorithm, namely the algorithm for the knapsack problem. The idea behind finding an FPAS for an NP-hard problem is typical to all problems for which a pseudopolynomial time algorithm exists. Starting from such an algorithm A, scaling and rounding are applied to the input values in an instance I to obtain an instance I'. Then, the same algorithm A is applied to the modified instance I' to obtain an answer that is an approximation of the optimal solution. In this section, we will investigate an FPAS for the subset-sum problem.

14.6.1   *The subset-sum problem*

The subset-sum problem is a special case of the knapsack problem in which the item values are identical to their sizes. Thus, the subset-sum problem can be defined as follows. Given n items of sizes $s_1, s_2, \ldots, s_n$, and a positive integer C, the knapsack capacity, the objective is to find a subset of the items that maximizes the total sum of their sizes without exceeding the knapsack capacity C. Incidentally, this problem is a variant of the partition problem (see Sec. 9.4.5). The algorithm to solve this problem is almost identical to that for the knapsack problem described in Sec. 6.6. It is shown below as Algorithm SUBSETSUM.

Algorithm 14.4 SUBSETSUM
Input: A set of items $U = \{u_1, u_2, \ldots, u_n\}$ with sizes $s_1, s_2, \ldots, s_n$ and a knapsack capacity C.
Output: The maximum value of the function $\sum_{u_i \in S} s_i$ subject to $\sum_{u_i \in S} s_i \leq C$ for some subset of items $S \subseteq U$.

1. **for** $i \leftarrow 0$ **to** n
2. $T[i, 0] \leftarrow 0$
3. **end for**
4. **for** $j \leftarrow 0$ **to** C
5. $T[0, j] \leftarrow 0$
6. **end for**
7. **for** $i \leftarrow 1$ **to** n
8.   **for** $j \leftarrow 1$ **to** C
9. $T[i, j] \leftarrow T[i - 1, j]$
10.   **if** $s_i \leq j$ **then**
11. $x \leftarrow T[i - 1, j - s_i] + s_i$
12.   **if** $x > T[i, j]$ **then** $T[i, j] \leftarrow x$
13.   **end if**
14.   **end for**
15. **end for**
16. **return** $T[n, C]$

Clearly, the time complexity of Algorithm SUBSETSUM is exactly the size of the table, $\Theta(nC)$, as filling each entry requires $\Theta(1)$ time. Now, we develop an approximation algorithm A_ϵ, where $\epsilon = 1/k$ for some positive integer k. The algorithm is such that for any instance I,

$$R_{A_\epsilon}(I) = \frac{OPT(I)}{A_\epsilon(I)} \leq 1 + \frac{1}{k}.$$

Let

$$K = \frac{C}{2(k + 1)n}.$$

First, we set $C' = \lfloor C/K \rfloor$ and $s'_j = \lfloor s_j/K \rfloor$ for all $j, 1 \leq j \leq n$, to obtain a new instance I'. Next, we apply Algorithm SUBSETSUM on I'. The running time is now reduced to $\Theta(nC/K) = \Theta(kn^2)$. Now, we estimate the error in the approximate solution. Since an optimal solution cannot contain more than all the n items, we have the following relationship between the two optimum values $OPT(I)$ and $OPT(I')$ corresponding to the original instance I and the new instance I':

$$OPT(I) - K \times OPT(I') \leq Kn.$$

That is, if we let the approximate solution be K times the output of the algorithm when presented with instance I', then we have

$$OPT(I) - A_\epsilon(I) \leq Kn,$$

or

$$A_\epsilon(I) \geq OPT(I) - Kn = OPT(I) - \frac{C}{2(k+1)}.$$

We may assume without loss of generality that $OPT(I) \geq C/2$. This is because it is easy to obtain the optimal solution if $OPT(I) < C/2$ (see Exercise 14.7). Consequently,

$$
\begin{aligned}
R_{A_\epsilon}(I) &= \frac{OPT(I)}{A_\epsilon(I)} \\
&\leq \frac{A_\epsilon(I) + C/2(k+1)}{A_\epsilon(I)} \\
&\leq 1 + \frac{C/2(k+1)}{OPT(I) - C/2(k+1)} \\
&\leq 1 + \frac{C/2(k+1)}{C/2 - C/2(k+1)} \\
&= 1 + \frac{1}{k+1-1} \\
&= 1 + \frac{1}{k}.
\end{aligned}
$$

Thus, the algorithm's performance ratio is $1 + \epsilon$, and its running time is $\Theta(n^2/\epsilon)$. For example, if we let $\epsilon = 0.1$, then we obtain a quadratic algorithm with performance ratio of $11/10$. If we let $\epsilon = 1/n^r$ for some $r \geq 1$, then we have an approximation algorithm that runs in time $\Theta(n^{r+2})$ with performance ratio of $1 + 1/n^r$.

14.7 Practice Problems

14.1. Give an instance I of the BIN PACKING problem such that $FF(I) \geq \frac{3}{2}OPT(I)$.

14.2. Show that the number of vertices of odd degree in an undirected graph is even.

14.3. Consider the following algorithm for finding a vertex cover in an undirected graph. Execute the following step until all edges are deleted. Pick a vertex of highest degree that is incident to at least one edge in the remaining graph, add it to the cover and delete all edges incident to that vertex. Show that this greedy approach does not always result in a vertex cover of minimum size.

14.4. Consider the following approximation algorithm for the problem of finding a maximum clique in a given graph G. Repeat the following step until the resulting graph is a clique. Delete from G a vertex that is not connected to every other vertex in G and also delete all its incident edges. Show that this greedy approach does not always result in a clique of maximum size.

14.5. Consider the following approximation algorithm for the problem of finding a maximum clique in a given graph G. Set $C = \{\}$ and repeat the following step until G has no vertex that is not in C and is connected to every other vertex in C. Add to C a vertex that is not in C and is connected to every other vertex in C. Show that this greedy approach does not always result in a clique of maximum size.

14.6. Show that Algorithm VCOVERAPPROX does not always give an optimal vertex cover by giving a counterexample of a graph consisting of at least three vertices.

14.7. Consider the SUBSET-SUM problem discussed in Sec. 14.6.1. Show that if $OPT(I) < C/2$, then it is straightforward to obtain the optimal solution. Hint: Show that $\sum_{j=1}^{n} s_j < C$.

14.8 Exercises

14.1. Show that the performance ratio of the MST heuristic is achievable. In other words, give an instance of the Euclidean traveling salesman problem on which the MST heuristic results in a performance ratio of 2.

14.2. Show that the performance ratio of the NN approximation algorithm for the Euclidean traveling salesman problem is unbounded.

14.3. Show that the performance ratio of Algorithm KNAPSACKGREEDY for the knapsack problem is 2.

14.4. Show that $\sum_{j=0}^{k} \binom{n}{j} = O(kn^k)$.

14.5. Theorem 14.4 states that the running time of Algorithm A_ϵ is $O(kn^{k+1})$, where $k = 1/\epsilon$ is part of the input. Explain why this is an exponential algorithm.

14.6. Let $G = (V, E)$ be an undirected graph. By Lemma 9.3, a subset $S \subseteq V$ is an independent set of vertices if and only if $V - S$ is a vertex cover for G. Show that if S is of maximum cardinality, then $V - S$ is a vertex cover of minimum cardinality.

14.7. Show that the performance ratio of the approximation algorithm in Exercise 14.3 for the vertex cover problem is unbounded.

14.8. Show that the performance ratio of the approximation algorithm in Exercise 14.4 for the maximum clique problem is unbounded.

14.9. Show that the performance ratio of the heuristic algorithm in Exercise 14.5 for the maximum clique problem is unbounded.

14.10. Give an approximation algorithm for the COLORING problem: Find the minimum number of colors needed to color an undirected graph so that adjacent vertices are assigned different colors. Prove or disprove that its performance ratio is bounded.

14.11. Give an approximation algorithm for the INDEPENDENT SET problem: Find the maximum number of vertices that are mutually disconnected from each other. Prove or disprove that its performance ratio is bounded.

14.12. Give an $O(n)$ time algorithm that finds a minimum vertex cover in a tree in linear time.

14.13. Show in more detail that the running time of the polynomial approximation scheme for the knapsack problem discussed in the proof of Theorem 14.4 is $O(kn^{k+1})$. You should take into account the time needed to generate the subsets.

14.14. Consider the optimization version of the SET COVER problem defined in Sec. 9.4.5: Given a set X of n elements, a family $\mathcal{F}$ of subsets of X, find a subset $\mathcal{C} \subseteq \mathcal{F}$ of minimum size that covers all the elements in X. An approximation algorithm to solve this problem is outlined as follows. Initialize $S = X$, and $C = \{\}$, and repeat the following step until $S = \{\}$. Choose a subset $Y \in \mathcal{F}$ that maximizes $|Y \cap S|$, add Y to $\mathcal{C}$ and set $S = S - Y$. Show that this greedy algorithm does not always produce a set cover of minimum size.

14.15. Show that the performance ratio of the approximation algorithm described in Exercise 14.14 for the set cover problem is unbounded.

14.16. Show that the performance ratio of the approximation algorithm described in Exercise 14.14 for the set cover problem is $O(\log n)$.

14.17. Consider the optimization version of the MULTIPROCESSOR SCHEDULING problem defined in Sec. 9.4.5: Given n jobs $J_1, J_2, \ldots, J_n$, each having a run time t_i and a positive integer m (number of processors), schedule those jobs on the m processors so as to minimize the finishing time. The finishing time is defined to be the maximum execution time among all the m processors. An approximation algorithm to solve this problem is similar to the *FF* algorithm: The jobs are considered in their order $J_1, J_2, \ldots, J_n$, each job is assigned to the next available processor (ties are broken arbitrarily). In other words, the next job is assigned to that processor with the least finishing time. Show that the performance ratio of this algorithm is $2 - 1/m$.

14.18. Show that the $2 - 1/m$ bound of the approximation algorithm in Exercise 14.17 is tight by exhibiting an instance that achieves this ratio.

14.19. Consider modifying the approximation algorithm described in Exercise 14.17 for the MULTIPROCESSOR SCHEDULING problem by first ordering the jobs by decreasing value of their run times. Prove that in this case the performance ratio becomes

$$\frac{4}{3} - \frac{1}{3m}.$$

14.9   Bibliographic Notes

Garey and Johnson (1979) provides a good exposition to approximation algorithms. Other introductions to approximation algorithms can also be found in Horowitz *et al.* (1978) and Papadimitriou and Steiglitz (1982). The 17/10 bound for the *FF* algorithm for the BIN PACKING problem is due to Johnson *et al.* (1974). The 11/9 bound for the *FFD* algorithm for the BIN PACKING problem is due to Johnson (1973). The approximation algorithm for the TRAVELING SALESMAN problem appears in Rosenkrantz *et al.* (1977). The 3/2 bound is due to Christofides (1976). Lawler *et al.* (1985) provide an extensive treatment of the TRAVELING SALESMAN problem. The PAS for the KNAPSACK problem can be found in Sahni (1975). The FPAS for the SUBSET-SUM problem is based on that for the knapsack problem due to Ibarra and Kim (1975). Sahni (1977) gives general techniques for constructing PAS and FPAS. An asymptotic PAS for the BIN PACKING problem is given by Vega and Lueker (1981).

PART 6

Iterative Improvement for Domain-Specific Problems

In this part of the book, we study an algorithm design technique that we will refer to as iterative improvement. In its simplest form, this technique starts with a simple-minded (usually a greedy) solution and continues to improve on that solution in stages until an optimal solution is found. One more aspect of problem-specificity characterizes this technique. Some marking characteristics of the iterative improvement technique are in order. First, devicing new data structures to meet the data access requirements of the algorithm effectively, e.g., splay trees and Fibonacci heaps. Second, the introduction of innovative analysis techniques to carefully account for the true cost of the computation. This will be evident when, for example, counting the number of phases or augmentations in network flow and matching algorithms. Third, exploiting the problem specific observations to improve upon the existing solution.

As examples of this design technique, we will study in detail two problems: finding a maximum flow in a network and finding a maximum matching in undirected graphs. Both of these problems have received a great

433

amount of attention by researchers, and as a result many algorithms have been developed. Beside being interesting in their own right, these problems arise as subproblems in many practical applications.

For the maximum flow problem, which is the subject of Chapter 15, we present a sequence of increasingly efficient algorithms, starting from an algorithm with unbounded time complexity to an algorithm that runs in cubic time.

Chapter 16 is devoted to the problem of finding a maximum matching in an undirected graph. We will give algorithms for bipartite graphs and general graphs. We close this chapter with an elegant matching algorithm in bipartite graphs that runs in time $O(n^{2.5})$.

Chapter 15

Network Flow

15.1 Introduction

Let $G = (V, E)$ be a directed graph with two distinguished vertices s and t called, respectively, the *source* and *sink*, and a capacity function $c(u, v)$ defined on all pairs of vertices. Throughout this chapter, the 4-tuple (G, s, t, c), or simply G, will denote a *network*. Also, n and m will denote, respectively, the number of vertices and edges in G, that is, $n = |V|$ and $m = |E|$. In this chapter, we consider the problem of finding a maximum flow in a given network (G, s, t, c) from s to t. This problem is called the *max-flow problem*. We will present a series of algorithms to solve this problem starting from a method of unbounded time complexity to an algorithm that runs in time $O(n^3)$.

15.2 Preliminaries

Let $G = (V, E)$ be a directed graph with two distinguished vertices s and t called, respectively, the *source* and *sink*, and a capacity function $c(u, v)$ defined on all pairs of vertices with $c(u, v) > 0$ if $(u, v) \in E$ and $c(u, v) = 0$ otherwise.

Definition 15.1 A *flow* in G is a real-valued function f on vertex pairs having the following three conditions:

C1. *Skew symmetry.* $\forall\, u, v \in V$, $f(u, v) = -f(v, u)$. We say there is a flow from u to v if $f(u, v) > 0$.

435

C2. *Capacity constraints.* $\forall \, u, v \in V, \; f(u, v) \leq c(u, v)$. We say edge (u, v) is *saturated* if $f(u, v) = c(u, v)$.

C3. *Flow conservation.* $\forall \, u \in V - \{s, t\}, \; \sum_{v \in V} f(u, v) = 0$. In other words, the *net flow* (total flow out minus total flow in) at any interior vertex is 0.

C4. $\forall \, v \in V, \; f(v, v) = 0$.

Definition 15.2   A *cut* $\{S, T\}$ is a partition of the vertex set V into two subsets S and T such that $s \in S$ and $t \in T$. The *capacity of the cut* $\{S, T\}$, denoted by $c(S, T)$, is

$$c(S, T) = \sum_{u \in S, v \in T} c(u, v).$$

The *flow across the cut* $\{S, T\}$, denoted by $f(S, T)$, is

$$f(S, T) = \sum_{u \in S, v \in T} f(u, v).$$

Thus, the flow across the cut $\{S, T\}$ is the sum of the positive flow on edges from S to T minus the sum of the positive flow on edges from T to S. For any vertex u and any subset $A \subseteq V$, let $f(u, A)$ denote $f(\{u\}, A)$ and $f(A, u)$ denote $f(A, \{u\})$. For a capacity function c, $c(u, A)$ and $c(A, u)$ are defined similarly.

Definition 15.3   The *value* of a flow f, denoted by $|f|$, is defined to be

$$|f| = f(s, V) = \sum_{v \in V} f(s, v).$$

Lemma 15.1   *For any cut* $\{S, T\}$ *and a flow* f, $|f| = f(S, T)$.

Proof.   By induction on the number of vertices in S. If $S = \{s\}$, then it is true by definition. Assume it is true for the cut $\{S, T\}$. We show that it also holds for the cut $\{S \cup \{w\}, T - \{w\}\}$ for $w \in T - \{t\}$. Let $S' = S \cup \{w\}$

and $T' = T - \{w\}$. Then,

$$
\begin{aligned}
f(S', T') &= f(S, T) + f(w, T) - f(S, w) - f(w, w) \\
&= f(S, T) + f(w, T) + f(w, S) - 0 \quad \text{(by conditions C1 and C4)} \\
&= f(S, T) + f(w, V) \\
&= f(S, T) + 0 \quad \text{(by condition C3)} \\
&= f(S, T) \\
&= |f|. \quad \text{(by induction)} \qquad \square
\end{aligned}
$$

Definition 15.4 Given a flow f on G with capacity function c, the *residual capacity function for f* on the set of pairs of vertices is defined as follows. For each pair of vertices $u, v \in V, r(u, v) = c(u, v) - f(u, v)$. The *residual graph for the flow f* is the directed graph $R = (V, E_f)$, with capacities defined by r and

$$
E_f = \{(u, v) | r(u, v) > 0\}.
$$

The residual capacity $r(u, v)$ represents the amount of additional flow that can be pushed along the edge (u, v) without violating the capacity constraints C2. If $f(u, v) < c(u, v)$, then both (u, v) and (v, u) are present in R. If there is no edge between u and v in G, then neither (u, v) nor (v, u) are in E_f. Thus, $|E_f| \leq 2|E|$.

Figure 15.1 shows an example of a flow f on a network G with its residual graph R. In Fig. 15.1(a), the capacity of each edge and its assigned flow are separated by comma. The edge (s, a) in G induces two edges in R, namely (s, a) and (a, s). The residual capacity of (s, a) is equal to $c(s, a) - f(s, a) = 6 - 2 = 4$. This means that we can push 4 additional units of flow along the edge (s, a). The residual capacity of (a, s) is equal to the flow along

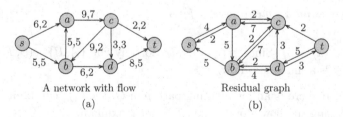

A network with flow   Residual graph

(a)   (b)

Fig. 15.1.   A network with flow and its residual graph.

the edge $(s, a) = 2$. This means that we can push 2 units of *backward* flow along the edge (s, a). The edge (s, b) is not present in the residual graph R, since its residual capacity is zero.

Let f and f' be any two flows in a network G. Define the function $f + f'$ by $(f + f')(u, v) = f(u, v) + f'(u, v)$ for all pairs of vertices u and v. Similarly, define the function $f - f'$ by $(f - f')(u, v) = f(u, v) - f'(u, v)$.

The following two lemmas, which appear to be intuitive, provide the basis for the iterative improvement technique in network flow. Their proofs are left for the exercises.

Lemma 15.2   *Let f be a flow in G and f' the flow in the residual graph R for f. Then, the function $f + f'$ is a flow in G of value $|f| + |f'|$.*

Lemma 15.3   *Let f be any flow in G and f^* a maximum flow in G. If R is the residual graph for f, then the value of a maximum flow in R is $|f^*| - |f|$.*

Definition 15.5   Given a flow f in G, an *augmenting path* p is a directed path from s to t in the residual graph R. The *bottleneck capacity* of p is the minimum residual capacity along p. The number of edges in p will be denoted by $|p|$.

In Fig. 15.1(b), the path s, a, c, b, d, t is an augmenting path with bottleneck capacity 2. If two additional units of flow are pushed along this path, then the flow becomes maximum.

Theorem 15.1   (*max-flow min-cut theorem*). *Let (G, s, t, c) be a network and f a flow in G. The following three statements are equivalent:*

(a) *There is a cut $\{S, T\}$ with $c(S, T) = |f|$.*
(b) *f is a maximum flow in G.*
(c) *There is no augmenting path for f.*

Proof.   (a)→(b). Since $|f| \leq c(A, B)$ for any cut $\{A, B\}$, $c(S, T) = |f|$ implies f is a maximum flow.

(b)→(c). If there is an augmenting path p in G, then $|f|$ can be increased by increasing the flow along p, i.e., f is not maximum.

(c)→(a). Suppose there is no augmenting path for f. Let S be the set of vertices reachable from s by paths in the residual graph R. Let $T = V - S$. Then, R contains no edges from S to T. Thus, in G, all edges from S to T are saturated. It follows that $c(S, T) = |f|$. ☐

The proof of the implication (c)→(a) suggests an algorithm for finding a minimum cut in a given network.

15.3 The Ford–Fulkerson Method

Theorem 15.1 suggests a way to construct a maximum flow by iterative improvement: One keeps finding an augmenting path *arbitrarily* and increases the flow by its bottleneck capacity. This is known as the Ford–Fulkerson method.

Algorithm 15.1 FORD–FULKERSON
Input: A network (G, s, t, c).
Output: A flow in G.

1. Initialize the residual graph: Set $R = G$.
2. **for** each edge $(u, v) \in E$
3. $f(u, v) \leftarrow 0$
4. **end for**
5. **while** there is an augmenting path $p = s, \ldots, t$ in R
6.   Let Δ be the bottleneck capacity of p.
7.   **for** each edge (u, v) in p
8. $f(u, v) \leftarrow f(u, v) + \Delta$
9.   **end for**
10.   Update the residual graph R.
11. **end while**

Step 1 initializes the residual graph to the original network. The **for** loop in Step 2 initializes the flow in G to the zero flow. The **while** loop is executed for each augmenting path found in the residual graph R. Each time an augmenting path is found, its bottleneck capacity Δ is computed and the flow is increased by Δ. This is followed by updating the residual graph R. Updating R may result in the addition of new edges or the deletion of some of the existing ones. It should be emphasized that the selection of the augmenting path in this method is arbitrary.

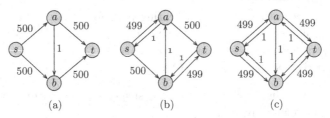

Fig. 15.2. An example of a graph on which the FORD-FULKERSON method performs badly.

The Ford–Fulkerson method may not halt if the capacities are irrational. If the flow does converge, however, it may converge to a value that is not necessarily maximum. If the capacities are integers, this method always computes the maximum flow f^* in at most $|f^*|$ steps, since each augmentation increases the flow by at least 1. As each augmenting path can be found in $O(m)$ time (e.g., using depth-first search), the overall time complexity of this method (when the input capacities are integers) is $O(m|f^*|)$. Notice that this time complexity is dependent on the input values. As an example, consider the network shown in Fig. 15.2(a). If the method alternately selects the augmenting paths s, a, b, t and s, b, a, t, the number of augmenting steps is 1000. The first two residual graphs are shown in Figs. 15.2(b) and 15.2(c).

15.4 Maximum Capacity Augmentation

In this section, we consider improving the Ford–Fulkerson method by selecting among all possible augmenting paths that path with maximum bottleneck capacity. This heuristic is due to Edmonds and Karp. As an example, consider the original graph with zero flow of the network shown in Fig. 15.1(a). According to this heuristic, the augmenting path s, a, c, b, d, t with bottleneck capacity 6 is first selected. This is followed by choosing the augmenting path s, b, c, t with bottleneck capacity 2. If the augmenting path s, b, c, d, t with bottleneck capacity 2 is next selected, then the flow becomes maximum. As to the network shown in Fig. 15.2, a maximum flow can be found using this method after exactly two augmentations.

To analyze the time complexity of this method, which we will refer to as the *maximum capacity augmentation* (MCA) method, we first show that there always exists a sequence of at most m augmentations that lead to a maximum flow. Next, we show that if the input capacities are integers, then its time complexity is polynomial in the input size, which is a significant improvement on the Ford–Fulkerson method.

Lemma 15.4   *Starting from the zero flow, there is a sequence of at most m augmentations that lead to a maximum flow.*

Proof.   Let f^* be a maximum flow. Let G^* be the subgraph of G induced by the edges (u, v) such that $f^*(u, v) > 0$. Initialize i to 1. Find a path p_i from s to t in G^*. Let Δ_i be the bottleneck capacity of p_i. For every edge (u, v) on p_i, reduce $f^*(u, v)$ by Δ_i deleting those edges whose flow becomes zero. Increase i by 1 and repeat the above procedure until t is no longer reachable from s. This algorithm halts after at most m steps, since at least one edge is deleted in each iteration. It produces a sequence of augmenting paths $p_1, p_2, \ldots$ with flows $\Delta_1, \Delta_2, \ldots$. Now, beginning with the zero flow, push Δ_1 units along p_1, Δ_2 units along $p_2, \ldots$ to construct a maximum flow in at most m steps.   □

This lemma is not constructive in the sense that it does *not* provide a way of finding this sequence of augmenting paths; it only proves the existence of such a sequence.

Theorem 15.2   *If the edge capacities are integers, then the MCA constructs a maximum flow in $O(m \log c^*)$ augmenting steps, where c^* is the maximum edge capacity.*

Proof.   Let R be the residual graph corresponding to the initial zero flow. Since the capacities are integers, there is a maximum flow f^* that is an integer. By Lemma 15.4, f^* can be achieved in at most m augmenting paths, and hence there is an augmenting path p in R with bottleneck capacity at least f^*/m. Consider a sequence of $2m$ consecutive augmentations using the MCA heuristic. One of these augmenting paths must have bottleneck capacity of $f^*/2m$ or less. Thus, after at most $2m$ augmentations, the maximum bottleneck capacity is reduced by a factor of at least 2. After at most $2m$ more augmentations, the maximum bottleneck capacity is reduced *further* by a factor of at least 2. In general, after at most $2km$ augmentations, the maximum bottleneck capacity is reduced by a factor of at least 2^k. Since the maximum bottleneck capacity is at least one, k cannot exceed $\log c^*$. This means the number of augmentations is $O(m \log c^*)$.   □

A path of maximum bottleneck capacity can be found in $O(n^2)$ time using a modification of Dijkstra's algorithm for the single-source shortest path problem (see Sec. 7.2). Therefore, the MCA heuristic finds a maximum flow in $O(mn^2 \log c^*)$ time.

The time complexity is now polynomial in the input size. However, it is undesirable that the running time of an algorithm be dependent on its input values. This dependence will be removed using the algorithms presented in the following three sections.

15.5　Shortest Path Augmentation

In this section, we consider another heuristic, also due to Edmonds and Karp, that puts some order on the selection of augmenting paths. It results in a time complexity that is not only polynomial but also independent of the input values.

Definition 15.6　The *level* of a vertex v, denoted by *level(v)*, is the least number of edges in a path from s to v. Given a directed graph $G = (V, E)$, the level graph L is (V, E'), where $E' = \{(u, v) \mid level(v) = level(u) + 1\}$.

Given a directed graph G and a source vertex s, its level graph L can easily be constructed using breadth-first search. As an example of the construction of the level graph, see Figs. 15.3(a) and 15.3(b). In these figures, the graph shown in (b) is the level graph of the network shown in (a). Here, $\{s\}$, $\{a, b\}$, $\{c, d\}$ and $\{t\}$ constitute levels 0, 1, 2 and 3, respectively. Observe that edges (a, b), (b, a) and (d, c) are not present in the level graph, as they connect vertices in the same level. Also the edge (c, b) is not included since it is directed from a vertex of higher level to a vertex of lower level.

This heuristic, which we will refer to as *minimum path length augmentation* (MPLA) method, selects an augmenting path of minimum length and increases the current flow by an amount equal to the bottleneck capacity of that path. The algorithm starts by initializing the flow to the zero flow and setting the residual graph R to the original network. It then proceeds in phases. Each phase consists of the following two steps:

(1) Compute the level graph L from the residual graph R. If t is not in L, then halt; otherwise, continue.

(2) As long as there is a path p from s to t in L, augment the current flow by p, remove saturated edges from L and R and update them accordingly.

Note that augmenting paths in the same level graph are of the same length. Moreover, as will be shown later, the length of an augmenting path in any phase after the first is strictly longer than the length of an augmenting path in the preceding phase. The algorithm terminates as soon as t does not appear in the newly constructed level graph. An outline of the algorithm is shown as Algorithm MPLA (see Fig. 15.3 for an example).

Algorithm 15.2 MPLA
Input: A network (G, s, t, c).
Output: The maximum flow in G.

1. **for** each edge $(u, v) \in E$
2. $f(u, v) \leftarrow 0$
3. **end for**
4. Initialize the residual graph: Set $R = G$.
5. Find the level graph L of R.
6. **while** t is a vertex in L
7.   **while** t is reachable from s in L
8.   Let p be a path from s to t in L.
9.   Let Δ be the bottleneck capacity on p.
10.   Augment the current flow f by Δ.
11.   Update L and R along the path p.
12.   **end while**
13.   Use the residual graph R to compute a new level graph L.
14. **end while**

To analyze the running time of the algorithm, we need the following lemma.

Lemma 15.5 *The number of phases in the* MPLA *algorithm is at most n.*

Proof. We show that the number of level graphs computed using the algorithm is at most n. First, we show that the sequence of lengths of augmenting paths using the MPLA algorithm is strictly increasing. Let p be any augmenting path in the current level graph. After augmenting using p, at least one edge will be saturated and will disappear in the residual graph. At most $|p|$ new edges will appear in the residual graph, but they are back edges and hence will not contribute to a shortest path from s to t.

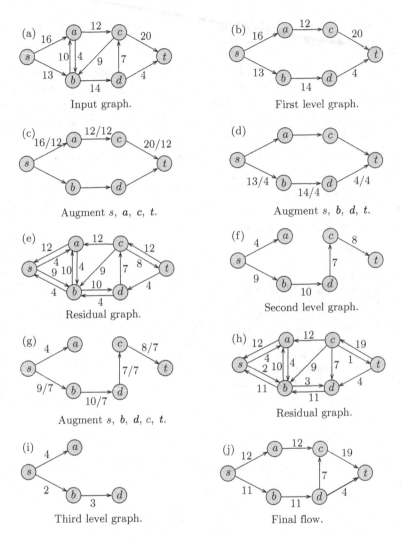

Fig. 15.3.　Example of the MPLA algorithm.

There can be at most m paths of length $|p|$ since each time an edge in the level graph disappears. When t is no longer reachable from s in the level graph, any augmenting path must use a back edge or a cross edge, and hence must be of length strictly greater than $|p|$. Since the length of any augmenting path is between 1 and $n - 1$, the number of level graphs used for augmentations is at most $n - 1$. Since one more level graph is computed in which t does not appear, the total number of level graphs computed is at most n. □

The running time of the MPLA algorithm is computed as follows. Since there can be at most m augmentations along paths of the same length, and since by Lemma 15.5 the number of level graphs computed that are used for augmenting is at most $n - 1$, the number of augmenting steps is at most $(n - 1)m$. Finding a shortest augmenting path in the level graph takes $O(m)$ time using breadth-first search. Thus, the total time needed to compute all augmenting paths is $O(nm^2)$. Computing each level graph takes $O(m)$ using breadth-first search, and hence the total time required to compute all level graphs is $O(nm)$. It follows that the overall running time of Algorithm MPLA is $O(nm^2)$.

As to the correctness of the algorithm, note that after computing at most $n - 1$ level graphs, there are no more augmenting paths in the original network. By Theorem 15.1, this implies that the flow is maximum. Hence, we have the following theorem:

Theorem 15.3 *The* MPLA *algorithm finds a maximum flow in a network with n vertices and m edges in $O(nm^2)$ time.*

15.6 Dinic's Algorithm

In Sec. 15.5, it was shown that finding the maximum flow can be achieved in $O(nm^2)$ time. In this section, we show that the time complexity can be reduced to $O(mn^2)$ using a method due to Dinic. In the MPLA algorithm, after a level graph is computed, augmenting paths are found individually. In contrast, the algorithm in this section finds all these augmenting paths more efficiently, and this is where the improvement in the running time comes from.

Definition 15.7 Let (G, s, t, c) be a network and H a subgraph of G containing both s and t. A flow f in H is a *blocking flow* (with respect to H) if every path in H from s to t contains at least one saturated edge.

In Fig. 15.4(c), the flow is a blocking flow with respect to the level graph shown in Fig. 15.4(b). Dinic's method is shown in Algorithm DINIC. As in

---

Algorithm 15.3 DINIC
Input: A network (G, s, t, c).

Output: The maximum flow in G.

```
 1. for each edge (u, v) ∈ E
 2.     f(u, v) ← 0
 3. end for
 4. Initialize the residual graph: Set R = G.
 5. Find the level graph L of R.
 6. while t is a vertex in L
 7.     u ← s
 8.     p ← u
 9.     while outdegree(s) > 0      {begin phase}
10.         while u ≠ t and outdegree(s) > 0
11.             if outdegree(u) > 0 then      {advance}
12.                 Let (u, v) be an edge in L.
13.                 p ← p, v
14.                 u ← v
15.             else      {retreat}
16.                 Delete u and all adjacent edges from L.
17.                 Remove u from the end of p.
18.                 Set u to the last vertex in p (u may be s).
19.             end if
20.         end while
21.         if u = t then      {augment}
22.             Let Δ be the bottleneck capacity along p. Augment
                the current flow along p by Δ. Adjust capacities
                along p in both residual graph and level graph, delet-
                ing saturated edges. Set u to the last vertex on p
                reachable from s. Note that u may be s.
23.         end if
24.     end while
25.     Compute a new level graph L from the current residual graph R.
26. end while
```

---

the MPLA algorithm, Dinic's algorithm is divided into at most n phases. Each phase consists of finding a level graph, a blocking flow with respect to that level graph and increasing the current flow by that blocking flow. By Lemma 15.5, the number of phases is at most n. Each iteration of the outer **while** loop corresponds to one phase. The intermediate **while** loop is essentially a depth-first search in which augmenting paths are found and used to increase the flow. Here, $p = s, \ldots, u$ is the current path found so far. There are two basic operations in the inner **while** loop. If u, which is the end of the current path, is not t and there is at least one edge out of u, say (u, v), then an *advance* operation takes place. This operation consists of appending v to p and making it the current endpoint of p. If, on the other hand, u is not t and there is no edge out of it, a *retreat* operation takes place. This operation simply amounts to removing u from the end of p and removing it and all adjacent edges in the current level graph L, as there cannot be any augmenting path that passes by u. The inner **while** loop terminates if either t is reached or the search backs up to s and all edges out of s have been explored. If t is reached, then this is an indication that an augmenting path has been discovered and augmenting by that path is carried out in the steps following the inner **while** loop. If, on the other hand, s has been reached and all edges out of it have been deleted, then no augmentation takes place and processing the current level graph is complete. An example of the execution of the algorithm is given in Fig. 15.4.

We compute the running time in each phase as follows. The number of augmentations is at most m since at least one edge of the level graph is deleted in each augmentation. Each augment costs $O(n)$ time to update the flow values and to delete edges in both the level graph, the residual graph and the path p used in the algorithm and possibly to add edges to the residual graph. Hence, the total cost of all augments in each phase is $O(mn)$. The number of retreats (the **else** part of the inner **while** loop) is at most $n - 2$ since each retreat results in the deletion of one vertex other than s or t. The total number of edges deleted from the level graph in the retreats is at most m. This means that the total cost of all retreats is $O(m + n)$ in each phase. The number of advances (the **if** part of the inner **while** loop) before each augment or retreat cannot exceed $n - 1$; for otherwise, one vertex will be visited more than once before an augment or retreat. Consequently, the total number of advances is $O(mn)$ in each phase. It follows that the overall cost of each phase is $O(mn)$, and since there are at most n phases, the overall running time of the algorithm is $O(mn^2)$.

As to the correctness of the algorithm, note that after computing at most $n - 1$ level graphs, there are no more augmenting paths in the residual graph. By Theorem 15.1, this implies that the flow is maximum. Hence, we have the following theorem:

Theorem 15.4 *Dinic's algorithm finds a maximum flow in a network with n vertices and m edges in $O(mn^2)$ time.*

Fig. 15.4.   Example of Dinic's algorithm.

15.7   The MPM Algorithm

In this section, we outline an $O(n^3)$ time algorithm to find the maximum flow in a given network. The algorithm is due to Malhotra, Pramodh-Kumar and Maheshwari. It is an improvement on Dinic's algorithm. The $O(n^3)$ bound is due to a faster $O(n^2)$ time method for computing a blocking flow.

In this section, we will consider only the method of finding such a blocking flow. The rest of the algorithm is similar to Dinic's algorithm. For this, we need the following definition.

Definition 15.8 For a vertex v in a network (G, s, t, c) different from s and t, we define the throughput of v as the minimum of the total capacity of incoming edges and the total capacity of outgoing edges. That is, for $v \in V - \{s, t\}$,

$$throughput(v) = \min \left\{ \sum_{u \in V} c(u, v), \sum_{u \in V} c(v, u) \right\}.$$

The throughputs of s and t are defined by

$$throughput(s) = \sum_{v \in V - \{s\}} c(s, v) \quad \text{and} \quad throughput(t) = \sum_{v \in V - \{t\}} c(v, t).$$

As in Dinic's algorithm, updating the residual graph, computing the level graph and finding a blocking flow comprise one phase of the algorithm. Finding a blocking flow from the level graph L can be described as follows. First, we find a vertex v such that $g = throughput(v)$ is minimum among all other vertices in L. Next, we "push" g units of flow from v all the way to t and "pull" g units of flow all the way from s. When pushing a flow out of a vertex v, we saturate some of its outgoing edges to their capacity and leave at most one edge partially saturated. We then delete all outgoing edges that are saturated. Similarly, when pulling a flow into a vertex v, we saturate some of its incoming edges to their capacity and leave at most one edge partially saturated. We then delete all incoming edges that are saturated. Either all incoming edges or all outgoing edges will be saturated. Consequently, vertex v and all its adjacent edges are removed from the level graph and the residual graph R is updated accordingly. The flow out of v is pushed through its outgoing edges to (some of) its adjacent vertices and so on until t is reached. Note that this is always possible, as v has minimum throughput among all other vertices in the current level graph. Similarly, the flow into v is propagated backward until s is reached. Next, another vertex of minimum throughput is found and the above procedure is repeated. Since there are n vertices, the above procedure is repeated at most $n - 1$ times. The method is outlined in Algorithm MPM.

Algorithm 15.4 MPM
Input: A network (G, s, t, c).
Output: The maximum flow in G.

  1. **for** each edge $(u, v) \in E$
  2. $f(u, v) \leftarrow 0$
  3. **end for**
  4. Initialize the residual graph: Set $R = G$.
  5. Find the level graph L of R.
  6. **while** t is a vertex in L
  7.   **while** t is reachable from s in L
  8.   Find a vertex v of minimum throughput $= g$.
  9.   Push g units of flow from v to t.
10.   Pull g units of flow from s to v.
11.   Update f, L and R.
12.   **end while**
13.   Use the residual graph R to compute a new level graph L.
14. **end while**

The time required by each phase of the algorithm is computed as follows. The time required to find the level graph L is $O(m)$ using breadth-first search. Finding a vertex of minimum throughput takes $O(n)$ time. Since this is done at most $n - 1$ times, the total time required by this step is $O(n^2)$. Deleting all saturated edges takes $O(m)$ time. Since at most one edge is partially saturated for each vertex, the time required to partially saturate edges in each iteration of the inner **while** loop takes $O(n)$ time. Since there are at most $n - 1$ iterations of the inner **while** loop, the total time required to partially saturate edges is $O(n^2)$. It follows that the total time required to push flow from v to t and to pull flow from s to v is $O(n^2)$. The time required to update the flow function f and the residual graph R is no more than the time required to push and pull flows, i.e., $O(n^2)$. As a result, the overall time required by each phase is $O(n^2 + m) = O(n^2)$.

As there are at most n phases (in the final phase, t is not a vertex of L), the overall time required by the algorithm is $O(n^3)$. Finally, note that after computing at most $n - 1$ level graphs, there are no more augmenting paths in the residual graph. By Theorem 15.1, this implies that the flow is maximum. Hence, we have the following theorem:

Theorem 15.5 *The* MPM *algorithm finds a maximum flow in a network with n vertices and m edges in $O(n^3)$ time.*

Fig. 15.5.   A network with capacities.

15.8   Practice Problems

15.1. Use the Ford–Fulkerson method to find a maximum flow in the network shown in Fig. 15.5. Show your work.

15.2. Find a minimum cut in the network shown in Fig. 15.5. Show your work.

15.3. Use the maximum capacity augmentation (MCA) method to find a maximum flow in the network shown in Fig. 15.5. Show your work.

15.4. Use the minimum path length augmentation (MPLA) method to find a maximum flow in the network shown in Fig. 15.5. Show your work.

15.5. Use Dinic's algorithm to find a maximum flow in the network shown in Fig. 15.5. Show your work.

15.6. Prove or disprove the following statement. If all capacities in a network are distinct, then there exists a unique flow function that gives the maximum flow.

15.7. Prove or disprove the following statement. If all capacities in a network are distinct, then there exists a unique min-cut that separates the source from the sink.

15.8. Explain how to solve the max-flow problem with multiple sources and multiple edges.

15.9   Exercises

15.1. Give an $O(m)$ time algorithm to construct the residual graph of a given network with positive edge capacities.

15.2. Show how to find efficiently an augmenting path in a given residual graph.

15.3. Adapt the Ford–Fulkerson algorithm to the case where the vertices have capacities as well.

15.4. Give an efficient algorithm to find a path of maximum bottleneck capacity in a given directed acyclic graph.

15.5. Give an efficient algorithm to find the level graph of a given directed acyclic graph.

15.6. Show by example that a blocking flow in the level graph of a residual graph need not be a blocking flow in the residual graph.

15.7. Let $G = (V, E)$ be a directed acyclic graph, where $|V| = n$. Give an algorithm to find a minimum number of directed vertex-disjoint paths which cover all the vertices, i.e., every vertex is in exactly one path. There are no restrictions on the lengths of the paths, where they start and end. To do this, construct a flow network $G' = (V', E')$, where

$$V' = \{s, t\} \cup \{x_1, x_2, \ldots, x_n\} \cup \{y_1, y_2, \ldots, y_n\},$$

$$E' = \{(s, x_i) \mid 1 \le i \le n\} \cup \{(y_i, t) \mid 1 \le i \le n\}$$

$$\cup \{(x_i, y_j) \mid (v_i, v_j) \in E\}.$$

Let the capacity of all edges be 1. Finally, show that the number of paths which cover V is $|V| - |f|$, where f is the maximum flow in G'.

15.8. Let $G = (V, E)$ be a directed graph with two distinguished vertices $s, t \in V$. Give an efficient algorithm to find the maximum number of edge-disjoint paths from s to t.

15.9. Let $G = (V, E)$ be an undirected weighted graph with two distinguished vertices $s, t \in V$. Give an efficient algorithm to find a minimum weight cut that separates s from t.

15.10. Let $G = (X \cup Y, E)$ be a bipartite graph. An *edge cover* C for G is a set of edges in E such that each vertex of G is incident to at least one edge in C. Give an algorithm to find an edge cover for G of minimum size.

15.11. Let $G = (X \cup Y, E)$ be a bipartite graph. Let C be a minimum edge cover (see Exercise 15.10) and I a maximum independent set. Show that $|C| = |I|$.

15.12. The vertex connectivity of a graph $G = (V, E)$ is defined as the minimum number of vertices whose removal disconnects G. Prove that if G has vertex connectivity k, then $|E| \geq k |V|/2$.

15.10   Bibliographic Notes

Some references for network flow include Even (1979), Lawler (1976), Papadimitriou and Steiglitz (1982) and Tarjan (1983). The Ford–Fulkerson method is due to Ford and Fulkerson (1956). The two heuristics of augmenting by paths with maximum bottleneck capacity and augmenting by paths of shortest lengths are due to Edmonds and Karp (1972). Dinic's algorithm is due to Dinic (1970). The $O(n^3)$ MPM algorithm is due to Malhotra *et al.* (1978). The $O(n^3)$ bound remains the best known for general graphs. In the case of sparse graphs, faster algorithms can be found in Ahuja *et al.* (1989), Galil (1980), Galil and Tardos (1988), Goldberg and Tarjan (1988), Sleator (1980) and Tardos (1985).

Chapter 16

Matching

16.1 Introduction

In this chapter, we study in detail another example of a problem whose existing algorithms use the iterative improvement design technique: the problem of finding a maximum matching in an undirected graph. In its most general setting, given an undirected graph $G = (V, E)$, the maximum matching problem asks for a subset $M \subseteq E$ with the maximum number of nonoverlapping edges, that is, no two edges in M have a vertex in common. This problem arises in many applications, particularly in the areas of communication and scheduling. While the problem is interesting in its own right, it is indispensable as a building block in the design of more complex algorithms. That is, the problem of finding a maximum matching is often used as a subroutine in the implementation of many practical algorithms.

16.2 Preliminaries

Let $G = (V, E)$ be a connected undirected graph. Throughout this chapter, we will let n and m denote, respectively, the number of vertices and edges in G, that is, $n = |V|$ and $m = |E|$.

A *matching* in G is a subset $M \subseteq E$ such that no two edges in M have a vertex in common. We will assume throughout this chapter that the graph is connected, and hence the modifier "connected" will be dropped. An edge $e \in E$ is *matched* if it is in M, and *unmatched* or *free* otherwise. A vertex $v \in V$ is *matched* if it is incident to a matched edge, and *unmatched* or

455

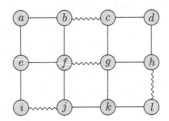

Fig. 16.1.   A matching in an undirected graph.

free otherwise. The *size* of a matching M, i.e., the number of matching edges in it, will be denoted by $|M|$. A *maximum matching* in a graph is a matching of maximum cardinality. A *perfect* matching is one in which every vertex in V is matched. Given a matching M in an undirected graph $G = (V, E)$, an *alternating path p with respect to M* is a simple path that consists of alternating matched and unmatched edges. The length of p is denoted by $|p|$. If the two endpoints of an alternating path coincide, then it is called an *alternating cycle*. An alternating path with respect to M is called an *augmenting path with respect to M* if all the matched edges in p are in M and its endpoints are free. Clearly, the number of edges in an augmenting path is odd, and as a result, it cannot be an alternating cycle. These definitions are illustrated in Fig. 16.1 in which matched edges are shown as jagged edges.

In Fig. 16.1, $M = \{(b, c), (f, g), (h, l), (i, j)\}$ is a matching. The edge (a, b) is unmatched or free and the edge (b, c) is matched. Vertex a is free and vertex b is matched. The path a, b, c, d is an alternating path. It is also an augmenting path (with respect to M). Another augmenting path with respect to M is a, b, c, g, f, e. Clearly, the matching M is neither maximum nor perfect.

Let M_1 and M_2 be two matchings in a graph G. Then,

$$M_1 \oplus M_2 = (M_1 \cup M_2) - (M_1 \cap M_2)$$
$$= (M_1 - M_2) \cup (M_2 - M_1).$$

That is, $M_1 \oplus M_2$ is the set of edges that are in M_1 or in M_2 but not in both. Consider the matching shown in Fig. 16.1 and the augmenting path

$$p = a, b, c, g, f, e.$$

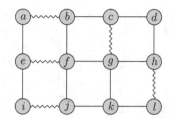

Fig. 16.2.   An augmented matching.

Reversing the roles of edges in p (matched to unmatched and vice-versa) results in the matching shown in Fig. 16.2. Moreover, the size of the new matching is exactly the size of the old matching plus one. This illustrates the following lemma whose proof is easy:

Lemma 16.1   *Let M be a matching and p an augmenting path with respect to M. Then, $M \oplus p$ is a matching of size $|M \oplus p| = |M| + 1$.*

The following corollary characterizes a maximum matching.

Corollary 16.1   *A matching M in an undirected graph G is maximum if and only if G contains no augmenting paths with respect to M.*

Theorem 16.1   *Let M_1 and M_2 be two matchings in an undirected graph $G = (V, E)$ such that $|M_1| = r$, $|M_2| = s$ and $s > r$. Then, $M_1 \oplus M_2$ contains $k = s - r$ vertex-disjoint augmenting paths with respect to M_1.*

Proof.   Consider the graph $G' = (V, M_1 \oplus M_2)$. Each vertex in V is incident to at most one edge in $M_2 - M_1$ and at most one edge in $M_1 - M_2$. Thus, each connected component in G' is either

- an isolated vertex,
- a cycle of even length,
- a path of even length, or
- a path of odd length.

Moreover, the edges of all paths and cycles in G' are alternately in $M_2 - M_1$ and $M_1 - M_2$, which means that all cycles and even-length paths have the same number of edges from M_1 as the number of edges from M_2.

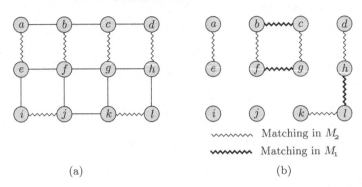

wwwwww Matching in M_2

wwwwww Matching in M_1

(a)   (b)

Fig. 16.3.   Illustration of Theorem 16.1. (a) M_2. (b) $M_1 \oplus M_2$.

Since there are k more M_2 edges than M_1 edges in G', it must be the case that G' contains k odd-length paths with one more edge from M_2. But these odd-length paths are augmenting paths with respect to M_1 since their endpoints are free with respect to M_1. Consequently, $M_1 \oplus M_2$ contains $k = s - r$ augmenting paths with respect to M_1.   □

Example 16.1   Consider the matching M_1 shown in Fig. 16.1 and the matching M_2 shown in Fig. 16.3(a) for the same graph. As shown in Fig. 16.3(b), $G' = (V, M_1 \oplus M_2)$ consists of an even length cycle, two isolated vertices and two augmenting paths with respect to M_1. Moreover, $|M_2| - |M_1| = 2$.

16.3   The Network Flow Method for Bipartite Graphs

Recall that an undirected graph is called bipartite if it contains no cycles of odd length. For example the graph in Fig. 16.1 is bipartite. Let $G = (X \cup Y, E)$ be a bipartite graph. We can utilize one of the maximum network flow algorithms to find a maximum matching in G as shown in Algorithm BIMATCH1.

The correctness of the algorithm is easy to verify. It is also easy to see that the construction of the flow network takes no more than $O(m)$ time, where $m = |E|$. Its running time is dependent on the maximum flow algorithm used. If, for example, Algorithm MPM is used, then the running time is $O(n^3)$, where $n = |X| + |Y|$.

Algorithm 16.1 BIMATCH1

Input: A bipartite graph $G = (X \cup Y, E)$.

Output: A maximum matching M in G.

1. Direct all edges in G from X to Y.
2. Add a source vertex s and a directed edge (s, x) from s to x for each vertex $x \in X$.
3. Add a sink vertex t and a directed edge (y, t) from y to t for each vertex $y \in Y$.
4. Assign a capacity $c(u, v) = 1$ to each (directed) edge (u, v).
5. Use one of the maximum network flow algorithms to find a maximum flow for the constructed network. M consists of those edges connecting X to Y whose corresponding directed edge carries a flow of one unit.

16.4 The Hungarian Tree Method for Bipartite Graphs

Let $G = (V, E)$ be an undirected graph. Lemma 16.1 and Corollary 16.1 suggest a procedure for finding a maximum matching in G. Starting from an arbitrary (e.g., empty) matching, we find an augmenting path p in G, invert the roles of the edges in p (matched to unmatched and vice-versa), and repeat the process until there are no more augmenting paths. At that point, the matching, by Corollary 16.1, is maximum. Finding an augmenting path in the case of bipartite graphs is much easier than in the case of general graphs.

Let $G = (X \cup Y, E)$ be a bipartite graph with $|X| + |Y| = n$ and $|E| = m$. Let M be a matching in G. We call a vertex in X an x-vertex. Similarly a y-vertex denotes a vertex in Y. First, we pick a free x-vertex, say r, and label it *outer*. From r, we grow an *alternating path tree*, i.e., a tree in which each path from the root r to a leaf is an alternating path. This tree, call it T, is constructed as follows. Starting from r, add each unmatched edge (r, y) connecting r to the y-vertex y and label y *inner*. For each y-vertex y adjacent to r, add *the* matched edge (y, z) to T if such a matched edge exists and label z *outer*. Repeat the above procedure and extend the tree until either a free y-vertex is encountered or the tree is blocked, i.e., cannot be extended any more (note that no vertex is added to the tree more than once). If a free y-vertex is found, say v, then the alternating path from the root r to v is an augmenting path. On the other hand, if the tree is blocked, then in this case the tree is called a *Hungarian tree*. Next, we start from another free x-vertex, if any, and repeat the above procedure.

If T is a Hungarian tree, then it cannot be extended; each alternating path traced from the root is stopped at some *outer* vertex. The only free vertex in T is its root. Notice that if (x, y) is an edge such that x is in T and y is not in T, then x must be labeled *inner*. Otherwise, x must be connected to a free vertex or T is extendable through x. It follows that no vertex in a Hungarian tree can occur in an augmenting path. For suppose that p is an alternating path that shares at least one vertex with T. If p "enters" T, then it must be through a vertex labeled *inner*. If it "leaves" T, then it must also be through a vertex labeled *inner*. But then, p is not an alternating path; a contradiction. This implies the following important observation:

Observation 16.1   If, in the process of searching for an augmenting path, a Hungarian tree is found, then it can be removed permanently without affecting the search.

Example 16.2   Consider the bipartite graph shown in Fig. 16.4. Starting from vertex c, the alternating path tree shown in the figure is constructed. Note that the vertices on any path from c to a leaf are alternately labeled o (outer) and i (inner). In this alternating path tree, the augmenting path $p = c, f, g, j$ is discovered. Augmenting the current matching by p results in the matching shown in Fig. 16.5. Now, if we try to grow another alternating path tree from the free x-vertex i, the search becomes blocked and results in the Hungarian tree shown in the figure. Since there are no more free x-vertices, we conclude that the matching shown in Fig. 16.5 is maximum.

The algorithm for finding a maximum matching in a bipartite graph is outlined in Algorithm BIMATCH2.

The running time of the algorithm is computed as follows. The construction of each alternating tree costs $O(m)$ time using breadth-first search. Since at most $|X| = O(n)$ trees are constructed, the overall running time is $O(nm)$. The correctness of the algorithm follows from Corollary 16.1 and Observation 16.1. Thus, we have the following theorem:

Theorem 16.2   *Algorithm* BIMATCH2 *finds a maximum matching in a bipartite graph with n vertices and m edges in $O(nm) = O(n^3)$ time.*

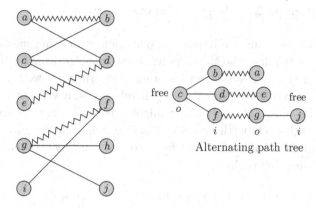

Fig. 16.4. A matching with an alternating path tree rooted at c.

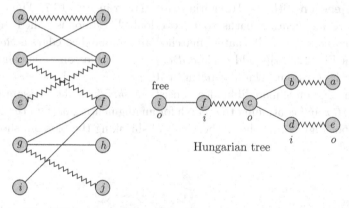

Fig. 16.5. A matching with a Hungarian tree rooted at i.

Algorithm 16.2 BIMATCH2
Input: A bipartite graph $G = (X \cup Y, E)$.
Output: A maximum matching M in G.

1. Initialize M to any arbitrary (possibly empty) matching.
2. **while** there exists a free x-vertex and a free y-vertex
3.   Let r be a free x-vertex. Using breadth-first search, grow an alternating path tree T rooted at r.
4.   **if** T is a Hungarian tree **then** let $G \leftarrow G - T$ {remove T}
5.   **else** find an augmenting path p in T and let $M = M \oplus p$.
6. **end while**

16.5　Maximum Matching in General Graphs

In this section, we consider finding a maximum matching in general graphs. Edmonds was the first who gave a polynomial time algorithm for this problem. Here, we study a variant of his original algorithm. If we try to apply Algorithm BIMATCH2 in Sec. 16.4 on general graphs, it will not work. The culprit is the odd-length cycles that might exist in a general graph (there are no odd cycles in bipartite graphs). Consider Fig. 16.6. If we start searching for an augmenting path at the free vertex a, we may not detect any of the two augmenting paths

$$a, b, c, d, e, f, g, h \quad \text{or} \quad a, b, c, g, f, e, d, i.$$

If we try to grow an alternating path tree starting at the free vertex a, we may end up with the Hungarian tree shown in Fig. 16.7. This causes the above augmenting paths to be overlooked. Edmonds called an odd cycle that consists of alternately matched and unmatched edges a *blossom*. Thus, in Fig. 16.6, the odd cycle c, d, e, f, g, c is a blossom. c is called the *base* of the blossom. The alternating path a, b, c is called the *stem* of the blossom. Edmonds incredible idea consists in *shrinking* the blossom into a *supervertex* and continuing the search for an augmenting path in the resulting graph. Figure 16.8 shows the result of shrinking the blossom shown in Fig. 16.6.

Fig. 16.6.　A blossom.

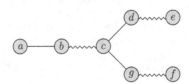

Fig. 16.7.　A Hungarian tree.

Fig. 16.8. A shrunken blossom.

In the resulting graph, there are two augmenting paths a, b, B, h and a, b, B, i. In Fig. 16.6, vertex g divides the odd cycle into two simple paths: an odd-length path c, g, and an even-length path c, d, e, f, g. To find an augmenting path in the original graph, we replace B in the augmenting path a, b, B, h by the even-length simple path c, d, e, f, g to obtain the augmenting path a, b, c, d, e, f, g, h. We may equally replace B in the augmenting path a, b, B, h by the even-length simple path c, g, f, e, d to obtain the augmenting path a, b, c, g, f, e, d, i. This procedure is in fact general and always detects those augmenting paths that would otherwise be overlooked.

Let $G = (V, E)$ be an undirected graph and B a blossom in G (we use B to denote both the odd cycle and the supervertex). Let G' denote G in which B is shrunk into a supervertex B. By shrinking a blossom, we mean the deletion of its vertices and connecting all their incident edges to B, as shown in Fig. 16.8. The following theorem is fundamental to the correctness of the matching algorithm to be presented.

Theorem 16.3 *Let $G = (V, E)$ be an undirected graph, and suppose that G' is formed from G by shrinking a blossom B. Then, G' contains an augmenting path if and only if G does.*

Proof. We prove the *only if* part. The proof of the *if* part is rather complicated and therefore omitted (see the bibliographic notes). Suppose that G' contains an augmenting path p'. If p' avoids B, then p' is an augmenting path in G. So, suppose that p' passes by B. We expand p' into an augmenting path p in G as follows. Let (u, B) be the matched edge incident to B, and (B, x) the unmatched edge incident to B that is on the path p' (see Fig. 16.9(a)). The matched edge corresponds in G to the edge (u, v) incident to the base of the blossom. Similarly, the unmatched edge corresponds to an unmatched edge (w, x) incident to the blossom. We modify p' to obtain p as follows:

(1) Replace (u, B) with (u, v).
(2) Replace (B, x) with (w, x).

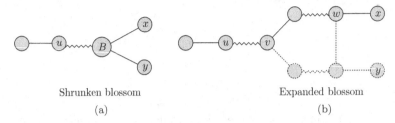

Shrunken blossom   Expanded blossom

(a)   (b)

Fig. 16.9.   Illustration of the proof of Theorem 16.3.

(3) Insert between v and w the even-length portion of the blossom between these two vertices (see Fig. 16.9(b)).   □

The above proof is constructive in the sense that it describes how an augmenting path in G' can be transformed into an augmenting path in G. Before presenting the algorithm, we illustrate in the following example the process of finding an augmenting path by shrinking and expanding blossoms.

Example 16.3   Consider Fig. 16.10 in which the augmenting path

$$a, b, c, d, k, l, v, u, e, f, g, h$$

is not so obvious.

First, we start at the free vertex a and begin to trace an augmenting path. As in the algorithm for bipartite graphs, the matched vertices are alternately labeled *outer* and *inner* starting from a free vertex. We label a *outer* and try to grow an alternating path tree rooted at a. We add the two edges (a, b) and (b, c) to the tree and label b *inner* and c *outer*. Next, we add the two edges (c, d) and (d, k) to the tree and label d *inner* and k *outer*. Again, we add the two edges (k, j) and (j, i) to the tree and label j *inner* and i *outer*. At this point, if we try to explore the edge (i, c), we find that its endpoints have been labeled *outer*. This is an indication of the existence of an odd cycle, i.e., a blossom. Thus, we have discovered the blossom c, d, k, j, i, c and therefore proceed by shrinking it to a single vertex W and label it *outer*, as shown in Fig. 16.11(a). Now, we continue the search from an outer vertex. As W is labeled *outer*, we continue the search from it and add the two edges (W, e) and (e, u) labeling e *inner* and u *outer*. Again, we find another odd cycle, namely u, v, l, u. We reduce this blossom into an *outer* vertex and call it X. This is shown in Fig. 16.11(b). This, in

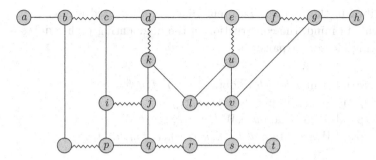

Fig. 16.10.   A matching that is not maximum.

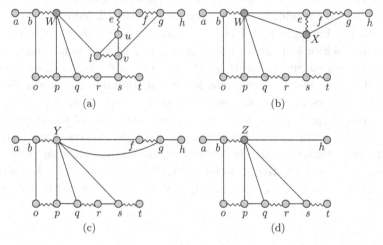

(a)   (b)

(c)   (d)

Fig. 16.11.   Finding an augmenting path.

turn, results in the odd cycle W, e, X, W, which we reduce into one vertex
Y and label it *outer*. This is shown in Fig. 16.11(c). It should be noted at
this point that we have *nested* blossoms, i.e., a blossom, in this case Y, that
contains other blossoms, namely W and X. The process of nesting blossoms
continues when the odd cycle Y, f, g, Y is detected. We call the blossom Z
and label it *outer* (see Fig. 16.11(d)). Finally, from the outer vertex Z, we
discover a free vertex h, which signals the existence of an augmenting path.

Now, we trace the augmenting path a, b, Z, h backward starting at h in
order to construct the augmenting path in the original graph. The rule of
expanding blossoms is that we *interpolate* the even-length path starting at
the vertex at which we enter the blossom to the base of the blossom as

described in the proof of Theorem 16.3 and illustrated in Fig. 16.9. With this rule in mind, the construction of the augmenting path reduces to the following blossom expansions

(1) Expand Z in a, b, Z, h to obtain a, b, Y, f, g, h.
(2) Expand Y to obtain a, b, W, X, e, f, g, h.
(3) Expand X to obtain $a, b, W, l, v, u, e, f, g, h$
(4) Expand W to obtain $a, b, c, d, k, l, v, u, e, f, g, h$.

The algorithm for matching in general graphs is described more formally in Algorithm GMATCH. This algorithm is similar to Algorithm BIMATCH2 of Sec. 16.4 with the addition of the necessary steps for handling blossoms as described in Example 16.3. First, the matching is initialized to be empty. The outer **while** loop iterates as long as the matching is not maximum. In each iteration, an augmenting path is found and the matching is augmented by that path. The intermediate **while** loop iterates for at most all the free vertices until an augmenting path is found. In each iteration of this **while** loop, a free vertex is chosen to be the root of the alternating path tree. From this root, exploration of the graph commences in the inner **while** loop, whose function is to grow an alternating path tree two edges at a time. In each iteration, it picks arbitrarily an *outer* vertex x and a corresponding edge (x, y). If such an edge exists, then we have the following cases:

(1) If y is *inner*, then that edge is useless, as it forms an even-length cycle.
(2) If y is *outer*, then this is an indication that a blossom has been found. This blossom is pushed on top of the stack and shrunk into a supervertex so that it can be expanded later on when an augmenting path is discovered. If the blossom contains the root, then it is labeled *free*.
(3) If y is labeled *free*, then an augmenting path has been found. In this case, the inner **while** loop is terminated and augmenting by the augmenting path found takes place. Note that the augmenting path may contain blossoms that are stored in the stack. These blossoms are popped off the stack, expanded and the appropriate even-length path is inserted into the augmenting path.
(4) Otherwise, the alternating path tree T is extended by two more edges, and the search for an augmenting path continues.

Algorithm 16.3 GMATCH
Input: An undirected graph $G = (V, E)$.

Output: A maximum matching M in G.

1. $M \leftarrow \{\}$ {*Initialize M to the empty matching*}
2. *maximum* $\leftarrow$ **false**
3. **while not** *maximum*
4.   determine the set of *free* vertices F with respect to M
5.   *augment* $\leftarrow$ **false**
6.   **while** $F \neq \{\}$ **and not** *augment*
7.   Empty stack, unmark edges and remove labels from vertices.
8.   Let x be a vertex in F; $F \leftarrow F - \{x\}$; $T \leftarrow x$
9.   Label x *outer*   {*initialize the alternating path tree*}
10.   *hungarian* $\leftarrow$ **false**
11.   **while not** *augment*
12.   Choose an *outer* vertex x and an unmarked edge (x, y).
13.   **if** (x, y) exists **then** Mark (x, y)
14.   **else**
15.   *hungarian* $\leftarrow$ **true**
16.   **exit** this **while** loop
17.   **end if**
18.   **if** y is *inner* **then** do nothing {*even-length cycle found*}
19.   **else if** y is *outer* **then**   {*a blossom found*}
20.   Place the blossom on top of the stack, shrink it.
21.   Replace the blossom with a vertex w and label w *outer*.
22.   If the blossom contains the root, then label w *free*.
23.   **else if** y is *free* **then**
24.   *augment* $\leftarrow$ **true**
25. $F \leftarrow F - \{y\}$
26.   **else**
27.   Let (y, z) be in M. Add (x, y) and (y, z) to T.
28.   Label y *inner* and z *outer*.
29.   **end if**
30.   **end while**
31.   **if** *hungarian* **then** remove T from G.
32.   **else if** *augment* **then**
33.   Construct p by popping blossoms from the stack,
34.   expanding them and adding the even-length portion.
35.   Augment G by p.
36.   **end if**
37.   **end while**
38.   **if not** *augment* **then** *maximum* $\leftarrow$ **true**
39. **end while**

If, however, the edge (x, y) does not exist, then T is Hungarian. By Observation 16.1, T can be removed from G permanently in the current iteration and all subsequent iterations.

To analyze the running time of the algorithm, we note that there can be no more than $\lfloor n/2 \rfloor$ augmentations. With careful handling of blossoms (shrinking and expanding blossoms), which we will not describe here, searching for an augmenting path and augmenting the current matching by that path costs $O(m)$ time. The $O(m)$ bound includes the time needed to shrink and expand blossoms. It follows that the time complexity of the algorithm is $O(nm) = O(n^3)$. The correctness of the algorithm follows from Theorem 16.3, Corollary 16.1 and Observation 16.1. This implies the following theorem.

Theorem 16.4 *Algorithm* GMATCH *finds a maximum matching in an undirected graph with n vertices and m edges in $O(nm) = O(n^3)$ time.*

16.6   An $O(n^{2.5})$ Algorithm for Bipartite Graphs

In this section, we study an algorithm that finds a maximum matching in a bipartite graph $G = (X \cup Y, E)$ in time $O(m\sqrt{n})$, where $n = |X| + |Y|$ and $m = |E|$. The algorithm is due to Hopcroft and Karp. In this algorithm, instead of starting at a free x-vertex and finding one augmenting path, the algorithm carries out the breadth-first search starting at *all* the free x-vertices. It then finds a *maximal* set of vertex-disjoint augmenting paths *of minimum length* and simultaneously augments the current matching by all these augmenting paths. The process of finding a maximal set of vertex-disjoint augmenting paths and augmenting the current matching by them constitutes one *phase* of the algorithm. The above time complexity follows from an upper bound of $O(\sqrt{n})$ on the number of phases whose cost is $O(m)$ each. This is reminiscent of Dinic's algorithm for finding a maximum flow in a network.

Lemma 16.2 *Let M be a matching, p an augmenting path with respect to M and p' an augmenting path with respect to $M \oplus p$. Let $M' = M \oplus p \oplus p'$. Then, $M \oplus M' = p \oplus p'$.*

Proof.   Clearly, we only need to consider edges in $p \cup p'$. Let e be an edge in $p \cup p'$. If e is in $p \oplus p'$, then its status (matched or unmatched) in M is different from its status in M' since its status will change only once: either by p or p'. Consequently, e is in $M \oplus M'$. On the other hand, if e is in $p \cap p'$, then its status is the same in both M and M' since its status will change twice: first by p and then by p', that is, e is not in $M \oplus M'$. Consequently, $M \oplus M' = p \oplus p'$. □

Lemma 16.3 *Let M be a matching, p a shortest augmenting path with respect to M and p' an augmenting path with respect to $M \oplus p$. Then,*

$$|p'| \geq |p| + 2|p \cap p'|.$$

Proof. Let $M' = M \oplus p \oplus p'$. By Lemma 16.1, M' is a matching and $|M'| = |M| + 2$. By Theorem 16.1, $M \oplus M'$ contains two vertex-disjoint augmenting paths p_1 and p_2 with respect to M. Since, by Lemma 16.2, $M \oplus M' = p \oplus p'$, we have

$$|p \oplus p'| \geq |p_1| + |p_2|.$$

Since p is of shortest length, $|p_1| \geq |p|$ and $|p_2| \geq |p|$. Therefore,

$$|p \oplus p'| \geq |p_1| + |p_2| \geq 2|p|.$$

From the identity

$$|p \oplus p'| = |p| + |p'| - 2|p \cap p'|,$$

we obtain

$$|p'| \geq |p| + 2|p \cap p'|.$$ □

Let M be a matching, k the length of a shortest augmenting path with respect to M and S a *maximal* set of vertex-disjoint augmenting paths with respect to M of length k. Let M' be obtained from M by augmenting M by all the augmenting paths in S. Let p be an augmenting path in M'. We have the following important corollary of Lemma 16.3.

Corollary 16.2 $|p| \geq k + 2$.

Thus, by Corollary 16.2, starting from the empty matching M_0, we obtain the matching M_1 by finding a maximal set of augmenting paths of length one and simultaneously augmenting by these paths. In general, we construct a sequence of matchings $M_0, M_1, \ldots$, where matching M_{i+1} is obtained from matching M_i by finding a maximal set of augmenting paths of the same length with respect to M_i and simultaneously augmenting by these paths. As stated before, we will denote by a *phase* the procedure of finding a maximal set of augmenting paths of the same length with respect to the current matching and augmenting by these paths. By Corollary 16.2, the length of augmenting paths increases from one phase to the next by at least 2. The following theorem establishes an upper bound on the number of phases.

Theorem 16.5   *The number of phases required to find a maximum matching in a bipartite graph is at most* $3\lfloor\sqrt{n}\rfloor/2$.

Proof.   Let M be the matching obtained after at least $\lfloor\sqrt{n}\rfloor/2$ phases and M^* a maximum matching. Since the length of augmenting paths increases from one phase to the next by at least 2, the length of any augmenting path in M is at least $\lfloor\sqrt{n}\rfloor + 1$. By Theorem 16.1, there are *exactly* $|M^*| - |M|$ vertex-disjoint augmenting paths with respect to M. Since the length of each path is at least $\lfloor\sqrt{n}\rfloor + 1$, and hence each path consists of at least $\lfloor\sqrt{n}\rfloor + 2$ vertices, we must have

$$|M^*| - |M| \leq \frac{n}{\lfloor\sqrt{n}\rfloor + 2} < \frac{n}{\sqrt{n}} = \sqrt{n}.$$

Since each phase contributes at least one augmenting path, the remaining number of phases is at most $\lfloor\sqrt{n}\rfloor$. It follows that the total number of phases required by the algorithm is at most $3\lfloor\sqrt{n}\rfloor/2$.   □

The above analysis implies Algorithm BIMATCH3. The algorithm starts with the empty matching. It then iterates through the **while** loop until the matching becomes maximum. During each iteration, a directed acyclic graph (dag) D is constructed from which a maximal set of vertex-disjoint augmenting paths is constructed. The current matching is then augmented by these paths and the procedure is repeated. To construct a dag, we use breadth-first search to find the sets of vertices $L_0, L_1, \ldots$ and sets of edges $E_0, E_1, \ldots$ as follows:

(1) L_0 is the set of free vertices in X.
(2) L_1 is the set of vertices in Y connected by an unmatched edge to the set of free vertices in X.
(3) If L_1 contains at least one free vertex, then the construction of the dag is complete, as there is at least one augmenting path consisting of exactly one edge.

Algorithm 16.4 BIMATCH3

Input: A bipartite graph $G = (X \cup Y, E)$.

Output: A maximum matching M in G.

1. Start with the empty matching $M = \{\}$.
2. $maximum \leftarrow false$
3. **while not** $maximum$ { Construct a dag D}
4. $L_0 \leftarrow$ Set of free vertices in X.
5. $L_1 \leftarrow \{y \in Y \mid (x,y) \in E$ for some $x \in L_0\}$
6. $E_0 = \{(x,y) \in E \mid x \in L_0, y \in L_1\}$
7.   Mark all vertices in L_0 and L_1.
8. $i \leftarrow 0$
9.   **while** L_{i+1} contains no free vertices and is not empty
10. $i \leftarrow i + 2$
11. $L_i \leftarrow \{x \in X \mid x$ is unmarked and is joined by
12.   a matched edge to a vertex $y \in L_{i-1}\}$
13. $E_{i-1} = \{(x,y) \in E \mid y \in L_{i-1}, x \in L_i\}$
14. $L_{i+1} \leftarrow \{y \in Y \mid y$ is unmarked and is joined by
15.   an unmatched edge to a vertex $x \in L_i\}$
16. $E_i = \{(x,y) \in E \mid x \in L_i, y \in L_{i+1}\}$
17.   Mark all vertices in L_i and L_{i+1}.
18.   **end while**
19.   **if** L_{i+1} is empty **then** $maximum \leftarrow true$
20.   **else**
21.   **for** each free vertex $y \in L_{i+1}$ {augment}
22.   Starting at y, use depth-first search to find an augmenting path p that ends at a free vertex $x \in L_0$. Remove all vertices on p and incident edges from the dag D. Set $M = M \oplus p$.
23.   **end for**
24.   **end if**
25. **end while**

---

(4) If L_1 does not contain free vertices, two more sets are constructed, namely L_2 and L_3, where L_2 consists of the set of vertices in X connected by matched edges to elements of L_1 and L_3 consists of those vertices in $Y - L_1$ connected to elements of L_2 by unmatched edges.

(5) If L_3 contains at least one free vertex, then the construction is complete, as there is at least one augmenting path connecting a free vertex in L_3 to a free vertex in L_0.

(6) If L_3 does not contain any free vertices, the process is repeated to construct sets $L_4, L_5, \ldots$. The construction ends whenever a set L_{2i+1}

of y-vertices is found to contain at least one free vertex or when L_{2i+1} is empty.

(7) After the construction of each set $L_i, i \geq 1$, a set of edges E_{i-1} is added. E_{i-1} consists of the set of edges connecting those vertices in L_{i-1} and L_i. The sets $E_0, E_1, \ldots$ consist alternately of unmatched and matched edges.

Note that whenever a vertex is added to a set L_i, it is marked so that it is not added later on to another set $L_j, j > i$. Incidentally, note that a *maximal* set does not necessarily imply *maximum*. If a set is maximal, then no more vertex-disjoint augmenting paths *of the same length* can be added.

Example 16.4   Consider the bipartite graph shown in Fig. 16.12(a). The matching shown is the result of the first phase of the algorithm. In the first phase, the algorithm found a maximal set of three augmenting paths (see Fig. 16.12(a)). As noted above, this set is maximal, but *not* maximum, as there are more than three augmenting paths in the original graph. Figure 16.12(b) shows the dag created in the second phase. In this dag, there are two vertex-disjoint augmenting paths of shortest length. Augmenting by these two augmenting paths results in a maximum matching of size 5. Thus, the number of phases required to achieve a maximum matching for this graph is 2.

Fig. 16.12.   An example of the algorithm.

As to the time complexity of the algorithm, Theorem 16.5 guarantees that the number of iterations of the outer **while** loop is at most $3\lfloor\sqrt{n}\rfloor/2$, that is, the number of iterations is $O(\sqrt{n})$. It is not hard to see that the construction of the dag in each iteration takes $O(m)$ time. The time taken for augmentations is also $O(m)$. It follows that the running time of the entire algorithm is $O(m\sqrt{n}) = O(n^{2.5})$.

Theorem 16.6 *Algorithm* BIMATCH3 *finds a maximum matching in a bipartite graph with n vertices and m edges in $O(m\sqrt{n}) = O(n^{2.5})$ time.*

16.7 Practice Problems

16.1. Use the network flow method to find a maximum matching in the bipartite graph shown in Fig. 16.13. Show your work.

16.2. Use the Hungarian tree method to find a maximum matching in the bipartite graph shown in Fig. 16.13. Show your work.

16.3. Use the $O(n^{2.5})$ algorithm for matching in bipartite graphs to find a maximum matching in the bipartite graph shown in Fig. 16.13. Show your work.

16.4. Hall's theorem: If $G = (X \cup Y, E)$ is a bipartite graph, then all vertices in X can be matched to a subset of Y if and only if $|\Gamma(S)| \geq |S|$ for all subsets S of X. Here, $\Gamma(S)$ is the set of all vertices in Y

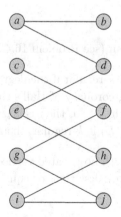

Fig. 16.13. A bipartite graph.

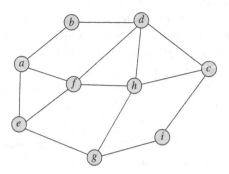

Fig. 16.14.   An undirected graph.

adjacent to at least one vertex in S. Hall's theorem is sometimes called the *marriage theorem* since it can be rephrased as follows. Given a set of n men and a set of n women, let each man make a list of the women he is willing to marry. Then each man can be married to a woman on his list if and only if the union of any k of the mens' lists contains at least k women. Verify Hall's theorem on the bipartite graph shown in Fig. 16.13.

16.5. Find a maximum matching in the general graph shown in Fig. 16.14.

16.6. Use Hall's theorem to show that there is no perfect matching in the bipartite graph shown in Fig. 16.5.

16.8   Exercises

16.1. Prove Hall's theorem (see Problem 16.4).

16.2. A graph G is called k-regular if the degree of each vertex of G is k. Prove the following corollary of Hall's theorem: If G is a k-regular bipartite graph with $k > 0$, then G has a perfect matching. Note that if $G = (X \cup Y, E)$ is k-regular, then $|X| = |Y|$.

16.3. Let G be a graph with no isolated vertices. Prove that the size of a maximum matching is less than or equal to the size of a minimum vertex cover for G.

16.4. Use the max-flow min-cut theorem to prove König's theorem: If G is a bipartite graph, then the size of a maximum matching in G is equal to the size of a minimum vertex cover for G.

16.5. How many perfect matchings are there in the graph $K_{n,n}$, the complete bipartite graph with $2n$ vertices?

16.6. Prove or disprove the following statement. Using an algorithm for finding a maximum matching by finding augmenting paths and augmenting using these paths, whenever a vertex becomes matched, then it will remain matched throughout the algorithm.

16.7. Prove that a (free) tree has at most one perfect matching. Give a linear time algorithm to find such a matching.

16.8. Give an algorithm that finds an independent set of vertices of maximum cardinality in a bipartite graph.

16.9. Give a recursive algorithm that finds an independent set of vertices of maximum cardinality in an arbitrary graph.

16.10. Show that Observation 16.1 applies in the case of general graphs.

16.11. Let G be a bipartite graph, and let M be a matching in G. Show that there is a maximum matching M^* such that every vertex matched in M is also matched in M^*.

16.12. Let G be a graph and S_1 and S_2 be two disjoint subsets of its vertices. Show how to find the maximum number of vertex-disjoint paths between S_1 and S_2 by modeling the problem as a matching problem. For simplicity, you may assume that S_1 and S_2 have the same size.

16.13. The *stable marriage problem.* In a group of n boys and n girls, each boy ranks the n girls according to his preference and each girl ranks the n boys according to her preference. A marriage corresponds to a perfect matching between the boys and girls. A marriage is *unstable* if there is a pair of one boy and one girl who are unmarried to each other but like each other more than their respective spouses. A marriage is *stable* if it is not unstable. Show that a stable marriage always exists. Give an efficient algorithm to find one stable marriage.

16.14. Show that the bound of Algorithm BIMATCH2 is tight by exhibiting a bipartite graph that requires $\Theta(n)$ iterations each taking $\Theta(m)$ time.

16.15. Let $G = (V, E)$ be a graph with no isolated vertices. An *edge cover* C for G is a subset of its edges that cover all its vertices, i.e., each vertex in V is incident to at least one edge in C. Show that if M is a matching, then there exists an edge cover C such that $|C| = |V| - |M|$.

16.16. Use the result of Exercise 16.15 to show that the problem of finding an edge cover of minimum size can be reduced to the problem of matching. In other words, show how to use matching techniques to find an edge cover of minimum cardinality.

16.17. Let $S_1, S_2, \ldots, S_n$ be n sets. A set $\{r_1, r_2, \ldots, r_n\}$ is called a *system of distinct representatives* (SDR) if $r_j \in S_j, 1 \leq j \leq n$. Give an algorithm for finding an SDR, if one exists, by defining a bipartite graph and solving a matching problem.

16.18. Let $S_1, S_2, \ldots, S_n$ be n sets. Prove that an SDR exists for these sets (see Exercise 16.17) if and only if the union of any k sets contains at least k elements, for $1 \leq k \leq n$. (*Hint*: See Problem 16.4.)

16.9 Bibliographic Notes

Algorithms for maximum matching and maximum-weight matching can be found in several books including Lawler (1976), McHugh (1990), Minieka (1978), Moret and Shapiro (1991), Papadimitriou and Steiglitz (1982) and Tarjan (1983). Algorithms for bipartite matching were studied a long time ago; see for example Hall (1956). Corollary 1.1 was proved independently by both Berge (1957) and Norman (1959). The idea of the algorithm for matching in general graphs is due to the pioneering work of Edmonds (1965).

Edmonds' proposed implementation requires $O(n^4)$ time. Improvements in the efficiency of blossom handling are due to Gabow (1976), whose implementation requires $O(n^3)$ time. The $O(m\sqrt{n})$ algorithm for matching in bipartite graphs is due to Hopcroft and Karp (1973). In Even and Tarjan (1975), it was first pointed out that this algorithm is a special case of the maximum flow algorithm applied to simple networks. An algorithm for maximum matching in general graphs with the same time complexity is described in Micali and Vazirani (1980).

PART 7

Techniques in Computational Geometry

Computational geometry is defined as the study of problems that are inherently geometric in nature. There are several techniques to solve geometric problems, some of them we have already covered in the previous chapters. There are, however, standard techniques that are specific to solving geometric problems. It is important to have fast geometric algorithms in many fields like computer graphics, scientific visualization and graphical user interfaces. Also, speed is fundamental in real-time applications in which the algorithm receives its input dynamically.

In Chapter 17, we will study an important design technique generally referred to as *geometric sweeping*. We will show how this technique can be employed to solve fundamental problems in computational geometry such as finding the maxima of a set of points, finding the intersection of line segments, computing the convex hull of a point set and finally computing the diameter of a set of points.

Chapter 18 will be devoted to the study of two variants of Voronoi diagrams: the nearest-point Voronoi diagram and the farthest-point Voronoi diagram. We will demonstrate the power of the former by presenting solutions to problems that are concerned with "nearness", and show how the latter can be used to solve problems that have to do with "farthness". Some of these solutions include linear time algorithms for the following problems:

(1) The convex hull problem.
(2) The all nearest neighbors problem.
(3) The Euclidean minimum spanning tree problem.
(4) The all farthest neighbors problem.
(5) Finding the smallest enclosing circle that enclose a planar point set.

Chapter 17

Geometric Sweeping

17.1 Introduction

In geometric algorithms, the main objects considered are usually points, line segments, polygons and others in two-dimensional, three-dimensional and higher-dimensional spaces. Sometimes, a solution to a problem calls for "sweeping" over the given input objects to collect information in order to find a feasible solution. This technique is called *plane sweep* in the two-dimensional plane and *space sweep* in the three-dimensional space. In its simplest form, a vertical line sweeps from left to right in the plane stopping at each object, say a point, starting from the leftmost object to the rightmost object.

17.2 A Simple Example: Computing the Maximal Points of a Point Set

We illustrate the method of geometric sweeping in connection with a simple problem in computational geometry: Computing the maximal points of a set of points in the plane.

Definition 17.1   Let $p_1 = (x_1, y_1)$ and $p_2 = (x_2, y_2)$ be two points in the plane. p_2 is said to dominate p_1, denoted by $p_1 \prec p_2$, if $x_1 \leq x_2$ and $y_1 \leq y_2$.

Definition 17.2 Let S be a set of points in the plane. A point $p \in S$ is a *maximal point* or a *maximum* if there does not exist a point $q \in S$ such that $p \neq q$ and $p \prec q$.

The following problem has a simple algorithm, which is a good example of a geometric sweeping algorithm.

MAXIMAL POINTS: Given a set S of n points in the plane, determine the maximal points in S.

This problem can easily be solved as follows. First, we sort all the points in S in nonincreasing order of their x-coordinates. The rightmost point (the one with maximum x-value) is clearly a maximum. The algorithm *sweeps* the points from right to left and for each point p it determines whether it is dominated on the y-coordinate by any of the previously scanned points. The algorithm is given as Algorithm MAXIMA.

Algorithm 17.1 MAXIMA
Input: A set S of n points in the plane.
Output: The set M of maximal points in S.

1. Let A be the points in S sorted in nonincreasing order of their x-coordinates. If two points have the same x-coordinate then the one with larger y-coordinate appears first in the ordering.
2. $M \leftarrow \{A[1]\}$
3. $maxy \leftarrow y$-coordinate of $A[1]$
4. **for** $j \leftarrow 2$ **to** n
5. $(x, y) \leftarrow A[j]$
6.   **if** $y > maxy$ **then**
7. $M \leftarrow M \cup \{A[j]\}$
8. $maxy \leftarrow y$
9.   **end if**
10. **end for**

Figure 17.1 illustrates the behavior of the algorithm on a set of points. As shown in the figure, the set of maxima $\{a, b, c, d\}$ forms a staircase. Note that, for example, e is dominated by a only, whereas f is dominated by both a and b, and g is dominated by c only.

It is easy to see that the running time of the Algorithm MAXIMA is dominated by the sorting step and hence is $O(n \log n)$.

The above example reveals the two basic components of a plane sweep algorithm. First, there is the *event point schedule*, which is a sequence of the

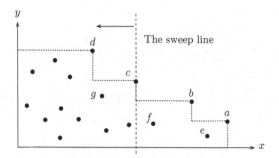

Fig. 17.1. A set of points with their maxima.

x-coordinates ordered from right to left. These points define the "stopping" positions of the sweeping line, which in this case is a vertical line. Unlike the case in the previous example, in some plane sweep algorithms, the event point schedule may be updated dynamically, and thus data structures that are more complex than a simple array or a queue may be required for efficient implementation.

The other component in the plane sweep method is the *sweep line status*. This is an appropriate description of the geometric objects at the sweeping line. In the above example, the sweep line status consists of a "description" of the most recent maximal point detected. This description is simply the value of its y-coordinate. In other geometric algorithms, the sweep line status may require storing the relevant information needed in the form of a stack, a queue, a heap, etc.

17.3 Geometric Preliminaries

In this section, we present the definitions of some of the fundamental concepts in computational geometry that will be used in this chapter. Most of these definitions are within the framework of the two-dimensional space; their generalization to higher dimensions is straightforward. A *point p* is represented by a pair of coordinates (x, y). A *line segment* is represented by two points called its *endpoints*. If p and q are two distinct points, we denote by $\overline{pq}$ the line segment whose endpoints are p and q. A *polygonal path* π is a sequence of points $p_1, p_2, \ldots, p_n$ such that $\overline{p_i p_{i+1}}$ is a line segment for $1 \leq i \leq n - 1$. If $p_1 = p_n$, then π (together with the closed region bounded by π) is called a *polygon*. In this case, the points $p_i, 1 \leq i \leq n$, are called

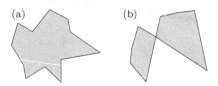

Fig. 17.2.   (a) A simple polygon. (b) A nonsimple polygon.

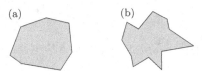

Fig. 17.3.   (a) A convex polygon. (b) A nonconvex polygon.

the *vertices* of the polygon, and the line segments $\overline{p_1p_2}, \overline{p_2p_3}, \ldots, \overline{p_{n-1}p_n}$ are called its *edges*. A polygon can conveniently be represented using a circular linked list to store its vertices. In some algorithms, it is represented by a circular doubly linked list. As defined above, technically, a polygon refers to the closed connected region called the *interior* of the polygon plus the *boundary* that is defined by the closed polygonal path. However, we will mostly write "polygon" to mean its boundary. A polygon P is called *simple* if no two of its edges intersect except at its vertices; otherwise, it is *nonsimple*. Figure 17.2 shows two polygons, one is simple and the other is not.

Henceforth, it will be assumed that a polygon is simple unless otherwise stated, and hence the modifier "simple" will be dropped. A polygon P is said to be *convex* if the line segment connecting any two points in P lies entirely inside P. Figure 17.3 shows two polygons, one is convex and the other is not.

Let S be a set of points in the plane. The *convex hull* of S, denoted by $CH(S)$, is defined as the smallest convex polygon enclosing all the points in S. The vertices of $CH(S)$ are called *hull vertices* and are also referred to as the *extreme points* of S.

Let $u = (x_1, y_1)$, $v = (x_2, y_2)$ and $w = (x_3, y_3)$. The *signed area* of the triangle formed by these three points is half the determinant

$$D = \begin{vmatrix} x_1 & y_1 & 1 \\ x_2 & y_2 & 1 \\ x_3 & y_3 & 1 \end{vmatrix}.$$

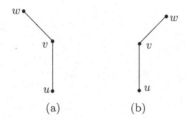

Fig. 17.4. (a) A left turn. (b) A right turn.

D is positive if u, v, w, u form a counterclockwise cycle, in which case we say that the path u, v, w is a *left turn*. It is negative if u, v, w, u form a clockwise cycle, in which case we say that the path u, v, w is a *right turn*. (see Fig. 17.4). $D = 0$ if and only if the three points are collinear, i.e., lie on the same line.

17.4 Computing the Intersections of Line Segments

In this section, we consider the following problem. Given a set $L = \{l_1, l_2, \ldots, l_n\}$ of n line segments in the plane, find the set of points at which they intersect. We will assume that no line segment is vertical and no three line segments intersect at the same point. Removing these assumptions will only make the algorithm more complicated.

Let l_i and l_j be any two line segments in L. If l_i and l_j intersect the vertical line with x-coordinate x at two distinct points p_i and p_j, respectively, then we say that l_i *is above* l_j at x, denoted by $l_i >_x l_j$, if p_i lies above p_j on the vertical line with x-coordinate x. The relation $>_x$ defines a total order on the set of all line segments intersecting the vertical line with x-coordinate x. Thus, in Fig. 17.5, we have

$$l_2 >_x l_1, l_2 >_x l_3, l_3 >_y l_2 \quad \text{and} \quad l_4 >_z l_3.$$

The algorithm starts by sorting the $2n$ endpoints of the n line segments in nondecreasing order of their x-coordinates. Throughout the algorithm, a vertical line sweeps all endpoints of the line segments and their intersections from left to right. Starting from the empty relation, each time an endpoint or an intersection point is encountered, the order relation

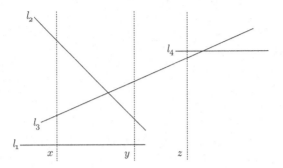

Fig. 17.5.   Illustration of the relation $>_x$.

changes. Specifically, the order relation changes whenever one of the following "events" occurs while the line is swept from left to right.

(1) When the left endpoint of a line segment is encountered.
(2) When the right endpoint of a line segment is encountered.
(3) When the intersection point of two line segments is encountered.

The sweep line status S is completely described by the order relation $>_x$. As to the event point schedule E, it includes the sorted endpoints plus the intersections of the line segments, which are added dynamically while the line is swept from left to right.

The actions taken by the algorithm on each event are as follows.

(1) When the left endpoint of a line segment l is encountered, l is added to the order relation. If there is a line segment l_1 immediately above l and l and l_1 intersect, then their intersection point is inserted into the event point schedule E. Similarly, if there is a line segment l_2 immediately below l and l and l_2 intersect, then their intersection point is inserted into E.
(2) When the right endpoint p of a line segment l is encountered, l is removed from the order relation. In this case, the two line segments l_1 and l_2 immediately above and below l are tested for a possible intersection at a point q *to the right of* p. If this is the case, q is inserted into E.
(3) When the intersection point p of two line segments is encountered, their relative order in the relation is reversed. Thus, if $l_1 >_x l_2$ to the left of their intersection, the order relation is modified so that $l_2 >_x l_1$. Let l_3 and l_4 be the two line segments immediately above and below the

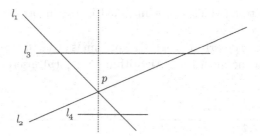

Fig. 17.6.   Reversing the order of two line segments at an intersection point.

intersection point p, respectively (see Fig. 17.6). In other words, l_3 is above l_2 and l_4 is below l_1 *to the right of* the intersection point (see Fig. 17.6). In this case, we check for the possibility of l_2 intersecting with l_3 and l_1 intersecting with l_4. As before, we insert their intersection points into E, if any.

It remains to specify the data structures needed to implement the event point schedule and the sweep line status. To implement the event point schedule E, we need a data structure that supports the following operations:

- *insert*(p, E): Insert point p into E.
- *delete-min*(E): Return the point with minimum x-coordinate and delete it from E.

These two operations are clearly supported by the heap data structure in $O(\log n)$ time. Thus, E is implemented as a heap that initially contains the $2n$ sorted points. Each time the sweep line is to be moved to the right, the point with minimum x-coordinate is extracted. As explained above, when the algorithm detects an intersection point p, it inserts p into E.

As we have seen in the description of the algorithm above, the sweep line status S must support the following operations:

- *insert*(l, S): Insert line segment l into S.
- *delete*(l, S): Delete line segment l from S.
- above(l, S): Return the line segment immediately above l.
- below(l, S): Return the line segment immediately below l.

A data structure known as a *dictionary* supports each of the above operations in $O(\log n)$ time. Note that above(l, S) or below(l, S) may not exist; a simple test (which is not included in the algorithm) is needed to handle these two cases.

A more precise description of the algorithm is given in Algorithm INTER-SECTIONSLS. In the algorithm, Algorithm process(p) inserts p into E and outputs p.

Algorithm 17.2 INTERSECTIONSLS

Input: A set $L = \{l_1, l_2, \ldots, l_n\}$ of n line segments in the plane.

Output: The intersection points of the line segments in L.

1. Sort the endpoints in nondecreasing order of their x-coordinates and insert them into a heap E (the event point schedule).
2. **while** E is not empty
3. $p \leftarrow delete\text{-}min(E)$
4.   **if** p is a left endpoint **then**
5.   let l be the line segment whose left endpoint is p
6. $insert(l, S)$
7. $l_1 \leftarrow \text{above}(l, S)$
8. $l_2 \leftarrow \text{below}(l, S)$
9.   **if** l intersects l_1 at point q_1 **then** process(q_1)
10.   **if** l intersects l_2 at point q_2 **then** process(q_2)
11.   **else if** p is a right endpoint **then**
12.   let l be the line segment whose right endpoint is p
13. $l_1 \leftarrow \text{above}(l, S)$
14. $l_2 \leftarrow \text{below}(l, S)$
15. $delete(l, S)$
16.   **if** l_1 intersects l_2 at point q *to the right of* p **then** process(q)
17.   **else** $\{p$ is an intersection point$\}$
18.   Let the two intersecting line segments at p be l_1 and l_2
19.   where l_1 is above l_2 to the left of p
20. $l_3 \leftarrow \text{above}(l_1, S)$ {to the left of p}
21. $l_4 \leftarrow \text{below}(l_2, S)$ {to the left of p}
22.   **if** l_2 intersects l_3 at point q_1 **then** process(q_1)
23.   **if** l_1 intersects l_4 at point q_2 **then** process(q_2)
24.   interchange the ordering of l_1 and l_2 in S
25.   **end if**
26. **end while**

As regards the running time of the algorithm, we observe the following. The sorting step takes $O(n \log n)$ time. Let the number of intersections be m. Then, there are $2n + m$ event points to be processed. Each point requires $O(\log(2n + m))$ processing time. Hence, the total time required by the algorithm to process all intersection points is $O((2n + m) \log(2n + m))$.

Since $m \leq n(n-1)/2 = O(n^2)$, the bound becomes $O((n+m)\log n)$. Since the naïve approach to find all intersections runs in time $O(n^2)$, the algorithm is not suitable to process a set of line segments whose number of intersections is known *a priori* to be $\Omega(n^2/logn)$. On the other hand, if $m = O(n)$, then the algorithm runs in $O(n \log n)$ time.

17.5   The Convex Hull Problem

In this section, we consider, perhaps, the most fundamental problem in computational geometry: Given a set S of n points in the plane, find $CH(S)$, the convex hull of S. We describe here a well-known geometric sweeping algorithm called "Graham scan".

In its simplest form, Graham scan uses a line centered at a certain point and makes one rotation that sweeps the whole plane stopping at each point to decide whether it should be included in the convex hull or not. First, in one scan over the list of points, the point with minimum y-coordinate is found, call it p_0. If there are two or more points with the minimum y-coordinate, p_0 is chosen as the rightmost one. Clearly, p_0 belongs to the convex hull. Next, the coordinates of all points are transformed so that p_0 is at the origin. The points in $S - \{p_0\}$ are then sorted by polar angle about the origin p_0. If two points p_i and p_j form the same angle with p_0, then the one that is closer to p_0 precedes the other in the ordering. Note that here, we do not have to calculate the real distance from the origin, as it involves computing the square root which is costly; instead, we only need to compare the squares of the distances. Let the sorted list be $T = \{p_1, p_2, \ldots, p_{n-1}\}$, where p_1 and p_{n-1} form the least and greatest angles with p_0, respectively. Figure 17.7 shows an example of a set of 13 points after sorting them by polar angle about p_0.

Now, the scan commences with the event point schedule being the sorted list T and the sweep line status being implemented using a stack St. The stack initially contains (p_{n-1}, p_0), with p_0 being on top of the stack. The algorithm then traverses the points starting at p_1 and ending at p_{n-1}. At any moment, let the stack content be

$$St = (p_{n-1}, p_0, \ldots, p_i, p_j)$$

(i.e., p_i and p_j are the most recently pushed points), and let p_k be the next point to be considered. If the triplet p_i, p_j, p_k forms a left turn, then p_k is

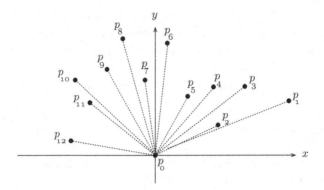

Fig. 17.7.   A set of points sorted in polar angle about p_0.

Fig. 17.8.   The convex hull after processing point p_5.

pushed on top of the stack and the sweep line is moved to the next point. If p_i, p_j, p_k form a right turn or are collinear, then p_j is popped off the stack and the sweep line is kept at point p_k.

Figure 17.8 shows the resulting convex hull just after p_5 has been processed. At this point, the stack content is

$$(p_{12}, p_0, p_1, p_3, p_4, p_5).$$

After processing point p_6, the points p_5, p_4 and p_3 are successively popped off the stack, and the point p_6 is pushed on top of the stack (see Fig. 17.9). The final convex hull is shown in Fig. 17.10.

Fig. 17.9. The convex hull after processing point p_6.

Fig. 17.10. The final convex hull.

Given below is a more formal description of the algorithm. At the end of the algorithm, the stack St contains the vertices of $CH(S)$, so it can be converted into a linked list to form a convex polygon.

The running time of Algorithm CONVEXHULL is computed as follows. The sorting step costs $O(n \log n)$ time. As to the **while** loop, we observe that each point is pushed exactly once and is popped at most once. Moreover, checking whether three points form a left turn or a right turn amounts to computing their signed area in $\Theta(1)$ time. Thus, the cost of the while loop is $\Theta(n)$. It follows that the time complexity of the algorithm is $O(n \log n)$. See Exercise 17.7 for an alternative approach that avoids computing the polar angles. Other algorithms for computing the convex hull are outlined in Exercises 17.3 and 17.8.

Algorithm 17.3 CONVEXHULL
Input: A set S of n points in the plane.
Output: $CH(S)$, the convex hull of S stored in a stack St.

1. Let p_0 be the rightmost point with minimum y-coordinate.
2. $T[0] \leftarrow p_0$
3. Let $T[1..n-1]$ be the points in $S - \{p_0\}$ sorted in increasing polar angle about p_0. If two points p_i and p_j form the same angle with p_0, then the one that is closer to p_0 precedes the other in the ordering.
4. **push** $(St, T[n-1]);$ **push** $(St, T[0])$
5. $k \leftarrow 1$
6. **while** $k < n-1$
7.   Let $St = (T[n-1], \ldots, T[i], T[j])$, $T[j]$ is on top of the stack.
8.   **if** $T[i], T[j], T[k]$ is a left turn **then**
9.   **push** $(St, T[k])$
10. $k \leftarrow k+1$
11.   **else pop** (St)
12.   **end if**
13. **end while**

17.6 Computing the Diameter of a Set of Points

Let S be a set of points in the plane. The diameter of S, denoted by $Diam(S)$, is defined to be the maximum distance realized by two points in S. A straightforward algorithm to solve this problem compares each pair of points and returns the maximum distance realized by two points in S. This approach leads to a $\Theta(n^2)$ time algorithm. In this section, we study an algorithm to find the diameter of a set of points in the plane in time $O(n \log n)$.

We start with the following observation, which seems to be intuitive (see Fig. 17.11):

Observation 17.1 The diameter of a point set S is equal to the diameter of the vertices of its convex hull, i.e., $Diam(S) = Diam(CH(S))$.

Consequently, to compute the diameter of a set of points in the plane, we only need to consider the vertices on its convex hull. Therefore, in what follows, we will be concerned primarily with the problem of finding the diameter of a convex polygon.

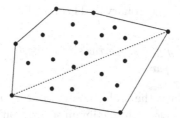

Fig. 17.11. The diameter of a set of points is the diameter of its convex hull.

Fig. 17.12. Some supporting lines of a convex polygon.

Fig. 17.13. Two parallel supporting lines with largest separation.

Definition 17.3   Let P be a convex polygon. A *supporting line* of P is a straight line l passing through a vertex of P such that the interior of P lies entirely on one side of l (see Fig. 17.12).

A useful characterization of the diameter of a convex polygon is given in the following theorem (see Fig. 17.13).

Theorem 17.1   *The diameter of a convex polygon P is equal to the greatest distance between any pair of parallel supporting lines of P.*

Definition 17.4   Any two points that admit two parallel supporting lines are called *antipodal pair*.

We have the following corollary of Theorem 17.1:

Corollary 17.1 *Any pair of vertices realizing the diameter in a convex polygon is an antipodal pair.*

By the above corollary, the problem now reduces to finding *all* antipodal pairs and selecting the one with maximum separation. It turns out that we can accomplish that in optimal linear time.

Definition 17.5 We define the distance between a point p and a line segment $\overline{qr}$, denoted by $dist(q, r, p)$ to be the distance of p from the straight line on which the line segment $\overline{qr}$ lies. A vertex p is *farthest* from a line segment $\overline{qr}$ if $dist(q, r, p)$ is maximum.

Consider Fig. 17.14(a) in which a convex polygon P is shown. From the figure, it is easy to see that p_5 is the farthest vertex from edge $\overline{p_{12}p_1}$. Similarly, vertex p_9 is the farthest from edge $\overline{p_1p_2}$.

It can be shown that a vertex p forms an antipodal pair with p_1 if and only if it is one of the vertices $p_5, p_6, \ldots, p_9$. In general, let the vertices on the convex hull of the point set be $p_1, p_2, \ldots, p_m$ for some $m \leq n$, in counterclockwise ordering. Let p_k be the first farthest vertex from edge $\overline{p_mp_1}$ and p_l the first farthest vertex from edge $\overline{p_1p_2}$ when traversing the boundary of $CH(S)$ in counterclockwise order (see Fig. 17.14(b)). Then, any

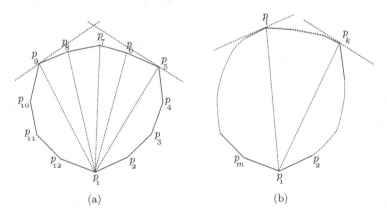

Fig. 17.14. Computing the set of antipodal pairs.

vertex between p_k and p_l (including p_k and p_l) forms an antipodal pair with p_1. Moreover, all other vertices do *not* form an antipodal pair with p_1.

This important observation suggests the following method for finding all antipodal pairs. First, we traverse the boundary of $CH(S)$ in counterclockwise order starting at p_2 until we find p_k, the farthest vertex from $\overline{p_m p_1}$. We add the pair (p_1, p_k) to an initially empty set for holding the antipodal pairs. We then keep traversing the boundary and include the pair (p_1, p_j) for each vertex p_j encountered until we reach p_l, the vertex farthest from $\overline{p_1 p_2}$. It may be the case that $l = k+1$ or even $l = k$, i.e., $p_l = p_k$. Next, we advance to the edge $\overline{p_2 p_3}$ to find the vertices that form antipodal pairs with p_2. Thus, we are simultaneously doing two counterclockwise traversals of the boundary: one from p_1 to p_k and the other from p_k to p_m. The traversal ends when the antipodal pair (p_k, p_m) is detected. Finally, a linear scan over the set of antipodal pairs is clearly sufficient to find the diameter of the convex hull, which by Observation 17.1 is the desired diameter of the point set. This method is described more formally in Algorithm DIAMETER.

If the convex hull contains no parallel edges, the number of antipodal pairs will be exactly m, which is the size of the convex hull. If there are pairs of parallel edges, then their number is at most $\lfloor m/2 \rfloor$ and hence the total number of antipodal pairs is at most $\lfloor 3m/2 \rfloor$.

Algorithm 17.4 DIAMETER

Input: A set S of n points in the plane.

Output: $Diam(S)$, the diameter of S.

1. $\{p_1, p_2, \ldots, p_m\} \leftarrow CH(S)$ {Compute the convex hull of S}
2. $A \leftarrow \{\}$ {Initialize the set of antipodal pairs}
3. $k \leftarrow 2$
4. **while** $dist(p_m, p_1, p_{k+1}) > dist(p_m, p_1, p_k)$ {Find p_k}
5. $k \leftarrow k+1$
6. **end while**
7. $i \leftarrow 1$; $j \leftarrow k$
8. **while** $i \leq k$ **and** $j \leq m$
9. $A \leftarrow A \cup \{(p_i, p_j)\}$
10.   **while** $dist(p_i, p_{i+1}, p_{j+1}) \geq dist(p_i, p_{i+1}, p_j)$ **and** $j < m$
11. $A \leftarrow A \cup \{(p_i, p_j)\}$
12. $j \leftarrow j+1$
13.   **end while**
14. $i \leftarrow i+1$
15. **end while**
16. Scan A to obtain an antipodal pair (p_r, p_s) with maximum separation.
17. **return** the distance between p_r and p_s.

When comparing the distance between a vertex and a line segment, we do not compute the actual distance (which involves taking the square roots); instead, we compare the signed area since it is proportional to the actual distance (see Sec. 17.3 for the definition of the signed area). For example, the comparison

$$dist(p_i, p_{i+1}, p_{j+1}) \geq dist(p_i, p_{i+1}, p_j)$$

in the algorithm can be replaced with the comparison

$$area(p_i, p_{i+1}, p_{j+1}) \geq area(p_i, p_{i+1}, p_j),$$

where $area(q, r, p)$ is the area of the triangle formed by the line segment $\overline{qr}$ and the point p. This area is half the magnitude of the signed area of these three points.

The running time of the algorithm is computed as follows. Finding the convex hull requires $O(n \log n)$ time. Since the two nested **while** loops consist of two concurrent sweeps of the boundary of the convex hull, the time taken by these nested **while** loops is $\Theta(m) = O(n)$, where m is the size of the convex hull. It follows that the overall running time of the algorithm is $O(n \log n)$.

17.7 Practice Problems

17.1. Let I be a set of intervals on the horizontal line. Design an algorithm to report all those intervals that are contained in another interval from I. What is the running time of your algorithm?

17.2. Consider the decision problem version of the line segment intersection problem: Given n line segments in the plane, determine whether two of them intersect. Give an $O(n \log n)$ time algorithm to solve this problem.

17.3. Give an efficient algorithm to report all intersecting pairs of a set of n horizontal line segments. What is the time complexity of the algorithm?

17.4. Explain how to determine whether a given polygon is simple. Recall that a polygon is simple if and only if no two of its edges intersect except at its vertices.

17.5. Let P and Q be two simple polygons whose total number of vertices is n. Give an $O(n \log n)$ time algorithm to determine whether P and Q intersect.

17.6. Give an $O(n)$ time algorithm to solve the problem in Problem 17.5 in the case where the two polygons are convex.

17.7. In Graham scan for finding the convex hull of a point set, the points are sorted by their polar angles. However, computing the polar angles is costly. One alternative to computing the convex hull is to sort using the sines or cosines of the angles instead. Another alternative is to sort the points around the point $(0, -\infty)$ instead. This is equivalent to sorting the points by x-coordinates. Explain how to use this idea to come up with another algorithm for computing the convex hull.

17.8 Exercises

17.1. Let S be a set of n points in the plane. Design an iterative $O(n \log n)$ time algorithm to compute for each point p the number of points in S dominated by p. A recursive algorithm to solve this problem was given in Sec. 5.12. *Hint*: Use a line sweep algorithm to scan the points in ascending x-coordinates while maintaining a (dynamic) binary search tree for the points already scanned in sorted y-coordinates. When a new point is scanned, you just search in the BST and count the number of points whose y-coordinates are less than (or equal to) that of the current point.

17.2. Give an efficient algorithm to report all intersecting pairs of a given set of n horizontal and vertical line segments. What is the time complexity of the algorithm?

17.3. Another algorithm for finding the convex hull is known as *Jarvis march*. In this algorithm, the edges of the convex hull are found instead of its vertices. The algorithm starts by finding the point with the least y-coordinate, say p_1, and finding the point p_2 with the least polar angle with respect to p_1. Thus, the line segment $\overline{p_1 p_2}$ defines an edge of the convex hull. The next edge is determined by finding the point p_3 with the least polar angle with respect to p_2, and so on. From its description, the algorithm resembles Algorithm SELECTIONSORT. Give the details of this method. What is its time complexity?

17.4. What are the merits and demerits of Jarvis march for finding the convex hull as described in Exercise 17.3?

17.5. Let P be a convex polygon. A line segment *tangent* to P, or a *supporting line* for P, is a line segment L that intersects P at one vertex or an edge, so P lies on one side of L. How many supporting lines for P that pass through a point p external to P?

17.6. Let P and Q be two disjoint convex polygons. A supporting line for both P and Q is one that is tangent to both P and Q (see Exercise 17.5). How many supporting lines for P and Q are possible?

17.7. Let p be a point external to a convex polygon P. Explain how to compute in $O(\log n)$ time the convex hull of their union, i.e., the convex hull of $P \cup \{p\}$. (*Hint*: Find the supporting lines of p and P (see Exercise 17.5).)

17.8. Use the result of Exercise 17.7 to devise an incremental algorithm for computing the convex hull of a set of points. The algorithm builds the convex hull by testing one point at a time and deciding whether it belongs to the current convex hull or not. The algorithm should run in time $O(n \log n)$.

17.9. Design an $O(n)$ time algorithm to find the convex hull of two given convex polygons P and Q, that is, the union of $CH(P)$ and $CH(Q)$.

17.10. Let S be a set of points in the plane. Derive a divide-and-conquer $O(n \log n)$ time algorithm to compute $CH(S)$. First, the algorithm divides S into two subsets S_1 and S_2 of approximately equal size. Then, it finds $CH(S_1)$ and $CH(S_2)$ recursively. The combine step consists of finding the two tangent lines (supporting lines) above and below $CH(S_1)$ and $CH(S_2)$, and concatenating the appropriate parts of these two hulls (see Exercises 17.5 and 17.9).

17.11. Give an $O(n)$ time algorithm that decides whether a point p is inside a simple polygon P. (*Hint*: Draw a horizontal line passing by p and count the number of intersections it has with P.)

17.12. Give an $O(n)$ time algorithm that decides whether a point p is inside a convex polygon P. (*Hint*: Draw a horizontal line passing by p and count the number of intersections it has with P or traverse the boundary of the polygon counterclockwise testing for left turns with the point p.)

17.13. Prove or disprove the following statement: Given a set of points S in the plane, there is only one unique simple polygon whose vertices are the points in S.

17.14. Given a set of n points in the plane, show how to construct a simple polygon having them as its vertices. The algorithm should run in time $O(n \log n)$.

17.15. Referring to the algorithm for finding the diameter of a given point set S in the plane, prove that the diameter is the distance between two points on their convex hull.

17.16. Let P be a simple polygon with n vertices. P is called *monotone with respect to the y-axis* if for any line l perpendicular to the y-axis, the intersection of l and P is either a line segment or a point. For example, any convex polygon is monotone with respect to the y-axis. A *chord* in P is a line segment that connects two nonadjacent vertices in P and lies entirely inside P. The problem of *triangulating* a simple polygon is to partition the polygon into $n - 2$ triangles by drawing $n - 3$ nonintersecting chords inside P. Give an algorithm to triangulate a simple and monotone polygon P. What is the time complexity of your algorithm?

17.9 Bibliographic Notes

Some books on computational geometry include de Berg *et al.* (1997), Edelsbrunner (1987), Mehlhorn (1984c), O'Rourke (1994), Preparata and Shamos (1985) and Toussaint (1984). The algorithm for computing line segment intersections is due to Shamos and Hoey (1975). The convex hull algorithm is due to Graham (1972). Theorem 17.1 is due to Yaglom and Boltyanskii (1986). The algorithm of finding the diameter can be found in

Preparata and Shamos (1985). The problem of triangulating a simple polygon is fundamental in computational geometry. The solution to the problem of triangulating a monotone polygon in $\Theta(n)$ time (Exercise 17.16) can be found in Garey *et al.* (1978). In this paper, it was also shown that triangulating a simple polygon can be achieved in $O(n \log n)$ time. Later, Tarjan and Van Wyk (1988) gave an $O(n \log \log n)$ time algorithm for triangulating a simple polygon. Finally, Chazelle (1990, 1991) gave a linear time algorithm, which is quite complicated.

Chapter 18

Voronoi Diagrams

18.1 Introduction

In this chapter, we study a fundamental geometric structure that aids in solving numerous proximity problems in computational geometry. This structure is referred to as the *Voronoi diagram*. Although there are many types of Voronoi diagrams, the phrase "Voronoi diagram" with no modifiers is commonly used to refer to the nearest-point Voronoi diagram. This construct is usually used to solve problems that are concerned with "nearness". In this chapter, we will also study another type of Voronoi diagram called the farthest-point Voronoi diagram. This construct is basically used to solve problems that have to do with "farthness". We will demonstrate the power of these two diagrams by outlining some of their important applications.

18.2 Nearest-Point Voronoi Diagram

Let $S = \{p_1, p_2, \ldots, p_n\}$ be a set of n points in the plane. The locus of all points in the plane closer to a point p_i in S than to any other point in S defines a polygonal region $V(p_i)$ called the *Voronoi region* of p_i. It is a convex polygon that may be unbounded. It has at most $n - 1$ edges with each edge lying on the perpendicular bisector of p_i and another point in S. Figure 18.1(a) shows the Voronoi region $V(p)$ of a point p. The collection of all n Voronoi regions, one for each point, constitute the *nearest-point Voronoi diagram*, or simply the *Voronoi diagram*, of the point set S,

501

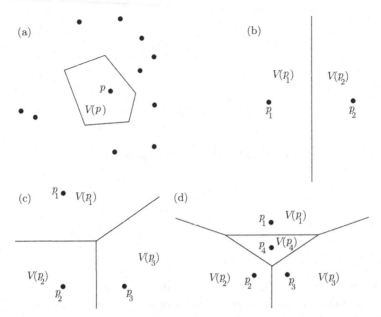

Fig. 18.1. (a) Voronoi region. (b)–(d) Voronoi diagrams of two, three and four points.

denoted by $\mathcal{V}(S)$. The Voronoi diagrams of sets of two, three and four points are shown in Figs. 18.1(b)–18.1(d). The Voronoi diagram of two points p_1 and p_2 is just the perpendicular bisector of the line segment $\overline{p_1 p_2}$. As shown in Fig. 18.1(c), the Voronoi diagram of three points that are not collinear consists of three bisectors that meet at one point. The region $V(p_4)$ associated with p_4 in Fig. 18.1(d) is bounded.

In general, let p_i and p_j be two points in S. The *half plane* $H(p_i, p_j)$ containing p_i and defined by the perpendicular bisector of p_i and p_j is the locus of all points in the plane closer to p_i than to p_j. The Voronoi region $V(p_i)$ associated with point p_i is the intersection of $n-1$ half-planes. That is,

$$V(p_i) = \bigcap_{i \neq j} H(p_i, p_j).$$

The Voronoi regions $V_1, V_2, \ldots, V_n$ define $\mathcal{V}(S)$, the Voronoi diagram of S. Figure 18.2 shows the Voronoi diagram of a number of points chosen randomly in the plane.

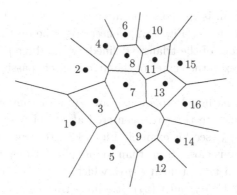

Fig. 18.2.   The Voronoi diagram of a set of points.

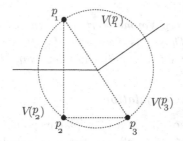

Fig. 18.3.   The Voronoi diagram of three points.

The Voronoi diagram of a point set S is a planar graph whose vertices and edges are respectively called *Voronoi vertices* and *Voronoi edges*. By construction, each point $p \in S$ belongs to a unique region $V(p)$, and hence for any point q in the interior of $V(p)$, q is closer to p than to any other point in S. The Voronoi diagram of a point set enjoys a number of interesting properties and can be used to answer several questions that have to do with proximity relationships. To simplify the discussion and make the justifications easier, we will assume henceforth that the points are in *general position* in the sense that no three points are collinear and no four points are cocircular, i.e., lie on the circumference of a circle.

Consider Fig. 18.3, which is Fig. 18.1(c) redrawn with more details. It is well known that the three perpendicular bisectors of the three sides of the triangle defined by the three points intersect at one point, the center of the circle that passes through these three points. Indeed, every vertex of the Voronoi diagram is the common intersection of exactly three edges of the Voronoi diagram (see Fig. 18.2). These edges lie on the perpendicular bisectors of the sides of the triangle defined by the three points, and hence that Voronoi vertex is the center of the unique circle passing through these three points.

Let v be a vertex in a Voronoi diagram $\mathcal{V}(S)$ for some planar point set S, and let $C(v)$ denote the circle centered at v and passing through the points p_1, p_2 and p_3 (see for example Fig. 18.3). If some other point p_4 is inside $C(v)$, then v is closer to p_4 than to any of the three points p_1, p_2 and p_3. This means that v must lie in $V(p_4)$, which contradicts the fact that v is common to $V(p_1), V(p_2)$ and $V(p_3)$. It follows that $C(v)$ contains no other point in S. These facts are summarized in the following theorem (here S is the original point set):

Theorem 18.1 *Every Voronoi vertex v is the common intersection of three Voronoi edges. Thus, v is the center of a circle $C(v)$ defined by three points in S. Moreover, $C(v)$ contains no other point in S.*

18.2.1 *Delaunay triangulation*

Let $\mathcal{V}(S)$ be a Voronoi diagram of a planar point set S. Consider the straight-line dual $\mathcal{D}(S)$ of $\mathcal{V}(S)$, i.e., the graph embedded in the plane obtained by adding a straight-line segment between each pair of points in S whose Voronoi regions share an edge. The dual of an edge in $\mathcal{V}(S)$ is an edge in $\mathcal{D}(S)$, and the dual of a vertex in $\mathcal{V}(S)$ is a triangular region in $\mathcal{D}(S)$. $\mathcal{D}(S)$ is a triangulation of the original point set and is called the *Delaunay triangulation* after Delaunay who proved this result in 1934. Figure 18.4 shows the dual of the Voronoi diagram in Fig. 18.2, i.e., the Delaunay triangulation of the set of points in Fig. 18.2. Figure 18.5 shows the Delaunay triangulation superimposed on its corresponding Voronoi diagram. Note that an edge in the Voronoi diagram and its dual in the Delaunay triangulation need not intersect, as is evident in the figure. In a Delaunay triangulation, the minimum angle of its triangles is maximum over all possible triangulations. Another property of the Delaunay triangulation $\mathcal{D}(S)$ of a planar point set S is that its boundary is $CH(S)$, the convex hull of S.

Let m and r be the number of edges and regions in a Delaunay triangulation $\mathcal{D}(S)$, respectively, where $|S| = n$. Clearly, $\mathcal{D}(S)$ is a planar graph,

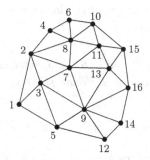

Fig. 18.4. The Delaunay triangulation of a set of points.

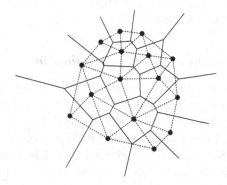

Fig. 18.5. The Voronoi diagram and Delaunay triangulation of a set of points.

and hence by Euler's formula (page 83), we have

$$n - m + r = 2$$

and, for $n \geq 3$,

$$m \leq 3n - 6.$$

Thus, its number of regions satisfies the inequality

$$r \leq 2n - 4.$$

Since each edge in a Delaunay triangulation is the dual of an edge in its corresponding Voronoi diagram, the number of edges in the latter is also no more than $3n - 6$. Since each region (except the unbounded region) in a Delaunay triangulation is the dual of a vertex in its corresponding Voronoi diagram, the number of vertices of the latter is at most $2n - 5$. Thus, we have the following theorem:

Theorem 18.2 *Let $\mathcal{V}(S)$ and $\mathcal{D}(S)$ be, respectively, the Voronoi diagram and Delaunay triangulation of a planar point set S, where $|S| = n \geq 3$. Then,*

(1) *the number of vertices and edges in $\mathcal{V}(S)$ is at most $2n - 5$ and $3n - 6$, respectively, and*
(2) *the number of edges in $\mathcal{D}(S)$ is at most $3n - 6$.*

It follows that the size of $\mathcal{V}(S)$ or $\mathcal{D}(S)$ is $\Theta(n)$, which means that both diagrams can be stored using only $\Theta(n)$ of space.

18.2.2 *Construction of the Voronoi diagram*

A straightforward approach to the construction of the Voronoi diagram is the construction of each region one at a time. Since each region is the intersection of $n - 1$ half-planes, the construction of each region can be achieved in $O(n^2)$ time, leading to an $O(n^3)$ algorithm to construct the Voronoi diagram. Indeed, the intersection of $n - 1$ half-planes can be constructed in $O(n \log n)$ time, thereby resulting in an overall time complexity of $O(n^2 \log n)$.

It turns out that the entire Voronoi diagram can be constructed in $O(n \log n)$ time. One method that we will describe in this section uses the divide-and-conquer technique to construct the diagram in $O(n \log n)$ time. In what follows, we will illustrate the method in connection with an example and give only the high-level description of the algorithm. More detailed description of the algorithm can be found in the references (see the bibliographic notes).

Let S be a set of n points in the plane. If $n = 2$, then the Voronoi diagram is the perpendicular bisector of the two points (see Fig. 18.1(b)). Otherwise, S is partitioned into two subsets S_L and S_R consisting of $\lfloor n/2 \rfloor$ and $\lceil n/2 \rceil$ points, respectively. The Voronoi diagrams $\mathcal{V}(S_L)$ and $\mathcal{V}(S_R)$ are then computed and merged to obtain $\mathcal{V}(S)$ (see Fig. 18.6).

In this figure, a set of 16 points $\{1, 2, \ldots, 16\}$ is partitioned into two subsets $S_L = \{1, 2, \ldots, 8\}$ and $S_R = \{9, 10, \ldots, 16\}$ using the median x-coordinate as a separator, that is, the x-coordinate of any point in S_L is

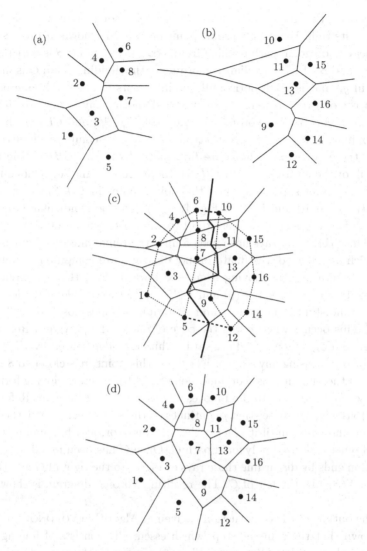

Fig. 18.6.   Construction of the Voronoi diagram.

less than the x-coordinate of any point in S_R. Figures 18.6(a) and 18.6(b) show $\mathcal{V}(S_L)$ and $\mathcal{V}(S_R)$, the Voronoi diagrams of S_L and S_R, respectively. Figure 18.6(c) shows how the merge step is carried out. The basic idea of this step is to find the *dividing chain* C, which is a polygonal curve with the property that any point to its left is closest to some point in S_L and any point to its right is closest to some point in S_R. C is shown in Fig. 18.6(c) as a heavy polygonal path running from $+\infty$ to $-\infty$. Since S is partitioned into S_L and S_R by the median x-coordinate, the dividing chain C is monotonic in y, that is, each horizontal line intercepts C at exactly one point. C consists of a ray, some line segments, and another ray, which are all part of the final constructed Voronoi diagram. Let $CH(S_L)$ and $CH(S_R)$ be the convex hulls of S_L and S_R, respectively. In order to compute the dividing chain, these two convex hulls are first merged to form $CH(S)$, the convex hull of the entire set S. In $CH(S)$, there are two line segments on the upper and lower supporting lines that join a point in $CH(S_L)$ to a point in $CH(S_R)$ ($\overline{6,10}$ and $\overline{5,12}$ in Fig. 18.6(c)). The perpendicular bisectors of these two edges are precisely the two rays of C extending to $+\infty$ and $-\infty$. Once these two rays have been found, the remaining line segments of C, which are edges of the final Voronoi diagram, are computed as follows. We imagine a point p moving from $+\infty$ inward along the ray extending to $+\infty$. Initially, p lies in $V(6)$ and $V(10)$ and proceeds along the locus of points equidistant from points 6 and 10 until it becomes closer to a different point. This occurs when p hits the edge of one of the polygons. Referring to Fig. 18.6(c), as p moves downward, it hits the edge shared by $V(6)$ and $V(8)$ before crossing any edge of $V(10)$. At this point, p is closer to 8 than to 6, and therefore it must continue along the 8,10 bisector. Moving further, p crosses an edge of $V(10)$ and moves off along the 8,11 bisector. Referring again to the figure, we see that p continues on the 8,11 bisector, then the 7,11 bisector and so on until it reaches the 5,12 bisector, at which point it has traced out the desired polygonal path C. Once C has been found, the construction ends by discarding those rays of $\mathcal{V}(S_L)$ to the right of C and those rays of $\mathcal{V}(S_R)$ to the left of C. The resulting Voronoi diagram is shown in Fig. 18.6(d).

The outline of the construction is given in Algorithm VORONOID. It can be shown that the combine step, which essentially consists of finding the dividing chain, takes $O(n)$ time. Since the sorting step takes $O(n \log n)$ time, the overall time taken by the algorithm is $O(n \log n)$. This implies the following theorem:

Theorem 18.3 *The Voronoi diagram of a set of n points in the plane can be constructed in $O(n \log n)$ time.*

Algorithm 18.1 VORONOID
Input: A set S of n points in the plane.

Output: $\mathcal{V}(S)$, the Voronoi diagram of S.

1. Sort S by nondecreasing order of x-coordinates.
2. $\mathcal{V}(S) \leftarrow vd(S, 1, n)$

Algorithm $vd(S, low, high)$
1. If $|S| \leq 3$, then compute $\mathcal{V}(S)$ by a straightforward method and **return** $\mathcal{V}(S)$; otherwise, continue.
2. $mid \leftarrow \lfloor (low + high)/2 \rfloor$
3. $S_L \leftarrow S[low..mid]$; $S_R \leftarrow S[mid + 1..high]$
4. $\mathcal{V}(S_L) \leftarrow vd(S, low, mid)$
5. $\mathcal{V}(S_R) \leftarrow vd(S, mid + 1, high)$
6. Construct the dividing chain C.
7. Remove those rays of $\mathcal{V}(S_L)$ to the right of C and those rays of $\mathcal{V}(S_R)$ to the left of C.
8. **return** $\mathcal{V}(S)$

18.3 Applications of the Voronoi Diagram

The Voronoi diagram of a point set is a versatile and powerful geometric construct that contains almost all the proximity information. In this section, we list some of the problems that can be solved efficiently if the (nearest-point) Voronoi diagram is already available. Some problems can be solved efficiently by first computing the Voronoi diagram.

18.3.1 *Computing the convex hull*

An important property of the Voronoi diagram $\mathcal{V}(S)$ of a point set S is given in the following theorem:

Theorem 18.4 *A Voronoi region $V(p)$ is unbounded if and only if its corresponding point p is on the boundary of $CH(S)$, the convex hull of S.*

Equivalently, the convex hull of S is defined by the boundary of $\mathcal{D}(S)$, the Delaunay triangulation of S. Thus, in $O(n)$ time, it is possible to construct $CH(S)$ from either $\mathcal{V}(S)$ or $\mathcal{D}(S)$. An outline of an algorithm that constructs the convex hull from the Voronoi diagram is as follows. Starting from an arbitrary point p in S, we search for a point whose Voronoi region is unbounded. Once p has been found, its neighbor in $CH(S)$ is that point q whose Voronoi region is separated from that of p by a ray. Continuing this way, we traverse the boundary of the Voronoi diagram until we return back to the initial point p. At this point, the construction of the convex hull is complete.

18.3.2 *All nearest neighbors*

Definition 18.1   Let S be a set of points in the plane and p and q in S. q is said to be a *nearest neighbor* of p if q is closest to p among all points in $S - \{p\}$. That is, q is said to be a nearest neighbor of p if

$$d(p, q) = \min_{r \in S - \{p\}} d(p, r),$$

where $d(p, x)$ is the Euclidean distance between point p and point $x \in S$.

The "nearest neighbor" is a relation on a set S. Observe that this relation is not necessarily symmetric, as is evident from Fig. 18.7. In this figure, p is the nearest neighbor of q, while q is not the nearest neighbors of p.

The all nearest neighbors problem is as follows. Given a set S of n planar points, find a nearest neighbor for each point in S. The solution to this problem is immediate from the following theorem.

Theorem 18.5   *Let S be a set of points in the plane, and p in S. Every nearest neighbor of p defines an edge of the Voronoi region $V(p)$.*

By Theorem 18.5, given $\mathcal{V}(S)$ and a point p in S, its nearest neighbor can be found by examining all its neighbors and returning one with the smallest distance from p. This takes $O(n)$ time, as $V(p)$ may consist of $O(n)$ edges. To find a nearest neighbor for *every* point in S, we need to examine all the Voronoi edges. Since each edge is examined no more than twice (once for each Voronoi region sharing that edge), all nearest neighbors can be found in time proportional to the number of edges in $\mathcal{V}(S)$, i.e., $\Theta(n)$.

Fig. 18.7.   The nearest neighbor relation.

It is interesting that, in the worst case, the time complexity of finding one nearest neighbor is the same as that for finding all nearest neighbors.

18.3.3 *The Euclidean minimum spanning tree*

Given a set S of n points in the plane, the Euclidean minimum spanning tree (EMST) problem asks for a minimum cost spanning tree whose vertices are the given point set and such that the cost between two points is the Euclidean distance between them. The brute-force method is to compute the distance between each pair of points and use one of the known algorithms for computing the minimum cost spanning tree in general graphs (see Sec. 7.3). Using Prim's or Kruskal's algorithms results in time complexities $\Theta(n^2)$ and $O(n^2 \log n)$, respectively. If, however, we have the Delaunay triangulation of the point set, then we can compute the tree in $O(n \log n)$ time. Indeed, an algorithm exists for constructing the minimum spanning tree from the Delaunay triangulation in only $\Theta(n)$ time, but we will not discuss such an algorithm here. The key idea comes from the following theorem, which says that we do not have to examine all the $\Theta(n^2)$ distances between pairs of points; examining those pairs that are connected by a Delaunay triangulation edge is all that we need.

Theorem 18.6 *Let S be a set of points in the plane and let $\{S_1, S_2\}$ be a partition of S. If $\overline{pq}$ is the shortest line segment between points of S_1 and points of S_2, then $\overline{pq}$ is an edge in $\mathcal{D}(S)$, the Delaunay triangulation of S.*

Proof. Suppose that $\overline{pq}$ realizes the shortest distance between points in S_1 and points in S_2, where $p \in S_1$ and $q \in S_2$, but it is not in $\mathcal{D}(S)$. Let m be the midpoint of the line segment $\overline{pq}$. Suppose that $\overline{pq}$ intersects $V(p)$ at edge e. Let r be the neighbor of p such that $V(p)$ and $V(r)$ share the edge e (see Fig. 18.8). It is not hard to show that r lies in the interior of the disk centered at m with diameter $\overline{pq}$. Consequently, $\overline{pq} > \overline{pr}$ and $\overline{pq} > \overline{qr}$. We have two cases. If $r \in S_2$, then $\overline{pq}$ does not realize the shortest distance between S_1 and S_2, since $\overline{pr} < \overline{pq}$. If $r \in S_1$, then $\overline{pq}$ does not realize the shortest distance between S_1 and S_2, since $\overline{qr} < \overline{pq}$. As both cases lead to a contradiction, we conclude that p and q must be neighbors in $\mathcal{V}(S)$, i.e., $\overline{pq}$ is an edge in $\mathcal{D}(S)$. $\qquad\square$

Now, to obtain an $O(n \log n)$ time algorithm, we only need to apply Kruskal's algorithm to the Delaunay triangulation of the point set. Recall

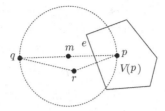

Fig. 18.8.   Illustration of the proof of Theorem 18.6.

that the time complexity of Kruskal's algorithm is $O(m \log m)$, where m is the number of edges, and in any Delaunay triangulation, $m = O(n)$ (Theorem 18.2).

18.4   Farthest-Point Voronoi Diagram

Let $S = \{p_1, p_2, \ldots, p_n\}$ be a set of n points in the plane. The locus of all points in the plane farthest from a point p_i in S than from any other point in S defines a polygonal region $V_f(p_i)$ called the *farthest-point Voronoi region* of p_i. It is an *unbounded* region and is defined only for points on the convex hull of S (see Exercises 18.6 and 18.7). The collection of all farthest-point Voronoi regions constitute the *farthest-point Voronoi diagram* of the point set, denoted by $\mathcal{V}_f(S)$. The Voronoi diagrams of sets of two and three points are shown in Fig. 18.9. The farthest-point Voronoi diagram of two points p_1 and p_2 is just the perpendicular bisector of the line segment $\overline{p_1 p_2}$. As shown in Fig. 18.9(b), the farthest-point Voronoi diagram of three points that are not collinear consists of three bisectors that meet at one point. Compare these two diagrams with the Voronoi diagrams shown in Figs. 18.1(b) and 18.1(c), in which the same point sets were used.

Figure 18.10 shows the farthest-point Voronoi diagram of a number of points chosen randomly in the plane. As in the case of Voronoi diagrams, we will assume that the points are in general position, that is, no three points are collinear and no four points are cocircular, i.e., lie on the circumference of a circle. The following theorem is similar to Theorem 18.1.

Theorem 18.7   *Every farthest-point Voronoi vertex v is the common intersection of three Voronoi edges. Thus, v is the center of a circle $C(v)$ defined by three points in S. Moreover, $C(v)$ contains all other points.*

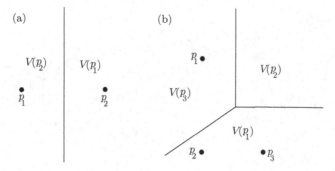

Fig. 18.9.   Farthest-point Voronoi diagrams of two and three points.

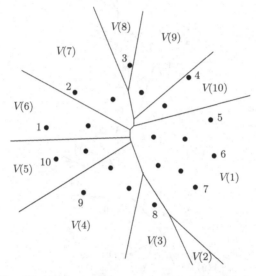

Fig. 18.10.   The farthest-point Voronoi diagram of a set of points.

18.4.1   *Construction of the farthest-point Voronoi diagram*

The construction of the farthest-point Voronoi diagram $\mathcal{V}_f(S)$ of a set of points S starts by discarding all points not on the convex hull, and the rest of the construction is similar to that of the nearest-point Voronoi diagram $\mathcal{V}(S)$ described in Sec. 18.2.2. There are minor modifications that reflect the transition from "nearness" to "farthness". These modifications will be clear from the construction shown in Fig. 18.11.

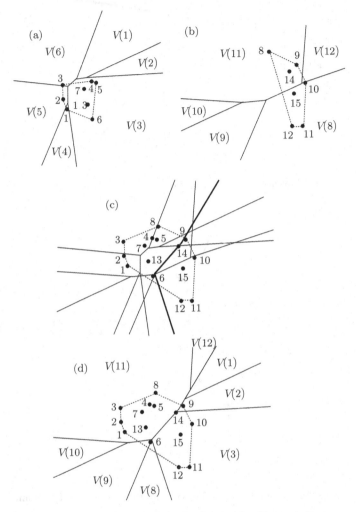

Fig. 18.11.   Construction of the farthest-point Voronoi diagram.

The first modification is in finding the dividing chain C (refer to Figs. 18.11(a)–18.11(c)). When constructing $\mathcal{V}_f(S)$ from $\mathcal{V}_f(S_L)$ and $\mathcal{V}_f(S_R)$, the ray coming from $+\infty$ inward is perpendicular to the *bottom* supporting line of $CH(S_L)$ and $CH(S_R)$, that is, the line segment connecting points 1 and 12 in the figure. This means the ray originates in $V(1)$ of $\mathcal{V}_f(S_L)$ and $V(12)$ of $\mathcal{V}_f(S_R)$. It then intersects the boundary between

$V(11)$ and $V(12)$ of $\mathcal{V}_f(S_R)$ and hence follows the 1,11 bisector. After that, it intersects the boundary between $V(1)$ and $V(2)$ of $\mathcal{V}_f(S_L)$ and hence follows the 2,11 bisector. The dividing chain continues this way until it finally becomes perpendicular to the *upper* supporting line that connects the points 3 and 8. It then continues in this direction indefinitely.

The second modification is in removing rays of $\mathcal{V}_f(S_L)$ and $\mathcal{V}_f(S_R)$ when merging them to obtain $\mathcal{V}_f(S)$. In this case, the rays of $\mathcal{V}_f(S_L)$ to the *left* of the dividing chain and the rays of $\mathcal{V}_f(S_R)$ to the *right* of the dividing chain are removed. The resulting farthest-point Voronoi diagram is shown in Fig. 18.11(d). Thus, the algorithm for the construction of the farthest-point Voronoi diagram is identical to that for constructing the Voronoi diagram except for the two modifications stated above.

The outline of the construction is given in Algorithm FPVORONOID.

Algorithm 18.2 FPVORONOID
Input: A set S of n points in the plane.

Output: $\mathcal{V}_f(S)$, the farthest-point Voronoi diagram of S.

1. Sort S by nondecreasing order of x-coordinates.
2. $\mathcal{V}_f(S) \leftarrow$ fpvd$(S, 1, n)$

Algorithm fpvd$(S, low, high)$
1. If $|S| \leq 3$, then compute $\mathcal{V}_f(S)$ by a straightforward method and **return** $\mathcal{V}_f(S)$; otherwise, continue.
2. $mid \leftarrow \lfloor (low + high)/2 \rfloor$
3. $S_L \leftarrow S[low..mid]$; $S_R \leftarrow S[mid+1..high]$
4. $\mathcal{V}_f(S_L) \leftarrow$ fpvd(S, low, mid)
5. $\mathcal{V}_f(S_R) \leftarrow$ fpvd$(S, mid+1, high)$
6. Construct the dividing chain C.
7. Remove those rays of $\mathcal{V}_f(S_L)$ to the left of C and those rays of $\mathcal{V}_f(S_R)$ to the right of C.
8. **return** $\mathcal{V}_f(S)$

18.5 Applications of the Farthest-Point Voronoi Diagram

The farthest-point Voronoi diagram is used to answer questions or compute some results that have to do with "farthness", e.g., clustering and covering. In this section, we touch on two problems that can be solved efficiently by means of the farthest-point Voronoi diagram.

18.5.1 *All farthest neighbors*

Definition 18.2 Let S be a set of points in the plane, and p and q in S. q is said to be a *farthest neighbor* of p if q is farthest from p among all other points in $S - \{p\}$. That is, q is said to be a farthest neighbor of p if

$$d(p, q) = \max_{r \in S - \{p\}} d(p, r),$$

where $d(p, x)$ is the Euclidean distance between point p and point $x \in S$.

The "farthest neighbor" is a relation on a set S that is not necessarily symmetric. For each point p, we need to find in what farthest-point Voronoi region p lies. If p lies in $V(q)$, then q is the farthest neighbor of p. Thus, the problem becomes a *point location* problem, which we will not pursue here. It suffices to say that the diagram can be preprocessed in $O(n \log n)$ time to produce a data structure that can be used to answer in $O(\log n)$ time any query of the form: Given any point x (not necessarily in S), return the region in which x lies. It follows that, after preprocessing $\mathcal{V}_f(S)$, the farthest neighbors of all the points in S can be computed in $O(n \log n)$ time.

18.5.2 *Smallest enclosing circle*

Consider the following problem. Given a set S of n points in the plane, find the smallest circle that encloses them. This problem has received a lot of attention and is familiar in operations research as the *facilities location problem*. The smallest enclosing circle is unique and is either the circumcircle of three points in S or is defined by two points as the diameter. The obvious brute-force approach, which considers all two-element and three-element subsets of S, leads to a $\Theta(n^4)$ time algorithm. Using $\mathcal{V}_f(S)$, finding the smallest enclosing circle becomes straightforward. First, find $CH(S)$ and compute $D = diam(S)$, the diameter of S (see Sec. 17.6). If the circle with diameter D encloses the points, then we are done. Otherwise, we test every *vertex* of $\mathcal{V}_f(S)$ as a candidate for the center of the enclosing circle and return the smallest circle; recall that a vertex of a farthest-point Voronoi diagram is the center of a circle that is defined by three points on $CH(S)$ and encloses all other points (Theorem 18.7). Computing $CH(S)$ takes $O(n \log n)$ time. Computing the diameter from $CH(S)$ takes $\Theta(n)$ time. Constructing $\mathcal{V}_f(S)$ from $CH(S)$ takes $O(n \log n)$ time. In fact, $\mathcal{V}_f(S)$ can be constructed from $CH(S)$ in $O(n)$ time. Finally, since the diagram

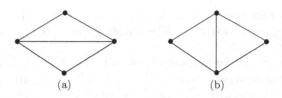

Fig. 18.12.   Two triangulations of a set of four points.

consists of $O(n)$ vertices, finding the smallest enclosing circle takes only $O(n)$ time. It follows that finding the smallest enclosing circle using the farthest-point Voronoi diagram takes $O(n \log n)$ time. Finally, we remark that finding the smallest enclosing circle can be solved in $\Theta(n)$ time by solving a variant of a three-dimensional linear programming problem.

18.6   Practice Problems

18.1 Draw the Voronoi diagram of four points that are the corners of a square.

18.2 Which of the two triangulations shown in Fig. 18.12 is a Delaunay triangulation? Explain.

18.3 The *one-dimensional* Voronoi diagram of a set of points $\{x_1, x_2, \ldots, x_n\}$ on the x-axis is a set of points $\{v_1, v_2, \ldots, v_{n-1}\}$ such that v_i is the midpoint of the line segment $\overline{x_i x_{i+1}}$. Give an efficient algorithm to determine whether a given point set $\{v_1, v_2, \ldots, v_{n-1}\}$ is a one-dimensional Voronoi diagram.

18.4 Let $\mathcal{V}(S)$ be the Voronoi diagram of a point set S. Let $x \in S$. Describe how to find the nearest neighbor(s) of x in S.

18.5 Give a brute-force algorithm to compute the Voronoi diagram of a planar point set.

18.6 Prove that the farthest neighbor of a point p in a point set S is one of the vertices of the convex hull of S.

18.7   Exercises

18.1. Give an example of a set S of n points in the plane such that one of the regions of $\mathcal{V}(S)$ has $n - 1$ vertices.

18.2. Show that the problem of computing $\mathcal{V}(S)$ for a point set S of n points requires $\Omega(n \log n)$ by reducing the problem of sorting to it.

18.3. Let $\mathcal{V}(S)$ be the Voronoi diagram of a point set S. Let x and y be two points such that $x \in S$ but $y \notin S$. Assume further that y lies in the Voronoi polygon of x. Explain how to construct efficiently $\mathcal{V}(S \cup \{y\})$.

18.4. Use the result of Exercise 18.3 to find an incremental algorithm that constructs $\mathcal{V}(S)$ by processing the points in S one point at a time. What is the time complexity of your algorithm?

18.5. Let $\mathcal{V}(S)$ be the Voronoi diagram of a planar point set S. Let $x \in S$. Explain how to construct efficiently $\mathcal{V}(S - \{x\})$.

18.6. Explain how to obtain the Euclidean minimum spanning tree of a set of points in the plane S directly from $\mathcal{D}(S)$ in $\Theta(n)$ time.

18.7. Prove that for any set of points in the plane, $\mathcal{V}_f(S) = \mathcal{V}_f(CH(S))$ (see Problem 18.6).

18.8. Let P be a convex polygon. Assume for simplicity that each of its vertices has only one farthest neighbor. For any vertex x of P, denote by $f(x)$ the farthest neighbor of x. Show that for two vertices x and y that are the endpoints of an edge, the two line segments $\overline{xf(x)}$ and $\overline{yf(y)}$ must intersect.

18.9. Modify Algorithm FPVORONOID for the construction of the farthest-point Voronoi diagram of a set of points S so that in each recursive call, the algorithm discards all points that are not on the convex hull.

18.10. Let S be a set of points in the plane. Assume for simplicity that each point has only one farthest neighbor. For each point $x \in S$ denote by $f(x)$ the farthest neighbor of x. Let $d(x, y)$ denote the Euclidean distance between x and y. Let x, y and z be three distinct points in S such that $f(x) = y$ and $f(y) = z$. Prove that

$$d(x, y) < d(y, z).$$

18.11. This exercise is a generalization of Exercise 18.10. For a point $x \in S$, show that the finite sequence

$$d(x, f(x)), d(f(x), f(f(x))), d(f(f(x)), f(f(f(x)))), \ldots.$$

is strictly increasing except the last two elements of the sequence, which must be equal.

18.8 Bibliographic Notes

The subject of Voronoi diagrams, especially the nearest-point Voronoi diagrams, can be found in several books on computational geometry, including de Berg *et al.* (1997), Edelsbrunner (1987), Mehlhorn (1984c), O'Rourke (1994), Preparata and Shamos (1985) and Toussaint (1984). The divide-and-conquer algorithm for the construction of Voronoi diagrams appeared first in Shamos and Hoey (1975). The Voronoi diagram can also be computed using line sweeping in $O(n \log n)$ time (Fortune, 1992). This algorithm appears in Fortune (1978). An algorithm for computing the Delaunay triangulation of a point set in the plane (and hence its Voronoi diagram) from three-dimensional convex hull is due to Edelsbrunner and Seidel (1986), although Brown (1979b) was the first to establish a connection of Voronoi diagrams to convex hulls in one higher dimension. This algorithm is detailed in O'Rourke (1994). A simple $O(n \log n)$ iterative algorithm for the construction of the farthest-point Voronoi diagram can be found in Skyum (1991). This algorithm was used to generate the drawings of the farthest point Voronoi diagrams in this chapter. It is a modification of a simple algorithm for computing the smallest enclosing circle. Two survey papers on Voronoi diagrams are Aurenhammer (1991) and Fortune (1992). The book by Okabe *et al.* (1992) covers algorithms as well as applications of Voronoi diagrams.

PART 8

Techniques in Parallel Algorithms

In the past few decades, there has been an interest in the study, design and analysis of parallel algorithms. This is mainly attributed to their importance in many fields like image processing, computer vision and weather forecasting, to mention a few.

Chapter 19 is concerned with the study of parallel algorithms. This chapter is intended to be an introduction to this field from both theoretical and practical points of view. In this chapter, the study of parallel computer architectures and the algorithms design techniques for these architectures will form the nucleus of study. The chapter starts with a study of the well-known PRAM model of computation and some of the algorithms designed for it. This is followed by a study of the most common computer architectures, the hypercube and the mesh. The parallel algorithms design techniques are either studied separately or are embedded in the descriptions of some algorithms.

Chapter 19

Parallel Algorithms

19.1 Introduction

In the previous chapters, we were interested in sequential algorithms, in which a single processor is used to execute an algorithm with the RAM as the main model of computation. In this chapter, we are concerned with parallel algorithms, those that make use of more than one processor. Parallel computing is a type of computing architecture in which several processors execute or process an application or computation simultaneously. Parallel computing helps in performing large computations by dividing the workload between more than one processor, all of which work through the computation at the same time. We start this chapter with two simple examples of parallel algorithms.

Example 19.1   Consider the problem of adding n numbers $s = a_1 + a_2 + \cdots + a_n$, where $n = 2^k$ for some nonnegative integer k. Sequentially, the expression can be computed by scanning the input from left to right in the obvious way using $n - 1$ additions. In parallel, $b_1 = a_1 + a_2, b_2 = a_3 + a_4, \ldots, b_{n/2} = a_{n-1} + a_n$ are computed in one parallel step using $n/2$ processors to produce a new expression $b_1 + b_2 + \cdots + b_{n/2}$ consisting of $n/2$ operands. Then, $c_1 = b_1 + b_2, c_2 = b_3 + b_4, \ldots, c_{n/4} = b_{n/2-1} + b_{n/2}$ are computed in one parallel step using $n/4$ processors to produce a new expression $c_1 + c_2 + \cdots + c_{n/4}$ consisting of $n/4$ operands. This process continues until there is only one value left. The total number of parallel steps is $k = \log n$ using $n/2$ processors.

Example 19.2   Recall the search problem: Given a set $X = \{x_1, x_2, \ldots, x_n\}$ of n unordered and distinct elements and an element y, determine j such that $y = x_j$ if $y \in X$ and $j = 0$ otherwise. n comparisons are needed in the worst case to solve this problem sequentially. In parallel, assume there are n processors $P_1, P_2, \ldots, P_n$, and that x_i is stored in P_i, $1 \le i \le n$. Initially, P_1 sets $j = 0$. Then, all processors P_i compare y with x_i simultaneously. If $y \in X$, only one processor P_k will succeed in setting $j = k$. It follows that the problem can be solved in two parallel steps using n processors. Notice that concurrent read capability is required, as all processors need to read y at the same time.

Unlike in sequential algorithms, the performance measures include the number of processors and communication cost. Let n be the input size, and p the number of processors. Then, $T(n, p)$, or simply $T(n)$ if p is known from the context, denotes the *running time* of the algorithm using p processors. If the algorithm has two parameters, n and m, then we write $T(n, m, p)$. We may also write $T(n, p)$ or $T(n, m)$ if m or p are known from the context. In Example 19.1, $T(n, n/2) = \Theta(\log n)$, while in Example 19.2, $T(n, n) = \Theta(1)$. The *cost* of an algorithm is the product of running time and number of processors, that is, $C(n, p) = pT(n, p)$. In Example 19.1, $C(n, n/2) = \Theta(n \log n)$, while in Example 19.2, $C(n, n) = \Theta(n)$. The *work* done by an algorithm is the total number of operations done by individual processors. It is less than or equal to the cost of the algorithm. In Example 19.1, $W(n, n/2) = n/2 + n/4 + \cdots + 1 = n - 1 = \Theta(n)$, while in Example 19.2, $W(n, n) = \Theta(n)$, since there are n comparisons.

The ratio $S(p) = T(n, 1)/T(n, p)$ is called the *speedup* of the algorithm, where $T(n, 1)$ should be taken from the best sequential algorithm. An algorithm achieves a *perfect speedup* if $S(p) = p$. In Example 19.1, $S(n/2) = \Theta(n/\log n)$, while in Example 19.2, $S(n) = \Theta(n)$. A useful measure of the utilization of the processors is the *efficiency* of a parallel algorithm, which is defined as $E(n, p) = S(p)/p = T(n, 1)/pT(n, p)$. The efficiency is the ratio of the time used by one processor with a sequential algorithm and the total time used by p processors, which is the cost of the algorithm. The efficiency indicates the percentage of the processors' time that is not wasted, compared to the sequential algorithm. If $E(n, p) = 1$, then the amount of work done by all processors throughout the execution of the algorithm is equal to the amount of work required by the sequential algorithm. In this case, we get the optimal use of the processors. So, the goal is to maximize the efficiency. In Example 19.1, $E(n, n/2) = \Theta(1/\log n)$, while in Example 19.2, $E(n, n) = \Theta(n)/n\Theta(1) = \Theta(1)$.

19.1.1 *Classifications of parallel architectures*

There are four classifications of parallel architectures based upon the number of concurrent instruction streams and data streams available in the architecture.

(1) Single instruction stream, single data stream (SISD): Most conventional computers with one CPU belong to this class. Examples of SISD architecture are the traditional uniprocessor machines like older personal computers and mainframe computers. By 2010, many personal computers had multiple cores.

(2) Single instruction stream, multiple data streams (SIMD): This category includes machines with a single program and multiple CPUs. In this class, a parallel computer consists of p identical processors. All processors operate under the control of a single instruction stream issued by a central control unit. Processors communicate among themselves during the computation in order to exchange data or intermediate results in two ways, giving rise to two subclasses: SIMD computers where communication is through a shared memory and those where it is done via an interconnection network.

(3) Multiple instruction streams, single data stream (MISD): This is an uncommon and unrealistic architecture.

(4) Multiple instruction streams, multiple data streams (MIMD): This class of computers is the most general and most powerful. In this class, there are p processors, p streams of instructions and p streams of data. The machines that fall into this category are capable of executing several programs independently. They include multi-core superscalar processors, and distributed systems, using either one shared memory space or a distributed memory space. In MIMD, processors may have multiple processing cores that can execute different instructions on different data. Most parallel computers, as of 2013, are MIMD systems.

19.2 Shared-Memory Computers (PRAM)

The PRAM was intended as the parallel-computing analogy to the random-access machine (RAM). It is used to model parallel algorithmic performance, such as time complexity, where the number of processors assumed is typically also stated. As in the RAM, the PRAM model neglects such issues as synchronization and communication but includes the number of processors. Algorithm cost, for instance, is estimated using two parameters: time × number of processors. Read/write conflicts are resolved by one of the following strategies:

- **Exclusive read exclusive write (EREW):** In this strategy, every processor can read or write to a memory cell at a time.
- **Concurrent read exclusive write (CREW):** Here, multiple processors can read a memory cell but only one can write to it at a time.
- **Exclusive read concurrent write (ERCW):** This is never considered.
- **Concurrent read concurrent write (CRCW):** In this strategy, multiple processors can read from or write to the same memory cell at the same time.

In the CRCW, the writes cause some discrepancies, and hence the write is further defined as:

- COMMON: If all processors write the same value, it is successful; otherwise, it is illegal.
- ARBITRARY: Only one arbitrary attempt by an arbitrary processor is successful.
- PRIORITY: Processors are ranked, and processor with the maximum rank can write.
- Array reduction binary operation like SUM, Logical AND or MAX of processor contents. For instance, only the maximum of processors' contents can be written.

In the PRAM, there is no limit on the number of processors in the machine. Any memory location is uniformly accessible from any processor, and there is no limit on the amount of shared memory in the system.

19.2.1 *The balanced tree method*

The balanced tree method is one of the parallel algorithmic design techniques usually implemented either as the main component or as a subtask of the parallel algorithm. Let ∘ be a binary associative operation (e.g., $+, \times, \min, \max$) and consider computing the expression

$$s = a_1 \circ a_2 \circ \cdots \circ a_n,$$

where $n = 2^k$ for some nonnegative integer k (see Example 19.1). Sequentially, the expression can be computed by scanning the input from left to right in the obvious way. In parallel, $b_1 = a_1 \circ a_2, b_2 = a_3 \circ a_4, \ldots, b_{n/2} = a_{n-1} \circ a_n$ are computed in one parallel step to produce a new expression $s = b_1 \circ b_2 \circ \ldots \circ b_{n/2}$ consisting of $n/2$ operands. This process continues until there is only one value to compute. This procedure defines a complete binary tree where the input is initially at its leaves, and each internal node corresponds to a subproblem, while the root corresponds to the overall problem. Each leaf node is assigned a processor $P_i, 1 \le i \le n$. The internal nodes at level $j, 0 \le j \le k - 1$, are assigned processors $P_1, P_2, \ldots, P_{2^j}$. The computations at the internal nodes of the same level are performed in one parallel step. Figure 19.1 depicts a typical complete binary tree for $n = 8$. It has $2n - 1$ nodes. Note that it is represented by the array $B[1..2n - 1]$, where the children for $B[j], 1 \le j \le n - 1$, are stored at $B[2j]$ and $B[2j+1]$ (see Sec. 2.6). For $j, 1 \le j \le n - 1$, if $B[2j] = x$ and $B[2j + 1] = y$, then $B[j] = x \circ y$.

Algorithm PARADDITION below performs the operation of addition on n numbers stored initially in array $A[1..n]$. The first **for** loop copies the numbers in A into $B[n], B[n + 1], \ldots, B[2n - 1]$, which correspond to the leaves of the binary tree. The **for** loop in Line 3 is repeated $k = \log n$ times, once for each internal level of the tree. The **for** loop at line 4 is for performing 2^i additions in parallel, $i = k - 1, k - 2, \ldots, 0$.

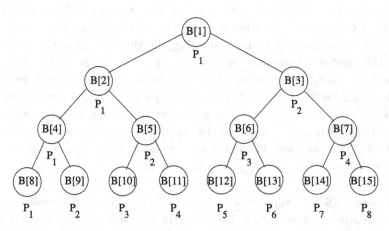

Fig. 19.1. The computation of $s = a_1 \circ a_2 \circ \ldots \circ a_n$.

Algorithm 19.1 PARADDITION
Input: $A[1..n]$, an array of n numbers, where $n = 2^k$.
Output: $A[1] + A[2] + \ldots + A[n]$.

1. **for** $j \leftarrow 1$ **to** n **do in parallel**
2. $\quad B[j + n - 1] \leftarrow A[j]$
3. **for** $i \leftarrow k - 1$ **downto** 0
4. $\quad$ **for** $j \leftarrow 2^i$ **to** $2^{i+1} - 1$ **do in parallel**
5. $\quad\quad B[j] \leftarrow B[2j] + B[2j + 1]$
6. $\quad$ **end for**
7. **end for**
8. **return** $B[1]$

The running time of the algorithm is equal to the depth of the binary tree, which is $\Theta(\log n)$. The work done by the algorithm is proportional to the number of additions performed in the internal nodes, which is $n - 1$. The cost of the algorithm is $\Theta(n \log n)$.

19.2.2 Brent theorem

Consider the algorithm for finding the maximum of n numbers on the EREW PRAM using the balanced tree method (see Fig. 19.1). The algorithm uses $n/2$ processors. Note that $n/2$ processors are actually required by the first step of the algorithm. In the second step, only $n/4$ processors are needed. In the third step, only $n/8$ processors are needed, and so on. Therefore, in a very short time, most of the processors will be idle. The running time of the algorithm is $\Theta(\log n)$. We can reduce the number of processors significantly without affecting the time complexity as follows. Let the number of processors be $n/\log n$, and assign $\log n$ numbers to each processor. Now, each processor finds the maximum in its group sequentially using $\log n - 1$ comparisons, and the parallel algorithm continues to find the maximum of the $n/\log n$ group maxima. Thus, the running time is still $\Theta(\log n)$, while the cost of the algorithm is reduced from $\Theta(n \log n)$ to $\Theta(n)$. The following theorem, known as Brent theorem, generalizes the above discussion.

Theorem 19.1 *Suppose an algorithm A_p performs t_p parallel steps using p processors on the PRAM such that the total number of operations over all processors is s, and let $q = s/t_p$. Then, there exists an algorithm*

A_q *that performs at most* $2t_p$ *parallel steps using* q *processors. Moreover, if the sequential time complexity is* $O(s)$*, then the cost of* A_q *is optimal.*

Proof. Let $s_i, 1 \leq i \leq t_p$, be the number of operations performed by all p processors in step i of Algorithm A_p. Let Algorithm A_q emulate A_p by replacing each parallel step i of A_p by $\lceil s_i/q \rceil$ parallel steps. The total number of parallel steps performed by algorithm A_q is thus

$$t_q = \sum_{i=1}^{t_p} \left\lceil \frac{s_i}{q} \right\rceil$$

$$= \sum_{i=1}^{t_p} \left\lceil \frac{s_i \times t_p}{s} \right\rceil$$

$$\leq \sum_{i=1}^{t_p} \left(\frac{s_i \times t_p}{s} + 1 \right)$$

$$= t_p + \frac{t_p}{s} \sum_{i=1}^{t_p} s_i$$

$$= 2t_p,$$

since $\sum_{i=1}^{t_p} s_i = s$. The new cost of the algorithm is $\leq 2t_p \times \frac{s}{t_p} = 2s = O(s)$. Hence, if the sequential time complexity is $O(s)$, then Algorithm A_q is cost-optimal. $\square$

Thus, in O-notation, if the original running time is $O(t_p)$, and the work is $O(s)$, then the number of processors can be reduced to $O(s/t_p)$ without increasing the running time. Recall Algorithm PARADDITION in Sec. 19.2.1 for the addition of n numbers using n processors. The running time of the algorithm is $\Theta(\log n)$ and it performs a total of $O(n)$ operations. Its cost is $\Theta(n \log n)$. By Brent theorem, the number of processors can be reduced to $n/\log n$ without changing the time complexity. The new cost is $\Theta(n)$, which is optimal.

19.2.3 *Parallel prefix*

Let $X = \langle x_1, x_2, \ldots, x_n \rangle$ be a sequences of n numbers, where $n = 2^k$ for a nonnegative integer k. Let $\circ$ be a binary associative operation defined on

•X. The *prefix sums* problem is to compute the n partial sums: $s_1 = x_1$, $s_2 = x_1 \circ x_2$, ..., $s_i = x_1 \circ x_2 \circ \cdots \circ x_i$, ..., $s_n = x_1 \circ x_2 \circ \cdots \circ x_n$. It is also called the *scan* or the *scan operation*. Algorithm PARPREFIX below is a simple iterative procedure to compute the prefix sums. The algorithm uses n processors. There are $k = \log n$ iterations in the outer loop in Step 5. Since the time needed for the loop in Step 6 is $\Theta(1)$, the running time of the algorithm is $\Theta(\log n)$. Its cost is $n \times \Theta(\log n) = \Theta(n \log n)$, which is not optimal in view of the $\Theta(n)$ time complexity for the sequential algorithm. The work can be computed as follows. The number of operations done by Step 6 in the first iteration is $n - 1$, and in the jth iteration, it is $n - 2^{j-1}$. Thus, $W(n) = \sum_{j=1}^{k}(n - 2^{j-1}) = \Theta(n \log n)$. The cost can be reduced to $\Theta(n)$ by reducing the number of processors to $n/\log n$ and making some simple modifications.

Algorithm 19.2 PARPREFIX
Input: $X = \langle x_1, x_2, \ldots, x_n \rangle$, a sequence of n numbers, where $n = 2^k$.
Output: $S = \langle s_1, s_2, \ldots, s_n \rangle$, the prefix sums of X.

1. **for** $i \leftarrow 1$ **to** n **do in parallel**
2. $s_i \leftarrow x_i$
3. **end for**
4. $t \leftarrow 1$
5. **for** $j \leftarrow 1$ **to** k
6.   **for** $i \leftarrow t + 1$ **to** n **do in parallel**
7. $s_i \leftarrow s_{i-t} \circ s_i$
8.   **end for**
9. $t \leftarrow 2t$
10. **end for**
11. **return** S

Another algorithm for computing the prefix sums is shown as Algorithm PARPREFIXREC, which is recursive. First, it computes the prefix sums $s_1, s_2, s_4, s_6 \ldots, s_n$. It then computes $s_3, s_5, s_7, \ldots, s_{n-1}$ in the combine step of divide and conquer. Except for the recursive call, the parallel time is $\Theta(1)$. Hence, $T(n) = \Theta(\log n)$. We compute the work done by the algorithm as follows. There are $n/2$ and $n/2 - 1$ iterations in the loops in Steps 3 and 7, respectively. Therefore, $W(n) = W(n/2) + \Theta(n) = \Theta(n)$. The cost, however, is not optimal since the number of processors needed is $n/2$ for a total cost of $\Theta(n \log n)$.

Algorithm 19.3 PARPREFIXREC
Input: $X = \langle x_1, x_2, \ldots, x_n \rangle$, a sequence of n numbers, where $n = 2^k$.
Output: $S = \langle s_1, s_2, \ldots, s_n \rangle$, the prefix sums of X.

1. $s_1 \leftarrow x_1$
2. **if** $n = 1$ **then return** $S = \langle x_1 \rangle$
3. **for** $i \leftarrow 1$ **to** $n/2$ **do in parallel**
4. $x_{2i} \leftarrow x_{2i-1} \circ x_{2i}$
5. **end for**
6. Recursively compute the prefix sums of $\langle x_2, x_4, \ldots, x_n \rangle$ and store them in $\langle s_2, s_4, \ldots, s_n \rangle$
7. **for** $i \leftarrow 2$ **to** $n/2$ **do in parallel**
8. $s_{2i-1} \leftarrow s_{2(i-1)} \circ x_{2i-1}$
9. **end for**
10. **return** $S = \langle s_1, s_2, \ldots, s_n \rangle$

There are no concurrent reads or writes in the above two algorithms, and hence they run on the EREW PRAM.

19.2.3.1 *Array packing*

Let $A = \langle a_1, a_2, \ldots, a_n \rangle$ be an array of n elements such that t of them are "marked" and the remaining $n - t$ elements are "unmarked". The *array packing* problem consists of creating another array D where all the marked elements are moved to the lower part of D and the unmarked ones to the upper part of the array D without changing their relative order. One method of packing consists of assigning a value of 1 to each of the marked elements and a value of 0 to each of the unmarked elements. A new array $B = \langle b_1, b_2, \ldots, b_n \rangle$ is used to hold the 0–1 values, with $b_i = 1$ if and only if a_i is marked. Now, if we apply the prefix sums algorithm to the array B and store the prefix sums in $C = \langle c_1, c_2, \ldots, c_n \rangle$, the ranks of the marked elements will be computed in C. Specifically, if a_i is marked, then it is stored in D at position c_i. So, the marked elements are moved to the first t cells of array D. Likewise, the ranks of the unmarked elements are computed by interchanging 0's and 1's in array B. Finally, the prefix computation is run again and the unmarked elements are moved to the last $n - t$ cells of array D.

Example 19.3 We now illustrate array packing explained above. Referring to Fig 19.2, the problem is to pack the even elements to the left.

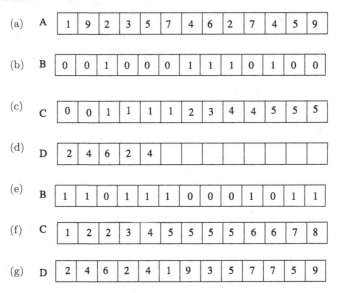

Fig. 19.2.   Example of array packing.

The first row, Fig 19.2(a), contains the input array A. The second row, Fig 19.2(b), contains the 0–1 values in array B. Array C in Fig 19.2(c) of the figure contains the result of applying parallel prefix on array B. Array D in Fig 19.2(d) contains the even numbers packed in their positions as given in array C. If we now interchange 0's and 1's in B, then we can pack the odd numbers using the same procedure to pack the even numbers. This is shown in Figs. 19.2(e)–19.2(g).

19.2.3.2   *Parallel quicksort*

Recall Algorithm QUICKSORT discussed in Sec. 5.6. A parallel version for the EREW PRAM with n processors is shown below as Algorithm PAR-QUICKSORT. As in the sequential quicksort algorithm, the pivot v is chosen as $A[1]$. First, the pivot is copied n times to avoid concurrent reads. This can be done by a broadcasting procedure in time $\Theta(\log n)$ (see Practice question 19.4). Next, array packing is used to partition the array A into two parts, one with elements less than v and one with elements greater than v. This takes $\Theta(\log n)$ as explained in Sec. 19.2.3.1. Next, these two parts are sorted recursively into A_1 and A_2, whose concatenation together with v is returned as the sorted array. In the worst case, the recursion depth can be as large as $\Theta(n)$, causing the running time to be $\Theta(n \log n)$. However, the average recursion depth is $\Theta(\log n)$, for a total running time of $\Theta(\log^2 n)$.

Algorithm 19.4 PARQUICKSORT
Input: An array $A[1..n]$ of n distinct numbers.

Output: A sorted in increasing order.

1. **if** $n = 1$ **then** return A
2. $v \leftarrow A[1]$
3. Let $B[i] = v$ for $1 \leq i \leq n$
4. **for** $i \leftarrow 1$ to n **do in parallel**
5.   **if** $A[i] < B[i]$ **then** $C[i] \leftarrow 1$
6.   **else if** $A[i] > B[i]$ **then** $C[i] \leftarrow 0$
7. **end for**
8. Pack the numbers in A marked 1 in C at the beginning of A followed by v followed by the numbers in A marked 0 in C
9. Let w be the position of v in A
10. **do in parallel**
11. $A_1 \leftarrow$ PARQUICKSORT$(A, 1, w - 1)$
12. $A_2 \leftarrow$ PARQUICKSORT$(A, w + 1, n)$
13. $A \leftarrow A_1 \| v \| A_2$, the concatenation of A_1, v and A_2
14. **return** A

19.2.4 *Parallel search*

Consider the search problem: Given a sequence $S = \langle a_1, a_2, \ldots, a_n \rangle$ of n distinct elements drawn from a linearly ordered set such that $a_1 < a_2 < \cdots < a_n$, and an element x, find the index $k, 1 \leq k \leq n$, such that $x = a_k$ if $x \in S$ and 0 otherwise. Assume that we have a CREW PRAM with p processors, $1 \leq p < n$. For convenience, let $n = (p+1)q$. First, the sequence S is divided into $p + 1$ subsequences of q elements each, and x is compared to the elements at the p internal boundaries of these subsequences. That is, the algorithm compares x with p elements simultaneously; processor P_i compares x with a_{iq} for $1 \leq i \leq p$. We have the following cases:

(1) If for some i, $1 \leq i \leq p$, $x = a_{iq}$, the algorithm returns $k = iq$ and halts.

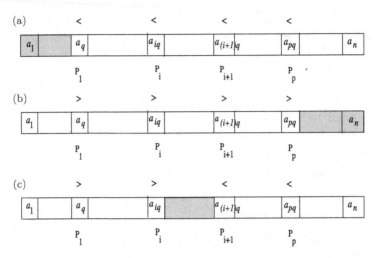

Fig. 19.3. Parallel search.

(2) $x < a_q$, and hence only the elements less than a_q are kept for the next stage. This is shown as the shaded area in Fig. 19.3(a). In this case, the algorithm returns the index of x in $\langle a_1, a_2, \ldots, a_{q-1} \rangle$.

(3) $x > a_{pq}$, and hence only the elements greater than a_{pq} are kept for the next stage. This is shown as the shaded area in Fig. 19.3(b). In this case, the algorithm returns pq plus the index of x in $\langle a_{pq+1}, a_{pq+2}, \ldots, a_n \rangle$.

(4) There exists an i, $1 \leq i < p$, such that $x > a_{iq}$ and $x < a_{(i+1)q}$. The next stage performs the search on $\langle a_{iq+1}, a_{iq+2}, \ldots, a_{(i+1)q-1} \rangle$. This is shown as the shaded area in Fig. 19.3(c). In this case, the algorithm returns iq plus the index of x in $\langle a_{iq+1}, a_{iq+2}, \ldots, a_{(i+1)q-1} \rangle$.

The above discussion is summarized in Algorithm PARSEARCH.

In Step 1, all processors read x simultaneously in one step. Step 2 is the stopping condition for recursion, which happens when the number of remaining elements drops as or below the number of processors. In this case, n processors are allocated, and each processor tests one element for equality against x. If one processor finds element $a_i = x$, it sets $k = i$. The remaining steps are as explained above.

The size of the recursive call is approximately $\frac{n}{p+1}$. Hence, the running time is given by the recurrence $T(n) = T(n/(p+1)) + \Theta(1)$ whose solution is $T(n) = \log_{p+1} n = \frac{\log n}{\log(p+1)}$. There are p element comparisons in each stage

---

Algorithm 19.5 PARSEARCH
Input: A sequence $S = \langle a_1, a_2, \ldots, a_n \rangle$ of n distinct elements such that
$\qquad a_1 < a_2 < \cdots < a_n$ and an element x.
Output: The index $k, 1 \leq k \leq n$, such that $x = a_k$ if $x \in S$ and 0 otherwise.

1. Initialize: $k \leftarrow 0$, All processors read x
2. **if** $n \leq p$ use n processors to compare x with $a_i, 1 \leq i \leq n$, and **return** k.
3. $q \leftarrow n/(p+1)$
4. **for** $i \leftarrow 1$ **to** p **do in parallel**
5. $\quad$ Processor P_i compares x with a_{iq}
6. $\quad$ **if** $x = a_{iq}$ **return** $k = iq$
7. **if** $x < a_q$ **then**
8. $\quad$ let $S' = \langle a_1, a_2, \ldots, a_{q-1} \rangle$
9. $\quad$ $k \leftarrow$ PARSEARCH(S', x)
10. $\quad$ **return** k
11. **else if** $x > a_{pq}$ **then**
12. $\quad$ let $S' = \langle a_{pq+1}, a_{pq+2}, \ldots, a_n \rangle$
13. $\quad$ $k \leftarrow$ PARSEARCH(S', x)
14. $\quad$ **return** $k + pq$
15. **else let** i be such that $x > a_{iq}$ and $x < a_{(i+1)q}$.
16. $\quad$ let $S' = \langle a_{iq+1}, a_{iq+2}, \ldots, a_{(i+1)q-1} \rangle$
17. $\quad$ $k \leftarrow$ PARSEARCH(S', x)
18. $\quad$ **return** $k + iq$
19. **end if**
20. **return** $k = 0$

---

for a total of $p \log_{p+1} n$, hence the work done by the algorithm is $W(n) = p \log_{p+1} n$. If $p = n^\epsilon, 0 < \epsilon < 1$, then $T(n) = \Theta(1)$ and $W(n) = \Theta(n^\epsilon)$.

19.2.5 *Pointer jumping*

Let L denote a linked list of n elements, and let us associate a processor with each element in the list. Each element x has two fields: $succ(x)$ and $dist(x)$. $succ(x)$ is a pointer that points to the next element in the list. The $succ$ field of the last element points to itself, that is, $succ(n) = n$. The other field $dist$ is initially 1 if $succ(x) \neq x$ and 0 if $succ(x) = x$. It is required to develop an algorithm to compute for each element x its distance from the end of the list and to store it in $dist(x)$. Algorithm PJUMPING below computes the distances from each node to the end of the list using a technique called *pointer jumping* or *doubling*.

Algorithm 19.6 PJUMPING
Input: A Linked list $L = (dist(x), succ(x))$, $1 \le x \le n$.
Output: $dist(x), 1 \le x \le n$, the distance of x from the end of the list.

1. **for** $x \leftarrow 1$ **to** n **do in parallel**
2. $s(x) \leftarrow succ(x)$
3.   **while** $s(x) \ne s(s(x))$
4. $dist(x) \leftarrow dist(x) + dist(s(x))$
5. $s(x) \leftarrow s(s(x))$
6.   **end while**
7. **end for**

Pointer jumping consists of updating the successor of each node by that node successor's successor. Thus, the distance between a node and its successor doubles unless it is its own successor. Hence, after k iterations, the distance between a node x and its successor is 2^k unless $succ(x)$ is the last element in the list. It follows that the **while** loop is executed $\lceil \log n \rceil$ times, which means the parallel time complexity of the algorithm is $T(n) = \Theta(\log n)$. Its cost, however, is $\Theta(n \log n)$ since there are n processors. Figure 19.4 illustrates the algorithm for a list of seven elements. Each pointer $s(x)$ is shown as an arc from one element to another, and the arc from element x is labeled with the current value of $dist(x)$. The top of the figure shows the original list, and the rest are the list after each one of the three iterations.

19.2.6 *Merging by ranking*

Given a sequence S and an element x, let rank(x, S) be the number of elements in S less than x. Equivalently, rank(x, S) is the index of the largest element in S less than x. It is not hard to modify Algorithm PARSEARCH given in Section 19.2.4 so that on input S and x, it returns rank(x, S). We will refer to the modified algorithm as Algorithm MODPARSEARCH.

19.2.6.1 *Computing ranks*

Let $A = \langle a_1, a_2, \ldots, a_n \rangle$ and $B = \langle b_1, b_2, \ldots, b_m \rangle$ be two sequences of $n + m$ distinct numbers, each sorted in increasing order. The problem of merging A and B into a new sequence $C = \langle c_1, c_2, \ldots, c_{m+n} \rangle$ may be solved in parallel by computing for each $x \in A \cup B$, $r_A = \text{rank}(x, A)$ and $r_B = \text{rank}(x, B)$,

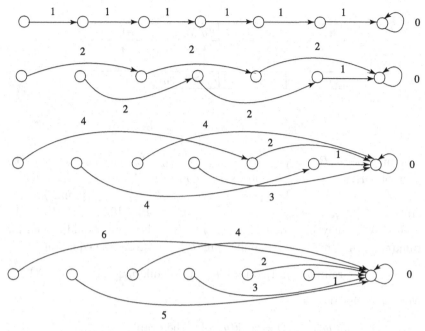

Fig. 19.4. Pointer jumping.

and setting $c_k = x$, where $k = r_A + r_B + 1$. The ranks of all items in B are found in parallel, where a processor P_i is assigned to each element $b_i \in B$. To find $\text{rank}(b_i, A)$, P_i performs binary search on A, and this is done for all $b_i \in B$ in parallel. To compute the rank of b_i in B, we use the identity $\text{rank}(b_i, B) = i - 1$. Next, we repeat the above procedure for all items $a_j \in A$ to find $\text{rank}(a_j, B)$ and set $\text{rank}(a_j, A) = j - 1$. The above algorithm works on the CREW PRAM in time $O(\max\{\log n, \log m\})$.

In what follows, we present a faster algorithm that runs in time $O(\log \log n)$ for the case $m = n$. First, we develop an algorithm for computing $\text{rank}(B, A) = \{\text{rank}(b, A) \mid b \in B\}$; finding $\text{rank}(A, B)$ can be achieved in a similar fashion. For clarity, let $s = \sqrt{m}$. First, use Algorithm MOD-PARSEARCH to compute in parallel the ranks of $b_s, b_{2s}, \ldots, b_m$, using $\sqrt{n}$ processors for each rank. Call these ranks $r(s), r(2s), \ldots, r(m)$. This divides the remaining elements in B into s subsequences $B_0, B_1, \ldots, B_{s-1}$ of $s - 1$ elements each, where $B_0 = \{b_1, b_2, \ldots, b_{s-1}\}$, $B_1 = \{b_{s+1}, b_{s+2}, \ldots, b_{2s-1}\}$,

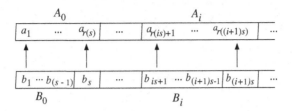

Fig. 19.5. Computing $\text{rank}(B, A)$.

and in general $B_i = \{b_{is+1}, b_{is+2}, \ldots, b_{(i+1)s-1}\}$. This induces a partition of $\{a_1, a_2, \ldots, a_{r(m)}\}$ into s subsequences $A_0, A_1, \ldots, A_{s-1}$, where $A_0 = \{a_1, a_2, \ldots, a_{r(s)}\}$, $A_1 = \{a_{r(s)+1}, a_{r(s)+2}, \ldots, a_{r(2s)}\}$ and in general $A_i = \{a_{r(is)+1}, a_{r(is)+2}, \ldots, a_{r((i+1)s)}\}$ (see Fig. 19.5). Note that $|A_i|$ may vary; it may be 0 or n. Let $b_{is+j} \in B_i$. Then, we should search for $\text{rank}(b_{is+j}, A_i)$ in A_i and compute $\text{rank}(b_{is+j}, A)$ from the equation

$$\text{rank}(b_{is+j}, A) = \text{rank}(b_{is}, A) + \text{rank}(b_{is+j}, A_i). \tag{19.1}$$

Note that this means

If $\text{rank}(b_{(i+1)s}, A) = \text{rank}(b_{is}, A)$, then $\text{rank}(b_{is+j}, A_i) = 0$.

Thus, the problem of computing the ranks of B in A reduces to computing the ranks of B_i in A_i, $0 \leq i \leq s-1$. Call the algorithm recursively on (A_i, B_i) to compute $\text{rank}(B_i, A_i)$ for $0 \leq i \leq s-1$. For $b_{is+j} \in B_i$, let $r_i(j) = \text{rank}(b_{is+j}, A_i)$. Thus, as stated in Eq. (19.1), $\text{rank}(b_{is+j}, A) = r(is) + r_i(j)$.

The above discussion is outlined in Algorithm PARRANK below. The algorithm returns $R = \{r(1), r(2), \ldots, r(m)\}$, a set of m ranks, where $r(i) = \text{rank}(b_i, A)$. In Line 7, the algorithm returns $R_i = \{r_i(1), r_i(2), \ldots, r_i(s-1)\}$, a set of $s-1$ ranks corresponding to $\text{rank}(B_i, A_i)$.

It is easy to see that the number of processors used by the algorithm is $O(\sqrt{m}\sqrt{n}) = O(m+n)$ as required by Steps 3 and 4 of the algorithm. Steps 1–4 take constant time. Step 9 takes at most $T(n, \sqrt{m})$ time since $|A_i|$ can be as large as n. Hence, the running time is given by the recurrence

$$T(n, m) \leq \begin{cases} O(1) & \text{if } m < 4 \\ T(n, \sqrt{m}) + O(1) & \text{if } m \geq 4, \end{cases}$$

whose solution is $T(n, m) = O(\log \log m)$. The work done by Steps 1 and 2 of the algorithm is $O(n)$. The number of operations done by Steps 3 and 4

Algorithm 19.7 PARRANK
Input: $A = \langle a_1, a_2, \ldots, a_n \rangle$ and $B = \langle b_1, b_2, \ldots, b_m \rangle$ are two sequences of
$\qquad n + m$ distinct numbers each sorted in increasing order.
Output: rank$(B, A) = \{\text{rank}(b_i, A) \mid b_i \in B\}$.

1. **if** $m < 4$ **then for** $i \leftarrow 1$ **to** m **do in parallel**
2. $\qquad$ Use Algorithm MODPARSEARCH to compute
$\qquad\quad r(i) = \text{rank}(b_i, A)$ using n processors.
3. **for** $i \leftarrow 1$ **to** s **do in parallel**
4. $\qquad$ Use Algorithm MODPARSEARCH to compute
$\qquad\quad r(is) = \text{rank}(b_{is}, A)$ using $\sqrt{n}$ processors.
5. $r(0) \leftarrow 0$
6. **for** $i \leftarrow 0$ **to** $s - 1$ **do in parallel**
7. $\qquad$ **if** $r(is) = r((i+1)s)$ **then** $R_i \leftarrow \{0, 0, \ldots, 0\}$
8. $\qquad$ **else**
9. $\qquad\qquad R_i \leftarrow$ PARRANK(A_i, B_i)
10. $\qquad\qquad$ **for** $j \leftarrow 1$ **to** $s - 1$ **do in parallel**
11. $\qquad\qquad\qquad r(is + j) \leftarrow r(is) + r_i(j)$
12. $\qquad$ **end if**
13. **end for**
14. **return** $R = \{r(1), r(2), \ldots, r(m)\}$

---

is $O(\sqrt{m}\sqrt{n}) = O(m + n)$ since the call to Algorithm MODPARSEARCH performs $O(\sqrt{n}) \times O(1) = O(\sqrt{n})$ operations. The work done by Steps 6–14 of the algorithm except for the recursive calls is $O(m)$. It follows that the overall work done by the algorithm is $W(n, m) = O((n + m) \log \log m)$.

Example 19.4 Let $A = \langle 10, 30, 40, 60, 70, 90, 110, 120 \rangle$ and $B = \langle 20, 50, 80, 100 \rangle$, so $m = 4$ and $n = 8$. $s = 2$, $b_2 = 50$ and $b_4 = 100$. First, the ranks of b_2 and b_4 are computed: $r(2) = 3$ and $r(4) = 6$. Next, B_0, B_1, A_0 and A_1 are computed: $B_0 = \{20\}, B_1 = \{80\}, A_0 = \{10, 30, 40\}$ and $A_1 = \{60, 70, 90\}$. Now, the algorithm recursively computes the ranks of B_0 in A_0 and B_1 in A_1: $r_0(1) = 1$ (which is the rank of 20 in A_0), so $R_0 = \{1\}$ and $r_1(1) = 2$ (which is the rank of 80 in A_1), so $R_1 = \{2\}$. Finally, we compute the ranks of B_0 in A and B_1 in A: $r(1) = r(0) + r_0(1) = 0 + 1 = 1$ and $r(3) = r(2) + r_1(1) = 3 + 2 = 5$. It follows that $R = R(B, A) = \{1, 3, 5, 6\}$.

Example 19.5 Suppose we change B in Example 19.4 to $B = \langle 7, 8, 80, 100 \rangle$. Then, $b_2 = 8$, $r(2) = 0$ and $B_0 = \{7\}$. Also, $A_0 = \{\}$ and $A_1 = \{10, 30, 40, 60, 70, 90\}$. By Step 7 of the algorithm, since $r(0) = r(2)$,

$R_0 = \{0\}$, and thus the algorithm will not be called recursively on A_0 and B_0. Consequently, $r(1) = r(0) + r_0(1) = 0 + 0 = 0$.

19.2.6.2 *Merging*

To merge A and B, we only need to compute $\text{rank}(B, A)$ and $\text{rank}(A, B)$. Algorithm PARMERGE below merges A and B into a sequence C. It is assumed here that $|A| = |B| = n$. Let $b_i \in B$. Then, the index of b_i in C is equal to $\text{rank}(b_i, B) + \text{rank}(b_i, A) + 1 = (i-1) + r(i) + 1 = r(i) + i$. Similarly, for $a_j \in A$, the index of a_j in C is equal to $\text{rank}(a_j, A) + \text{rank}(a_j, B) + 1 = (j-1) + r(j) + 1 = r(j) + j$.

Algorithm 19.8 PARMERGE
Input: $A = \langle a_1, a_2, \ldots, a_n \rangle$ and $B = \langle b_1, b_2, \ldots, b_n \rangle$ are two sequences of $2n$ distinct numbers each sorted in increasing order.
Output: A sequence $C = \langle c_1, c_2, \ldots, c_{2n} \rangle$ which is the merge of A and B.

1. $\{r(1), r(2), \ldots, r(n)\} \leftarrow$ PARRANK(A, B) (Find $\text{rank}(B, A)$)
2. $\{r'(1), r'(2), \ldots, r'(n)\} \leftarrow$ PARRANK(B, A) (Find $\text{rank}(A, B)$)
3. **for** $i \leftarrow 1$ **to** n **do in parallel**
4. $c_{i+r(i)} \leftarrow b_i$
5. $c_{i+r'(i)} \leftarrow a_i$
6. **end for**
7. **return** C

Clearly, the running time of Algorithm PARMERGE is $T(n) = O(\log\log n)$. The cost of the algorithm is $C(n) = O(n \log\log n)$.

19.2.6.3 *Parallel bottom-up merge sorting*

Recall Algorithm BOTTOMUPSORT in Sec. 1.7. The algorithm works by merging pairs of consecutive elements, then merging consecutive pairs to form 4-element sequences, and so on. This algorithm can easily be parallelized as shown below in Algorithm PARBOTTOMUPSORT. Note here that $n = 2^k$ for some positive integer k.

Algorithm PARBOTTOMUPSORT defines a (conceptual) complete binary tree whose nodes are the sequences $S_{i,j}$, $0 \le i \le k, 1 \le j \le 2^{k-i}$. Initially, the elements are stored at the leaves $S_{0,j}, 1 \le j \le n$. Subsequently, the sequence $S_{i,j}$ corresponding to an internal node is computed by merging its children $S_{i-1,2j-1}$ and $S_{i-1,2j}$. Now, we compute the running time

---

Algorithm 19.9 PARBOTTOMUPSORT
Input: $A = \langle a_1, a_2, \ldots, a_n \rangle$, a sequences of n distinct numbers, where $n = 2^k$.
Output: A sorted in increasing order.

1. **for** $j \leftarrow 1$ **to** n **do in parallel**
2. $S_{0,j} \leftarrow a_j$
3. **for** $i \leftarrow 1$ **to** k
4. $t \leftarrow n/2^i$
5.   **for** $j \leftarrow 1$ **to** t **do in parallel**
6. $S_{i,j} \leftarrow$ PARMERGE$(S_{i-1,2j-1}, S_{i-1,2j})$
7.   **end for**
8. **end for**
9. $A \leftarrow S_{k,1}$
10. **return** A

---

of the algorithm. Algorithm PARMERGE is called in Step 6, and it takes $O(\log \log |S_{i-1,2j-1}|) = O(\log \log 2^{i-1})$. This is repeated in the **for** loop in Step 3 k times, for sizes $1, 2, 4, \ldots, n/2$. Hence, the running time is

$$T(n) = \sum_{i=1}^{k} O(\log \log 2^{i-1})$$

$$= \sum_{i=1}^{k} O(\log(i-1))$$

$$= \sum_{i=1}^{k} O(\log k)$$

$$= O(k \log k)$$

$$= O(\log n \log \log n).$$

19.2.7 *The zero-one principle*

A sorting algorithm is called *oblivious* if it consists of comparison-exchange operations that are prescribed and independent of the input elements and results of comparisons between them. The zero-one principle states that if a comparison-based oblivious algorithm sorts any sequence of zeros and ones, then it sorts any sequence of arbitrary values. It really simplifies the proofs of correctness of many oblivious sorting algorithms.

Lemma 19.1   *If an oblivious comparison-exchange algorithm sorts any sequence of zeros and ones, then it sorts any sequence of arbitrary values.*

Proof.   Suppose for the sake of contradiction that an oblivious comparison-exchange algorithm sorts all sequences of zeros and ones but fails to sort the input sequence $\langle x_1, x_2, \ldots, x_n \rangle$ of arbitrary numbers. Let π be a permutation such that $x_{\pi(1)} \leq x_{\pi(2)} \leq \cdots \leq x_{\pi(n)}$, and for some permutation $\sigma \neq \pi$, let the output of the algorithm be $x_{\sigma(1)}, x_{\sigma(2)}, \ldots, x_{\sigma(n)}$. Then, there exists some integer j such that $x_{\sigma(i)} = x_{\pi(i)}$ for $i < j$ and $x_{\sigma(j)} > x_{\pi(j)}$. Hence, there must exist $k > j$ such that $x_{\sigma(k)} = x_{\pi(j)}$. For $1 \leq i \leq n$, define $y_i = 0$ if $x_i \leq x_{\pi(j)}$, and $y_i = 1$ if $x_i > x_{\pi(j)}$. Now, consider the action of the algorithm on input $\langle y_1, y_2, \ldots, y_n \rangle$ of 0s and 1s. The algorithm will perform the same set of comparison-exchange operations as it did for the original input $\langle x_1, x_2, \ldots, x_n \rangle$. In particular, the output of the algorithm on the y_i's input will be

$$y_{\sigma(1)}, y_{\sigma(2)}, \ldots, y_{\sigma(j-1)}, y_{\sigma(j)}, \ldots, y_{\sigma(k)} \ldots = 0, 0, \ldots, 0, 1, \ldots, 0, \ldots,$$

which is not sorted. This contradicts the assumption that the algorithm sorts all sequences of zeros and ones.   □

19.2.8   *Odd–even merging*

Let $A = \langle a_0, a_1, \ldots, a_{n-1} \rangle$ and $B = \langle b_0, b_1, \ldots, b_{n-1} \rangle$ be two sorted sequences of $2n$ distinct numbers, where n is a power of 2. The odd–even merging method is summarized in Algorithm ODDEVENMERGE.

After the execution of Step 6, we have $s_0 = \min\{c_0, d_0\}$, $s_1 = \max\{c_0, d_0\}$, $s_2 = \min\{c_1, d_1\}$, $s_3 = \max\{c_1, d_1\}$, $\ldots$, $s_{2n-2} = \min\{c_{n-1}, d_{n-1}\}$, $s_{2n-1} = \max\{c_{n-1}, d_{n-1}\}$.

The algorithm uses $2n$ processors on the EREW PRAM. Obviously, the time needed in each recursive call is $\Theta(1)$. Hence, the running time of the algorithm is governed by the recurrence $T(n) = T(n/2) + \Theta(1)$, whose solution is $T(n) = \Theta(\log n)$. The work done by the algorithm is given by the recurrence $W(n) = 2W(n/2) + \Theta(n)$, and hence $W(n) = \Theta(n \log n)$.

Example 19.6   Let $A = \langle 1, 3, 4, 7 \rangle$ and $B = \langle 2, 5, 6, 8 \rangle$. Then, $A_{\text{even}} = \{1, 4\}$, $A_{\text{odd}} = \{3, 7\}$, $B_{\text{even}} = \{2, 6\}$, $B_{\text{odd}} = \{5, 8\}$, $C = \langle 1, 4, 5, 8 \rangle$ and $D = \langle 2, 3, 6, 7 \rangle$. $E = \langle 1, 2, 4, 3, 5, 6, 8, 7 \rangle$. The pair $(4, 3)$ is out of order, so 4 and 3 are exchanged. The same applies to the pair $(8, 7)$. The sorted sequence is $S = \langle 1, 2, 3, 4, 5, 6, 7, 8 \rangle$. See Fig. 19.6.

Algorithm 19.10 ODDEVENMERGE

Input: Two sorted sequences $A = \langle a_0, a_1, \ldots, a_{n-1} \rangle$ and $B = \langle b_0, b_1, \ldots, b_{n-1} \rangle$ of n elements each sorted in ascending order, where $n = 2^k \geq 2$.

Output: The elements in $S = A \cup B$ in sorted order.

1. **if** $n \leq 2$ **return** the merge of A and B, and exit.
2. Let $A_{\text{even}} = \langle a_0, a_2, \ldots, a_{n-2} \rangle$ and $A_{\text{odd}} = \langle a_1, a_3, \ldots, a_{n-1} \rangle$ be the even and odd subsequences of A, respectively.
3. Let $B_{\text{even}} = \langle b_0, b_2, \ldots, b_{n-2} \rangle$ and $B_{\text{odd}} = \langle b_1, b_3, \ldots, b_{n-1} \rangle$ be the even and odd subsequences of B, respectively.
4. Recursively merge A_{even} and B_{odd} to obtain $C = \langle c_0, c_1, \ldots, c_{n-1} \rangle$.
5. Recursively merge A_{odd} and B_{even} to obtain $D = \langle d_0, d_1, \ldots, d_{n-1} \rangle$.
6. Let E be the shuffle of C and D, that is, $E = \langle c_0, d_0, c_1, d_1, \ldots, c_{n-1}, d_{n-1} \rangle$.
7. Traverse the pairs (c_i, d_i) in E, $0 \leq i \leq n - 1$, and interchange the elements in each pair if they are out of order to obtain the sorted sequence $S = \langle s_0, s_1, \ldots, s_{2n-1} \rangle$
8. **return** S

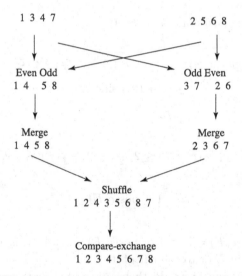

Fig. 19.6.   An example of odd–even merging.

Theorem 19.2   *Algorithm* ODDEVENMERGE *correctly merges A and B into S.*

Proof. Let A, B, C, D and E be as defined in Algorithm ODDEVEN-MERGE, and assume the elements in $A \cup B$ are distinct. Given a sequence X and an element x, recall that $\mathrm{rank}(x, X)$ is the number of elements in X less than x. For $x \in X$, let $\mathrm{pos}(x, X)$ be the position of x in the sequence X, where $\mathrm{pos}(x, X) \geq 0$. Thus, if X is sorted, then $\mathrm{pos}(x, X) = \mathrm{rank}(x, X)$. Let $x \in A \cup B$. Then,

$$\mathrm{rank}(x, C) = \left\lceil \frac{\mathrm{rank}(x, A)}{2} \right\rceil + \left\lfloor \frac{\mathrm{rank}(x, B)}{2} \right\rfloor,$$

and

$$\mathrm{rank}(x, D) = \left\lfloor \frac{\mathrm{rank}(x, A)}{2} \right\rfloor + \left\lceil \frac{\mathrm{rank}(x, B)}{2} \right\rceil.$$

For $c \in C$, let $r_1 = \mathrm{rank}(c, A)$ and $r_2 = \mathrm{rank}(c, B)$, and $r_c = r_1 + r_2$. Either $c \in A$ or $c \in B$. If $c \in A$, then r_1 is even since $\mathrm{pos}(c, A)$ is even, and it follows that the position of c in E is

$$\mathrm{pos}(c, E) = 2\,\mathrm{rank}(c, C) = 2\left\lceil \tfrac{r_1}{2} \right\rceil + 2\left\lfloor \tfrac{r_2}{2} \right\rfloor$$
$$\leq r_1 + (r_2) \text{ since } r_1 \text{ is even}$$
$$= r_c.$$

Since $r_c - 1 = r_1 + (r_2 - 1) \leq 2\left\lceil \tfrac{r_1}{2} \right\rceil + 2\left\lfloor \tfrac{r_2}{2} \right\rfloor = \mathrm{pos}(c, E)$, we have

$$r_c - 1 \leq \mathrm{pos}(c, E) \leq r_c. \tag{19.2}$$

Thus, either $\mathrm{pos}(c, E) = r_c - 1$ or $\mathrm{pos}(c, E) = r_c$. That is, either c is in its correct position in E or to the left of it.

On the other hand, if $c \in B$, then r_2 is odd since $\mathrm{pos}(c, B)$ is odd, and we get the same inequalities.

For $d \in D$, let $r_3 = \mathrm{rank}(d, A), r_4 = \mathrm{rank}(d, B)$ and $r_d = r_3 + r_4$. If $d \in A$, then r_3 is odd since $\mathrm{pos}(d, A)$ is odd. It follows that if $d \in A$, then

the position of d in E is

$$\begin{aligned}
\text{pos}(d, E) &= 2\,\text{rank}(d, D) + 1 = 2\left\lfloor \tfrac{r_3}{2} \right\rfloor + 2\left\lceil \tfrac{r_4}{2} \right\rceil + 1 \\
&\leq (r_3 - 1) + (r_4 + 1) + 1 \text{ since } r_3 \text{ is odd} \\
&= r_d + 1.
\end{aligned}$$

Since $r_d = (r_3 - 1) + (r_4) + 1 \leq 2\left\lfloor \tfrac{r_3}{2} \right\rfloor + 2\left\lceil \tfrac{r_4}{2} \right\rceil + 1 = \text{pos}(d, E)$, we have

$$r_d \leq \text{pos}(d, E) \leq r_d + 1. \tag{19.3}$$

Thus, either $\text{pos}(d, E) = r_d$ or $\text{pos}(d, E) = r_d + 1$. That is, either d is in its correct position in E or to the right of it.

If $d \in B$, then r_4 is even, and we get the same inequalities.

To finish the proof, we must show that the sorted sequence can be obtained by comparison-exchanges with elements neighbors. Suppose that E is not sorted. Then, by Eqs. (19.2) and (19.3), this happens if for some $c \in C$, $\text{pos}(c, E) = r_c - 1$, where $r_c = \text{rank}(c, A) + \text{rank}(c, B)$. So, assume that for some $c \in C$, $\text{pos}(c, E) = r_c - 1$. There must exist an element $d < c$ such that $\text{pos}(d, E) > r_c - 1$. First, note that d must belong to D, since it is to the right of its correct position. By Eq. (19.3), we must have $\text{pos}(d, E) \leq r_d + 1$, where $r_d = \text{rank}(d, A) + \text{rank}(d, B)$. Thus, we have $r_c - 1 < \text{pos}(d, E) \leq r_d + 1$. Since $d < c$, we must have $r_d < r_c$. Combining this with the above inequality yields $r_c - 1 < r_d + 1 < r_c + 1$, or $r_c - 2 < r_d < r_c$, whose solution is $r_d = r_c - 1$. That is, d should be at position $r_c - 1$, while now it is at position $r_d + 1 = (r_c - 1) + 1 = r_c$. In other words, $c \in C$ and $d \in D$, with $c > d$, are next to each other in E with $\text{pos}(c, E) = r_d$ and $\text{pos}(d, E) = r_c$. Their order will be fixed by exchanging them in Step 7 of the algorithm (see Fig. 19.7).

The algorithm for sorting is given as Algorithm ODDEVENSORT below. The running time of the algorithm is $\Theta(\log^2 n)$. Its work is $\Theta(n \log^2 n)$.

Fig. 19.7. Proof of Theorem 19.2. (a) Before exchange, (b) After exchange.

Algorithm 19.11 ODDEVENSORT

Input: A sequence $S = \langle a_0, a_1, \ldots, a_{n-1} \rangle$ where n is a power of 2.

Output: The elements in S in sorted order.

  1. $S_1 \leftarrow \langle a_0, a_1, \ldots, a_{n/2-1} \rangle$.
  2. $S_2 \leftarrow \langle a_{n/2}, a_{n/2+1}, \ldots, a_{n-1} \rangle$.
  3. $S_1' \leftarrow \text{ODDEVENSORT}(S_1)$
  4. $S_2' \leftarrow \text{ODDEVENSORT}(S_2)$
  5. $S \leftarrow \text{ODDEVENMERGE}(S_1', S_2')$
  6. **return** S

19.2.9 Bitonic merging and sorting

A sequence $S = \langle a_1, a_2, \ldots, a_n \rangle$ is *monotonically increasing* if $a_1 \leq a_2 \leq \cdots \leq a_n$ and is *monotonically decreasing* if $a_1 \geq a_2 \geq \cdots \geq a_n$. A sequence is *monotone* if it is monotonically increasing or monotonically decreasing. A monotone sequence can be represented pictorially as shown in Fig. 19.8(a), where there is a point for each item in the sequence. The sequence corresponding to this diagram is $T = \langle a_1, \ldots, a_i, \ldots, a_j, \ldots, a_n \rangle$, where $1 < i < j < n$. However, if we are not interested in the actual values of the items in the sequence but only in their relative order, then we can simply represent a monotone sequence by a line segment. An example is shown in Fig. 19.8(b) for the monotonically increasing sequence T above. Figure 19.8(c) shows a generic monotone sequence in which the items and their number are immaterial. Thus, the diagram shown in Fig. 19.8(c) is the representation of any monotonically increasing sequence. Similarly, a monotonically decreasing sequence can be represented by a line segment with negative slope.

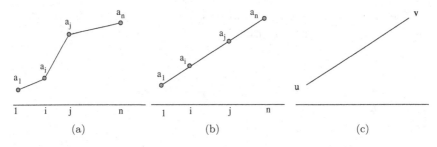

Fig. 19.8.   A monotone sequence.

A sequence $S = \langle a_1, a_2, \ldots, a_n \rangle$ is *bitonic* if it monotonically increases and then monotonically decreases, that is, there is an i, $1 \le i \le n$, such that

$$a_1 \le a_2 \le \cdots \le a_i \ge a_{i+1} \ge a_{i+2} \ge \cdots \ge a_n,$$

or can be circularly shifted to become monotonically increasing and then monotically decreasing. Thus, a sequence is also bitonic if it is monotone. For example, the sequence $\langle 1, 3, 5, 7, 4, 2 \rangle$ is bitonic while $\langle 1, 3, 1, 2 \rangle$ is not.

The sequence $\langle 7, 8, 3, 1, 0, 4 \rangle$ is also a bitonic sequence because it is a cyclic shift of $\langle 0, 4, 7, 8, 3, 1 \rangle$. We will represent a bitonic sequence by a diagram consisting of a polygonal chain composed of line segments intersecting at their internal endpoints with at most one local maximum and one local minimum. Each line segment represents a monotone sequence. Figure 19.9 shows the diagrams of two bitonic sequences. In part (a) there is one local maximum, and in part (b) there is one local maximum and one local minimum. If the number of line segments is 1 or 2, then the diagram is a bitonic sequence. If the number of line segments is more than 2, then the diagram is a bitonic sequence if and only if there does not exist a horizontal line that intersects the polygonal chain at more than 2 points. To see this, consider Fig. 19.10, which shows the diagram of a sequence with three intersections of the polygonal chain with a horizontal line.

The sequence corresponding to this diagram is $\langle a_1, \ldots, a_i, \ldots, a_j, \ldots, a_n \rangle$, where $1 < i < j < n$, with the following inequalities: $a_1 > a_i, a_i < a_j, a_j > a_n$ and $a_n < a_1$. If this sequence is bitonic, then the sequence $\alpha = \langle a_1, a_i, a_j, a_n \rangle$ such that $a_1 > a_i < a_j > a_n < a_1$ is bitonic.

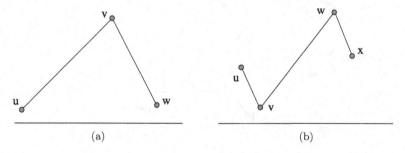

Fig. 19.9.   Bitonic sequences.

Then, it is possible through circular shifts to transform α into two monotonic sequences, one increasing followed by one decreasing. It can be shown, however, that α cannot be converted to such a sequence. It follows that it is not bitonic.

Now consider the sequence α' obtained from α by increasing the value of a_n so that $a_n > a_1$. Then, we have $a_1 > a_i < a_j > a_n > a_1$, and thus α' is bitonic, as it can be transformed into $\alpha'' = \langle a_i, a_j, a_n, a_1 \rangle$, which consists of two monotonic sequences. The diagram of α' is similar to the one shown in Fig. 19.9(b); there does not exist a horizontal line that intersects this diagram at more than 2 points. The diagram of α'' is similar to the one shown in Fig. 19.9(a).

Example 19.7 Consider the sequence $\alpha = \langle 4, 1, 6, 3 \rangle$. Its diagram is the one shown in Fig. 19.10. In this sequence, $4 > 1 < 6 > 3 < 4$, so obviously α is not a bitonic sequence. However, if we change 3 to 5 to obtain $\alpha' = \langle 4, 1, 6, 5 \rangle$, the new sequence is bitonic since in this case $4 > 1 < 6 > 5 > 4$. Its diagram is similar to the one shown in Fig. 19.9(b). With one cyclic shift α' is converted to $\alpha'' = \langle 1, 6, 5, 4 \rangle$, which consists of two monotonic sequences, one increasing and one decreasing. Its diagram is similar to the one shown in Fig. 19.9(a).

Let $S = \langle a_1, a_2, \ldots, a_n \rangle$ be a bitonic sequence. Define

$$S_1 = \langle \min(a_1, a_{n/2+1}), \min(a_2, a_{n/2+2}), \ldots, \min(a_{n/2}, a_n) \rangle, \qquad (19.4)$$

and

$$S_2 = \langle \max(a_1, a_{n/2+1}), \max(a_2, a_{n/2+2}), \ldots, \max(a_{n/2}, a_n) \rangle. \qquad (19.5)$$

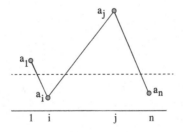

Fig. 19.10.   A nonbitonic sequence.

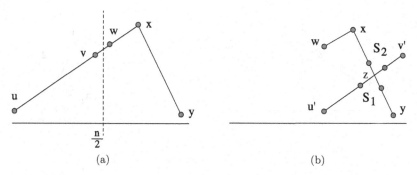

Fig. 19.11.   Bitonic sequences.

Then, both S_1 and S_2 are bitonic sequences. Moreover,

$$\max(S_1) \leq \min(S_2). \tag{19.6}$$

Consider, for example, the bitonic sequence u, v, w, x, y shown in Fig. 19.11(a). Here, the line segment $\overline{u,v}$ accounts for approximately half the elements in the sequence. Shift the line segment $\overline{u,v}$ to the right until the vertex u is aligned vertically with w. The resulting line segment $\overline{u',v'}$ intersects the line segment $\overline{x,y}$ at the vertex z. Then, $S_1 = u', z, y$ and $S_2 = w, x, z, v'$ as shown in Fig. 19.11(b) are bitonic. It is clear from the figure that $\max(S_1) \leq \min(S_2)$.

Example 19.8   Consider the bitonic sequence $S = \langle 2, 3, 5, 7, 9, 10, 8, 6, 4, 1 \rangle$ shown in Fig. 19.12(a). If we apply the procedure described above for splitting this sequence, we obtain the two bitonic sequences $S_1 = \langle 2, 3, 5, 4, 1 \rangle$ and $S_2 = \langle 9, 10, 8, 6, 7 \rangle$ shown in Fig. 19.12(b). S_2 is a cyclic shift of the sequence $\langle 10, 8, 6, 7, 9 \rangle$. Furthermore, $\max(S_1) = 5 \leq 6 = \min(S_2)$.

By Eq. (19.6), every element of the sequence S_1 is less than or equal to every element of the sequence S_2. Thus, the problem of sorting the elements in S is reduced to sorting the elements in S_1 and S_2 separately. This is summarized in Algorithm BITONICMERGE below. It is important to note that the input to the algorithm is a bitonic sequence S of length n, where n is a power of 2, and the output is the elements in S in sorted order. The algorithm first computes S_1 and S_2 as in Eqs. (19.4) and (19.5). Now, S_1 and S_2 are bitonic sequences, so the algorithm recursively computes the

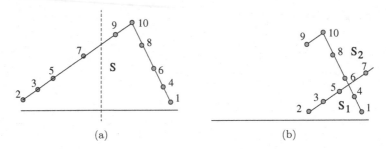

Fig. 19.12.   Bitonic sequences example.

Algorithm 19.12 BITONICMERGE

Input: A bitonic sequence $S = \langle a_1, a_2, \ldots, a_n \rangle$, where n is a power of 2.

Output: The elements in S in sorted order.

1. **if** $|S| = 1$ **then return** S
2. **for** $i \leftarrow 1$ **to** $n/2$ **do in parallel**
3.   **if** $a_i > a_{i+n/2}$ **then** interchange a_i and $a_{i+n/2}$
4. $S_1 = \langle a_1, a_2, \ldots, a_{n/2} \rangle$
5. $S_2 = \langle a_{n/2+1}, a_{n/2+2}, \ldots, a_n \rangle$
6. $S_1' \leftarrow$ BITONICMERGE(S_1)
7. $S_2' \leftarrow$ BITONICMERGE(S_2)
8. **return** $S_1' \| S_2'$, the concatenation of S_1' and S_2'

---

two sorted sequences S_1' and S_2' and returns their concatenation sequence $S_1' \| S_2'$.

Algorithm BITONICMERGE works on the EREW PRAM with n processors. The running time is $\Theta(\log n)$ and the total amount of work is $\Theta(n \log n)$, which is not optimal in view of the $O(n)$ time sequential algorithm.

Example 19.9   Consider the instance given in Fig. 19.13. Line 1 is the input bitonic sequence. Line 2 shows the first split into two bitonic sequences. Lines 3 and 4 show the second and third splits, respectively.

A *comparator* is a devise with two inputs x and y, and two outputs $\min(x, y)$ and $\max(x, y)$. It is either an *increasing* comparator, shown in Fig. 19.14(a), or *decreasing* comparator, shown in Fig. 19.14(b). A *network of comparators* is composed solely of wires and comparators. Algorithm BITONICMERGE can be implemented on a network of comparators, also

$$2\ 5\ 7\ 8\ 6\ 4\ 3\ 1$$
$$2\ 4\ 3\ 1\ |\ 6\ 5\ 7\ 8$$
$$2\ 1\ |\ 3\ 4\ |\ 6\ 5\ |\ 7\ 8$$
$$1\ |\ 2\ |\ 3\ |\ 4\ |\ 5\ |\ 6\ |\ 7\ |\ 8$$

Fig. 19.13. Bitonic merge example for $n = 8$.

x ——————○—————— min(x, y)   x ——————○—————— max(x, y)

y ——————○—————— max(x, y)   y ——————○—————— min(x, y)

(a)   (b)

Fig. 19.14. (a) Increasing comparator. (b) Decreasing comparator.

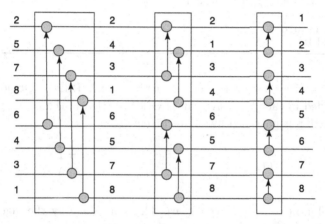

Fig. 19.15. Bitonic merge network for $n = 8$.

called a *merging network*, as illustrated in Fig. 19.15. A sample input of bitonic sequence is shown on the wires. The merging network with n inputs consists of $\log n$ columns, called stages.

19.2.9.1 *Bitonic sorting*

Bitonic sorting essentially works like Algorithm MERGESORT in that it divides the input into two halves, sorts each half recursively and uses Algorithm BITONICMERGE to merge the two sorted sequences. It is given in Algorithm BITONICSORT below. To merge two monotonic sequences S_1' and S_2'

sorted in ascending order, first reverse S_2' and form the bitonic sequence S_3 obtained by concatenating S_1' and S_2'', where S_2'' is the reverse of S_2'. Finally, apply Algorithm BITONICMERGE to S_3.

Algorithm 19.13 BITONICSORT
Input: A sequence S of n elements, where n is a power of 2.

Output: The elements in S in sorted order.

1. **if** $|S| > 1$ **then**
2. $\quad S_1 \leftarrow \langle a_1, a_2, \ldots, a_{n/2} \rangle$
3. $\quad S_2 \leftarrow \langle a_{n/2+1}, a_{n/2+2}, \ldots, a_n \rangle$
4. $\quad S_1' \leftarrow$ BITONICSORT(S_1)
5. $\quad S_2' \leftarrow$ BITONICSORT(S_2)
6. $\quad S_2'' \leftarrow$ Reverse of S_2'
7. $\quad S_3 \leftarrow S_1' || S_2''$, the concatenation of S_1' and S_2''
8. $\quad S \leftarrow$ BITONICMERGE(S_3)
9. $\quad$ **return** S
10. **end if**

The algorithm uses n processors on the EREW PRAM. Obviously, the time needed in each recursive call is $\Theta(\log n)$. Hence, the running time of the algorithm is governed by the recurrence

$$T(n) = \begin{cases} c & \text{if } n = 1 \\ T(n/2) + \Theta(\log n) & \text{if } n \geq 2, \end{cases}$$

whose solution is $T(n) = \Theta(\log^2 n)$. The work done by the algorithm is $W(n) = \Theta(n \log^2 n)$, which is not optimal.

Theorem 19.3 *Algorithm* BITONICSORT *correctly sorts a given sequence of numbers in ascending order.*

Proof.   By the zero-one principle (Lemma 19.1 in Sec. 19.2.7), we may assume that the input consists of 0s and 1s. Let A and B be two strings of 0's and 1s such that $|A| + |B| = n$, and assume without loss of generality that $n = 2^m \geq 2$. The proof is by induction on m. If $m = 1$, then clearly the input will be sorted, so assume that the algorithm correctly sorts its input for all powers h, $1 \leq h < m$, and let $|A| + |B| = 2^m$. First, A and B will be sorted separately, and B will be reversed, and so they will look like the following:

$$A = 0^i 1^j, \quad B = 1^k 0^l.$$

Next, some 1s in A will be swapped with 0s in B by Step 3 of Algorithm BITONICMERGE. Let A' and B' be A and B after swapping, respectively. If $j \leq l$, all 1s in A will be swapped with 0s in B, and A' will consist of 0s only. In this case, A' and B' will look like:

$$A' = 0^{i+j}, \quad B' = 1^k 0^{l-j} 1^j.$$

If, however, $j > l$, then l 1's in A will be swapped with l 0s in B, and A' and B' will look like the following:

$$A' = 0^i 1^{j-l} 0^l, \quad B' = 1^{k+l}.$$

Finally, A' and B' will be merged separately and concatenated by Algorithm BITONICMERGE to produce $A''\|B''$, which is sorted in ascending order. □

We can derive a sorting network by unrolling recursion as follows. Starting from $n = 1$, any sequence of length 1 is monotonic, and hence any sequence of length 2 is bitonic. In the first stage of bitonic sort, bitonic sequences of size 2 are merged to create ordered lists of size 2. If these sequences alternate between being ordered into increasing and decreasing order, then at the end of this stage of merging, we have $n/4$ bitonic sequences of size 4. In the next stage, bitonic sequences of size 4 are merged into sorted sequences of size 4, alternately into increasing and decreasing order, so as to form $n/8$ bitonic sequences of size 8. Given an unordered sequence of size n, exactly $\log n$ stages of merging are required to produce a completely ordered sequence. Figure 19.16 shows a bitonic sorting network with sample input of size 8. This network has three stages labeled Merge(2), Merge(4) and Merge(8). Stage 3 in the figure is identical to the merging network of Fig. 19.15.

19.2.10 *Pipelined merge sort*

Recall the parallel bottom-up merge sorting algorithm, Algorithm PAR-BOTTOMUPSORT, discussed in Sec. 19.2.6.3. The algorithm works by merging pairs of consecutive elements, then merging consecutive pairs to form 4-element sequences, and so on. The running time of the algorithm was shown to be $O(\log n \log \log n)$. In fact, there is an $\Omega(\log \log n)$ time lower

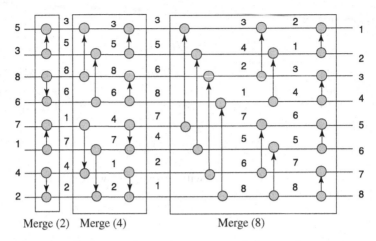

Fig. 19.16. Bitonic sort network for $n = 8$.

bound for merging two sorted sequences of n elements using n processors on the CREW PRAM. In this section, we sketch an optimal $\Theta(\log n)$ time algorithm for sorting n items on the CREW PRAM with $\Theta(n)$ processors. The algorithm can be modified to work on the EREW PRAM with the same time complexity. It is a modification of Algorithm PARBOTTOMUPSORT, in which merges are pipelined efficiently. We will assume in this section that the elements to be sorted are all distinct and that n is a power of 2.

Let a, b and c be three numbers such that $a < c$. We say that b is *between* a and c if $a \le b < c$. We also say that a and c *straddle* b. Given a sequence A and an element a, recall that $\text{rank}(a, A)$ denotes the number of elements in A less than a. We will assume that all sequences and arrays are implicitly augmented with $-\infty$ and ∞, so the rank of the minimum element is 1, not 0. Given two arrays A and B, the cross rank $R(A, B) = \langle \text{rank}(a, B) \mid a \in A \rangle$. Let a and b be two adjacent items in B (if necessary, we let $a = -\infty$ or $b = \infty$). We define the range $[a, b)$ to be the interval induced by item a (including the cases $a = -\infty$ and $b = \infty$). Let C be a sorted sequence of numbers. C will be called a *3-cover* or simply a *cover* of A if each interval induced by consecutive elements of C contains at most three elements from A. More precisely, for any two consecutive elements a and c in C_∞, the set $\{b \in A \mid a \le b < c\}$ has at most 3 elements, where $C_\infty = \{-\infty\} \cup C \cup \{+\infty\}$. For example, if C contains the numbers $9, 18$ and 30 while A contains $1, 5, 20, 23, 25$ and 35, then C is a 3-cover for A.

If, however, A also contains 28, then C is not a 3-cover for A, since in this case the number of elements between 18 and 30 is more than 3.

19.2.10.1   *The algorithm*

The sorting algorithm is described in terms of a complete binary tree T with n leaves. Initially, the n elements to be sorted are placed at the leaves of T, one element per leaf, and the internal nodes contain empty sequences. Let v be an internal node in the tree. L_v will denote the sequence of leaves of the subtree T_v rooted at v. In the course of the algorithm, the internal nodes of T will contain sorted sequences of elements. The task of node v is to sort the sequence L_v. The algorithm goes through stages $t, 1 \leq t \leq 3 \log n - 2$. By $A_v(t)$, we denote the sequence associated with node v at stage t. The items in $A_v(t)$ will be a rough sample of the items in $L(v)$. As the algorithm proceeds, the size of $A_v(t)$ increases, and $A_v(t)$ becomes a more accurate approximation of $L(v)$, and it will always be a sorted subsequence of L_v. We say that node v is *complete* at stage t if and only if $A_v(t) = L_v$; otherwise, v is said to be *active*. Throughout the algorithm, node v receives from its left son x a sorted sequence $B_x(t)$ and receives from its right son y a sorted sequence $B_y(t)$ and produces the sequence $B_v(t + 1)$, which is sent to the parent of v. In each of these sequences, the size of the next object is twice as big as the size of the preceding one. That is, for all nodes v,

$$|A_v(t + 1)| = 2|A_v(t)| \quad \text{and} \quad |B_v(t + 1)| = 2|B_v(t)|.$$

We explain the processing performed in one stage at an arbitrary internal node v of the tree. The array $A_v(t)$ is the array at hand at the start of the stage; $A_v(t + 1)$ is the array at hand at the start of the next stage, and $A_v(t - 1)$ is the array at hand at the start of the previous stage, if any. Also, in each stage, we will create an array $B_v(t)$ at node v; $B_v(t + 1)$ and $B_v(t - 1)$ are the corresponding arrays in the next and previous stages, respectively. $B_v(t)$ is a sorted array comprising every fourth item in $A_v(t)$, for active node v. The computation performed during each stage at each internal node v comprises the following two phases:

(1) Compute $B_v(t) \leftarrow \alpha(A_v(t))$ and send it to the parent of v, where $\alpha(A_v(t))$ is computed as follows. If v is active, then $\alpha(A_v(t))$ consists of every fourth element of $A_v(t)$. During the first stage after v becomes complete, $\alpha(A_v(t))$ consists of every fourth element of $A_v(t)$. During

the second stage after v becomes complete, $\alpha(A_v(t))$ consists of every second element of $A_v(t)$, while in the third stage, $\alpha(A_v(t))$ consists of every element of $A_v(t)$.

(2) If v is active, then merge $B_x(t)$ with $B_y(t)$ using the cover $A_v(t)$ to obtain $A_v(t+1)$. That is, $A_v(t+1) \leftarrow B_x(t) \cup B_y(t)$, where $\cup$ denotes merging. If v is complete, then v ignores its inputs $B_x(t)$ and $B_y(t)$.

By (1) above, three stages after node v becomes complete, its parent becomes complete too. The exception is in stage 1 in which the nodes at the level before the last merge their inputs and become complete in one stage. Hence, the total number of stages of the algorithm is $3 \log n - 2$.

Figure 19.17 illustrates the flow of the algorithm with $n = 8$ by depicting stages 2–7, that is, after nodes d, e, f and g become complete. Note that the total number of stages is $3 \log 8 - 2 = 7$. In Fig. 19.17(c) of this figure,

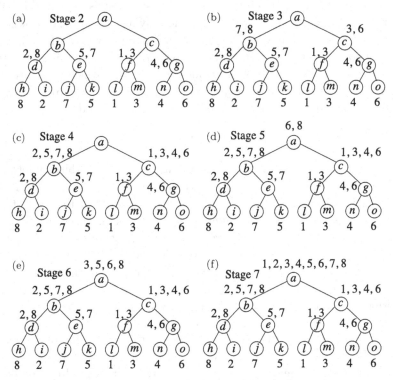

Fig. 19.17. The flow of the algorithm with $n = 8$.

we have $A_a(4) = \{\}, B_b(4) = \langle 8 \rangle$ and $B_c(4) = \langle 6 \rangle$. In Fig. 19.17(d) of this figure, we have $A_a(5) = \langle 6, 8 \rangle, B_b(5) = \langle 5, 8 \rangle$ and $B_c(5) = \langle 3, 6 \rangle$. The proof of the following theorem is omitted.

Theorem 19.4 $B_v(t)$ *is a 3-cover of* $B_v(t+1)$.

We will need the following observation to show that the merge can be performed in $O(1)$ time.

Observation 19.1   Let A and C be two sets such that C is a cover for A. Then, for any set D, $C \cup D$ is a cover for A.

By the above theorem, $B_x(t-1)$ is a 3-cover for $B_x(t)$ for each node x. By the above observation, since $A_v(t) = B_x(t-1) \cup B_y(t-1)$, we deduce $A_v(t)$ is a 3-cover for $B_x(t)$; similarly, $A_v(t)$ is a 3-cover for $B_y(t)$. We will assume that $R(A_v(t), B_x(t))$ and $R(A_v(t), B_y(t))$ are available. Let a be an item in $B_x(t)$; the rank of a in $A_v(t+1) = B_x(t) \cup B_y(t)$ is equal to the sum of its ranks in $B_x(t)$ and $B_y(t)$. So, to perform the merge, we compute the cross ranks $R(B_x(t), B_y(t))$ and $R(B_y(t), B_x(t))$ (the method is given below).

19.2.10.2 *Maintaining ranks*

We compute and maintain ranks as described in the following steps:

(1) The first step is to compute $R(B_x(t), A_v(t))$ and $R(B_y(t), A_v(t))$. For two adjacent items a and b with $a < b$, recall that the interval induced by item a is the range $[a, b)$ (including the cases $a = -\infty$ and $b = \infty$). Let u be an item in $A_v(t)$; u may be $-\infty$. Consider the interval $I(u)$ in $A_v(t)$ induced by u, and consider the set of items $X(u)$ in $B_x(t)$ contained in $I(u)$ (there are at most three items in $X(u)$ by the 3-cover property). $X(u)$ can be found in $O(1)$ time since $R(A_v(t), B_x(t))$ is available, which means $\text{rank}(u, B_x)$ is known. Each item a in $X(u)$ is given its rank in $A_v(t)$ as $\text{rank}(a, A_v(t)) = \text{rank}(u, A_v(t)) + 1$ (note that all elements are distinct, which means $a > u$). For example, in Fig. 19.17(d), with $t = 5$, we have $A_a(5) = \{6, 8\}, B_b(5) = \{5, 8\}$. If we let $u = -\infty$, then $I(u) = (-\infty, 6)$ and $X(u) = \{5\}$. Hence, $\text{rank}(5, A_a(5)) = 0 + 1 = 1$. This takes care of $R(B_x(t), A_v(t))$. We repeat the symmetrical procedure to compute $R(B_y(t), A_v(t))$. These

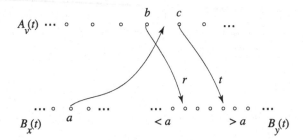

Fig. 19.18.   Computing $R(B_x(t), B_y(t))$.

ranks are needed for computing $R(B_x(t), B_y(t))$ and $R(B_y(t), B_x(t))$, which are required by the merge step $A_v(t+1) \leftarrow B_x(t) \cup B_y(t)$.

(2) Now, we show how to compute $R(B_x(t), B_y(t))$; $R(B_y(t), B_x(t))$ can be found in a similar fashion. Let a be an item in $B_x(t)$; we show how to compute its rank in $B_y(t)$ (see Fig. 19.18). We determine the two items b and c in $A_v(t)$ that straddle a, using $\text{rank}(a, A_v(t))$ computed above. Suppose that b and c have ranks r and t, respectively, in $B_y(t)$. Then, all items of rank r or less are smaller than item a (recall we assumed that all the inputs were distinct), while all items of rank greater than t are larger than item a; thus, the only items about which there is any doubt as to their size relative to a are the items with rank $s, r < s \le t$. But there are at most three such items by the 3-cover property. By means of at most two comparisons, the relative order of a and these (at most) three items can be determined.

(3) At this point, we find for each item a in $B_x(t)$, using its rank in $B_y(t)$ computed above, the two items b and c in $B_y(t)$ that straddle a, and the ranks of b and c in $A_v(t+1)$. Similarly, we find for each item d in $B_y(t)$, using its rank in $B_x(t)$, the two items e and f in $B_x(t)$ that straddle d, and the ranks of e and f in $A_v(t+1)$. This information is needed for computing $R(A_v(t+1), B_x(t+1))$ and $R(A_v(t+1), B_y(t+1))$.

(4) Now, we show how to compute $R(A_v(t+1), B_x(t+1))$; $R(A_v(t+1), B_y(t+1))$ can be found by a similar means. For each item a in $A_v(t+1)$, we want to determine its rank in $B_x(t+1)$. Given the ranks for an item from $A_v(t)$ in both $B_x(t)$ and $B_y(t)$, we can immediately deduce the rank of this item in $A_v(t+1) = B_x(t) \cup B_y(t)$ (the new rank is just the sum of the two old ranks). Similarly, we obtain the ranks for items from $A_x(t)$ in $A_x(t+1)$. This yields the ranks of items from $B_x(t)$

in $B_x(t+1)$ (for each item in $B_x(t)$ came from $A_x(t)$, and $B_x(t+1)$ comprises every fourth or second item in $A_x(t+1)$ or every item in $A_x(t+1)$). Consequently, for $a \in B_x(t), \text{rank}(a, B_x(t+1)) = \frac{1}{4}\text{rank}(a, A_x(t+1))$ if in stage $t+1$ x is active or in the first stage after being complete, $\text{rank}(a, B_x(t+1)) = \frac{1}{2}\text{rank}(a, A_x(t+1))$ if in stage $t+1$ x is in the second stage after being complete, and $\text{rank}(a, B_x(t+1)) = \text{rank}(a, A_x(t+1))$ if in stage $t+1$ x is in the third stage after being complete. For example, in Fig. 19.17, if $t=4$, then we have $A_b(4) = \{2, 5, 7, 8\}, B_b(4) = \{8\}, A_b(5) = A_b(4), B_b(5) = \{5, 8\}$, and $\text{rank}(8, B_b(5)) = \frac{1}{2}\text{rank}(8, A_b(5)) = 2$ (note that stages 4 and 5 are in Figs. 19.17(c) and 19.17(d)). Thus, for every item in $A_v(t+1)$ that came from $B_x(t)$, we have its rank in $B_x(t+1)$; it remains to compute the rank for those items in $A_v(t+1)$ that came from $B_y(t)$.

Let a be an item in $B_y(t)$. We compute $\text{rank}(a, B_x(t+1))$ as follows. Recall that for each item a from $B_y(t)$, we computed the straddling items b and c from $B_x(t)$ (see Fig. 19.19). We know the ranks r and t of b and c, respectively, in $B_x(t+1)$ (as asserted in the previous paragraph). Every item of rank r or less in $B_x(t+1)$ is smaller than a, while every item of rank greater than t is larger than a. Thus, the only items about which there is any doubt concerning their size relative to a are the items with rank $s, r < s \le t$. But there are at most three such items by the 3-cover property. As before, the relative order of a and these (at most) three items can be determined by means of at most two comparisons.

19.2.10.3 *Analysis of the algorithm*

It is not difficult to prove that the merge step takes $O(1)$ time at each stage of the algorithm given that we assign a processor to every array element.

Fig. 19.19. Computing $\text{rank}(a, B_x(t+1))$ for $a \in B_y(t)$.

Hence, the total running time is $\Theta(\log n)$. Now we estimate the number of processors needed, which is equal to the total array elements at any stage of the algorithm. First, we compute the total number of items in the $A(t)$ arrays. Let v be an internal node, and assume, as before, that x and y are the children of v. If $|A_v(t)| \neq 0$ and x is not complete, then

$$2|A_v(t)| = |A_v(t+1)| = |B_x(t)| + |B_y(t)| = \frac{1}{4}(|A_x(t)| + |A_y(t)|) = \frac{1}{2}|A_x(t)|,$$

that is, $|A_v(t)| = \frac{1}{4}|A_x(t)|$. So, the total size of the $A(t)$ arrays at v's level is $\frac{1}{8}$ of the size of the $A(t)$ arrays at x's level, if x is not complete (the number of nodes at v's level is $\frac{1}{2}$ of that at x's level). This need not be true at complete nodes x. It is true for the first stage in which x is complete; but for the second stage, $|A_v(t)| = \frac{1}{2}|A_x(t)|$, and so the total size of the $A(t)$ arrays at v's level is $\frac{1}{4}$ of the total size of the arrays at x's level; likewise, for the third stage, $|A_v(t)| = |A_x(t)|$, and so the total size of the $A(t)$ arrays at v's level is $\frac{1}{2}$ of the total size of the $A(t)$ arrays at x's level.

Thus, on the first stage in which x is complete, the total size of the $A(t)$ arrays is bounded above by $n + n/8 + n/64 + \cdots = n + n/7$; on the second stage, by $n + n/4 + n/32 + \cdots = n + 2n/7$; on the third stage, by $n + n/2 + n/16 + \cdots = n + 4n/7$. Using similar argument, it can be shown that on the first stage, the total size of the $B(t)$ arrays is bounded above by $2n/7$; on the second stage, by $4n/7$; on the third stage, by $8n/7$. We conclude that the algorithm needs $\Theta(n)$ processors (so as to have a processor standing by each item in the $A(t)$ and $B(t)$ arrays) and takes constant time for the merge step.

The following theorem summarizes the main result. Its proof follows from Theorem 19.4 and the algorithm's description and timing analysis. Recall that the algorithm can be modified to run on the EREW PRAM with the same complexities.

Theorem 19.5   *The pipelined merge sort algorithm sorts a sequence of n elements in $\Theta(\log n)$ time using $\Theta(n)$ processors on the EREW PRAM.*

19.2.11   *Selection*

Recall the problem of selection discussed in Sec. 5.5: Given a sequence $A = \langle a_1, a_2, \ldots, a_n \rangle$ of n elements and a positive integer $k, 1 \leq k \leq n$, find the kth smallest element in A. A straightforward solution would be to sort A in $\Theta(\log n)$ time and return the kth smallest element. However, the work done by this approach is $\Theta(n \log n)$, which is not optimal. In Sec. 5.5, we presented Algorithm SELECT, a sequential algorithm that runs in $\Theta(n)$ time. It can be shown that this algorithm can be parallelized to run on the PRAM in $\Theta(\log^2 n)$ time using $n/\log n$ processors. In this section, we present an algorithm, which is shown below as Algorithm PARSELECT, to solve the selection problem, that runs in time $O(\log n \log \log n)$ and uses $n/\log n$ processors. This algorithm is a modification of the parallel version of Algorithm SELECT.

Algorithm 19.14 PARSELECT
Input: A sequence $A = \langle a_1, \ldots, a_n \rangle$ of elements and an integer k, $1 \leq k \leq n$.
Output: The kth smallest element in A

1. $c \leftarrow 1/\log(4/3)$
2. **for** $j \leftarrow 1$ **to** $\lfloor c \log \log n \rfloor$
3.   Divide A into $|A|/\log|A|$ groups of $\log|A|$ elements each.
4.   Find the median of each group individually.
    Let the set of medians be M.
5.   Sort M and find its median m.
6.   Partition A into three sequences:
    $A_1 = \{a \mid a < m\}$
    $A_2 = \{a \mid a = m\}$
    $A_3 = \{a \mid a > m\}$
7.   **case**
        $|A_1| \geq k$: $A \leftarrow A_1$
        $|A_1| + |A_2| \geq k$: **return** m
        $|A_1| + |A_2| < k$:
8. $A = A_3$
9. $k \leftarrow k - |A_1| - |A_2|$
10.   **end case**
11. **end for**
12. Sort A and **return** the kth smallest element in A.

The **for** loop is executed $c \log \log n$ times, where $c = 1/\log(4/3)$, after which the number of elements in A drops to $O(n/\log n)$. The algorithm then sorts A using the pipelined merge sort algorithm and the kth smallest element is returned in $O(\log n)$ time using $O(n/\log n)$ processors. Within the **for** loop, first A is partitioned into $|A|/\log|A|$ blocks of $\log|A|$ elements each. The median of each block is found using one processor in $\Theta(|A|)$

sequential time, and the median of medians m is computed by sorting the set M using the pipelined merge sort algorithm in $\Theta(\log(|A|/\log|A|)) = O(\log n)$ time using $\Theta(|A|/\log|A|)$ processors. A is then partitioned to A_1 of elements smaller than m, A_2 of elements equal to m and A_3 of elements greater than m. If $|A_1| < k \leq |A_1| + |A_2|$, the algorithm terminates and returns m. Else, if $|A_1| \geq k$, A is set to A_1. Otherwise, if $|A_1| + |A_2| < k$, then A is set to A_3 and k is set to $k - |A_1| - |A_2|$.

Partitioning A can be achieved by labeling the elements in A with numbers $1, 2$ and 3 according to whether $a < m, a = m$ or $a > m$, respectively. Then, the parallel prefix algorithm can be used to extract and compact the arrays A_1, A_2 and A_3. This can be achieved in $\Theta(\log|A|)$ time using $O(|A|/\log|A|) = O(n/\log n)$ processors. It follows that the **for** loop takes $O(\log n)$ time in each iteration.

If we let $s = |A|/\log|A|$ denote the group size, then the median of medians m is smaller than (and greater than) at least $(|A|/2s)(s/2) = |A|/4$ elements. That is, it is greater than (and smaller than) at most $3|A|/4$ elements (see Sec. 5.5 for detailed analysis). Thus, in the second iteration, $|A| \leq 3n/4$, and in the jth iteration $|A| \leq (3/4)^j n$. Consequently, after $\lfloor c\log\log n\rfloor$ iterations, the size of A is at most

$$\left(\frac{3}{4}\right)^{c\log\log n} \times n$$

$$= (\log n)^{c\log(3/4)} \times n$$

$$= \frac{n}{(\log n)^{c\log(4/3)}}$$

$$= \frac{n}{(\log n)^{\log(4/3)/\log(4/3)}}$$

$$= \frac{n}{\log n}$$

$$= p.$$

Therefore, in Step 12, there will be enough processors to sort A in $O(\log p) = O(\log n)$ time. Since the time required in each iteration is $O(\log n)$, the running time of the algorithm is $O(\log n \log\log n)$. The work done in each iteration is $O(|A|)$. Hence, the total work done is at most

$$n + (3/4)n + (3/4)^2 n + \cdots + (3/4)^{\lfloor c\log\log n\rfloor} n = \Theta(n),$$

which is optimal. However, the cost, which is $O(n\log\log n)$, is not optimal.

19.2.12 *Multiselection*

Let $A = \langle a_1, a_2, \ldots, a_n \rangle$ be a sequence of n elements drawn from a linearly ordered set, and let $K = \langle k_1, k_2, \ldots, k_r \rangle$ be a sorted sequence of positive integers between 1 and n. The *multiselection* problem is to select the k_ith smallest element for all values of $i, 1 \le i \le r$. To make the presentation simple, we will assume that all elements in A are distinct. Consider Algorithm PARMULTISELECT1 shown below, which is the parallel version of Algorithm MULTISELECT in Sec. 5.8. The algorithm initially uses $n/\log n$ processors. In the two recursive calls, it uses $p|A_1|/|A|$ and $p|A_2|/|A|$ processors, where p is the current number of processors. The recurrence for the running time of this divide-and-conquer algorithm is $T(n, r) = T(n, r/2) + O(\log n \log \log n)$ since we used the parallel algorithm for selection, Algorithm PARSELECT, of Sec. 19.2.11. As the recursion depth is $\log r$, the solution to this recurrence is $T(n, r) = O(\log n \log \log n \log r)$.

Algorithm 19.15 PARMULTISELECT1
Input: A sequence $A = \langle a_1, a_2, \ldots, a_n \rangle$ of n elements and a sorted sequence
of r positive integers $K = \langle k_1, k_2, \ldots, k_r \rangle$. The number of processors p.
Output: The k_ith smallest element in A, $1 \le i \le r$.

1. $r \leftarrow |K|$
2. If $r > 0$ **then**
3.   Set $k = k_{\lceil r/2 \rceil}$.
4.   Use Algorithm PARSELECT to find a, the kth smallest element in A.
5.   Output a.
6.   Let $A_1 = \langle a_i \mid a_i < a \rangle$ and $A_2 = \langle a_i \mid a_i > a \rangle$.
7.   Let $K_1 = \langle k_1, k_2, \ldots, k_{\lceil r/2 \rceil - 1} \rangle$ and
       $K_2 = \langle k_{\lceil r/2 \rceil + 1} - k, k_{\lceil r/2 \rceil + 2} - k, \ldots, k_r - k \rangle$.
8.   PARMULTISELECT1$(A_1, K_1, p|A_1|/|A|)$.
9.   PARMULTISELECT1$(A_2, K_2, p|A_2|/|A|)$.
10. **end if**

In the remaining of this section, we present an efficient algorithm to solve this problem that runs in time

$$T(n, p) = O((n/p + t_s(p, p))(\log r + \log(n/p)))$$

on the PRAM with p processors, $r \le p < n$, where $t_s(p, p)$ is the time needed to sort p elements using p processors. If $p = n/\log n$, the running time becomes $T(n, n/\log n) = O(\log n(\log r + \log \log n))$.

In the algorithm to be presented, we will use the following notation to repeatedly partition A into smaller subsets. Let $a \in A$ with rank k_a. Partition A into two subsets $A' = \{x \in A \mid x \le a\}$ and $A'' = \{x \in A \mid x > a\}$. This partitioning of A induces the following bipartitioning of K: $B' = \{k \in K \mid k \le k_a\}$ and $B'' = \{k - k_a \mid k \in K \text{ and } k > k_a\}$. In this case, we will call each of (A', B') and (A'', B'') a *selection pair*. Let (A', B') be a selection pair. We will label (A', B') as "active" if $|B'| > 0$; otherwise, it will be called "inactive". The algorithm is given as Algorithm PARMULTISELECT2.

We turn to the analysis of the algorithm. First, we allocate a number of processors for each active set. Specifically, we assign $p' = (|A|/s)p$ processors for active set (A, B), where s is the number of remaining elements computed in Line 15. There are enough processors for all active sets. The set A is partitioned into p' groups of $w = |A|/p' = s/p$ elements each. Note that $w \le n/p = q$. The median of medians m is smaller than (and greater than) at least $(|A|/2w)(w/2) = |A|/4$ elements. That is, it is greater than (and smaller than) at most $3|A|/4$ elements. Hence, after $c \log r$ iterations, the size of each subset is at most

$$
\left(\frac{3}{4}\right)^{c \log r} \times n
$$

$$
= r^{c \log (3/4)} \times n
$$

$$
= \frac{n}{r^{c \log (4/3)}}
$$

$$
= \frac{n}{r^{\log (4/3)/\log (4/3)}}
$$

$$
= \frac{n}{r}.
$$

We observe that if A is partitioned into more than r subsets, then *at most* r of these subsets are active, and the rest are inactive, since the number of ranks in B is $\le r$. Consequently, after $c \log r$ iterations, there are at most r subsets of size at most n/r each. Clearly, after $c \log q$ additional iterations, the size of active subsets in the first stage will be reduced further by a factor of q, so that the size of each subset is upperbounded by $n/rq = p/r$. In other words, after $c \log q$ additional iterations, there are at most r subsets of size at most p/r each.

Algorithm 19.16 PARMULTISELECT2

Input: A sequence $A = \langle a_1, \ldots, a_n \rangle$ of elements and a sorted sequence of positive integers $B = \langle k_1, k_2, \ldots, k_r \rangle$, $1 \le k_i \le n$. The number of processors p.

Output: The k_ith smallest element in A, $1 \le i \le r$.

1. $\mathcal{L} \leftarrow \{(A, B)\}$; Mark (A, B) "active"; $s \leftarrow n$; $q \leftarrow n/p$.
2. $c \leftarrow 1/\log(4/3)$
3. Repeat Steps 4–16 $c(\log r + \log q)$ times.
4. **for each** active pair $(A, B) \in \mathcal{L}$ **do in parallel**
5.   Assign $p' = (|A|/s)p$ processors for active set (A, B).
6.   **if** $|A| \le p'$ **then** sort A and return the k_ith smallest element for $1 \le i \le |B|$.
7.   **else**
8. $w \leftarrow |A|/p' = s/p$. Partition A into p' subsequences $A_1, A_2, \ldots, A_{p'}$ of size at most $w \le q$ each. Find the median m_i of each A_i. Sort these medians to obtain the median of medians m.
9.   Find k, the rank of m in A.
10.   Partition A into A' and A'', where A' (resp. A'') is the set of elements in A less than or equal to (resp. greater than) m.
11.   Partition B into B' and B'', where B' (resp. B'') is the set of elements in B less than or equal to (resp. greater than) k. Subtract k from each rank in B''.
12.   Replace (A, B) in $\mathcal{L}$ by (A', B') and (A'', B'').
13.   If B' is empty, then mark (A', B') as "inactive"; otherwise, mark it as "active". If B'' is empty, then mark (A'', B'') as "inactive"; otherwise, mark it as "active". Discard inactive pairs.
14.   **end if**
15.   Let s be the number of all remaining elements.
16. **end for**
17. Sort all partitions A in all active pairs $(A, B) \in \mathcal{L}$, and for each element in B return its corresponding element in A.

Now, we compute the overall time needed by the algorithm in the first $\log r$ iterations. Consider an arbitrary iteration where there are a number of subsets of total size less than or equal to n. We analyze the running time of a subset (A, B) of maximum size, that is, $|A| \le n$ is maximum among all active subsets. Finding the medians m_i takes $O(q)$ sequential time. Sorting the medians can be done in $t_s(|A|/w, p') = t_s(p', p') \le t_s(p, p)$ parallel time. Computing k, the rank of m in A, and the sets A' and A'' can be achieved in $O(w + \log p') = O(q + \log p)$ parallel time using parallel prefix and compaction. Since K is sorted, both B' and B'' are computed using parallel p'-search in $O(\log_{p'} r) = O(\log r / \log p')$ time. Hence, the time needed by the first $\log r$ iterations is

$$O\left((q + t_s(p, p) + \log p) \log r + \frac{\log^2 r}{\log p'} \right).$$

Observe that $t_s(p, p) \geq \log p$ and since $r \leq p$, we have

$$\frac{\log^2 r}{\log p'} \leq \frac{\log p \log r}{\log p'} \leq \log p \log r.$$

Hence, the above expression reduces to

$$O((q + t_s(p, p)) \log r) = O((n/p + t_s(p, p)) \log r).$$

The time taken by the next $\log q$ iterations is asymptotically the same as that taken by the first $\log r$ iterations, except that the number of iterations $\log r$ is replaced by $\log q$. Hence, the remaining iterations can be completed in time $O((q + t_s(p, p)) \log q) = O((n/p + t_s(p, p)) \log(n/p))$.

As to the sorting step in Line 17 of the algorithm, we have at most r subsets of size at most $n/rq = p/r$ each to be sorted. If we allocate p/r processors to each of the r subsets, the time needed for sorting is $t_s(p/r, p/r)$, which is negligible.

It follows that the time complexity of the algorithm is

$$T(n, p) = O((n/p + t_s(p, p))(\log r + \log(n/p))).$$

If, for example, we set $p = n^{1-\epsilon}$, $0 < \epsilon < 1$, we may use a simple $O(\log^2 p)$ sorting algorithm, and the above expression reduces to

$$T(n, n^{1-\epsilon}) = O((n^\epsilon + \log^2 p)(\log r + \log(n^\epsilon)))$$

$$= O(n^\epsilon(\log r + \log(n^\epsilon))),$$

which is optimal for $r \geq \log n^\epsilon$, since the cost of the algorithm will be $O(n \log r)$. If, on the other hand, we set $p = n/\log n$ and use the pipelined mergesort algorithm of Sec. 19.2.10, the time complexity becomes

$$T(n, n/\log n) = O((\log n + \log(n/\log n))(\log r + \log\log n))$$
$$= O(\log n(\log r + \log\log n)),$$

which is optimal for $r \geq \log n$. This is superior to the running time of Algorithm PARMULTISELECT1. If we let $r = O(\log n)$, the time complexity becomes $O(\log n \log\log n)$, which is the same as the running time for classical selection of one element in Sec. 19.2.11. In the special case when $r = 1$ and $p = n/\log n$, the running time reduces to that of the $O(\log n \log\log n)$ parallel selection algorithm of Sec. 19.2.11.

19.2.13 *Matrix multiplication*

Given two $n \times n$ matrices A and B, consider the problem of computing the product $C = AB$, where $n = 2^k$ for some positive integer k. Assume that there are n^3 processors available, labeled $P_{i,j,l}, 1 \leq i, j, l \leq n$. Each entry $c_{i,j}$ of C is the dot product of two vectors: row i of A and column j of B. First, we present an algorithm for the dot product. Algorithm DOT-PRODUCT below computes the dot product of two given vectors row i of A and column j of B of dimension n each using n processors. Lines 1 and 2 compute $W = A[i, *]B[*, j]$ in $\Theta(1)$ time. The rest of the algorithm is similar to Algorithm PARADDITION in Sec. 19.2.1. The second **for** loop copies the numbers in W into $V[n], V[n+1], \ldots, V[2n-1]$, which correspond to the leaves of the binary tree. The **for** loop in Line 5 is repeated $k = \log n$ times, once for each internal level of the tree. The **for** loop at line 6 is for performing 2^r additions in parallel, $r = k - 1, k - 2, \ldots, 0$ (see Sec. 19.2.1).

The algorithm for matrix multiplication is a parallelization of the traditional $\Theta(n^3)$ time sequential algorithm. It is shown below as Algorithm PAR-MATRIXMULT. It uses n^3 processors. The n processors $P_{i,j,1}, P_{i,j,2}, \ldots, P_{i,j,n}$ compute $C[i, j]$ using Algorithm DOTPRODUCT.

Thus, the running time of the algorithm is dominated by the call to Algorithm DOTPRODUCT, which takes $\Theta(\log n)$ time. The work done by the algorithm can be computed as follows. Line 3 is executed n^2 times, and in each call to Algorithm DOTPRODUCT, it performs $\Theta(n)$ operations. Hence, the work done by the algorithm is $\Theta(n^3)$. Notice that the algorithm requires concurrent read capability, and hence it runs on the CREW PRAM.

Algorithm 19.17 DOTPRODUCT
Input: Two $n \times n$ matrices A and B and two indices i and j, $n = 2^k$.
Output: The dot product of row i of A and column j of B.

1. **for** $l \leftarrow 1$ **to** n **do in parallel**
2. $W[l] \leftarrow A[i, l] * B[l, j]$
3. **for** $l \leftarrow 1$ **to** n **do in parallel**
4. $V[l + n - 1] \leftarrow W[l]$
5. **for** $r \leftarrow k - 1$ **downto** 0
6.   **for** $t \leftarrow 2^r$ **to** $2^{r+1} - 1$ **do in parallel**
7. $V[t] \leftarrow V[2t] + V[2t + 1]$
8.   **end for**
9. **end for**
10. **return** $V[1]$

Algorithm 19.18 PARMATRIXMULT
Input: Two $n \times n$ matrices A and B, $n = 2^k$.
Output: The product $C = AB$.

1. **for** $i \leftarrow 1$ **to** n **do in parallel**
2.   **for** $j \leftarrow 1$ **to** n **do in parallel**
3. $C[i, j] \leftarrow$ DOTPRODUCT(A, B, i, j)
4.   **end for**
5. **end for**
6. **return** C

19.2.14 *Transitive closure*

Assume that an $n \times n$ adjacency matrix representation of a directed graph $G = (V, E)$ is given, where $|V| = n$. In such a representation, $A(i, j) = 1$ if and only if there is an edge from v_i to v_j in E, and $A(i, j) = 0$ if $(v_i, v_j) \notin E$. The *transitive closure* of A is represented as an $n \times n$ Boolean matrix A^* in which $A^*(i, j) = 1$ if and only if there is a path in G from v_i to v_j. $A^*(i, j) = 0$ if no such path exists. One way to obtain the transitive closure of A is to compute A^n by performing $\lceil \log n \rceil$ operations of squaring the matrix: $A \times A = A^2, A^2 \times A^2 = A^4$, and so on until a matrix A^m is obtained where $m \geq n$. Here, we use Boolean matrix multiplication method, in which the operations of scalar multiplication and addition in the standard matrix multiplication are replaced by the logical "AND" and "OR" operations, respectively. Since there are $\lceil \log n \rceil$ matrix multiplications, $A^* = A^n$ can be obtained in time $\Theta(\log^2 n)$ with $\Theta(n^3)$ processors on the CREW PRAM using Boolean matrix multiplication (see Sec. 19.2.13). The total number of operations is $\Theta(n^3 \log n)$.

19.2.15   *Shortest paths*

Let $G = (V, E)$ be a weighted directed graph on n vertices, in which each edge (i, j) has a weight $w[i, j]$. If there is no edge from vertex i to vertex j, then $w[i, j] = \infty$. For simplicity, we will assume that $V = \{1, 2, \ldots, n\}$. We assume that G does not have negative weight cycles, that is, cycles whose total weight is negative. The problem is to find the *distance* from each vertex to all other vertices, where the distance from vertex i to vertex j is the length of a shortest path from i to j. Let i and j be two different vertices in V. Define $d_{i,j}^k$ to be the length of a shortest path from i to j that contains at most k edges, $1 \le k \le n - 1$. Thus, for example, $d_{i,j}^1 = w[i, j]$, $d_{i,j}^2$ is the length of a shortest path from i to j that contains at most two edges, and so on. Then, by definition, $d_{i,j}^{n-1}$ is the length of a shortest path from i to j, i.e., the distance from i to j. Given this definition, we can compute $d_{i,j}^k$ recursively as follows:

$$d_{i,j}^k = \begin{cases} 0 & \text{if } i = j \\ w[i, j] & \text{if } k = 1 \\ \min_l \{d_{i,l}^{k/2} + d_{l,j}^{k/2}\} & \text{if } k \ge 2. \end{cases}$$

Let D^k be the matrix whose entries are $d_{i,j}^k$, $1 \le i, j \le n$. Then, D^k can be obtained from $D^{k/2}$ by squaring, except that the operations "+" and "min" replace the usual matrix operations "×" and "+", respectively. Letting $D^1 = (d_{i,j}^1)$, we can use the operations "+" and "min" to evaluate $D^2, D^4, \ldots, D^m$, where m is the smallest power of $2 \ge n - 1$. This takes $\lceil \log(n - 1) \rceil$ matrix multiplications. Hence, the running time is $\Theta(\log^2 n)$ using $\Theta(n^3)$ processors on the CREW PRAM (see Sec. 19.2.13). The total number of operations is $\Theta(n^3 \log n)$.

19.2.16   *Computing the convex hull of a set of points*

Let $S = \{p_1, p_2, \ldots, p_n\}$ be a set of n points in the plane, where n is a power of 2. The *convex hull* of S, denoted by $CH(S)$, is the smallest convex polygon containing all the points of S (see Sec. 17.3 for definitions

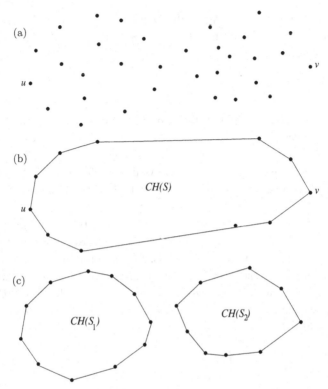

Fig. 19.20.   (a) The set of points S. (b) Convex hull of S. (c) Convex hulls of S_1 and S_2.

of geometric concepts). The convex hull is usually represented by a list of points, called vertices, ordered clockwise (or counterclockwise). See Figs. 19.20(a) and 19.20(b) for an example, in which S consists of 32 points. In what follows, we present a divide-and-conquer parallel algorithm to find $CH(S)$ in $\Theta(\log n)$ time using $O(n)$ processors on the CREW PRAM.

As a preprocessing step, the points in S are first sorted in ascending order of their x-coordinates in $\Theta(\log n)$ time using the pipelined merge sort algorithm. So, assume that $x(p_1) \leq x(p_2) \leq \cdots \leq x(p_n)$, where $x(p_i)$ denotes the x-coordinate of point p_i. We will assume for simplicity that no three points of S are collinear and no two points have the same x-coordinate. Next, the set of points S is divided into two halves: $S_1 = \langle p_1, p_2, \ldots, p_{n/2} \rangle$ and $S_2 = \langle p_{n/2+1}, p_{n/2+2}, \ldots, p_n \rangle$. Now, we recursively determine the two convex hulls of the two halves $CH(S_1)$ and $CH(S_2)$. Figure 19.20(c) shows the two convex hulls of the points in Fig. 19.20(a).

Consider the convex hull $CH(S)$ shown in Fig. 19.20(b). Here, u and v are the two points with minimum and maximum x-coordinates, respectively (recall that no two points have the same x-coordinate). These two points are clearly part of $CH(S)$. The polygonal chain defined by the edges from u to v in clockwise traversal is called the *upper hull* $UH(S)$. The *lower hull*, $LH(S)$, is defined similarly as the polygonal chain defined by the edges from v to u in clockwise traversal. The algorithm, after determining $CH(S_1)$ and $CH(S_2)$, proceeds by constructing the upper and lower hulls of S. The upper hull of S, $UH(S)$, is constructed by joining $UH(S_1)$ and $UH(S_2)$ by a line segment, called *tangent* such that $CH(S_1)$ and $CH(S_2)$ are below it. The lower hull $LH(S)$ is constructed in a similar manner to obtain the desired $CH(S)$. In what follows, we compute the upper tangent and upper hull $UH(S)$.

Let $\langle x_1, x_2, \ldots, x_r \rangle$ and $\langle y_1, y_2, \ldots, y_s \rangle$ be the upper hulls $UH(S_1)$ and $UH(S_2)$ of S_1 and S_2, respectively. We now show how to find the line of tangent $\overline{x^* y^*}$ with the property that both of $UH(S_1)$ and $UH(S_2)$ are below it. That is, $\overline{x^* y^*}$ is a tangent to both $UH(S_1)$ and $UH(S_2)$. The most crucial phase of the algorithm is the identification of the upper and lower tangents. We outline the steps of the algorithm for determining $\overline{x^* y^*}$ in the following two observations.

Observation 19.2 If x_i is a vertex of $UH(S_1)$, its tangent line $\overline{x_i v_i}$ with $UH(S_2)$ can be found in $\Theta(1)$ time using $\sqrt{s}$ processors.

Proof. We find the vertex v_i in $UH(S_2)$ such that $\overline{x_i v_i}$ is a tangent of $UH(S_2)$ as follows. Let y_j be any vertex in $UH(S_2)$, and let y_{j-1} and y_{j+1} be the two vertices to the left and right of y_j, respectively. If $x_i y_j y_{j-1}$ is a right turn and $x_i y_j y_{j+1}$ is a left turn, then v_i is to the right of y_j (see Fig. 19.21(a)). If $x_i y_j y_{j-1}$ is a left turn and $x_i y_j y_{j+1}$ is a right turn, then v_i is to the left of y_j (see Fig. 19.21(b)). If both $x_i y_j y_{j-1}$ and $x_i y_j y_{j+1}$ are right turns, then $v_i = y_j$ (see Fig. 19.21(c)). Hence, we do parallel search on the set of vertices of $UH(S_2)$ using $\sqrt{s}$ processors to identify the vertex y_k such that $v_i = y_k$. There are $\log_{\sqrt{s}} s = 2$ iterations in this search, which implies that the running time is $\Theta(1)$. $\qquad \square$

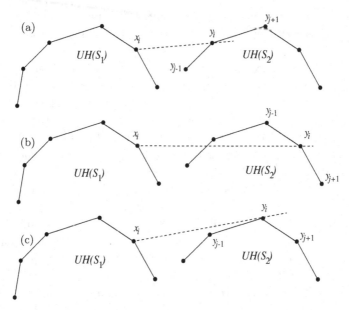

Fig. 19.21.   Tangents to $UH(S_2)$.

Observation 19.3   The common tangent $\overline{x^*y^*}$ of $UH(S_1)$ and $UH(S_2)$ can be determined in $\Theta(1)$ time using $\sqrt{r}\sqrt{s}$ processors.

Proof.   Let $\overline{x_i v_i}$ be a tangent to $UH(S_2)$ at v_i determined as described in Observation 19.2, and let x_{i-1} and x_{i+1} be the two vertices to the left and right of x_i, respectively. If $\overline{x_i v_i}$ is also a tangent to $UH(S_1)$, then $x^* = x_i$. If $x_{i-1}x_i v_i$ is a left turn, then x^* is to the left of x_i (see Fig. 19.22(a)). If $x_{i-1}x_i v_i$ is a right turn, then x^* is to the right of x_i (see Fig. 19.22(b)). This allows us to determine, for any given vertex x_i of $UH(S_1)$, whether the vertex x^* appears to the left of, to the right of, or equal to x_i in $\Theta(1)$ time. Thus, to locate x^*, we do double parallel search, the outer search is on the vertices of $UH(S_1)$, and for each vertex x_i in $UH(S_1)$, we do the inner parallel search on the vertices of $UH(S_2)$. The parallel search performed on the set of vertices of $UH(S_2)$ is done as outlined in Observation 19.2 to obtain the tangent $\overline{x_i v_i}$ and next apply the test for the location of x^* relative to x_i as stated above. We will use $\sqrt{r}$ processors for the outer search on the vertices of $UH(S_1)$, and so there are $\log_{\sqrt{r}} r = 2$ iterations

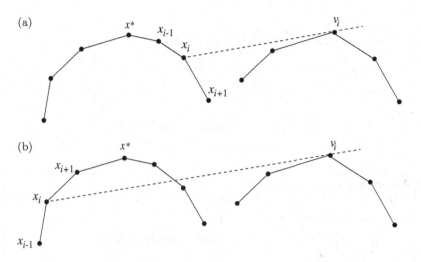

Fig. 19.22. Tangents to $UH(S_1)$.

in this search. We use $\sqrt{s}$ processors for the inner search on the vertices of $UH(S_2)$, which amounts to two iterations for the inner search. Thus, the total number of processors used is $\sqrt{r}\sqrt{s} \leq n$, that is, $\sqrt{s}$ processors for every vertex considered in $UH(S_1)$. It follows that the overall running time to find the upper tangent is $\Theta(1)$ using $\sqrt{r}\sqrt{s} \leq n$ processors. □

Observations 19.2 and 19.3 provide the steps for finding the upper common tangent $\overline{x^*y^*}$. The lower common tangent can be found in a similar fashion. It remains to finish the construction of $CH(S)$. Let $x_i = x^*$ and $y_j = y^*$. To construct $UH(S)$, first, we remove the vertices $x_{i+1}, x_{i+2}, \ldots, x_r$ from $UH(S_1)$ and remove the vertices $y_1, y_2, \ldots, y_{j-1}$ from $UH(S_2)$ to obtain $UH'(S_1)$ and $UH'(S_2)$, respectively. That is, $UH'(S_1) = \langle x_1, x_2, \ldots, x_i \rangle$ and $UH'(S_2) = \langle y_j, y_{j+1}, \ldots, y_s \rangle$. Next, connecting x_i in $UH'(S_1)$ to y_j in $UH'(S_2)$ by the edge $e = \overline{x^*y^*} = \overline{x_iy_j}$ yields the desired upper hull $UH(S)$ (see Fig. 19.23). Finally, the problem of computing $LH(S)$ can be solved in a similar fashion.

The above discussion is summarized in Algorithm PARCONVEXHULL below. The recurrence for the running time of the algorithm is $T(n) = T(n/2) + \Theta(1)$, which implies a running time of $\Theta(\log n)$. Clearly, there are concurrent read operations, and hence the algorithm works on the CREW PRAM.

Fig. 19.23. Upper hull of S, $UH(S)$.

Algorithm 19.19 PARCONVEXHULL
Input: A set $S = \{p_1, \ldots, p_n\}$ of n points in the plane, where n is a power of 2.
Output: The convex hull of S, $CH(S)$.

1. Sort the points in S in nondecreasing order of their x-coordinates.
2. $CH(S) \leftarrow ch(S)$
3. **return** $CH(S)$

Algorithm $ch(S)$
1. **if** $|S| \leq 4$ **then**
2.   compute $CH(S)$ by a straightforward method.
3.   **return** (CH(S))
4. **end if**
5. Divide S into two halves $S_1 = \langle p_1, p_2, \ldots, p_{n/2} \rangle$ and $S_2 = \langle p_{n/2+1}, p_{n/2+2}, \ldots, p_n \rangle$.
6. $CH(S_1) \leftarrow ch(S_1)$; $CH(S_2) \leftarrow ch(S_2)$
7. Let $UH(S_1) \leftarrow \langle x_1, x_2, \ldots, x_r \rangle$ and $UH(S_2) \leftarrow \langle y_1, y_2, \ldots, y_s \rangle$ be the upper hulls of S_1 and S_2, respectively.
8. Find the common upper tangent $\overline{x_i y_j}$.
9. $UH'(S_1) \leftarrow \langle x_1, x_2, \ldots, x_i \rangle$ and $UH'(S_2) \leftarrow \langle y_j, y_{j+1}, \ldots, y_s \rangle$.
10. $UH(S) \leftarrow UH'(S_1) \cup UH'(S_1) \cup \overline{x_i y_j}$.
11. Repeat Steps 7–10 to find the lower hull of S, $LH(S)$.
12. $CH(S) \leftarrow UH(S) \cup LH(S)$
13. **return** $CH(S)$

19.3 Interconnection-Network Computers

Interconnection networks or distributed memory machines are constructed as processor–memory pairs and connected to each other in a well-defined pattern. These processor–memory pairs are often referred to as *processing elements* or PEs, or sometimes just as *processors*. An interconnection network may be viewed as an undirected graph $G = (V, E)$, where V is the set of nodes or processors, and E is the set of two-way links. Processors communicate between each other by sending messages.

The topology of a network refers to its general infrastructure, the pattern in which multiple processors are connected. This pattern could either be regular or irregular, though many multi-core architectures today use highly regular interconnection networks. On one extreme, there is the complete graph, which models an interconnection network in which every processor is connected to every other processor. This kind of connection is prohibitive, as it is impractical. On the other extreme, the line graph, which models the linear array, connects each node to one or two other nodes. In between, there is a multitude of interconnection networks that have both advantages and disadvantages. For instance, there is the hypercube, the mesh, the tree, the pyramid to mention a few.

The degree of the network is the maximum degree of any vertex in the underlying graph. The degree of processor P corresponds to the number of processors directly connected to P. Naturally, networks of high degree become very difficult to manufacture. Therefore, it is desirable to use networks of low degree, especially if the network is to be scaled to extremely large number of processors. In a network with n processors, a constant degree is preferable to one that is a function of n. For example, the degree of the mesh is 4 while that of the hypercube is $\log n$.

The network diameter is defined as the maximum shortest path distance between any two processors. A low communication diameter is highly desirable, in that it allows for efficient communication between arbitrary processors. For instance, the diameter of the hypercube with n processors is $\log n$, while the diameter of a mesh with the same number of processors is $2\sqrt{n} - 2$.

The bisection width of an interconnection network is the minimum number of links that have to be removed in order to disconnect the network into two approximately equal size subnetworks. In general, machines with a high bisection width are difficult to build, but they provide users with the possibility of moving large amounts of data efficiently. The bisection width implies a lower bound on the computations in an interconnection network, especially in algorithms that require massive data movements. For instance, in the problem of sorting n elements, $\Omega(n)$ data items may have to be moved from one half of the network to the other. For example, the bisection width of the hypercube is $\Theta(n)$, and it admits sorting algorithms in the order of $\Theta(\log^2 n)$ and $\Theta(\log n \log n)$, while the bisection width of the mesh is $\Theta(\sqrt{n})$, which explains why sorting on the mesh is $\Omega(\sqrt{n})$.

19.4 The Hypercube

The hypercube is one of the most popular, versatile and efficient topological structures of interconnection networks. It has many excellent features, and thus became the first choice for the topological structure of parallel processing and computing systems. Let $d \geq 0$. The d-dimensional hypercube H_d has $p = 2^d$ nodes and $d2^{d-1}$ edges. Each node corresponds to a d-bit binary string, and two nodes are linked by an edge if and only if their binary strings differ in precisely one bit. Each node is incident to $d = \log p$ other nodes, one for each bit position. Figure 19.24 shows the d-dimensional hypercubes for $d = 1, 2, 3$.

An edge in the hypercube is called a *dimension k edge* if it links two nodes that differ in their kth bit position. In the d-dimensional hypercube H_d, for any $k \leq d$, the removal of the dimension k edges leaves two disjoint copies of a $(d-1)$-dimensional hypercube. Conversely, a d-dimensional hypercube H_d can be constructed from two $(d-1)$-dimensional hypercubes H_{d-1} by simply connecting the ith node of one H_{d-1} to the ith node of the other H_{d-1}. Thus, a hypercube has a simple recursive structure. For example, see Fig. 19.25. The d-dimensional hypercube H_d has a diameter d, which is low, and a high bisection width of 2^{d-1}.

Let $G_1 = (V_1, E_1)$ and $G_2 = (V_2, E_2)$ be two undirected graphs. The *Cartesian product* of G_1 and G_2 is an undirected graph, denoted by $G_1 \times G_2$,

Fig. 19.24. d-dimensional hypercubes for $d = 1, 2, 3$.

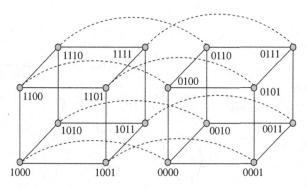

Fig. 19.25.   The construction of H_4 from two H_3's.

where $V(G_1 \times G_2) = V_1 \times V_2$, two distinct vertices $x_1 x_2$ and $y_1 y_2$, where $x_1, y_1 \in V(G_1)$ and $x_2, y_2 \in V(G_2)$, are linked by an edge in $G_1 \times G_2$ if and only if either $x_1 = y_1$ and $(x_2, y_2) \in E(G_2)$ or $x_2 = y_2$ and $(x_1, y_1) \in E(G_1)$. Examples of Cartesian products are shown in Figs. 19.24 and 19.25, where $H_2 = H_1 \times H_1$, $H_3 = H_2 \times H_1$ and $H_4 = H_3 \times H_1$. Let K_2 be the complete graph on two vertices. Then, H_d can be defined recursively as follows:

$$H_1 = K_2, \quad H_d = H_{d-1} \times H_1 = \underbrace{H_1 \times H_1 \times \cdots \times H_1}_{d}, \quad d \geq 2.$$

19.4.1 *The butterfly*

The butterfly interconnection network is closely related to the hypercube. Th d-dimensional butterfly B_d consists of $p = (d+1)2^d$ processors and $d2^{d+1}$ links. Each processor in B_d is represented by the pair (u, i), where i is the *level* or *dimension* of the processor, $0 \leq i \leq d$, and u is a d-bit binary number that denotes the row of the processor. Two processors (u, i) and (v, j) are connected by a link if and only if $j = i + 1$ and either u and v are identical or u and v differ in exactly the jth bit. Figure 19.26 shows the d-dimensional butterfly for $d = 1, 2, 3$. If u and v are identical, the link is said to be a *straight* link; otherwise, it is called a *cross* link. Edges connecting processors on levels i and $i + 1$ are called *level $i + 1$* edges.

There are structural similarities between the hypercube and the butterfly. In particular, the ith node of H_d corresponds naturally to the ith row of B_d, and the ith dimension edge (u, v) of H_d corresponds to cross edges

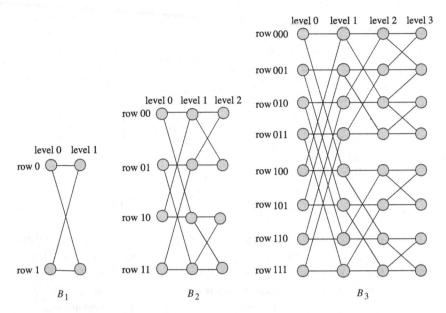

Fig. 19.26. d-dimensional butterfly for $d = 1, 2, 3$.

$((u, i - 1), (v, i))$ and $((v, i - 1), (u, i))$ in level i of B_d. We can obtain the hypercube H_d from the butterfly B_d by merging all nodes in the same row in B_d and then removing the extra copy of each edge.

The butterfly has a simple recursive structure. Figure 19.27 shows a three-dimensional butterfly with level 3 nodes removed. The result is two two-dimensional butterflies, one consisting of even rows (solid edges) and the other of odd rows (dashed edges). Alternatively, we could remove the level 0 nodes of B_d to obtain two identical B_{d-1}'s.

A useful property of the d-dimensional butterfly is that the level 0 processor in any row u is linked to the level d processor in any row v by a unique path of length d. The path traverses each level exactly once, using the cross edge from level i to level $i + 1$ if and only if u and v differ in the $(i + 1)$th bit. We will call this path the *greedy path*. Figure 19.28(a) shows the greedy path from $(000, 0)$ to $(110, 3)$. It follows that the diameter of the d-dimensional butterfly is $2d = \Theta(\log p)$.

Figure 19.28(b) shows a 2^d-leaf complete binary tree contained within the d-dimensional butterfly. The leaves of the tree are the level d nodes of the butterfly.

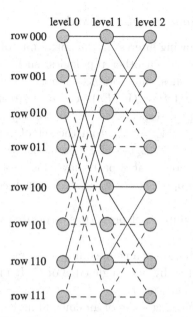

Fig. 19.27.   Recursive structure of the butterfly.

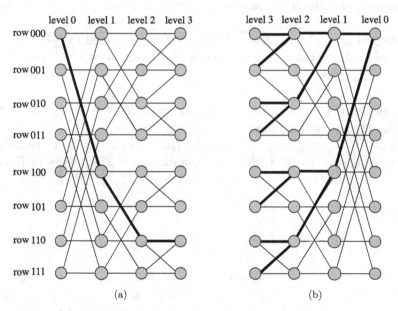

Fig. 19.28.   (a) The greedy path from $(000, 0)$ to $(110, 3)$. (b) A complete binary tree contained within B_3.

19.4.2   *Embeddings of the hypercube*

There is an ever-growing interest in the portability of algorithms developed for architectures based on other topologies, such as linear arrays, rings, two-dimensional meshes, and complete binary trees, into the hypercube. Let $G = (V_g, E_g)$ and $H = (V_h, E_h)$ be two undirected graphs, called the *guest* and *host* graphs, respectively. An *embedding* of G into H is defined by two mappings: $\phi : V_g \to V_h$ from the set of vertices of G to the set of vertices of H and $\psi : E_g \to \Pi(H)$ from the set of edges of G to the set of paths in H. Note that a path may consist of one edge, so in some embeddings, the mapping is $\psi : E_g \to E_h$ in which edges in G are mapped to edges in H.

There are some important properties associated with an embedding:

- **Dilation:** The dilation of an embedding is the maximum length of a path in $\Pi(H)$ mapped to by one single edge of G. It measures how much an edge in G is stretched in H.
- **Congestion:** The congestion of an embedding is the maximum number of edges in G mapped to one single edge in H. This counts the maximum number of paths in the image of ψ that pass through one particular edge in H.
- **Expansion:** The expansion of an embedding is defined by $\frac{|V_h|}{|V_g|}$.
- **Load:** This is the maximum number of nodes in G that are mapped to one single node in H.

Example 19.10   Consider the two graphs G and H shown in Fig. 19.29. Define the embedding functions ϕ and ψ by: $\phi(a) = w, \phi(b) = x, \phi(c) = z,$ $\psi((a,b)) = w, x, \psi((b,c)) = x, z,$ and $\psi((a,c)) = w, y, z.$ Since the edge (a, c) is mapped to the path $w, y, z,$ the dilation is 2. All edges of H are

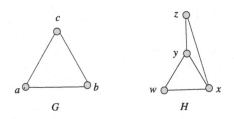

Fig. 19.29.   Example of graph embedding.

used at most once, and hence the congestion is 1. The expansion is 4/3. The load is 1.

19.4.2.1 *Gray codes*

A Gray code is an ordering of all possible d-bit binary sequences so that for all $k \geq 0, k$ and $k + 1$ differ in exactly one bit. The sequence of 3-bit numbers corresponding to $0, 1, \ldots, 7$ is $000, 001, 011, 010, 110, 111, 101, 100$. The Gray code of d bits is denoted by G_d, which is defined recursively as

$$G_1 = \{0, 1\} \quad \text{and} \quad G_{k+1} = \{0G_k, 1G_k^R\},$$

where $0G_k$ and $1G_k$ denote prefixing each element in the sequence G_k with 0 and 1, respectively, and G_k^R denotes G_k in reverse order. Thus, for example, to construct the sequence G_3, we do the following steps (see Fig. 19.30):

(1) Write down the sequence for G_1 columnwise, that is $\begin{smallmatrix}0\\1\end{smallmatrix}$.
(2) Next, construct G_2 as $\begin{smallmatrix}0G_1\\1G_1^R\end{smallmatrix}$.
(3) Repeat step 2 to get G_3 as $\begin{smallmatrix}0G_2\\1G_2^R\end{smallmatrix}$.

Figure 19.31 shows the recursive construction of G_3 pictorially. Note that this is a Hamiltonian cycle in H_3.

Fig. 19.30.   Construction of G_3.

Fig. 19.31.   Pictorial illustration of the construction of G_3.

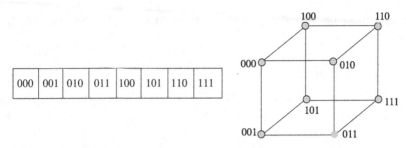

Fig. 19.32.   Embedding of a linear array into the hypercube.

19.4.2.2   *Embedding of a linear array into the hypercube*

The embedding of a linear array with $n = 2^d$ processors onto H_d is straight-forward (see Fig. 19.32). As we saw above, renumbering the hypercube processors using the Gray code induces a Hamiltonian cycle. Hence, a linear array or a ring with $n = 2^d$ processors can be embedded onto H_d with dilation 1 and congestion 1.

19.4.2.3   *Embedding of a mesh into the hypercube*

The linear array is really a one-dimensional mesh. Although the word mesh usually refers to the two-dimensional mesh, there are d-dimensional meshes in general with dimensions $r_1, r_2, \ldots, r_d$. A d-dimensional mesh is the cross product (Cartesian product) of d arrays. This is similar to the hypercube in which a d-dimensional hypercube is the cross product of d hypercubes of dimension 2. A two-dimensional mesh or two-dimensional array can be embedded by extending the idea discussed above for the case of linear arrays to two dimensions. Let M be a mesh with 2^r rows and 2^c columns. We treat each row independently as a linear array. Next, we generate the numbers $0, 1, \ldots, 2^c - 1$ in Gray code and prefix each processor number in row j with the number j in Gray code. Figure 19.33 provides an example of embedding a mesh with $2^1 \times 2^2$ nodes into H_3. First, label each node in row 0 with the numbers $0, 1, 2, 3(00, 01, 11, 10)$ using G_2 code. Do the same for row 1. Finally, prefix each node label in rows 0 and 1 with 0 and 1, respectively.

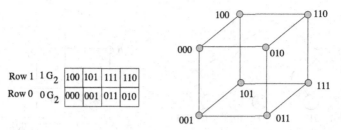

Fig. 19.33.   Embedding of a mesh into the hypercube.

19.4.2.4   *Embedding of a binary tree into the hypercube*

There are several embeddings of binary trees into hypercubes.

Theorem 19.6   *It is impossible to embed a complete binary tree T with $n - 1$ nodes into a hypercube H with $n \geq 8$ nodes with dilation 1.*

Proof.   Assume $n = 2^d$. Since T has $n - 1$ nodes, the number of leaves in T is $n/2$. Suppose for the sake of contradiction that a complete binary tree with $n - 1$ nodes is a subgraph of the d-dimensional hypercube H_d. A node in H_d has even parity if the number of ones in its binary string is even; otherwise, it has odd parity. It is easy to see that the number of nodes of even parity is $n/2$ and the number of nodes of odd parity is $n/2$. Assume without loss of generality that the hypercube node that contains the root of T has even parity. Since the neighbors of this node have odd parity, the children of the root of T are contained in odd parity hypercube nodes. Similarly, the grandchildren of the root of T are contained in even parity hypercube nodes, and so on. Hence, the leaves and their grandparents, which account for $n/2 + n/8 = 5n/8$ nodes, must all be contained in hypercube nodes of the same parity. This is impossible, as there are only $n/2$ nodes with the same parity in H_d. It follows that T is not a subgraph of H_d.   □

It is possible, however, to embed a complete binary tree T with n leaves into a hypercube H with n nodes with dilation 1. Note that the tree has a total of $2n-1$ nodes. In this embedding, the ith leaf of the binary tree T is mapped to the ith node of the hypercube, and each internal node of T is mapped to the same hypercube node as its leftmost descendant leaf. See Fig. 19.34.

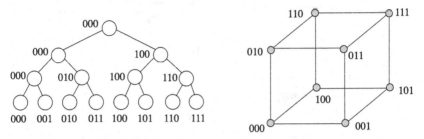

Fig. 19.34.   One possible embedding of a binary tree with n leaves into the hypercube with n nodes with dilation 1.

19.4.3   *Broadcasting on the hypercube*

Let H_d be a d-dimensional hypercube. Broadcasting a datum x from P_0 to all other processors can be achieved as follows. In the first step, P_0 sends x to P_1. In Step 2, P_0 and P_1 send in parallel x to P_2 and P_3. In Step 3, P_0, P_1, P_2 and P_3 send in parallel x to P_4, P_5, P_6 and P_7. The formal algorithm is shown as Algorithm HCBROADCAST below. The notation $j^{(i)}$ means j with the ith bit complemented, $0 \leq i \leq d - 1$. For example, $101^2 = 001$. The total number of steps in the algorithm is d.

Algorithm 19.20 HCBROADCAST
Input: x.
Output: Broadcast x from P_0 to all other processors.

  1. **for** $i \leftarrow 0$ **to** $d - 1$
  2.   **for all** $j < 2^i$ and $j < j^{(i)}$ **do in parallel**
  3.   Processor P_j sends x to processor $P_{j^{(i)}}$
  4.   **end for**
  5. **end for**

19.4.4   *Permutation routing in the hypercube*

Consider the problem of routing in the d-dimensional hypercube H_d with $p = 2^d$ processors. We consider the problem of *permutation routing* in which every processor tries to send to a different destination. Processor i wants to send a packet v_i to destination $\delta(i)$. We also assume *oblivious routing*, in which the route taken by packet v_i depends only on the destination $\delta(i)$ and not on any other packet's destination $\delta(j)$. A *collision* occurs when two packets arrive at the same processor at the same time, and try to leave at the same link. To deal with collisions, every processor has a queue and a prioritizing scheme for each incoming packet. If incoming packets try to leave along the same link, they are placed in a queue and sent off in different time steps.

19.4.4.1 *The greedy algorithm*

A straightforward method for oblivious routing is called *bit fixing*, which works by taking the bit address of the source processor and changing one bit at a time to the address of the destination processor. Each time a bit is changed, the packet is forwarded to a neighboring processor. Clearly, bit fixing is an optimal routing scheme for a single packet. If the source i and destination j differ by k bits, then the packet must traverse at least k links in the hypercube to get to its destination. Bit fixing takes exactly k steps.

19.4.4.2 *The randomized algorithm*

If we have to route many packets, bit fixing can cause collisions. In fact, so can any deterministic oblivious routing strategy. We have the following theorem, which is quite general:

Theorem 19.7 *Any deterministic oblivious permutation routing scheme for a parallel machine with p processors, each with d outward links, requires $\Omega(\sqrt{p/d})$ steps.*

Luckily, we can avoid this bad case by using a randomized routing scheme. In fact, most permutations cause very few collisions. So, the idea is to first route all the packets using a *random permutation*, and then from there to their final destination. That is,

(a) **Phase 1.** Choose a random permutation σ of $\{1, 2, \ldots, p\}$. Route packet v_i to destination $\sigma(i)$ using bit fixing.
(b) **Phase 2.** Route packet v_i from $\sigma(i)$ to destination $\delta(i)$ using bit fixing.

The following observation about bit fixing during one of the two phases above is important.

Observation 19.4 Two packets can come together along a route and then separate, but only once. That is, a pair of routes can look like Fig. 19.35(a), but 19.35(b) is impossible.

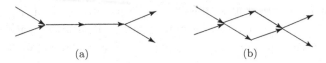

(a)   (b)

Fig. 19.35.   Packets collision.

To see this, notice that during bit fixing routing, an intermediate address is always of the form $y_1 \ldots y_k x_{k+1} \ldots x_d$, where x_i is a bit of the source address and y_j is a bit of the destination address. If two routes collide at the kth step, that means their destination addresses agree in their first k bits, and the source addresses agree in their $d-k$ bits. At each time step, we add one more bit of the destination address, which means we increment k. Eventually, the destination bits must disagree since the destinations are different. Let k_0 be the value of k at which this happens. Then, the y_{k_0} destination bit is different for the two packets. At this point, the two packets separate, and they will never collide again because all the later intermediate destinations will include the y_{k_0} bit. Observation 19.4 is the crux of the proof of the following theorem:

Theorem 19.8   *Let S be the set of packets whose routes intersect v_i's route. Then, the delay of packet v_i is $\leq |S|$.*

Notice that whenever the routes of two packets intersect, one of the packets may be delayed by one time step. Once that packet is delayed by one time step at the first shared node, it will flow along the shared route behind the other packet and will not be delayed any more by that packet. If the same route intersects other routes, each of them may add a delay of one time step. This happens either because another packet collides with the current packet along a shared route, or because another packet collides with a packet that is ahead of the current packet along a part of the route which is shared by all three. In either case, an extra delay of at most one results.

To get the running time of this scheme, we compute the expected value of the size of the set S above. Define the indicator random variable $X_{i,j}$ which is 1 when the routes of packets v_i and v_j share at least one edge, and $X_{i,j}$ is 0 otherwise. Then, by the above theorem, the expected delay of packet v_i is the expected size of S, which is $\mathbf{E}\left[\sum_{j=1}^p X_{i,j}\right]$. It is rather difficult to get an estimate of this quantity. It is easier to think of $Y(e)$, which is the number of routes that pass through a given edge e. Now, suppose the route of packet v_i consists of the edges $(e_1, e_2, \ldots, e_k)$. Then, we have $\sum_{j=1}^{p} X_{i,j} \le \sum_{l=1}^{k} Y(e_l)$. Hence,

$$\mathbf{E}\left[\sum_{j=1}^{p} X_{i,j}\right] \le \mathbf{E}\left[\sum_{l=1}^{k} Y(e_l)\right].$$

To use this bound, we next compute $\mathbf{E}[Y(e)]$. Notice that

$\mathbf{E}[Y(e)] = $ (sum of lengths of all routes)/(total edges in the network).

The sum of lengths of all routes is the expected length of a route times p (the number of all routes). The average length of a route is $d/2$ because a d-bit source differs from a random destination address in $d/2$ bits on average. So, the sum of route lengths is $pd/2$. The total number of edges in the network is the number of nodes times the number of outbound links, which is pd. So, $\mathbf{E}[Y(e)] = (pd/2)/(pd) = 1/2$. Thus, if the path for packet v_i has k edges along it, then

$$\mu = \mathbf{E}\left[\sum_{j=1}^{p} X_{i,j}\right] \le \mathbf{E}\left[\sum_{l=1}^{k} Y(e_l)\right] = \sum_{l=1}^{k} \mathbf{E}[Y(e_l)] = \frac{k}{2} \le d \times \frac{1}{2} = \frac{d}{2}.$$

Now, we can apply Chernoff bound in Theorem 13.6 to the probability of there being a substantial number of paths intersecting v_i's path. The Chernoff bound is

$$\mathbf{Pr}\left[\sum_{j=1}^{p} X_{i,j} > (1+\delta)\mu\right] < 2^{-\delta\mu}.$$

We now compute the probability that v_i is delayed at least $3d$ steps. So, we require that $(1+\delta)\mu = 3d$. Notice that we do not actually know what μ is, but we have a bound for it of $\mu \le d/2$. It follows that $\mu\delta \ge 2.5d$. Thus, the probability that v_i is delayed by at least $3d$ steps is bounded above by $2^{-2.5d}$.

This is a bound for the probability that a given packet is delayed more than $3d$ steps. But we want to get a bound for the probability that *no* packet gets delayed more than $3d$ steps. For that, it is enough to use Boole's inequality for probabilities as a bound:

Boole's inequality: For any finite sequence of events $\mathcal{E}_1, \mathcal{E}_2, \ldots, \mathcal{E}_n$,

$$\mathbf{Pr}[\mathcal{E}_1 \cup \mathcal{E}_2 \cup \cdots \cup \mathcal{E}_n] \leq \mathbf{Pr}[\mathcal{E}_1] + \mathbf{Pr}[\mathcal{E}_2] + \cdots + \mathbf{Pr}[\mathcal{E}_n]. \qquad (19.7)$$

There are $p = 2^d$ routes in total, and the probability that one of these takes more than $3d$ steps is bounded above by $2^d 2^{-2.5d} = 2^{-1.5d}$. So, we can make the following assertion: With probability at least $1 - 2^{-1.5d}$ every packet reaches its destination $\sigma(i)$ in $4d$ or fewer steps. The $4d$ comes from the delay time $3d$ plus the time for bit fixing steps, which is $\leq d$. Notice that all of this applies to just one phase of the algorithm. So, the full algorithm (two phases) routes all packets to their destinations with high probability in $8d$ or fewer steps.

19.4.5 *Permutation routing in the butterfly*

Consider the problem of sending packets from level 0 to level d in the d-dimensional butterfly B_d. Processor $(i, 0)$ in level 0 wants to send a packet v_i to destination $(\delta(i), d)$ in level d. We consider the problem of *permutation routing* in which every processor in level 0 tries to send to a different destination in level d. That is, the function $\delta(i)$ is a permutation.

A simple process for routing a single packet obliviously is called *bit fixing*. For definitions of bit fixing, its lower bound, collision and oblivious routing see Sec. 19.4.4. Next, we discuss in detail a randomized routing scheme for the butterfly. This scheme consists of three phases:

(a) **Phase 1.** Choose a random permutation σ of $\{1, 2, \ldots, 2^d\}$. Route packet v_i to destination $(\sigma(i), d)$ using the greedy path.

(b) **Phase 2.** Route packet v_i from $(\sigma(i), d)$ to destination row but in level 0 $(\delta(i), 0)$ using the greedy path.

(c) **Phase 3.** Route packet v_i from $(\delta(i), 0)$ in level 0 to $(\delta(i), d)$ in level d through direct links.

In what follows, we analyze phase 1; phase 2 is the reverse of phase 1, and phase 3 takes d steps.

Let S be the set of packets whose routes intersect v_i's route. Define the indicator random variable $X_{i,j}$ which is 1 when the routes of packets v_i and v_j share at least one edge, and $X_{i,j}$ is 0 otherwise. Then, by Theorem 19.8, the expected delay of packet v_i is the expected size of S, which is $\mathbf{E}\left[\sum_{j=1}^{2^d} X_{i,j}\right]$. It is rather difficult to get an estimate of this quantity. It is easier to think of $Y(e)$, which is the number of routes that pass through a given edge e. Now, suppose the route of packet v_i consists of the edges $(e_1, e_2, \ldots, e_d)$. Then, we have $\sum_{j=1}^{2^d} X_{i,j} \le \sum_{l=1}^{d} Y(e_l)$. Hence,

$$\mathbf{E}\left[\sum_{j=1}^{2^d} X_{i,j}\right] \le \mathbf{E}\left[\sum_{l=1}^{d} Y(e_l)\right].$$

To use this bound, we next compute $\mathbf{E}[Y(e_l)]$. Consider the link e_l at level l, which connects level $l-1$ node to level l node. The number of packets that can potentially go through e_l is 2^{l-1} since there are only 2^{l-1} processors at level 0 for which there are greedy paths through this link. In fact, if $e_l = ((u, l-1), (v, l))$, then u is the root of a complete binary tree with 2^{l-1} leaves in level 0. Now, we compute the probability that packet v_i will go through link e_l. Consider what happens to packet v_i in level 0, when it wants to move to level 1. There are two links to choose from to go to level 1, either the direct link or the cross link. Thus, it takes one of these two links with probability $1/2$. It follows that in order for packet v_i to go through link e_l, it has to go through l links with probability $(1/2)^l$. Clearly, $Y(e_l)$ has the binomial distribution with parameters 2^{l-1} and $(1/2)^l$ (see Sec. B.4.3). Hence, $\mathbf{E}[Y(e_l)] = 2^{l-1} \times (1/2)^l = 1/2$.

Thus,

$$\mathbf{E}\left[\sum_{j=1}^{2^d} X_{i,j}\right] \le \mathbf{E}\left[\sum_{l=1}^{d} Y(e_l)\right] = \sum_{l=1}^{d} \mathbf{E}[Y(e_l)] = \frac{d}{2}.$$

Now, we can apply Chernoff bound in Theorem 13.6 to the probability of there being a substantial number of paths intersecting v_i's path. The Chernoff bound is

$$\mathbf{Pr}\left[\sum_{j=1}^{2^d} X_{i,j} > (1+\delta)\mu\right] < 2^{-\delta\mu}.$$

We compute the probability that v_i is delayed at least $3d$ steps. So, we require that $(1+\delta)\mu = 3d$. Notice that we do not actually know what μ is, but we have a bound for it of $\mu \le d/2$. It follows that $\mu\delta \ge 2.5d$. Thus, the probability that v_i is delayed by at least $3d$ steps is bounded above by $2^{-2.5d}$.

This is a bound for the probability that a given packet is delayed more than $3d$ steps. But we want to get a bound for the probability that *no* packet gets delayed more than $3d$ steps. For that it is enough to use Boole's inequality for probabilities as a bound (Eq. 19.7): There are 2^d routes total, and the probability that one of these takes more than $3d$ steps is bounded above by $2^d 2^{-2.5d} = 2^{-1.5d}$. So, we can make the following assertion: With probability at least $1 - 2^{-1.5d}$ every packet v_i reaches its phase 1 destination $(\sigma(i), d)$ in $4d$ or fewer steps. The $4d$ comes from the delay time $3d$ plus the time for bit fixing steps, which is d. Notice that all of this applies to just one phase of the algorithm. So, the full algorithm (three phases) routes all packets to their destinations with high probability in $4d + 4d + d = 9d$ or fewer steps.

19.4.6   *Computing parallel prefix on the hypercube*

The parallel prefix problem was defined in Sec. 19.2.3. In this section, we show how to compute it on the hypercube. Let H_d be a d-dimensional hypercube, where each processor P_i contains item x_i, $0 \leq i \leq n - 1 = 2^d - 1$. Assume that each processor has two registers: s and z. The algorithm is shown as Algorithm HCPARPREFIX below. The notation $j^{(i)}$ means j with the ith bit complemented, $0 \leq i \leq d - 1$, where $i = 0$ corresponds to the rightmost least significant binary digit. For example, $100^1 = 110$. s_j computes the sum $x_0 \circ x_2 \circ \cdots \circ x_j$, and z_j is a temporary variable. Initially, $s_i = z_i = x_i$, $0 \leq i \leq n - 1$.

Algorithm 19.21 HCPARPREFIX
Input: $X = \langle x_0, x_1, \ldots, x_{n-1} \rangle$, a sequence of n numbers, where $n = 2^d$.
Output: $S = \langle s_0, s_1, \ldots, s_{n-1} \rangle$, the prefix sums of X.

1. **for** $i \leftarrow 0$ **to** $d - 1$
2.   **for all** $j < j^{(i)}$ **do in parallel**
3. $z_{j^{(i)}} \leftarrow z_{j^{(i)}} \circ z_j$
4. $s_{j^{(i)}} \leftarrow s_{j^{(i)}} \circ z_j$
5. $z_j \leftarrow z_{j^{(i)}}$
6.   **end for**
7. **end for**

Figure 19.36 illustrates the operation of the algorithm on the three-dimensional hypercube. For clarity, the intermediate calculations have been

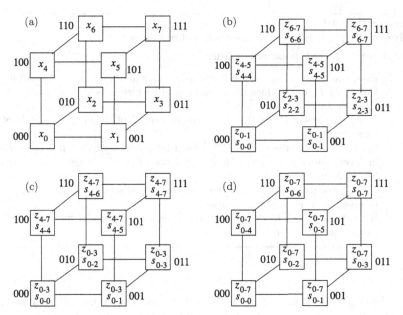

Fig. 19.36. Example of computing parallel prefix on the three-dimensional hypercube.

shown with indices of the form s_{i-j}, which is equal to $x_i \circ x_{i+1} \circ \ldots \circ x_j$, $0 \le i \le j \le n - 1$. The same thing applies to z_{i-j}. Figure 19.36(b) shows the contents of registers after the computations in the first iteration ($i = 0$). Figures 19.36(c) and 19.36(d) show the contents of registers after the computations in the second and third iterations ($i = 1$ and 2). There are $d = \log n$ iterations in the algorithm, each takes $\Theta(1)$ time. Hence, its running time is $\Theta(\log n)$.

19.4.7 *Hyperquicksort*

Quicksort is a very popular sorting algorithm. There have been numerous attempts to parallelize it for a variety of machines and models of computation; see Sec. 19.2.3.2 for an example. One attempt is hyperquicksort, which is targeted for the case of hypercubes with $p < n$. The algorithm is shown as Algorithm HCHYPERQUICKSORT below. Initially, it is assumed that the n elements are evenly distributed among the $p = 2^d$ processors, so that every processor contains n/p elements.

Algorithm 19.22 HCHYPERQUICKSORT
Input: $X = \langle x_1, x_2, \ldots, x_n \rangle$, a sequence of n numbers.

Output: X sorted in ascending order.

1. Each processor sorts its n/p items using a sequential sorting algorithm.
2. Processor P_0 determines the median m of its elements and broadcasts it to all other processors.
3. Every processor P_i partitions its items into X of items $\leq m$ and Y of items $> m$.
4. Let the two subcubes of size 2^{d-1} each be L and U. Every processor P_i in L sends its set Y to its adjacent processor P_j in U. Likewise, P_j sends its set X to P_i.
5. Every processor merges the elements that it already has with those it received from its adjacent processor.
6. Repeat Steps 2–5 to recursively sort L and U in parallel until the subcubes consist of one processor.

Clearly, Algorithm HCHYPERQUICKSORT sorts its input. It remains to find its running time. Assume that the data is balanced, so that after Step 5 is executed, each processor has $\Theta(n/p)$ elements. In this case, the recursion depth is $O(\log p) = O(d)$. Step 1 takes $\Theta((n/p)\log(n/p))$ time. Determining the median in Step 2 takes $\Theta(1)$ time since the items in each processor are sorted. Broadcasting m takes $\Theta(d)$ time in one recursive call for a total of $d + (d-1) + (d-2) + \cdots = \frac{d(d+1)}{2} = \Theta(d^2)$ in all recursive calls. Step 3 takes $\Theta(n/p)$ time. Step 4 of data transmission takes $\Theta(n/p)$ time. By the end of this step, every element in L is $\leq$ every element in U. Step 5 of merging the two sets takes $\Theta(n/p)$ time.

It can be shown that if the data is initially distributed in random fashion, the expected running time of the algorithm is

$$\Theta\left((n/p)\log(n/p) + d^2 + dn/p\right).$$

The $(n/p)\log(n/p)$ term represents the sorting step. The d^2 term represents broadcasting as stated above, and the dn/p term represents the time required for exchanging and merging sets of elements in all recursive calls. One disadvantage of the algorithm is that the elements may not be evenly distributed after the algorithm terminates.

19.4.8 *Selection on the hypercube*

Recall the problem of selection discussed in Secs. 5.5 and 19.2.11: Given a sequence $A = \langle a_1, a_2, \ldots, a_n \rangle$ of n elements and a positive integer $k, 1 \leq k \leq n$, find the kth smallest element in A. In this section, we develop an algorithm that runs on the hypercube with $p < n$ processors. The algorithm is shown as Algorithm HCSELECT.

Algorithm 19.23 HCSELECT

Input: A sequence $A = \langle a_1, \ldots, a_n \rangle$ of elements and an integer k, $1 \leq k \leq n$.

Output: The kth smallest element in A.

1. **if** $|A| \leq p$ **then** sort A and return the kth smallest element.
2. **for** $i \leftarrow 0$ **to** $p - 1$ **do in parallel**
3.   Processor P_i computes the median m_i of its local n/p elements using an optimal sequential algorithm for selection. Let the set of medians be M.
4. Sort M and find its median m.
5. Broadcast m to all p processors.
6. Partition A into three sequences:
   $A_1 = \{a \mid a < m\}$
   $A_2 = \{a \mid a = m\}$
   $A_3 = \{a \mid a > m\}$
7. **case**
8. $|A_1| \geq k$:
9.   Distribute A_1 evenly over all processors
10.   HCSELECT(A_1, k)
11. $|A_1| + |A_2| \geq k$: **return** m
12. $|A_1| + |A_2| < k$:
13.   Distribute A_3 evenly over all processors
14. $k \leftarrow k - |A_1| - |A_2|$
15.   HCSELECT(A_3, k)
16. **end case**

The time complexity of the algorithm can be computed as follows. Step 3 of the algorithm takes $O(n/p)$ time using an optimal sequential algorithm for selection. The sorting step in Line 4 takes $t_s(p, p)$ time, which is the time needed to sort p elements using p processors. Broadcasting m in Step 5 requires $O(\log p)$ time. Partitioning A into A_1, A_2 and A_3 can be done by first each processor splitting its data and then computing the global sizes of A_1, A_2 and A_3. This takes $O(n/p + \log p)$ time using parallel prefix and compaction. The load balancing problem is to redistribute data items stored in a hypercube such that the number of items in different processors differ by at most one after the redistribution. We use a load balancing algorithm that has a time complexity of $O(M + \log p)$, where M is the maximum number of items at any processor before the redistribution. Thus, data distribution in Steps 9 and 13 takes $O(n/p + \log p)$ time.

The median of medians m is smaller than (and greater than) at least $(|A|/2p)(p/2) = |A|/4$ elements. That is, it is greater than (and smaller than) at most $3|A|/4$ elements (see Sec. 5.5). Hence, the recursive call takes at most $T(3n/4)$. This implies the following recurrence for the running time:

$$T(n,p) = \begin{cases} O(n) & \text{if } p = 1 \\ O(t_s(p,p)) & \text{if } p \geq n \\ T(3n/4,p) + O(n/p + t_s(p,p)) & \text{if } 1 < p < n. \end{cases}$$

The recursion depth is $\log n - \log p$, and hence the solution to this recurrence is

$$T(n,p) = O(n/p + t_s(p,p)(\log n - \log p)) = O(n/p + t_s(p,p)\log(n/p)).$$

If, for example, we let $p = n/\log n$ and use the $O(\log p \log \log p)$ time sorting algorithm, then the time complexity becomes

$$\begin{aligned} T(n, n/\log n) &= O(\log n + \log p \log \log p \log(\log n)) \\ &= O(\log n + \log n (\log \log n)^2) \\ &= O(\log n (\log \log n)^2). \end{aligned}$$

19.4.9 *Multiselection on the hypercube*

Let $A = \langle a_1, a_2, \ldots, a_n \rangle$ be a sequence of n distinct elements drawn from a linearly ordered set, and let $K = \langle k_1, k_2, \ldots, k_r \rangle$ be a sequence of positive integers between 1 and n. The *multiselection* problem is to select the k_ith smallest element for all values of $i, 1 \leq i \leq r$. The hypercube structure lends itself well for parallel execution of balanced divide-and-conquer algorithms. This leads to the following idea of the multiselection algorithm. First use Algorithm HCSELECT to find the median m of A. Use m as a splitter to partition A into A_1 of items smaller than or equal to m and A_2 of items larger than m. This induces a bipartition of B into two subsequences B_1 of items less than $k = \lceil n/2 \rceil$ and B_2 of items greater than k. The algorithm is then recursively called in parallel with (A_1, B_1) and (A_2, B_2). Note that since the elements are distinct, $|A_1| = \lceil n/2 \rceil$ and $|A_2| = \lfloor n/2 \rfloor$. Following this idea, the algorithm is shown as Algorithm HCMULTISELECT. In $cube(s, d)$, s is the starting address of the cube and d is its dimension. Initially, the algorithm is called with HCMULTISELECT$(A, B, cube(0, \log p))$.

Algorithm 19.24 HCMULTISELECT

Input: A sequence $A = \langle a_1, \ldots, a_n \rangle$ of elements and a sequence of positive integers $B = \langle k_1, k_2, \ldots, k_r \rangle$, $1 \le k_i \le n$. $cube(s, d)$, the starting address of the cube s and its dimension d.

Output: The k_ith smallest element in A, $1 \le i \le r$.

1. $p \leftarrow 2^d$.
2. **if** $p = 1$ **then** use a sequential multiselection algorithm and exit.
3. **else if** $|A| \le p$ **then** sort A and return the k_ith smallest element, $1 \le i \le r$.
4. **else if** $|B| = 1$ **then** use Algorithm HCSELECT to find the k_1th smallest element.
5. **else** do Steps 6–24
6. Use Algorithm HCSELECT to find the median element m
7. Broadcast m to all p processors.
8. $k \leftarrow \lceil |A|/2 \rceil$.
9. Partition A into A_1 and A_2, where A_1 (resp. A_2) is the set of elements in A less than or equal to (resp. greater than) m.
10. Partition B into B_1 and B_2, where B_1 (resp. B_2) is the set of elements in B less than or equal to (resp. greater than) k. Subtract k from each item in B_2.
11. **case**
12.　　$|B_1| = 0$:
13.　　　　Distribute A_2 evenly over all processors
14.　　　　HCMULTISELECT(A_2, B_2, s, d)
15.　　$|B_2| = 0$:
16.　　　　Distribute A_1 evenly over all processors
17.　　　　HCMULTISELECT(A_1, B_1, s, d)
18.　　$|B_1| > 0$ and $|B_2| > 0$:
19.　　　　Distribute A_1 evenly over all processors in $L = cube(s, d - 1)$
20.　　　　Distribute A_2 evenly over all processors in $U = cube(s + 2^{d-1}, d - 1)$
21.　　　　**do in parallel**
22.　　　　　　HCMULTISELECT$(A_1, B_1, cube(s, d - 1))$
23.　　　　　　HCMULTISELECT$(A_2, B_2, cube(s + 2^{d-1}, d - 1))$
24. **end case**

In Step 13, A_1 is discarded, since $|B_1| = 0$. Similarly, in Step 16, A_2 is discarded, since $|B_2| = 0$. Let Q denote our hypercube with $p = 2^d$ processors. Q can be divided into two disjoint halves L and U, where L consists of processors with addresses $0x$, and U consists of processors with addresses $1x$. Now, we show how to move the elements in A_1 and A_2 to L and U, respectively, as stated in Steps 19 and 20. Every processor P in Q logically partitions its local set of data into two groups X and Y, where X contains those elements less than or equal to the median m, and Y contains those elements greater than m. This requires $O(n/p)$ sequential time. Now, each processor P_{0x} in L sends its set Y to its adjacent processor P_{1x} in U. Likewise, each processor P_{1x} in U sends its set X to its adjacent processor P_{0x} in L. Notice that when this step is complete, all elements less than or equal to m are in L, while all elements greater than m are in U. This step requires $O(n/p)$ time for the transmission of data. It is followed by load balancing. The load balancing problem is to redistribute data items stored in a hypercube such that the number of items in different processors differ by at most one after the redistribution. The load balancing algorithm has a time complexity of $O(M + \log p)$, where M is the maximum number of items at any processor before the redistribution. Thus, it runs in time $O(n/p + \log p)$.

The time complexity of the algorithm can be computed as follows. Finding the median m by Algorithm HCSELECT in Step 6 requires $O(n/p + t_s(p, p) \log(n/p))$ time, where $t_s(p, p)$ is the time needed to sort p elements using p processors. Partitioning A into A_1 and A_2 can be done by each processor splitting its data in time $O(n/p)$. Data redistribution takes $O(n/p + \log p)$ time. This implies the following recurrence for the running time:

$$T(n, r, p) \leq \begin{cases} O(n \log r) & \text{if } p = 1 \\ O(n/p + t_s(p, p) \log(n/p)) & \text{if } r = 1 \\ O(t_s(p, p)) & \text{if } p \geq n \\ T(n/2, r-1, p/2) + O(n/p + t_s(p, p) \log(n/p)) & \text{if } 1 < p, r < n. \end{cases}$$

In the worst case, the recursion depth is $\min\{r, \log p, \log n\} = \min\{r, \log p\}$ since $p < n$. It follows that the solution to this recurrence is

$$T(n, r, p) = O((n/p + t_s(p, p) \log(n/p)) \min\{r, \log p\}).$$

If we use the $O(\log p \log \log p)$ time sorting algorithm, then the time complexity becomes

$$T(n, r, p) = O((n/p + \log p \log \log p \log(n/p)) \min\{r, \log p\}).$$

If we let $p = n^{1-\epsilon}$ for $0 < \epsilon < 1$, then there is always a constant n_0 such that $n/p = n^\epsilon > \log p \log \log p \log(n/p)$ holds for all $n > n_0$. This shows that $T(n, r, n^{1-\epsilon}) = O(n^\epsilon \min\{r, \log n^{1-\epsilon}\})$. This bound is optimal for $r \geq n^{1-\epsilon}$.

19.4.10   *Computing parallel prefix on the butterfly*

The parallel prefix problem was defined in Sec. 19.2.3. In this section, we show how to compute it on the butterfly. For simplicity, we will assume addition as the binary operation. Recall from Sec. 19.4.1 that a complete binary tree with 2^d leaves corresponding to level 0 processors, and rooted at $(0, d)$ is a subgraph of the d-dimensional butterfly (see Fig. 19.28(b)). Assume that each processor has two registers: s and z. Register s at node v, denoted by $s(v)$, contains the sum of all items at the leaves of the subtree rooted at v, and $z(v)$ contains the sum of all items at the leaves of the subtree rooted at the left child of node v. Initially, the items $x_1, x_2, \ldots, x_n$ are input to the $n = 2^d$ processors at level 0 in registers z and s. The algorithm consists of two passes: Bottom-up and top-down. It is shown as Algorithm BFPARPREFIX.

Algorithm 19.25 BFPARPREFIX

Input: $X = \langle x_1, x_2, \ldots, x_n \rangle$, a sequence of n numbers, where $n = 2^d$.

Output: $S = \langle s_1, s_2, \ldots, s_n \rangle$, the prefix sums of X.

(a) Bottom-up phase. See Fig. 19.37(a). Each leaf node l sends its item $s(l)$ to its parent. Each internal node v upon receipt of two s-values $s(x)$ and $s(y)$ from its children x and y computes their sum and stores it in register $s(v)$. It also stores $s(x)$, the left child sum, in register $z(v)$.

(b) Top-down phase. See Figs. 19.37(b)–19.37(d). Initially, the root sends 0 to its left child and z to its right child. Each node v upon receipt of value y from its parent does the following: If v is a leaf, it sets $s(v) = s(v) + y$; otherwise, it sends y to its left child and sends $y + z(v)$ to its right child. At the end, the s value at the ith leaf contains $s_i = x_1 + x_2 + \cdots + x_i$, $1 \leq i \leq n$.

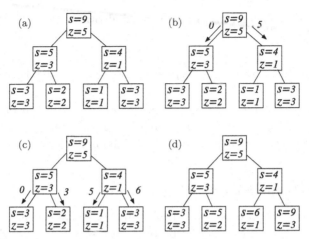

Fig. 19.37. Example of computing parallel prefix on the two-dimensional butterfly.

Obtaining the running time is straightforward; it is $\Theta(d)$ in both the bottom-up phase and the top-down phase.

19.5 The Linear Array and the Mesh

Linear arrays are the simplest example of a fixed-connection network. An example of a linear array is shown in Fig. 19.38(a). It consists of p processors $P_1, P_2, \ldots, P_p$, where each interior processor is connected with bidirectional links to its left neighbor and its right neighbor. The outermost processors P_1 and P_p have just one connection each. If we connect them by a link, we obtain a *ring*, which is a simple extension of the linear array (see Fig. 19.38(b)).

A two-dimensional *mesh* is an extension of the linear array to two dimensions. A mesh of size p consists of p simple processors arranged in a square lattice. To simplify exposition, it is assumed that $p = 4^k$ for some positive integer k. For all $i, j, 1 \leq i, j \leq \sqrt{p}$, processor $P_{i,j}$ representing the processor in row i and column j, is connected via bidirectional communication links to its four neighbors, processors $P_{i\pm 1,j}$ and $P_{i,j\pm 1}$, assuming they exist (see Fig. 19.38(c)).

The communication diameter of a mesh of size p is $2(\sqrt{p} - 1) = \Theta(\sqrt{p})$, as can be seen by examining the distance between processors in opposite

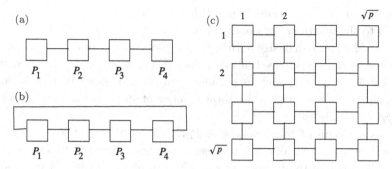

Fig. 19.38. (a) A linear array. (b) A ring. (c) A mesh.

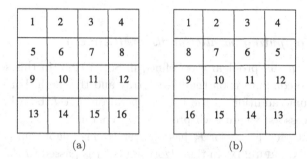

Fig. 19.39. Mesh indexing schemes. (a) Row-major. (b) Snakelike.

corners of the mesh. This means if a processor in one corner of the mesh needs data from a processor in another corner of the mesh sometime during the execution of an algorithm, then a lower bound on the running time of the algorithm is $\Omega(\sqrt{p})$. The bisection width of a mesh of size p can be seen to be $\sqrt{p}$.

There is no linear ordering on the set of processors in the mesh. However, there are several two-dimensional orderings, called indexing schemes, like row-major and snakelike shown in Fig. 19.39.

19.5.1 *Broadcasting in the linear array and the mesh*

Let L be a linear array of p processors. To broadcast a datum x from P_1 to all other processors, x is sent to $P_2, P_3, \ldots, P_p$ in this order. The number of steps is $p - 1 = \Theta(p)$. If the origin of broadcasting is not P_1, say $P_i(i < n)$,

x is sent in both directions in parallel. The number of steps in this case is equal to the maximum of the distances from P_i to P_1 and P_p.

Let M be a mesh of size p. Broadcasting a datum x from $P_{1,1}$ to all other processors can be achieved in two phases. First, x is sent to all processors in row 1. Next, x is sent in parallel from all processors in row 1 along all columns of the mesh. The total number of steps in the two phases is $2(\sqrt{p} - 1) = \Theta(\sqrt{p})$.

If the origin of broadcasting is $P_{i,j}$ that is different from $P_{1,1}$, then broadcasting of x to all other processors can be achieved in two phases. In phase 1, x is sent to all processors in row i. In phase 2, x is sent in parallel from all processors in row i along all columns in M. The running time is $\Theta(\sqrt{p})$.

19.5.2   *Computing parallel prefix on the mesh*

The parallel prefix problem was defined in Sec. 19.2.3. In this section, we show how to compute it on the linear array and the mesh. For simplicity, we will assume addition as the binary operation. Let L be a linear array with p processors, where each processor P_i contains item x_i, $1 \leq i \leq p$. Assume that each processor P_i has register s_i. The algorithm is shown as Algorithm LAPARPREFIX. In this algorithm, s_{i-1} is passed to $P_i, 2 \leq i \leq p$, where x_i is added to it to produce s_i, as in the sequential algorithm. The algorithm runs in time $\Theta(p)$.

Algorithm 19.26 LAPARPREFIX
Input: $X = \langle x_1, x_2, \ldots, x_p \rangle$, a sequence of p numbers.
Output: $S = \langle s_1, s_2, \ldots, s_p \rangle$, the prefix sums of X.

1. $s_1 \leftarrow x_1$
2. **for** $i \leftarrow 2$ **to** p
3.   Processor P_i computes $s_i \leftarrow s_{i-1} + x_i$.
4. **end for**

Now, we consider computing parallel prefix on the mesh. Let M be $\sqrt{p} \times \sqrt{p}$ mesh, and assume the row-major indexing scheme. The algorithm is given as Algorithm MESHPARPREFIX below. First, the individual prefix sums of all rows are computed using Algorithm LAPARPREFIX. For $1 \leq i \leq \sqrt{p}$, let the prefix sums of row i be $y_{i,1}, y_{i,2}, \ldots, y_{i,\sqrt{p}}$. Note that these are not the final prefix sums, except for row 1. Next, the prefix sums of column $\sqrt{p}$ are computed, again using Algorithm LAPARPREFIX. These are denoted by $s_{1,\sqrt{p}}, s_{2,\sqrt{p}}, \ldots, s_{\sqrt{p},\sqrt{p}}$, and they are the final prefix sums for column $\sqrt{p}$. Finally, for all processors $P_{i,j}, 2 \leq i \leq \sqrt{p}, 1 \leq j \leq \sqrt{p} - 1$, we set $s_{i,j} \leftarrow y_{i,j} + s_{i-1,\sqrt{p}}$. This implies broadcasting $s_{i-1,\sqrt{p}}$ to row i.

Steps 1 and 2 take $\Theta(\sqrt{p})$ time. Step 3 takes $\Theta(\sqrt{p})$ time too. Steps 4–8 take $\Theta(1)$ time plus the time needed for broadcasting, which is $\Theta(\sqrt{p})$. Hence, the total running time of the algorithm is $\Theta(\sqrt{p})$.

Algorithm 19.27 MESHPARPREFIX
Input: $X = \langle x_{i,j} \mid 1 \leq i,j \leq \sqrt{p}\rangle$, a sequence of p numbers.
Output: $S = \langle s_{i,j} \mid 1 \leq i,j \leq \sqrt{p}\rangle$, the prefix sums of X.

1. **for** $i \leftarrow 1$ **to** $\sqrt{p}$ **do in parallel**
2.   Use Algorithm LAPARPREFIX to compute the prefix sums of row i. Let these be $y_{i,1}, y_{i,2}, \ldots, y_{i,\sqrt{p}}$.
3.   Use Algorithm LAPARPREFIX to compute the prefix sums of column $\sqrt{p}$. Let these be $s_{1,\sqrt{p}}, s_{2,\sqrt{p}}, \ldots, s_{\sqrt{p},\sqrt{p}}$.
4. **for** $i \leftarrow 2$ **to** $\sqrt{p}$ **do in parallel**
5.   **for** $j \leftarrow 1$ **to** $\sqrt{p} - 1$ **do in parallel**
6. $s_{i,j} \leftarrow y_{i,j} + s_{i-1,\sqrt{p}}$
7.   **end for**
8. **end for**

19.5.3 *Odd–even transposition sort*

This sorting algorithm is for linear arrays (and rows and columns of meshes). The algorithm is very simple. It alternates between odd steps and even steps. At odd steps, we compare the contents of processors P_1 and P_2, P_3 and P_4, and so on exchanging values if necessary. At even steps, we repeat the same procedure on processors P_2 and P_3, P_4 and P_5, and so on. The algorithm takes p steps to sort its input $\langle x_1, x_2, \ldots, x_p\rangle$, one item x_i per processor P_i, $1 \leq i \leq p$. Hence, its running time is $\Theta(p)$. An example of the algorithm is shown in Fig. 19.40.

Theorem 19.9 *Odd–even transposition sort correctly sorts any sequence of numbers.*

Proof. By Lemma 19.1 in Sec. 19.2.7, we may assume that the input sequence X consists of 0s and 1s. We prove by induction on $|X|$ that the

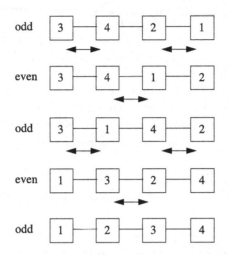

Fig. 19.40.   Example of odd–even transposition sort.

algorithm sorts the binary sequence X. If $p = 1$ or 2, then the hypothesis is true. So, assume it is true for all sequences of size $k, 1 \leq k \leq p - 1$. Let $X = \langle x_1, x_2, \ldots, x_p \rangle$ stored in processors $P_1, P_2, \ldots, P_p$. Let x_j be the rightmost 1, where $1 \leq j \leq p$. x_j will start moving rightward in the first or second step of the algorithm. Once it starts moving, it will subsequently move rightward in each step until it reaches the right end, that is, until $x_p = 1$. Now, it remains to sort $X' = \langle x_1, x_2, \ldots, x_{p-1} \rangle$ in processors $P_1, P_2, \ldots, P_{p-1}$. By induction, X' will be sorted by the algorithm. It follows that X will be sorted correctly by the algorithm. $\qquad\square$

19.5.4   *Shearsort*

This sorting algorithm is for meshes, and it sorts in snakelike order. It consists of $\log p + 1$ phases, where p is the number of processors. The algorithm alternates between odd and even phases. At odd phases, it sorts the rows of the mesh, and at even phases, it sorts its columns. The odd rows are sorted so that smaller numbers move leftward, and the even rows are sorted so that smaller numbers move rightward. The columns are sorted so that smaller numbers move upward. Odd–even transposition sort may be used to sort the rows and columns. In this case, the running time of the algorithm is $\Theta(\sqrt{p} \log p)$.

Theorem 19.10 *Algorithm* SHEARSORT *correctly sorts any sequence of numbers in* $\log p + 1$ *phases.*

Proof. By Lemma 19.1 in Sec. 19.2.7, we may assume that the input consists of 0s and 1s. So, let the input be initially stored in the $\sqrt{p} \times \sqrt{p}$ mesh, one number per processor. A row of the mesh will be called *dirty* if it consists of 0s and 1s, and *clean* if it consists of only 0s or only 1s. Initially, there may be as many as $\sqrt{p}$ dirty rows. During the execution of the algorithm, there will be rows all 0s followed by dirty rows followed by rows with all 1s. After the algorithm terminates, there will be at most one dirty row. Let an iteration of the algorithm consist of two phases, a row sort phase and a column sort phase.

We will show that after each iteration, at least half of the dirty rows become clean. This will imply that after $\log(\sqrt{p})$ iterations there will be at most one dirty row, which can be sorted using an additional sorting phase for a total of $2\log(\sqrt{p}) + 1 = \log p + 1$ phases. Thus, it remains to show that the number of dirty rows will decrease by a factor of at least 2 in each iteration.

Consider two adjacent rows in an iteration after the phase of row sorting. There are three possibilities according to whether there are more 0s than 1s (Fig. 19.41(a)), more 1s than 0s (Fig. 19.41(b)), or an equal number of 0s and 1s (Fig. 19.41(c)).

Now, after sorting the columns of the mesh, each one of these three cases will contribute at least one clean row. If there are more 0s than 1s (Fig. 19.41(a)), then after sorting the columns, there will be at least one more clean row consisting of all 0s. If there are more 1s than 0s (Fig. 19.41(b)), then after sorting the columns, there will be at least one more clean row consisting of all 1s. If there are equal number of 0s and 1s (Fig. 19.41(c)), then after sorting the columns, there will be two more clean rows one consisting of all 0s and one consisting of all 1s. Thus, the number of dirty rows will decrease by a factor of at least 2 in each iteration. $\square$

0 ...... 01.... 1	0 ... 01.........1	0 .....01......1
1....10.........0	1.........10.....0	1......10.......0
(a) **more 0s**	(b) **more 1s**	(c) **equal 0s & 1s**

Fig. 19.41. Dirty rows after rows are sorted.

19.5.5　Odd–even merging and sorting on the mesh

In this section, we implement odd–even merging and sorting on a $\sqrt{n} \times \sqrt{n}$ mesh; odd–even merging and sorting on the PRAM were discussed in Sec. 19.2.8. Let $A = \langle a_0, a_1, \ldots, a_{n/2-1} \rangle$ and $B = \langle b_0, b_1, \ldots, b_{n/2-1} \rangle$ be two sorted sequences of n distinct numbers, where n is a power of 4. Initially, A and B are input in the first and second $\sqrt{n}/2$ columns of the mesh. The odd–even merging method is outlined in Algorithm MESHOD-DEVENMERGE. k, the number of columns, is input to the algorithm. In the beginning, $k = \sqrt{n}$, which is a power of 2. The algorithm divides the input into A_{even}, A_{odd}, B_{even} and B_{odd}, and each part occupies $k/4$ columns. Next, A_{odd} and B_{odd} are interchanged, and the algorithm recursively merges A_{even} with B_{odd} to produce C, and recursively merges B_{even} with A_{odd} to produce D. C and D are then shuffled into E, which is scanned from left to right for pairs that are out of order, which are ordered, if necessary.

Algorithm 19.28 MESHODDEVENMERGE
Input: Two sorted sequences $A = \langle a_0, a_1, \ldots, a_{n/2-1} \rangle$ and $B = \langle b_0, b_1, \ldots, b_{n/2-1} \rangle$ of $n/2$ elements each sorted in ascending order, where $n = 4^k \geq 4$, number of columns k, $2 \leq k \leq \sqrt{n}$.
Output: The elements in $S = A \cup B$ in sorted order.

1. **if** $k = 2$, **then** merge the two columns using an algorithm for the linear array to produce a sorted snake with two columns and $\sqrt{n}$ rows. Exit.
2. Let $A_{\text{even}} = \langle a_0, a_2, \ldots, a_{n/2-2} \rangle$ and $A_{\text{odd}} = \langle a_1, a_3, \ldots, a_{n/2-1} \rangle$ be the even and odd subsequences of A, respectively. A_{even} and A_{odd} are snakes with $k/4$ columns and $\sqrt{n}$ rows each.
3. Let $B_{\text{even}} = \langle b_0, b_2, \ldots, b_{n/2-2} \rangle$ and $B_{\text{odd}} = \langle b_1, b_3, \ldots, b_{n/2-1} \rangle$ be the even and odd subsequences of B, respectively. B_{even} and B_{odd} are snakes with $k/4$ columns and $\sqrt{n}$ rows each.
4. Interchange A_{odd} with B_{odd}. Thus, A_{even} and B_{odd} occupy the first $k/2$ columns, and B_{even} and A_{odd} occupy the next $k/2$ columns.
5. Recursively merge A_{even} and B_{odd} to obtain $C = \langle c_0, c_1, \ldots, c_{n/2-1} \rangle$, a mesh of $k/2$ columns and $\sqrt{n}$ rows.
6. Recursively merge A_{odd} and B_{even} to obtain $D = \langle d_0, d_1, \ldots, d_{n/2-1} \rangle$, a mesh of $k/2$ columns and $\sqrt{n}$ rows.
7. Let E be the shuffle of C and D, that is, $E = \langle c_0, d_0, c_1, d_1, \ldots, c_{n/2-1}, d_{n/2-1} \rangle$.
8. Traverse the pairs (c_i, d_i) in E, $0 \leq i \leq n/2 - 1$, and interchange the elements in each pair if they are out of order to obtain the sorted sequence $S = \langle s_0, s_1, \ldots, s_{n-1} \rangle$ in a mesh with k columns and $\sqrt{n}$ rows.
9. **return** S

Notice that the algorithm is general for any mesh with k columns and $\sqrt{n}$ rows, where k is a power of 2. We express the running time of the algorithm in terms of the number of columns k, $2 \leq k \leq \sqrt{n}$. Step 1 takes $T(2) = \Theta(\sqrt{n})$, which is the time needed to merge in a linear array with $2\sqrt{n}$ processors. Steps 2 and 3 take $\Theta(k)$, as data has to be routed from left to right and from right to left. Step 4 of interchanging columns takes $\Theta(k)$. Steps 5 and 6 take $T(k/2)$ time. Step 7 of shuffling columns takes $\Theta(k)$. Step 8 takes $\Theta(1)$. Hence, the running time of the algorithm is governed by the recurrence $T(k) = T(k/2) + \Theta(k)$, whose solution is $T(k) = \Theta(k) + T(2)$. When $k = \sqrt{n}$, $T(\sqrt{n}) = \Theta(\sqrt{n})$. The proof of correctness is given by Theorem 19.2 in Sec. 19.2.8.

Example 19.11   Consider the mesh shown in Fig. 19.42. It consists of four rows and four columns. The first input A is in the first half of the mesh, in the first two columns in a snakelike order. The second input B is in the last two columns in a snakelike order. $A = \langle 3, 5, 6, 9, 11, 13, 14, 16 \rangle$ and $B = \langle 1, 2, 4, 7, 8, 10, 12, 15 \rangle$. First, we partition A and B into their even on odd parts. The even are shown in shaded squares of Fig. 19.42(a). Thus, $A_{even} = \{3, 6, 11, 14\}$ is in the first column (see Fig. 19.42(b)), $A_{odd} = \{5, 9, 13, 16\}$ is in the second column. $B_{even} = \{1, 4, 8, 12\}$ is shown in the third column and $B_{odd} = \{2, 7, 10, 15\}$ is in the last column. These are shown in Fig. 19.42(b). In 19.42(c), A_{odd} is interchanged with B_{odd}. So, the first two

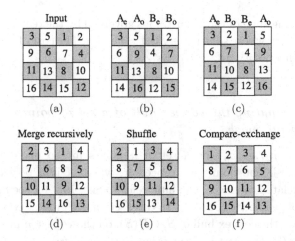

Fig. 19.42.   An example of odd–even merging on the mesh.

columns are merged recursively to produce $C = \langle 2, 3, 6, 7, 10, 11, 14, 15 \rangle$ in snakelike order, and the last two columns are merged recursively to produce $D = \langle 1, 4, 5, 8, 9, 12, 13, 16 \rangle$ in snakelike order. In Fig. 19.42(e), C and D are shuffled to produce $E = \langle 2, 1, 3, 4, 6, 5, 7, 8, 10, 9, 11, 12, 14, 13, 15, 16 \rangle$, which spans the four columns in a snakelike order. The pair (2, 1) is out of order, so 2 and 1 are exchanged. The same applies to the pair (6, 5), etc. The sorted sequence is $S = \langle 1, 2, 3, 4, 5, 6, 7, 8, 9, 10, 11, 12, 13, 14, 15, 16 \rangle$ shown in Fig. 19.42(f).

The algorithm for sorting is given as Algorithm MESHODDEVENSORT below. It is similar to Algorithm ODDEVENSORT for the PRAM in Sec. 19.2.8.

Algorithm 19.29 MESHODDEVENSORT
Input: A sequence $S = \langle a_0, a_1, \ldots, a_{n-1} \rangle$ where n is a power of 4.
Output: The elements in S in sorted order.

1. $S_1 \leftarrow \langle a_0, a_1, \ldots, a_{n/2-1} \rangle$.
2. $S_2 \leftarrow \langle a_{n/2}, a_{n/2+1}, \ldots, a_{n-1} \rangle$.
3. $S_1' \leftarrow$ MESHODDEVENSORT(S_1)
4. $S_2' \leftarrow$ MESHODDEVENSORT(S_2)
5. $S \leftarrow$ MESHODDEVENMERGE(S_1', S_2')
6. **return** S

The running time of the algorithm is governed by the recurrence $T(n) = T(n/2) + \Theta(\sqrt{n})$, whose solution is $T(n) = \Theta(\sqrt{n})$. The cost of the algorithm is $\Theta(\sqrt{n}) \times n = \Theta(n^{1.5})$.

19.5.6 *Computing the convex hull of a set of points on the mesh*

Let $S = \{p_1, p_2, \ldots, p_n\}$ be a set of n points in the plane stored in a $\sqrt{n} \times \sqrt{n}$ mesh one point per processor, where n is a power of 4. For definitions related to the convex hull, refer to Sec. 19.2.16; see Sec. 17.3 for definitions of geometric concepts. In this section, we present two algorithms for computing the convex hull of S, $CH(S)$, on the $\sqrt{n} \times \sqrt{n}$ mesh; the first runs in time $O(\sqrt{n} \log n)$ and the other in time $\Theta(\sqrt{n})$.

19.5.6.1 *The first algorithm*

The first algorithm is almost a straightforward implementation of the PRAM algorithm presented in Sec. 19.2.16 and given in Algorithm PAR-CONVEXHULL. The algorithm consists of repeated applications of the steps given in Observations 19.2 and 19.3.

As a preprocessing step, the points in S are first sorted in ascending order of their x-coordinates in $\Theta(\sqrt{n})$ time. So, assume that $x(p_1) \leq x(p_2) \leq \cdots \leq x(p_n)$, where $x(p_i)$ denotes the x-coordinate of point p_i. We will assume for simplicity that no three points of S are collinear and no two points have the same x-coordinate. Next, the set of points S is divided into four parts $S_1 = \langle p_1, p_2, \ldots, p_{n/4} \rangle$, $S_2 = \langle p_{n/4+1}, p_{n/4+2}, \ldots, p_{n/2} \rangle$, $S_3 = \langle p_{n/2+1}, p_{n/2+2}, \ldots, p_{3n/4} \rangle$ and $S_4 = \langle p_{3n/4+1}, p_{3n/4+2}, \ldots, p_n \rangle$, and arranged in the mesh, as shown in Fig. 19.43(b). Now, we recursively determine the four convex hulls of the four parts $CH(S_1)$, $CH(S_2)$, $CH(S_3)$ and $CH(S_4)$. Figure 19.43(c) shows the four convex hulls of the points in Fig. 19.43(a).

From $CH(S_1)$ and $CH(S_2)$, we identify $CH(S_1 \cup S_2)$, and denote the set of vertices representing $S_1 \cup S_2$ as P. From $CH(S_3)$ and $CH(S_4)$, we identify $CH(S_3 \cup S_4)$ and denote the set of vertices representing $S_3 \cup S_4$ as Q. From $CH(P)$ and $CH(Q)$, we identify $CH(P \cup Q)$, which is the desired convex hull $CH(S)$. In what follows, we turn our attention to computing the upper hull of P, $UH(P)$. Computing the lower hull of P, $LH(P)$, and hence $CH(P)$ can be determined in a similar fashion and in parallel with $UH(P)$. Finally, finding $CH(Q)$, and hence $CH(S)$ can be achieved by a similar means.

The steps for finding $UH(P)$ and hence $LH(P)$ are similar to those described in Sec. 19.2.16. In each iteration of the binary search, vertex x_i of $UH(S_1)$ is broadcast to the processors holding the vertices of $UH(S_2)$ and one of those processors succeeds in finding its tangent line $\overline{x_i v_i}$ with $UH(S_2)$. Clearly, this takes $\Theta(\sqrt{n})$ time on the $\frac{\sqrt{n}}{2} \times \frac{\sqrt{n}}{2}$ mesh. Since there are $O(\log n)$ iterations in the binary search for finding the upper common tangent, the overall running time for finding this tangent is $O(\sqrt{n} \log n)$. Recall that the computation of $LH(P)$ is done in parallel with that of $UH(P)$. Clearly, the remaining work of finding $UH(P)$ and then $CH(P)$ takes $\Theta(\sqrt{n})$ time. Hence, the overall running time for finding $CH(P)$ from $CH(S_1)$ and $CH(S_2)$ is $O(\sqrt{n} \log n)$. It should be noted that finding $CH(P)$ and $CH(Q)$ are done concurrently, and it remains to find $CH(S)$, which

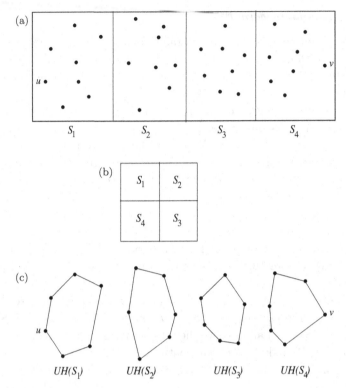

Fig. 19.43.   (a) The set of points S. (b) Arrangement of the subsets on the mesh. (c) Convex hulls of S_1, S_2, S_3 and S_4.

asymptotically takes the same running time. It follows that the running time of the algorithm obeys the recurrence $T(n) = T(n/4) + O(\sqrt{n} \log n) = O(\sqrt{n} \log n)$.

19.5.6.2   *The second algorithm*

The algorithm to be presented is similar to the first algorithm. However, the main difference is in the binary search and how it is conducted. In this algorithm, the number of elements considered in iteration i is $O(\sqrt{n/2^i})$, which results in $\Theta(\sqrt{n})$ running time for the binary search. This is to be contrasted to the first algorithm in which each iteration takes $O(\sqrt{n})$ for a total of $O(\sqrt{n} \log n)$.

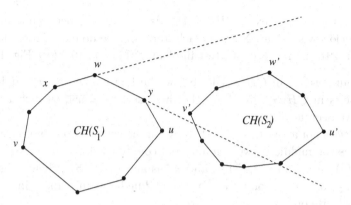

Fig. 19.44. Proof of Lemma 19.2.

In what follows, we describe in detail finding the tangents using binary search for the two sets S_1 and S_2. The rest of the algorithm is similar to that of the first algorithm.

The correctness of the algorithm hinges on the following lemma (see Fig. 19.44). Here, v and u are the vertices with minimum and maximum x-coordinate in $CH(S_1)$, respectively, and v' and u' are the vertices with minimum and maximum x-coordinate in $CH(S_2)$, respectively.

Lemma 19.2 *Let w be a vertex of $CH(S_1)$. If there is another vertex w' of $CH(S_2)$ such that $\overline{ww'}$ is the common upper tangent of $CH(S_1)$ and $CH(S_2)$, then all vertices in $CH(S_2)$ must lie below the line passing by $\overline{xw}$ and some points in $CH(S_2)$ must lie above the line passing by $\overline{wy}$, where x and y are the two vertices in $CH(S_1)$ immediately succeeding and preceding w in counterclockwise order.*

Proof. The tangent line must lie entirely within the wedge defined by $\overline{xw}$ and $\overline{wy}$. If $\overline{xw}$ is not above all points in $CH(S_2)$, then any line that passes by w and lies entirely inside the wedge either intersects $CH(S_2)$ at more than one point or lies below the line $\overline{v'u'}$. On the other hand, if $\overline{wy}$ is above $CH(S_2)$, then this wedge does not contain a point from $CH(S_2)$. In both cases, there does not exist a common upper tangent $\overline{ww'}$ of $CH(S_1)$ and $CH(S_2)$. $\square$

Lemma 19.2 suggests the following method for identifying the vertex w. We perform binary search on the set of vertices of $CH(S_1)$. Initially, w is assigned the hull vertex in $CH(S_1)$ that is half the way between u and v in counterclockwise order. Next, in each iteration, we do one of the following according to the result of the test implied by Lemma 19.2 (see Fig. 19.44).

(a) If all vertices in $CH(S_2)$ lie below the line passing by $\overline{xw}$ and some points in $CH(S_2)$ lie above the line passing by $\overline{wy}$, then w, x and y have been identified.
(b) If $\overline{xw}$ is not above $CH(S_2)$, then assign the vertex x to u and recompute w as the middle between u and v in counterclockwise order.
(c) If (a) above is not satisfied and $\overline{xw}$ is above $CH(S_2)$, then assign vertex y to v and recompute w as the middle between u and v in counterclockwise order.

Example 19.12   Consider Fig. 19.45 in which the steps of binary search are shown. In Fig. 19.45(a), the two convex hulls are shown. w is set half the way between v and u, in counterclockwise order. The extension of the line $\overline{xw}$ crosses $CH(S_2)$ at more than one point. Hence, the vertex x is assigned to u. w is recomputed as half the way between u and v and x and y are relocated as shown in Fig. 19.45(b). y is assigned to the vertex before w in counterclockwise order, which happens to be u. Next, since the extensions of both $\overline{xw}$ and $\overline{wy}$ are above $CH(S_2)$, v is set equal to y in Fig. 19.45(c). Then, w, x and y are recomputed as shown in Fig. 19.45(c). In this part of the figure, $u = v = w$, and the test in (a) above is satisfied, so the search is halted, and w is declared as one end of the tangent line.

After the end of each iteration of the binary search, the remaining vertices in $CH(S_1)$ and $CH(S_2)$ are compressed into the smallest square set of processors using parallel prefix. Thus, in the ith iteration, the binary search is performed on $\Theta(n/2^i)$ vertices, which means that the ith iteration takes $\Theta(\sqrt{n/2^i})$ time, including the time required for broadcasting and data compression. This implies that the total running time for the binary search is $\sum_{i=0}^{O(\log n)} \Theta(\sqrt{n/2^i})$, which is $\Theta(\sqrt{n})$.

Note that in each iteration, w, x and y are broadcast to the processors holding hull vertices in $CH(S_2)$ above the line $\overline{u'v'}$. Then, the equations of the two lines $\overline{xw}$ and $\overline{wy}$ are computed. The results of the tests given in (a)–(c) above are sent to the vertices of $CH(S_1)$ above the line $\overline{vu}$.

Similar computations of all the above are performed to identify $w', \overline{w'x'}, \overline{y'w'}$ for $CH(S_2)$. It is important that identifying w and w' be done simultaneously, and so is data compression for the remaining data of

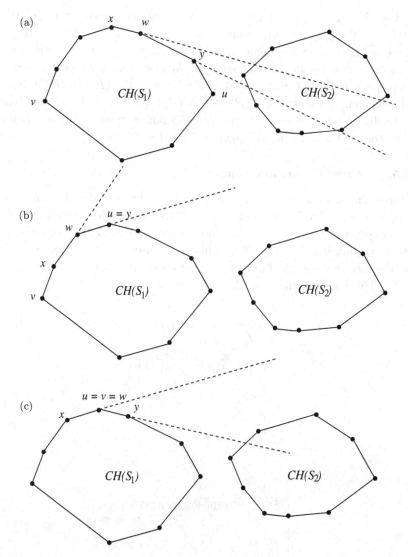

Fig. 19.45.   Example of binary search.

$CH(S_1)$ and $CH(S_2)$. This is to ensure that half the number of hull vertices after compression in $CH(S_1)$ between v and u and in $CH(S_2)$ between v' and u' are eliminated from further inspection in subsequent iterations of the two binary searches.

Let $P = S_1 \cup S_2$ and $Q = S_3 \cup S_4$. Now, we construct $CH(P) = CH(S_1) \cup CH(S_2)$ by connecting w and w' and z and z' by two edges, where $\overline{zz'}$ is the lower tangent. Also, the vertices inside the quadrilateral defined by w, w', z and z' are removed. At the same time, we construct $CH(Q) = CH(S_3) \cup CH(S_4)$, and finally CH(S)$= CH(P) \cup CH(Q)$. Note that the computations of $CH(P)$ and $CH(Q)$ are done concurrently. The above discussion implies that the overall running time of the algorithm obeys the recurrence $T(n) = T(n/4) + \Theta(\sqrt{n}) = \Theta(\sqrt{n})$.

19.5.7 *Three-dimensional mesh*

A three-dimensional mesh of sides $m = n^{1/3}$ can be viewed as a connection of m successive levels of two-dimensional meshes of size $m \times m$. It has $n = m^3$ processors and $3m^3 - 3m^2$ links. Two processors are connected by a two-way link if and only if they differ in precisely one coordinate and if the absolute value of the difference in that coordinate is 1 (see Fig. 19.46). In this figure, $m = 4$ and $n = 64$.

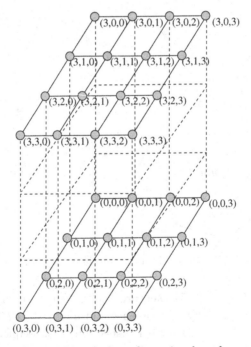

Fig. 19.46.   A three-dimensional mesh.

In three-dimensional mesh, the degree of each node is between 3 and 6, and the diameter is $3(m - 1) = \Theta(n^{1/3})$, so meshes are not regular. Of course, the degree of a corner vertex is less than the degree of an internal vertex.

19.5.7.1 *Sorting on three-dimensional meshes*

Consider the problem of sorting $n = m^3$ numbers on a three-dimensional mesh with n processors in lexicographic zyx-order. In a zyx-ordering, elements of processors in the plane with coordinate $z = 0$ come first, followed by those with $z = 1$, and so on. The xy-planes are sorted in yx-order, that is, in columnwise order. The following algorithm needs just five steps, where each step sorts numbers within two-dimensional meshes. These steps are outlined in Algorithm THREEDMESHSORT.

Algorithm 19.30 THREEDMESHSORT
Input: $n = m^3$ elements stored in a three-dimensional mesh.
Output: The elements sorted in ascending zyx-order.

1. Sort all xz-planes in zx-order.
2. Sort all yz-planes in zy-order.
3. Sort all xy-planes in yx-order. Reverse the order on every other plane.
4. Perform one odd–even and one even–odd transposition within all columns in parallel.
5. Sort all xy-planes in yx-order.

Recall that a dirty row is a row consisting of 0s and 1s. A dirty plane is one containing at least one dirty row or column. A z-column is a column of processors parallel to the z-axis. A 0-row is a row of 0s and no 1s.

Theorem 19.11 *Algorithm* THREEDMESHSORT *correctly sorts a given sequence of numbers in zyx-order.*

Proof. By the zero-one principle (Lemma 19.2.7), we may consider any input sequence of 0's and 1's. After Step 1 is completed, in every xz-plane, there is at most one dirty row, and therefore the difference in the number of zeroes between any two z-columns in the same xz-plane is at most one. Hence, any two yz-planes can differ in at most m 0's. It follows that after Step 2 is completed, the difference in the number of 0-rows between any two yz-planes is at most one, which means that all dirty rows can span at most two adjacent xy-planes. If there is only one dirty xy-plane, we can go directly to Step 5 and we are done. If there are two dirty xy-planes, Steps 3 and 4 eliminate at least one of them and Step 5 completes the sorting. □

Example 19.13   Figure 19.47 illustrates the algorithm on a sequence of 0s and 1s shown in Fig. 19.47(a). First, the xz-planes are sorted in Fig. 19.47(b). Next, the yz-planes are sorted in Fig. 19.47(c). In this part of the figure, both the middle and top xy-planes are dirty, and so Steps 3 and 4 are needed, as shown in Fig. 19.47(d) and 19.47(e). Finally, Fig. 19.47(f) shows the result after Step 5 is executed, in which the input is sorted. Note that there is only one dirty plane, the middle xy-plane.

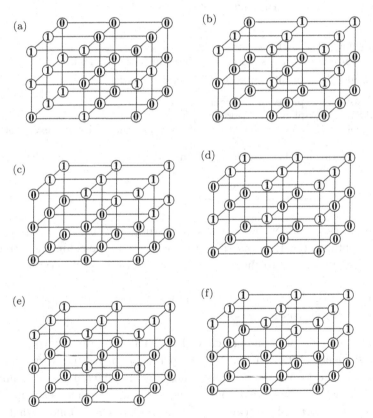

Fig. 19.47.   Sorting in the three-dimensional mesh of 0s and 1s.

Example 19.14 Figure 19.48 illustrates the algorithm on a sequence of integers shown in Fig. 19.48(a). First, the xz-planes are sorted in Fig. 19.48(b). Next, the yz-planes are sorted in Fig. 19.48(c). The xy-planes are then sorted in reverse order according to Step 3 of the algorithm as shown in Fig. 19.48(d). Next, two iterations of odd–even sort are executed, and the result is shown in Fig. 19.48(e). Finally, Fig. 19.48(f) shows the result after Step 5 is executed, in which the input is sorted.

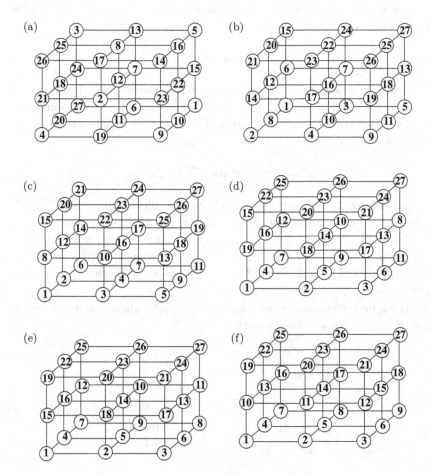

Fig. 19.48. Sorting in the three-dimensional mesh of arbitrary numbers.

19.5.8 *Fast Fourier transform*

The Fourier transform has a wide range of applications in science and engineering. We will describe a version of Fourier transform called *discrete Fourier transform* (DFT) and present a fast method for computing the DFT, called the *fast Fourier transform* (FFT).

Let r and θ be the polar coordinates of the point (x, y) corresponding to the complex number $z = x + iy$, where $i = \sqrt{-1}$. Since $x = r \cos \theta$ and $y = r \sin \theta$, z can be written in polar form as $z = r(\cos \theta + i \sin \theta)$. Using Euler's formula $e^{i\theta} = \cos \theta + i \sin \theta$, z can also be written as $z = re^{i\theta}$.

For $n \geq 2$, the n distinct roots of the equation $x^n - 1 = 0$ are called the n roots of unity. Define the complex number

$$\omega = e^{i2\pi/n} = \cos \frac{2\pi}{n} + i \sin \frac{2\pi}{n}.$$

ω is called a *primitive* nth root of unity, which means $\omega^n = 1$ and $\omega^j \neq 1$ for $0 < j < n$. If $\omega^n = 1$, then $(\omega^j)^n = (\omega^n)^j = 1$. Hence, the remaining complex roots of unity are the powers of ω. That is, $1 = \omega^0, \omega, \omega^2, \ldots, \omega^{n-1}$ constitute the n *distinct roots of unity*, where

$$\omega^k = e^{i2\pi k/n} = \cos \frac{2\pi k}{n} + i \sin \frac{2\pi k}{n}.$$

Pictorially, these roots are distributed in the complex plane evenly around the circumference of the unit circle. Figure 19.49 illustrates the n roots of unity for $n = 2, 4, 8$, which are powers of 2. As shown in the figure, the pairs ω^j and $\omega^{j+n/2}$ are symmetrically located with respect to the origin. Algebraically, we have $\omega^{j+n/2} = -\omega^j$ (Property 2), and in particular, $\omega^{n/2} = -1$.

Let $\mathbf{a}$ be the column vector $[a_0, a_1, \ldots, a_{n-1}]^T$, where n is a power of 2. Let F_n be the Vandermonde matrix

$$\begin{bmatrix} 1 & 1 & 1 & \ldots & 1 \\ 1 & \omega & \omega^2 & \ldots & \omega^{n-1} \\ 1 & \omega^2 & \omega^4 & \ldots & \omega^{2n-2} \\ \vdots & \vdots & \vdots & \vdots & \vdots \\ 1 & \omega^{n-2} & \omega^{2(n-2)} & \ldots & \omega^{(n-1)(n-2)} \\ 1 & \omega^{n-1} & \omega^{2(n-1)} & \ldots & \omega^{(n-1)^2} \end{bmatrix}.$$

Then, the product $\mathbf{b} = F_n \mathbf{a}$ is called the DFT of $\mathbf{a}$.

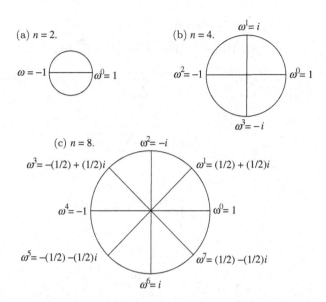

Fig. 19.49. The n roots of unity for $n = 2, 4, 8$.

Thus, computing the DFT **b** of a vector **a** is equivalent to evaluating the polynomial $P(x) = a_0 + a_1 x + \cdots + a_{n-1} x^{n-1}$ at the points $1, \omega, \omega^2, \ldots, \omega^{n-1}$.

It is easy to see that the DFT of a vector **a** can be computed in $\Theta(n^2)$ sequential time and $\Theta(\log n)$ parallel time using $n^2 / \log n$ processors on the PRAM. We now show that it can be computed in optimal $\Theta(n \log n)$ sequential time and $\Theta(\log n)$ parallel time using n processors on the PRAM. The efficiency of the algorithm is based on the following properties of the n roots of unity.

Property 1   For even n, if ω is an nth root of unity, then ω^2 is an $(n/2)$th root of unity.

Property 2   For even n, $\omega^{k+n/2} = -\omega^k$.

For $0 \le i < n/2$, b_i can be expressed as

$$b_i = \sum_{j=0}^{n-1} (\omega^i)^j a_j$$
$$= (\omega^i)^0 a_0 + (\omega^i)^1 a_1 + \cdots + (\omega^i)^{n-1} a_{n-1}$$

$$= (\omega^i)^0 a_0 + (\omega^i)^2 a_2 + \cdots + (\omega^i)^{n-2} a_{n-2}$$
$$+ (\omega^i)^1 a_1 + (\omega^i)^3 a_3 + \cdots + (\omega^i)^{n-1} a_{n-1}$$

$$= \sum_{j=0}^{(n/2)-1} (\omega^i)^{2j} a_{2j} + \sum_{j=0}^{(n/2)-1} (\omega^i)^{2j+1} a_{2j+1}$$

$$= \sum_{j=0}^{(n/2)-1} (\omega^{2i})^j a_{2j} + \omega^i \sum_{j=0}^{(n/2)-1} (\omega^{2i})^j a_{2j+1}. \tag{19.8}$$

Since

$$(\omega^{i+(n/2)})^k = \begin{cases} \omega^{ki} & \text{if } k \text{ is even} \\ -\omega^{ki} & \text{if } k \text{ is odd}, \end{cases}$$

we have

$$b_{i+(n/2)} = \sum_{j=0}^{(n/2)-1} (\omega^{2i})^j a_{2j} - \omega^i \sum_{j=0}^{(n/2)-1} (\omega^{2i})^j a_{2j+1}. \tag{19.9}$$

By Eqs. (19.8) and (19.9), $F_n\mathbf{a}$ is computed recursively from $F_{(n/2)}\mathbf{a}_e$ and $F_{(n/2)}\mathbf{a}_o$, where $\mathbf{a}_e$ and $\mathbf{a}_o$ are, respectively, the even and odd parts of $\mathbf{a}$. On the PRAM, this gives rise to the recurrence $T(n) = T(n/2) + \Theta(1)$, which solves for $T(n) = \Theta(\log n)$. The number of processors needed is $\Theta(n)$.

19.5.8.1 *Implementation on the butterfly*

Let

$$\mathbf{c} = F_{(n/2)} \begin{bmatrix} a_0 \\ a_2 \\ a_4 \\ \vdots \\ a_{n-2} \end{bmatrix} \quad \text{and} \quad \mathbf{d} = F_{(n/2)} \begin{bmatrix} a_1 \\ a_3 \\ a_5 \\ \vdots \\ a_{n-1} \end{bmatrix}.$$

Then, for $0 \le i < n/2$, Eqs. (19.8) and (19.9) can be rewritten as

$$b_i = c_i + \omega^i d_i \tag{19.10}$$

and

$$b_{i+n/2} = c_i - \omega^i d_i. \tag{19.11}$$

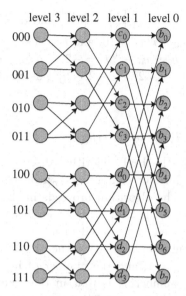

level 3   level 2   level 1   level 0

Fig. 19.50.   Implementation of FFT on the butterfly for $n = 8$.

By Eqs. (19.10) and (19.11), the implementation of the Fourier transform on the d-dimensional butterfly, where $n = 2^d$, is straightforward. These two equations are implemented naturally on the butterfly, as shown in Fig. 19.50 for $n = 8$. The b_i's are computed recursively in level 0, and c_i's and d_i's are computed recursively in level 1, and so on. As an example in the figure, b_3 is computed as $b_3 = c_3 + \omega^3 d_3$ and b_6 is computed as $b_6 = c_2 - \omega^2 d_2$.

Each parallel step is carried out by one level of the butterfly. Hence, the number of parallel steps can be expressed by the recurrence $T(n) = T(n/2) + 1$, whence the number of steps is equal to $d = \log n$.

Example 19.15   Let $\mathbf{a} = [1, 2, 3, 4]^T$. In this example, we compute $F_4 \mathbf{a}$, where

$$
F_4 = \begin{bmatrix} 1 & 1 & 1 & 1 \\ 1 & i & -1 & -i \\ 1 & -1 & 1 & -1 \\ 1 & -i & -1 & i \end{bmatrix}.
$$

Since $F_2 = \begin{bmatrix} 1 & 1 \\ 1 & -1 \end{bmatrix}$, $\mathbf{c} = \begin{bmatrix} 1 & 1 \\ 1 & -1 \end{bmatrix} \begin{bmatrix} 1 \\ 3 \end{bmatrix} = \begin{bmatrix} 4 \\ -2 \end{bmatrix}$ and $\mathbf{d} = \begin{bmatrix} 1 & 1 \\ 1 & -1 \end{bmatrix} \begin{bmatrix} 2 \\ 4 \end{bmatrix} = \begin{bmatrix} 6 \\ -2 \end{bmatrix}$.
By Eq. (19.10), $b_0 = c_0 + i^0 d_0 = 10$, and $b_1 = c_1 + i^1 d_1 = -2 - 2i$, since $\omega = i$. By Eq. (19.11), $b_2 = c_0 - i^0 d_0 = -2$, and $b_3 = c_1 - i^1 d_1 = -2 + 2i$. Hence, $\mathbf{b} = F_4 \mathbf{a} = [10, -2 - 2i, -2, -2 + 2i]^T$, as can be verified by direct multiplication.

19.5.8.2 *Iterative FFT on the butterfly*

Unfolding recursion in the FFT algorithm discussed above results in a simple iterative procedure for computing $F_n \mathbf{a}$ on the d-dimensional butterfly, where $n = 2^d$. The algorithm proceeds in the reverse order, from level d to level 0, where the processors in level d contain the input. If $\mathbf{a} = [a_1, a_2, \ldots, a_n]^T$, then a_j is stored in node (j^R, d), where j^R is the number whose representation in binary is the reverse of the representation of j. For example, if $j = 1$, and the number of bits is 3, then $j^R = 4$. The reason for this renumbering is that in the recursive algorithm, the items are divided into even and odd. The items are divided into two halves; those even in the upper half have 0 as their most significant bit, and those odd in the lower half have 1 as their most significant bit. Appending 0s and 1s is repeated recursively with repeated divisions into even and odd halves.

The algorithm proceeds in d phases corresponding to levels $d - 1, d - 2, \ldots, 0$, where the output of each phase except the last is the input to the next. Each phase is carried out in one parallel step, for a total of d parallel steps. In phase 1, the algorithm starts by evaluating the contents of the processors at level $d - 1$. Each pair of consecutive processors perform the multiplication $F_2 \mathbf{u}$, where $\mathbf{u}$ is the vector of corresponding pair of values entered at level d. $F_2 \mathbf{u}$ is not computed using the recursive algorithm discussed above, or using direct matrix multiplication; it is computed using Eqs. 19.10 and 19.11. There are $n/2$ computations of the products $F_2 \mathbf{u}$. Next, in phase 2, each group of four consecutive processors in level $d - 2$ perform the multiplication $F_4 \mathbf{v}$ using Eqs. (19.10) and (19.11), where $\mathbf{v}$ is the vector of corresponding four elements computed in phase 1 while processing level $d - 1$. There are $n/4$ computations of the products $F_4 \mathbf{v}$. This process of doubling the group size in each phase and computing the Fourier transforms using Eqs. (19.10) and (19.11) is repeated in the following phases,

phases $3, 4, \ldots, d$, until the final product $F_n \mathbf{a}$ is computed. In general, in phase j, $n/2^j$ computations of $F_{2^j} \mathbf{w}$ in level $d - j$ are carried out using Eqs. (19.10) and (19.11).

Example 19.16 (see Fig. 19.51) As in Example 19.15, let $\mathbf{a} = [1, 2, 3, 4]^T$. We compute $F_4 \mathbf{a}$. The input is entered into level $d = 2$, where a_j is stored in node (j^R, d), as explained above. In phase 1 of the algorithm, the contents of the processors at level $d - 1 = 1$ are evaluated. Each pair of consecutive processors perform the multiplication $F_2 \mathbf{u}$ using Eqs. (19.10) and (19.11), where $\mathbf{u}$ is the vector of corresponding pair of values entered at level 2. For example, the contents of node $(0, 1)$ is computed as $c_0 + (-1)^0 d_0 = 1 + (-1)^0 3 = 4$ (here, $\omega = -1$). Similarly, the contents of node $(1, 1)$ is computed as $c_0 - (-1)^0 d_0 = 1 - (-1)^0 3 = -2$. Hence, $F_2 \mathbf{u} = \begin{bmatrix} 1 & 1 \\ 1 & -1 \end{bmatrix} \begin{bmatrix} 1 \\ 3 \end{bmatrix} = \begin{bmatrix} 4 \\ -2 \end{bmatrix}$. Likewise, in the lower half of level 1, $\begin{bmatrix} 1 & 1 \\ 1 & -1 \end{bmatrix} \begin{bmatrix} 2 \\ 4 \end{bmatrix} = \begin{bmatrix} 6 \\ -2 \end{bmatrix}$. Next, in phase 2, the group of four consecutive processors in level 0 perform the multiplication $F_4 \mathbf{v}$ using Eqs. (19.10) and

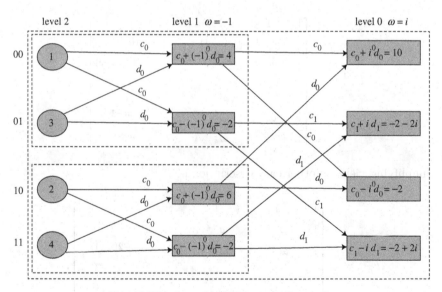

Fig. 19.51. Iterative FFT on the butterfly.

(19.11), where $\mathbf{v} = [4, -2, 6, -2]^T$ is the vector of corresponding four cle
ments computed in phase 1. For example, the contents of node $(0,0)$ is
computed as $c_0 + i^0 d_0 = 4 + i^0 6 = 10$ (here, $\omega = i$). Similarly, the contents
of node $(1,0)$ is computed as $c_1 + i d_1 = -2 + i(-2) = -2 - 2i$. Likewise,
the contents of nodes $(2,0)$ and $(3,0)$ are computed as -2 and $-2 + 2i$,
respectively. Hence,

$$
F_4 \mathbf{a} = F_4 \mathbf{v} =
\begin{bmatrix}
1 & 1 & 1 & 1 \\
1 & i & -1 & -i \\
1 & -1 & 1 & -1 \\
1 & -i & -1 & i
\end{bmatrix}
\begin{bmatrix}
4 \\
-2 \\
6 \\
-2
\end{bmatrix}
=
\begin{bmatrix}
10 \\
-2 - 2i \\
-2 \\
-2 + 2i
\end{bmatrix}.
$$

This conforms with the result obtained in Example 19.15.

19.5.8.3 *The inverse Fourier transform*

The inverse of the matrix F_n turns out to be easy to describe: for $1 \leq k < n$,
the kth row of $n F_n^{-1}$ is the $n - k$th row of F_n:

$$
F_n^{-1} = \frac{1}{n}
\begin{bmatrix}
1 & 1 & 1 & \cdots & 1 \\
1 & \omega^{n-1} & \omega^{2(n-1)} & \cdots & \omega^{(n-1)^2} \\
1 & \omega^{n-2} & \omega^{2(n-2)} & \cdots & \omega^{(n-1)(n-2)} \\
\vdots & \vdots & \vdots & \vdots & \vdots \\
1 & \omega^2 & \omega^4 & \cdots & \omega^{2n-1} \\
1 & \omega & \omega^2 & \cdots & \omega^{n-1}
\end{bmatrix}.
$$

Simplifying yields another easy description of F_n^{-1}:

$$
F_n^{-1} = \frac{1}{n}
\begin{bmatrix}
1 & 1 & 1 & \cdots & 1 \\
1 & \omega^{-1} & \omega^{-2} & \cdots & \omega^{-(n-1)} \\
1 & \omega^{-2} & \omega^{-4} & \cdots & \omega^{-2(n-1)} \\
\vdots & \vdots & \vdots & \vdots & \vdots \\
1 & \omega^{-(n-2)} & \omega^{-2(n-2)} & \cdots & \omega^{-(n-2)(n-1)} \\
1 & \omega^{-(n-1)} & \omega^{-2(n-1)} & \cdots & \omega^{-(n-1)^2}
\end{bmatrix}.
$$

That is,

$$(F_n^{-1})_{ij} = \frac{\omega^{-ij}}{n}.$$

So, the inverse of F_n is $1/n$ times the Fourier transform matrix of a different primitive root of unity, namely ω^{-1}.

To show that it is indeed the inverse of F_n, we need the following property.

Property 3   Since

$$\sum_{j=0}^{n-1} \omega^j = \frac{\omega^n - 1}{\omega - 1} = \frac{1-1}{\omega - 1} = 0,$$

we have

$$\sum_{j=0}^{n-1} \omega^{ij} = \begin{cases} 0 & \text{if } i \not\equiv 0 (\text{mod n}) \\ n & \text{if } i \equiv 0 (\text{mod n}). \end{cases}$$

By Property 3, we have

$$(F_n \times F_n^{-1})_{ij} = \frac{1}{n} \sum_{k=0}^{n-1} \omega^{ik} \omega^{-kj}$$

$$= \frac{1}{n} \sum_{k=0}^{n-1} \omega^{k(i-j)}$$

$$= 1 \text{ if } i = j \text{ and } 0 \text{ otherwise.}$$

Example 19.17

Since $F_4 = \begin{bmatrix} 1 & 1 & 1 & 1 \\ 1 & i & -1 & -i \\ 1 & -1 & 1 & -1 \\ 1 & -i & -1 & i \end{bmatrix}$, $F_4^{-1} = \frac{1}{4} \begin{bmatrix} 1 & 1 & 1 & 1 \\ 1 & -i & -1 & i \\ 1 & -1 & 1 & -1 \\ 1 & i & -1 & -i \end{bmatrix}$

as can be easily verified.

Clearly, the algorithm for the inverse Fourier transform is the same as the algorithm for FFT described above.

19.5.8.4 *Applications of FFT*

We list here two of the many applications of FFT.

19.5.8.5 *Product of polynomials*

Let $f(x)$ and $g(x)$ be two polynomials of degree $n - 1$, where

$$f(x) = \sum_{j=0}^{n-1} a_j x^j \quad \text{and} \quad g(x) = \sum_{j=0}^{n-1} b_j x^j,$$

where n is a power of 2. The product polynomial $h(x)$ is given by

$$h(x) = f(x)g(x) = \sum_{j=0}^{2n-1} c_j x^j,$$

where $c_{2n-1} = 0$.

Recall that if $\mathbf{a}$ is a vector of n coefficients of the polynomial $f(x)$, then $F_n \mathbf{a}$ denotes the vector consisting of the values of $f(x)$ evaluated at the n roots of unity. Likewise, $F_n \mathbf{b}$ denotes the vector consisting of the values of $g(x)$ evaluated at the n roots of unity. That is,

$$
\begin{bmatrix} f(\omega^0) \\ f(\omega^1) \\ \vdots \\ f(\omega^{n-1}) \end{bmatrix} = F_n \begin{bmatrix} a_0 \\ a_1 \\ \vdots \\ a_{n-1} \end{bmatrix} \quad \text{and} \quad \begin{bmatrix} g(\omega^0) \\ g(\omega^1) \\ \vdots \\ g(\omega^{n-1}) \end{bmatrix} = F_n \begin{bmatrix} b_0 \\ b_1 \\ \vdots \\ b_{n-1} \end{bmatrix}.
$$

By inverting F_n, we can perform the process of *interpolation*, which in the above functions obtains the a_i's from the vector of $f(\omega_i)$'s and the b_i's from the vector of $g(\omega_i)$'s. That is,

$$
\begin{bmatrix} a_0 \\ a_1 \\ \vdots \\ a_{n-1} \end{bmatrix} = F_n^{-1} \begin{bmatrix} f(\omega^0) \\ f(\omega^1) \\ \vdots \\ f(\omega^{n-1}) \end{bmatrix} \quad \text{and} \quad \begin{bmatrix} b_0 \\ b_1 \\ \vdots \\ b_{n-1} \end{bmatrix} = F_n^{-1} \begin{bmatrix} g(\omega^0) \\ g(\omega^1) \\ \vdots \\ g(\omega^{n-1}) \end{bmatrix}.
$$

The componentwise product of vectors $F_n \mathbf{a}$ and $F_n \mathbf{b}$ is defined as

$$\begin{bmatrix} f(\omega^0)g(\omega^0) \\ f(\omega^1)g(\omega^1) \\ \vdots \\ f(\omega^{n-1})g(\omega^{n-1}) \end{bmatrix},$$

where $f(\omega^i)g(\omega^i) = h(\omega^i)$, $0 \leq i \leq n - 1$. By taking the inverse Fourier transform of the componentwise product of vectors $F_n \mathbf{a}$ and $F_n \mathbf{b}$, we can obtain $h(x)$ in its coefficient form. There is a little difficulty, however. Given a polynomial $p(x)$ of degree m in its (point, value) pairs, it is well known that $m + 1$ points are needed in order to reconstruct $p(x)$ in its coefficient form. The componentwise product of $F_n \mathbf{a}$ and $F_n \mathbf{b}$ provides the values of $h(x)$ at only n points, but $h(x)$ is of degree $2n - 2$. Hence, we extend $f(x)$ and $g(x)$ to degree $2n - 1$ by adding zeros for the terms with degree n through $2n - 1$. Thus, define $\mathbf{a}' = [a_0, a_1, a_2, \ldots, a_{n-1}, 0, 0, \ldots, 0]^T$ and $\mathbf{b}' = [b_0, b_1, b_2, \ldots, b_{n-1}, 0, 0, \ldots, 0]^T$. We compute the coefficients of $h(x)$ as

$$\begin{bmatrix} c_0 \\ c_1 \\ \vdots \\ c_{2n-1} \end{bmatrix} = F_{2n}^{-1} \begin{bmatrix} f(\omega^0)g(\omega^0) \\ f(\omega^1)g(\omega^1) \\ \vdots \\ f(\omega^{2n-1})g(\omega^{2n-1}) \end{bmatrix}.$$

Note here that ω is the $2n$th primitive root of unity. In summary, to construct the product $h(x) = f(x)g(x)$, we do the following steps:

(1) Compute $\mathbf{c_1} = F_{2n}\mathbf{a}'$ and $\mathbf{c_2} = F_{2n}\mathbf{b}'$.
(2) Perform the componentwise product $\mathbf{c_1} \odot \mathbf{c_2}$.
(3) Interpolate by computing the inverse Fourier transform $\mathbf{c} = F_{2n}^{-1}(\mathbf{c_1} \odot \mathbf{c_2})$.
(4) Output $\mathbf{c} = [c_0, c_1, c_2, \ldots, c_{2n-1}]^T$.

Steps 1 and 3 take $\Theta(\log n)$ parallel time on the d-dimensional butterfly using $\Theta(n \log n)$ operations. Step 2 takes $\Theta(1)$ parallel time. Hence, the algorithm for computing the product of two polynomials requires $\Theta(n \log n)$ operations and runs in $\Theta(\log n)$ parallel time on the $\log n$-dimensional butterfly. This is much more efficient than the $\Theta(n^2)$ direct multiplication algorithm.

Example 19.18   Let $f(x) = 1 + 2x$ and $g(x) = 1 + 3x$. We will compute the product $h(x) = f(x)g(x)$ using fast Fourier transform. Write $f(x) = \mathbf{ax}$, where $\mathbf{a} = [1, 2]$, and $\mathbf{x} = [1, x]^T$, and $g(x) = \mathbf{bx}$, where $\mathbf{b} = [1, 3]$. Let $\mathbf{a}' = [1, 2, 0, 0]^T$ and $\mathbf{b}' = [1, 3, 0, 0]^T$. Then,

$$
\mathbf{c_1} = F_4\mathbf{a}' = \begin{bmatrix} 1 & 1 & 1 & 1 \\ 1 & i & -1 & -i \\ 1 & -1 & 1 & -1 \\ 1 & -i & -1 & i \end{bmatrix} \begin{bmatrix} 1 \\ 2 \\ 0 \\ 0 \end{bmatrix} = \begin{bmatrix} 3 \\ 1 + 2i \\ -1 \\ 1 - 2i \end{bmatrix}.
$$

Similarly,

$$
\mathbf{c_2} = F_4\mathbf{b}' = \begin{bmatrix} 1 & 1 & 1 & 1 \\ 1 & i & -1 & -i \\ 1 & -1 & 1 & -1 \\ 1 & -i & -1 & i \end{bmatrix} \begin{bmatrix} 1 \\ 3 \\ 0 \\ 0 \end{bmatrix} = \begin{bmatrix} 4 \\ 1 + 3i \\ -2 \\ 1 - 3i \end{bmatrix}.
$$

Now, we compute $\mathbf{c_1} \odot \mathbf{c_2}$, which is the componentwise multiplication of $\mathbf{c_1}$ and $\mathbf{c_2}$.

$$
\mathbf{c_1} \odot \mathbf{c_2} = \begin{bmatrix} 3 \\ 1 + 2i \\ -1 \\ 1 - 2i \end{bmatrix} \odot \begin{bmatrix} 4 \\ 1 + 3i \\ -2 \\ 1 - 3i \end{bmatrix} = \begin{bmatrix} 12 \\ -5 + 5i \\ 2 \\ -5 - 5i \end{bmatrix}.
$$

Next, we interpolate.

$$
\mathbf{c} = F_4^{-1}(\mathbf{c_1} \odot \mathbf{c_2}) = \frac{1}{4} \begin{bmatrix} 1 & 1 & 1 & 1 \\ 1 & -i & -1 & i \\ 1 & -1 & 1 & -1 \\ 1 & i & -1 & -i \end{bmatrix} \begin{bmatrix} 12 \\ -5 + 5i \\ 2 \\ -5 - 5i \end{bmatrix} = \frac{1}{4} \begin{bmatrix} 4 \\ 20 \\ 24 \\ 0 \end{bmatrix} = \begin{bmatrix} 1 \\ 5 \\ 6 \\ 0 \end{bmatrix}.
$$

Hence, $h(x) = 1 + 5x + 6x^2$, as can be verified by direct multiplication.

19.5.8.6   *Computing the convolution of two vectors*

Given two sequences of numbers

$$
A = a_0, a_1, \ldots, a_{n-1} \quad \text{and} \quad B = b_0, b_1, \ldots, b_{n-1},
$$

the *convolution* of A and B denoted by $A \oplus B$ is defined as

$$
a_0b_0, \ a_0b_1 + a_1b_0, \ a_0b_2 + a_1b_1 + a_2b_0, \ldots, a_0b_{n-1} + a_1b_{n-2} + \cdots + a_{n-1}b_0.
$$

So, if

$$f(x) = \sum_{j=0}^{n-1} a_j x^j \quad \text{and} \quad g(x) = \sum_{j=0}^{n-1} b_j x^j,$$

then the kth term in $f(x)g(x)$ is the kth element in the sequence $A \oplus B$.

Example 19.19 As in Example 19.18, let $\mathbf{a}' = [1, 2, 0, 0]^T$ and $\mathbf{b}' = [1, 3, 0, 0]^T$. Then,

$$(a_0 b_0) + (a_0 b_1 + a_1 b_0)x + (a_0 b_2 + a_1 b_1 + a_2 b_0)x^2 = 1 + 5x + 6x^2.$$

It follows that $a_0 b_0 = 1$, $a_0 b_1 + a_1 b_0 = 5$, and $a_0 b_2 + a_1 b_1 + a_2 b_0 = 6$, as can be verified by direct evaluation.

19.6 Systolic Computation

Systolic computation refers to one in which the processors, usually called processing elements, are arranged in a very regular way (most often, as one- or two-dimensional arrays), and the data move through them in a regular fashion. Processors are usually primitive and perform very simple operations on the data they receive, e.g., computing the maximum and minimum of two items.

19.6.1 *An on-chip bubble sorter*

The basic component of the bubble sorter is the compare/steer unit, which is shown in Fig. 19.52. It consists of four interconnected cells: A, B, C and D. The sorter consists of a stack of n comparators that work synchronously in one of two modes: downward and upward (see Fig. 19.53). In the downward mode, cell A in every unit receives its input from the unit above or from outside, the content of C is routed to B, and the content of D, which is the larger of the two numbers, is moved to the next comparator below. Next, the contents of A and B are compared, and the minimum and maximum are delivered to C and D, respectively. That is, $C = \min\{A, B\}$ and $D = \max\{A, B\}$. In the upward mode, an outside key is loaded from the bottom into cell B of the unit, and an inside key previously at D is loaded into A. After loading, the comparison is executed, and the minimum is delivered to C and the maximum to D. Loading and comparison are executed almost

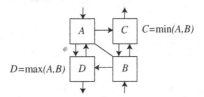

Fig. 19.52.   A compare/steer unit (comparator).

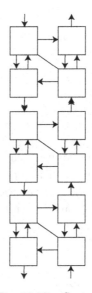

Fig. 19.53.   Sorter.

simultaneously, so all these operations are performed in all comparators in every period, which we will take for convenience as one unit.

During the downward input phase, n keys are loaded into n units in $2n$ periods. During the upward output phase, each unit delivers the smaller key to its upper unit in every period, outputting one item per period from the sorted keys. The sorting time is completely absorbed in the input/output time. So, it takes $2n$ periods to sort n numbers.

Example 19.20   Figures 19.54 and 19.55 illustrate the action of the sorter during the sorting of an input of six numbers, 4, 3, 1, 6, 2 and 5 in the downward and upward phases, respectively. Initially, at time t_0, the

Fig. 19.54.   Up-down sorter.

Fig. 19.55.   Bottom-up sorter.

contents of the buffer cells in each comparator are all set to ∞. During the
first cycle, the first number 4 is compared to ∞ and routed to the upper
right cell. During the second cycle, the number 3 is loaded and compared
to 4; then, the number 3 is routed to the upper right cell and 4 is routed
to the lower left cell of the first unit. During the third cycle, as the third
number is being loaded into the first unit, the number 4 is loaded into the

second unit. In other words, the larger of the two numbers will be pushed out of the comparator in which it resides. At the end of time t_3, the upper right cell of the first unit contains 1 and the lower left cell contains 3; and the upper right cell of the second unit contains 4 and the lower left cell contains ∞. At the end of time t_6, all the six numbers have been loaded into the sorter, thus completing the input downward phase. From time t_7 on, the output upward phase begins. Note that in the input phase, the ∞'s are pushed out of the bottom of the sorter; in the output phase, the ∞'s are pushed back into the sorter from the bottom. At the end of time t_7, the smallest number 1 is out and the second smallest 2 is in the upper right cell of the first unit awaiting to be output. In this output phase, the smaller of the two numbers within each comparator is popped up, leaving the unit it resides in and entering the unit on top of it. In the case of the top unit, the smaller number is delivered as output. Thus, the sorter continues to put out the numbers in order. At the end of time t_{12}, all data in the sorter will have been output in ascending order as desired. At the same time, the sorter is automatically reset to its initial state (all ∞) and is ready to accept the next input sequence.

Theorem 19.12 *The sorter correctly sorts the input numbers.*

Assume the elements to be sorted are distinct, and n is even. Let C_i and D_i denote the contents stored in cells C and D of the ith comparator. First, we show that $\min\{C_{i+1}, D_{i+1}\} \geq \min\{C_i, D_i\}$. In input phase, C_{i+1} and D_{i+1} are obtained by comparing the contents of the ith comparator and hence must be greater than or equal to the keys in it. Similarly, in output phase, C_i and D_i are obtained by comparing the contents of the $(i + 1)$st comparator and hence must be less than or equal to the keys in it, that is, C_{i+1} and D_{i+1}. In both cases, $\min\{C_{i+1}, D_{i+1}\} \geq \min\{C_i, D_i\}$. Consequently, the kth smallest element is in one of the top k comparators. To see this, assume that the kth smallest element x is not in the first k comparators, that is, it is in comparator j for some $j > k$. Then, since $\min\{C_1, D_1\} \leq \min\{C_2, D_2\} \leq \cdots \leq \min\{C_j, D_j\} \leq x$, at least k elements are smaller than x, which is a contradiction. It follows that after n keys have been read into the sorter, the minimum must be in the top comparator, the second smallest must be either in the first or second comparator, and so on. Thus, the first element to be output must be the smallest, followed by the second smallest, etc.

19.7 Practice Problems

19.1. Give a parallel algorithm to compute the maximum of n numbers in the sequence $\langle x_1, x_2, \ldots, x_n \rangle$ on the EREW PRAM. What is the running time of your algorithm?

19.2. Use parallel prefix to compute the sequence of maximums $x_1, \max\{x_1, x_2\}, \max\{x_1, x_2, x_3\}, \ldots, \max\{x_1, x_2, \ldots, x_n\}$ for the sequence $S = \langle x_1, x_2, \ldots, x_n \rangle$.

19.3. Let $S = \langle x_1, x_2, \ldots, x_n \rangle$ be a sequence of integers. Give an algorithm to rearrange the elements of S so that all negative integers precede all positive integers. For example, if $S = \langle 3, -2, 1, -5, 4, -6, 7 \rangle$, the result should be $\langle -2, -5, -6, 3, 1, 4, 7 \rangle$.

19.4. Give an algorithm to broadcast an item x stored in processor P_0 to all other processors in the EREW PRAM with $n = 2^k$ processors. What is the running time of your algorithm?

19.5. Consider Algorithm PARQUICKSORT in Sec. 19.2.3.2 for parallel quicksort. What is the cost of the algorithm on average? How about in the worst case?

19.6. Carry out the algorithm for parallel search using two processors on the sequence

$$S = \langle 1, 3, 4, 6, 9, 12, 14, 15, 20 \rangle, \quad \text{and} \quad x = 8.$$

How many parallel steps are there?

19.7. Illustrate the operation of Algorithm PARRANK in Sec. 19.2.6.1 for computing the ranks of B in A on the input:

$$A = \langle 1, 4, 7, 10, 12, 14, 19, 20 \rangle \quad \text{and} \quad B = \langle 5, 11, 15, 18 \rangle.$$

19.8. Illustrate the operation of Algorithm ODDEVENMERGE in Sec. 19.2.8 for odd–even merging on the input:

$$A = \langle 2, 5, 6, 8 \rangle \quad \text{and} \quad B = \langle 1, 3, 7, 9 \rangle.$$

19.9. Do Problem 19.8 with the following modification. Merge A_{odd} with B_{odd} and A_{even} with B_{even} (see Exercise 19.21).

19.10. Illustrate the operation of the bitonic sort network shown in Fig. 19.16 on the input sequence $\langle 6, 7, 1, 4, 2, 5, 8, 3 \rangle$.

19.11. Give an example of a bitonic sequence with one local maximum and one local minimum.

19.12. Consider Algorithm PARMULTISELECT1 for multiselection discussed in Sec. 19.2.12. Compare the algorithm given with direct application of Algorithm PARSELECT given in Sec. 19.2.11.

19.13. Repeat Problem 19.12 with the second algorithm for multiselection for the PRAM, Algorithm PARMULTISELECT2.

19.14. Suggest an algorithm for sorting using multisession. What is the time complexity of your algorithm?

19.15. Consider the algorithm for matrix multiplication discussed in Sec. 19.2.13. What is the cost of the algorithm? What modification should be done in order to make the total cost $O(n^3)$.

19.16. Design a recursive algorithm for parallel prefix on the hypercube. What is the time complexity of your algorithm?

19.17. Describe how to implement the odd–even merge sort on a hypercube of dimension $d = 2^k$.

19.18. Consider the algorithm for permutation routing in the hypercube discussed in Sec. 19.4.4. What is the probability that the algorithm will route all packets to their destinations in $8d$ steps or fewer?

19.19. Consider Algorithm HCMULTISELECT for multiselection on the hypercube discussed in Sec. 19.4.9. Compare the algorithm given with direct application of Algorithm HCSELECT given in Sec. 19.4.8.

19.20. Explain how to broadcast an item in an arbitrary processor to all other processors in the ring.

19.21. One method to smooth a picture is as follows. Let p be the pixel in the middle of a square of a 3×3 square of pixels. Replace the value of p by the average of all the 3×3 pixels. Suggest a network computation model to solve this problem, and show how to solve it.

19.22. Let P be a simple polygon (that is not necessarily convex) with n vertices, and let x be a point. Assume that there are n processors, each assigned to one edge. Give an *efficient* parallel algorithm to decide whether x is in the interior of P. (*Hint*: Draw a horizontal line L such that x lies on L. Count how many times L intersects with the edges of P.)

19.23. The tree-connected computer with n leaf processors consists of $2n - 1$ processors connected in the form of a complete binary tree. Design an algorithm to find the sum of n numbers on a tree-connected computer with n leaf processors. The input numbers are stored at the leaves, and the output is to be stored in the root processor. What is the time complexity of your algorithm?

19.24. Design an algorithm to find the maximum of n numbers on a tree-connected computer with $O(\log n)$ processors. The input numbers are stored at the leaves, and the output is to be stored in the root processor. What is the time complexity of your algorithm?

19.25. The d-dimensional cube-connected cycles (CCC) is constructed from the d-dimensional hypercube by replacing each node with a cycle of length d (see Fig. 19.56). The nodes in the cycle corresponding to node x in the hypercube are labeled as $(x, 1), (x, 2), \ldots, (x, d)$. Node (x, i) is connected to node (y, j) if and only if $x = y$ and $|i - j| = 1 \pmod d$ or $i = j$ and x and y are connected in the hypercube. The CCC has $d2^d$ nodes. Derive an algorithm to find the sum of $n = d2^d$ numbers stored in the CCC, one number per processor. The resulting sum should be stored in processor $P_{(0^d, 1)}$.

19.26. What are the degree, diameter and bisection width of the d-dimensional cube-connected cycles described in Problem 19.25?

19.27. Give an algorithm for computing parallel prefix on the d-dimensional cube-connected cycles described in Problem 19.25. Your algorithm should run in $O(d) = O(\log n)$ time.

19.28. Give an embedding function from the d-dimensional hypercube to the cube-connected cycles (CCC) network described in Problem 19.25. What are the expansion, dilation and congestion of the embedding?

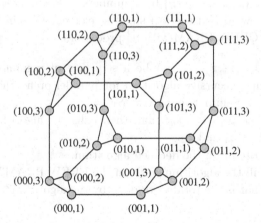

Fig. 19.56.   Three-dimensional cube-connected cycles (CCC).

19.8 Exercises

19.1. Let $x_1, x_2, \ldots, x_n$ be n Boolean variables. Show how to find the logical OR of these variables in $O(1)$ time on the COMMON CRCW PRAM with n processors.

19.2. Let $\langle x_1, x_2, \ldots, x_n \rangle$ be a sequence of n distinct numbers. Show how to find the maximum of these numbers in $O(1)$ time on the CRCW PRAM with n^2 processors.

19.3. Let $\langle x_1, x_2, \ldots, x_n \rangle$ be a sequence of n distinct numbers. Show how to find the maximum of these numbers in $O(\log \log n)$ time on the CRCW PRAM with n processors. (*Hint*: Partition the input into $\sqrt{n}$ parts and recursively find the maximum in each part. Use Exercise 19.2.)

19.4. Let S be a sequence of n distinct numbers and $x \in S$. The rank of x in S is the number of elements in S less than x. Show how to compute the rank of x in S in $O(\log n)$ time on the CREW PRAM with n processors.

19.5. Let S be a sequence of n integers and x an integer. Show how to compute $\text{rank}(x, S)$, the rank of x in S, in $O(\log n)$ time on the EREW PRAM using $O(n)$ operations.

19.6. Let $S = \{x_1, x_2, \ldots, x_n\}$ be n numbers and k an integer, $1 \leq k \leq n$. Show how to find the kth smallest element in S in $O(\log n)$ time on the CREW PRAM with n^2 processors.

19.7. Let $S = \langle x_1, x_2, \ldots, x_n \rangle$ be a sequence of n numbers. Consider the simple recursive algorithm for parallel prefix that divides the sequence S into two halves: $S_1 = \langle x_1, x_2, \ldots, x_{n/2} \rangle$ and $S_2 = \langle x_{n/2+1}, x_{n/2+2}, \ldots, x_n \rangle$, and then calls the algorithm recursively on each of S_1 and S_2.
    (a) Write down the detailed algorithm.
    (b) Will the algorithm work on the EREW PRAM?
    (c) What is the total work done by the algorithm?

(d) Will Brent theorem (Theorem 19.1) help in reducing the number of processors without increasing the running time complexity?

19.8. Let $\langle x_1, x_2, \ldots, x_n \rangle$ be a sequence of n numbers. The *prefix minima* is to compute for each i, $1 \leq i \leq n$, the minimum among the elements $\{x_1, x_2, \cdots, x_i\}$. Develop an algorithm to compute the prefix minima that runs in time $O(\log n)$ on the EREW PRAM.

19.9. Do Exercise 19.8 using *suffix minima* instead, that is, compute for each i, $1 \leq i \leq n$, the minimum among the elements $\{x_i, x_{i+1}, \ldots, x_n\}$.

19.10. Let $\langle x_1, x_2, \ldots, x_n \rangle$ be a sequence of n numbers. The *suffix computation problem* is to compute the suffixes $x_n, x_{n-1} \circ x_n, \ldots, x_1 \circ x_2 \circ \cdots \circ x_n$. Give an $O(\log n)$ time algorithm to solve this problem on the CREW PRAM with n processors.

19.11. Do Exercise 19.10 for the case of EREW PRAM.

19.12. Let $X = \langle x_1, x_2, \ldots, x_n \rangle$ be a sequences of n numbers, where $n = 2^k$ for a nonnegative integer k. Explain how to perform the prefix computation on the sequence X using p processors, where $p < n$. Assume the binary operation of addition.

19.13. Let $T_1, T_2, \ldots, T_m$ be m directed and rooted binary trees on n vertices. Each node has a pointer to its parent, except the root which points to itself. Design a parallel algorithm to allow each vertex to know the identity of the tree to which it belongs (the trees are identified by their roots. The roots are numbered $1, 2, \ldots, m$).

19.14. Parallelize Horner's rule to evaluate a polynomial of degree n under the EREW PRAM in time $O(\log n)$.

19.15. Let $\langle x_1, x_2, \ldots, x_n \rangle$ be a sequence of n distinct numbers. Design a parallel algorithm for the CREW PRAM to sort this sequence in time $O(\log n)$. Assume an unlimited number of processors.

19.16. Let n be a positive integer. Consider the problem of computing the polynomials $y_i = x^i$, for $1 \le i \le n$. Show how to compute the y_i's in $O(\log n)$ time. Specify the PRAM model used.

19.17. Let A be a sequence of integers and x an integer. Develop an EREW PRAM algorithm to find all occurrences, if any, of x in A. Your algorithm should run in time $O(\log n)$ and use a linear number of operations.

19.18. Consider Algorithm PARQUICKSORT presented in Sec. 19.2.3.2. Suppose we always select the median as the pivot (see Sec. 19.2.11). What will be the running time of the algorithm?

19.19. Let A and B be two sequences of distinct number sorted in ascending order. Design an $O(1)$ time algorithm to merge A and B on the CRCW PRAM. Assume an unlimited number of processors.

19.20. Apply Brent theorem on Algorithm PARMERGE presented in Sec. 19.2.6.2.

19.21. In Algorithm ODDEVENMERGE in Sec. 19.2.8, A_{even} is merged with B_{odd} and A_{odd} is merged with B_{even}. Rewrite the algorithm with the modification that it merges A_{odd} with B_{odd} and A_{even} with B_{even}. It is important to know that this will change the step of traversing the shuffle of C and D.

19.22. Let $G = (V, E)$ be an undirected graph with n vertices. Give an algorithm to decide whether G contains a triangle, that is, three mutually adjacent vertices. Assume that G is represented by its adjacency matrix. Your algorithm should run in $O(\log n)$ time on the CRCW PRAM with n^3 processors.

19.23. Illustrate the operation of the pipelined mergesort algorithm on the input $\langle 6, 7, 1, 4, 2, 5, 8, 3 \rangle$.

19.24. Parallelize Algorithm SELECT given in Sec. 5.5 using $n/\log n$ processors on the PRAM. Analyze your algorithm.

19.25. Explain how to make Algorithm PARSELECT of Sec. 19.2.11 cost optimal.

19.26. Rewrite Algorithm PARSELECT for selection discussed in Sec. 19.2.11 for the case when the number of processors is $p < n$. Derive its running time.

19.27. Let $A = \langle a_1, a_2, \ldots, a_n \rangle$ be a sequence of numbers and let k be a given integer between 1 and n. Design and analyze a parallel algorithm to find all k smallest items in A. Do not use multiselection. What model of computation did you use?

19.28. Compute the bisection width of the d-dimensional butterfly B_d.

19.29. Give an $O(d)$ time algorithm for broadcasting in the d-dimensional hypercube H_d if the origin of the message is an arbitrary processor.

19.30. Design an algorithm to compute the sum of n numbers on the hypercube with p processors, $1 \leq p < n$. Is your algorithm always optimal?

19.31. Give an $O(pd)$ time algorithm for the problem of routing in the d-dimensional hypercube if every processor has a packet to be sent to every other processor, where $p = 2^d$. (*Hint*: Use randomized routing p times.)

19.32. Give an $O(p)$ time algorithm for the problem in Exercise 19.31.

19.33. Give an algorithm to evaluate the polynomial $a_{n-1}x^{n-1} + a_{n-2}x^{n-2} + \cdots + a_1 x + a_0$ at the point x_0 on the d-dimensional hypercube H_d with $n = 2^d$ processors. Assume that each a_i is stored in processor P_i, $0 \leq i \leq n - 1$.

19.34. Let $S = \langle x_0, x_1, \ldots, x_{n-1} \rangle$ be a sequence of numbers stored in a hypercube with n processors, where x_i is stored in P_i, $0 \leq i < n$, and let y be stored in P_0. Give an algorithm to count the number of elements in S that are larger than y.

19.35. Consider running odd–even transposition sort on a p-processor linear array if each item in the input is known to start within distance d from its final position. What is the number of steps needed to sort p items in this case?

19.36. Consider Algorithm MERGE-SPLIT, which is a generalization of odd–even transposition sort for the case $p < n$. Let S be a sequence of numbers to be sorted, and assume that each of the p processors in the linear array holds a subsequence S of length n/p. In Algorithm MERGE-SPLIT, the comparison-exchange operations of odd–even transposition sort are now replaced with merge-split operations on subsequences. Let S_i denote the subsequence held by processor P_i. Initially, the S_i's are random subsequences of S. In step 1, each P_i sorts S_i using a sequential algorithm. In Step 2 each odd-numbered processor P_i merges the two subsequences S_i and S_{i+1}, into a sorted sequence S_i'. It retains the first half of S_i' and assigns to its neighbor P_{i+1}, the second half. Step 3 is identical to 2 except that it is performed by all even-numbered processors. Steps 2 and 3 are repeated alternately. After $\lceil p/2 \rceil$ iterations, no further exchange of elements can take place between two processors, where an iteration consists of Steps 2 and 3. Analyze the running time of this algorithm.

19.37. Do Exercise 19.36 for the case $p = \log n$. Is the algorithm optimal?

19.38. Show how to compute the prefix sums on the mesh for the snakelike indexing scheme.

19.39. Give an algorithm to evaluate the polynomial $a_{n-1}x^{n-1} + a_{n-2}x^{n-2} + \cdots + a_1 x + a_0$ at the point x_0 on the $\sqrt{n} \times \sqrt{n}$ mesh. Assume that each a_i is stored in processor P_i, $0 \leq i \leq n - 1$ (the processors are indexed as $P_0, P_1, \ldots, P_{n-1}$). What is the running time of your algorithm?

19.40. Consider the following method for sorting on the mesh. The method alternately sorts all rows from left to right and all columns from top to bottom. Will this method always work in sorting any input? Assume an unlimited amount of time.

19.41. Consider sorting the rows and then the columns of a $2 \times n$ mesh. Does this leave the rows in sorted order?

19.42. This is a generalization of Exercise 19.41. Consider sorting the rows and then the columns of a general $n \times n$ mesh. Does this leave the rows in sorted order?

19.43. Let $A = \langle a_1, a_2, \ldots, a_n \rangle$ be a sequence of elements stored in the processors of a $\sqrt{n} \times \sqrt{n}$ mesh, one element per processor, and let x be a given element. Design an algorithm for the search problem in the mesh: If $a_i = x$ for some i, $1 \leq i \leq n$, then return i, else return 0. Analyze its running time.

19.44. Outline an algorithm for broadcasting an item x stored in processor $P_{0,0,0}$ in a three-dimensional mesh with n processors to all other processors. How many steps in your algorithm?

19.45. Give an algorithm to find the maximum in a set of numbers stored in a three-dimensional mesh with n processors. How many steps in your algorithm?

19.46. What is the bisection width of a three-dimensional mesh with $n = m^3$ processors if m is even?

19.47. Illustrate the operation of Algorithm THREEDMESHSORT for sorting the 0s and 1s shown in Fig. 19.57.

19.48. Illustrate the operation of Algorithm THREEDMESHSORT for sorting the numbers shown in Fig. 19.58.

Fig. 19.57. Exercise 19.47.

Fig. 19.58. Exercise 19.48.

19.49. Use the FFT to compute $F_4\mathbf{a}$, where $\mathbf{a} = [2, 1, -1, 3]^T$.

19.50. Use the iterative FFT on the butterfly to compute the product $F_4\mathbf{a}$, where $\mathbf{a} = [2, 1, -1, 3]^T$.

19.51. Use FFT to compute the product $f(x)g(x)$, where $f(x) = 1 + 3x$ and $g(x) = 1 + 4x$.

19.52. Explain how to use FFT to compute $(1 + x)^n$ efficiently, where n is a power of 2. What is the time complexity of your algorithm?

19.53. Explain how to make the bubble sorter output the numbers in descending order.

19.9   Bibliographic Notes

There are a number of books on parallel algorithms. These include Akl (1989, 1997), Horowitz *et al.* (1998), JáJá (1992), Leighton (1992), Gibbons and Rytter (1990) and Miller and Boxer (2000). The $O(\log \log n)$ time algorithm for merging on the PRAM is due to Kruscal (1983). Bitonic and odd–even sorting networks were described in Batcher (1968). Multiselection on the PRAM is a modification of an algorithm in Alsuwaiyel (2001). The pipelined mergesort algorithm is due to Cole (1988). The ideas for selection on the PRAM are from Akl (1984) and Vishkin (1987). Randomized routing in the hypercube and the butterfly are based on Valiant (1982) and Valiant and Brebner (1981). Selection on the hypercube is from Chandran and Rosenfeld (1988). Hyperquicksort is due to Wagar (1987). Multiselection on the hypercube is from Shen (1997, 2000). The $O(\log n \log \log n)$ time algorithm for sorting on the hypercube is due to Cyphcr and Plaxton (1990). The load balancing problem is to redistribute data items stored in a hypercube such that the number of items in different processors differ by at most one after the redistribution. We used the load balancing algorithm in JáJá and Ryu (1990), and Plaxton (1989). It has a time complexity of $O(M + \log p)$, where M is the maximum number of items at any processor before the redistribution. Shearsort was presented independently by Sado and Igarashi (1986) and Scherson *et al.* (1986). The odd–even mergesort on the mesh can be found in Thompson and Kung (1977). Bubble sorter of Sec. 19.6.1 is from Lee *et al.* (1981).

19.10   Solutions

19.1. Let $x_1, x_2, \ldots, x_n$ be n Boolean variables. Show how to find the logical OR of these variables in $O(1)$ time on the COMMON CRCW PRAM with n processors.

Let y hold the output. Initially, set $y = 0$. Each processor P_i executes the command: **if** $x_i = 1$ **then** $y = 1$. Then all processors P_j with $x_j = 1$ will write the same value. Hence, the output is $y = 1$ using the COMMON PRAM if and only if at least one x_i is 1.

19.2. Let $\langle x_1, x_2, \ldots, x_n \rangle$ be a sequence of n distinct numbers. Show how to find the maximum of these numbers in $O(1)$ time on the CRCW PRAM with n^2 processors.

Assume the x_i's are distinct. Label the n^2 processors as $P_{i,j}$, $1 \leq i, j \leq n$. Let processors $P_{i,1}, P_{i,2}, \ldots, P_{i,n}$ define group i, $1 \leq i \leq n$. Then, group i will find the OR of $x'_{i,1}, x'_{i,2}, \ldots, x'_{i,n}$, where $x'_{i,j} = x_i < x_j$, as shown in the solution of Exercise 19.1. The output of group i is 0 if and only if x_i is the maximum. Each processor P_i executes the command: **if** $x_i = 0$ **then** output x_i. Only one processor will succeed and output its element. The reason concurrent writes are needed is the computation of the OR's.

19.3. Let $\langle x_1, x_2, \ldots, x_n \rangle$ be a sequence of n distinct numbers. Show how to find the maximum of these numbers in $O(\log \log n)$ time on the CRCW PRAM with n processors. (*Hint*: Partition the input into $\sqrt{n}$ parts and recursively find the maximum in each part. Use Exercise 19.2.)

Partition the input into $\sqrt{n}$ parts and recursively find the maximum in each part. Each part is assigned $\sqrt{n}$ processors to find the maximum recursively (number of elements equals number of processors). Let the maximums be $x'_1, x'_2, \ldots, x'_{\sqrt{n}}$. Use Exercise 19.2 to find the maximum of $x'_1, x'_2, \ldots, x'_{\sqrt{n}}$ using n processors in $O(1)$ time. The running time is given by the recurrence $T(n) = T(\sqrt{n}) + O(1)$ whose solution is $T(n) = O(\log \log n)$.

19.4. Let S be a sequence of n distinct numbers and $x \in S$. The rank of x in S is the number of elements in S less than x. Show how to compute the rank of x in S in $O(\log n)$ time on the CREW PRAM with n processors.

Let $S = \langle a_1, a_2, \ldots, a_n \rangle$. Compute $A[i] = a_i < x$ for $1 \leq i \leq n$. Let r be the sum of the 1's in array A. Output r. r can be found by addition or parallel prefix in $O(\log n)$ time. The reason concurrent reads are required is that all processors read x at the same time.

19.5. Let S be a sequence of n integers, and x an integer. Show how to compute rank(x, S), the rank of x in S, in $O(\log n)$ time on the EREW PRAM using $O(n)$ operations.

To adapt the solution of the previous exercise to the EREW PRAM, first broadcast x to all processors, say $B[i] = x$ for $1 \leq i \leq n$, then compute $A[i] < B[i]$ for $1 \leq i \leq n$. To broadcast x, first P_1 copies $B[1] = x$ to $B[2]$. Next, P_1 and P_2 copy $B[1]$ and $B[2]$ to $B[3]$ and $B[4]$, respectively. Next, P_1, P_2, P_3 and P_4 copy $B[1], B[2], B[3]$ and $B[4]$ to $B[5], B[6], B[7]$ and $B[8]$, respectively, and so on. The number of writes is equal to $1 + 2 + 4 + \cdots + 2^k = 2n - 1$, where $k = \log n$. The number of comparisons ($A[i] < B[i]$) is n, which is equal to the number of assignments. Hence, the total number of operations is $\Theta(n)$.

19.6. Let $S = \{x_1, x_2, \ldots, x_n\}$ be n numbers and k an integer, $1 \leq k \leq n$. Show how to find the kth smallest element in S in $O(\log n)$ time on the CREW PRAM with n^2 processors.

Assume the x_i's are distinct. Label the n^2 processors as $P_{i,j}$, $1 \leq i, j \leq n$. Let processors $P_{i,1}, P_{i,2}, \ldots, P_{i,n}$ define group i, $1 \leq i \leq n$. For $i = 1, 2, \ldots, n$, we use Exercise 19.4 to find the rank of x_i in group i and store it in $B[i]$, $1 \leq i \leq n$. Now, for $i = 1, 2, \ldots, n$, processor $P_{i,1}$ outputs x_i if its rank $B[i]$ is equal to $k - 1$. Note that exactly one processor will output the kth smallest element, so there are no concurrent writes. The running time is $O(\log n)$ and the fact that it runs on the CREW PRAM follows from Exercise 19.4.

19.7. Let $S = \langle x_1, x_2, \ldots, x_n \rangle$ be a sequence of n numbers. Consider the simple recursive algorithm for parallel prefix that divides the sequence S into two halves: $S_1 = \langle x_1, x_2, \ldots, x_{n/2} \rangle$ and $S_2 = \langle x_{n/2+1}, x_{n/2+2}, \ldots, x_n \rangle$, and then calls the algorithm recursively on each of S_1 and S_2.

(a) Write down the detailed algorithm.

(b) Will the algorithm work on the EREW PRAM?

(c) What is the total work done by the algorithm?

(d) Will Brent theorem (Theorem 19.1) help in reducing the number of processors without increasing the running time complexity?

(a) The algorithm is shown below as Algorithm PARPREFIX2.

Algorithm 19.31 PARPREFIX2
Input: $X = \langle x_1, x_2, \ldots, x_n \rangle$, a sequence of n numbers, where $n = 2^k$.
Output: $S = \langle s_1, s_2, \ldots, s_n \rangle$, the prefix sums of X.

1. **if** $n = 1$ **then return** x_1
2. **else**
3. $X_1 = \langle x_1, x_2, \ldots, x_{n/2} \rangle$
4. $X_2 = \langle x_{n/2+1} x_{n/2+2}, \ldots, x_n \rangle$
5. $S_1 \leftarrow$ PARPREFIX2(X_1)
6. $S_2 \leftarrow$ PARPREFIX2(X_2)
7.   **for** $j \leftarrow (n/2 + 1)$ **to** n
8. $s_j \leftarrow s_j + s_{n/2}$
9.   **end for**
10. **return** $S_1 \cup S_2$

(b) The algorithm will not work on the EREW PRAM. There are concurrent reads of $s_{n/2}$.

(c) The total number of operations (additions) done by the algorithm is given by the recurrence $W(n) = 2W(n/2) + n/2$, whose solution is $W(n) = \Theta(n \log n)$, which is the total work performed by the algorithm.

(d) Brent theorem does not help in reducing the number of processors without increasing the running time complexity, since the total number of operations is $\Theta(n \log n)$.

19.8. Let $\langle x_1, x_2, \ldots, x_n \rangle$ be a sequence of n numbers. The *prefix minima* is to compute for each i, $1 \leq i \leq n$, the minimum among the elements $\{x_1, x_2, \ldots, x_i\}$. Develop an algorithm to compute the prefix minima that runs in time $O(\log n)$ on the EREW PRAM.

This is the parallel prefix problem using the associative binary operation MIN.

19.9. Do Exercise 19.8 using *suffix minima* instead, that is, compute for each i, $1 \le i \le n$, the minimum among the elements $\{x_i, x_{i+1}, \ldots, x_n\}$.

The algorithm is similar to Algorithm PARPREFIXREC. It is shown as Algorithm PSMINIMA.

Algorithm 19.32 PSMINIMA
Input: $X = \langle x_1, x_2, \ldots, x_n \rangle$, a sequence of n numbers, where $n = 2^k$.
Output: $S = \langle s_1, s_2, \ldots, s_n \rangle$, where $s_i = \min\{x_i, x_{i+1}, \ldots, x_n\}$ are the suffix minima.

1. $s_n \leftarrow x_n$
2. **if** $n = 1$ **then return** $S = \langle x_n \rangle$
3. **for** $i \leftarrow 1$ **to** $n/2$ **do in parallel**
4. $x_{2i-1} \leftarrow \min\{x_{2i-1}, x_{2i}\}$
5. **end for**
6. Recursively compute the prefix minima of $\langle x_1, x_3, \ldots, x_{n-1} \rangle$ and store them in $\langle s_1, s_3, \ldots, s_{n-1} \rangle$
7. **for** $i \leftarrow 1$ **to** $(n/2) - 1$ **do in parallel**
8. $s_{2i} \leftarrow \min\{x_{2i}, s_{2i+1}\}$
9. **end for**
10. **return** $S = \langle s_1, s_2, \ldots, s_n \rangle$

19.10. Let $\langle x_1, x_2, \ldots, x_n \rangle$ be a sequence of n numbers. The *suffix computation problem* is to compute the suffixes $x_n, x_{n-1} \circ x_n, \ldots, x_1 \circ x_2 \circ \ldots \circ x_n$. Give an $O(\log n)$ time algorithm to solve this problem on the CREW PRAM with n processors.

The algorithm is similar to Algorithm PARPREFIX2 in the solution of Exercise 19.7. It is shown below as Algorithm PARSUFFIX.

Algorithm 19.33 PARSUFFIX
Input: $X = \langle x_1, x_2, \ldots, x_n \rangle$, a sequence of n numbers, where $n = 2^k$.
Output: $S = \langle s_1, s_2, \ldots, s_n \rangle$, where $s_i = x_i \circ x_{i+1} \circ \ldots \circ x_n$.

1. **if** $n = 1$ **then return** x_1
2. **else**
3. $X_1 = \langle x_1, x_2, \ldots, x_{n/2} \rangle$
4. $X_2 = \langle x_{n/2+1} x_{n/2+2}, \ldots, x_n \rangle$
5. $S_1 \leftarrow$ PARSUFFIX(X_1)
6. $S_2 \leftarrow$ PARSUFFIX(X_2)
7.   **for** $j \leftarrow 1$ **to** $n/2$
8. $s_j \leftarrow s_j \circ s_{(n/2)+1}$
9.   **end for**
10. **return** $S_1 \cup S_2$

19.11. Do Exercise 19.10 for the case of EREW PRAM.

The algorithm is a generalization of Algorithm PSMINIMA in the solution of Exercise 19.9. Replace the MIN operator with ∘.

19.12. Let $X = \langle x_1, x_2, \ldots, x_n \rangle$ be a sequence of n numbers, where $n = 2^k$ for a nonnegative integer k. Explain how to perform the prefix computation on the sequence X using p processors, where $p < n$. Assume the binary operation of addition.

Split the sequence X into p subsequences $X_1, X_2, \ldots, X_p$ of $q = n/p$ elements each, where $X_i = \langle x_{(i-1)q+1}, x_{(i-1)q+2}, \ldots, x_{iq} \rangle$. First, in parallel, processor $P_i, 1 \leq i \leq p$, computes sequentially the prefix sums of sequence X_i in time $\Theta(n/p)$. Let the prefix sums of processor P_i be $Y_i = \langle y_{(i-1)q+1}, y_{(i-1)q+2}, \ldots, y_{iq} \rangle$. Next, all processors find the prefix sums of $\langle y_q, y_{2q}, \ldots, y_{pq} \rangle$ in time $\Theta(\log p)$. Finally, for $2 \leq i \leq p$, processor P_i adds $y_{(i-1)q}$ to the elements of the sequence Y_i. This takes $\Theta(n/p)$ time. The resulting prefix sums are $y_1, y_2, \ldots, y_n$, and the overall running time is $\Theta(n/p + \log p)$.

19.13. Let $T_1, T_2, \ldots, T_m$ be m directed and rooted binary trees on n vertices. Each node has a pointer to its parent, except the root which points to itself. Design a parallel algorithm to allow each vertex to know the identity of the tree to which it belongs (the trees are identified by their roots. The roots are numbered $1, 2, \ldots, m$).

Use pointer jumping to let each node point to its root. Then assign $root(s) \leftarrow succ(s)$ for all nodes s.

19.14. Parallelize Horner's rule to evaluate a polynomial of degree n under the EREW PRAM in time $O(\log n)$.

$$a_0 + x(a_1 + x(a_2 + x((\ldots x(a_{n-2} + a_{n-1}x)\ldots))))$$
$$= a_0 + x(a_1 + x(a_2 + x((\ldots x(a_{n/2-2} + a_{n/2-1}x)\ldots))))$$
$$+ x^{n/2}(a_{n/2} + x(a_{n/2+1} + x(a_{n/2+2}$$
$$+ x((\ldots x(a_{n-2} + a_{n-1}x)\ldots)))).$$

Thus, recursively compute the two halves and multiply the right half by $x^{n/2}$, which is computed by doubling in each recursive call: $x \leftarrow x * x$.

19.15. Let $\langle x_1, x_2, \ldots, x_n \rangle$ be a sequence of n distinct numbers. Design a parallel algorithm for the CREW PRAM to sort this sequence in time $O(\log n)$. Assume an unlimited number of processors.

Use n groups of processors. Each group g_k, $1 \le k \le n$, consists of n^2 processors and uses Exercise 19.6 to find the kth smallest element on the CREW PRAM.

19.16. Let n be a positive integer. Consider the problem of computing the polynomials $x_i' = x^i$, for $1 \le i \le n$. Show how to compute the x_i''s in $O(\log n)$ time. Specify the PRAM model used.

Use parallel prefix.

19.17. Let A be a sequence of integers and x an integer. Develop an EREW PRAM algorithm to find all the occurrences, if any, of x in A. Your algorithm should run in time $O(\log n)$ and use a linear number of operations.

Define $B[i], 1 \le i \le n$, to be 1 if $A[i] = x$ and 0 otherwise. Apply parallel prefix on A so as to move all x's to the beginning of A (array packing). Output $A[1], A[2], \ldots, A[j]$, where j is the number of occurrences of x. The number of operations is $O(n)$ if we use $n / \log n$ processors (the detailed description is skipped here).

19.18. Consider Algorithm PARQUICKSORT presented in Sec. 19.2.3.2. Suppose we always select the median as the pivot (see Sec. 19.2.11). What will be the running time of the algorithm?

We will use $n / \log n$ processors. The running time for finding the median is that for selection, which is $O(\log n \log \log n)$. Since there are $\log n$ levels, the overall running time is $O(\log^2 n \log \log n)$.

19.19. Let A and B be two sequences of distinct number sorted in ascending order. Design an $O(1)$ time algorithm to merge A and B on the CRCW PRAM. Assume an unlimited number of processors.

There is no need for concurrent writes, so we will adopt the CREW PRAM. Assume $|A| = |B| = n$, and let C be the array that will hold the merge of A and B. We will use n-ary search (parallel search using n processors for each element-search). Associate n processors with each element of A and B. Let $P_{i,1}, P_{i,2}, \ldots, P_{i,n}$ be the n processors associated with $A[i]$. Processor $P_{i,j}$ tests whether $B[j] < A[i]$ and $B[j+1] > A[i]$. If this is the case, then $\mathrm{rank}(A[i], B) = j$, and we set $C[i+j] = A[i]$. This is done for each element of A. We repeat the procedure in parallel for array B. The total number of processors needed is $2n^2$.

19.20. Apply Brent theorem on Algorithm PARMERGE presented in Sec. 19.2.6.2.

The amount of work done by Algorithm PARMERGE is $O(n \log \log n)$, assuming $n = m$. Since the work is equal to the cost, Brent theorem is of no help in reducing the cost by reducing the number of processors.

19.21. In Algorithm ODDEVENMERGE in Sec. 19.2.8, A_{even} is merged with B_{odd} and A_{odd} is merged with B_{even}. Rewrite the algorithm with the modification that it merges A_{odd} with B_{odd} and A_{even} with B_{even}. It is important to know that this will change the step of traversing the shuffle of C and D.

In this case, we traverse E starting from d_0. Thus, we compare d_0 with c_1, d_1 with c_2, and so on.

19.22. Let $G = (V, E)$ be an undirected graph with n vertices. Give an algorithm to decide whether G contains a triangle, that is, three mutually adjacent vertices. Assume that G is represented by its adjacency matrix. Your algorithm should run in $O(\log n)$ time on the CRCW PRAM with n^3 processors.

Let A be the $n \times n$ adjacency matrix. There is a triangle in G if and only if there is a 1 in the diagonal of A^3. Thus, to test for the presence of a triangle, compute A^3 in $\Theta(\log n)$ time, and test its diagonal for the occurrence of 1 by taking the OR of the diagonal in $O(1)$ time as explained in Exercise 19.1.

Similar to the example in Fig. 19.16.

19.23. Illustrate the operation of the pipelined mergesort algorithm on the input $\langle 6, 7, 1, 4, 2, 5, 8, 3 \rangle$.

Similar to the example in Fig. 19.17.

19.24. Parallelize Algorithm SELECT given in Sec. 5.5 using $n/\log n$ processors on the PRAM. Analyze your algorithm.

Each step of the sequential algorithm is done in parallel using the available processors. Dividing the inputs into groups of five elements will be changed to $\log n$ elements. Sorting the $\log n$-element groups takes $\Theta(\log n)$ sequential time (each group is assigned one processor). Computing A_1, A_2 and A_3 takes $\Theta(\log n)$ time using parallel prefix and packing as explained in the parallel quicksort algorithm. The recursive calls take $T(n/5)$ and at most $T(3n/4)$. Hence, the running time is given by the recurrence $T(n) \leq T(3n/4) + T(n/5) + \Theta(\log n)$, whose solution is $T(n) = O(\log^2 n)$.

19.25. Explain how to make Algorithm PARSELECT of Sec. 19.2.11 cost optimal.

Apply Brent theorem (Theorem 19.1). Since the work done is $O(n)$, we may reduce the number of processors to $O(n)/O(\log n \log \log n) = O(n/(\log n \log \log n))$. The running time will remain unchanged, that is, $O(\log n \log \log n)$. However, the new cost is

$$O\left(\frac{n}{\log n \log \log n}\right) O(\log n \log \log n) = O(n).$$

19.26. Rewrite Algorithm PARSELECT for selection discussed in Sec. 19.2.11 for the case when the number of processors is $p < n$. Derive its running time.

The modified algorithm is shown as Algorithm PARSELECT2. First, we count the number of iterations of the **for** loop. In the second iteration, $|A| \leq 3n/4$, and in the jth iteration $|A| \leq (3/4)^j n$. Hence, after $c \log(n/p)$ iterations, the size of A is at most

$$\left(\frac{3}{4}\right)^{c \log(n/p)} \times n$$

$$= (n/p)^{c \log (3/4)} \times n$$

$$= \frac{n}{(n/p)^{c \log (4/3)}}$$

$$= \frac{n}{(n/p)^{\log (4/3)/ \log (4/3)}}$$

$$= \frac{n}{n/p}$$

$$= p.$$

Therefore, in Step 12, there will be enough processors to sort A in $O(\log p)$ time. In Step 4, the median of each block is found using one processor in $O(|A|/p)$ sequential time. We have to be careful about estimating the time taken by Step 4. The time taken by Step 4 throughout the algorithm is

$$O\left(\frac{n}{p} + \left(\frac{3}{4}\right)\frac{n}{p} + \left(\frac{3}{4}\right)^2 \frac{n}{p} + \cdots\right) = O(n/p).$$

The median of medians m (Step 5) is computed by sorting the set M using the pipelined merge sort algorithm in $O(\log p)$ time. Partitioning A (Step 6) can be achieved in $O(\log p)$ time using p processors. Hence, the total time taken by these two steps is $O(\log p \log(n/p))$ throughout the algorithm. Therefore, the **for** loop takes $O(n/p + \log p \log(n/p))$. When the **for** loop terminates, A is sorted using the pipelined merge sort algorithm and the kth smallest element is returned in $O(\log p)$ time using the available p processors. It follows that the running time of the algorithm is $O(n/p + \log(n/p) \log p))$.

Algorithm 19.34 PARSELECT2
Input: A sequence $A = \langle a_1, \ldots, a_n \rangle$ of elements and an integer k, $1 \leq k \leq n$.
Output: The kth smallest element in A.

1. $c \leftarrow 1/\log(4/3)$
2. **for** $j \leftarrow 1$ **to** $c\log(n/p)$
3. $q = \lfloor |A|/p \rfloor$. Divide A into p groups of q elements each.
4.   Find the median of each of the p groups individually.
       Let the set of medians be M.
5.   Sort M and find its median m.
6.   Partition A into three sequences:
       $A_1 = \{a \mid a < m\}$
       $A_2 = \{a \mid a = m\}$
       $A_3 = \{a \mid a > m\}$
7.   **case**
           $|A_1| \geq k$: $A \leftarrow A_1$
           $|A_1| + |A_2| \geq k$: **return** m
           $|A_1| + |A_2| < k$:
8. $A = A_3$
9. $k \leftarrow k - |A_1| - |A_2|$
10.   **end case**
11. **end for**
12. Sort A and **return** the kth smallest element in A.

19.27. Let $A = \langle a_1, a_2, \ldots, a_n \rangle$ be a sequence of numbers and let k be a given integer between 1 and n. Design and analyze a parallel algorithm to find all k smallest items in A. Do not use multiselection. What model of computation did you use?

Use Exercise 19.6 to find the kth smallest element on the CREW PRAM with n^2 processors, call it x. For $1 \leq i \leq n$, let $B[i] = 1$ if $a_i \leq x$ and $B[i] = 0$ otherwise. Now, use parallel prefix and packing to move the k smallest elements to the beginning of A or to any other location. The model used is the CREW PRAM.

19.28. Compute the bisection width of the d-dimensional butterfly B_d.

Figure 19.26 shows the d-dimensional butterfly for $d = 1, 2, 3$. From the figure, it is clear that for $j > 1$, B_j can be divided into two halves with $2 \times 2^{d-1} = 2^d$ connections between them. Hence, the bisection width is 2^d.

19.29. Give an $O(d)$ time algorithm for broadcasting in the d-dimensional hypercube H_d if the origin of the message is an arbitrary processor.

Let P_i be the origin of broadcasting datum x. First, transfer x from P_i to P_0 using bit fixing in $O(d)$ steps, then broadcast it to all other processors in $O(d)$ time as shown in Algorithm HCBROADCAST.

19.30. Design an algorithm to compute the sum of n numbers on the hypercube with p processors, $1 \leq p < n$. Is your algorithm always optimal?

Assume that each processor P_i contains at least one number; if not then, let P_i contain 0. First, compute the sum of the numbers in each processors. Next, compute the sum of the $p = 2^d$ resulting numbers using the technique of *reduction*, which is a method similar to that used in broadcasting in the hypercube but in reverse order. This is shown in Algorithm HCSUM below. Here, the notation $j^{(i)}$ means j with the ith bit complemented, $0 \leq i \leq d - 1$. If the numbers are distributed evenly among the p processors, so that each processor contains n/p numbers, then the running time is $O(\max\{\frac{n}{p}, d\})$, which is optimal. Otherwise, the algorithm is not optimal, as the running time may be as large as $\Theta(n)$. In this case data redistribution may be helpful if it takes $o(m)$, where m is the maximum number of elements in all processors.

Algorithm 19.35 HCSUM

Input: $x_0, x_1, \ldots, x_{2^d - 1}$.

Output: The sum of the numbers $x_0, x_1, \ldots, x_{2^d - 1}$ stored in processors $P_0, P_1, \ldots, P_{2^d - 1}$ of H_d.

1. **for** $i \leftarrow d - 1, d - 2, \ldots, 1, 0$
2.   **for all** $j < 2^i$ and $j < j^{(i)}$ **do in parallel**
3. $x_j \leftarrow x_j + x_{j^{(i)}}$
4.   **end for**
5. **end for**

19.31. Give an $O(pd)$ time algorithm for the problem of routing in the d-dimensional hypercube if every processor has a packet to be sent to every other processor, where $p = 2^d$. Note that the total number of packets to be routed is $p(p-1)$. (*Hint*: Use randomized routing p times.)

Use randomized routing sequentially p times. Each run takes $O(d)$ time for a total of $O(pd)$.

19.32. Give an $O(p)$ time algorithm for the problem in Exercise 19.31.

Use randomized routing in parallel p times. This takes $O(d)$ time if we ignore the delays. However, there are queues that will expand the running time. There are $p(p-1)$ paths, and hence each node of the hypercube is included in $\frac{p(p-1)}{p} = p - 1$ paths. This results in a queue of size $O(p)$ at each node. This means the running time will be expanded to $O(p) + O(d) = O(p)$.

19.33. Give an algorithm to evaluate the polynomial $a_{n-1}x^{n-1} + a_{n-2}x^{n-2} + \cdots + a_1 x + a_0$ at the point x_0 on the d-dimensional hypercube H_d with $n = 2^d$ processors. Assume that each a_i is stored in processor P_i, $0 \le i \le n - 1$.

First, use parallel prefix to compute $1, x_0, x_0^2, \ldots, x_0^{n-1}$ in processors $P_0, P_1, \ldots, P_{n-1}$. Next, within each processor, multiply $a_i \times x_0^i$, $0 \le i \le n - 1$. Finally, use Algorithm HCSUM in Exercise 19.30 above to find the desired sum. The running time is $\Theta(\log n)$.

19.34. Let $S = \langle x_0, x_1, \ldots, x_{n-1} \rangle$ be a sequence of numbers stored in a hypercube with n processors, where x_i is stored in P_i, $0 \le i < n$, and let y be stored in P_0. Give an algorithm to count the number of elements in S that are larger than y.

First, broadcast y to all processors. Next, each processor P_i sets $z_i = 1$ if $x_i > y$ and $z_i = 0$ if $x_i \le y$. Finally, find the sum of $z_i, 0 \le i \le n - 1$ in all processors, and store the sum, which is the number of 1s, in P_0. Use Algorithm HCSUM in Exercise 19.30 above.

19.35. Consider running odd–even transposition sort on a p-processor linear array if each item in the input is known to start within distance d from its final position. What is the number of steps needed to sort p items in this case?

Consider the input: 5 7 8 6 1 3 2 4. If we run the algorithm on this input, 6 will move two steps to the left away from its final position. This shows that the number of steps may be more than d. However, we will show that this is not the case, that is, the number of steps will be at most d. Let the input be $a_1, a_2, \ldots, a_p$, which is a permutation of the numbers $1, 2, \ldots, p$. Thus, the position of a_i is i, and the final position of a_i is a_i itself. For instance, in the above example, the position of 6 is 4, while its final position is 6. Define $\delta(a_i, t)$ to be an upper bound on the distance of a_i from its final position at the end of step t of the algorithm, where $1 \leq t \leq T$ (T is the total number of steps). Thus, $\delta(a_i, T) = 0$ for all $i, 1 \leq i \leq n$, since the input is sorted, and $\delta(a_i, 0) = d$, which is given.

We will prove our claim by contradiction. Suppose that a_i is the leftmost number such that for some $t_1 > 1$, $\delta(a_i, t_1) > d$. Assume without loss of generality that $a_i - i > 0$, that is, a_i is initially to the left of its sorted position a_i. Since $\delta(a_i, t_1) > d$, there exists a step number $t_0 < t_1$ such that $\delta(a_i, t_0) = d$. Going from step t_0 to step t_1, it must be the case that $a_{i-1} > a_i$, that is, a_{i-1} is larger than a_i (e.g., $a_{i-1} = 8$ and $a_i = 6$ in the above example). But this implies that $\delta(a_{i-1}, t_1) > \delta(a_i, t_1) > d$. This contradicts the assumption that a_i is the leftmost number such that for some $t_1 > 1$, $\delta(a_i, t_1) > d$.

19.36. Consider Algorithm MERGE-SPLIT, which is a generalization of odd–even transposition sort for the case $p < n$. Let S be a sequence of numbers to be sorted, and assume that each of the p processors in the linear array holds a subsequence of S of length n/p. In Algorithm MERGE-SPLIT, the comparison-exchange operations of odd–even transposition sort are now replaced with merge-split operations on subsequences. Let S_i denote the subsequence held by processor P_i. Initially, the S_i's are random subsequences of S. In Step 1, each P_i sorts S_i using a sequential algorithm. In Step 2, each odd-numbered processor P_i merges the two subsequences S_i and S_{i+1}, into a sorted sequence S_i'. It retains the first half of S_i' and assigns to its neighbor P_{i+1}, the second half. Step 3 is identical to 2 except that it is performed by all even-numbered processors. Steps 2 and 3 are repeated alternately. After $\lceil p/2 \rceil$ iterations no further exchange of elements can take place between two processors, where an iteration consists of Steps 2 and 3. Analyze the running time of this algorithm.

There are p phases, where an iteration consists of two phases. The first phase, the sorting step, takes $O(\frac{n}{p} \log \frac{n}{p})$ time. The merge-split phases after that take $O(\frac{n}{p})$ each for a total of $O(n)$ time. Hence, the running time is $O(\max\{\frac{n}{p} \log \frac{n}{p}, n\})$.

19.37. Do Exercise 19.36 for the case $p = \log n$. Is the algorithm optimal?

If $p = \log n$, then the running time is $\Theta(n)$, which is optimal.

19.38. Show how to compute the prefix sums on the mesh for the snakelike indexing scheme.

Modify Algorithm MESHPARPREFIX discussed in Sec. 19.5.2.

19.39. Give an algorithm to evaluate the polynomial $a_{n-1}x^{n-1} + a_{n-2}x^{n-2} + \cdots + a_1 x + a_0$ at the point x_0 on the $\sqrt{n} \times \sqrt{n}$ mesh. Assume that each a_i is stored in processor P_i, $0 \le i \le n-1$ (the processors are indexed as $P_0, P_1, \cdots, P_{n-1}$). What is the running time of your algorithm?

Compute the sequence $1, x_0, x_0^2, \ldots, x_0^{n-1}$ using parallel prefix. Each x_0^j is stored in P_j, $0 \le j \le n-1$. Next, compute the products $a_j \times x_0^j$, $0 \le j \le n-1$. Finally, compute the sum $a_0 + a_1 x_0 + a_2 x_0^2 + \cdots + a_{n-1}x_0^{n-1}$. The total running time is $\Theta(\sqrt{n})$.

19.40. Consider the following method for sorting on the mesh. The method alternately sorts all rows from left to right and all columns from top to bottom. Will this method always work in sorting any input? Assume an unlimited amount of time.

The method will not work in sorting any input. We will succeed in showing that if we can exhibit an example in which the method does not terminate or terminates before sorting the input. We will choose the latter. Let $\mathbf{M} = \begin{vmatrix} x_{1,1} & x_{1,2} \\ x_{2,1} & x_{2,2} \end{vmatrix}$, where $x_{1,1} = 3, x_{1,2} = 2, x_{2,1} = 1$ and $x_{2,2} = 4$. After sorting by rows and then by columns, M becomes:

$$\mathbf{M_h} = \begin{vmatrix} 2 & 3 \\ 1 & 4 \end{vmatrix} \quad \mathbf{M_v} = \begin{vmatrix} 1 & 3 \\ 2 & 4 \end{vmatrix}.$$

Clearly, M_v is sorted by rows and by columns, but the input is not sorted. So, the method terminated without sorting the input.

19.41. Consider sorting the rows and then the columns of a $2 \times n$ mesh M. Does this leave the rows in sorted order?

Call a column C_j of the mesh "good" if sorting that column leaves the rows sorted. We prove by induction on the number of columns that all columns are good, and hence sorting the mesh by columns leaves the rows sorted. If all columns are unsorted, then there is nothing to prove, as exchanging the two rows leaves them sorted. So, assume without loss of generality that column $C_1 = \langle x_{1,1}, x_{2,1} \rangle$ is sorted, that is, $x_{1,1} < x_{2,1}$. Hence, column C_1 is good by assumption. Assume for the induction hypothesis that column C_{k-1} is good, $1 < k < n$. We show that column C_k is also good. We have the following situation:

$$\mathbf{M} = \begin{vmatrix} x_{1,1} & \cdots & x_{1,k-1} & x_{1,k} & \cdots \\ x_{2,1} & \cdots & x_{2,k-1} & x_{2,k} & \cdots \end{vmatrix}.$$

By induction, $x_{1,k-1} < x_{2,k-1} < x_{2,k}$. If $x_{1,k} > x_{2,k}$, then we have the following situation after sorting column C_k:

$$\mathbf{M} = \begin{vmatrix} x_{1,1} & \cdots & x_{1,k-1} & x_{2,k} & \cdots \\ x_{2,1} & \cdots & x_{2,k-1} & x_{1,k} & \cdots \end{vmatrix}.$$

In this case, we have $x_{1,k-1} < x_{2,k-1} < x_{2,k} < x_{1,k}$, whence $x_{1,k-1} < x_{2,k}$ and $x_{2,k-1} < x_{1,k}$. Thus, column C_k is good and, by induction, all columns are good. It follows that if all columns are sorted, then the rows will remain sorted.

19.42. This is a generalization of Exercise 19.41. Consider sorting the rows and then the columns of a general $n \times n$ mesh. Does this leave the rows in sorted order?

Call a column C_j of the mesh "good" if sorting that column leaves the rows sorted. We prove by induction on the number of columns that all columns are good, and hence sorting the mesh by columns leaves the rows sorted. Let the first column be $C_1 = \langle x_{1,1}, x_{2,1}, \ldots, x_{n,1} \rangle$ and let C_1 after sorting be $C_1' = \langle x_{1,1}', x_{2,1}', \ldots, x_{n,1}' \rangle$. Thus, we have $x_{j,1}' \leq x_{j,1}$ for $1 \leq j \leq n$. Since row i is sorted, and since $x_{i,1}' \leq x_{i,1}$, we have $x_{i,1}' \leq x_{i,2}$. Therefore, we may assume without loss of generality that column C_1 is sorted. Hence, column C_1 is good by assumption. Assume for the induction hypothesis that column C_{k-1} is good, $1 < k < n$. We show that column C_k is also good. We have the following situation:

$$
\mathbf{M} = \begin{vmatrix} & \vdots & \vdots & \\ \cdots & x_{i,k-1} & x_{i,k} & \cdots \\ & \vdots & \vdots & \\ \cdots & x_{j,k-1} & x_{j,k} & \cdots \\ & \vdots & \vdots & \end{vmatrix}.
$$

We show that sorting column k leaves the rows sorted. We will use Algorithm SELECTIONSORT to sort column k. Recall that this algorithm sorts by interchanging the elements to be sorted if they are out of order. Let $x_{i,k}$ and $x_{j,k}$, where $i < j$, be the next two numbers in column k to be interchanged by Algorithm SELECTIONSORT because $x_{i,k} > x_{j,k}$. We have the following situation for columns $k - 1$ and k after the interchange of $x_{i,k}$ and $x_{j,k}$:

$$
\mathbf{M} = \begin{vmatrix} & \vdots & \vdots & \\ \cdots & x_{i,k-1} & x_{j,k} & \cdots \\ & \vdots & \vdots & \\ \cdots & x_{j,k-1} & x_{i,k} & \cdots \\ & \vdots & \vdots & \end{vmatrix},
$$

where $x_{i,k-1} < x_{i,k}$ and $x_{j,k-1} < x_{j,k}$ since the rows are sorted. By Exercise 19.41, exchanging $x_{i,k}$ and $x_{j,k}$ will leave the two rows i and j sorted. Now, the procedure is repeated for each pair $x_{i',k}$ and $x_{j',k}$ that are out of order until column k is sorted. Thus, column C_k is good and, by induction, all columns are good.

It follows that if all columns are sorted, then the rows will remain sorted.

19.43. Let $A = \langle a_1, a_2, \ldots, a_n \rangle$ be a sequence of elements stored in the processors of a $\sqrt{n} \times \sqrt{n}$ mesh, one element per processor, and let x be a given element. Design an algorithm for the search problem in the mesh: If $a_i = x$ for some i, $1 \leq i \leq n$, then return i, else return 0. Analyze its running time.

Assume the processors are numbered $P_1, P_2, \ldots, P_n$. First, initialize the search index $k \leftarrow 0$, which is stored in P_1. Next, broadcast x to all processors in $\Theta(\sqrt{n})$ time. Each processor P_j now compares a_j with x. If $a_j = x$, then processor P_j sends j to P_1 in $\Theta(\sqrt{n})$ time, which sets $k \leftarrow j$. Note that we have assumed here that the a_j's are distinct. The total running time is $\Theta(\sqrt{n})$.

19.44. Outline an algorithm for broadcasting an item x stored in processor $P_{0,0,0}$ in a three-dimensional mesh with n processors to all other processors. How many steps are there in your algorithm?

First, broadcast x to all processors along the x-axis in the row $z = 0, y = 0$. Next, broadcast in parallel all occurrences of x in row $z = 0, y = 0$ to all processors in the two-dimensional mesh $y = 0$. Finally, broadcast x in parallel from all processors in the two-dimensional mesh $y = 0$ to all other processors. The number of steps executed is $3(n^{1/3}-1)$ steps.

19.45. Give an algorithm to find the maximum in a set of numbers stored in a three-dimensional mesh with n processors. How many steps in your algorithm?

We use reduction. First, find the maximum in each two-dimensional mesh and store it in the respective processor with $x = 0, y = 0$. Next, find the maximum in the z-column $x = 0, y = 0$. The number of steps executed is $3(n^{1/3}-1)$ steps.

19.46. What is the bisection width of a three-dimensional mesh with $n = m^3$ processors if m is even?

The bisection width is m^2 if m is even.

Fig. 19.59.   Exercise 19.47.

Fig. 19.60.   Exercise 19.48.

19.47. Illustrate the operation of Algorithm THREEDMESHSORT for sorting the 0s and 1s shown in Fig. 19.59.

Similar to Example 19.13.

19.48. Illustrate the operation of Algorithm THREEDMESHSORT for sorting the numbers shown in Fig. 19.60.

Similar to Example 19.14.

19.49. Use the fast Fourier transform (FFT) to compute $F_4\mathbf{a}$, where $\mathbf{a} = [2, 1, -1, 3]^T$.

Similar to Example 19.15.

19.50. Use the iterative FFT on the butterfly to compute the product $F_4\mathbf{a}$, where $\mathbf{a} = [2, 1, -1, 3]^T$.

Similar to Example 19.16.

19.51. Use FFT to compute the product $f(x)g(x)$, where $f(x) = 1 + 3x$ and $g(x) = 1 + 4x$.

Similar to Example 19.18.

19.52. Explain how to use FFT to compute $(1 + x)^n$ efficiently, where n is a power of 2. What is the time complexity of your algorithm?

We compute $(1 + x)^2, (1 + x)^4, (1 + x)^8, \ldots, (1 + x)^n$ in this order using FFT. There are $\log n$ applications of FFT costing $\Theta(\log 2) + \Theta(\log 4) + \cdots + \Theta(\log n) = \Theta(\log^2 n)$ in parallel. The sequential time complexity is $\Theta(n \log^2 n)$.

19.53. Explain how to make the bubble sorter output the numbers in descending order.

We propose two possibilities. The first approach is that we still use the same sorting mechanism except that on top of the sorter we add a multiplier which multiplies each input/output datum by -1. The second approach is to exchange the input and output ports. That is, let the input data enter the sorter from the lower right end (i.e., where the number ∞ enters) and output data come out from the lower left end (i.e., where ∞ comes out). In addition to the I/O port exchange, the sorter must be initialized to contain a number known to be smaller than the input data.

Appendix A

Mathematical Preliminaries

When analyzing an algorithm, the amount of resources required is usually expressed as a function of the input size. A nontrivial algorithm typically consists of repeating a set of instructions either iteratively, e.g., by executing a **for** or **while** loop, or recursively by invoking the same algorithm again and again, each time reducing the input size until it becomes small enough, in which case the algorithm solves the input instance using a straightforward method. This implies that the amount of resources used by an algorithm can be expressed in the form of summation or recursive formula. This mandates the need for the basic mathematical tools that are necessary to deal with these summations and recursive formulas in the process of analyzing an algorithm.

In this appendix, we review some of the mathematical preliminaries and discuss briefly some of these mathematical tools that are frequently employed in the analysis of algorithms.

A.1 Sets, Relations and Functions

When analyzing an algorithm, its input is considered to be a set drawn from some particular domain e.g., the set of integers. An algorithm, in the formal sense, can be thought of as a function, which is a constrained relation, that maps each possible input to a specific output. Thus, sets and functions are at the heart of algorithmic analysis. In this section, we briefly review some of the basic concepts of sets, relations and functions that arise naturally in the design and analysis of algorithms. More detailed treatments can be found in most books on set theory and discrete mathematics.

A.1.1 *Sets*

The term *set* is used to refer to any collection of objects, which are called *members* or *elements* of the set. A set is called *finite* if it contains n elements, for some constant $n \geq 0$, and *infinite* otherwise. Examples of infinite sets include the set of natural numbers $\{1, 2, \ldots\}$ and the sets of integers, rationals and reals.

Informally, an infinite set is called *countable* if its elements can be listed as the first element, second element, and so on; otherwise, it is called *uncountable*. For example, the set of integers $\{0, 1, -1, 2, -2, \ldots\}$ is countable, while the set of real numbers is uncountable.

A finite set is described by listing ITS elements in some way and enclosing this list in braces. If the set is countable, three dots may be used to indicate that not all the elements have been listed. For example, the set of integers between 1 and 100 can be stated as $\{1, 2, 3, \ldots, 100\}$ and the set of natural numbers can be stated as $\{1, 2, 3, \ldots\}$. A set may also be denoted by specifying some property. For example, the set $\{1, 2, \ldots, 100\}$ can also be denoted by $\{x \mid 1 \leq x \leq 100 \text{ and } x \text{ is integer}\}$. An uncountable set can only be described this way. For example, the set of real numbers between 0 and 1 can be expressed as $\{x \mid x \text{ is a real number and } 0 \leq x \leq 1\}$. The *empty* set is denoted by $\{\ \}$ or ϕ.

If A is a finite set, then the cardinality of A, denoted by $|A|$, is the number of elements in A. We write $x \in A$ if x is a member of A, and $x \notin A$ otherwise. We say that a set B is a *subset* of a set A, denoted by $B \subseteq A$, if each element of B is an element of A. If, in addition, $B \neq A$, we say that B is a *proper subset* of A, and we write $B \subset A$. Thus, $\{a, \{2, 3\}\} \subset \{a, \{2, 3\}, b\}$, but $\{a, \{2, 3\}\} \not\subseteq \{a, \{2\}, \{3\}, b\}$. For any set A, $A \subseteq A$ and $\phi \subseteq A$. We observe that if A and B are sets such that $A \subseteq B$ and $B \subseteq A$, then $A = B$. Thus, to prove that two sets A and B are equal, we only need to prove that $A \subseteq B$ and $B \subseteq A$.

The *union* of two sets A and B, denoted by $A \cup B$, is the set $\{x \mid x \in A \text{ or } x \in B\}$. The *intersection* of two sets A and B, denoted by $A \cap B$, is the set $\{x \mid x \in A \text{ and } x \in B\}$. The *difference* of a set A from a set B, denoted by $A - B$, is the set $\{x \mid x \in A \text{ and } x \notin B\}$. The *complement* of a set A, denoted by $\overline{A}$, is defined as $U - A$, where U is the *universal set* containing A, which is usually understood from the context. If A, B and C are sets, then $A \cup (B \cup C) = (A \cup B) \cup C$ and $A \cap (B \cap C) = (A \cap B) \cap C$. We say that two sets A and B are *disjoint* if $A \cap B = \phi$. The *power set* of a set A, denoted by $P(A)$, is the set of all subsets of A. Note that $\phi \in P(A)$ and $A \in P(A)$. If $|A| = n$, then $|P(A)| = 2^n$.

A.1.2 Relations

An *ordered n-tuple* $(a_1, a_2, \ldots, a_n)$ is an ordered collection that has a_1 as its first element, a_2 as its second element, $\ldots$, and a_n as its nth element. In particular, 2-tuples are called *ordered pairs*. Let A and B be two sets. The *Cartesian product* of A and B, denoted by $A \times B$, is the set of all ordered pairs (a, b) where $a \in A$ and $b \in B$. In set notation,

$$A \times B = \{(a, b) \mid a \in A \quad \text{and} \quad b \in B\}.$$

More generally, the Cartesian product of $A_1, A_2, \ldots, A_n$ is defined as

$$A_1 \times A_2 \times \cdots \times A_n = \{(a_1, a_2, \ldots, a_n) \mid a_i \in A_i, 1 \leq i \leq n\}.$$

Let A and B be two nonempty sets. A *binary relation*, or simply a *relation*, *R from A to B* is a set of ordered pairs (a, b), where $a \in A$ and $b \in B$, that is, $R \subseteq A \times B$. If $A = B$, we say that R is a relation *on the set A*. The *domain* of R, sometimes written $\text{Dom}(R)$, is the set

$$\text{Dom}(R) = \{a \mid \text{ for some } b \in B \ (a, b) \in R\}.$$

The *range* of R, sometimes written $\text{Ran}(R)$, is the set

$$\text{Ran}(R) = \{b \mid \text{ for some } a \in A, (a, b) \in R\}.$$

Example A.1 Let $R_1 = \{(2,5), (3,3)\}$, $R_2 = \{(x,y) \mid x, y \text{ are positive integers and } x \leq y\}$ and $R_3 = \{(x,y) \mid x, y \text{ are real numbers and } x^2 + y^2 \leq 1\}$. Then, $\text{Dom}(R_1) = \{2,3\}$ and $\text{Ran}(R_1) = \{5,3\}$, $\text{Dom}(R_2) = \text{Ran}(R_2)$ is the set of natural numbers, and $\text{Dom}(R_3) = \text{Ran}(R_3)$ is the set of real numbers in the interval $[-1..1]$.

Let R be a relation *on a set A*. R is said to be *reflexive* if $(a, a) \in R$ for all $a \in A$. It is *irreflexive* if $(a, a) \notin R$ for all $a \in A$. It is *symmetric* if $(a, b) \in R$ implies $(b, a) \in R$. It is *asymmetric* if $(a, b) \in R$ implies $(b, a) \notin R$. It is *antisymmetric* if $(a, b) \in R$ and $(b, a) \in R$ implies $a = b$. Finally, R is said to be *transitive* if $(a, b) \in R$ and $(b, c) \in R$ implies $(a, c) \in R$. A relation that is reflexive, antisymmetric and transitive is called a *partial order*.

Example A.2 Let $R_1 = \{(x, y) \mid x, y \text{ are positive integers and } x \text{ divides } y\}$. Let $R_2 = \{(x, y) \mid x, y \text{ are integers and } x \leq y\}$. Then, both R_1 and R_2 are reflexive, antisymmetric and transitive, and hence both are partial orders.

A.1.2.1 *Equivalence relations*

A relation R on a set A is called an *equivalence relation* if it is reflexive, symmetric and transitive. In this case, R partitions A into *equivalence classes* $C_1, C_2, \ldots, C_k$ such that any two elements in one equivalence class are related by R. That is, for any $C_i, 1 \leq i \leq k$, if $x \in C_i$ and $y \in C_i$, then $(x, y) \in R$. On the other hand, if $x \in C_i$ and $y \in C_j$ and $i \neq j$, then $(x, y) \notin R$.

Example A.3 Let x and y be two integers, and let n be a positive integer. We say that x and y are *congruent modulo* n, denoted by

$$x \equiv y \pmod{n}$$

if $x - y = kn$ for some integer k. In other words, $x \equiv y \pmod{n}$ if both x and y leave the same (positive) remainder when divided by n. For example, $13 \equiv 8 \pmod 5$ and $13 \equiv -2 \pmod 5$. Now, define the relation

$$R = \{(x, y) \mid x, y \text{ are integers} \quad \text{and} \quad x \equiv y \pmod{n}\}.$$

Then, R is an equivalence relation. It partitions, the set of integers into n classes $C_0, C_1, \ldots, C_{n-1}$ such that $x \in C_i$ and $y \in C_i$ if and only if $x \equiv y \pmod{n}$.

A.1.3 *Functions*

A *function* f is a (binary) relation such that for every element $x \in \text{Dom}(f)$ there is *exactly* one element $y \in \text{Ran}(f)$ with $(x, y) \in f$. In this case, one usually writes $f(x) = y$ instead of $(x, y) \in f$ and says that y is the *value* or *image* of f at x.

Example A.4 The relation $\{(1,2),(3,4),(2,4)\}$ is a function, while the relation $\{(1,2),(1,4)\}$ is not. The relation $\{(x,y) \mid x, y$ are positive integers and $x = y^3\}$ is a function, while the relation $\{(x,y) \mid x$ is a positive integer, y is integer and $x = y^2\}$ is not. In Example A.1, R_1 is a function, while R_2 and R_3 are not.

Let f be a function such that $\mathrm{Dom}(f) = A$ and $\mathrm{Ran}(f) \subseteq B$ for some nonempty sets A and B. We say that f is *one to one* if for no different elements x and y in A, $f(x) = f(y)$. That is, f is one to one if $f(x) = f(y)$ implies $x = y$. We say that f is *onto* B if $\mathrm{Ran}(f) = B$. f is said to be a *bijection* or *one to one correspondence between A and B* if it is both one to one and onto B.

A.2 Proof Methods

Proofs constitute an essential component in the design and analysis of algorithms. The correctness of an algorithm and the amount of resources needed by the algorithm such as its computing time and space usage are all established by proving postulated assertions. In this section, we briefly review the most common methods of proof used in the analysis of algorithms.

A.2.1 *Notation*

A *proposition* or an *assertion* P is simply a statement that can be either *true* or *false* but not both. The symbol "$\neg$" is the negation symbol. For example, $\neg P$ is the converse of proposition P. The symbols "$\rightarrow$"and "$\leftrightarrow$" are used extensively in proofs. "$\rightarrow$" is read "implies" and "$\leftrightarrow$" is read "if and only if". Thus, if P and Q are two propositions, then the statement "$P \rightarrow Q$" stands for "P implies Q" or "if P then Q", and the statement "$P \leftrightarrow Q$", stands for "P if and only if Q", that is, "P is *true* if and only if Q is *true*". The statement "$P \leftrightarrow Q$" is usually broken down into two implications: "$P \rightarrow Q$" and "$Q \rightarrow P$", and each statement is proven separately. If $P \rightarrow Q$, we say that Q is a *necessary condition* for P, and P is a *sufficient condition* for Q.

A.2.2 Direct proof

To prove that "$P \rightarrow Q$", a direct proof works by assuming that P is *true* and then deducing the truth of Q from the truth of P. Many mathematical proofs are of this type.

Example A.5 We wish to prove the assertion: If n is an even integer, then n^2 is an even integer. A direct proof for this claim is as follows. Since n is even, $n = 2k$ for some integer k. So, $n = 4k^2 = 2(2k^2)$. It follows that n^2 is an even integer.

A.2.3 Indirect proof

The implication "$P \rightarrow Q$" is logically equivalent to the *contrapositive* implication "$\neg Q \rightarrow \neg P$". For example the statement "if it is raining then it is cloudy" is logically equivalent to the statement "if it is not cloudy then it is not raining". Sometimes, proving "if not Q then not P" is much easier than using a direct proof for the statement "if P then Q".

Example A.6 Consider the assertion: If n^2 is an even integer, then n is an even integer. If we try to use the direct proof technique to prove this theorem, we may proceed as in the proof in Example A.5. An alternative approach, which is much simpler, is to prove the logically equivalent assertion: If n is an odd integer, then n^2 is an odd integer. We prove the truth of this statement using the direct proof method as follows. If n is an odd integer, then $n = 2k + 1$ for some integer k. Thus, $n^2 = (2k + 1)^2 = 4k^2 + 4k + 1 = 2(2k^2 + 2k) + 1$. That is, n^2 is an odd integer.

A.2.4 Proof by contradiction

This is an extremely powerful method and is widely used to make proofs short and simple to follow. To prove that the statement "$P \rightarrow Q$" is true using this method, we start by assuming that P is *true* but Q is *false*. If this assumption leads to a contradiction, it means that our assumption that "Q is *false*" must be wrong, and hence Q must follow from P. This method is based on the following logical reasoning. If we know that $P \rightarrow Q$ is true and Q is *false*, then P must be *false*. So, if we assume at the beginning that P is *true*, Q is *false*, and reach the conclusion that P is *false*, then we have that P is both *true* and *false*. But P cannot be both *true* and *false*, and hence this is a contradiction. Thus, we conclude that our assumption that Q is *false* is wrong, and it must be the case that Q is *true* after all. It should be noted that this is not the only contradiction that may result; for example, after assuming that P is *true* and Q is *false*, we may reach the conclusion that, say, $1 = -1$. The following example illustrates this method of proof. In this example, we make use of the following theorem. If a, b and c are integers such that a divides both b and c, then a divides their difference, that is, a divides $b - c$.

Example A.7   We prove the assertion: There are infinitely many primes. We proceed to prove this assertion by contradiction as follows. Suppose to the contrary that there are only k primes $p_1, p_2, \ldots, p_k$, where $p_1 = 2$, $p_2 = 3, p_3 = 5$, etc. and that all other integers greater than 1 are composite. Let $n = p_1 p_2 \ldots p_k + 1$ and let p be a prime divisor of n (recall that n is not a prime by assumption since it is larger than p_k). Since n is not a prime, one of $p_1, p_2, \ldots, p_k$ must divide n. That is, p is one of the numbers $p_1, p_2, \ldots, p_k$, and hence p divides $p_1 p_2 \ldots p_k$. Consequently, p divides $n - p_1 p_2 \ldots p_k$. But $n - p_1 p_2 \ldots p_k = 1$, and p does not divide 1 since it is greater than 1, by definition of a prime number. This is a contradiction. It follows that the number of primes is infinite.

The proof of Theorem A.3 provides an excellent example of the method of proof by contradiction.

A.2.5   *Proof by counterexample*

This method provides quick evidence that a postulated statement is false. It is usually employed to show that a proposition that holds true quite often is not always true. When we are faced with a problem that requires proving or disproving a given assertion, we may start by trying to disprove the assertion with a counterexample. Even if we suspect that the assertion is true, searching for a counterexample might help to see why a counterexample is impossible. This often leads to a proof that the given statement is true. In the analysis of algorithms, this method is frequently used to show that an algorithm does not always produce a result with certain properties.

Example A.8   Let $f(n) = n^2 + n + 41$ be a function defined on the set of nonnegative integers. Consider the assertion that $f(n)$ is always a prime number. For example, $f(0) = 41, f(1) = 43, \ldots f(39) = 1601$ are all primes. To falsify this statement, we only need to find one positive integer n such that $f(n)$ is composite. Since $f(40) = 1681 = 41^2$ is composite, we conclude that the assertion is false.

Example A.9   Consider the assertion that $\lceil \sqrt{\lfloor x \rfloor} \rceil = \lceil \sqrt{x} \rceil$ holds for all nonnegative real numbers. For example, $\lceil \sqrt{\lfloor \pi \rfloor} \rceil = \lceil \sqrt{\pi} \rceil$. To prove that this assertion is false, we only need to come up with a counterexample, that is, a nonnegative real number x for which the equality does not hold. This counterexample is left as an exercise (Exercise A.11).

A.2.6   *Mathematical induction*

Mathematical induction is a powerful method for proving that a property holds for a sequence of natural numbers $n_0, n_0 + 1, n_0 + 2, \ldots$. Typically, n_0 is taken to be 0 or 1, but it can be any natural number. Suppose we want to prove a property $P(n)$ for $n = n_0, n_0 + 1, n_0 + 2, \ldots$ whose truth follows from the truth of property $P(n-1)$ for all $n > n_0$. First, we prove that the property holds for n_0. This is called the *basis step*. Then, we prove that whenever the property is true for $n_0, n_0 + 1, \ldots, n - 1$, then it must follow that the property is true for n. This is called the *induction step*. We then conclude that the property holds for all values of $n \geq n_0$. In general, if we want to prove $P(n)$ for $n = n_k, n_{k+1}, n_{k+2}, \ldots$ whose truth follows from the truth of properties $P(n-1), P(n-2), \ldots, P(n-k)$, for some $k \geq 1$, then we must prove $P(n_0), P(n_0+1), \ldots, P(n_0+k-1)$ directly before proceeding to the induction step. The following examples illustrate this proof technique.

Example A.10   We prove Bernoulli's inequality: $(1 + x)^n \geq 1 + nx$ for every real number $x \geq -1$ and every natural number n.
Basis step: If $n = 1$, then $1 + x \geq 1 + x$.
Induction step: Suppose the hypothesis holds for all $k, 1 \leq k < n$, where $n > 1$. Then,

$$(1 + x)^n = (1 + x)(1 + x)^{n-1}$$
$$\geq (1 + x)(1 + (n - 1)x) \quad \{\text{by induction and since } x \geq -1\}$$

$$= (1+x)(1+nx-x)$$
$$= 1 + nx - x + x + nx^2 - x^2$$
$$= 1 + nx + (nx^2 - x^2)$$
$$\geq 1 + nx. \qquad \{\text{since } (nx^2 - x^2) \geq 0 \text{ for } n \geq 1\}$$

Hence, $(1+x)^n \geq 1 + nx$ for all $n \geq 1$.

Example A.11 Consider the Fibonacci sequence $1, 1, 2, 3, 5, 8, \ldots$, defined by

$$f(1) = f(2) = 1, \quad \text{and} \quad f(n) = f(n-1) + f(n-2) \text{ if } n \geq 3,$$

and let

$$\phi = \frac{1 + \sqrt{5}}{2}.$$

We prove that $f(n) \leq \phi^{n-1}$ for all $n \geq 1$.

Basis step: If $n = 1$, we have $1 = f(1) \leq \phi^0 = 1$. If $n = 2$, we have $1 = f(2) \leq \phi^1 = (1 + \sqrt{5})/2$.

Induction step: Suppose the hypothesis holds for all $k, 1 \leq k < n$, where $n > 2$. First, note that

$$\phi^2 = \left(\frac{1 + \sqrt{5}}{2}\right)^2 = \left(\frac{1 + 2\sqrt{5} + 5}{4}\right) = \left(\frac{2 + 2\sqrt{5} + 4}{4}\right) = \phi + 1.$$

Consequently,

$$f(n) = f(n-1) + f(n-2) \leq \phi^{n-2} + \phi^{n-3} = \phi^{n-3}(\phi + 1) = \phi^{n-3}\phi^2 = \phi^{n-1}.$$

Hence, $f(n) \leq \phi^{n-1}$ for all $n \geq 1$.

Example A.12 This example shows that if the problem has two or more parameters, then the choice of the parameter on which to use induction is important. Let n, m and r denote, respectively, the number of vertices, edges and regions in an embedding of a connected planar graph (see Sec. 2.3.2). We will prove Euler's formula:

$$n - m + r = 2$$

stated on page 83. We prove the formula by induction on m, the number of edges.

Basis step: If $m = 1$, then there is only one region and two vertices; so $2 - 1 + 1 = 2$.

Induction step: Suppose the hypothesis holds for $1, 2, \ldots, m - 1$. We show that it also holds for m. Let G be a connected planar graph with n vertices, $m - 1$ edges and r regions, and assume that $n - (m - 1) + r = 2$. Suppose we add one more edge. Then, we have two cases to consider. If the new edge connects two vertices that are already in the graph, then one more region will be introduced and consequently the formula becomes $n - m + (r + 1) = n - (m - 1) + r = 2$. If, on the other hand, the added edge connects a vertex in the graph with a new added vertex, then no more regions are introduced, and the formula becomes $(n + 1) - m + r = n - (m - 1) + r = 2$. Thus, the hypothesis holds for m and hence for all connected planar graphs with $m \geq 1$.

A.3   Logarithms

Let b be a positive real number greater than 1, x a real number, and suppose that for some positive real number y, we have $y = b^x$. Then, x is called the *logarithm of y to the base b*, and we write this as

$$x = \log_b y.$$

Here, b is referred to as the *base of the logarithm*. For any real numbers x and y greater than 0, we have

$$\log_b xy = \log_b x + \log_b y,$$

and

$$\log_b (c^y) = y \log_b c, \quad \text{if } c > 0.$$

When $b = 2$, we will write $\log x$ instead of $\log_2 x$.

Another useful base is e, which is defined by

$$e = \lim_{n \to \infty} \left(1 + \frac{1}{n} \right)^n = 1 + \frac{1}{1!} + \frac{1}{2!} + \frac{1}{3!} + \cdots = 2.7182818\ldots. \quad \text{(A.1)}$$

It is common to write $\ln x$ instead of $\log_e x$. The quantity $\ln x$ is called the *natural logarithm of x*. The natural logarithm is also defined by

$$\ln x = \int_1^x \frac{1}{t} \, dt.$$

To convert from one base to another, we use the *chain rule*:

$$\log_a x = \log_b x \, \log_a b \quad \text{or} \quad \log_b x = \frac{\log_a x}{\log_a b}.$$

For example,

$$\log x = \frac{\ln x}{\ln 2} \quad \text{and} \quad \ln x = \frac{\log x}{\log e}.$$

The following important identity can be proven by taking the logarithms of both sides:

$$x^{\log_b y} = y^{\log_b x}, \quad x, y > 0. \tag{A.2}$$

A.4 Floor and Ceiling Functions

Let x be a real number. The *floor of x*, denoted by $\lfloor x \rfloor$, is defined as the greatest integer less than or equal to x. The *ceiling of x*, denoted by $\lceil x \rceil$, is defined as the least integer greater than or equal to x. For example,

$$\lfloor \sqrt{2} \rfloor = 1, \ \lceil \sqrt{2} \rceil = 2, \lfloor -2.5 \rfloor = -3, \ \lceil -2.5 \rceil = -2.$$

We list the following identities without proofs.

$$\lceil x/2 \rceil + \lfloor x/2 \rfloor = x.$$
$$\lfloor -x \rfloor = -\lceil x \rceil.$$
$$\lceil -x \rceil = -\lfloor x \rfloor.$$

The following theorem is useful.

Theorem A.1 *Let $f(x)$ be a monotonically increasing function such that if $f(x)$ is integer, then x is integer. Then,*

$$\lfloor f(\lfloor x \rfloor) \rfloor = \lfloor f(x) \rfloor \quad \text{and} \quad \lceil f(\lceil x \rceil) \rceil = \lceil f(x) \rceil.$$

For example,

$$\left\lceil \sqrt{\lceil x \rceil} \right\rceil = \left\lceil \sqrt{x} \right\rceil \quad \text{and} \quad \lfloor \log \lfloor x \rfloor \rfloor = \lfloor \log x \rfloor.$$

The following formula follows from Theorem A.1.

$$\lfloor \lfloor x \rfloor / n \rfloor = \lfloor x/n \rfloor \quad \text{and} \quad \lceil \lceil x \rceil / n \rceil = \lceil x/n \rceil, \quad n \text{ a positive integer.}$$

(A.3)

For example,

$$\lfloor \lfloor \lfloor n/2 \rfloor / 2 \rfloor / 2 \rfloor = \lfloor \lfloor n/4 \rfloor / 2 \rfloor = \lfloor n/8 \rfloor.$$

A.5 Factorial and Binomial Coefficients

In this section, we briefly list some of the important combinatorial properties that are frequently used in the analysis of algorithms, especially those designed for combinatorial problems. We will limit the coverage to permutations and combinations, which lead to the definitions of factorials and binomial coefficients.

A.5.1 *Factorials*

A *permutation* of n distinct objects is defined to be an arrangement of the objects in a row. For example, there are 6 permutations of a, b and c, namely:

$$a\,b\,c, \quad a\,c\,b, \quad b\,a\,c, \quad b\,c\,a, \quad c\,a\,b, \quad c\,b\,a.$$

In general, let there be $n > 0$ objects, and suppose we want to count the number of ways to choose k objects and arrange them in a row, where $1 \le k \le n$. Then, there are n choices for the first position, $n - 1$ choices for the second position, ..., and $n - k + 1$ choices for the kth position. Therefore, the number of ways to choose $k \le n$ objects and arrange them in a row is

$$n(n - 1) \cdots (n - k + 1).$$

This quantity, denoted by P_k^n, is called the *number of permutations of n objects taken k at a time*. When $k = n$, the quantity becomes

$$P_n^n = n \times (n - 1) \times \cdots \times 1$$

and is commonly called *the number of permutations of n objects*. Because of its importance, this quantity is denoted by $n!$, read "n factorial". By convention, $0! = 1$, which gives the following simple recursive definition of $n!$:

$$0! = 1, \quad n! = n(n-1)! \quad \text{if } n \geq 1.$$

$n!$ is an extremely fast growing function. For example,

$$30! = 265252859812191058636308480000000.$$

A useful approximation to $n!$ is *Stirling's formula*:

$$n! \approx \sqrt{2\pi n} \left(\frac{n}{e}\right)^n, \tag{A.4}$$

where $e = 2.7182818\ldots$ is the base of the natural logarithm. For example, using Stirling's formula, we obtain

$$30! \approx 264517095922964306151924784891709,$$

with relative error of about 0.27%.

A.5.2 *Binomial coefficients*

The possible ways to choose k objects out of n objects, disregarding order, is customarily called the *combinations of n objects taken k at a time*. It is denoted by C_k^n. For example, the combinations of the letters a, b, c and d taken three at a time are

$$a\,b\,c, \quad a\,b\,d, \quad a\,c\,d, \quad b\,c\,d.$$

Since order does not matter here, the combinations of n objects taken k at a time is equal to the number of permutations of n objects taken k at a time divided by $k!$. That is,

$$C_k^n = \frac{P_k^n}{k!} = \frac{n(n-1)\ldots,(n-k+1)}{k!} = \frac{n!}{k!(n-k)!}, \quad n \geq k \geq 0.$$

This quantity is denoted by $\binom{n}{k}$, read "n choose k", which is called the *binomial coefficient*. For example, the number of combinations of 4 objects taken 3 at a time is

$$\binom{4}{3} = \frac{4!}{3!(4-3)!} = 4.$$

Equivalently, $\binom{n}{k}$ is the number of k-element subsets in a set of n elements. For example, the 3-element subsets of the set $\{a, b, c, d\}$ are

$$\{a, b, c\}, \quad \{a, b, d\}, \quad \{a, c, d\}, \quad \{b, c, d\}.$$

Since the number of ways to choose k elements out of n elements is equal to the number of ways *not* to choose $n - k$ elements out of n elements, we have the following identity:

$$\binom{n}{k} = \binom{n}{n-k}, \text{ in particular } \binom{n}{n} = \binom{n}{0} = 1. \qquad \text{(A.5)}$$

The following identity is important:

$$\binom{n}{k} = \binom{n-1}{k} + \binom{n-1}{k-1}. \qquad \text{(A.6)}$$

Equation (A.6) can be proven using the following argument. Let $A = \{1, 2, \ldots, n\}$. Then, the k-element subsets can be partitioned into those subsets containing n and those that do not contain n. The number of subsets not containing n is the number of ways to choose k elements from the set $\{1, 2, \ldots, n-1\}$, which is $\binom{n-1}{k}$. The number of subsets containing n is the number of ways to choose $k-1$ elements from the set $\{1, 2, \ldots, n-1\}$, which is $\binom{n-1}{k-1}$. This establishes the correctness of Eq. (A.6).

The *binomial theorem*, stated below, is one of the fundamental tools in the analysis of algorithms. For simplicity, we will state only the special case when n is a positive integer.

Theorem A.2　*Let n be a positive integer. Then,*

$$(1 + x)^n = \sum_{j=0}^{n} \binom{n}{j} x^j.$$

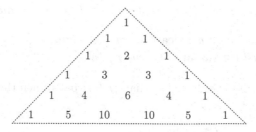

Fig. A.1. The first six rows of Pascal triangle.

If we let $x = 1$ in Theorem A.2, we obtain

$$\binom{n}{0} + \binom{n}{1} + \cdots + \binom{n}{n} = 2^n.$$

In terms of combinations, this identity states that the number of all subsets of a set of size n is equal to 2^n, as expected. If we let $x = -1$ in Theorem A.2, we obtain

$$\binom{n}{0} - \binom{n}{1} + \binom{n}{2} - \cdots \pm \binom{n}{n} = 0$$

or

$$\sum_{j \text{ even}} \binom{n}{j} = \sum_{j \text{ odd}} \binom{n}{j}.$$

Letting $n = 1, 2, 3, \ldots$ in Theorem A.2, we obtain the expansions: $(1 + x) = 1 + x$, $(1 + x)^2 = 1 + 2x + x^2$, $(1 + x)^3 = 1 + 3x + 3x^2 + x^3$, and so on. If we continue this way indefinitely, we obtain Pascal triangle, which is shown in Fig. A.1. In this triangle, each row after the first is computed from the previous row using Eq. (A.6).

A.6   The Pigeonhole Principle

This principle, although easy and intuitive, is extremely powerful and is indispensable in the analysis of algorithms.

Theorem A.3   *If n balls are distributed into m boxes, then*

(1) *one box must contain* at least $\lceil n/m \rceil$ *balls and*
(2) *one box must contain* at most $\lfloor n/m \rfloor$ *balls.*

Proof.   (1) If all boxes have less than $\lceil n/m \rceil$ balls, then the total number of balls is at most

$$m\left(\left\lceil \frac{n}{m} \right\rceil - 1\right) \leq m\left(\left(\frac{n}{m} + \frac{m-1}{m}\right) - 1\right) = n + m - 1 - m = n - 1 < n,$$

which is a contradiction.

(2) If all boxes have greater than $\lfloor n/m \rfloor$ balls, then the total number of balls is at least

$$m\left(\left\lfloor \frac{n}{m} \right\rfloor + 1\right) \geq m\left(\left(\frac{n}{m} - \frac{m-1}{m}\right) + 1\right) = n - m + 1 + m = n + 1 > n,$$

which is also a contradiction. $\qquad\qquad\qquad\qquad\qquad\qquad\qquad\qquad\square$

Example A.13   Let $G = (V, E)$ be a connected undirected graph with m vertices (see Sec. 2.3). Let p be a path in G that visits $n > m$ vertices. We show that p must contain a cycle. Since $\lceil n/m \rceil > 2$, there is at least one vertex, say v, that is visited by p more than once. Thus, the portion of the path that starts and ends at v constitutes a cycle.

A.7   Summations

A *sequence* $a_1, a_2, \ldots, \ldots$ is defined formally as a function whose domain is the set of natural numbers. It is useful to define a *finite sequence* $\{a_1, a_2, \ldots, a_n\}$ as a function whose domain is the set $\{1, 2, \ldots, n\}$. Throughout this book, we will assume that a sequence is finite, unless stated otherwise. Let $S = a_1, a_2, \ldots, a_n$ be any sequence of numbers. The sum $a_1 + a_2 + \cdots + a_n$ can be expressed compactly using the notation

$$\sum_{j=1}^{n} a_{f(j)} \quad \text{or} \quad \sum_{1 \leq j \leq n} a_{f(j)},$$

where $f(j)$ is a function that defines a permutation of the elements $1, 2, \ldots, n$. For example, the sum of the elements in the above sequence can be stated as

$$\sum_{j=1}^{n} a_j \quad \text{or} \quad \sum_{1 \le j \le n} a_j.$$

Here, $f(j)$ is simply j. If, for example, $f(j) = n - j + 1$, then the sum becomes

$$\sum_{j=1}^{n} a_{n-j+1}.$$

This sum can be simplified as follows:

$$\sum_{j=1}^{n} a_{n-j+1} = a_{n-1+1}, a_{n-2+1}, \ldots, a_{n-n+1} = \sum_{j=1}^{n} a_j.$$

Using the other notation, it is simpler to change indices, as in the following example.

Example A.14

$$\sum_{j=1}^{n} a_{n-j} = \sum_{1 \le j \le n} a_{n-j} \qquad \text{(Rewrite summation in other form.)}$$

$$= \sum_{1 \le n-j \le n} a_{n-(n-j)} \qquad \text{(Substitute } n - j \text{ for } j.)$$

$$= \sum_{1-n \le n-j-n \le n-n} a_{n-(n-j)} \qquad \text{(Subtract } n \text{ from inequalities.)}$$

$$= \sum_{1-n \le -j \le 0} a_j \qquad \text{(Simplify)}$$

$$= \sum_{0 \le j \le n-1} a_j \qquad \text{(Multiply inequalities by } -1.)$$

$$= \sum_{j=0}^{n-1} a_j.$$

The above procedure applies to any permutation function $f(j)$ of the form $k \pm j$, where k is an integer that does not depend on j.

In what follows, we list closed form formulas for some of the summations that occur quite often when analyzing algorithms. The proofs of these formulas can be found in most standard books on discrete mathematics.

The arithmetic series:

$$\sum_{j=1}^{n} j = \frac{n(n+1)}{2} = \Theta(n^2). \tag{A.7}$$

The sum of squares:

$$\sum_{j=1}^{n} j^2 = \frac{n(n+1)(2n+1)}{6} = \Theta(n^3). \tag{A.8}$$

The geometric series:

$$\sum_{j=0}^{n} c^j = \frac{c^{n+1}-1}{c-1} = \Theta(c^n), \quad c \neq 1. \tag{A.9}$$

If $c = 2$, we have

$$\sum_{j=0}^{n} 2^j = 2^{n+1} - 1 = \Theta(2^n). \tag{A.10}$$

If $c = 1/2$, we have

$$\sum_{j=0}^{n} \frac{1}{2^j} = 2 - \frac{1}{2^n} < 2 = \Theta(1). \tag{A.11}$$

When $|c| < 1$ and the sum is infinite, we have the infinite geometric series

$$\sum_{j=0}^{\infty} c^j = \frac{1}{1-c} = \Theta(1), \quad |c| < 1. \tag{A.12}$$

Differentiating both sides of Eq. (A.9) and multiplying by c yields

$$\sum_{j=0}^{n} jc^j = \sum_{j=1}^{n} jc^j = \frac{nc^{n+2} - nc^{n+1} - c^{n+1} + c}{(c-1)^2} = \Theta(nc^n), \quad c \neq 1. \tag{A.13}$$

Letting $c = 1/2$ in Eq. (A.13) yields

$$\sum_{j=0}^{n} \frac{j}{2^j} = \sum_{j=1}^{n} \frac{j}{2^j} = 2 - \frac{n+2}{2^n} = \Theta(1). \tag{A.14}$$

Differentiating both sides of Eq. (A.12) and multiplying by c yields

$$\sum_{j=0}^{\infty} jc^j = \frac{c}{(1-c)^2} = \Theta(1), \quad |c| < 1. \tag{A.15}$$

A.7.1 *Approximation of summations by integration*

Let $f(x)$ be a continuous function that is monotically decreasing or increasing, and suppose we want to evaluate the summation

$$\sum_{j=1}^{n} f(j).$$

We can obtain upper and lower bounds by approximating the summation by integration as follows.

If $f(x)$ is decreasing, then we have (see Fig. A.2 for example)

$$\int_{m}^{n+1} f(x)\ dx \leq \sum_{j=m}^{n} f(j) \leq \int_{m-1}^{n} f(x)\ dx.$$

If $f(x)$ is increasing, then we have (see Fig. A.3 for example)

$$\int_{m-1}^{n} f(x)\ dx \leq \sum_{j=m}^{n} f(j) \leq \int_{m}^{n+1} f(x)\ dx.$$

Example A.15 We derive an upper and lower bounds for the summation

$$\sum_{j=1}^{n} j^k, \quad k \geq 1$$

as follows. Since j^k is increasing, we have

$$\int_{0}^{n} x^k\ dx \leq \sum_{j=1}^{n} j^k \leq \int_{1}^{n+1} x^k\ dx.$$

That is,

$$\frac{n^{k+1}}{k+1} \leq \sum_{j=1}^{n} j^k \leq \frac{(n+1)^{k+1} - 1}{k+1}.$$

Hence, by definition of the Θ-notation, we have

$$\sum_{j=1}^{n} j^k = \Theta(n^{k+1}), \qquad k \geq 1.$$

Example A.16 In this example, we derive upper and lower bounds for the harmonic series

$$H_n = \sum_{j=1}^{n} \frac{1}{j}.$$

From Fig. A.2(a), it is clear that

$$\sum_{j=1}^{n} \frac{1}{j} = 1 + \sum_{j=2}^{n} \frac{1}{j}$$

$$\leq 1 + \int_{1}^{n} \frac{dx}{x}$$

$$= 1 + \ln n.$$

Similarly, from Fig. A.2(b), we obtain

$$\sum_{j=1}^{n} \frac{1}{j} \geq \int_{1}^{n+1} \frac{dx}{x}$$

$$= \ln(n+1).$$

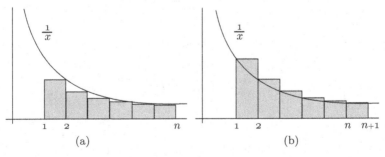

Fig. A.2.   Approximation of the sum $\sum_{j=1}^{n} \frac{1}{j}$.

It follows that

$$\ln(n+1) \le \sum_{j=1}^{n} \frac{1}{j} \le \ln n + 1, \tag{A.16}$$

or

$$\frac{\log(n+1)}{\log e} \le \sum_{j=1}^{n} \frac{1}{j} \le \frac{\log n}{\log e} + 1. \tag{A.17}$$

Hence, by definition of the Θ-notation, we have

$$H_n = \sum_{j=1}^{n} \frac{1}{j} = \Theta(\log n).$$

Example A.17 In this example, we derive upper and lower bounds for the series

$$\sum_{j=1}^{n} \log j.$$

From Fig. A.3(a), it is clear that

$$\sum_{j=1}^{n} \log j = \log n + \sum_{j=1}^{n-1} \log j$$

$$\le \log n + \int_{1}^{n} \log x \, dx$$

$$= \log n + n \log n - n \log e + \log e.$$

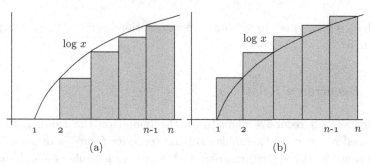

Fig. A.3. Approximation of the sum $\sum_{j=1}^{n} \log j$.

Similarly, from Fig. A.3(b), we obtain

$$\sum_{j=1}^{n} \log j = \sum_{j=2}^{n} \log j$$

$$\geq \int_{1}^{n} \log x \, dx$$

$$= n \log n - n \log e + \log e.$$

It follows that

$$n \log n - n \log e + \log e \leq \sum_{j=1}^{n} \log j \leq n \log n - n \log e + \log n + \log e.$$

$$(A.18)$$

Hence, by definition of the Θ-notation, we have

$$\sum_{j=1}^{n} \log j = \Theta(n \log n).$$

This is the same bound derived in Example 1.12. However, the derivation here is more precise. For example, taking exponentials in Eq. (A.18) yields

$$2^{n \log n - n \log e + \log e} \leq n! \leq 2^{n \log n - n \log e + \log n + \log e},$$

or

$$e \left(\frac{n}{e} \right)^{n} \leq n! \leq ne \left(\frac{n}{e} \right)^{n},$$

which is fairly close to Stirling approximation formula (Eq. (A.4) on page 673).

A.8   Recurrence Relations

In virtually all recursive algorithms, the bound on the running time is expressed recursively. This makes solving *recursive formulas* of paramount importance to the algorithm analyst. A recursive formula is simply a formula that is defined in terms of itself. In this case, we call such a definition a *recurrence relation* or simply a *recurrence*. For example, the sequence of odd positive integers can be described by the recurrence

$$f(n) = f(n-1) + 2, \text{ if } n > 1 \quad \text{and} \quad f(1) = 1.$$

Computing $f(n)$ for large values of n using the recurrence directly is tedious, and hence it is desirable to express the sequence in a *closed form* from which $f(n)$ can be computed directly. When such a closed form is found, we say that the recurrence has been solved. In what follows, we give some techniques for solving some elementary recurrences.

A recurrence relation is called *linear homogeneous with constant coefficients* if it is of the form

$$f(n) = a_1 f(n-1) + a_2 f(n-2) + \cdots + a_k f(n-k).$$

In this case, $f(n)$ is said to be of degree k. When an additional term involving a constant or a function of n appears in the recurrence, then it is called *inhomogeneous*.

A.8.1 *Solution of linear homogeneous recurrences*

Let

$$f(n) = a_1 f(n-1) + a_2 f(n-2) + \cdots + a_k f(n-k). \qquad (A.19)$$

The general solution to A.19 involves a sum of individual solutions of the form $f(n) = x^n$. Substituting x^n for $f(n)$ in (A.19) yields

$$x^n = a_1 x^{n-1} + a_2 x^{n-2} + \cdots + a_k x^{n-k}.$$

Dividing both sides by x^{n-k} yields

$$x^k = a_1 x^{k-1} + a_2 x^{k-2} + \cdots + a_k,$$

or equivalently

$$x^k - a_1 x^{k-1} - a_2 x^{k-2} - \cdots - a_k = 0. \qquad (A.20)$$

Equation (A.20) is called the *characteristic equation* of the recurrence relation (A.19).

In what follows, we will confine our attention to first and second linear homogeneous recurrences. The solution to a first-order homogeneous recurrence is straightforward. Let $f(n) = af(n-1)$, and suppose that the sequence starts from $f(0)$. Since

$$f(n) = af(n-1) = a^2 f(n-2) = \cdots = a^n f(0),$$

it is easy to see that $f(n) = a^n f(0)$ is the solution to the recurrence.

If the degree of the recurrence is 2, then the characteristic equation becomes $x^2 - a_1 x - a_2 = 0$. Let the roots of this quadratic equation be r_1 and r_2. Then, the solution to the recurrence is

$$f(n) = c_1 r_1^n + c_2 r_2^n, \text{ if } r_1 \neq r_2 \quad \text{and} \quad f(n) = c_1 r^n + c_2 n r^n \text{ if } r_1 = r_2 = r.$$

Here, c_1 and c_2 are determined by the initial values of the sequence: $f(n_0)$ and $f(n_0 + 1)$.

Example A.18　　Consider the sequence $1, 4, 16, 64, 256, \ldots$, which can be expressed by the recurrence $f(n) = 3f(n-1) + 4f(n-2)$ with $f(0) = 1$ and $f(1) = 4$. The characteristic equation is $x^2 - 3x - 4 = 0$, and hence $r_1 = -1$ and $r_2 = 4$. Thus, the solution to the recurrence is $f(n) = c_1(-1)^n + c_2 4^n$. To find the values of c_1 and c_2, we solve the two simultaneous equations:

$$f(0) = 1 = c_1 + c_2 \quad \text{and} \quad f(1) = 4 = -c_1 + 4c_2.$$

Solving the two simultaneous equations, we obtain $c_1 = 0$ and $c_2 = 1$. It follows that $f(n) = 4^n$.

Example A.19　　Consider the sequence $1, 3, 5, 7, 9, \ldots$ of odd integers, which can be expressed by the recurrence $f(n) = 2f(n-1) - f(n-2)$ with $f(0) = 1$ and $f(1) = 3$. The characteristic equation is $x^2 - 2x + 1 = 0$, and hence $r_1 = r_2 = 1$. Thus, the solution to the recurrence is $f(n) = c_1 1^n + c_2 n 1^n = c_1 + c_2 n$. To find the values of c_1 and c_2, we solve the two simultaneous equations:

$$f(0) = 1 = c_1 \quad \text{and} \quad f(1) = 3 = c_1 + c_2.$$

Solving the two simultaneous equations, we obtain $c_1 = 1$ and $c_2 = 2$. It follows that $f(n) = 2n + 1$.

Example A.20　　Consider the Fibonacci sequence $1, 1, 2, 3, 5, 8, \ldots$, which can be expressed by the recurrence $f(n) = f(n-1) + f(n-2)$ with $f(1) = f(2) = 1$. To simplify the solution, we may introduce the extra term $f(0) = 0$. The characteristic equation is $x^2 - x - 1 = 0$, and hence

$r_1 = (1 + \sqrt{5})/2$ and $r_2 = (1 - \sqrt{5})/2$. Thus, the solution to the recurrence is

$$f(n) = c_1 \left(\frac{1 + \sqrt{5}}{2} \right)^n + c_2 \left(\frac{1 - \sqrt{5}}{2} \right)^n.$$

To find the values of c_1 and c_2, we solve the two simultaneous equations:

$$f(0) = 0 = c_1 + c_2 \quad \text{and} \quad f(1) = 1 = c_1 \left(\frac{1 + \sqrt{5}}{2} \right) + c_2 \left(\frac{1 - \sqrt{5}}{2} \right).$$

Solving the two simultaneous equations, we obtain $c_1 = 1/\sqrt{5}$ and $c_2 = -1/\sqrt{5}$. It follows that

$$f(n) = \frac{1}{\sqrt{5}} \left(\frac{1 + \sqrt{5}}{2} \right)^n - \frac{1}{\sqrt{5}} \left(\frac{1 - \sqrt{5}}{2} \right)^n.$$

Since $(1 - \sqrt{5})/2) \approx -0.618034$, when n is large the second term approaches 0, and hence when n is large enough,

$$f(n) \approx \frac{1}{\sqrt{5}} \left(\frac{1 + \sqrt{5}}{2} \right)^n \approx 0.447214(1.61803)^n.$$

The quantity $\phi = (1 + \sqrt{5})/2 \approx 1.61803$ is called the *golden ratio*. In Example A.11, we have proven that $f(n) \leq \phi^{n-1}$ for all $n \geq 1$.

A.8.2 *Solution of inhomogeneous recurrences*

Unfortunately, there is no convenient method for dealing with inhomogeneous recurrences in general. Here, we will confine our attention to some elementary inhomogeneous recurrences that arise frequently in the analysis of algorithms. Perhaps, the simplest inhomogeneous recurrence is

$$f(n) = f(n - 1) + g(n), \quad n \geq 1, \tag{A.21}$$

where $g(n)$ is another sequence. It is easy to see that the solution to recurrence (A.21) is

$$f(n) = f(0) + \sum_{i=1}^{n} g(i).$$

For example, the solution to the recurrence $f(n) = f(n-1)+1$ with $f(0) = 0$ is $f(n) = n$.

Now, consider the homogeneous recurrence

$$f(n) = g(n)f(n-1), \quad n \geq 1. \tag{A.22}$$

It is also easy to see that the solution to recurrence (A.22) is

$$f(n) = g(n)g(n-1)\ldots g(1)f(0)$$

For example, the solution to the recurrence $f(n) = nf(n-1)$ with $f(0) = 1$ is $f(n) = n!$.

Next, consider the inhomogeneous recurrence

$$f(n) = g(n)f(n-1) + h(n), \quad n \geq 1. \tag{A.23}$$

where $h(n)$ is also another sequence. We define a new function $f'(n)$ as follows. Let

$$f(n) = g(n)g(n-1)\ldots g(1)f'(n), \quad n \geq 1; f'(0) = f(0).$$

Substituting for $f(n)$ and $f(n-1)$ in recurrence (A.23), we obtain

$$g(n)g(n-1)\ldots g(1)f'(n) = g(n)(g(n-1)\ldots g(1)f'(n-1)) + h(n),$$

which simplifies to

$$f'(n) = f'(n-1) + \frac{h(n)}{g(n)g(n-1)\ldots g(1)}, \quad n \geq 1.$$

Consequently,

$$f'(n) = f'(0) + \sum_{i=1}^{n} \frac{h(i)}{g(i)g(i-1)\ldots g(1)}, \quad n \geq 1.$$

It follows that

$$f(n) = g(n)g(n-1)\ldots g(1)\left(f(0) + \sum_{i=1}^{n} \frac{h(i)}{g(i)g(i-1)\ldots g(1)}\right), \quad n \geq 1. \tag{A.24}$$

Example A.21   Consider the sequence $0, 1, 4, 18, 96, 600, 4320, 35280\ldots$, which can be expressed by the recurrence

$$f(n) = nf(n-1) + n!, \quad n \geq 1; f(0) = 0.$$

We proceed to solve this inhomogeneous recurrence as follows. Let $f(n) = n!f'(n)$ $(f'(0) = f(0) = 0)$. Then,

$$n!f'(n) = n(n-1)!f'(n-1) + n!,$$

which simplifies to

$$f'(n) = f'(n-1) + 1,$$

whose solution is

$$f'(n) = f'(0) + \sum_{i=1}^{n} 1 = 0 + n.$$

Hence,

$$f(n) = n!f'(n) = nn!.$$

Example A.22   Consider the sequence $0, 1, 4, 11, 26, 57, 120, \ldots$, which can be expressed by the recurrence

$$f(n) = 2f(n-1) + n, \quad n \geq 1; f(0) = 0.$$

We proceed to solve this inhomogeneous recurrence as follows. Let $f(n) = 2^n f'(n)$ $(f'(0) = f(0) = 0)$. Then,

$$2^n f'(n) = 2(2^{n-1} f'(n-1)) + n,$$

which simplifies to

$$f'(n) = f'(n-1) + \frac{n}{2^n},$$

whose solution is

$$f'(n) = f'(0) + \sum_{i=1}^{n} \frac{i}{2^i}.$$

Hence (since $f'(0) = f(0) = 0$),

$$f(n) = 2^n f'(n) = 2^n \sum_{i=1}^{n} \frac{i}{2^i}.$$

By Eq. (A.14) on page 678,

$$f(n) = 2^n \sum_{i=1}^{n} \frac{i}{2^i} = 2^n \left(2 - \frac{n+2}{2^n} \right) = 2^{n+1} - n - 2.$$

A.9 Divide-and-Conquer Recurrences

See Sec. 1.15.

A.10 Exercises

A.1. Let A and B be two sets. Prove the following properties, which are known as *De Morgan's laws*.
   (a) $\overline{A \cup B} = \overline{A} \cap \overline{B}$.
   (b) $\overline{A \cap B} = \overline{A} \cup \overline{B}$.

A.2. Let A, B and C be finite sets.
   (a) Prove the *principle of inclusion–exclusion for two sets*:

$$|A \cup B| = |A| + |B| - |A \cap B|.$$

   (b) Prove the *principle of inclusion–exclusion for three sets*:

$$|A \cup B \cup C| = |A| + |B| + |C| - |A \cap B| - |A \cap C| - |B \cap C|$$
$$+ |A \cap B \cap C|.$$

A.3. Show that if a relation R on a set A is transitive and irreflexive, then R is asymmetric.

A.4. Let R be a relation on a set A. Then, R^2 is defined as $\{(a, b) \mid (a, c) \in R \text{ and } (c, b) \in R \text{ for some } c \in A\}$. Show that if R is symmetric, then R^2 is also symmetric.

A.5. Let R be a *nonempty* relation on a set A. Show that if R is symmetric and transitive, then R is *not* irreflexive.

A.6. Let A be a finite set and $P(A)$ the power set of A. Define the relation R on the set $P(A)$ by $(X, Y) \in R$ if and only if $X \subseteq Y$. Show that R is a partial order.

A.7. Let $A = \{1, 2, 3, 4, 5\}$ and $B = A \times A$. Define the relation R on the set B by $\{((x, y), (w, z)) \in B\}$ if and only if $xz = yw$.

    (a) Show that R is an equivalence relation.

   (b) Find the equivalence classes induced by R.

A.8. Given the sets A and B and the function f from A to B, determine whether f is one to one, onto B or both (i.e., a bijection).

    (a) $A = \{1, 2, 3, 4, 5\}$, $B = \{1, 2, 3, 4\}$ and
      $f = \{(1, 2), (2, 3), (3, 4), (4, 1), (5, 2)\}$.

   (b) A is the set of integers, B is the set of even integers and $f(n) = 2n$.

   (c) $A = B$ is the set of integers and $f(n) = n^2$.

   (d) $A = B$ is the set of real numbers with 0 excluded and $f(x) = 1/x$.

   (e) $A = B$ is the set of real numbers and $f(x) = |x|$.

A.9. A real number r is called *rational* if $r = p/q$, for some integers p and q; otherwise, it is called *irrational*. The numbers $0.25, 1.3333333\ldots$ are rational, while π and $\sqrt{p}$, for any prime number p, are irrational. Use the proof by contradiction method to prove that $\sqrt{7}$ is irrational.

A.10. Prove that for any positive integer n

$$\lfloor \log n \rfloor + 1 = \lceil \log(n + 1) \rceil.$$

A.11. Give a counterexample to disprove the assertion given in Example A.9.

A.12. Use mathematical induction to show that $n! > 2^n$ for $n \geq 4$.

A.13. Use mathematical induction to show that a tree with n vertices has exactly $n - 1$ edges.

A.14. Prove that $\phi^n = \phi^{n-1} + \phi^{n-2}$ for all $n \geq 2$, where ϕ is the golden ratio (see Example A.11).

A.15. Prove that for every positive integer k, $\sum_{i=1}^{n} i^k \log i = O(n^{k+1} \log n)$.

A.16. Show that

$$\sum_{j=1}^{n} j \log j = \Theta(n^2 \log n)$$

(a) using algebraic manipulations.
(b) using the method of approximating summations by integration.

A.17. Show that

$$\sum_{j=1}^{n} \log(n/j) = O(n),$$

(a) using algebraic manipulations.
(b) using the method of approximating summations by integration.

A.18. Solve the following recurrence relations.
(a) $f(n) = 3f(n-1)$ for $n \geq 1$; $f(0) = 5$.
(b) $f(n) = 2f(n-1)$ for $n \geq 1$; $f(0) = 2$.
(c) $f(n) = 5f(n-1)$ for $n \geq 1$; $f(0) = 1$.

A.19. Solve the following recurrence relations.
(a) $f(n) = 5f(n-1) - 6f(n-2)$ for $n \geq 2$; $f(0) = 1, f(1) = 0$.
(b) $f(n) = 4f(n-1) - 4f(n-2)$ for $n \geq 2$; $f(0) = 6, f(1) = 8$.
(c) $f(n) = 6f(n-1) - 8f(n-2)$ for $n \geq 2$; $f(0) = 1, f(1) = 0$.
(d) $f(n) = -6f(n-1) - 9f(n-2)$ for $n \geq 2$; $f(0) = 3, f(1) = -3$.
(e) $2f(n) = 7f(n-1) - 3f(n-2)$ for $n \geq 2$; $f(0) = 1, f(1) = 1$.
(f) $f(n) = f(n-2)$ for $n \geq 2$; $f(0) = 5, f(1) = -1$.

A.20. Solve the following recurrence relations:
(a) $f(n) = f(n-1) + n^2$ for $n \geq 1$; $f(0) = 0$.
(b) $f(n) = 2f(n-1) + n$ for $n \geq 1$; $f(0) = 1$.
(c) $f(n) = 3f(n-1) + 2^n$ for $n \geq 1$; $f(0) = 3$.
(d) $f(n) = 2f(n-1) + n^2$ for $n \geq 1$; $f(0) = 1$.
(e) $f(n) = 2f(n-1) + n + 4$ for $n \geq 1$; $f(0) = 4$.
(f) $f(n) = -2f(n-1) + 2^n - n^2$ for $n \geq 1$; $f(0) = 1$.
(g) $f(n) = nf(n-1) + 1$ for $n \geq 1$; $f(0) = 1$.

Appendix B

Introduction to Discrete Probability

B.1 Definitions

The *sample space* Ω is the set of all possible outcomes (also called occurrences or points) of an experiment. An *event* $\mathcal{E}$ is a subset of the sample space. For example, when tossing a die, $\Omega = \{1, 2, 3, 4, 5, 6\}$ and $\mathcal{E} = \{1, 3, 5\}$ is one possible event.

Let $\mathcal{E}_1$ and $\mathcal{E}_2$ be two events. Then, $\mathcal{E}_1 \cup \mathcal{E}_2$ is the event consisting of all points either in $\mathcal{E}_1$ or in $\mathcal{E}_2$ or both, and $\mathcal{E}_1 \cap \mathcal{E}_2$ is the event consisting of all points that are in both $\mathcal{E}_1$ and $\mathcal{E}_2$. Other set operations are defined similarly. $\mathcal{E}_1$ and $\mathcal{E}_2$ are called *mutually exclusive* if $\mathcal{E}_1 \cap \mathcal{E}_2 = \phi$.

Let $x_1, x_2, \ldots, x_n$ be the set of all n possible outcomes of an experiment. Then, we must have $0 \leq \mathbf{Pr}[x_i] \leq 1$ for $1 \leq i \leq n$ and $\sum_{i=1}^{n} \mathbf{Pr}[x_i] = 1$. Here, $\mathbf{Pr}$, the function from the set of all events of the sample space to a subset of $[0..1]$ is called a *probability distribution*. For many experiments, it is natural to assume that all outcomes have the same probability. For example, in the experiment of tossing a die, $\mathbf{Pr}[k] = \frac{1}{6}$ for $1 \leq k \leq 6$.

B.2 Conditional Probability and Independence

Let $\mathcal{E}_1$ and $\mathcal{E}_2$ be two events. Then, the *conditional probability* of $\mathcal{E}_1$ given $\mathcal{E}_2$, denoted by $\mathbf{Pr}[\mathcal{E}_1 \mid \mathcal{E}_2]$, is defined as

$$\mathbf{Pr}[\mathcal{E}_1 \mid \mathcal{E}_2] = \frac{\mathbf{Pr}[\mathcal{E}_1 \cap \mathcal{E}_2]}{\mathbf{Pr}[\mathcal{E}_2]}. \tag{B.1}$$

$\mathcal{E}_1$ and $\mathcal{E}_2$ are called *independent* if

$$\mathbf{Pr}[\mathcal{E}_1 \cap \mathcal{E}_2] = \mathbf{Pr}[\mathcal{E}_1]\mathbf{Pr}[\mathcal{E}_2],$$

and they are called *dependent* if they are not independent. Equivalently, $\mathcal{E}_1$ and $\mathcal{E}_2$ are independent if

$$\mathbf{Pr}[\mathcal{E}_1 \mid \mathcal{E}_2] \times \mathbf{Pr}[\mathcal{E}_2] = \mathbf{Pr}[\mathcal{E}_1]\mathbf{Pr}[\mathcal{E}_2].$$

Example B.1 Consider the experiment of flipping two coins, where all outcomes are assumed to be equally likely. The sample space is $\{HH, HT, TH, TT\}$. Let $\mathcal{E}_1$ be the event that the first coin lands heads and let $\mathcal{E}_2$ be the event that at least one coin lands tails. Now, $\mathbf{Pr}[\mathcal{E}_1] = \mathbf{Pr}[\{HT, HH\}] = \frac{1}{2}$, and $\mathbf{Pr}[\mathcal{E}_2] = \mathbf{Pr}[\{HT, TH, TT\}] = \frac{3}{4}$. Hence,

$$\mathbf{Pr}[\mathcal{E}_1 \mid \mathcal{E}_2] = \frac{\mathbf{Pr}[\{HT, HH\} \cap \{HT, TH, TT\}]}{\mathbf{Pr}[\{HT, TH, TT\}]} = \frac{\mathbf{Pr}[\{HT\}]}{\mathbf{Pr}[\{HT, TH, TT\}]} = \frac{1}{3}.$$

Since $\mathbf{Pr}[\mathcal{E}_1 \cap \mathcal{E}_2] = \frac{1}{4} \neq \frac{3}{8} = \mathbf{Pr}[\mathcal{E}_1]\mathbf{Pr}[\mathcal{E}_2]$, we conclude that $\mathcal{E}_1$ and $\mathcal{E}_2$ are not independent.

Now, consider changing $\mathcal{E}_2$ to the event that the second coin lands tails. Then, $\mathbf{Pr}[\mathcal{E}_2] = \mathbf{Pr}[\{HT, TT\}] = \frac{1}{2}$. Hence,

$$\mathbf{Pr}[\mathcal{E}_1 \mid \mathcal{E}_2] = \frac{\mathbf{Pr}[\{HT, HH\} \cap \{HT, TT\}]}{\mathbf{Pr}[\{HT, TT\}]} = \frac{\mathbf{Pr}[\{HT\}]}{\mathbf{Pr}[\{HT, TT\}]} = \frac{1}{2}.$$

Since $\mathbf{Pr}[\mathcal{E}_1 \cap \mathcal{E}_2] = \frac{1}{4} = \frac{1}{2} \times \frac{1}{2} = \mathbf{Pr}[\mathcal{E}_1]\mathbf{Pr}[\mathcal{E}_2]$, we conclude that $\mathcal{E}_1$ and $\mathcal{E}_2$ are independent.

Example B.2 Consider the experiment of tossing two dice, where all outcomes are assumed to be equally likely. The sample space is $\{(1,1), (1,2), \ldots, (6,6)\}$. Let $\mathcal{E}_1$ be the event that the sum of the two dice is 6 and let $\mathcal{E}_2$ be the event that the first die equals 4. Then, $\mathbf{Pr}[\mathcal{E}_1] = \mathbf{Pr}[\{(1,5), (2,4), (3,3), (4,2), (5,1)\}] = \frac{5}{36}$, and $\mathbf{Pr}[\mathcal{E}_2] = \mathbf{Pr}[\{(4,1), (4,2), (4,3), (4,4), (4,5), (4,6)\}] = \frac{1}{6}$. Since $\mathbf{Pr}[\mathcal{E}_1 \cap \mathcal{E}_2] = \mathbf{Pr}[\{(4,2)\}] = \frac{1}{36} \neq \frac{5}{36} \times \frac{1}{6} = \frac{5}{216} = \mathbf{Pr}[\mathcal{E}_1]\mathbf{Pr}[\mathcal{E}_2]$, we conclude that $\mathcal{E}_1$ and $\mathcal{E}_2$ are not independent.

Now, change $\mathcal{E}_1$ to the event that the sum of the two dice equals 7. Then, $\mathbf{Pr}[\mathcal{E}_1] = \mathbf{Pr}[\{(1,6), (2,5), (3,4), (4,3), (5,2), (6,1)\}] = \frac{1}{6}$. Since $\mathbf{Pr}[\mathcal{E}_1 \cap \mathcal{E}_2] = \mathbf{Pr}[\{(4,3)\}] = \frac{1}{36} = \frac{1}{6} \times \frac{1}{6} = \mathbf{Pr}[\mathcal{E}_1]\mathbf{Pr}[\mathcal{E}_2]$, we conclude that $\mathcal{E}_1$ and $\mathcal{E}_2$ are independent.

B.2.1 *Multiplication rule for conditional probability*

Rearranging (B.1), one obtains

$$\mathbf{Pr}[\mathcal{E}_1 \cap \mathcal{E}_2] = \mathbf{Pr}[\mathcal{E}_1 \mid \mathcal{E}_2]\mathbf{Pr}[\mathcal{E}_2]$$

or

$$\mathbf{Pr}[\mathcal{E}_1 \cap \mathcal{E}_2] = \mathbf{Pr}[\mathcal{E}_1]\mathbf{Pr}[\mathcal{E}_2 \mid \mathcal{E}_1]. \tag{B.2}$$

In the case of three events, (B.2) can be extended to

$$\mathbf{Pr}[\mathcal{E}_1 \cap \mathcal{E}_2 \cap \mathcal{E}_3] = \mathbf{Pr}[\mathcal{E}_1]\,\mathbf{Pr}[\mathcal{E}_2 \mid \mathcal{E}_1]\,\mathbf{Pr}[\mathcal{E}_3 \mid \mathcal{E}_1 \cap \mathcal{E}_2].$$

In general, we have

$$\mathbf{Pr}[\mathcal{E}_1 \cap \cdots \cap \mathcal{E}_n] = \mathbf{Pr}[\mathcal{E}_1]\,\mathbf{Pr}[\mathcal{E}_2 \mid \mathcal{E}_1]\cdots\mathbf{Pr}[\mathcal{E}_n \mid \mathcal{E}_1 \cap \mathcal{E}_2 \cap \cdots \cap \mathcal{E}_{n-1}]. \tag{B.3}$$

B.3 Random Variables and Expectation

A *random variable* X is a function from the sample space to the set of real numbers. For example, we may let X denote the number of heads appearing when throwing three coins. Then, the random variable X takes on one of the values 0, 1, 2 and 3 with probabilities
$\mathbf{Pr}[X = 0] = \mathbf{Pr}[\{TTT\}] = \frac{1}{8}$, $\mathbf{Pr}[X = 1] = \mathbf{Pr}[\{HTT, THT, TTH\}] = \frac{3}{8}$, $\mathbf{Pr}[X = 2] = \mathbf{Pr}[\{HHT, HTH, THH\}] = \frac{3}{8}$ and $\mathbf{Pr}[X = 3] = \mathbf{Pr}[\{HHH\}] = \frac{1}{8}$.

The *expected value* of a (discrete) random variable X with range S is defined as

$$\mathbf{E}[X] = \sum_{x \in S} x\mathbf{Pr}[X = x].$$

For example, if we let X denote the number appearing when throwing a die, then the expected value of X is

$$\mathbf{E}[X] = \sum_{k=1}^{6} k\mathbf{Pr}[X = k] = \frac{1}{6}(1 + 2 + 3 + 4 + 5 + 6) = \frac{7}{2}. \tag{B.4}$$

$\mathbf{E}[X]$ represents the *mean* of the random variable X and is often written as μ_X or simply μ. An important and useful property is *linearity of expectation*:

$$\mathbf{E}\left[\sum_{i=1}^{n} X_i\right] = \sum_{i=1}^{n} \mathbf{E}[X_i],$$

which is always true regardless of independence.

Another important measure is the *variance* of X, denoted by $\mathbf{var}[X]$ or σ_X^2, which is defined as

$$\mathbf{var}[X] = \mathbf{E}[(X - \mu)^2] = \sum_{x \in S}(x - \mu)^2 \mathbf{Pr}[X = x],$$

where S is the range of X. It can be shown that $\mathbf{var}[X] = \mathbf{E}[X^2] - \mu^2$. For example, in the experiment of throwing a die,

$$\mathbf{var}[X] = \left(\sum_{k=1}^{6} k^2 \mathbf{Pr}[X = k]\right) - \left(\frac{7}{2}\right)^2$$

$$= \frac{1}{6}(1 + 2^2 + 3^2 + 4^2 + 5^2 + 6^2) - \left(\frac{7}{2}\right)^2$$

$$= \frac{91}{6} - \frac{49}{4}$$

$$= \frac{35}{12}.$$

σ_X, or simply σ, is called the *standard deviation*. So, in the above example, $\sigma = \sqrt{35/12} \approx 1.7$.

B.4   Discrete Probability Distributions

B.4.1   *Uniform distribution*

The *uniform distribution* is the simplest of all probability distributions in which the random variable assumes all its values with equal probability. If X takes on the values $x_1, x_2, \ldots, x_n$ with equal probability, then for all k, $1 \leq k \leq n$, $\mathbf{Pr}[X = k] = \frac{1}{n}$. The random variable denoting the number that appears when a die is rolled is an example of such a distribution.

B.4.2 Bernoulli distribution

A *Bernoulli trial* is an experiment with exactly two outcomes, e.g., flipping a coin. These two outcomes are often referred to as success and failure with probabilities p and $q = 1 - p$, respectively. Let X be the random variable corresponding to the toss of a biased coin with probability of heads $\frac{1}{3}$ and probability of tails $\frac{2}{3}$. If we label the outcome as success when heads appear, then

$$X = \begin{cases} 1 & \text{if the trial succeeds} \\ 0 & \text{if it fails.} \end{cases}$$

A random variables that assumes only the numbers 0 and 1 is called an *indicator random variable*. The expected value and variance of an indicator random variable with probability of success p are given by

$$\mathbf{E}[X] = p \quad \text{and} \quad \mathbf{var}[X] = pq = p(1 - p).$$

B.4.3 Binomial distribution

Let $X = \sum_{i=1}^{n} X_i$, where the X_i's are indicator random variables corresponding to n *independent* Bernoulli trials with parameter p (identically distributed). Then, X is said to have the *binomial distribution* with parameters p and n. The probability that there are *exactly* k successes is given by

$$\mathbf{Pr}[X = k] = \binom{n}{k} p^k q^{n-k},$$

where $q = 1 - p$. The expected value and variance of X are given by

$$\mathbf{E}[X] = np \quad \text{and} \quad \mathbf{var}[X] = npq = np(1 - p).$$

The first equality follows from the linearity of expectations, and the second follows from the fact that all $X_i's$ are pairwise independent.

For example, the probabilities of getting k heads, $0 \le k \le 4$, when tossing a fair coin four times are

$$\frac{1}{16}, \frac{1}{4}, \frac{3}{8}, \frac{1}{4}, \frac{1}{16}.$$

$\mathbf{E}[X] = 4 \times (1/2) = 2$, and $\mathbf{var}[X] = 4 \times (1/2) \times (1/2) = 1$.

B.4.4 *Geometric distribution*

Suppose we have a (biased) coin with probability p of heads. Let the random variable X denote the number of coin tosses until heads appears for the first time. Then, X is said to have the *geometric distribution* with parameter p. The probability of having a success after $k \geq 1$ trials is $P[X = k] = q^{k-1}p$, where $q = 1 - p$. The expected value of X is $\mathbf{E}[X] = 1/p$ and its variance is $\mathbf{var}[X] = q/p^2$.

 Consider the experiment of tossing a coin until heads appear for the first time. Suppose we toss a coin 10 times with no success, that is, tails appears 10 times. What is the probability of getting heads in the 11th toss? The answer is $\frac{1}{2}$. This observation about the geometric distribution is called the *memoryless property*: the probability of having an event in the future is independent of the past.

B.4.5 *Poisson distribution*

A discrete random variable X that takes on one of the values 0, 1, 2, ... is called a Poisson random variable with parameter $\lambda > 0$ if

$$\mathbf{Pr}[X = k] = \frac{e^{-\lambda}\lambda^k}{k!}; \quad k \geq 0.$$

If X is a Poisson random variable with parameter λ, then $\mathbf{E}[X] = \mathbf{var}[X] = \lambda$. That is, both the expected value and variance of a Poisson random variable with parameter λ are equal to λ.

Bibliography

Aho, A. V., Hopcroft, J. E., and Ullman, J. D. (1974) *The Design and Analysis of Computer Algorithms*, Addison-Wesley, Reading, MA.

Aho, A. V., Hopcroft, J. E., and Ullman, J. D. (1983) *Data Structures and Algorithms*, Addison-Wesley, Reading, MA.

Ahuja, R. K., Orlin, J. B., and Tarjan, R. E. (1989) "Improved time bounds for the maximum flow problem", *SIAM Journal on Computing*, 18, 939–954.

Akl, S. G. (1984) "An optimal algorithm for parallel selection", *Information Processing Letters*, 19 (1984), 47–50.

Akl, S. G. (1989) *The Design and Analysis of Parallel Algorithms*, Prentice Hall, Englewood Cliffs, New Jersey.

Akl, S. G. (1997) *Parallel Computation: Models and Methods*, Prentice-Hall, Englewood Cliffs, NJ.

Alsuwaiyel, M. H. (2001) "An Efficient and Adaptive Algorithms for Multiselection on the PRAM", *Proceedings of the International Conference on Software Engineering, Artificial Intelligence, Networking and Parallel/Distributed Computing (SNPD01)*, Nagoya, Japan, pp. 140–143.

Alsuwaiyel, M. H. (2006) "A random algorithm for multiselection", *Journal of Discrete Mathematics and Applications*, **16**(2), 175–180.

Aurenhammer, F. (1991) "Voronoi diagrams: A survey of a fundamental data structure", *ACM Computing Surveys*, **23**, 345–405.

Batcher, K. (1968) "Sorting networks and their applications", *AFIPS Spring Joint Computing Conference*, Atlantic City, NJ, pp. 307–314.

Baase, S. (1988) *Computer Algorithms: Introduction to Design and Analysis*, 2nd edn. Addison-Wesley, Reading, MA.

Balcazar, J. L., Diaz, J., and Gabarro J. (1988) *Structural Complexity I*, Springer-Verlag, Berlin.

Balcazar, J. L., Diaz, J., and Gabarro J. (1990) *Structural Complexity II*, Springer-Verlag, Berlin.

Banachowski, L., Kreczmar, A., and Rytter, W. (1991) *Analysis of Algorithms and Data Structures*, Addison-Wesley, Reading, MA.

Bellman, R. E. (1957) *Dynamic Programming*, Princeton University Press, Princeton, NJ.

Bellman, R. E., and Dreyfus, S. E. (1962) *Applied Dynamic Programming*, Princeton University Press, Princeton, NJ.

Bellmore, M., and Nemhauser, G. (1968) "The traveling salesman problem: A survey", *Operations Research*, **16**(3), 538–558.

Ben-Or, M. (1983) "Lower bounds for algebraic computation trees", *Proceedings of the 15th ACM Annual Symposium on Theory of Computation*, pp. 80–86.

Blum, M., Floyd, R. W., Pratt, V. R., Rivest, R. L., and Tarjan, R. E. (1973) "Time bounds for selection", *Journal of Computer and System Sciences*, **7**, 448–461.

Berge, C. (1957) "Two theorems in graph theory", *Proceedings of the National Academy of Science*, **43**, 842–844.

Bovet, D. P., and Crescenzi, P. (1994) *Introduction to the Theory of Complexity*, Prentice-Hall, Englewood Cliffs, NJ.

Brassard, G., and Bratley, P. (1988) *Fundamentals of Algorithmics*, Prentice-Hall, Englewood Cliffs, NJ.

Brassard, G., and Bratley, P. (1996) *Algorithmics: Theory and Practice*, Prentice-Hall, Englewood Cliffs, NJ.

Brown, K. (1979a) *Dynamic Programming in Computer Science*, Carnegie-Mellon University, Pittsburgh, PA, USA.

Brown, K. (1979b) "Voronoi diagrams from convex hulls", *Information Processing Letters*, **9**, 223–228.

Burge, W. H. (1975) *Recursive Programming Techniques*, Addison-Wesley, Reading, MA.

Chandran, S., and Rosenfeld, A. (1988) "Order statistics on a hypercube", *Information Processing Letters*, **27**, 129–132.

Chazelle, B. (1990) "Triangulating a simple polygon in linear time", *Proceedings of 31th Annual IEEE Symposium on the Foundations of Computer Science*, pp. 220–230.

Chazelle, B. (1991) "Triangulating a simple polygon in linear time", *Discrete & Computational Geometry*, **6**, 485–524.

Cheriton, D., and Tarjan, R. E. (1976) "Finding minimum spanning trees", *SIAM Journal on Computing*, **5**(4), 724–742.

Christofides, N. (1976) "Worst-case analysis of a new heuristic for the traveling salesman problem", Technical Report, Graduate School of Industrial Administration, Carnegie-Mellon University, Pittsburgh, PA.

Cole, R. (1988) "Parallel merge sort", *SIAM Journal on Computing*, **17**(4), 770–785.

Cook, S. A. (1971) "The complexity of theorem-proving procedures", *Proceedings of 3rd Annual ACM Symposium on the Theory of Computing*, pp. 151–158.

Cook, S. A. (1973) "An observation on time-storage trade off", *Proceedings of 5th Annual ACM Symposium on the Theory of Computing*, pp. 29–33.

Cook, S. A. (1974) "An observation on time-storage trade off", *Journal of Computer and System Sciences*, **7**, 308–316.

Cook, S. A. (1983) "An overview of computational complexity", *Communication of the ACM*, **26**(6), 400–408 (Turing Award Lecture).

Cook, S. A. (1985) "A taxonomy of problems with fast parallel algorithms", *Information and Control*, **64**, 2–22.

Cook, S. A., and Sethi, R. (1976) "Storage requirements for deterministic polynomial time recognizable languages", *Journal of Computer and System Sciences*, **13**(1), 25–37.

Cormen, T. H., Leiserson, C. E., Rivest, R. L., and Stein, C. (2009) *Introduction to Algorithms*, MIT Press, Cambridge, MA.

Cyphcr, R., and Plaxton, G. (1990) "Deterministic sorting in nearly logarithmic time on the hypercube and related computers", *Proceedings of the 22nd ACM Symp. Theory of Computing*, ACM Press.

de Berg, M., van Kreveld, M., Overmars, M., and Schwarzkopf, O. (1997) *Computational Geometry: Algorithms and Applications*, Springer, Berlin.

Dijkstra, E. W. (1959) "A note on two problems in connexion with graphs", *Numerische Mathematik*, **1**, 269–271.

Dinic, E. A. (1970) "Algorithm for solution of a problem of maximal flow in a network with power estimation", *Soviet Mathematics Doklady*, **11**, 1277–1280.

Dobkin, D., and Lipton, R. (1979) "On the complexity of computations under varying set of primitives", *Journal of Computer and System Sciences*, **18**, 86–91.

Dobkin, D., Lipton, R., and Reiss, S. (1979) "Linear programming is log-space hard for P", *Information Processing Letters*, **8**, 96–97.

Dreyfus, S. E. (1977) *The Art and Theory of Dynamic Programming*, Academic Press, New York, NY.

Dromey, R. G. (1982) *How to Solve It by Computer*, Prentice-Hall, Englewood Cliffs, NJ.

Edelsbrunner, H. (1987) *Algorithms in Combinatorial Geometry*, Springer-Verlag, Berlin.

Edelsbrunner, H., and Seidel, R. (1986) "Voronoi diagrams and arrangements", *Discrete Computation Geometry*, **1**, 25–44.

Even, S. (1979) *Graph Algorithms*, Computer Science Press, Rockville, MD.

Even, S., and Tarjan, R. E. (1975) "Network flow and testing graph connectivity", *SIAM Journal on Computing*, **4**, 507–512.

Edmonds, J. (1965) "Paths, trees and flowers", *Canadian Journal of Mathematics*, **17**, 449–467.

Edmonds, J., and Karp, R. M. (1972) "Theoretical improvements in algorithmic efficiency for network problems", *Journal of the ACM*, **19**, 248–264.

Fischer, M. J. (1972) "Efficiency of equivalence algorithms", in R. E. Miller and J. W. Thatcher, eds., *Complexity and Computations*, Plenum Press, New York, pp. 153–168.

Fischer, M. J., and Salzberg, S. L. (1982) "Finding a majority among n votes", *Journal of Algorithms*, **3**, 375–379.

Floyd, R. W. (1962) "Algorithm 97: Shortest Path", *Communications of the ACM*, **5**, 345.

Floyd, R. W. (1964) "Algorithm 245: Treesort 3", *Communications of the ACM*, **7**, 701.

Floyd, R. W. (1967) "Assigning meanings to programs", *Symposium on Applied Mathematics, American Mathematical Society*, pp. 19–32.

Ford, L. R., Jr., and Fulkerson, D. R. (1956) "Maximal flow through a network", *Canadian Journal of Mathematics*, **8**, 399–404.

Ford, L. R., Jr., and Johnson, S. (1959) "A tournament problem", *American Mathematical Monthly*, **66**, 387–389.

Fortune, S. (1978) "A sweeping algorithm for Voronoi diagrams", *Algorithmica*, **2**, 153–174.

Fortune, S. (1992) "Voronoi diagrams and Delaunay triangulations", in Du, D. Z. and Hwang, F. eds., *Computing in Euclidean Geometry*, Lecture Notes Series on Computing, Vol. 1, World Scientific, Singapore, pp. 193–234.

Fredman, M. L., and Tarjan, R. E. (1987) "Fibonacci heaps and their uses in network optimization", *Journal of the ACM*, **34**, 596–615.

Friedman, N. (1972) "Some results on the effect of arithmetics on comparison problems", *Proceedings of the 13th Symposium on Switching and Automata Theory, IEEE*, pp. 139–143.

Fussenegger, F., and Gabow, H. (1976) "Using comparison trees to derive lower bounds for selection problems", *Proceedings of the 17th Found. C. S., IEEE*, pp. 178–182.

Gabow, H. N. (1976) "An efficient implementation of Edmonds' algorithm for maximum matching on graphs", *Journal of the ACM*, **23**, 221–234.

Galil, Z. (1980) "An $O(V^{5/3}E^{2/3})$ algorithm for the maximal flow problem", *Acta Informatica*, **14**, 221–242.

Galil, Z., and Tardos, E. (1988) "An $O(n^2(m + n \log n) \log n)$ min-cost flow algorithm", *Journal of the ACM*, **35**, 374–386.

Galler, B. A., and Fischer, M. J. (1964) "An improved equivalence algorithm", *Communications of the ACM*, **7**, 301–303.

Garey, M. R., and Johnson, D. S. (1979) *Computers and Intractability: A Guide to the Theory of NP-Completeness*, W. H. Freeman and Co., San Francisco, CA.

Garey, M. R. Johnson, D. S., Preparata, F. P., and Tarjan, R. E. (1978) "Triangulating a simple polygon", *Information Processing Letters*, **7**, 175–179.

Gibbons, A., and Rytter, W. (1990) *Efficient Parallel Algorithms*, Cambridge University Press, London.

Gilmore, P. C. (1977) "Cutting stock, linear programming, knapsack, dynamic programming and integer programming, some interconnections", IBM Research Report RC6528.

Gilmore, P. C., and Gomory, R. E. (1966) "The theory and computation of knapsack functions", *Journal of Operations Research*, **14**(6), 1045–1074.

Godbole, S. (1973) "On efficient computation of matrix chain products", *IEEE Transactions on Computers*, **C-22**(9), 864–866.

Goldberg, A. V., and Tarjan, R. E. (1988) "A new approach to the maximum flow problem", *Journal of the ACM*, **35**, 921–940.

Goldschlager, L., Shaw, L., and Staples, J. (1982) "The maximum flow problem is log space complete for P", *Theoretical Computer Science*, **21**, 105–111.

Golomb, S., and Brumert, L. (1965) "Backtrack programming", *Journal of the ACM*, **12**(4), 516–524.

Gonnet, G. H. (1984) *Handbook of Algorithms and Data Structures*, Addison-Wesley, Reading, MA.

Graham, R. L. (1972) "An efficient algorithm for determining the convex hull of a finite planar set", *Information Processing Letters*, **1**, 132–133.

Graham, R. L., and Hell, P. (1985) "On the history of the minimum spanning tree problem", *Annals of the History of Computing*, **7**(1), 43–57.

Greene, D. H., and Knuth, D. E. (1981) *Mathematics for the Analysis of Algorithms*, Birkhauser, Boston, MA.

Greenlaw, R., Hoover, J., and Ruzzo, W. (1995), *Limits to Parallel Computation: P-completeness Theory*, Oxford University Press, New York.

Gupta, R., Smolka, S., and Bhaskar, S. (1994) "On randomization in sequential and distributed algorithms", *ACM Computer Surveys*, **26**(1), 7–86.

Hall, M., Jr. (1956) "An Algorithm for distinct representatives", *American Mathematical Monthly*, **63**, 716–717.

Hartmanis, J., and Stearns, R. E. (1965) "On the computational complexity of algorithms", *Transactions of American Mathematical Society*, **117**, 285–306.

Held, M., and Karp, R. M. (1967) "Finite-State Process and Dynamic programming", *SIAM Journal on Computing*, **15**, 693–718.

Hoare, C. A. R. (1961) "Algorithm 63 (partition) and Algorithm 65 (find)", *Communication of the ACM*, **4**(7), 321–322.

Hoare, C. A. R. (1962) "Quicksort", *Computer Journal*, **5**, 10–15.

Hofri, M. (1987) *Probabilistic Analysis of Algorithms*, Springer Verlag, Berlin.

Hopcroft, J. E., and Karp, R. M. (1973) "A $n^{5/2}$ algorithm for maximum matching in bipartite graphs", *SIAM Journal on Computing*, **2**, 225–231.

Hopcroft, J. E., and Tarjan, R. E. (1973) "Dividing a graph into triconnected components", *SIAM Journal on Computing*, **2**, 135–158.

Hopcroft, J. E., and Tarjan, R. E. (1973a) "Efficient algorithms for graph manipulation", *Communication of the ACM*, **16**(6), 372–378.

Hopcroft, J. E., and Ullman, J. D. (1973) "Set merging algorithms", *SIAM Journal on Computing*, **2**(4), 294–303.

Hopcroft, J. E., and Ullman, J. D. (1979) *Introduction to Automata Theory, Languages, and Computation*, Addison-Wesley, Reading, MA.

Horowitz, E., Sahni, S., and Rajasekaran, S. (1998) *Computer Algorithms*, Computer Science Press, Rockville, MD.

Hromkovic, J. (2005) *Design and Analysis of Randomized Algorithms: Introduction to Design Paradigms*, Springer-Verlag, Berlin.

Hu, T. C. (1969) *Integer Programming and Network Flows*, Addison-Wesley, Reading, MA.

Hu, T. C. (1982) *Combinatorial Algorithms*, Addison-Wesley, Reading, MA.

Hu, T. C., and M. T. Shing (1980) "Some theorems about matrix multiplication", *Proceedings of the 21st Annual Symposium on Foundations of Computer Science*, pp. 28–35.

Hu, T. C., and Shing, M. T. (1982) "Computation of matrix chain products", Part 1, *SIAM Journal on Computing*, **11**(2), 362–373.

Hu, T. C., and Shing, M. T. (1984) "Computation of matrix chain products", Part 2, *SIAM Journal on Computing*, **13**(2), 228–251.

Huffman, D. A. (1952) "A method for the construction of minimum redundancy codes", *Proceedings of the IRA*, **40**, 1098–1101.

Hwang, F. K., and Lin, S. (1972) "A simple algorithm for merging two disjoint linearly ordered sets", *SIAM Journal on Computing*, **1**, 31–39.

Hyafil, L. (1976) "Bounds for selection", *SIAM Journal on Computing*, **5**(1), 109–114.

Ibarra, O. H., and Kim, C. E. (1975) "Fast approximation algorithms for the knapsack and sum of subset problems", *Journal of the ACM*, **22**, 463–468.

JáJá, J. (1992) *An Introduction to Parallel Algorithms*, Addison-Wesley, Reading, MA.

JáJá, J., and Ryu, K. W. (1990) "Load balancing on the hypercube and related networks", *Proceedings of the 1990 International Conference on Parallel Processing*, pp. I203–I210.

Johnson, D. B. (1975) "Priority queues with update and finding minimum spanning trees", *Information Processing Letters*, **4**(3), 53–57.

Johnson, D. B. (1977) "Efficient algorithms for shortest paths in sparse networks", *Journal of the ACM*, **24**(1), 1–13.

Johnson, D. S. (1973) "Near-optimal bin packing algorithms", Doctoral thesis, Department of Mathematics, MIT, Cambridge, MA.

Johnson, D. S., Demers, A., Ullman, J. D., Garey, M. R., and Graham, R. L. (1974) "Worst-case performance bounds for simple one-dimensional packing algorithm", *SIAM Journal on Computing*, **3**, 299–325.

Jones, D. W. (1986) "An empirical comparison of priority-queue and event-set implementations", *Communications of the ACM*, **29**, 300–311.

Jones, N. D. (1975) "Space-bounded reducibility among combinatorial problems", *Journal of Computer and System Sciences*, **11**(1), 68–85.

Jones, N. D., Lien, E., and Lasser, W. T. (1976) "New problems complete for nondeterministic log space", *Mathematical System Theory*, **10**(1), 1–17.

Jones, N. D., and Lasser, W. T. (1976) "Complete problems for deterministic polynomial time", *Theoretical Computer Science*, **3**(1), 105–118.

Karatsuba, A., and Ofman, Y. (1962) "Multiplication of multidigit numbers on automata" (in Russian), *Doklady Akademii Nauk SSSR*, **145**, 293–294.

Karp, R. (1972) "Reducibility among combinatorial problems", in Miller, R. E. and Thatcher, J. W., eds., *Complexity of Computer Computations*, Plenum Press, New York, NY, pp. 85–104.

Karp, R. M. (1986) "Combinatorics, complexity, and randomness", *Communications of the ACM*, **29**, 98–109 (Turing Award Lecture).

Karp, R. M. (1991) "An introduction to randomized algorithms", *Discrete Applied Mathematics*, **34**, 165–201.

Khachiyan, L. G. (1979) "A polynomial algorithm in linear programming", *Soviet Mathematics Doklady*, **20**, 191–194.

Knuth, D. E. (1968) *The Art of Computer Programming, 1: Fundamental Algorithms* (second edition, 1973), Addison-Wesley, Reading, MA.

Knuth, D. E. (1969) *The Art of Computer Programming, 2: Seminumerical Algorithms* (second edition, 1981), Addison-Wesley, Reading, MA.

Knuth, D. E. (1973) *The Art of Computer Programming, 3: Sorting and Searching*, Addison-Wesley, Reading, MA.

Knuth, D. E. (1975) "Estimating the efficiency of backtrack programs", *Mathematics of Computation*, **29**, 121–136.

Knuth, D. E. (1976) "Big omicron and big omega and big theta", *SIGACT News, ACM*, **8**(2), 18–24.

Knuth, D. E. (1977) "Algorithms", *Scientific American*, **236**(4), 63–80.

Kruskal, J. B., Jr. (1956) "On the shortest spanning subtree of a graph and the traveling salesman problem", *Proceedings of the American Mathematical Society*, **7**(1), 48–50.

Kruscal, C. (1983) "Searching, merging and sorting in parallel computation", *IEEE Transactions on Computers*, **C-32**(10), 942–946.

Lander, R. E. (1975) "The circuit value problem is log-space complete for P", *SIGACT News, ACM*, **7**(1), 18–20.

Lawler, E. L. (1976) *Combinatorial Optimization: Networks and Matroids*, Holt, Rinehart and Winston, New York.

Lawler, E. L., and Wood, D. W. (1966) "Branch-and-bound methods: A survey", *Operations Research*, **14**(4), 699–719.

Lawler, E. L, Lenstra, J. K., Rinnooy Kan, A. H. G., and D. B. Shmoys, eds., (1985) *The Traveling Salesman Problem*, John Wiley & Sons.

Lee, C. Y. (1961) "An algorithm for path connection and its applications", *IRE Transactions on Electronic Computers*, **EC-10**(3), 346–365.

Lee, D. T, Hsu, C., and Wong, C. K. (1981) "An on-chip compare/steer bubble sorter", *IEEE Transactions on Computers*, **c-30**(6), 396–404.

Leighton, F. T. (1992) *Introduction to Parallel Algorithms and Architectures: Arrays. Trees. Hypercubes*, Morgan Kaufmann Publishers, San Mateo, CA.

Lewis, H. R., and Papadimitriou, C. H. (1978) "The efficiency of algorithms", *Scientific American*, **238**(1), 96–109.

Lewis, P. M., Stearns, R. E., and Hartmanis, J. (1965) "Memory bounds for recognition of context-free and context sensitive languages", *Proceedings of the 6th Annual IEEE Symposium on Switching Theory and Logical Design*, pp. 191–202.

Little, J. D. C., Murty, K. G., Sweeney, D. W., and Karel, C. (1963) "An algorithm for the traveling salesman problem", *Operations Research*, **11**, 972–989.

Malhotra, V. M., Pramodh-Kumar, M., and Maheshwari, S. N. (1978) "An $O(V^3)$ algorithm for finding maximum flows in networks", *Information Processing Letters*, **7**, 277–278.

Manber, U. (1988) "Using induction to design algorithms", *Communication of the ACM*, **31**, 1300–1313.

Manber, U. (1989) *Introduction to Algorithms: A Creative Approach*, Addison-Wesley, Reading, MA.

Martìnez, C., and Roura, S. (2001) "Optimal Sampling Strategies in Quicksort and Quickselect", *SIAM Journal on Computing*, **6**(3), 683–705.

McHugh, J. A. (1990) *Algorithmic Graph Theory*, Prentice-Hall, Englewood Cliffs, NJ.

Mehlhorn, K. (1984a) *Data Structures and Algorithms, 1: Sorting and Searching*, Springer-Verlag, Berlin.

Mehlhorn, K. (1984b) *Data Structures and Algorithms, 3: Multi-Dimensional Searching and Computational Geometry*, Springer-Verlag, Berlin.

Micali, S., and Vazirani, V. V. (1980) "An $O(\sqrt{V}.E)$ algorithm for finding maximum matching in general graphs", *Proceedings of the Twenty-first Annual Symposium on the Foundation of Computer Science*, IEEE, Long Beach, California pp. 17–27.

Miller, R., and Boxer, L. (2000) *Algorithms Sequential & Parallel*, Prentice-Hall, Englewood Cliffs, NJ.

Minieka, E. (1978) *Optimization Algorithms for Networks and Graphs*, Marcel Dekker, NY.

Misra, J., and Gries, D. (1982) "Finding repeated elements", *Science of Computer Programming*, **2**, 143–152.

Mitzenmacher, M., and Upfal, E. (2005) *Probability and Computing: Randomized Algorithms and Probabilistic Analysis*, Cambridge University Press, New York, NY.

Moore, E. F. (1959) "The shortest path through a maze", *Proceedings of the International Symposium on the Theory of Switching*, Harvard University Press, pp. 285–292.

Moret, B. M. E., and Shapiro, H. D. (1991) *Algorithms from P to NP, 1: Design and Efficiency*, Benjamin/Cummings, Redwood City, CA.

Motwani, R., and Raghavan, P. (1995) *Randomized Algorithms*, Cambridge University Press, New York, NY, USA.

Nemhauser, G. (1966) *Introduction to Dynamic Programming*, John Wiley & Sons, Inc., New York, NY.

Norman, R. Z. (1959) "An algorithm for a minimum cover of a graph", *Proceedings of the American Mathematical Society*, **10**, 315–319.

Okabe, A., Boots, B., and Sugihara, K. (1992) *Spatial Tessellations: Concepts and Applications of Voronoi Diagrams*, John Wiley, Chichester, England.

O'rourke, J. (1994) *Computational Geometry in C*, Cambridge University Press, New York, NY.

Pan, V. (1978) "Strassen's algorithm is not optimal", *Proceedings of 9th Annual IEEE Symposium on the Foundations of Computer Science*, pp. 166–176.

Papadimitriou, C. H. (1994) *Computational Complexity*, Addison-Wesley, Reading, MA.

Papadimitriou, C. H., and Steiglitz, K. (1982) *Combinatorial Optimization: Algorithms and Complexity*, Prentice-Hall, Englewood Cliffs, NJ.

Paull, M. C. (1988) *Algorithm Design: A Recursion Transformation Framework*, John Wiley & Sons, Inc., New York, NY.

Plaxton, C. G. (1989) "Load balancing, selection and sorting on the hypercube", *Proceedings of the 1989 ACM Symposium on Parallel Algorithms and Archetictures*, pp. 64–73.

Preparata, F. P., and Shamos, M. I. (1985) *Computational Geometry: An introduction*, Springer-Verlag, New York, NY.

Prim, R. C. (1957) "Shortest connection networks and some generalizations", *Bell System Technical Journal*, **36**, 1389–1401.

Purdom, P. W., Jr., and Brown, C. A. (1985) *The Analysis of Algorithms*, Holt, Rinehart and Winston, New York, NY.

Rabin, M. O. (1960) "Degree of difficulty of computing a function and a partial ordering of recursive sets", Technical Report 2, Hebrew University, Jerusalem.

Rabin, M. O. (1976) "Probabilistic Algorithms", in Traub, J. F., ed., *Algorithms and Complexity: New Directions and Recent Results*, Academic Press, New York, pp. 21–39.

Reif, J. (1985) "Depth first search is inherently sequential", *Information Processing Letters*, **20**(5), 229–234.

Reingold, E. M. (1971) "Computing the maximum and the median", *Proceedings of the 12th Symposium on Switching and Automata Theory, IEEE*, 216–218.

Reingold, E. M. (1972) "On the optimality of some set algorithms", *Journal of the ACM*, **23**(1), 1–12.

Reingold, E. M., and Hansen, W. J. (1983) *Data Structures*, Little, Brown, Boston, MA.

Reingold, E. M., Nievergelt, J., and Deo, N. (1977) *Combinatorial Algorithms: Theory and Practice*, Prentice-Hall, Englewood Cliffs, NJ.

Rosenkrantz, D. J., Stearns, R. E., and Lewis, P. M. (1977) "An analysis of several heuristics for the traveling salesman problem", *SIAM Journal on Computing*, **6**, 563–581.

Sado, K., and Igarashi, Y. (1986) "Some parallel sorts on a mesh-connected processor array and their time efficiency", *Journal of Parallel and Distributed Computing*, 3, 398–410.

Sahni, S. (1975) "Approximation Algorithms for the 0/1 knapsack problem", *Journal of the ACM*, **22**, 115–124.

Sahni, S. (1977) "General techniques for combinatorial approximation", *Operations Research*, **25**(6), 920–936.

Savitch, W. J. (1970) "Relationships between nondeterministic and deterministic tape complexities", *Journal of Computer and System Sciences*, **4**(2), 177–192.

Scherson, I., Sen, S., and Shamir, A. (1986) "Shear-sort: A true two-dimensional sorting technique for VLSI networks", *Proceedings of the International Conference on Parallel Processing*, pp. 903–908.

Sedgewick, R. (1988) *Algorithms*, Addison-Wesley, Reading, MA.

Shamos, M. I., and Hoey, D. (1975) "Geometric intersection problems", *Proceedings of the 16th Annual Symposium on Foundation of Computer Science*, pp. 208–215

Sharir, M. (1981) "A strong-connectivity algorithm and its application in data flow analysis", *Computers and Mathematics with Applications*, **7**(1), 67–72.

Shen, H. (1997) "Efficient parallel multiselection on hypercubes", *Proceedings of the 1997 International Symposium on Parallel Architectures, Algorithms and Networks (I-SPAN)*, IEEE CS Press, pp. 338–342.

Shen, H. (2000) "Optimal multiselection in hypercubes", *Parallel Algorithms and Applications*, 14, 203–212.

Skyum, S. (1991) "A simple algorithm for computing the smallest enclosing circle", *Information Processing Letters*, **37**, 121–125.

Sleator, D. D. (1980) "An $O(nm \log n)$ algorithm for maximum network flow", Technical Report STAN-CS-80-831, Stanford University.

Solovay, R., and Strassen, V. (1977) "A fast Monte-Carlo test for primality", *SIAM Journal on Computing*, **6**(1), 84–85.

Solovay, R., and Strassen, V. (1978) "Erratum: A fast Monte-Carlo test for primality", *SIAM Journal on Computing*, **7**(1), 118.

Springsteel, F. N. (1976) "On the pre-AFL of [log n] space and related families of languages", *Theoretical Computer Science*, **2**(3), 295–304.

Standish, T. A. (1980) *Data Structure Techniques*, Addison-Wesley, Reading, MA.

Stearns, R. E., Hartmanis, J., and Lewis, P. M. (1965) "Hierarchies of memory-limited computations", *Conference Record on Switching Circuit Theory and Logical Design*, 191–202.

Strassen, V. (1969) "Gaussian elimination is not optimal", *Numerical Mathematics* **13**, 354–356.

Stockmeyer, L. J. (1974) "The complexity of decision problems in automata theory and logic", MAC TR-133, Project MAC, MIT, Cambridge, Mass.

Stockmeyer, L. J. (1976) "The polynomial hierarchy", *Theoretical Computer Science*, **3**, 1–22.

Stockmeyer, L. J., and Meyer, A. R. (1973) "Word problems requiring exponential time", *Proceedings of ACM Symposium on Theory of Computing*, pp. 1–9.

Sudborough, I. H. (1975a) "A note on tape-bounded complexity classes and linear context-free languages", *Journal of the ACM*, **22**(4), 499–500.

Sudborough, I. H. (1975b) "On tape-bounded complexity classes and multihead finite automata", *Journal of Computer and System Sciences*, **10**(1), 62–76.

Tardos, E. (1985) "A strongly polynomial minimum cost circulation algorithm", *Combinatorica*, **5**, 247–255.

Tarjan, R. E. (1972) "Depth-first search and linear graph algorithms", *SIAM Journal on Computing*, **1**, 146–160.

Tarjan, R. E. (1975) "On the efficiency of a good but not linear set merging algorithm", *Journal of the ACM*, **22**(2), 215–225.

Tarjan, R. E. (1983) *Data Structures and Network Algorithms*, SIAM, Philadelphia, PA.

Tarjan, R. E. (1987) "Algorithm design", *Communications of the ACM*, **30**, 204–212 (Turing Award Lecture).

Tarjan, R. E., and Van Wyk, C. J. (1988) "An $O(n \log \log n)$-time algorithm for triangulating a simple polygon", *SIAM Journal on Computing*, **17**, 143–178. Erratum in **17**, 106.

Thompson, C., and Kung, H. (1977) "Sorting on a mesh-connected parallel computer", *Communication of the ACM*, **20**(4), 263–271.

Toussaint, G. (1984) *Computational Geometry*, North Holland, Amsterdam.

Valiant, L. G. (1982) "A scheme for fast parallel communication", *SIAM Journal on Computing*, **11**, 350–361.

Valiant, L. G., and Brebner, G. L. (1981) "Universal schemes for parallel communication", *Proceedings of the 13th ACM Symposium on Theory of Computing*, Milwaukee, WI, pp. 263–277.

Vega, W., and Lueker, G. S. (1981) "Bin packing can be solved within $1 + \epsilon$ in linear time", *Combinatorica*, **1**, 349–355.

Vishkin, U. (1987) "An optimal parallel algorithm for selection", *Advances in Computing Research*, JAI Press Inc., Greenwich, CT.

Wagar, B. (1987) "Hyperquicksort: A fast sorting algorithm for hypercubes", in M.T. Health, ed., *Hypercube Multiprocessors*, SIAM, Philadelphia, PA, pp. 292–299.

Weide, B. (1977) "A survey of analysis techniques for discrete algorithms", *Computing Surveys*, **9**, 292–313.

Welsh, D. J. A. (1983) "Randomized algorithms", *Discrete Applied Mathematics*, **5**, 133–145.

Wilf, H. S. (1986) *Algorithms and Complexity*, Prentice-Hall, Englewood Cliffs, NJ.

Williams, J. W. J. (1964) "Algorithm 232: Heapsort", *Communications of the ACM*, **7**, 347–348.

Wirth, N. (1986) *Algorithms & Data Structures*, Prentice-Hall, Englewood Cliffs, NJ.

Wrathall, C. (1976) "Complete sets for the polynomial hierarchy", *Theoretical Computer Science*, **3**, 23–34.

Yaglom, I. M., and Boltyanskii, V. G. (1986) *Convex Figures*, Holt, Rinehart and Winston, New York.

Yao, A. C. (1975) "An $0(|E| \log \log |V|)$ algorithm for finding minimum spanning trees", *Information Processing Letters*, **4**(1), 21–23.

Index

A

adjacency lists, 82, 91

adjacency matrix, 82, 259

algebraic decision tree

  connected component, 330

  definition of, 329

  height of, 330

  linear, 329–330

  model of computation, 329, 331

  order of, 329

algorithm

  adaptive, 190

  analysis of (*see also* algorithm analysis), 44

  cryptography, 52

  definition of, 3

  deterministic, 3, 268

  exact order of, 26

  exponential, 53–54

  graph, 46, 52

  network, 46

  nondeterministic, 269, 280

  number theory, 52

  optimal (*see also* optimal algorithm), 32

  probabilistic, 409

  randomized (*see also* randomized algorithm), 363

  recursive, 43

algorithm analysis, 44, 52

  amortized (*see also* amortized analysis), 48

  average case (*see also* average case analysis), 45

  worst case (*see also* worst case analysis), 45

algorithm design technique

  approximation algorithms, 411

  backtracking, 345

  divide and conquer, 121, 145

  dynamic programming, 121, 193

  geometric sweeping, 481

  graph traversal, 245

  greedy approach, 219

  induction, 121, 143

  iterative improvement (flow in network), 435

  iterative improvement (matching), 455

  randomized algorithms, 363

  Voronoi diagrams, 501

all-pairs shortest path problem, 205, 207, 211–212, 215

almost-complete binary tree, 86, 94

alternating path, 456
    augmenting (*see also* augmenting
        path), 456
    cycle, 456
    length of, 456
alternating path tree, 459
amortized analysis, 48, 52
ancestor (of a vertex), 84
antipodal pair, 493–494
applications of the farthest-point
    Voronoi diagram, 515, 517
    computing all farthest neighbors,
        516
    computing the smallest enclosing
        circle, 516–517
applications of the Voronoi diagram,
    509, 512
    computing all nearest neighbors,
        510–511
    computing the convex hull,
        509–510
    computing the Euclidean minimum
        spanning tree, 511–512
approximation algorithm, 411
    definition of, 412
    difference bound, 413–414
    fully polynomial approximation
        scheme, 426, 428, 432
    performance bound, 411
    polynomial approximation scheme,
        422, 425, 432
    relative bound, 414, 422
array packing, 531
ARTICPOINTS algorithm, 251–253
articulation point, 251, 254, 259–260
assignment problem, 361
asymptotic running time, 21, 23
augmenting path, 438, 456–457
    bottleneck capacity of, 438
    vertex-disjoint, 457, 468–469, 475
average case analysis, 45, 47–49, 78

B

backtracking, 345, 362

advance step, 353
backtrack step, 354
depth-first search, 347
general method, 352, 354
search tree, 347
BACKTRACKITER algorithm, 354–355
BACKTRACKREC algorithm, 354
balanced tree method, 526
basic operation, 40–41
Bernoulli distribution, 695
Bernoulli trial, 695
best case, 45
BFPARPREFIX algorithm, 597
BFS algorithm, 255–257, 260–261
BIMATCH1 algorithm, 458–459
BIMATCH2 algorithm, 460–462, 466,
    476
BIMATCH3 algorithm, 470–471, 473
BIN PACKING problem, 280, 284, 412,
    415–417, 429, 432
    approximation algorithms for, 415,
        417
binary search, 6, 10, 41, 46
    randomized, 405
    recursive algorithm, 147, 149
binary search tree, 87–88, 91
binary tree, 85, 87
    almost-complete (*see also*
        almost-complete binary tree), 86
    complete (*see also* complete binary
        tree), 86
    full (*see also* full binary tree), 86
    height of (*see also* height (of a
        binary tree)), 87
    levels in (*see also* levels (in binary
        tree)), 86
    quantitative aspects of, 87
BINARYSEARCH algorithm, 7–8, 10,
    31–32, 41, 43–44, 46, 68, 324–325,
    405
BINARYSEARCHREC algorithm,
    147–149, 154, 186, 188
binomial coefficient, 195, 210, 673
binomial distribution, 695

binomial theorem, 674
bipartite graph, 82, 90, 261
 complete ($K_{m,n}$), 82
 edge cover for, 452
 independent set in, 453, 475
birthday paradox, 377
bisection width, 575
bitonic merging and sorting, 546, 553
bitonic sorting, 551
BITONICMERGE algorithm, 549–553
BITONICSORT algorithm, 551–552
blossom, 462, 477
 expanding of, 464
 shrinking of, 462–464
Boole's inequality, 387
bottom-up merge sorting, 15, 19
 parallel (*see also* parallel
  bottom-up merge sorting), 540
BOTTOMUPSORT algorithm, 16–19,
 26–27, 31–33, 40, 66, 69, 113, 120,
 141, 149, 151, 153–154, 171, 187,
 190, 540
bound
 exact, 26, 33, 48–49
 lower, 33, 46
 tight, 33
 upper, 33, 46
branch and bound, 354, 359, 362
breadth-first search, 255, 257,
 259–261
 applications of, 257
 back edge, 255
 cross edge, 255
 time complexity, 257
 tree edge, 255
Brent theorem, 528
broadcasting on the hypercube, 584
BRUTE-FORCE PRIMALITYTEST
 algorithm, 29, 53
BUBBLESORT algorithm, 70–71,
 140–141, 190
bucketsort, 141
butterfly, 577
 permutation routing in, 588

C

2-COLORING problem, 269, 283, 319
3-COLORING problem, 267, 279, 342,
 345, 347, 349, 352, 359
3-COLORITER algorithm, 348–349
3-COLORREC algorithm, 347–348
Carmichael numbers, 402, 409
CCC (*see also* cube-connected
 cycles), 633
ceiling function, 671–672
Chebyshev inequality, 380–381
Chernoff bounds, 381, 384
 lower tail, 381, 383
 upper tail, 383
child (of a vertex), 84
chromatic number, 267
CHROMATIC NUMBER problem, 267,
 316–317
Church Thesis, 4
Church, A., 4
CIRCUIT VALUE problem, 311, 322
class of problems
 co-NP (*see also* co-NP), 280
 DEXT (*see also* DEXT), 290
 EXPTIME (*see also* EXPTIME),
  290
 LOGSPACE (*see also*
  LOGSPACE), 293
 NC (*see also* NC), 310
 NEXPTIME (*see also*
  NEXPTIME), 290
 NEXT (*see also* NEXT), 290
 NLOGSPACE (*see also*
  NLOGSPACE), 293
 NP (*see also* NP), 269, 290
 NSPACE (*see also* NSPACE),
  293
 P (*see also* P), 268, 290
 POLYLOGSPACE (*see also*
  POLYLOGSPACE), 320
 PSPACE (*see also* PSPACE),
  293
CLIQUE problem, 267, 276–277, 279,
 283–284, 421

clique, 267
  maximum (*see also* max-clique),
    429
closed form, 683
closest pair problem, 178, 182,
    191–192, 335, 338
  1-dimensional, 191
  lower bound on, 335
CLOSESTPAIR algorithm, 181–182
closure of a class of problems, 303
co-NP (class of problems), 280–281
co-NP-complete, 280–281
collinear, 485
COLORING problem, 267, 270, 279,
    283, 316, 421, 430
coloring
  of planar graph, 413
combine step, 155
complete binary tree, 86
complete bipartite graph, 260–261
complete problem, 306, 313
  definition of, 306
  for co-NP (*see also*
    co-NP-complete), 280
  for LOGSPACE (*see also*
    LOGSPACE-complete), 307
  for NLOGSPACE (*see also*
    NLOGSPACE-complete), 307
  for NP (*see also* NP-complete),
    271
  for P (*see also* P-complete), 309
  for PSPACE (*see also*
    PSPACE-complete), 308
complexity
  space (*see also* space complexity),
    31
  time (*see also* time complexity), 19
complexity classes, 30–31
computability theory, 5
computational complexity, 5, 19, 287,
    294, 321–322
computational geometry, 52, 499
computer science, 3
conditional probability, 691

connected component, 81
  finding, 259
  listing vertices in, 259
connected graph, 81
CONVEX HULL problem, 334–335
conquer step, 154
convex hull, 484, 504
  computing the, 489, 491, 499
  on the mesh, 606, 612
  parallel algorithm, 569, 573
convex hull problem
  lower bound on, 334–335
CONVEXHULL algorithm, 491–492
CSG RECOGNITION problem, 309, 321
cube-connected cycles, 633
  bisection width of, 633
  degree of, 633
  diameter of, 633
  embedding of hypercube in, 633
  parallel prefix on, 633
cycle (in a graph), 81
  even-length, 81
  odd-length, 81
  of shortest length, 261

D

3-dimensional mesh, 612
  sorting on, 613
decidability, 5
decision problem, 266, 287, 329
decision tree, 9
  height of, 326
  model of computation, 324
degree of the network, 575
Delaunay triangulation, 504, 506
DELETE algorithm, 98
delete operation, 94, 487–488
delete-max operation, 94, 102, 113
delete-min operation, 487–488
DELETEMAX algorithm, 98
depth (of a vertex), 84
depth-first search, 245, 255, 258–259,
    261
  back edge, 247–248

cross edge, 248
forward edge, 248
in directed graphs, 247
in undirected graphs, 247
iterative, 259
postorder numbering, 247
preorder numbering, 247
spanning tree, 247, 260–261
time complexity of, 249
tree edge, 247–248
depth-first search applications, 250, 255
depth-first search applications of
articulation points (*see also* articulation point), 251
connected components (*see also* connected component), 259
graph acyclicity, 250
strongly connected components (*see also* strongly connected component), 254
topological sorting (*see also* topological sorting), 250
descendant (of a vertex), 84
DEXT (class of problems), 290
DFS algorithm, 246, 249–251, 259
diameter, 575
DIAMETER algorithm, 495
diameter of a point set
lower bound on, 336
diameter of a set of points, 492, 499
computing the, 492, 496, 499
dice problem, 372, 375
DIJKSTRA algorithm, 223–225, 235, 239–240, 242, 244
DINIC algorithm, 445–446
disjoint sets data structure, 49, 104, 112, 117
divide and conquer
combine step, 155
conquer step, 154
divide step, 154
general format, 156

paradigm, 154
threshold in, 156
divide and conquer recurrence, 54, 65
change of variables, 63, 65
expanding of, 54, 58
substitution, 58, 63
divide step, 154
dominance problem, 183, 191
dominance relation, 481
DOTPRODUCT algorithm, 567–568
DTIME, 290
dynamic programming, 193, 219
paradigm, 204–205
principle of optimality (*see also* principle of optimality), 204

E

edge
free, 455
matched, 455
unmatched, 455
edge cover, 452, 476
effective procedure, 4
element assignment, 12
element comparison, 11, 40
ELEMENT UNIQUENESS problem, 74, 266, 331–333, 335
lower bound on, 331
elementary operation, 22–23, 33, 40
embedding of a binary tree, 583
embeddings of the hypercube, 580
equivalence relation, 30, 664
ETSPAPPROX algorithm, 418–419
ETSP problem, 417
EUCLID algorithm, 74–75
Euclidean minimum spanning tree problem
lower bound on, 335–336
EUCLIDEAN MINIMUM SPANNING TREE problem, 335–336
EUCLIDEAN TRAVELING SALESMAN problem, 417–419
approximation algorithm for, 417, 419

minimum spanning tree heuristic,
    417, 429
nearest neighbor heuristic, 417, 430
Euler's formula, 83, 505
event, 691
event point schedule, 482
EXP algorithm, 124, 139–140
expectation, 693–694
expected value, 693
EXPMOD algorithm, 400–403, 405
exponentiation
    integer, 123–124
EXPREC algorithm, 123–124, 139–140
EXPTIME (class of problems), 290
extreme points, 484

F

factorial, 672–673
farthest-point Voronoi diagram,
    512–513
    a simple algorithm for, 519
    applications of (*see also*
        applications of the farthest-point
        Voronoi diagram), 515
    construction of, 513, 515
    regions, 512
    vertices, 512
fast Fourier transform, 616, 627
Fermat's theorem, 401
Fibonacci sequence, 64, 140, 193–194,
    210, 669, 684
file compression, 237, 239, 244
FIND algorithm, 108
find operation, 104–113, 115–116, 230
fixed points, 376
floor function, 671–672
flow in network
    augmenting path (*see also*
        augmenting path), 438
    blocking flow, 445
    cut, 436
    definition of, 435
    Dinic's algorithm, 445, 448
    Ford-Fulkerson method, 439–440
    level graph, 442
    maximum capacity augmentation,
        440, 442
    MPM algorithm, 448, 451
    residual capacity, 437
    residual graph, 437
    shortest path augmentation, 442,
        445
    value of, 436
FLOYD algorithm, 206
FORD–FULKERSON algorithm, 439
FORD-FULKERSON algorithm, 440
forest, 84
formula
    satisfiable, 269, 272, 275
    tautology, 281
    unsatisfiable, 281
FPVORONOID algorithm, 515, 518
full binary tree, 86–87
function, 664–665
    cubic, 22
    linear, 22
    logarithmic, 22
    quadratic, 22
    space constructible, 295
    sublinear, 22
    subquadratic, 22
    time constructible, 295, 318

G

GAP problem, 293–294, 298, 307–308,
    319–320, 322
Gödel, K., 4
geometric distribution, 696
GMATCH algorithm, 466–468
golden ratio, 195
Graham scan, 489, 497
graph, 80, 83
    2-colorable, 413
    3-colorable (*see also* 3-color), 413
    4-colorable, 413
    acyclic, 81
    acyclicity, 250

bipartite (*see also* bipartite graph), 82

bridge, 260

chromatic number of, 267

clique in, 267

coloring, 266–267

complete (K_n), 81

connected (*see also* connected graph), 81

connected component in (*see also* connected component), 81

connectivity of, 453

cycle in (*see also* cycle (in a graph)), 81

directed, 80

disconnected, 81

k-regular, 474

path in (*see also* path (in a graph)), 81

planar (*see also* planar graph), 83, 504

representation of, 82

strongly connected (*see also* strongly connected component), 81

triangulated (*see also* triangulated graph), 83

undirected, 80

GRAPH ACCESSIBILITY problem, 322

graph representation

adjacency lists (*see also* adjacency lists), 82

adjacency matrix (*see also* adjacency matrix), 82

graph traversal, 40, 261

breadth-first search, *see* breadth-first search, 255

depth-first search (*see also* depth-first search), 245, 261

Gray Codes, 581

greatest common divisor, 74, 143

H

Hall's theorem, 473–474

HAMILTONIAN CYCLE problem, 274, 360, 421

HAMILTONIAN PATH problem, 279

harmonic series, 680

hashing, 406

HCBROADCAST algorithm, 584, 651

HCHYPERQUICKSORT algorithm, 591–592

HCMULTISELECT algorithm, 595, 632

HCPARPREFIX algorithm, 590

HCSELECT algorithm, 593–596, 632

heap, 93, 103, 117

creating a, 99, 102, 117

delete-max, 98

deletion, 98

d-heap, 115

insertion, 97

min and max-heaps, 103

operations on, 95, 99

property, 94

variants of, 117

heapsort, 102–103, 117

HEAPSORT algorithm, 2, 33, 103, 113–115, 141, 166, 190, 326

height (of a binary tree), 87

height (of a tree), 84

height (of a vertex), 84

height of a binary tree, 191

HORNER algorithm, 125

Horner's rule, 124, 139, 142, 191

HUFFMAN algorithm, 238–241, 244

Huffman tree, 237–238

Hungarian tree, 460

removal of, 460

hypercube, 576

broadcasting on, 584

embedding of a linear array in, 582

embedding of a mesh in, 582

permutation routing in, 584

hyperquicksort, 591

I

independent set, 430

in bipartite graph, 475

of maximum cardinality, 475

INDEPENDENT SET problem, 278–279, 421, 430
indepenence, 691–692
indicator random variable, 695
induction design technique, 121
inorder traversal, 85
input
  distribution, 52
  order, 52
  size, 52
INSERT algorithm, 97
insert operation, 94, 113, 487–488
insertion sort, 13, 15
  average case analysis of, 47
INSERTIONSORT algorithm, 13–15, 23–25, 27, 31, 41–42, 44–48, 52, 66, 69, 89, 140–141, 155, 187, 190, 326, 337
interconnection network, 574
internal vertex, 84
intersections of line segments, 485, 489, 499
INTERSECTIONSLS algorithm, 488
intractable problem, 265

J

Jarvis march, 497–498

K

König's theorem, 475
k-clique problem, 310, 318
KNAPSACK algorithm, 208, 213
KNAPSACK problem, 207, 210–215, 279, 284, 361, 413, 422, 432
  0/1, 207
  another version of, 213
  fractional, 220
  hardness result, 413–414
  polynomial approximation scheme for, 422, 425
  two dimensional, 215
KNAPSACKGREEDY algorithm, 423–424, 430
knight tour problem, 360

Knuth, D. E., 3
KRUSKAL algorithm, 2, 229–231, 240, 242, 244

L

LBA ACCEPTANCE problem, 309, 321
λ-calculus, 4
LAPARPREFIX algorithm, 600–601
LCS algorithm, 197, 210–212
leading constants, 21
leaf vertex, 84
left turn, 485
levels (in binary tree), 86
line segment, 483
linear array, 598
  broadcasting on, 599
LINEAR PROGRAMMING problem, 286, 311, 322
linear search, 6, 41, 46
  average case analysis of, 47
linearity of expectation, 694
LINEARSEARCH algorithm, 6, 31, 46–47, 184, 324–325, 337
linked list, 79
logarithm, 670–671
LOGSPACE (class of problems), 293
LOGSPACE-complete, 307
longest common subsequence, 195, 197
LONGEST PATH problem, 280, 285
longest simple path, 204, 211
  in a directed acyclic graph, 215
lower bound, 46
  for finding the maximum, 327
  for finding largest and second largest, 327
  for sorting, 325
  on a problem, 323
  trivial, 323
lower order terms, 20–21

M

MINIMUM EQUIVALENT EXPRESSION problem, 317

MAJORITY algorithm, 123, 139–140
majority element, 122–123, 143, 407
MAKEHEAP algorithm, 101–103, 114
Markov inequality, 379–380
marriage theorem, 474
MATCHAIN algorithm, 202–203, 210, 212
matching
    alternating path (*see also* alternating path), 456
    definition of, 455
    in bipartite graph (*see also* matching in bipartite graph), 458
    in general graph (*see also* matching in general graph), 458
MAX-CLIQUE problem, 267, 321
MAX-FLOW problem, 311–322
    maximum, 456–457, 476
    maximum-weight, 476
    perfect, 456, 475
    size of, 456
matching in bipartite graph
    algorithms for, 476
    an improved algorithm for, 468, 473
    maximum, 460, 473
    the Hungarian tree algorithm for, 459–460
    the network flow method, 458
matching in general graph
    an algorithm for, 462, 468
    blossom (*see also* blossom), 462
    maximum, 468
mathematical notations, 23
    examples, 27, 30
    O-notation (*see also* O-notation), 23
    o-notation (*see also* o-notation), 30
    Ω-notation, (*see also* Ω-notation), 24
    Θ-notation, (*see also* Θ-notation), 26

matrix chain multiplication, 198, 204, 212, 215
matrix multiplication, 34, 40, 175, 177, 324
    comparison of algorithms for, 177
    parallel, 567
    randomized verification of, 407
    Strassen's algorithm, 176–177, 191–192
    traditional algorithm, 176, 186
max-clique, 429
max-flow (*see also* flow in network), 435
max-flow min-cut theorem, 438, 475
max-flow problem, 435
MAXIMA algorithm, 482
maximal matching, 420
maximal point, 482
MCA algorithm, 440–442
mean, 693
median, 157
median finding algorithm (*see also* selection), 156
memoryless property, 696
MERGE algorithm, 11–12, 17–18, 31–32, 39–41, 150, 155, 165, 187, 241
merge sort
    pipelined merge sort, 553, 560
mergesort, 149, 154, 185, 187, 192
MERGESORT algorithm, 120, 150–156, 161, 165, 171, 181, 183, 185, 187, 189–192, 326–327, 337, 551
merging, 10, 12, 540
    lower bound on, 339
    merging by ranking, 536
mesh, 598
    3-dimensional, 612
    broadcasting on, 599
    odd-even merging and sorting, 604
MESHODDEVENMERGE algorithm, 604, 606
MESHODDEVENSORT algorithm, 606

MESHPARPREFIX algorithm, 600–601, 654

minimum spanning tree
  Euclidean (*see also* Euclidean minimum spanning tree problem), 335
minimum-cost spanning tree, 227, 237, 245
  an efficient algorithm for, 235, 237
  Kruskal's algorithm, 227, 230
  Prim's algorithm, 231, 235
MINMAX algorithm, 146, 185–186
model of computation, 268
  algebraic decision tree, 329, 331
  decision tree, 324
  λ-calculus, 4
  parallel, 5
  Post machines, 4
  RAM, 4
  recursive functions, 4
  Turing machine, 4, 268, 287
MODPARSEARCH algorithm, 536–537, 539
money change problem, 214, 220, 239–240, 361
MPLA algorithm, 442–446
MPM algorithm, 449–450, 458
MST algorithm, 235–236
multiplication
  matrix chain (*see also* matrix chain multiplication), 198
  of complex numbers, 190
  of large integers, 174–175, 192
  of matrices (*see also* matrix multiplication), 175
MULTISELECT algorithm, 172–174, 563
multiselection, 172, 384
  analysis of randomized, 387, 390
  parallel (*see also* parallel multiselection), 563
  randomized algorithm for, 384, 387
multiselection on the hypercube, 594

MULTIPROCESSOR SCHEDULING problem, 280, 422, 431–432
mutually exclusive event, 691

N

NC (class of problems), 310
NEAREST POINT problem, 338
neighbor
  farthest, 516–518
  nearest, 510
network, 435
network flow (*see also* flow in network), 435
NEXPTIME (class of problems), 290
NEXT (class of problems), 290
NEXTPERM algorithm, 137–139
NEXTSUBSET algorithm, 131–132, 139
NLOGSPACE (class of problems), 293
NLOGSPACE-complete, 307–308
NP (class of problems), 269, 280, 290
  definition of, 270–271
NP-complete, 265, 271–272, 280, 285–286, 306
NP-hard, 272, 412
NP-hard problems, 193
NSPACE (class of problems), 293
NTIME, 290

O

O-notation, 23–24
o-notation, 30–31
occupancy problems, 375, 379
odd-even merging, 542
odd-even merging and sorting, 604
odd-even transposition sort, 601
ORDERED DEPTH-FIRST SEARCH problem, 311–322
ODDEVENMERGE algorithm, 542–544, 546, 631, 636, 647
ODDEVENSORT algorithm, 545–546, 606
Ω-notation, 24–25, 78
on-chip bubble sorter, 627

operation
  amortized running time of, 49
  average cost of, 49
  basic (*see also* basic operation), 40
  element assignment (*see also*
    element assignment), 40
  element comparison (*see also*
    element comparison), 40
  elementary (*see also* elementary
    operation), 22
optimal algorithm, 32–33, 323
optimal solution, 219–220, 412
optimization problem, 193, 204, 219,
  266, 411
oracle Turing machine, 313
order of growth, 19, 23

P

Pascal
triangle, 195
P (class of problems), 268–269, 290
  definition of, 268, 271
P-complete, 309, 311, 322
  definition of, 310–311
padding argument, 300, 302
PARADDITION algorithm, 527–529, 567
parallel architectures
  classifications of, 525
parallel bottom-up merge sorting, 540
parallel multiselection, 563, 567
parallel prefix, 529
parallel prefix on the butterfly,
  597
parallel prefix on the hypercube,
  590
parallel prefix on the mesh, 600
parallel quicksort, 532
parallel search, 533
parallel selection, 560
PARBOTTOMUPSORT algorithm,
  540–541, 553–554
PARCONVEXHULL algorithm, 573–574,
  607
parent (of a vertex), 84

PARMATRIXMULT algorithm, 567–568
PARMERGE algorithm, 540–541, 636,
  647
PARMULTISELECT1 algorithm, 563,
  567, 632
PARMULTISELECT2 algorithm,
  564–565, 632
PARPREFIX algorithm, 530
PARPREFIXREC algorithm, 530–531,
  644
PARQUICKSORT algorithm, 532–533,
  631, 636, 646
PARRANK algorithm, 538–540, 631
PARSEARCH algorithm, 534–536
PARSELECT algorithm, 561, 563, 632,
  636–637, 648
partial order, 664
partitioning
  a set of points, 338
PARTITION problem, 279, 284, 353,
  360
path
  alternating (*see also* alternating
    path), 456
  augmenting (*see also* augmenting
    path), 438
  longest (*see also* longest simple
    path), 204
  shortest (*see also* shortest path),
    204
path (in a graph), 81
  length of, 81
  simple, 81
path compression heuristic, 105, 107,
  109–113, 115–117
pattern matching, 397, 399
PATTERNMATCHING algorithm, 398
performance ratio
  absolute, 415
  asymptotic, 415
  constant, 415
  relative, 414
permutation, 32, 133
  algorithms for generating, 133, 137

generating using backtracking, 360
random, 406
permutation routing in the butterfly,
588
permutation routing in the
hypercube, 584
permutations
iterative algorithm, 137
PERMUTATIONS1 algorithm, 133–134,
142
PERMUTATIONS2 algorithm, 135–136,
142–143
PERMUTATIONS3 algorithm, 138–139
pigeonhole principle, 675–676
pipelined merge sort, 553, 560
PJUMPING algorithm, 535–536
planar graph, 83
coloring of, 413
Euler's formula (*see also* Euler's
formula), 83
point, 483
maximal, 482
Poisson approximation, 376
Poisson distribution, 376, 696
polygon, 483
boundary of, 484
chord in, 499
convex, 484
edges of, 484
interior of, 484
monotone, 499
nonsimple, 484
simple, 484, 496
vertices of, 484
polygonal path, 483
POLYLOGSPACE (class of
problems), 320
polynomial
representation of, 89
testing, 364, 405
polynomial evaluation
Horner's rule, 124–125, 139, 143
polynomial time hierarchy, 313, 317,
322

definition of, 314
problems in the, 316
properties of, 314
Post machines, 4
Post, E. L., 4
postorder traversal, 85
PRAM, 525
≺ relation, 31
preorder traversal, 85, 245
PRIM algorithm, 233–235, 240,
242–244
primality test, 400, 405, 409
primality test problem, 29
PRIMALITYTEST algorithm, 404–405
principle
of inclusion-exclusion, 688
of optimality (*see also* principle of
optimality), 204
pigeonhole (*see also* pigeonhole
principle), 675
principle of optimality, 204
priority queue, 93, 117
probability distribution, 691
problem complete (*see also* complete
problem), 306
decision, 266, 287
intractable, 265
lower bound on, 25
NP-hard (*see also* NP-hard
problems), 193
optimization (*see also* optimization
problem), 193, 266
solvable, 4–5
tractable, 265
unsolvable, 4–5
well-parallelizable, 310
problem instance, 52
proof method, 665, 670
by contradiction, 666–667
by counterexample, 667–668
direct, 666
indirect, 666
induction, 668, 670
PSPACE (class of problems), 293

PSPACE-complete, 308–309
PTEST1 algorithm, 401–402
PTEST2 algorithm, 402, 404
PTEST3 algorithm, 403–404

Q

4-QUEENS algorithm, 350–351, 360
4-QUEENS problem, 350
8-QUEENS problem, 349, 352, 360
queue, 80
QUANTIFIED BOOLEAN FORMULA
  problem, 308–309
QUICKMULTISELECT algorithm,
  385–386
quickselect, 171, 374
QUICKSELECT algorithm, 171–172,
  185–186, 190, 192, 369
quicksort, 161, 171, 185, 190, 192
  expected running time, 368
  partitioning algorithm for, 162
  randomized algorithm, 366, 369,
    410
QUICKSORT algorithm, 120, 156, 161,
  164–168, 170–171, 185, 189–190,
  192, 342, 366–367, 406, 532

R

radix sort, 125, 127, 143
RADIXSORT algorithm, 126–127, 139,
  141, 190
RAM, 4
random sampling, 390, 392
random variables, 693–694
randomized algorithm, 363–364, 409
  definition of, 363
  expected running time of, 365
  Las Vegas, 364, 366, 407
  Monte Carlo, 364–365, 406
randomized select
  expected running time, 369, 371
RANDOMIZEDQUICKSORT algorithm,
  367, 369, 405
RANDOMSAMPLING algorithm,
  390–391, 408

ranks
  computing, 536
rate of growth (*see also* order of
  growth), 20
recurrence relation, 43–44, 65, 682
  definition of, 683
  degree of, 683
  divide and conquer (*see also* divide
    and conquer recurrence), 54
  homogeneous, 683
  linear, 683
  linear homogeneous, 683, 685
  linear inhomogeneous, 685, 688
  with constant coefficients, 683
recursive function, 4
reduction, 302, 306
  definition of, 302
  linear time, 333–334
  log space, 303
  NC, 310
  polynomial time, 271, 273, 303
  Turing, 313
relation, 663–664
  equivalence (*see also* equivalence
    relation), 664
  partial order (*see also* partial
    order), 664
right turn, 485
RQUICKSELECT algorithm, 369–371,
  374, 406
running time, 19, 31, 33–34
  asymptotic (*see also* asymptotic
    running time), 21
  counting basic operations, 39, 42
  counting number of iterations, 33,
    39
  dependent on input values, 44
  estimate of, 33, 44
  exact bound of, 26, 33
  lower bound on, 24–25, 33
  upper bound on, 23, 33

S

2-SAT problem, 269

3-SAT problem, 275, 283, 285
sample space, 691
sampling (*see also* random sampling),
    377, 390
SATISFIABILITY problem, 272–273,
    275–278, 280–281, 283–286,
    308–309, 317
scaling and rounding, 213, 426
searching, 34, 40, 52
    lower bound on, 324–325
second largest element, 186
    algorithm for, 328
    lower bound for, 331
SELECT algorithm, 120, 157–159, 161,
    171–172, 185, 187–189, 342, 369,
    561, 636, 648
selection, 156, 161, 188–189, 192
    lower bound on, 339
    on the hypercube, 593
    parallel (*see also* parallel selection),
        560
    randomized algorithm, 369, 410
selection sort, 12–13
SELECTIONSORT algorithm, 12–15, 19,
    26–27, 31, 44, 66, 68–69, 102,
    140–141, 190, 497
sequence, 676
    finite, 676
sequential search (*see also* linear
    search), 6
set, 662–663
SET COVER problem, 280, 285, 431
SET DISJOINTNESS problem, 268, 283,
    333, 336
    lower bound on, 333
SET EQUALITY problem, 332
    lower bound on, 332
SET INCLUSION problem, 332
    lower bound on, 332
shared-memory computers, 525
shearsort, 602
shortest path, 204, 211, 219, 221, 227,
    231, 244–245

all-pairs (*see also* all-pairs shortest
    path problem), 205
    an efficient algorithm for, 225, 227
    Dijkstra's algorithm, 221, 225
    tree (*see also* shortest path tree),
        242
SHORTEST PATH problem, 268
shortest path tree, 242, 244
shortest paths
    parallel, 569
SHORTESTPATH algorithm, 225–227,
    235, 236, 242
siblings, 84
SIFT-DOWN algorithm, 96–98,
    101–103, 114–115
sift-down operation, 96–97, 103
SIFT-UP algorithm, 95, 97–98, 115
sift-up operation, 95–96
signed area, 484
simple polygon
    triangulation of (*see also*
        triangulation of a simple
        polygon), 499
solvability, 5
solvable problem, 4–5
sorting, 5, 34, 40, 44, 52, 78
    bitonic sorting, 551
    bottom-up merge (*see also*
        bottom-up merge sorting), 15
    bucketsort (*see also* bucketsort),
        141
    by comparisons, 325
    comparison of algorithms for, 170
    comparison-based, 25, 32
    comparison-based algorithm for,
        327
    heapsort (*see also* heapsort), 102
    hyperquicksort, 591
    insertion sort (*see also* insertion
        sort), 13
    lower bound on, 325, 327, 331, 339
    mergesort (*see also* mergesort), 149
    odd-even, 542
    on 3-dimensional mesh, 613

parallel bottom-up, 540
parallel quicksort, 532
pipelined merge sort, 553, 560
quicksort (*see also* quicksort), 161
radix sort (*see also* radix sort), 125
selection sort (*see also* selection
  sort), 12
stable, 141, 190
topological (*see also* topological
  sorting), 250
SORTING problem, 268, 283, 326, 334,
  336, 338
space
  complexity (*see also* space
    complexity), 31
  definition of, 31
  hierarchy (*see also* space and time
    hierarchy theorems), 298
  hierarchy theorems, 298, 301, 321
  work, 31–32
space and time hierarchy theorems,
  298, 300
space complexity, 31–33
spanning tree
  depth-first search, 246–247
  minimum-cost (*see also*
    minimum-cost spanning tree),
    227
SPLIT algorithm, 162–165, 167, 185,
  189, 367
stable marriage problem, 475
stack, 80
standard deviation, 380, 694
string equality, 395, 397
STRINGEQUALITYTEST algorithm, 396
STRONGCONNECTCOMP algorithm,
  254, 261
strongly connected component, 81,
  254–255, 259, 261
subset-sum problem, 422, 429, 432
  fully polynomial approximation
    scheme for, 426, 428
subsets
  algorithms for generating, 127, 133

SUBSETS1 algorithm, 128, 142
SUBSETS2 algorithm, 130, 142
SUBSETS3 algorithm, 131–132
SUBSETSUM algorithm, 427
subtree, 84
summation, 676, 682
  approximation by integration, 679,
    682
  formulas, 677, 679
supporting line, 493, 498
sweep line status, 483
system of distinct representatives,
  476
systolic computation, 627

T

tail bounds, 379, 384
tail recursion, 121
tangent, 498
TAUTOLOGY problem, 281, 285
theory of computation, 5, 19
Θ-notation, 26–27, 78
tight bound, 33
time
  complexity (*see also* time
    complexity), 19
  hierarchy (*see also* space and time
    hierarchy theorems), 298
  hierarchy theorems, 298–299, 321
time complexity, 19, 31
time-space tradeoff, 32
topological sorting, 250–251
topology, 575
tournament, 328
tractable problem, 265
transformation (*see also* reduction),
  302
transitive closure, 568
traveling salesman problem, 193
  branch and bound solution, 355
  hardness result, 420, 422
TRAVELING SALESMAN problem, 274,
  280, 283, 285, 355–356, 358,
  361–362, 421, 432

tree, 84, 88
  binary (*see also* binary tree), 85
  binary search (*see also* also binary
    search tree), 87
  height of (*see also* height (of a
    tree)), 84
  Hungarian (*see also* Hungarian
    tree), 460
  root of, 84
  rooted, 84
  siblings (*see also* siblings), 84
  subtree (*see also* subtree), 84
  traversal (*see also* tree traversal),
    85
tree traversal, 85
  inorder (*see also* inorder traversal),
    85
  postorder (*see also* postorder
    traversal), 85
  preorder (*see also* preorder
    traversal), 85
tree-connected computer, 632
triangulated graph, 83
triangulation
  of a set of points, 338
triangulation of a simple polygon,
  499
  $O(n)$ time algorithm, 500
  $O(n \log \log n)$ time algorithm, 500
  $O(n \log n)$ time algorithm, 500
Turing machine, 4, 52, 268, 287–288
  configuration of, 289
  deterministic, 289
  encoding of, 298
  k-tape, 288, 291
  off-line, 291, 293
  space used by, 292
  standard, 288
  time taken by, 290
Turing reduction, 313
Turing, A. M., 4

U

uniform distribution, 694

UNION algorithm, 108–109
union by rank heuristic, 105, 107,
  110, 112–113, 115–117
union operation, 104–113, 115–117,
  230
union-find algorithms, 49, 108, 112
  analysis of, 110, 112
unsolvable problem, 5
upper bound, 46

V

variance, 380, 694
VCOVERAPPROX algorithm, 420–421,
  429
vertex (in a graph), 80
  adjacent, 81
  degree of, 81
  free, 456
  indegree of, 81
  matched, 455
  outdegree of, 81
  reachable, 81
  unmatched, 455
VERTEX COVER problem, 277–279,
  283–285, 421
vertex (in a tree)
  ancestor of (*see also* ancestor (of a
    vertex)), 84
  child of (*see also* child (of a
    vertex)), 84
  depth of (*see also* depth (of a
    vertex)), 84
  descendant of (*see also* descendant
    (of a vertex)), 84
  height of (*see also* height (of a
    vertex)), 84
  internal (*see also* internal vertex),
    84
vertex cover, 429–430
  in a tree, 430
  minimum size of, 474
vertex cover problem
  approximation algorithm for,
    419–420

Voronoi diagram, 501–502, 504, 519
  applications of (*see also*
    applications of the Voronoi
    diagram), 509
  computing from three-dimensional
    convex hull, 519
  construction of, 506, 508
  divide-and-conquer algorithm for,
    519
  dividing chain, 507
  edges, 503
  line sweeping algorithm for, 519
  regions, 501
  vertices, 503
VORONOID algorithm, 508–509

W

weight-balancing rule, 116
word length, 23
work space, 31–32
worst case analysis, 45, 47

Z

zero-one principle, 541

Printed in the United States
by Baker & Taylor Publisher Services